Lecture Notes in Computer Science 11257

Commenced Publication in 1973
Founding and Former Series Editors:
Gerhard Goos, Juris Hartmanis, and Jan van Leeuwen

More information about this series at http://www.springer.com/series/7412

Jian-Huang Lai · Cheng-Lin Liu
Xilin Chen · Jie Zhou · Tieniu Tan
Nanning Zheng · Hongbin Zha (Eds.)

Pattern Recognition and Computer Vision

First Chinese Conference, PRCV 2018
Guangzhou, China, November 23–26, 2018
Proceedings, Part II

 Springer

Editors
Jian-Huang Lai
Sun Yat-sen University
Guangzhou, China

Cheng-Lin Liu
Institute of Automation
Chinese Academy of Sciences
Beijing, China

Xilin Chen
Institute of Computing Technology
Chinese Academy of Sciences
Beijing, China

Jie Zhou
Tsinghua University
Beijing, China

Tieniu Tan
Institute of Automation
Chinese Academy of Sciences
Beijing, China

Nanning Zheng
Xi'an Jiaotong University
Xi'an, China

Hongbin Zha
Peking University
Beijing, China

ISSN 0302-9743 ISSN 1611-3349 (electronic)
Lecture Notes in Computer Science
ISBN 978-3-030-03334-7 ISBN 978-3-030-03335-4 (eBook)
https://doi.org/10.1007/978-3-030-03335-4

Library of Congress Control Number: 2018959435

LNCS Sublibrary: SL6 – Image Processing, Computer Vision, Pattern Recognition, and Graphics

This Springer imprint is published by the registered company Springer Nature Switzerland AG
The registered company address is: Gewerbestrasse 11, 6330 Cham, Switzerland

Preface

Welcome to the proceedings of the First Chinese Conference on Pattern Recognition and Computer Vision (PRCV 2018) held in Guangzhou, China!

PRCV emerged from CCPR (Chinese Conference on Pattern Recognition) and CCCV (Chinese Conference on Computer Vision), which are both the most influential Chinese conferences on pattern recognition and computer vision, respectively. Pattern recognition and computer vision are closely inter-related and the two communities are largely overlapping. The goal of merging CCPR and CCCV into PRCV is to further boost the impact of the Chinese community in these two core areas of artificial intelligence and further improve the quality of academic communication. Accordingly, PRCV is co-sponsored by four major academic societies of China: the Chinese Association for Artificial Intelligence (CAAI), the China Computer Federation (CCF), the Chinese Association of Automation (CAA), and the China Society of Image and Graphics (CSIG).

PRCV aims at providing an interactive communication platform for researchers from academia and from industry. It promotes not only academic exchange, but also communication between academia and industry. In order to keep track of the frontier of academic trends and share the latest research achievements, innovative ideas, and scientific methods in the fields of pattern recognition and computer vision, international and local leading experts and professors are invited to deliver keynote speeches, introducing the latest advances in theories and methods in the fields of pattern recognition and computer vision.

PRCV 2018 was hosted by Sun Yat-sen University. We received 397 full submissions. Each submission was reviewed by at least two reviewers selected from the Program Committee and other qualified researchers. Based on the reviewers' reports, 178 papers were finally accepted for presentation at the conference, including 24 oral and 154 posters. The acceptance rate is 45%. The proceedings of the PRCV 2018 are published by Springer.

We are grateful to the keynote speakers, Prof. David Forsyth from University of Illinois at Urbana-Champaign, Dr. Zhengyou Zhang from Tencent, Prof. Tamara Berg from University of North Carolina Chapel Hill, and Prof. Michael S. Brown from York University.

We give sincere thanks to the authors of all submitted papers, the Program Committee members and the reviewers, and the Organizing Committee. Without their contributions, this conference would not be a success. Special thanks also go to all of the sponsors and the organizers of the special forums; their support made the conference a success. We are also grateful to Springer for publishing the proceedings and especially to Ms. Celine (Lanlan) Chang of Springer Asia for her efforts in coordinating the publication.

We hope you find the proceedings enjoyable and fruitful reading.

September 2018

Tieniu Tan
Nanning Zheng
Hongbin Zha
Jian-Huang Lai
Cheng-Lin Liu
Xilin Chen
Jie Zhou

Organization

Steering Chairs

Tieniu Tan	Institute of Automation, Chinese Academy of Sciences, China
Hongbin Zha	Peking University, China
Jie Zhou	Tsinghua University, China
Xilin Chen	Institute of Computing Technology, Chinese Academy of Sciences, China
Cheng-Lin Liu	Institute of Automation, Chinese Academy of Sciences, China
Long Quan	Hong Kong University of Science and Technology, SAR China
Yong Rui	Lenovo Group

General Chairs

Tieniu Tan	Institute of Automation, Chinese Academy of Sciences, China
Nanning Zheng	Xi'an Jiaotong University, China
Hongbin Zha	Peking University, China

Program Chairs

Jian-Huang Lai	Sun Yat-sen University, China
Cheng-Lin Liu	Institute of Automation, Chinese Academy of Sciences, China
Xilin Chen	Institute of Computing Technology, Chinese Academy of Sciences, China
Jie Zhou	Tsinghua University, China

Organizing Chairs

Liang Wang	Institute of Automation, Chinese Academy of Sciences, China
Wei-Shi Zheng	Sun Yat-sen University, China

Publicity Chairs

Huimin Ma	Tsinghua University, China
Jian Yu	Beijing Jiaotong University, China
Xin Geng	Southeast University, China

International Liaison Chairs

Jingyi Yu	ShanghaiTech University, China
Pong C. Yuen	Hong Kong Baptist University, SAR China

Publication Chairs

Zhouchen Lin   Peking University, China
Zhenhua Guo   Tsinghua University, China

Tutorial Chairs

Huchuan Lu   Dalian University of Technology, China
Zhaoxiang Zhang   Institute of Automation, Chinese Academy of Sciences, China

Workshop Chairs

Yao Zhao   Beijing Jiaotong University, China
Yanning Zhang   Northwestern Polytechnical University, China

Sponsorship Chairs

Tao Wang   iQIYI Company, China
Jinfeng Yang   Civil Aviation University of China, China
Liang Lin   Sun Yat-sen University, China

Demo Chairs

Yunhong Wang   Beihang University, China
Junyong Zhu   Sun Yat-sen University, China

Competition Chairs

Xiaohua Xie   Sun Yat-sen University, China
Jiwen Lu   Tsinghua University, China

Website Chairs

Ming-Ming Cheng   Nankai University, China
Changdong Wang   Sun Yat-sen University, China

Finance Chairs

Huicheng Zheng   Sun Yat-sen University, China
Ruiping Wang   Institute of Computing Technology, Chinese Academy
                       of Sciences, China

Program Committee

Haizhou Ai   Tsinghua University, China
Xiang Bai   Huazhong University of Science and Technology, China

Xiaochun Cao	Institute of Information Engineering, Chinese Academy of Sciences, China
Hong Chang	Institute of Computing Technology, China
Songcan Chen	Chinese Academy of Sciences, China
Xilin Chen	Institute of Computing Technology, China
Hong Cheng	University of Electronic Science and Technology of China, China
Jian Cheng	Chinese Academy of Sciences, China
Ming-Ming Cheng	Nankai University, China
Yang Cong	Chinese Academy of Science, China
Dao-Qing Dai	Sun Yat-sen University, China
Junyu Dong	Ocean University of China, China
Yuchun Fang	Shanghai University, China
Jianjiang Feng	Tsinghua University, China
Shenghua Gao	ShanghaiTech University, China
Xinbo Gao	Xidian University, China
Xin Geng	Southeast University, China
Ping Guo	Beijing Normal University, China
Zhenhua Guo	Tsinghua University, China
Huiguang He	Institute of Automation, Chinese Academy of Sciences, China
Ran He	National Laboratory of Pattern Recognition, China
Richang Hong	Hefei University of Technology, China
Baogang Hu	Institute of Automation, Chinese Academy of Sciences, China
Hua Huang	Beijing Institute of Technology, China
Kaizhu Huang	Xi'an Jiaotong-Liverpool University, China
Rongrong Ji	Xiamen University, China
Wei Jia	Hefei University of Technology, China
Yunde Jia	Beijing Institute of Technology, China
Feng Jiang	Harbin Institute of Technology, China
Zhiguo Jiang	Beihang University, China
Lianwen Jin	South China University of Technology, China
Xiao-Yuan Jing	Wuhan University, China
Xiangwei Kong	Dalian University of Technology, China
Jian-Huang Lai	Sun Yat-sen University, China
Hua Li	Institute of Computing Technology, Chinese Academy of Sciences, China
Peihua Li	Dalian University of Technology, China
Shutao Li	Hunan University, China
Wu-Jun Li	Nanjing University, China
Xiu Li	Tsinghua University, China
Xuelong Li	Xi'an Institute of Optics and Precision Mechanics, Chinese Academy of Sciences, China
Yongjie Li	University of Electronic Science and Technology of China, China
Ronghua Liang	Zhejiang University of Technology, China
Zhouchen Lin	Peking University, China

Cheng-Lin Liu	Institute of Automation, Chinese Academy of Sciences, China
Huafeng Liu	Zhejiang University, China
Huaping Liu	Tsinghua University, China
Qingshan Liu	Nanjing University of Information Science and Technology, China
Wenyin Liu	Guangdong University of Technology, China
Wenyu Liu	Huazhong University of Science and Technology, China
Yiguang Liu	Sichuan University, China
Yue Liu	Beijing Institute of Technology, China
Guoliang Lu	Shandong University, China
Jiwen Lu	Tsinghua University, China
Yue Lu	East China Normal University, China
Bin Luo	Anhui University, China
Ke Lv	Chinese Academy of Sciences, China
Huimin Ma	Tsinghua University, China
Zhanyu Ma	Beijing University of Posts and Telecommunications, China
Deyu Meng	Xi'an Jiaotong University, China
Qiguang Miao	Xidian University, China
Zhenjiang Miao	Beijing Jiaotong University, China
Weidong Min	Nanchang University, China
Bingbing Ni	Shanghai Jiaotong University, China
Gang Pan	Zhejiang University, China
Yuxin Peng	Peking University, China
Jun Sang	Chongqing University, China
Nong Sang	Huazhong University of Science and Technology, China
Shiguang Shan	Institute of Computing Technology, Chinese Academy of Sciences, China
Linlin Shen	Shenzhen University, China
Wei Shen	Shanghai University, China
Guangming Shi	Xidian University, China
Fei Su	Beijing University of Posts and Telecommunications, China
Jian Sun	Xi'an Jiaotong University, China
Jun Sun	Fujitsu R&D Center Co., Ltd., China
Zhengxing Sun	Nanjing University, China
Xiaoyang Tan	Nanjing University of Aeronautics and Astronautics, China
Jinhui Tang	Nanjing University of Science and Technology, China
Jin Tang	Anhui University, China
Yandong Tang	Shenyang Institute of Automation, Chinese Academy of Sciences, China
Chang-Dong Wang	Sun Yat-sen University, China
Liang Wang	National Laboratory of Pattern Recognition, China
Ruiping Wang	Institute of Computing Technology, Chinese Academy of Sciences, China
Shengjin Wang	Tsinghua University, China
Shuhui Wang	Institute of Computing Technology, Chinese Academy of Sciences, China

Tao Wang	iQIYI Company, China
Yuanquan Wang	Hebei University of Technology, China
Zengfu Wang	University of Science and Technology of China, China
Shikui Wei	Beijing Jiaotong University, China
Wei Wei	Northwestern Polytechnical University, China
Jianxin Wu	Nanjing University, China
Yihong Wu	Institute of Automation, Chinese Academy of Sciences, China
Gui-Song Xia	Wuhan University, China
Shiming Xiang	Institute of Automation, Chinese Academy of Sciences, China
Xiaohua Xie	Sun Yat-sen University, China
Yong Xu	South China University of Technology, China
Zenglin Xu	University of Electronic and Technology of China, China
Jianru Xue	Xi'an Jiaotong University, China
Xiangyang Xue	Fudan University, China
Gongping Yang	Shandong University, China
Jie Yang	ShangHai JiaoTong University, China
Jinfeng Yang	Civil Aviation University of China, China
Jufeng Yang	Nankai University, China
Qixiang Ye	Chinese Academy of Sciences, China
Xinge You	Huazhong University of Science and Technology, China
Jian Yin	Sun Yat-sen University, China
Xu-Cheng Yin	University of Science and Technology Beijing, China
Xianghua Ying	Peking University, China
Jian Yu	Beijing Jiaotong University, China
Shiqi Yu	Shenzhen University, China
Bo Yuan	Tsinghua University, China
Pong C. Yuen	Hong Kong Baptist University, SAR China
Zheng-Jun Zha	University of Science and Technology of China, China
Daoqiang Zhang	Nanjing University of Aeronautics and Astronautics, China
Guofeng Zhang	Zhejiang University, China
Junping Zhang	Fudan University, China
Min-Ling Zhang	Southeast University, China
Wei Zhang	Shandong University, China
Yanning Zhang	Northwestern Polytechnical University, China
Zhaoxiang Zhang	Institute of Automation, Chinese Academy of Sciences, China
Qijun Zhao	Sichuan University, China
Huicheng Zheng	Sun Yat-sen University, China
Wei-Shi Zheng	Sun Yat-sen University, China
Wenming Zheng	Southeast University, China
Jie Zhou	Tsinghua University, China
Wangmeng Zuo	Harbin Institute of Technology, China

Contents – Part II

Deep Learning

Deep Learning

An Interpretation
of Forward-Propagation and
Back-Propagation of DNN

Guotian Xie[1,2] and Jianhuang Lai[1,2,3(✉)]

[1] The School of Data and Computer Science, Sun Yat-sen University,
Guangzhou 510006, China
guotian.xgt@alibaba-inc.com
[2] Guangdong Key Laboratory of Information Security Technology,
Guangzhou 510006, China
[3] The School of Information Science and Technology, Xinhua College,
Sun Yat-sen University, Guangzhou, People's Republic of China
stsljh@mail.sysu.edu.cn

Abstract. Deep neural network (DNN) is hard to understand because the objective loss function is defined on the last layer, not directly on the hidden layers. To best understand DNN, we interpret the forward-propagation and back-propagation of DNN as two network structures, fp-DNN and bp-DNN. Then we introduce the direct loss function for hidden layers of fp-DNN and bp-DNN, which gives a way to interpret the fp-DNN as an encoder and bp-DNN as a decoder. Using this interpretation of DNN, we do experiments to analyze that fp-DNN learns to encode discriminant features in the hidden layers with the supervision of bp-DNN. Further, we use bp-DNN to visualize and explain DNN. Our experiments and analyses show the proposed interpretation of DNN is a good tool to understand and analyze the DNN.

Keywords: Forward-propagation · Back-propagation · Encoder Decoder

1 Introduction

In recent years, with the assist of hard-ware development, more and more applications are based on Deep learning, e.g., Compute vision [18], Audio Analysis [2], Nature Language Processing [8], Robots [13] and so on. Encouraging by its successes in widespread applications, Deep Learning (DL) and Deep Neural Networks (DNN) become a hot research topic among researchers and show its power comparing to other machine learning model, e.g., in these years, DL wins the first place on machine learning competitions on real data challenges [6,10] and even surpasses human beings on some tasks [7]. Despite such successes, we still know little about DNN, though it bases on a simple optimization techniques, Gradient Back-Propagation [11]. Although there are some feedback mechanisms

© Springer Nature Switzerland AG 2018
J.-H. Lai et al. (Eds.): PRCV 2018, LNCS 11257, pp. 3–15, 2018.
https://doi.org/10.1007/978-3-030-03335-4_1

proposed to train DNN [14,16,19], BP is still a popular way and DNN is still a black box [9,17,20].

The major obstacle of understanding how DNN learns knowledge is that, the objective function of the DNN is defined on last layer of DNN. It's not directly defined on the hidden layers. A loss function directly defining on the hidden layers could help us to understand what knowledge will be learned. For example, researchers know that the objective loss function of SVM [5] is to learn a hyperplane to segment the dataset into two classes. That's because the objective loss function is defined directly on the linear model $y = \mathbf{W}\mathbf{x} + b$.

Inspire by that, we define a direct loss function for the hidden layers of DNN. First, we interpret the forward-propagation and back-propagation of DNN as two network structures, denoted as fp-DNN and bp-DNN. Then we define direct loss function for the hidden layers of fp-DNN and bp-DNN respectively, which uncovers the fact that fp-DNN acts as a role of encoder, while bp-DNN acts as a role of decoder. In this interpretation, fp-DNN and bp-DNN generate targets to supervise the training of each other, as showing in Fig. 2. Here, the word "targets", which is also used in [3,12], represents the signal to supervise the training.

In experiments, we use the proposed interpretation of fp-DNN and bp-DNN to analyze DNN. First, we analyze the bp-DNN generate discriminant targets to supervise the fp-DNN to learn to encode the discriminant features. Then, we visualize the distribution of the encoded features of fp-DNN to verify that fp-DNN does learn to encode discriminant features. Finally, we use bp-DNN to visualize the DNN to do some analyses. The experimental results show that the proposed interpretation is a good tool for analyzing DNN.

Our contributions in this paper are as follows,

1. We interpret the forward-propagation and the backward-propagation of DNN as two network structures, fp-DNN and bp-DNN, respectively. By defining the direct loss function for hidden layers of fp-DNN and bp-DNN, we think that the fp-DNN acts as a role of an encoder, supervising the training of the bp-DNN, while the bp-DNN acts as a role of a decoder, supervising the training of the fp-DNN. This interpretation helps us to understand the DNN. For example, we could explain why the hidden layers of fp-DNN learns to encode the discriminant features.
2. Since the bp-DNN acts as a decoder, It could be used to visualized what knowledge the DNN have learned. However, the bp-DNN has some disadvantages for visualization. So we propose the guided-bp-DNN for knowledge visualization of DNN, and our experiments show that the visualization using guided-bp-DNN could focus on the important patterns for recognition.

Notation: We use bold lower case letters to represent a column based vector, e.g., $\mathbf{x}$, bold capital letters to represent a matrix, e.g., $\mathbf{W}$. we denote a function as $f_{\Theta}(\mathbf{x})$, where Θ is the parameters of this function and $\mathbf{x}$ is the input.

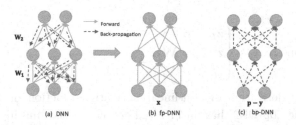

Fig. 1. (a) The normal DNN training procedure contains two steps, forward(blue) and backward(red), which forms two network sharing weights. (b) The network fp-DNN represents the forward pass, extracting features (c) The network bp-DNN has the inverted structure of fp-DNN, but sharing the same parameters, which is for transporting the gradients (or label information) from top to the bottom. (Color figure online)

2 Formulation of Deep Neural Networks

Classification is a basic task for Machine Learning. In this paper, we use DNN to model the classification task and analyze how DNN is trained. We assume a classification task with C classes, with a training data set $\{\mathbf{x}_i, \mathbf{y}_i\}_{i=1}^N$ that contains N training samples. Where $\mathbf{x} \in R^S$ is the input signal and $\mathbf{y} \in \{0, 1\}^C$ is the class label of $\mathbf{x}$, with $y_c = 1$ if $\mathbf{x}$ belongs to the cth class and otherwise $y_i = 0, i \neq c$. The classification task for this data set is to train a DNN to predict the conditional distribution $p(\mathbf{y}|\mathbf{x}) = f_\Theta(\mathbf{x})$, where $f_\Theta(\mathbf{x})$ is the function of DNN. We denote $\mathbf{p} = [p_0, p_1, \ldots, p_C]^T \subset R^C$ as the output of $f_\Theta(\mathbf{x})$ for convenience, with $p_i = p(y_i|\mathbf{x})$.

To solve this classification task, we construct a model of deep neural network with L hidden layers, and formulate it as [1], (Fig. 1(a))

$$\text{DNN} = \begin{cases} \ell_\Theta(\mathbf{x}, \mathbf{y}) = \sum_i^C y_i \log p_i \\ p_i = \frac{e^{z_{L,i}}}{\sum_j^C e^{z_{L,j}}} \\ \mathbf{z}_1 = \mathbf{W}_1 \mathbf{x} + \mathbf{b}_1 \\ \mathbf{z}_l = \mathbf{W}_l \sigma(\mathbf{z}_{l-1}) + \mathbf{b}_l, 2 \leq l \leq L \end{cases} \tag{1}$$

where $\mathbf{W}_l \in R^{C_l \times C_{l-1}}$ and $\mathbf{b}_l \in R^{C_l}$ is the parameters of the lth layer of DNN, and $\ell_\Theta(\mathbf{x}, \mathbf{y})$ is the softmax loss function. Θ is all the parameters of DNN. $\mathbf{z}_L = [z_{L,1}, z_{L,2}, \ldots, z_{L,C}]^T$ is the linear output of DNN. $\mathbf{z}_l \in R^{C_l}$ is the linear output of the lth hidden layer, and $\mathbf{p} = [p_1, p_2, \cdots, p_C]^T$ is the final prediction of this DNN.

We define two network structures corresponding to the training process with forward and back-propagation,

$$\text{fp-DNN} = \begin{cases} \mathbf{z}_0 = \mathbf{x} \\ \mathbf{z}_1 = \mathbf{W}_1 \mathbf{z}_0 + \mathbf{b}_1 \\ \mathbf{z}_l = \mathbf{W}_l \sigma(\mathbf{z}_{l-1}) + \mathbf{b}_l, 2 \leq l \leq L \end{cases} \tag{2}$$

$$\text{bp-DNN} = \begin{cases} \tilde{\mathbf{z}}_L = \mathbf{p} - \mathbf{y} \\ \tilde{\mathbf{z}}_{L-1} = \mathbf{W}_L^T \tilde{\mathbf{z}}_L \\ \tilde{\mathbf{z}}_{l-1} = \mathbf{W}_l^T (\tilde{\mathbf{z}}_l \odot \tilde{\mathbf{b}}_l), L-1 \geq l \geq 1 \end{cases} \tag{3}$$

where $\tilde{\mathbf{b}}_l$ is the derivation of non-linear activation function of the lth layer, $\tilde{\mathbf{b}}_l = \frac{\partial \sigma(\mathbf{z}_l)}{\partial \mathbf{z}_l}$. Since bp-DNN has an inverted structure, showing in Fig. 1, we use an inverted order to number the layers of bp-DNN, i.e., the Lth layer is the first layer of bp-DNN, while the 0th layer is the last layer of bp-DNN.

As the definition of fp-DNN and bp-DNN shows, they share the parameters $\mathbf{W}_l, l = 1, \cdots, L$. See Fig. 1(b) and (c) for specification. Compare (b) and (c), the structure of fp-DNN and bp-DNN is similar but inverted. For convenience, we denoted $\mathbf{o}_l$ and $\tilde{\mathbf{o}}_l$ as the non-linear output of the lth layer of fp-DNN and bp-DNN, respectively,

$$\mathbf{o}_l = \begin{cases} \mathbf{z}_0, l = 0 \\ \sigma(\mathbf{z}_l), \text{otherwise} \end{cases} , \tilde{\mathbf{o}}_l = \begin{cases} \tilde{\mathbf{z}}_L, l = L \\ \tilde{\mathbf{z}}_l \odot \tilde{\mathbf{b}}_l, \text{otherwise} \end{cases} \tag{4}$$

Since bp-DNN is an interpretation of back-propagation of DNN, we have $\frac{\partial \ell_\Theta}{\partial \mathbf{z}_l} = \tilde{\mathbf{o}}_l$.

The symmetrical but inverted structures of fp-DNN and bp-DNN remind us the auto-encoder network structures, which contain a part of network acting as a role of encoder, and another part of network acting as a role of decoder. In analyses of the next section, we will found that fp-DNN does act as a role of encoder, while bp-DNN does act as a role of decoder.

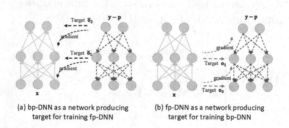

(a) bp-DNN as a network producing target for training fp-DNN

(b) fp-DNN as a network producing target for training bp-DNN

Fig. 2. fp-DNN and bp-DNN are supervisor for each other. (a) From the view of fp-DNN, bp-DNN generates targets to supervise the training of each hidden layers of fp-DNN. (b) From the view of bp-DNN, fp-DNN generates targets to supervise the training of each hidden layers of bp-DNN.

3 fp-DNN and bp-DNN vs Encoder and Decoder

In this section, we will give an interpretation that bp-DNN acts as a role of decoder and fp-DNN acts as a role of encoder, by defining the direct loss function for hidden layers of fp-DNN and bp-DNN respectively.

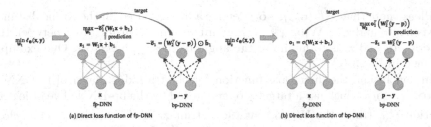

Fig. 3. The direct loss function for fp-DNN is $\tilde{\ell}^{fp}_{\mathbf{W}_l}(\mathbf{o}_{l-1}, -\tilde{\mathbf{o}}_l) = -\tilde{\mathbf{o}}_l^T(\mathbf{W}_l\mathbf{o}_{l-1} + \mathbf{b}_l)$, while the direct loss function for bp-DNN is $\tilde{\ell}^{bp}_{\mathbf{W}_l}(-\tilde{\mathbf{o}}_l, \mathbf{o}_{l-1}) = -\mathbf{o}_{l-1}^T(\mathbf{W}_l^T\tilde{\mathbf{o}}_l)$. Here we show an instance of the direct loss function of the DNN network described in Fig. 1. The fp-DNN and bp-DNN in both (a) and (b) are shown only part of the fp-DNN and bp-DNN in Fig. 1. (a) The bp-DNN generates the targets $\tilde{\mathbf{o}}_1$ to supervise the fp-DNN to learn the $\mathbf{W}_1$. (b) The fp-DNN generates the targets $\mathbf{o}_1$ to supervise the bp-DNN to learn the $\mathbf{W}_2$.

3.1 Direct Loss Function for Hidden Layer of fp-DNN

The DNN is optimized on the loss function $\ell_\Theta(\mathbf{x}, \mathbf{y}) = \sum_i^C y_i \log p_i$. If we interpret $\ell_\Theta(\mathbf{x}, \mathbf{y})$ into a direct loss function of hidden layer, we can understand easily how the hidden layer is trained. We define the direct loss function $\ell^{fp}_{\mathbf{W}_l}$ of lth hidden layer, so that it has the same gradient w.r.t $\mathbf{W}_l$, i.e., $\frac{\partial \ell^{fp}_{\mathbf{W}_l}}{\partial \mathbf{W}_l} = \frac{\partial \ell_\Theta(\mathbf{x}, \mathbf{y})}{\partial \mathbf{W}_l}$.

When we want to optimize the parameters $\mathbf{W}_l$ of l_{th} hidden layer, we use the gradient descent, $\mathbf{W}_l = \mathbf{W}_l - \eta \Delta \mathbf{W}_l$, where η is the learning rate and $\Delta \mathbf{W}_l$ is the gradient back-propagated from the top layer, and has the form as follows,

$$\Delta \mathbf{W}_l = \frac{\partial \ell_\Theta}{\partial \mathbf{z}_l} \frac{\partial \mathbf{z}_l^T}{\partial \mathbf{W}_l} = \frac{\partial \ell_\Theta}{\partial \mathbf{z}_l} \sigma(\mathbf{z}_{l-1})^T = \tilde{\mathbf{o}}_l \mathbf{o}_{l-1}^T$$

$$\Delta \mathbf{b}_l = \frac{\partial \ell_\Theta}{\partial \mathbf{z}_l} \frac{\partial \mathbf{z}_l^T}{\partial \mathbf{b}_l} = \frac{\partial \ell_\Theta}{\partial \mathbf{z}_l} = \tilde{\mathbf{o}}_l$$

$$(5)$$

By observation, we found that the gradient $\Delta \mathbf{W}_l$ and $\Delta \mathbf{b}_l$ is equivalent to the gradient of the loss function $\tilde{\ell}^{fp}_{\mathbf{W}_l}(\mathbf{o}_{l-1}, \tilde{\mathbf{o}}_l)$ w.r.t. $\mathbf{W}_l$ and $\mathbf{b}_l$,

$$\tilde{\ell}^{fp}_{\mathbf{W}_l}(\mathbf{o}_{l-1}, \tilde{\mathbf{o}}_l) = \tilde{\mathbf{o}}_l^T(\mathbf{W}_l\mathbf{o}_{l-1} + \mathbf{b}_l) \qquad (6)$$

where $\mathbf{o}_{l-1} = \sigma(\mathbf{z}_{l-1})$ is the input signal and $\tilde{\mathbf{o}}_l = \frac{\partial \ell_\Theta(\mathbf{x}, \mathbf{y})}{\partial \mathbf{z}_l}$ is the new target of the lth hidden layer, and we view $\mathbf{o}_{l-1}$ and $\tilde{\mathbf{o}}_l$ as constants w.r.t. $\mathbf{W}_l$ and $\mathbf{b}_l$. Obviously,

$$\Delta \mathbf{W}_l = \frac{\partial \tilde{\ell}^{fp}_{\mathbf{W}_l}(\mathbf{o}_{l-1}, \tilde{\mathbf{o}}_l)}{\partial \mathbf{W}_l} = \frac{\partial \ell_\Theta(\mathbf{x}, \mathbf{y})}{\partial \mathbf{W}_l}$$

$$\Delta \mathbf{b}_l = \frac{\partial \tilde{\ell}^{fp}_{\mathbf{W}_l}(\mathbf{o}_{l-1}, \tilde{\mathbf{o}}_l)}{\partial \mathbf{b}_l} = \frac{\partial \ell_\Theta(\mathbf{x}, \mathbf{y})}{\partial \mathbf{b}_l}$$

$$(7)$$

$$\min_{\mathbf{W}_l, \mathbf{b}_l} \ell_\Theta(\mathbf{x}, \mathbf{y}) \equiv \min_{\mathbf{W}_l, \mathbf{b}_l} \tilde{\ell}^{fp}_{\mathbf{W}_l}(\mathbf{o}_{l-1}, \tilde{\mathbf{o}}_l) \equiv \max_{\mathbf{W}_l, \mathbf{b}_l} \tilde{\ell}^{fp}_{\mathbf{W}_l}(\mathbf{o}_{l-1}, -\tilde{\mathbf{o}}_l) \qquad (8)$$

Please note that, $\tilde{\ell}^{fp}_{\mathbf{W}_l}(\mathbf{o}_{l-1}, -\tilde{\mathbf{o}}_l)$ defines a metric based on the cosine distance between $-\tilde{\mathbf{o}}_l$ and $\mathbf{z}_l = \mathbf{W}_l\mathbf{o}_{l-1} + \mathbf{b}_l$. Maximizing the cosine distance between the vectors $-\tilde{\mathbf{o}}_l$ and $\mathbf{z}_l$ is to minimize the angle of these two vectors. One example is shown in Fig. 3 (a).

In conclusion, the direct loss function for the lth hidden layer of fp-DNN is $\tilde{\ell}^{fp}_{\mathbf{W}_l}(\mathbf{o}_{l-1}, -\tilde{\mathbf{o}}_l)$, which use a target $-\tilde{\mathbf{o}}_l$ generated by the bp-DNN. The objective function $\tilde{\ell}^{fp}_{\mathbf{W}_l}$ trains the $\mathbf{W}_l$ so that the output $\mathbf{z}_l$ of this hidden layer is close to the target $-\tilde{\mathbf{o}}_l$ in cosinc distance metric. The fp-DNN is going to map to information of the output label $\mathbf{y}$ layer by layer during the training process, with the supervision of bp-DNN. As a result, fp-DNN could be interpreted as acting the role of the encoder, encoding the information of input $\mathbf{x}$ into the information of label signal $\mathbf{y}$.

3.2 Direct Loss Function for Hidden Layer of bp-DNN

Similar to the definition of direct loss function of fp-DNN, we define the direct loss function of bp-DNN to have the same gradient w.r.t. $\mathbf{W}_l$.

$$\tilde{\ell}^{bp}_{\mathbf{W}_l}(-\tilde{\mathbf{o}}_l, \mathbf{o}_{l-1}) = -\mathbf{o}^T_{l-1}(\mathbf{W}^T_l\tilde{\mathbf{o}}_l) \tag{9}$$

$$\min_{\mathbf{W}_l} \ell_{\Theta}(\mathbf{x}, \mathbf{y}) \equiv \max_{\mathbf{W}_l} \tilde{\ell}^{bp}_{\mathbf{W}_l}(-\tilde{\mathbf{o}}_l, \mathbf{o}_{l-1}) \tag{10}$$

Comparing to Eq. (6), It's a symmetric form of $\tilde{\ell}^{fp}_{\mathbf{W}_l}(\mathbf{o}_{l-1}, -\tilde{\mathbf{o}}_l)$. $\tilde{\ell}^{bp}_{\mathbf{W}_l}(-\tilde{\mathbf{o}}_l, \mathbf{o}_{l-1})$ also defines a metric based on the cosine distance between $\mathbf{o}_{l-1}$ and $-\tilde{\mathbf{z}}_{l-1} = -\mathbf{W}_l\tilde{\mathbf{o}}_l$. It minimizes the angle of these two vectors. On example is shown in Fig. 3(b).

In conclusion, the direct loss function for the lth hidden layer of bp-DNN is $\tilde{\ell}^{bp}_{\mathbf{W}_l}(-\tilde{\mathbf{o}}_l, \mathbf{o}_{l-1})$, which use a target $\mathbf{o}_{l-1}$ generated by the fp-DNN. The objective function $\tilde{\ell}^{bp}_{\mathbf{W}_l}$ trains the $\mathbf{W}_l$ so that the output $-\tilde{\mathbf{z}}_{l-1}$ of this hidden layer is close to the target $\mathbf{o}_{l-1}$ in cosine distance metric. The bp-DNN is going to reconstruct the information of the input signal $\mathbf{x}$ layer by layer during the training process, with the supervision of fp-DNN. As a result, bp-DNN could be interpreted as acting the role of decoder, decoding the information of label $\mathbf{y}$ into the information of input signal $\mathbf{x}$.

3.3 Interpretation of Forward-Propagation and Back-Propagation

As discussion above, we first interpret the forward-propagation and back-propagation of DNN to be corresponding to two network structures, fp-DNN and bp-DNN. Using the direct loss function for hidden layers of fp-DNN and bp-DNN, we further interpret training process of DNN as the process of collaboration of training the encoder and decoder, i.e., the targets generated by bp-DNN (decoder) supervises the training of fp-DNN (encoder), while the targets generated by fp-DNN supervises the training of bp-DNN, see Fig. 2 for specification. The structures of this interpretation shows a similar form as the stacked auto-encoder [4], both with the encoder and decoder network structures. However, the major difference between our interpretation and stacked auto-encoder is that the input signal for the decoder. The input signal for decoder of stacked auto-encoder is the code $\mathbf{p}$ generated by encoder, while the input signal for the decoder (bp-DNN) of our interpretation contains the label information, $\mathbf{p} - \mathbf{y}$. With the supervision of label information, the encoder (fp-DNN) of our interpretation learns to encode the discriminant features, while encoder of stacked auto-encoder learns to encode features with maximum information for reconstruction.

This interpretation could help us understand the training process of DNN. For example, by analyzing the distribution of the targets $\tilde{o}_l$ generated by bp-DNN, we can know how the bp-DNN guides the fp-DNN to encode discriminant features layer by layer; by analyzing the reconstruction of input signal $\mathbf{x}$ from the bp-DNN, we can learn what the network have learned. In next section, we use this interpretation of DNN to do some analyses.

4 Experiments

We designed a DNN with six layers, denoted as DNN-6, of which all layers are fully connection layers. The number of output channels of each hidden layers of DNN-6 is set as 100, and we use ReLU as the non-linear activation function. We train DNN-6 on MNIST [11] digits dataset and use it to show the collaboration of training process of the encoder and decoder. We train DNN-6 for totally 10000 iterations, with batch size as 64. The final accuracy of DNN-6 on the test set of MNIST is 97.51%.

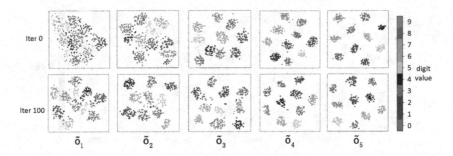

Fig. 4. In the 0th and 100th iteration, the targets $\tilde{o}_l$ generated by bp-DNN have the discriminant property. This shows that targets generated by bp-DNN preserve the discriminant property of label information during training. Here, points with the same color come from the same category, e.g., red points belong to the category of digit 0. (Color figure online)

4.1 Explanation of the Encoder (fp-DNN)

Why fp-DNN learns to encode discriminant features? We think the reason is that the targets generated by bp-DNN, which supervise the training of fp-DNN, are discriminant. In this discussion, we conduct experiments to verify the targets generated by bp-DNN are discriminant, even when the weights of bp-DNN are initialized randomly.

The direct loss function for fp-DNN is $\tilde{\ell}^{fp}_{\mathbf{W}_l}(\mathbf{o}_{l-1}, -\tilde{\mathbf{o}}_l) = -\tilde{\mathbf{o}}_l^T(\mathbf{W}_l\mathbf{o}_{l-1} + \mathbf{b}_l)$, where $\tilde{\mathbf{o}}_l$ is the supervised information generated by bp-DNN and $\mathbf{z}_l = \mathbf{W}_l\mathbf{o}_{l-1} + \mathbf{b}_l$ is the learned encoded features of fp-DNN. Since the fp-DNN is supervised by the bn-DNN, analyzing the properties of the target $\tilde{\mathbf{o}}_l$ generated by the bp-DNN can tell us what a kind of fp-DNN will be trained using bp-DNN as supervisor. The input of bp-DNN is the label information $\mathbf{p}-\mathbf{y}$, so the target $\tilde{\mathbf{o}}_l$ generated by bp-DNN is a function of the label information. As we know, the most important property of label information is the discriminant property. Here we want to use the t-SNE [15] technique to visualize the target $\tilde{\mathbf{o}}_l$ to explore whether $\tilde{\mathbf{o}}_l$ preserve the discriminant property of label information $\mathbf{p} - \mathbf{y}$. We use the DNN-6 to generate the corresponding bp-DNN and fp-DNN, and use them to extract the target $\tilde{\mathbf{o}}_l$ and the encoded feature $\mathbf{z}_l$.

First, we will conduct experiments that to show the $\tilde{\mathbf{o}}_l$ preserve the discriminant property of label information during training.

Then we further visualize the distribution of the encoded feature $\mathbf{z}_l$, to verify that the encoded features are discriminant under the supervision of the discriminant target $\tilde{\mathbf{o}}_l$ generated by bp-DNN.

Since the direct loss function is based on the cosine distance metric, we also set the distance metric of t-SNE as cosine distance metric for reducing dimension.

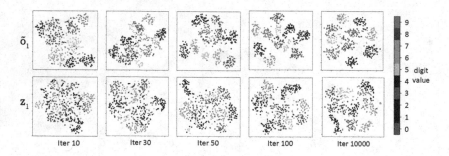

Fig. 5. The learned feature $\mathbf{z}_1$ of fp-DNN is going to be more discriminant during the training, under the supervision of the discriminant target $\tilde{\mathbf{o}}_1$. Finally, the distribution of $\mathbf{z}_1$ is close to the distribution of $\tilde{\mathbf{o}}_1$ in the iteration 10000.

Visualize the Discriminant Target $\tilde{\mathbf{o}}_l$. This experiment is to show that the target $\tilde{\mathbf{o}}_l$ generated by bp-DNN is discriminant in varying degrees. We visualize the $\tilde{\mathbf{o}}_l, l = 1, \cdots, 5$ in the 2D plane, using t-SNE to reduce dimension, as showing in Fig. 4. In Fig. 4, we show the distribution of the target of 5 layers, with $l = 1, \cdots, 5$, with the first column showing the distribution of the target of $l = 1$th layer, the second column showing the distribution of the target of the $l = 2$th layer and so on. We also show the distribution of the target in different training iteration, and specifically, we show the distribution in 0th iteration and the 100th iteration. More distributions in other iterations are not shown for the limitation of paper length, but we are sure that distribution in other iterations shows consistent agreements with those in the 0th iteration and 100th iteration.

In Fig. 4, points with the same colour are in the same category. The points in the same cluster are more close to each other, then the distribution of these points are more discriminant. From the visualization in Fig. 4, we have such observation,

First, the target $\tilde{o}_l$ generated from bp-DNN does have the discriminant property for all layers $l = 1, \cdots, 5$. But the degree of discriminant properties of each layer are varying, where the distribution of target in higher layers ($l \geq 3$) seems more discriminant than that of bottom layers ($l \leq 3$).

Second, the discriminant property is preserved during training, for example, in the iteration 100, $\tilde{o}_l$ preserve the discriminant property as well, as Fig. 4 showing. Specifically, after training, the target has the trends to be more discriminant. For example, the targets $\tilde{o}_1$ and $\tilde{o}_2$ in 100th iteration are more discriminant than those in the 0th iteration.

In conclusion, the targets generated by bp-DNN preserve the discriminant property of label information in varying degrees. Naturally, the encoded feature z_l of fp-DNN is expected to be discriminant after training, since it's supervisor is discriminant. Next, we conduct experiments to visualize the encoded features to verify this assumption.

Visualize the Discriminant Feature z_l. First, we show the encoded features z_1 in the first layer during the training iteration 10, 30, 50, 100 and 10000, as showing in the second row of Fig. 5. For comparison, we show the corresponding targets $\tilde{o}_1$ for supervision in the first row of Fig. 5. In Fig. 5, the distribution of the learned features z_1 becomes more and more discriminant during the training. When the training iteration is finished, the learned feature z_1 run into a distribution similar to the target $\tilde{o}_l$. Specifically, in iteration 10000, the distribution of z_1 achieves a similar degree of discriminant property as the distribution of $\tilde{o}_1$. The fp-DNN does learn to encode the input signal to a feature space with discriminant property.

Then, in the second row of Fig. 6, we show the distribution of $z_l, l = 1, \cdots, 5$ after training for 10000 iteration. For comparison, the corresponding distribution of $z_l, l = 1, \cdots, 5$ in the iteration 0 is shown in the first row of Fig. 6, which are far from discriminant. Comparing to the distribution of $z_l, l = 1, \cdots, 5$ in iteration 0, the distribution of $z_l, l = 1, \cdots, 5$ in iteration 10000 does show the discriminant property as Fig. 6 showing. And we think that the reason of fp-DNN learning discriminant features in hidden layer is the target generated by

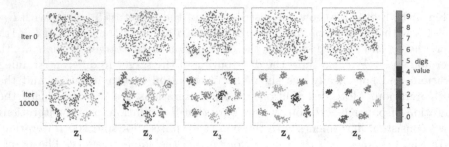

Fig. 6. Before training, features of fp-DNN don't have discriminant property. After training, features of all hidden layers of fp-DNN have varying degrees of discriminant property. This is because fp-DNN learns to encode features under the supervision of discriminant targets generated by bp-DNN.

bp-DNN, which preserve the discriminant property and supervise the fp-DNN to learn discriminant features.

4.2   Explanation of the Decoder (bp-DNN)

Since bp-DNN is a decoder network, we can use bp-DNN to map $\mathbf{y}$ back into the input signal space $\hat{\mathbf{x}}$. By visualizing the reconstruction $\hat{\mathbf{x}}$, we can know which part of $\mathbf{x}$ is important for the DNN to recognize that it belongs to the category $\mathbf{y}$. However, the direct reconstruction loss function of bp-DNN is to train $\mathbf{W}_l$ to reconstruct all training samples $\mathbf{o}_{l-1}$ as much as possible. This leads the reconstruction to be an average version of $\mathbf{o}_{l-1}$ and not only relative to the specific input signal $\mathbf{x}$. An average version of $\mathbf{o}_{l-1}$ could be a bad visualization for human.

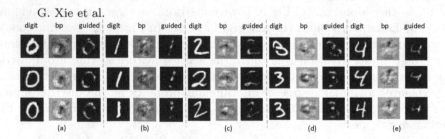

Fig. 7. Visualization using guided-bp-DNN could show clearly which parts of the digit images are important for DNN to recognize, while visualization of bp-DNN is not clear and hard to read.

To only visualize those reconstructions that are relative to a specific signal $\mathbf{x}_i$, we need to add some constrains. Here, we select the reconstructions that are mostly matched with the input. To achieve this objective, we introduce an indicator to measure the degree of matching between the reconstructed feature $\tilde{z}_{l-1}$ and the feature z_{l-1}, that is, $1_{sign(z_l)=sign(\tilde{z}_l)}$. Let's give an example. If $z_l = [0.5, 0.3, -0.1, -0.2]^T$ and $\tilde{z}_l = [0.5, -0.3, -0.1, 0.2]^T$, the $1_{sign(z_l)=sign(\tilde{z}_l)} = [1, 0, 1, 0]^T$. With the $1_{sign(z_l)=sign(\tilde{z}_l)}$ to measure the degree of matching, we select the reconstructed feature as $\hat{z}_l = 1_{sign(z_l)=sign(\tilde{z}_l)} \odot \tilde{z}_l$. The bp-DNN could be modified as, denoted as guided-bp-DNN,

$$
\text{Guided-bp-DNN} = \begin{cases} \tilde{z}_L = y \\ \tilde{z}_{L-1} = W_L^T \tilde{z}_L \\ \hat{z}_l = 1_{sign(z_l)=sign(\tilde{z}_l)} \odot \tilde{z}_l, l \geq 0 \\ \tilde{z}_{l-1} = W_l^T(\hat{z}_l \odot \tilde{b}_l), L-1 \geq l \geq 1 \end{cases} \tag{11}
$$

We will give experiments to show the advantages of guided-bp-DNN for visualization. By the way, when using ReLU as non-linear activation function, guided-bp-DNN is the same as the guided-Back-Propagation proposed in paper [21] for visualization. That is, guided-Back-Propagation is a specific case of our guided-bp-DNN.

Comparison Between bp-DNN and Guided-bp-DNN. We use DNN-6 for visualization on the MNIST. In Fig. 7, we show the visualization results using bp-DNN and guided-bp-DNN respectively, showing the visualization results of five digits $(0, 1, 2, 3, 4)$, each digit with three instances. The first column shows the origin images of the digit, while the second column and third column shows the visualization results using bp-DNN and guided-bp-DNN respectively. From Fig. 7, we can be found that the visualization results of bp-DNN could be a mess and hard for us to understand. Only the visualization of digit 1 and digit 3 could be recognized to has a shape of digit 1 and digit 3. As mentioned previously, this mess is caused by the fact that bp-DNN is trained to reconstruct an average version of all training samples.

On the contrary, guided-bp-DNN use $1_{sign(z_l)=sign(\tilde{z}_l)}$ to guide the reconstruction to be close to the specific input signal. The visualization of guided-bp-DNN in Fig. 7 could be readably for human. In Fig. 7, The highlight in visualization of guided-bp-DNN shows that the part of the digit covering by the highlight is an important pattern for the DNN to recognize this digit. In next section, we use guided-bp-DNN to analyze what DNN have learned to recognize the digit.

What Patterns are Important for DNN to Recognize? In Fig. 8, we use guided-bp-DNN to visualize what part of the digit the DNN think is important to recognize. In Fig. 8, the column 'digit' is the origin image of those digits, and the column 'guided' is the visualization results of guided-bp-DNN. In the origin images of digits, we use a green/red box to mark out the part that is highlighted by the guided-bp-DNN visualization. In Fig. 8, we show two types of patterns that is important to recognize digits. One is the intersection part where two or more strokes intersect, which is marked with red box in Fig. 8. The other is the

Fig. 8. Through the visualization using guided-bp-DNN, we found that two types of patterns are important for DNN to recognize digits, i.e., the intersection parts of strokes (red box) and the turning parts of strokes (green box). These two types of patterns contain rich information for recognition. (Color figure online)

turning part where the strokes change the direction suddenly, which is marked with green box. The DNN learns these two types of patterns to recognize digits is reasonable, because there are rich information in the intersection parts and the turning parts.

5 Conclusion

We proposed an interpretation of DNN into two networks structures, fp-DNN and bp-DNN. By introducing direct loss function for hidden layers of fp-DNN and bp-DNN, fp-DNN could be interpreted to act as a role of encoder while bp-DNN acts as a role of decoder. Using this interpretation, we could explain how DNN learn discriminant features in the hidden layer. We also use the proposed guided-bp-DNN to analyze what have learned in DNN.

Acknowledgments. This project is supported by the Natural Science Foundation of China (61573387) and Guangdong Project (2017B030306018).

References

1. An, S., Boussaid, F., Bennamoun, M., Hu, J.: From deep to shallow: transformations of deep rectifier networks. arXiv preprint arXiv:1703.10355 (2017)
2. Arik, S.O., et al.: Deep voice: real-time neural text-to-speech. arXiv preprint arXiv:1702.07825 (2017)
3. Bengio, Y.: How auto-encoders could provide credit assignment in deep networks via target propagation. arXiv preprint arXiv:1407.7906 (2014)
4. Bengio, Y., et al.: Learning deep architectures for Ai. Found. Trends® Mach. Learn. **2**(1), 1–127 (2009)
5. Cortes, C., Vapnik, V.: Support-vector networks. Mach. Learn. **20**(3), 273–297 (1995)
6. He, K., Zhang, X., Ren, S., Sun, J.: Deep residual learning for image recognition. arXiv preprint arXiv:1512.03385 (2015)

7. He, K., Zhang, X., Ren, S., Sun, J.: Delving deep into rectifiers: surpassing human-level performance on imagenet classification. In: Proceedings of the IEEE International Conference on Computer Vision, pp. 1026–1034 (2015)
8. Joulin, A., Grave, E., Bojanowski, P., Douze, M., Jégou, H., Mikolov, T.: Fast-text.zip: compressing text classification models. arXiv preprint arXiv:1612.03651 (2016)
9. Koh, P.W., Liang, P.: Understanding black-box predictions via influence functions. arXiv preprint arXiv:1703.04730 (2017)
10. Krizhevsky, A., Sutskever, I., Hinton, G.E.: ImageNet classification with deep convolutional neural networks. In: Advances in Neural Information Processing Systems, pp. 1097–1105 (2012)
11. LeCun, Y., Bottou, L., Bengio, Y., Haffner, P.: Gradient-based learning applied to document recognition. Proc. IEEE **86**(11), 2278–2324 (1998)
12. Lee, D.-H., Zhang, S., Fischer, A., Bengio, Y.: Difference target propagation. In: Appice, A., Rodrigues, P.P., Santos Costa, V., Soares, C., Gama, J., Jorge, A. (eds.) ECML PKDD 2015. LNCS (LNAI), vol. 9284, pp. 498–515. Springer, Cham (2015). https://doi.org/10.1007/978-3-319-23528-8_31
13. Levine, S., Pastor, P., Krizhevsky, A., Ibarz, J., Quillen, D.: Learning hand-eye coordination for robotic grasping with deep learning and large-scale data collection. Int. J. Robot. Res. **37**, 421–436 (2016). https://doi.org/10.1177/0278364917710318
14. Lillicrap, T.P., Cownden, D., Tweed, D.B., Akerman, C.J.: Random feedback weights support learning in deep neural networks. arXiv preprint arXiv:1411.0247 (2014)
15. van der Maaten, L., Hinton, G.: Visualizing data using t-SNE. J. Mach. Learn. Res. **9**(Nov), 2579–2605 (2008)
16. Nøkland, A.: Direct feedback alignment provides learning in deep neural networks. In: Advances in Neural Information Processing Systems, pp. 1037–1045 (2016)
17. Pei, K., Cao, Y., Yang, J., Jana, S.: Deepxplore: automated whitebox testing of deep learning systems. In: Proceedings of the 26th Symposium on Operating Systems Principles, pp. 1–18. ACM (2017)
18. Redmon, J., Farhadi, A.: Yolo9000: better, faster, stronger. arXiv preprint arXiv:1612.08242 (2016)
19. Scellier, B., Bengio, Y.: Equilibrium propagation: bridging the gap between energy-based models and backpropagation. Front. Comput. Neurosci. **11**, 24 (2017)
20. Shwartz-Ziv, R., Tishby, N.: Opening the black box of deep neural networks via information. arXiv preprint arXiv:1703.00810 (2017)
21. Springenberg, J.T., Dosovitskiy, A., Brox, T., Riedmiller, M.: Striving for simplicity: the all convolutional net. arXiv preprint arXiv:1412.6806 (2014)

Multi-attention Guided Activation Propagation in CNNs

Xiangteng He and Yuxin Peng[(⊠)]

Institute of Computer Science and Technology, Peking University, Beijing, China
pengyuxin@pku.edu.cn

Abstract. CNNs compute the activations of feature maps and propagate them through the networks. Activations carry various information with different impacts on the prediction, thus should be handled with different degrees. However, existing CNNs usually process them identically. Visual attention mechanism focuses on the selection of regions of interest and the control of information flow through the network. Therefore, we propose a multi-attention guided activation propagation approach (MAAP), which can be applied into existing CNNs to promote their performance. Attention maps are first computed based on the activations of feature maps, vary as the propagation goes deeper and focus on different regions of interest in the feature maps. Then multi-level attention is utilized to guide the activation propagation, giving CNNs the ability to adaptively highlight pivotal information and weaken uncorrelated information. Experimental results on fine-grained image classification benchmark demonstrate that the applications of MAAP achieve better performance than state-of-the-art CNNs.

Keywords: Multiple attention · Activation propagation
Convolutional Neural Networks

1 Introduction

Neural networks have advanced the state of the art in many domains, such as computer vision, speech recognition and natural language processing. Convolutional Neural Networks (CNNs) [1], one type of the popular and classical neural networks, have been widely used in computer vision due to its strong power in feature learning, and have achieved state-of-the-art performance in image classification [2], object detection [3], semantic segmentation [4] and so on.

Recent advances of CNNs focus on designing deeper neural network structure, which promote the performance of image classification. In 2012, Krizhevsky et al. designed an 8-layer convolutional neural network, called AlexNet [5], which contains 5 convolutional layers and 3 fully-connected layers. In 2014, VGGNet [2] was designed and its depth was increased to 16/19 layers by using an architecture with very small (3 × 3) convolutional filters, which achieved significant

© Springer Nature Switzerland AG 2018
J.-H. Lai et al. (Eds.): PRCV 2018, LNCS 11257, pp. 16–27, 2018.
https://doi.org/10.1007/978-3-030-03335-4_2

improvement on image classification. In 2016, He et al. designed a residual network with the depth of up to 152 layers, 8 times deeper than VGGNet, called ResNet [6], which also had a 1000-layer version.

These popular CNNs take images as inputs, conduct convolutional operation on each pixel, compute the activations of feature maps and propagate the activations through the networks layer by layer. Activations carry various information with different impacts on prediction, thus should be handled with different degrees of attention. However, existing CNNs usually process the activations identically in the propagation process, leading to the fact that the pivotal information is not highlighted and the uncorrelated information is not weakened, which is contradictory with visual attention mechanism that pays high attention to pivotal information, such as regions of interest. For addressing above problems, an intuitive idea is to adaptively highlight or weaken the activations based on their importance degrees for final prediction. The importance degree can be defined as attention.

Attention is a behavioral and cognitive process of selectively concentrating on a discrete aspect of information [7]. Tsotsos et al. state that visual attention mechanism seems to involve at least the following basic components [8]: (1) the selection of regions of interest in the visual field, (2) the selection of feature dimensions and values of interest and (3) the control of information flow through the network. Therefore, we apply visual attention mechanism to guide the activation propagation in CNNs, selecting the activations of interest and feature values of interest, as well as controlling the activation propagation through the network based on the attention. Karklin et al. indicate that neurons in primary visual cortex (V1) respond to the edge over a range of positions, and neurons in higher visual areas, such as V2 and V4, are more invariant to image properties and might encode shape [9]. According to the studies on visual attention mechanism, different level attentions focus on different attributes of objects.

Inspired by these discoveries about visual attention mechanism, we propose a multi-attention guided activation propagation approach (MAAP), which can be applied into existing CNNs to improve the performance, and give CNNs the ability to adaptively highlight pivotal information and weaken uncorrelated information. The main contributions of the proposed approach can be summarized as follows:

(i) **Low-level Attention Guided Activation Propagation (LAAP).** Neurons in primary visual cortex (V1) respond to the edge over a range of positions, which is significant for discovering the shape of the object. Inspired by this discovery, we first extract the attention map based on the activations of feature maps output from the first convolutional layer as the low-level attention, and then guide the activation propagation based on the low-level attention, enhancing the pivotal activations that carry key information such as the edge of the object. Low-level attention guided activation propagation feeds such key information forward to the high-level convolutional layer, which helps to localize the object as well as learn discriminative features.

(ii) **High-level Attention Guided Activation Propagation (HAAP).**
Neurons in higher visual areas (V2 and V4) might encode shape, which is
significant for recognition. Inspired by this discovery, we first extract the
attention map output from high-level convolutional layer, and then apply
the high-level attention to guide the activation propagation, preserving
the pivotal activations that carry key information such as the object and
removing the uncorrelated activations that carry less significant information such as background noise. Then we feedback the activations to the
input data to eliminate the background noise, which carries uncorrelated
information. High-level attention guide activation propagation to feed activations backward to the input data, which finds the region of interest and
boosts discriminative feature learning.

(iii) **Multi-level Attention Activation Propagation (MAAP).** Low-level
attention and high-level attention jointly guide activation propagation in
CNNs to promote the discriminative feature learning, and enhance their
mutual promotions to achieve better performance. The two activation propagation strategies have different but complementary focuses: LAAP focuses
on enhancing the pivotal activations, while HAAP focuses on reducing the
uncorrelated activations. With the guide of multi-level attention, activations are propagated through CNNs with different weights, where the key
information is enhanced through the forward propagation and the uncorrelated information is removed through the backward propagation, which
boost the performance of CNNs.

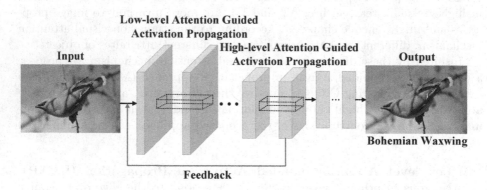

Fig. 1. Overview of the multi-attention guided activation propagation approach.

2 Multi-attention Guided Activation Propagation

Researchers state discovery of visual attention mechanism: different level visual
areas of cerebral cortex concentrate on different aspects of the visual information
[10]. Like neurons in V1 and V2 respond to the edge and shape of the object

respectively [9], neurons in convolutional layers have similar functions. For example, neurons in low-level convolutional layers focus on the edge of the object and neurons in high-level convolutional layers pay attention to the shape of the object. Inspired by this discovery, we propose a multi-attention guided activation propagation approach (MAAP), applying the low-level and high-level visual attention into activation propagation, which can be inserted into the CNNs, and its overview is shown in Fig. 1.

For a CNN, in the training phase: (1) We adopt the low-level attention guided activation propagation (LAAP) after the first convolutional layer to give the activations variant weights based on their attention values. (2) We employ the high-level attention guided activation propagation (HAAP) after the last convolutional layer, and feedback the activations to the input data, which is to drop the background noise and preserve the region of interest at the same time. (3) We utilize alternative training strategy to train the CNNs with LAAP and HAAP. The three components are presented in the following paragraphs. The high-level attention is performed on the input data, and frequent data modification is time-consuming and not sensible, so only LAAP is adopted in the testing phase.

2.1 Low-Level Attention Guided Activation Propagation

Neurons in convolutional layers have higher activation to some specific spatial positions of the input data, and have the pattern that focusing on the significant and discriminative features which is help for recognizing the image. We extract the feature maps from some specific convolutional layers in the widely-used CNN, e.g. VGGNet [2], and visualize their average feature map in Fig. 2. We can observe that: (1) Low-level convolutional layer focuses on the edge of the object just like neurons in primary visual cortex (V1). (2) Average feature map generated from middle-level convolutional layers has some noises, which are not helpful for recognition.

Therefore, we consider enhancing the significance of the key information, such as the edge shown in the sub figure of "Conv1_1" in Fig. 2. An intuitive idea is to give the pivotal activations with higher weights. We propose low-level

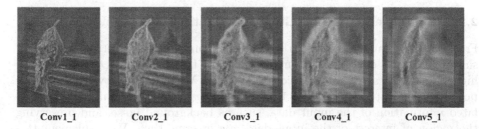

| Conv1_1   Conv2_1   Conv3_1   Conv4_1   Conv5_1 |

Fig. 2. Visualization of average feature maps in convolutional layers. "Conv1_1" to "Conv5_1" indicate the name of the convolutional layers in VGGNet [2].

attention activation propagation approach, which consists of attention extraction and activation enhancement. The detailed processing is shown in Fig. 3.

Attention Extraction. For a given image I, we first extract its feature maps $F = \{F_1, F_2, \ldots, F_n\}$ from the first convolutional layer in the CNN, such as AlexNet [5], VGGNet [2] and ResNet [6]. n indicates the number of neurons in this convolutional layers, and F_n indicates the feature map extracted from the first convolutional layer responding to the n-th neuron. Each feature map is a 2D matrix with the size of $mh \times mw$. Then we calculate their average feature map, denoted as FA, its definition is:

$$FA = \frac{1}{n}\sum_{1}^{n} F_i \tag{1}$$

For each element in the average feature map FA, we perform sigmoid function to normalize it to the range of $[0, 1]$. Then we get the attention map, where the element indicates the importance of each activation in the feature maps to the recognition. Each element in attention map A is calculated as follows:

$$A_{i,j} = \frac{1}{1 + e^{-FA_{i,j}}} \tag{2}$$

where i and j indicate the spatial position of element in the attention map A.

Activation Enhancement. After generating the attention map A, we apply it to guide the activation propagation. For each feature map $F_i \in F$, we calculate the new feature map F_i' based on the attention map as follows:

$$F_i' = (1 + A) * F_i \tag{3}$$

where $*$ denotes element wise product. Through the activation enhancement manipulation, we infuse the attention information to the feature outputs of convolutional layer, in order to guide the feature learning processing by highlighting the pivotal activations.

2.2   High-Level Attention Guided Activation Propagation

From Fig. 2 we can observe that the high-level convolutional layer (as "Conv5_1" shown in Fig. 2) concentrates on the shape of the whole-object, just like the higher visual areas of cerebral cortex (V2 and V4). Inspired by this, we propose high-level attention guided activation propagation, dropping the uncorrelated information of the input data, such as background noise, and preserving the region of interest of the input data at the same time. We implement this through attention extraction and activation elimination, which are presented in the following paragraphs.

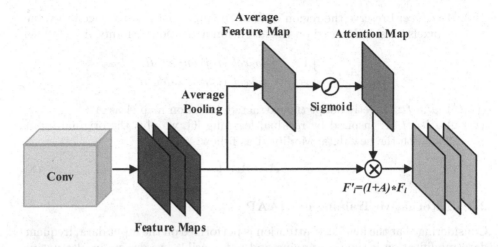

Fig. 3. Overview of low-level attention guided activation propagation approach.

Attention Extraction. The attention extraction is the same with the process in LAAP. First, we extract the attention map A from the last convolutional layer. Second, we perform binarization operation on the attention map with an adaptive threshold, which is obtained by OTSU algorithm [11], and take the bounding box that covers the largest connected region as the discriminative region R.

Activation Elimination. We propagate the attention activation backward to modify the input data D to the new data D^* as follows:

$$D_i^* = A^* * D_i \tag{4}$$

where i indicates the i-th channel of the input data. We experiment with 6 definitions of A^*:

(i) *A-RoI*: Retrain the region of R and remove the uncorrelated region.
(ii) *A-uncorrelated*: Set values of pixels outside the region of R as 0. Modify A as follow:

$$A_{i,j} = \begin{cases} 1 & , \ pixel \ (i,j) \ inside \ R \\ 0 & , \ pixel \ (i,j) \ outside \ R \end{cases} \tag{5}$$

(iii) *A-enhance*: Enhance the region of R in the input data and set values of pixels outside R as 0. Modify A as follow:

$$A_{i,j} = \begin{cases} A_{i,j} + 1 & , \ pixel \ (i,j) \ inside \ R \\ 0 & , \ pixel \ (i,j) \ outside \ R \end{cases} \tag{6}$$

(iv) *A-reduce*: Preserve the region of R in the input data and reduce the value of pixels outside R based on the attention activations. Modify A as follow:

$$A_{i,j} = \begin{cases} 1 & , \; pixel \; (i,j) \; inside \; R \\ A_{i,j} & , \; pixel \; (i,j) \; outside \; R \end{cases} \tag{7}$$

(v) *A-allsoft*: Directly adopt the extracted attention map A as A^*.

(vi) *A-allsoft*+1: Inspired by residual learning [6], we plus the original input data with the new data. Modify A as follow:

$$A = A + 1 \tag{8}$$

2.3   Alternative Training of MAAP

Considering that the high-level attention is performed on the input data, frequent data modification is time-consuming and not sensible, we design an alternative training strategy for the application of MAAP in CNNs, which is described as Algorithm 1.

Algorithm 1. Alternative Training

Input: Training data D, maximal iterative epoch it_m.
Output: Trained CNN model N.
 1: Initialize N, such as pre-training on the large scale dataset, ImageNet [12].
 2: **for** $epoch = 1, ..., it_m$ **do**
 3:    Compute attention map A and feature maps F of first convolutional layer.
 4:    Modify feature maps F as formula (3).
 5:    Perform a feed-forward pass.
 6:    Compute the loss and perform back-propagate manipulation.
 7:    **if** loss is converged **then**
 8:        Stop this phase of training.
 9:    **end if**
10: **end for**
11: Perform feed-forward pass to compute attention map A of last convolutional layer.

12: Modify input data D as formula (4).
13: Repeat 2 to 10.
14: **return** N.

---

3   Experiments

Fine-grained image classification task aims to recognize hundreds of subcategories belonging to the same basic-level category, such as 200 subcategories belonging to the category of bird. It is a challenging task due to the large variances in the same subcategory and small variances among different similar subcategories. It covers a lot of domains, such as animal species [13], plant breeds

Table 1. Classification results on CUB-200-2011 dataset.

Method	Accuracy (%)		
	AlexNet	VGGNet	ResNet
Baseline	59.0	72.2	76.0
+LAAP	59.7	72.9	76.4
+HAAP	62.2	78.0	78.1
+MAAP	**63.0**	**78.2**	**78.7**

[14], car types [15] and aircraft models [16]. We choose fine-grained image classification to evaluate the effectiveness of our MAAP approach. We conduct experiments on the widely-used CUB-200-2011 [13] dataset for fine-grained image classification. Accuracy is adopted to evaluate the effectiveness of our proposed approach, which is widely used in fine-grained image classification [17,18].

CUB-200-2011 dataset [13] is the most widely-used dataset in fine-grained image classification task, which contains 11788 images of 200 subcategories belonging to the same basic-level category of bird. It is split into training and test sets, with 5994 images and 5794 images respectively. For each image, detailed annotations are provided: an image-level subcategory label, a bounding box of object, and 15 part locations. In our experiments, only image-level subcategory label is utilized to train the CNNs.

3.1   Implementation

We implement our MAAP approach as two layers: *enhancement layer* and *elimination layer*, which are corresponding to low-level attention guided activation propagation and high-level attention guided activation propagation respectively. We implement the two layers based on the open source framework Caffe[1] [19].

Table 2. Results of adopting dropout in different convolutional layers of AlexNet.

Net	**AlexNet**	conv1	conv2	conv3	conv4	conv5
Accuracy (%)	**59.0**	57.8	58.7	58.7	57.9	58.7

To verify the effectiveness of our proposed MAAP approach, we insert MAAP into the state-of-the-art CNNs: AlexNet with 8 layers [5], VGGNet with 19 layers [2] and ResNet with 152 layers [6]. Following Algorithm 1, it consists of 3 steps in the training phase. (1) Each of these CNNs is pre-trained on the 1.3M training data of ImageNet [12]. (2) We make some modifications for each CNN. In general, for each CNN, we follow the original settings, only incorporate it

---

[1] http://caffe.berkeleyvision.org/.

Table 3. Comparisons of different definitions of A^* in high-level attention guided activation propagation.

Net	AlexNet	**A-RoI**	A-uncorrelated	A-enhance	A-reduce	A-allsoft	A-allsoft+1
Accuracy (%)	59.0	**62.2**	58.2	52.6	59.5	55.3	55.3

with our MAAP approach. Specifically, we make the following modifications: For AlexNet, we insert our implemented enhancement layer after "relu1", resulting in a mapping resolution of 55 × 55. For VGGNet, we insert enhancement layer after "relu1_1", resulting in a mapping resolution of 224 × 224. For ResNet, we insert enhancement layer after "conv1_relu", resulting in a mapping resolution of 112 × 112. And then we fine-tune each CNN on CUB-200-2011 dataset, obtaining the first CNN with enhancement layer. (3) We further insert our implemented elimination layer. For AlexNet, we insert elimination layer after "relu5", resulting in a mapping resolution of 13 × 13. For VGGNet, we insert elimination layer after "relu5_4", resulting in a mapping resolution of 14 × 14. For ResNet, we insert elimination layer after "res4b2_branch2b_relu", resulting in a mapping resolution of 14 × 14. And then we fine-tune each CNN on CUB-200-2011 dataset. Finally, we obtain the final CNNs.

3.2 Effectiveness of MAAP in State-of-the-Art CNNs

This subsection presents the experimental results and analyses of adopting our MAAP in 3 state-of-the-art CNNs, and analyzes the effectivenesses of the components in our MAAP. Table 1 shows the results of MAAP incorporated with AlexNet, VGGNet and ResNet respectively on CUB-200-2011 dataset. From the experimental results, we can observe:

(i) The application of low-level attention guided activation propagation (LAAP) improves the classification accuracy via enhancing the pivotal information in the forward propagation to help the high-level convolutional layers learn the shape of the object, which boosts the discriminative feature learning. Compared with the results of CNNs themselves, without adopting our proposed MAAP approach, LAAP improves 0.7%, 0.7%, and 0.4% respectively.

(ii) The application of high-level attention guided activation propagation (HAAP) improves the classification accuracy, via retaining the region of interest and removing the background noise of the input data at the same time. Comparing with the results of CNNs themselves, HAAP improves 3.2%, 5.8%, and 2.1% respectively.

(iii) Combination of LAAP and HAAP via alternative training achieves more accurate results than only one of them is adopted, e.g. 63.0% vs. 59.7% and 62.2% of AlexNet, which shows the complementarity of LAAP and HAAP. The two activation propagations have different but complementary focuses: LAAP focuses on enhancing the discriminative features, while

HAAP focuses on dropping the background noise. Both of them are jointly employed to boost the discriminative feature learning, and enhance their mutual promotion to achieve the better performance.

3.3 Comparison with Dropout

Low-level attention guided activation propagation can be regarded as weighting activations of feature maps. Dropout [20,21] randomly drops units from the neural networks during training. It can be regarded as weighting activations, which is a special case of low-level attention guided activation propagation with weights equal to 0 or 1. So we present the results of adopting traditional dropout in different convolutional layers of AlexNet in Table 2. For AlexNet, we add dropout layer after "relu1", "relu2", "relu3", "relu4", "relu5" respectively, which are denoted as "conv1" to "conv5" respectively in Table 2. We can observe that no matter where to add dropout layer, the classification accuracy is not improved. It is because that dropout is performed randomly on units, which may lead to that key information is lost in a large probability in convolutional layers. The experimental results of comparison with dropout show that our proposed MAAP is highly useful for improving the performance of CNNs.

3.4 Effectivenesses of A^* in HAAP

In high-level attention guided activation propagation, we conduct experiments with 6 definitions of A^*. From Table 3, we can see that A-RoI and A-$reduce$ bring improvements for classification performance. It is because that they all focus on reducing the impact of background noise and preserving the key information simultaneously. The other definitions retain negative impact of background noise more or less.

4   Conclusion

In this paper, the multi-attention guided activation propagation approach (MAAP) has been proposed to improve the performance of CNNs, which explicitly allows CNNs to adaptively highlight or weaken activations of feature maps in the propagation process. The activation propagation can be inserted into state-of-the-art CNNs, enhancing the key information and dropping the less significant information. Experimental results show that the application of MAAP approach achieves better performance on fine-grained image classification benchmarks than the state-of-the-art CNNs.

The future work lies in two aspects: First, we will adopt the low-level attention to guide the feature learning of higher convolutional layers and vice versa. Second, we will also attempt to apply the attention mechanism to compress the neural networks. Both of them will be employed to further improve the effectiveness and efficiency of CNNs.

Acknowledgments. This work was supported by National Natural Science Foundation of China under Grant 61771025 and Grant 61532005.

References

1. LeCun, Y., Bottou, L., Bengio, Y., Haffner, P.: Gradient-based learning applied to document recognition. In: Proceedings of the IEEE, vol. 86, pp. 2278–2324. IEEE (1998)
2. Simonyan, K., Zisserman, A.: Very deep convolutional networks for large-scale image recognition. arXiv:1409.1556 (2014)
3. Ren, S., He, K., Girshick, R., Sun, J.: Faster R-CNN: towards real-time object detection with region proposal networks. In Advances in Neural Information Processing Systems (NIPS), pp. 91–99 (2015)
4. Liu, X., Xia, T., Wang, J., Lin, Y.: Fully convolutional attention localization networks: efficient attention localization for fine-grained recognition. arXiv:1603.06765 (2016)
5. Krizhevsky, A., Sutskever, I., Hinton, G.E.: Imagenet classification with deep convolutional neural networks. In: Neural Information Processing Systems (NIPS), pp. 1097–1105 (2012)
6. He, K., Zhang, X., Ren, S., Sun, J.: Deep residual learning for image recognition. In: Proceedings of the IEEE Conference on Computer Vision and Pattern Recognition (CVPR), pp. 770–778 (2016)
7. Anderson, J.R.: Cognitive Psychology and Its Implications. WH Freeman/Times Books/Henry Holt & Co., New York (1990)
8. Tsotsos, J.K., Culhane, S.M., Wai, W.Y.K., Lai, Y., Davis, N., Nuflo, F.: Modeling visual attention via selective tuning. Artif. Intell. **78**(1–2), 507–545 (1995)
9. Karklin, Y., Lewicki, M.S.: Emergence of complex cell properties by learning to generalize in natural scenes. Nature **457**(7225), 83–86 (2009)
10. Zhang, X., Zhaoping, L., Zhou, T., Fang, F.: Neural activities in V1 create a bottom-up saliency map. Neuron **73**(1), 183–192 (2012)
11. Otsu, N.: A threshold selection method from gray-level histograms. IEEE Trans. Syst. Man Cybern. **9**(1), 62–66 (1979)
12. Deng, J., Dong, W., Socher, R., Li, L-J., Li, K., Fei-Fei, L.: ImageNet: a large-scale hierarchical image database. In: Proceedings of the IEEE Conference on Computer Vision and Pattern Recognition (CVPR), pp. 248–255 (2009)
13. Wah, C., Branson, S., Welinder, P., Perona, P., Belongie, S.: The Caltech-UCSD birds-200-2011 dataset (2011)
14. Nilsback, M.E., Zisserman, A.: Automated flower classification over a large number of classes. In: Sixth Indian Conference on Computer Vision, Graphics & Image Processing, pp. 722–729 (2008)
15. Krause, J., Stark, M., Deng, J., Fei-Fei, L.: 3D object representations for fine-grained categorization. In: International Conference of Computer Vision Workshop (ICCV), pp. 554–561 (2013)
16. Maji, S., Rahtu, E., Kannala, J., Blaschko, M., Vedaldi, A.: Fine-grained visual classification of aircraft. arXiv:1306.5151 (2013)
17. He, X., Peng, Y.: Fine-grained image classification via combining vision and language. In: The IEEE Conference on Computer Vision and Pattern Recognition (CVPR), July 2017
18. Fu, J., Zheng, H., Mei, T.: Look closer to see better: recurrent attention convolutional neural network for fine-grained image recognition. In: The IEEE Conference on Computer Vision and Pattern Recognition (CVPR), July 2017
19. Jia, Y., et al.: Caffe: convolutional architecture for fast feature embedding. In: Proceedings of the 22nd ACM International Conference on Multimedia, pp. 675–678. ACM (2014)

20. Hinton, G.E., Srivastava, N., Krizhevsky, A., Sutskever, I., Salakhutdinov, R.R.: Improving neural networks by preventing co-adaptation of feature detectors. arXiv preprint arXiv:1207.0580 (2012)
21. Srivastava, N., Hinton, G.E., Krizhevsky, A., Sutskever, I., Salakhutdinov, R.: Dropout: a simple way to prevent neural networks from overfitting. J. Mach. Learn. Res. **15**(1), 1929–1958 (2014)

GAN and DCN Based Multi-step Supervised Learning for Image Semantic Segmentation

Jie Fang[1,2](✉) and Xiaoqian Cao[3]

[1] Center for OPTical IMagery Analysis and Learning (OPTIMAL),
Xi'an Institute of Optics and Precision Mechanics, Chinese Academy of Sciences,
Xi'an 710119, Shaanxi, People's Republic of China
fangjie2015@opt.cn
[2] University of Chinese Academy of Sciences,
19A Yuquanlu, Beijing 100049, People's Republic of China
[3] College of Electrical and Information Engineering,
Shaanxi University of Science and Technology,
Xi'an 710021, Shaanxi, People's Republic of China
caoxiaoqian@sust.edu.cn

Abstract. Image semantic segmentation contains two sub-tasks, segmenting and labeling. However, the recent *fully convolutional network* (FCN) based methods often ignore the first sub-task and consider it as a direct labeling one. Even though these methods have achieved competitive performances, they obtained spatially fragmented and disconnected outputs. The reason is that, pixel-level relationships inside the deepest layers become inconsistent since traditional FCNs do not have any explicit pixel grouping mechanism. To address this problem, a multi-step supervised learning method, which contains image-level supervised learning step and pixel-level supervised learning step, is proposed. Specifically, as for the visualized result of image semantic segmentation, it is actually an image-to-image transformation problem, from RGB domain to category label domain. The recent *conditional generative adversarial network* (cGAN) has achieved significant performance for image-to-image generation task, and the generated image remains good regional connectivity. Therefore, a cGAN supervised by RGB-category label map is used to obtain a coarse segmentation mask, which avoids generating disconnected segmentation results to a certain extent. Furthermore, an interaction information (II) loss term is proposed for cGAN to remain the spatial structure of the segmentation mask. Additionally, *dilated convolutional networks* (DCNs) have achieved significant performance in object detection field, especially for small objects because of its special receptive field settings. Specific to image semantic segmentation, if each pixel is seen as an object, this task can be transformed to object detection. In this case, combined with the segmentation mask from cGAN, a DCN supervised by the pixel-level label is used to finalize the category recognition of each pixel in the image. The proposed method achieves satisfactory performances on three public and challenging datasets for image semantic segmentation.

© Springer Nature Switzerland AG 2018
J.-H. Lai et al. (Eds.): PRCV 2018, LNCS 11257, pp. 28–40, 2018.
https://doi.org/10.1007/978-3-030-03335-4_3

Keywords: cGAN · DCN · Image semantic segmentation
Multi-step supervised learning

Image semantic segmentation, which aims to parse image into several semantic regions, specifically, attach one of the annotated semantic category labels to each pixel or super-pixel in the image automatically, is an important task for understanding objects in a scene. As a bridge towards high-level tasks, image semantic segmentation is adopted in various applications, such as human pose estimation [11], visual tracking [9], *etc.* Even though remarkable efforts [7, 12, 20] have been made for image semantic segmentation during the past decades, this task is still a challenging problem (Fig. 1).

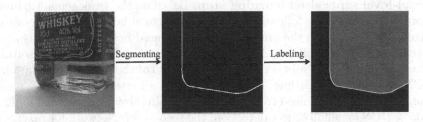

Fig. 1. The task of image semantic segmentation, which includes two steps: segmenting and labeling.

Most recent methods for image semantic segmentation are formulated to solve structured pixel-wise labeling problem on CNNs [1, 14, 21]. These methods convert an existing CNN architecture for classification to a *fully convolutional network* (FCN) [15]. They obtain a coarse label map from the network by classifying each local region in the image, and perform a simple deconvolution for pixel-level labeling. *Conditional random field* (CRF) [24] is optionally applied to output map for better segmentation. The main advantage of the FCN based methods that the network accepts a whole image as an input and performs fast and accurate inference. Adopting the FCN, many present subsequent methods have solved the challenging task to a certain extent and achieved even better performance. However, all of these methods still rely on traditional FCN architecture. As a result, their segmentation maps are spatially fragmented and disconnected, because traditional FCNs do not any explicit pixel grouping mechanism and then pixel-level relationships inside the deepest layers are inconsistent.

Actually, the task of image semantic segmentation includes two sub-tasks: image segmenting and semantic category labeling, the former focus on the relationships among different pixels while the latter emphasizes on the labeling for each pixel. Inspired by the strong image transformation capacity of cGAN [4] and description capacity for small objects of DCN [13], a multi-step supervised learning method is proposed for image semantic segmentation in this paper, which contains image-level and pixel-level supervised learning steps. Specifically, the image-level supervised learning step focus on segmenting while the pixel-level supervised learning step aims to consider the labeling precisely. The details of the proposed method can be described as follows:

– **Image-level supervised learning step.** Category label map is considered as a RGB image, and it is used as the ground truth of the image-level supervision to train the cGAN model for transforming original images to region-based ones. Furthermore, in order to remain the spatial structure information of region-based segmented mask, a novel information interaction (II) loss term is incorporated in the framework, which enhances the pixel-to-pixel interaction through considering the 2-order information of generated map. Actually, because the category label map has only few kinds of colors, the generated image from cGAN owns weak semantic information to a certain extent.
– **Pixel-level supervised learning step.** Based on the weak semantic image from cGAN, a DCN is followed to complete the final label recognition of each pixel or super-pixel in the image. As we introduced before, this part is pixel-level supervision. Similar to FCN, multi convolutional layers and a softmax layer are used in this subtask. However, because of the inherent limitation of FCN aforementioned before, in order to obtain a better segmentation result, the FCN architecture need to be modified. Inspired by the successful application of DCN for small object detection, the second sub-Network for pixel-level supervision learning is builded up with dilated kernels, which can remain the spatial information from original image to predicted category label map well.

Even though the proposed method is introduced as two separated parts, the network guided by our method is still builded as the popular end-to-end fashion. The loss functions of the two sub-Networks are summed as the final loss of the overview network, and the parameters of the two sub-Networks are optimized simultaneously. In summary, the contributions of this work are listed as follows:

1. A multi-step supervised learning based approach is proposed for image semantic segmentation, which divides this challenging task into two much simpler ones, image-level supervised learning (segmenting) and pixel-level supervised learning (labeling).
2. A cGAN is used to generated the weak semantic map of the original image. Additionally, a novel information interaction (II) loss term incorporated to the cGAN framework, which can enhance the global and detail structure information of the generated map.
3. A DCN is used to predict the final semantic category label, which has strong discriminative capacity and can remain the spatial information of the image well.

The rest of paper is organized as follows: In Sect. 1, we introduce the related works to image semantic segmentation. Section 2 describes the proposed method. We report the experiment results in Sect. 3 and conclude the paper in Sect. 4.

1   Related Work

This section details some related works for the task of image semantic segmentation. First of all, we introduce some previous works for image semantic segmentation. Additionally, because generative adversarial network and dilated network are used as the sub-Networks of the proposed method, they are also introduced in this section.

1.1   Previous Works

In the past years, image semantic segmentation has attract a lot attentions, because its wide applications. The recent fully convolutional network (FCN) has led to remarkable results in image semantic segmentation task. However, due to the operation and many pooling layers, the FCN typically suffers from low spatial resolution predictions, which causes inconsistent relationships between the neighboring pixels inside the deepest layers. Recently, there has many attempts to address these problems, all of this subsequent work can be divided into several groups. The works in [2,3] used FCN learned potentials, in the separated globalization framework to refine the original FCN results. The methods in [5,23] integrated a CRF-like inference procedure into their network, which allowed to train such models in an end-to-end fashion and achieve satisfactory performances. Even so, these methods did not fix the core problem, such as the lack of consistent mechanism in the deep layers inside the network.

1.2   Generative Adversarial Network

Generative adversarial networks (GAN) [4] is recently introduced as alternative frameworks for training generative models in order to sidestep the difficulty of approximating many intractable probabilistic computations. Adversarial networks have the advantages that Markov chains are never needed, only the backpropagation is used to obtain gradients, no inference is required during learning, and a wide variety of factors and interactions can easily be incorporated into the model. Furthermore, as demonstrated in [4], it can provide state-of-the-art log-likelihood estimated and realistic samples. In an unconditioned generative model, there is no control on models of the data being generated. However, by conditioning the model on additional information it is possible to direct the data generation process. Such conditioning could be based on class labels, on some part of data for inpainting, or data from different modality.

1.3   Dilated Convolutional Network

Dilated convolution [8,17] was original applied for wavelet decomposition in signal processing. It supports exponential expanding of receptive filed. Yu and Koltun developed a convolutional network for dense prediction in [22], in which dilated convolution was adopted to systematically combine multi-scale contextual information without sacrificing resolution or coverage. The method can be mainly attributed to the expansion of receptive field by dilated convolution, and their work provides a simple yet effective way to enlarge receptive field for CNN. The dilated convolution operator has been referred to in the past as "convolution with a dilated filter". The convolution operator itself is modified to use the parameters in a different way. The dilated convolution operator can apply the same filter as different ranges using different dilation factors, and it enlarges the receptive field without reducing the size of feature map, so it can remain the spatial resolution of image even though many convolutional layers.

2 Proposed Method

This section details the proposed method with two important components, *conditional generative adversarial network* (cGAN) and *dilated convolutional network* (DCN). The cGAN is used to generate the weak semantic map of the image, which considers the category label map as another style of the input image, and this operation is called the image-level supervised learning step. Additionally, based on the generated map from cGAN, The DCN is used to recognize the real semantic category label map of the image while remaining the spatial resolution, which is called the pixel-level supervised learning step. The overview framework of the proposed method is shown in Fig. 2 and the procedures are described as follows:

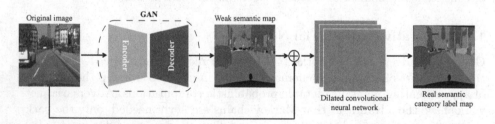

Fig. 2. The overview of the proposed method, including two important components, GAN and dilated convolutional neural network.

- Image-level supervised learning. cGAN equipped with a novel information interaction(II) loss term is used to generate the weak semantic (regional connected) map of original image.
- Pixel-level supervised learning. Combined with the generated weak semantic map from cGAN, a dilated convolutional network is used to recognize the semantic category label of each pixel in the image.
- The aforementioned two supervised learning steps are incorporated into a whole, and the two sub-Networks are optimized simultaneously in an end-to-end way.

2.1 Image-Level Supervised Learning Step

Image-level supervised learning step is mainly to finish the "segmentation" sub-task of the image semantic segmentation. There are many unsupervised methods can complete this subtask, such as cluster and super-pixel-based methods. However, these unsupervised methods are depended on the initial conditions seriously, and the segmentation results are not stable. In this work, we transform segmentation to a generation problem in an appropriate way. Recently, GANs have achieved significant performances for image generation task, especially the successful application of *conditional generative adversarial network* (cGAN), it can transform the image from one style to another very well. Actually, the segmented map is another style of the original image, from a pixel-based one to a region-based one. In this case, cGAN can be used to generate the region based maps with weak semantic information. The loss function of the conditional cGAN used in this paper is shown as Eq. 1.

$$\ell_{cGAN} = \min_{G} \max_{D} \left\{ \mathrm{E}_{x \sim p_d(x)} \left[\log D\left(x\,|y\right) \right] + \mathrm{E}_{z \sim p_z(z)} \left[\log \left(1 - D\left(G\left(z\,|y\right)\right)\right) \right] \right\},$$

$$(1)$$

where G is the generator and D is the discriminator. G tries to minimize this objective against an adversarial D that tries to maximize it. For instance, $G^* = $ arg $\min_{G} \max_{D} L_{cGAN}\left(G, D\right)$.

Additionally, specific to the image segmenting subtask, besides the probability distribution information, spatial structure information should be considered in the proposed model as well. To address this issue, we mixed the cGAN objective with another two loss terms: L_1 distance term and the proposed information interaction (II) loss term. The L_1 and II loss terms are shown as Eqs. 2 and 3 respectively,

$$L_1(G) = \mathrm{E}_{x,y,z} \left[\|y - G\left(x, z\right)\|_1 \right], \tag{2}$$

$$II(G) = \mathrm{E}_{x,y,z} \left[\|y^2 - G^2\left(x, z\right)\|_1 \right], \tag{3}$$

where L_1 is to ensure the 1st-order information of the generated weak semantic map. In other words, it aims to estimate the label of each single pixel accurately as much as possible. II is to ensure the 2nd-order information of the generated weak semantic map. Specifically, as is shown in Fig. 4, corresponding elements in two matrices with small L_1 distance are closer. As for small II distance, besides the accurate single pixel information, the similar relationships among different elements are needed. That is to say, if we incorporate L_1 and II distances in the cGAN loss, the generated map will have the similar intensity and spatial structure information with the groundtruth. Therefore, the final objective the cGAN here is shown as Eq. 4,

$$G^* = \arg \min_{G} \max_{D} \mathrm{E}_{x,y,z} L_{cGAN} + \lambda_1 \cdot L_1 + \lambda_2 \cdot II, \tag{4}$$

where λ_1 and λ_2 are two regulation parameters, which are used to balance the relationships of three loss terms.

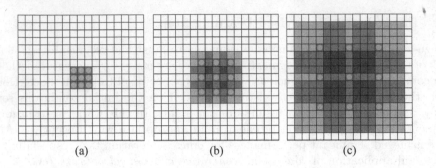

(a)   (b)   (c)

Fig. 3. Different receptive fields with different factors in dilated convolutional neural networks. (a), (b), (c) are 1-dilated, 2-dilated and 3-dilated, respectively, and the receptive field sizes of them are 3×3, 7×7 and 15×15, respectively.

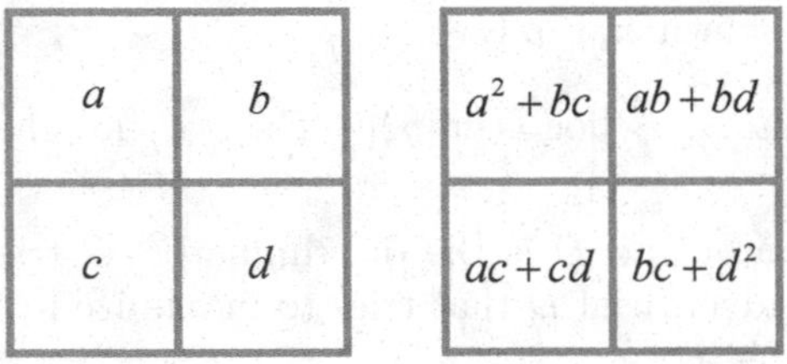

a	b
c	d

$a^2 + bc$	$ab + bd$
$ac + cd$	$bc + d^2$

Fig. 4. *The details of L_1 and II.* Two matrices with small L_1 distance means that corresponding element-pair is close to each other. For instance, the first element in another matrix is close to 'a' if this matrix has small L_1 distance with the left one. Additionally, II is the 2nd-order of the matrix. Two matrices with small II distance means that, their structure interaction information is similar. For example, the first element in another matrix is close to $a^2 + bc$ if this matrix has small II distance with the left one. As can be seen, $a^2 + bc$ not only contains the information of the first element 'a' in the left matrix, but also contains the interaction information of 'b' and 'c'.

2.2   Pixel-Level Supervised Learning Step

Pixel-level supervised learning step is mainly to complete the semantic category labeling subtask of the image semantic segmentation. Most recent methods consider the semantic segmentation task as a direct classification one and they have achieved competitive performance. In order to obtain the global information of the image, traditional CNNs pooling layers to enlarge the receptive field, even though this strategy have gained satisfactory performance for classification and recognition tasks, the experiment results are not in accordance with our expectations when we apply this architecture to semantic segmentation task. Investigate its reasons, the pooling layers result in severe lose spatial information of the image when it enlarge the receptive field by narrowing down the size of the feature map. Even though some FCN-based methods adopt the strategy of pooling-unpooling to make the output of the network has the same size with the original image, the visualized prediction results are still coarse due to the loss of detailed spatial information.

In this paper, to address the problem aforementioned, we use dilated convolutional kernel (Fig. 3) to replace the traditional kernel, which can enlarge the receptive field without narrowing down the size of feature map. Additionally, a softmax layer is followed by several dilated convolutional layers to recognize the category label of each pixel in the image. The loss function is shown as Eq. 5,

$$
L_c = -\frac{1}{n^2}\left[\sum_{i=1}^{n^2}\sum_{j=1}^{k} \mathrm{I}\left\{y^i = j\right\}\log\frac{e^{\theta_j^T x^i}}{\sum_{l=1}^{k} e^{\theta_l^T x^i}}\right],
\tag{5}
$$

where n is the size of the input image, k is the category number of the dataset. y^i and j are the predicted category label and the real category label of i_{th} image respectively. $\mathrm{I}\{\cdot\}$ is the indicator function and θ represents the parameters of the network.

2.3   Network Architecture and Optimization Strategy

The cGAN used in this paper is a traditional encoder-decoder architecture, which has 10 convolutional layers, 5 layers for encoder and the others for decoder. The dilated network contains five dilation convolution layers and a softmax classifier layer. Additionally, the overall loss function for the proposed network is shown as Eq. 6,

$$
\ell = L_{cGAN} + \lambda_1 \cdot L_1 + \lambda_2 \cdot II + \lambda_3 L_c,
\tag{6}
$$

where L_{cGAN} is the loss function of the conditional GAN. L_c is the loss function of the dilated convolutional network. L_1 is the 1-norm distance. II is the proposed interaction information loss term. And λ_1, λ_2 and λ_3 are three formulation parameters to balance these four loss terms. Two sub-Networks used in this paper are optimized simultaneously in an end-to-end fashion.

Implementation: In order to speed up the convergence, we adopted the "separated & combined" training strategy. Specifically, we obtained the initial parameters of cGAN and DCN by training them separately. Then, combined these two sub-Networks together and obtained the final parameters of the model through joint training in an end-to-end way.

3   Experiments

The section details of the experiment, including datasets, experiment settings, contrasting methods, evaluation metrics and results & analysis.

3.1 Datasets

The proposed method is tested on three public and challenging datasets: SIFT Flow [19], NYUDv2 [18] and SIFT Flow [19] and PASCAL VOC 2012 [6].

NYUDv2 is a RGB-D dataset collected using the Microsoft Kinect, and it has 1449 RGB-D images with pixel-wise labels. This dataset is challenging, because the additional depth information increases the structure complexity of the image.

SIFT Flow is a dataset of 2,688 images with pixel labels for 33 semantic classes.

PASCAL VOC 2012 dataset for semantic segmentation includes 2913 label images for 21 semantic categories. Some samples of the dataset is shown in Fig. 5.

Fig. 5. *Samples of the PASCAL VOC2012 dataset.* The dataset consists of 2913 images from 20 classes.

3.2 Experiment Settings

In this paper, we choose 80% images of the dataset to train the network, and use the others to be the testing set. We train the network using mini-batch SGD with patch size 224×224 and batch size 10. The initial learning rate is set to 2.5×10^{-4}, weight decay is set to 5×10^{-4}, momentum is 0.9 and the network is trained for 200 epoches. Additionally, the formulation parameters λ_1, λ_2 and λ_3 are set to 1 in our experiments.

3.3 Contrasting Methods

To verify the effectiveness of the proposed method, four state-of-the-art methods are used as the contrasting methods: FCN8s, Deconv, cGAN and cGAN+DCN.

FCN8s [15] is one version of the original FCN methods, which achieves the best performance in this series because it uses more information from lower layers of the network.

Deconv [16] is a method based on the encoder-decoder architecture, which achieves the satisfactory performance for image semantic segmentation with double parameters compared to FCN8s.

cGAN [10] is a method which uses conditional generative adversarial network to generate a continuous fake "label map", and then discretizes the fake "label map" as the semantic category label of the image.

cGAN + DCN (Ours1) is a method that uses traditional conditional generate adversarial network to generate a weak semantic "label map", then integrates the original image and weak semantic "label" map information by a dilated convolutional network to finalize the category recognition of each pixel in the image. Additionally, this method trains two sub-Networks separately and the II loss term is not used in the image-level supervised step.

3.4 Evaluation Metrics

Pixel classification accuracy (Pix.acc) and mean intersection over union (Mean IoU) are used to verify the methods.

3.5 Results and Analysis

This section details the experiments on NYUDv2 [18], SIFT Flow [19] and PASCAL VOC 2012 [6]. The experiment results are shown in Table 1.

Table 1. Experiment results on three datasets (%).

Dataset	NYUDv2		SIFT flow		PASCAL VOC 2012	
Method	Pix.acc	Mean IoU	Pix.acc	Mean IoU	Pix.acc	Mean IoU
FCN8s [15]	66.84	40.91	85.82	44.75	92.56	66.48
Deconv [16]	68.30	42.78	87.43	45.59	92.84	69.37
cGAN [10]	55.76	37.35	74.82	39.40	67.36	43.55
Ours1	69.52	44.84	88.07	47.28	93.43	72.69
Ours2	**71.35**	**47.06**	**90.53**	**50.21**	**94.18**	**75.82**

From Table 1 we can see that, Deconv method achieves better performance than FCN8s. Specifically, it obtains 1.46% and 1.87% improvement in terms of pixel.acc and mean IoU on NYUDv2 dataset, respectively. The reason is that, compared to FCN8s, Deconv uses a strategy by enlarging the prediction map gradually by a stride of 2 in each step, this avoids the loss of spatial structure information in a certain extent.

Additionally, the results of cGAN method are not satisfactory as we expected. The reason is that, even though the result through descretizing the output of the traditional cGAN have semantic information in a certain extent, it is coarse since no classification mechanism is used in this framework. Compared to the cGAN method, Ours1 (cGAN + DCN) method achieves better performance. For example, Ours1 method obtains surprising 13.25% Pix.acc improvement and 7.88% Mean IoU improvement on SIFT Flow dataset. This is because Ours1 method divides the complex image semantic segmentation into two simpler ones with a multi-step supervised learning ones, segmentation supervised by image-level and category labeling by pixel-level. Specifically, cGAN is used to generate a region-based weak semantic map of the original image, and based on this weak-semantic map, a dilated convolutional network is used to predict the precise category label of each pixel while remaining the spatial information of the original image well. This also demonstrates the importance of classification mechanism for image semantic segmentation task.

Finally, Ours2 method gains better performance than Ours1 method. Specifically, our method achieves 0.75% pix.acc improvement and 3.13% mean IoU improvement on PASCAL VOC 2012 dataset, compared to the Ours1 method. The reason is that, compared to Ours1 method which uses two sub-Networks separately, Ours2 method optimizes two sub-Networks simultaneously, this enhances the joint representation capability of the model. Besides, the novel information interaction (II) loss term is vital for the image-level supervised step, which considers the interaction information among different pixels and makes the structure information more precise.

In general, the proposed method achieves the satisfactory performances, and this demonstrates the effectiveness of the proposed framework for the image semantic segmentation task.

4   Conclusion

In this work, a cGAN and DCN based multi-step supervised learning method is proposed for image semantic segmentation task. Specifically, the cGAN used in image-level supervised learning step is to generate initial weak semantic map, and the DCN used in pixel-level supervised learning step is to finalize the category label recognition of each pixel in the image. Additionally, a novel information interaction (II) loss term is proposed to obtain a segmentation map with more precise spatial structure in image-level supervised learning step. Finally, the experiment results on three public and challenging datasets have verified the rationality and effectiveness of the proposed method.

References

1. Dai, J., He, K., Sun, J.: BoxSup: exploiting bounding boxes to supervise convolutional networks for semantic segmentation, pp. 1635–1643 (2015)
2. Donahue, J., et al.: DeCAF: a deep convolutional activation feature for generic visual recognition. In: International Conference on Machine Learning, p. I-647 (2014)
3. Eigen, D., Puhrsch, C., Fergus, R.: Depth map prediction from a single image using a multi-scale deep network, pp. 2366–2374 (2014)

4. Goodfellow, I.J., et al.: Generative adversarial nets. In: International Conference on Neural Information Processing Systems, pp. 2672–2680 (2014)
5. Gupta, S., Girshick, R., Arbeláez, P., Malik, J.: Learning rich features from RGB-D images for object detection and segmentation. In: Fleet, D., Pajdla, T., Schiele, B., Tuytelaars, T. (eds.) ECCV 2014. LNCS, vol. 8695, pp. 345–360. Springer, Cham (2014). https://doi.org/10.1007/978-3-319-10584-0_23
6. Hariharan, B., Arbelaez, P., Bourdev, L., Maji, S., Malik, J.: Semantic contours from inverse detectors. In: International Conference on Computer Vision, pp. 991–998 (2011)
7. He, Y., Chiu, W.C., Keuper, M., Fritz, M.: STD2P: RGBD semantic segmentation using spatio-temporal data-driven pooling, pp. 7158–7167 (2016)
8. Holschneider, M., Kronland-Martinet, R., Morlet, J., Tchamitchian, P.: A real-time algorithm for signal analysis with the help of the wavelet transform. In: Combes, J.M., Grossmann, A., Tchamitchian, P. (eds.) Wavelets. IPTI, pp. 286–297. Springer, Heidelberg (1990). https://doi.org/10.1007/978-3-642-75988-8_28
9. Hong, S., You, T., Kwak, S., Han, B.: Online tracking by learning discriminative saliency map with convolutional neural network, pp. 597–606 (2015)
10. Isola, P., Zhu, J.Y., Zhou, T., Efros, A.A.: Image-to-image translation with conditional adversarial networks. In: IEEE Conference on Computer Vision and Pattern Recognition, pp. 5967–5976 (2017)
11. Ji, S., Xu, W., Yang, M., Yu, K.: 3d convolutional neural networks for human action recognition. IEEE Trans. Pattern Anal. Mach. Intell. **35**(1), 221 (2013)
12. Kemker, R., Salvaggio, C., Kanan, C.: High-resolution multispectral dataset for semantic segmentation (2017)
13. Li, J., Wu, Y., Zhao, J., Guan, L., Ye, C., Yang, T.: Pedestrian detection with dilated convolution, region proposal network and boosted decision trees. In: International Joint Conference on Neural Networks, pp. 4052–4057 (2017)
14. Lin, G., Shen, C., Van Den Hengel, A., Reid, I.: Efficient piecewise training of deep structured models for semantic segmentation, pp. 3194–3203 (2015)
15. Long, J., Shelhamer, E., Darrell, T.: Fully convolutional networks for semantic segmentation. In: IEEE Conference on Computer Vision and Pattern Recognition, pp. 3431–3440 (2015)
16. Noh, H., Hong, S., Han, B.: Learning deconvolution network for semantic segmentation. In: IEEE International Conference on Computer Vision, pp. 1520–1528 (2015)
17. Shensa, M.J.: The discrete wavelet transform: wedding the a trous and Mallat algorithms. IEEE Trans. Sig. Process. **40**(10), 2464–2482 (1992)
18. Silberman, N., Hoiem, D., Kohli, P., Fergus, R.: Indoor segmentation and support inference from RGBD images. In: Fitzgibbon, A., Lazebnik, S., Perona, P., Sato, Y., Schmid, C. (eds.) ECCV 2012. LNCS, vol. 7576, pp. 746–760. Springer, Heidelberg (2012). https://doi.org/10.1007/978-3-642-33715-4_54
19. Tighe, J., Lazebnik, S.: SuperParsing: scalable nonparametric image parsing with superpixels. In: Daniilidis, K., Maragos, P., Paragios, N. (eds.) ECCV 2010. LNCS, vol. 6315, pp. 352–365. Springer, Heidelberg (2010). https://doi.org/10.1007/978-3-642-15555-0_26
20. Wang, P., et al.: Understanding convolution for semantic segmentation (2017)
21. Yasrab, R.: DCSeg: decoupled CNN for classification and semantic segmentation. In: IEEE Sponsored International Conference on Knowledge and Smart Technologies (2017)
22. Yu, F., Koltun, V.: Multi-scale context aggregation by dilated convolutions (2015)

23. Zheng, S., et al.: Conditional random fields as recurrent neural networks, pp. 1529–1537 (2015)
24. Zhou, H., Zhang, J., Lei, J., Li, S., Tu, D.: Image semantic segmentation based on FCN-CRF model. In: International Conference on Image, Vision and Computing, pp. 9–14 (2016)

Predicting Aesthetic Radar Map Using a Hierarchical Multi-task Network

Xin Jin[1,2] , Le Wu[1], Xinghui Zhou[1], Geng Zhao[1], Xiaokun Zhang[1],
Xiaodong Li[1], and Shiming Ge[3(✉)]

[1] Department of Cyber Security,
Beijing Electronic Science and Technology Institute, Beijing 100070, China
jinxin@besti.edu.cn
[2] CETC Big Data Research Institute Co., Ltd., Guiyang 550018, Guizhou, China
[3] Institute of Information Engineering,
Chinese Academy of Sciences, Beijing 100093, China
geshiming@iie.ac.cn

Abstract. The aesthetic quality assessment of images is a challenging
work in the field of computer vision because of its complex subjective
semantic information. The recent research work can utilize the deep convolutional neural network to evaluate the overall score of the image.
However, the focus in the field of aesthetic is often not limited to the
total score of image, and multiple attribute of the aesthetic evaluation
can obtain image richer aesthetic characteristics. The multi-attribute rating called Aesthetic Radar Map. In addition, traditional deep learning
methods can only be predicted by classification or simple regression, and
cannot output multi-dimensional information. In this paper, we propose
a hierarchical multi-task dense network to make multiple regression of
the properties of images. According to the total score, the scoring performance of each attribute is enhanced, and the output effect is better
by optimizing the network structure. Through this method, the more
sufficient aesthetic information of the image can be obtained, which is
of certain guiding significance to the comprehensive evaluation of image
aesthetics.

Keywords: Aesthetic evaluation · Neural network · Computer vision

1 Introduction

Recently, deep convolutional neural network technology has made great progress
in the field of computer vision, especially object recognition and semantic recognition. However, the aesthetic quality of using computer to identify or evaluate
images is far from practical. Image Aesthetic Quality Assessment (IAQA) is still
a challenging task [1], the reasons are: large-scale data set of aesthetic is less in
this field, aesthetic features are difficult for learning and generalization, evaluation of human subjectivity, etc. The aesthetic quality evaluation of images is a

J.-H. Lai et al. (Eds.): PRCV 2018, LNCS 11257, pp. 41–50, 2018.
https://doi.org/10.1007/978-3-030-03335-4_4

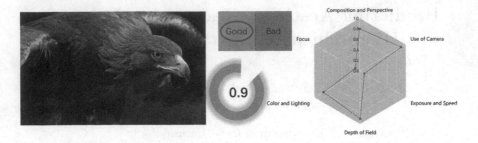

Fig. 1. Aesthetic radar map and other assessment methods.

hot topic in the field of computer vision, computational aesthetics and computational photography.

In terms of the data set we use the PCCD aesthetic data set to train proposed by Chang et al. [22], which provided 7 kinds of aesthetic characteristics of the image, and we use these characteristics to compute the multiply scores. As shown in Fig. 1, according to the Aesthetic Radar Map we can get more complete and multi-angle evaluation aesthetic information. We will think it is a very good photo by scoring one number or classification, but it has some disadvantages in focus and exposure, which is very important for people's aesthetic understanding, and the general one score regression or classification can not implement.

This paper presents a new hierarchical multi-task dense network architecture. Compared with the traditional learning method, this network can be strengthened from both global and attribute scoring, and finally get the total score of the image and the score of each attribute. In the feature extraction part of the convolution neural network, this paper use dense block structure [20] with different aesthetic characteristics in learning step, to reduce the phenomenon of vanishing-gradient and strengthens the use and transfer of feature information, and reduce the numbers of parameters to a certain extent. Behind the network part, we combine the study of the characteristics of global score and attribute score by fusion connection operation, to realize the global score effective utilization, and strengthens the attribute. Finally, through the combination of loss function, the network performs better. In the experimental part, this paper makes a comparison between the simple regression model and the non-hierarchical multi-task method, and proves that the proposed network and method have better performance. The main contributions of this paper are as follows:

- This is the first time to put forward the concept of the Aesthetic Radar Map and it fully show the aesthetic features with the Aesthetic Radar Map;
- Use the structure of the dense block in the aesthetic task to return the aesthetic score;
- For the first time, multi-task regression learning is applied to the aesthetic task, and a new feature fusion strategy is proposed to make the network selectively extract aesthetic features.

This paper predicts that the multi-attribute scoring of image aesthetic quality can be used for aesthetic image retrieval, photography technical guidance, video cover automatic generation and other applications. The evaluation of the quality of image aesthetics has a guiding effect on the application of UAV shooting, robot intelligence, and so on. Only by making the machine have the eyes of beauty can we serve the human beings better.

2 Related Work

As mentioned in [2], the early work of image aesthetic quality evaluation mainly focuses on the manual design of various image aesthetic features and uses pattern recognition algorithm to make aesthetic quality prediction. Another research route tries to directly fit the quality of image aesthetics with some hand-designed universal image features. Recently, the study from big data depth image characteristics shows good performance [3–15], and the performance beyond the traditional manual design features. The training data for image aesthetic quality assessment usually comes from the online professional photography community, such as photo.net and dpchallenge.com. People can rate photos on these sites (1–7 or 1–10). The higher the score means the higher the aesthetic quality of the image [17].

Although aesthetic quality evaluation exists in a certain sense, it is still an inherent subjective visual task. The quality evaluation of image aesthetics is ambiguous [18], and there are different methods for quality evaluation of aesthetic images.

In the field of aesthetic classification, people usually use two value labels, such as good image and bad image, which are usually used to represent the quality of image aesthetics. In the field of aesthetic scoring, some regression network begins to get the score aesthetics of image, these models designed by convolution neural network to present image aesthetic quality of binary classification results or one-dimensional numerical evaluation [16,23,24]. Before the depth of neural network and mass aesthetic image quality evaluation dataset AVA [19] release, such as Wu et al. [17] training on small data sets, which is proposed based on support vector machine (SVM) prediction methods of the aesthetic image quality evaluation of distribution. Jin et al. [14] began to put forward an aesthetic histogram to better represent aesthetic quality, and Chang et al. [22] began to perform aesthetic image caption.

On aesthetic data set, Murray et al. [19] first puts forward the most massive data sets in aesthetics field, AVA, and gaussian distribution to fitting all the AVA data samples, the rest of the image evaluation scores can better be gamma distribution fitting [19]. Then, in view of the imbalance of AVA samples, Kong et al. [12] proposed the AADB data set to make the aesthetic data set more balanced and better proper in the normal distribution. Chang et al. [22] proposed the PCCD data set, which is a relatively comprehensive small-scale data set.

3   Hierarchical Multi-task Network

3.1   Aesthetics Radar

For aesthetic image evaluation, the evaluation of a score is often incomplete. Through the evaluation of the pictures through several aesthetic indicators, a more comprehensive and a richer evaluation can be obtained. Usually such evaluation is also more meticulous.

The data set we use is called PCCD. It is based on the evaluation of the basic score, in the meantime, it considered the influence of Subject of Photo, Composition & Perspective, Use of Camera, Exposure & Speed, Depth of Field, Color & Lighting, Focus on the evaluation of the picture is also considered, and finally it is plotted in the form of a radar chart.

The composition of the picture evaluation will be updated from low dimension to high dimension, and some of the features with clear features can also be well represented by radar charts (Fig. 2).

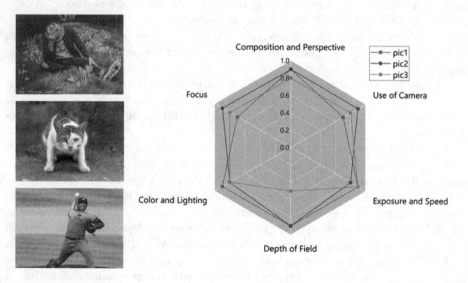

Fig. 2. Samples in the Photo Critique Captioning Dataset (PCCD)

The PCCD (Photo Critique Captioning Dataset) data set is a model for verifying the problems arising from the proposed aesthetic image evaluation, provided by Chang et al. [22]. The dataset is based on the professional photo review website[1] and provides experienced photographers' comments on the photos. On the website, photos were displayed and some professional reviews were provided in the following seven areas: general impressions, composition and perspective, color and lighting, photo theme, depth of field, focus and camera usage, exposure and speed.

---

[1] https://grushots.com/.

3.2 Dense Module

The dense module neural network was proposed in CVPR2017 [20]. Its algorithm is based on ResNet [21], but its network structure is completely new. Dense module can effectively reduce the number of features in a neural network while achieving better results. In each Dense Model, the input for each layer comes from the output of all previous layers. At the same time, each layer can relate to the input data and the loss, which can alleviate over-fitting and the problem of gradient disappearing when the network is too deep (Fig. 3).

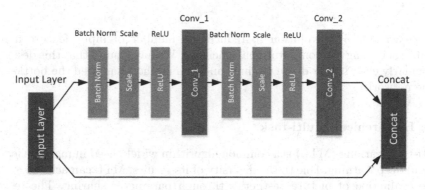

Fig. 3. Dense module

In ResNet, the relationship between two adjacent layers can be expressed by the following formula:

$$X_l = H_l(X_{l-1}) + X_{l-1} \tag{1}$$

where l denotes the layer, X_l denotes the output of layer l, and H_l denotes a nonlinear transform. So for ResNet, the output of layer l is the output of layer $l - 1$ plus the nonlinear transformation of the output of layer $l - 1$.

By changing the way information is transmitted between layers, dense module proposes a new connection method. Any one of them needs to relate to its subsequent layer. Its mathematical expression is as follows:

$$X_l = H_l([X_0, X_1, \ldots, X_{l-1}]) \tag{2}$$

where $[X_0, X_1, \ldots, X_{l-1}]$ refers to the concatenation of the feature-maps produced in layers $0, .., l - 1$ (Fig. 4).

There H_l as a composite function of three consecutive operations: batch normalization (BN), a rectified linear unit (ReLU) and a convolution (Conv). Due to the dense connectivity of the network, we refer to this network architecture as a dense convolutional network (DenseNet).

Dense module produces k output maps for each layer, but there are more inputs. In a specific application, a 1×1 convolution is added as a bottleneck

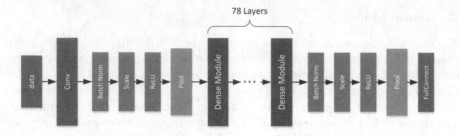

Fig. 4. The structure of feature extract network

before each 3×3 convolution to reduce the number of input feature maps, thereby increasing the computational efficiency. We have found that this design is particularly effective for dense module, and this method has been the bottleneck in the network.

3.3   Hierarchical Multi-task

Multi-task learning (MTL) is a common algorithm widely used in machine learning and deep learning. Due to the diversity of its results, MTL can achieve multi-angle evaluation of picture aesthetics through parameter sharing. The results of picture evaluation under different angles are relatively independent, but the model training process is the same. The Hierarchical MTL structure used in the experiment like Fig. 5.

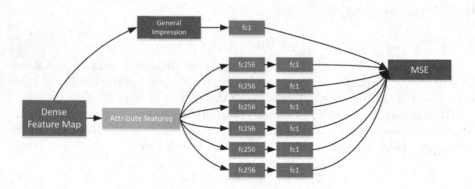

Fig. 5. The multi-task part of HMDnet (hierarchical multi-task dense network)

The dense module output at the last full-connection level is divided into seven parts, general impression and another six aesthetic attributes. Next, we split six aesthetic properties on the output by full-connection operation and perform the same operation to create the general impression. For the final result, the calculation of the mean-square error (MSE) is performed and returned as a model loss parameter to the previous network.

Hierarchical multi-task is a joint learning method. It learns multiple attributes of a picture, solves multiple problems at the same time, and performs regression prediction on multiple problems. A typical Multi-task, for example, in the business area, the personalized problem, from analysing multiple hobbies of a person to get a more comprehensive evaluation plan.

Hierarchical multi-task image processing methods have two advantages over traditional statistical methods:

- The radar image can display multi-angled and multi-leveled image information. In this experiment, pictures often have different levels of picture attributes and can be vividly represented by Multi-task;
- Multi-task evaluation pictures are often more specific and detailed. Multi-task analysis pictures can show the advantages and disadvantages of the picture in all aspects.

4   Experiment

4.1   Implementation Details

We fix the parameters of the layers before the first full connected layer of a pre-trained densenet model on the ImageNet [2] and fine-tune the all full connected layers on the training set of the PCCD dataset. We use the Keras framework[2] to train and test our models. The learning policy is set to step. Stochastic gradient descent is used to train our model with a mini-batch size of 16 images, a momentum of 0.9, a learning rate of 0.001 and a weight decay of 1e−6. The max number of iterations is 160. The training time is about 40 min using Titan X Pascal GPU.

4.2   Predict Result

For the data output by our model, dimension reduction is performed through the full connect layer, and regression calculations are performed on the known scores to obtain the predicted values of six aesthetic attributes of a picture and a total score estimate. The size of the Test data set is 500 pictures.

The experimental prediction results and test dataset data fitting results are better. Among them, the Color and Lighting attribute and the Composition and Perspective attribute have better results, and the other four attributes have larger deviations. The overall result is accurate. Some predict demo shown in Fig. 6.

---

[2] https://github.com/keras-team/keras/.

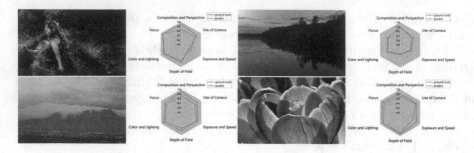

Fig. 6. Predicted results of test data set photos and ground truth.

4.3 Compare with Other Methods

To verify the effectiveness of our experimental results, we compared the algorithm (HMDNet) with other algorithms. The regression method uses densenet to make a simple regression to the score, without adding multi-attribute and multilayer full-connection structure, multi-task method uses multi-attribute combination method but does not use the total score. For the same data set, we get a better fit for the model predictions and the real data. Compared with other methods, we can prove that our method has more advantages in multi-task picture aesthetic reviews.

Table 1. The predictions' MSE of HMDNet and other methods.

Methods	GI	SP	CP	UES	DF	CL	FO
Regression	0.086801	0.13978	0.109241	0.111274	0.204511	0.122637	0.223453
Multi-task	0.079941	0.14742	0.094143	0.127399	0.150707	0.094961	0.173752
HMDNet	**0.079646**	**0.12789**	**0.076158**	**0.109694**	**0.128662**	**0.088098**	**0.142878**

As Shown in Table 1, the GI means General Impression, it's a general evaluate of a picture. The SP which in the Table 1 means Subject of Photo, the CP means Composition & Perspective, the UES means Use of Camera, Exposure & Speed, the DF means Depth of Field, the CL means Color & Lighting, the FO means Focus. Our methods can get best performance in overall score and all attribute scores.

5   Conclusions

This paper puts forward a new Hierarchical Multitasking convolution neural network architecture. We present a new aesthetic task and goal of Aesthetic Radar Map, and predict it through the multi-task regression network. Compared with the traditional regression network, this paper makes full use of the global aesthetic rating to make the overall score and attribute rating interact with each other, thus realizing the accurate prediction of multi-attribute tasks. Experiments show that this method makes the prediction closer to the real label. As an interdisciplinary subject of computer vision, photography and iconography, aesthetic evaluation has more interesting discoveries waiting for people to explore, and many blind areas await our in-depth discovery.

Acknowledgments. We thank all the reviewers and ACs. This work is partially supported by the National Natural Science Foundation of China (grant numbers 61772047, 61772513, 61402021), the open funding project of CETC Big Data Research Institute Co.,Ltd., (grant number W-2018022), the Science and Technology Project of the State Archives Administrator (grant number 2015-B-10), the Open Research Fund of Beijing Key Laboratory of Big Data Technology for Food Safety (grant number BTBD-2018KF-07), Beijing Technology and Business University, and the Fundamental Research Funds for the Central Universities (grant numbers. 328201803, 328201801).

References

1. Mai, L., Jin, H., Liu, F.: Composition-preserving deep photo aesthetics assessment. In: Proceedings of the IEEE Conference on Computer Vision and Pattern Recognition, pp. 497–506 (2016)
2. Deng, J., Dong, W., Socher, R., et al.: ImageNet: a large-scale hierarchical image database. In: 2009 IEEE Conference on Computer Vision and Pattern Recognition, CVPR 2009, pp. 248-255. IEEE (2009)
3. Karaycv, S., Trentacoste, M., Han, H., et al.: Recognizing image style. arXiv preprint arXiv:1311.3715 (2013)
4. Lu, X., Lin, Z., Jin, H., et al.: RAPID: rating pictorial aesthetics using deep learning. In: Proceedings of the 22nd ACM International Conference on Multimedia, pp. 457–466. ACM (2014)
5. Kao, Y., Wang, C., Huang, K.: Visual aesthetic quality assessment with a regression model. In: 2015 IEEE International Conference on Image Processing (ICIP), pp. 1583–1587. IEEE (2015)
6. Lu, X., Lin, Z., Shen, X., et al.: Deep multi-patch aggregation network for image style, aesthetics, and quality estimation. In: Proceedings of the IEEE International Conference on Computer Vision, pp. 990–998 (2015)
7. Lu, X., Lin, Z., Jin, H.: Rating image aesthetics using deep learning. IEEE Trans. Multimed. **17**(11), 2021–2034 (2015)
8. Dong, Z., Tian, X.: Multi-level photo quality assessment with multi-view features. Neurocomputing **168**, 308–319 (2015)
9. Kao, Y., Huang, K., Maybank, S.: Hierarchical aesthetic quality assessment using deep convolutional neural networks. Sig. Process. Image Commun. **47**, 500–510 (2016)
10. Wang, W., Zhao, M., Wang, L.: A multi-scene deep learning model for image aesthetic evaluation. Sig. Process. Image Commun. **47**, 511–518 (2016)
11. Ma, S., Liu, J., Chen, C.W.: A-Lamp: adaptive layout-aware multi-patch deep convolutional neural network for photo aesthetic assessment. CoRR abs/1704.00248. URL: http://arxiv.org/abs/1704.00248 (2017)

12. Kong, S., Shen, X., Lin, Z., Mech, R., Fowlkes, C.: Photo aesthetics ranking network with attributes and content adaptation. In: Leibe, B., Matas, J., Sebe, N., Welling, M. (eds.) ECCV 2016. LNCS, vol. 9905, pp. 662–679. Springer, Cham (2016). https://doi.org/10.1007/978-3-319-46448-0_40
13. Jin, X., Chi, J., Peng, S., et al.: Deep image aesthetics classification using inception modules and fine-tuning connected layer. In: 2016 8th International Conference on Wireless Communications Signal Processing (WCSP), pp. 1–6. IEEE (2016)
14. Jin, X., Wu, L., Song, C., et al.: Predicting aesthetic score distribution through cumulative jensen-shannon divergence. In: Proceedings of the 32th International Conference of the America Association for Artificial Intelligence (AAAI 2018), New Orleans, Louisiana, 2–7 February 2018 (2017)
15. Kao, Y., He, R., Huang, K.: Deep aesthetic quality assessment with semantic information. IEEE Trans. Image Process. **26**(3), 1482–1495 (2017)
16. Wang, Z., Liu, D., Chang, S., et al.: Image aesthetics assessment using Deep Chatterjee's machine. In: 2017 International Joint Conference on Neural Networks (IJCNN), pp. 941–948. IEEE (2017)
17. Wu, O., Hu, W., Gao, J.: Learning to predict the perceived visual quality of photos. In: 2011 IEEE International Conference on Computer Vision (ICCV), pp. 225–232. IEEE (2011)
18. Ke, Y., Tang, X., Jing, F.: The design of high-level features for photo quality assessment. In: 2006 IEEE Computer Society Conference on Computer Vision and Pattern Recognition, vol. 1, pp. 419–426. IEEE (2006)
19. Murray, N., Marchesotti, L., Perronnin, F.: AVA: a large-scale database for aesthetic visual analysis. In: 2012 IEEE Conference on Computer Vision and Pattern Recognition (CVPR), pp. 2408–2415. IEEE (2012)
20. Iandola, F., Moskewicz, M., Karayev, S., et al.: DenseNet: implementing efficient convnet descriptor pyramids. arXiv preprint arXiv:1404.1869 (2014)
21. He, K., Zhang, X., Ren, S., et al.: Deep residual learning for image recognition. In: Proceedings of the IEEE Conference on Computer Vision and Pattern Recognition (2016)
22. Chang, K.Y., Lu, K.H., Chen, C.S.: Aesthetic critiques generation for photos. In: 2017 IEEE International Conference on Computer Vision (ICCV) pp. 3534–3543. IEEE (2017)
23. Jin, B., Segovia, M.V.O., Süsstrunk, S.: Image aesthetic predictors based on weighted CNNs. In: 2016 IEEE International Conference on Image Processing (ICIP), pp. 2291–2295. IEEE (2016)
24. Hou, L., Yu, C.P., Samaras, D.: Squared earth mover's distance-based loss for training deep neural networks. arXiv preprint arXiv:1611.05916 (2016)

Blind Image Quality Assessment via Deep Recursive Convolutional Network with Skip Connection

Qingsen Yan[1,3], Jinqiu Sun[2(✉)], Shaolin Su[1], Yu Zhu[1], Haisen Li[1], and Yanning Zhang[1]

[1] School of Computer Science and Engineering,
Northwestern Polytechnical University, Xi'an, China
[2] School of Astronautics, Northwestern Polytechnical University, Xi'an, China
sunjinqiu@nwpu.edu.cn
[3] School of Computer Science, The University of Adelaide,
South Australia, Australia

Abstract. The performance of traditional image quality assessment (IQA) methods are not robust, due to those methods exploit shallow hand-designed features. It has been demonstrated that deep neural network can learn more effective features compared with the traditional methods. In this paper we propose a multi-scale recursive deep neural network to accurately predict image quality. In order to learn more effective feature representations for IQA, many deep learning based works focus on using more layers and deeper network structure. However, deeper network layers introduce large numbers of parameters, which causes huge difficulty in training. The proposed recursive convolution layer ensures both the depth of the network and the light of parameters, which guarantees the convergence of training procedure. Moreover, extracting multi-scale features is the most prevalent approach in IQA. Based on this criteria, we using skip connection to combine information among layers, and it further enriches the coarse and fine features for quality assessment. The experimental results on the LIVE, CISQ and TID2013 databases show that the proposed algorithm outperforms all of the state-of-the-art methods, which verifies the effectiveness of our network architecture.

Keywords: Image quality assessment (IQA) · Feature extraction
Deep learning · Convolutional neural networks (CNN) · Skip layer
No-reference (NR)

1 Introduction

Image quality assessment (IQA) aims to evaluate image quality in various types of distortion during image acquisition, compression, transmission and restoration [23,29,34]. Typical ways of IQA include subjective quality assessment and

© Springer Nature Switzerland AG 2018
J.-H. Lai et al. (Eds.): PRCV 2018, LNCS 11257, pp. 51–61, 2018.
https://doi.org/10.1007/978-3-030-03335-4_5

objective quality assessment. The former requires manual intervention, which is usually time consuming. In this case, image quality should be automatically generated and consistent with human perception. Therefore, objective image quality assessment obtains great attention in research. However, objective IQA has been a challenging issue in computer vision due to the variety of image distortion types and the difficulty in understanding the visual mechanisms of human perception.

Generally, objective IQA methods could be divided into three categories: full-reference (FR) IQA, reduced-reference (RR) IQA and no-reference (NR) IQA. FR-IQA methods are based on the full accessibility of raw image, and use this information to evaluate how much the distorted image has deviated from the origin one. The state-of-the-art FR-IQA methods include SSIM [24], MS-SSIM [26], FSIM [32], VIF [19] and GMSD [28]. The RR-IQA methods, including [25] and [22], extract only partial information of the reference image to predict the target image quality. However, in most cases, raw image is not available, therefore the NR-IQA methods that do not require a reference image becomes very necessary. Therefore, the NR-IQA method becomes very attractive in practical applications. Nevertheless, the lack of prior information has forced NR-IQA methods to work in different manners, making it the most challenging one among the three categories.

Early NR-IQA researches focus on extracting features from distorted images [11–14,17], based on the observation that some features are distinguishable from the distortion free images. Although huge efforts have been devoted in designing feature forms, the performance improved rather slow, which shows the limitations and drawbacks of these hand-crafted features. On the other hand, deep learning methods have shown great ability in many computer vision [3,7,18,30,33], it also can be applied in NR-IQA research field, being expected to achieve better performances. Deep learning methods can use convolutional layer and pooling layer to extract features for IQA, and fully connected layers are used to mapping features to quality score. Based on the superiority that image features could be trained automatically instead of manually designed, deep learning frameworks are supposed to extract more capable features with higher efficiency. Not surprisingly, many deep learning based IQA works have achieved good performances following [6].

The motivation of our method is that learning the complex relationship between visual content and the perceived quality via a novel recursive convolutional neural network. In [21], it has been demonstrated that deep convolutional neural networks (CNNs) with more layers outperform shallow network architectures. Based on this, we train a deep neural network with 7 convolutional layers (including recursive layer) and 3 pooling layers for IQA feature extraction. Since the learned features are based on a data-driven approach, they are able to describe the changes in local image which are relevant to quality perception.

In this paper we propose a new framework for IQA. The contributions of this work are summarized as follows. First, we propose a deep convolutional neural network to obtain effective features from different distortions types for the estimation image quality based on training samples. Second, our network repeatedly applies the same convolutional layer as many times as desired. The convolution layers have drawback which will introduce more parameters and the pooling layers discard too much information. Since the parameters are shared in our network, the number of parameters does not increase. Third, we employ a skip-connection between layers to combines coarse and fine information. Extracting multi-scale feature is the most prevalent approach in IQA. How to fusion different scale information is the problem should be considered in quality assessment. The experimental results show that the proposed network is accurate compared with the existing IQA methods.

2   Related Work

NR-IQA methods can be generally classified into two groups: natural scene statistic (NSS) approaches and learning based approaches. NSS approaches are based on the observation that statistic features of an image changes with the presence of distortion. These approaches first extract the features from the query image, and then a regression model, which is learned previously to map the features with corresponding subjective perception scores, is used to predict the final quality score. In [14], BIQI was proposed to first estimate the distortion type, then a distortion-associated metric is applied to evaluate image quality. Later, Moorthy et al. improved BIQI into DIIVINE [13] by extracting features in wavelet domain. However, these distortion-specific methods may not perform well dealing with a generalized problem, since only certain types of distortions are considered. In [17], Saad et al. came up with an approach, called BLINDS-II, solve the problem by combining contrast and structure information in DCT. After realizing the potential of spatial features, BRISQUE [11] was proposed to capture the statistics of locally normalized illumination coefficients. NIQE [12] works in spatial domain as well, but uses a multivariate model (MVG) to fit the local features.

For learning approaches, image features are learned to map with subjective scores directly. To capture the relevant features, lots of training samples are needed. In [31], spatial features of training images are extracted to construct a codebook, and the raw image quality is estimated via encoding and pooling. In [27], FR-IQA method was used to build a training database, where image patches of similar quality are clustered to evaluate the target image quality. In [10], a generalized regression neural network was deployed to train the IQA model. Inspired by the recent success of CNNs for classification and detection tasks, Kang [6] proposed a shallow CNN consisting of a convolutional layer with max and min pooling and contrasting the normalized image patches as input. Gu [4] introduced sparse autoencoder based Image Quality Index (DIQI) for blind quality assessment. Bianco [1] estimated the image quality by average-pooling the scores predicted on multiple sub-regions of the original image. But those networks cannot make full use the information of different layers. Hou [5] learned qualitative evaluations directly and outputs numerical scores for general utilization. Actually, images are represented by natural scene statistics features, some information is lost in this method. Bosse [2] constructed a network consisting of 10 convolutional layers and 5 pooling layers for feature extraction, and 2 fully connected layers for regression. Because it is more deeper than other networks, more parameters are introduced. In contrast, the proposed method considers taking the various advantages of different layer features while reducing the number of parameters.

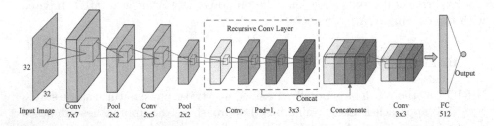

Fig. 1. The framework of our recursive convolutional neural network. Features are extracted from the distorted patch image by a convolutional neural network in order to generate the score of distortion image. The dashed-boxed represents a recursive convolution layer which share the same parameters. The layers with different colors capture different information of distorted patch images.

3   Deep Neural Network for NR-IQA

The proposed network takes an RGB image as input. Given a distortion image, our goal is to get the quality score by estimating the mapping from the images to numerical ratings. The framework of our convolutional neural network is shown in Fig. 1. We sample non-overlapping patches from a given image, then the quality score of each patch can be estimated by multi-scale network with skip connection. The score of full size image is calculated by average the patch scores.

3.1   Network Architecture for NR-IQA

The proposed network consists of 12 layers as shown in Fig. 1. The layers are organized as conv7-32, max pool, conv5-32, max pool, conv3-32, conv3-32, conv3-32, conv3-32 (four layers have same parameters), concatenate, conv3-128, FC-512, FC-1. This makes about 34 thousand trainable parameters in the network.

The convolution layers consist of filter banks. The response of each convolution layer is given by $f_n^{l+1} = \sum_m (f_m^l * k_{m,n}^{l+1} + b_n^{l+1})$, where $k_{m,n}^{l+1}$ is the convolution kernel of the l layer m-th feature map to the $l+1$ layer n-th feature map, f_m^l denotes the m-th feature of the l layer, and similar for f_n^{l+1}. The network use convolutional to learn effective feature representations. The first part of network is conv7-32, max pooling, conv5-32 and max pooling to capture the effective semantic information, then further refined by the recursive convolution layer. In order to obtain an output of the same size as the previous input in recursive convolution layer, padding is used for convolutions layers.

Instead of traditional sigmoid or tanh neurons, all convolutional layers are activated through the rectified linear unit (ReLU) activation function:

$$g = max(0, \sum_{n=1} w_n f_n) \tag{1}$$

where g, w_n, f_n denote the output of the ReLU, the weights of the ReLU and the output of the previous layer, respectively [15]. ReLUs enable the network to train several times faster compared tanh units. The input is 32×32 image patches. All the max pooling layers have 2×2 pixel-sized kernels in network. The network is trained end-to-end, the last layer is a linear regression with one output which is the quality score of the image patches. More detail will be explained in the following subsection.

3.2 Recursive Convolution Layer

Recursive convolution layer [8] takes the input matrix R_0 (after conv7-32, max pool, conv5-32 and max pool layer) and computes the matrix output R_1, R_2, R_3, R_4. The same weight W_r and bias b_r are used for all operations in this step. For example, R_1 is calculated by

$$R_1 = max(0, W_r * R_0 + b_r) \tag{2}$$

Similar operation are performed in the following layers. The recurrence relation is

$$R_d = max(0, W_r * R_{d-1} + b_r) \tag{3}$$

where, $d = 1, 2, 3, 4$. Then, we will get four feature matrices with different kinds of information. The *concat* layer is used to concatenate R_1, R_2, R_3, R_4 with skip structure in order to fuse coarse and fine information. As we can see, recursive convolution layer increases the depth of network and reduces the number of parameters simultaneously.

3.3 Training

Due to training need more samples for network, We train our network on non-overlapping 32×32 patches taken from large images, thus we have numbers of patches for training. However it may cause one problem that we only have the ground truth score of full image. Fortunately, the dataset of training images in our experiments have homogeneous distortions, we put the source images quality score to each patch of image. In the process of testing, the full size images quality score calculated by average the predicted patch scores.

$$q = \frac{1}{N_p} \sum_{i=1}^{N_p} f(x_i; w) \tag{4}$$

where, x_i denotes the input patch, $f(x_i; w)$ represents the predicted score of patch x_i with parameters w and N_p is the number of patches sampled from the image.

Learning the mapping between distortion images and scores are achieved by minimizing the loss between the predicted score $f(x_i; w)$ and the corresponding ground truth y_i. We adopt a similar objective function as [6]:

$$min_w \quad \frac{1}{N} \sum_{i=1}^{N} \|f(x_i; w) - y_i\|_{l_1} \tag{5}$$

where N is the number of images in the training set. We optimize the regression objective using the mini-batches gradient descent method based on the back-propagation learning rule. We implement our model using the Chainer package.

Table 1. LCC on LIVE dataset. The best two results are presented with bold face and italic fonts.

Method	JP2K	JPEG	WN	GBlur	FF	ALL
PSNR	0.896	0.860	0.986	0.783	0.890	0.824
SSIM	0.937	0.928	0.970	0.874	0.943	0.863
IFC	0.903	0.905	0.958	0.961	0.961	0.911
VIF	0.962	0.943	0.984	0.974	0.962	0.950
NSS	0.929	0.427	0.835	0.597	0.895	0.504
BIQI	0.942	0.922	0.945	0.941	0.856	0.902
BLIINDS-II	*0.963*	0.979	0.985	0.948	0.944	0.923
DIIVINE	0.922	0.921	0.988	0.923	0.888	0.917
SRNSS	0.936	0.939	0.940	0.936	0.947	0.932
BRISQUE	0.936	0.937	0.958	0.935	0.898	0.917
CORNIA	0.915	0.902	0.952	0.940	0.913	0.903
DLIQA	0.953	0.948	0.961	0.950	0.892	0.934
CNN	0.953	**0.981**	0.984	*0.953*	0.933	0.953
SOM	0.952	0.961	*0.991*	**0.974**	*0.954*	*0.962*
Proposed	**0.977**	*0.980*	**0.994**	0.949	**0.972**	**0.971**

4 Experiments and Results

4.1 Datasets and Evaluation

Datasets: The following image quality datasets LIVE [20], TID2013 [16] and CSIQ [9] are used in our experiments. The LIVE dataset comprises 779 distorted images with five different types of distortions JPEG 2000 compression

(JP2K), JPEG compression (JPEG), White Gaussian Noise (WN), Gaussian blur (GBlur) and Fast Fading (FF) based on 29 source reference images. Distortion types have 7–8 degradation levels. Quality ratings were captured use a single-stimulus methodology. Differential Mean Opinion Scores (DMOS) of each image quality score is in a range of [0 100], where a higher DMOS means lower quality of the image.

The TID2013 image quality dataset include 3000 distorted images by 24 different distortions which derived from 25 reference images at 5 degradation levels each. The distortion types cover a wide range for real world, which makes TID2013 to be a challenging database. Each image is associated with a Mean Opinion Score (MOS) values lie in the range [0, 9], where a lower MOS denotes bad visual quality.

The CSIQ image quality dataset also contains of a corresponding set of 866 distorted images based on 30 reference images from 35 different observers reported in the form of DMOS. For the proposed Deep Quality system, the DMOS scores are mapped into 5 different levels of image quality for evaluation purposes. After alignment and normalization the DMOS values range in [0 1], where a higher DMOS presents lower quality.

Evaluation: Random segmentation of the data set was repeated 10 times to eliminate bias from individual data. For each repetition we calculate the Linear Correlation Coefficient (LCC), Root Mean Square Error (RMSE) and Spearman Rank Order Correlation Coefficient (SROCC) between the predicted quality score and the ground truth, then compute the average of metrics. The value of correlation metrics close to 1, or RMSE close to 0 indicates high performance.

Table 2. RMSE on LIVE dataset.

Method	JP2K	JPEG	WN	GBlur	FF	ALL
PSNR	7.187	8.170	2.680	9.772	7.516	9.124
SSIM	5.671	5.947	3.916	7.639	5.485	8.126
IFC	6.972	6.813	4.574	4.360	4.528	6.656
VIF	4.449	5.321	2.851	3.533	4.502	5.024
NSS	8.911	21.25	12.13	17.22	9.821	19.69
BIQI	8.213	9.233	7.005	**6.566**	11.38	9.849
BLIINDS-II	7.257	9.103	6.825	7.894	9.709	8.800
DIIVINE	9.660	12.25	*5.310*	7.070	12.93	10.90
SRNSS	7.892	7.948	7.971	7.591	*7.157*	*7.618*
BRISQUE	8.150	9.230	7.273	7.516	9.536	9.538
CORNIA	9.666	10.32	6.541	7.689	8.917	9.935
DLIQA	*7.250*	*7.596*	5.881	*6.570*	9.540	8.149
Proposed	**4.785**	**4.793**	**2.288**	6.749	**5.129**	**5.514**

Table 3. SROCC on LIVE dataset.

Method	JP2K	JPEG	WN	GBlur	FF	ALL
PSNR	0.890	0.841	0.985	0.782	0.890	0.820
SSIM	0.932	0.903	0.963	0.894	0.941	0.851
IFC	0.892	0.866	0.938	0.959	0.963	0.913
VIF	0.953	0.913	0.986	0.973	0.965	0.953
NSS	0.882	0.247	0.852	0.644	0.859	0.339
BIQI	0.940	0.915	0.971	0.947	0.831	0.903
BLIINDS-II	0.951	0.942	0.978	0.944	0.927	0.920
DIIVINE	0.913	0.910	*0.984*	0.921	0.863	0.916
SRNSS	0.928	0.931	0.938	0.933	*0.941*	0.930
BRISQUE	0.910	0.919	0.955	0.941	0.874	0.920
CORNIA	0.903	0.889	0.958	0.946	0.915	0.906
DLIQA	0.933	0.914	0.968	0.947	0.857	0.929
CNN	*0.952*	**0.977**	0.978	0.962	0.908	0.956
SOM	0.947	*0.952*	*0.984*	**0.976**	0.937	*0.964*
Proposed	**0.966**	0.949	**0.989**	*0.963*	**0.973**	**0.965**

4.2   Consistency Experiment

In this subsection, we consider how the proposed network corresponds to human assessment on the LIVE database. We train and test on images of all five distortions (JP2K, JPEG, WN, BLUR and FF) together without providing a distortion type. Since machine learning requires training samples, we randomly divide into several groups and the rest are used as test sets. To eliminate effects from the separated data, the random division of the data set was repeated 10 times. Other learning-based BIQA approaches are all executed in this way.

We employ four traditional full-reference IQA methods as the benchmarks, including PSNR, SSIM, IFC, and VIF. In addition, there are 10 kinds of BIQA methods for comparison: (1) NSS; (2) BIQI; (3) BLIINDS-II; (4) DIIVINE; (5) SRNSS; (6) BRISQUE; (7) CORNIA; (8) DLIQA; (9) CNN; (10) SOM. All of these methods are based on machine learning and can be found in [5] and [2]. The results are evaluated by using 90% of the data for training, then testing on the other 10% of the data.

Tables 1, 2 and 3 show the experimental results of different methods on the LIVE dataset with different distortion types. The best two results are shown in bold face and italic fonts. Our proposed network outperforms all previous NR-IQA methods. From LCC and SROCC we can see that the proposed network works well on the entire database, especially on JP2K, WN and FF. SOM method ranks second in the entire database. In particular, our RMSE is significantly reduced compared to other methods. This phenomenon comes from recursive convolution and skip structure. We have reason to believe that the proposed network can obtain more useful features for describing image quality.

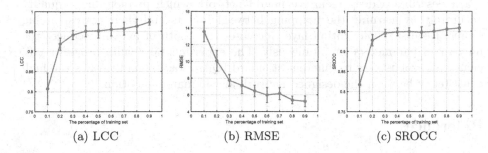

(a) LCC   (b) RMSE   (c) SROCC

Fig. 2. Performance of the proposed network versus the percentage of training sets

Figure 2 shows the relationship between the percentage of training sets and the performance of proposed network. The random split of the LIVE II dataset is repeated 10 times, each group include training and testing data. The average score of LCC, RMSE and SROCC are calculated according this datasets. As can be seen, the RMSE curve decreases slowly with the increases of the training set. The trend of LCC and SROCC curves is consistent. The new network can get better results even when the training sets are fewer.

4.3 Extensibility Experiment

To evaluate the performance of generalization we perform a cross-dataset evaluation as shown in Table 4. The subset of CSIQ and TID2013 includes only four types of distortions that are shared with LIVE dataset. Unfortunately, no results are available for the other methods. All models are trained on the full LIVE dataset and evaluated on subset of CSIQ and TID2013 or full set. We can see that our network is superior to previous state of the art methods on full dataset.

Table 4. SROCC results of the cross-dataset evaluations.

Method	Subset		Full	
	CSIQ	TID2013	CSIQ	TID2013
DIIVINE	-	-	0.596	0.355
DLIINDS-II	-	-	0.577	0.393
BRISQUE	0.899	0.882	0.557	0.367
CORNIA	**0.899**	0.892	0.603	0.429
CNN	-	**0.920**	-	-
Proposed	0.897	0.889	**0.609**	**0.412**

5 Conclusion

This paper develops a CNN for no-reference image quality assessment. Our approach describes a deep recursive neural network which predict image quality accurately by learning the mapping between images and their corresponding scores. Recursive convolution layer increases the depth of net and reduces the number of parameters simultaneously. The experimental results prove its efficiency and robustness to different standard IQA datasets, and verifies the high consistency between the designed network and human perception.

References

1. Bianco, S., Celona, L., Napoletano, P., Schettini, R.: On the use of deep learning for blind image quality assessment. Signal Image Video Process. **3**, 1–8 (2016)
2. Bosse, S., Maniry, D., Müller, K.R., Wiegand, T., Samek, W.: Deep neural networks for no-reference and full-reference image quality assessment. IEEE Trans. Image Process. **27**(1), 206–219 (2018)
3. Gong, D., et al.: From motion blur to motion flow: a deep learning solution for removing heterogeneous motion blur. In: Computer Vision and Pattern Recognition, pp. 1827–1836 (2017)
4. Gu, K., Zhai, G., Yang, X., Zhang, W.: Deep learning network for blind image quality assessment. In: IEEE International Conference on Image Processing, pp. 511–515 (2014)
5. Hou, W., Gao, X., Tao, D., Liu, W.: Blind image quality assessment via deep learning **26**(6), 1275–1286 (2015)
6. Kang, L., Ye, P., Li, Y., Doermann, D.: Convolutional neural networks for no-reference image quality assessment. In: Computer Vision and Pattern Recognition, pp. 1733–1740 (2014)
7. Kavukcuoglu, K., Boureau, Y.L., Gregor, K., Lecun, Y.: Learning convolutional feature hierarchies for visual recognition. In: International Conference on Neural Information Processing Systems, pp. 1090–1098 (2010)
8. Kim, J., Lee, J.K., Lee, K.M.: Deeply-recursive convolutional network for image super-resolution. In: 2016 IEEE Conference on Computer Vision and Pattern Recognition (CVPR), pp. 1637–1645 (2016)
9. Larson, E.C., Chandler, D.M.: Most apparent distortion: full-reference image quality assessment and the role of strategy. J. Electron. Imaging **19**(1), 6–11 (2010)
10. Li, C., Bovik, A.C., Wu, X.: Blind image quality assessment using a general regression neural network. IEEE Trans. Neural Netw. **22**(5), 793–799 (2011)
11. Mittal, A., Moorthy, A.K., Bovik, A.C.: No-reference image quality assessment in the spatial domain. IEEE Trans. Image Process. Publ. IEEE Signal Process. Soc. **21**(12), 4695–4708 (2012)
12. Mittal, A., Soundararajan, R., Bovik, A.C.: Making a completely blind image quality analyzer. IEEE Signal Process. Lett. **20**(3), 209–212 (2013)
13. Moorthy, A.K., Bovik, A.C.: Blind image quality assessment: from natural scene statistics to perceptual quality. IEEE Trans. Image Process. Publ. IEEE Signal Process. Soc. **20**(12), 3350 (2011)
14. Moorthy, A.K., Bovik, A.C.: A two-step framework for constructing blind image quality indices. IEEE Signal Process. Lett. **17**(5), 513–516 (2010)

15. Nair, V., Hinton, G.E.: Rectified linear units improve restricted Boltzmann machines. In: International Conference on International Conference on Machine Learning, pp. 807–814 (2010)
16. Ponomarenko, N., et al.: Color image database TID2013: peculiarities and preliminary results. In: European Workshop on Visual Information Processing, pp. 106–111 (2013)
17. Saad, M.A., Bovik, A.C., Charrier, C.: Blind image quality assessment: a natural scene statistics approach in the DCT domain. IEEE Trans. Image Process. Publ. IEEE Signal Process. Soc. 21(8), 3339–3352 (2012)
18. Schmidhuber, J.: Multi-column deep neural networks for image classification. In: Computer Vision and Pattern Recognition, pp. 3642–3649 (2012)
19. Sheikh, H.R., Bovik, A.C.: Image information and visual quality. IEEE Trans. Image Process. Publ. IEEE Signal Process. Soc. 15(2), 430 (2006)
20. Sheikh, H.R., Sabir, M.F., Bovik, A.C.: A statistical evaluation of recent full reference image quality assessment algorithms. IEEE Trans. Image Process. 15(11), 34–51 (2006)
21. Simonyan, K., Zisserman, A.: Very deep convolutional networks for large-scale image recognition. In: International Conference on Learning Representations (2015)
22. Soundararajan, R., Bovik, A.C.: RRED indices: reduced reference entropic differencing for image quality assessment. IEEE Trans. Image Process. Publ. IEEE Signal Process. Soc. 21(2), 517–526 (2012)
23. Wang, Z., Bovik, A.: Modern Image Quality Assessment. Morgan and Claypool, San Rafael (2006)
24. Wang, Z., Bovik, A.C., Sheikh, H.R., Simoncelli, E.P.: Image quality assessment: from error visibility to structural similarity. IEEE Trans. Image Process. 13(4), 600–612 (2004)
25. Wang, Z., Simoncelli, E.P.: Reduced-reference image quality assessment using a wavelet-domain natural image statistic model. Proc. SPIE 56, 149–159 (2005)
26. Wang, Z., Simoncelli, E.P., Bovik, A.C.: Multi-scale structural similarity for image quality assessment (2004)
27. Xue, W., Zhang, L., Mou, X.: Learning without human scores for blind image quality assessment. In: Computer Vision and Pattern Recognition, pp. 995–1002 (2013)
28. Xue, W., Zhang, L., Mou, X., Bovik, A.C.: Gradient magnitude similarity deviation: a highly efficient perceptual image quality index. IEEE Trans. Image Process. Publ. IEEE Signal Process. Soc. 23(2), 684–695 (2013)
29. Yan, Q., Sun, J., Li, H., Zhu, Y., Zhang, Y.: High dynamic range imaging by sparse representation. Neurocomputing 269, 160–169 (2017)
30. Yang, J., Gong, D., Liu, L., Shi, Q.: Seeing deeply and bidirectionally: a deep learning approach for single image reflection removal. In: European Conference on Computer Vision (2018)
31. Ye, P., Kumar, J., Kang, L., Doermann, D.: Unsupervised feature learning framework for no-reference image quality assessment. In: IEEE Conference on Computer Vision and Pattern Recognition, pp. 1098–1105 (2012)
32. Zhang, D.: FSIM: a feature similarity index for image quality assessment. IEEE Trans. Image Process. Publ. IEEE Signal Process. Soc. 20(8), 2378–2386 (2011)
33. Zhang, L., et al.: Adaptive importance learning for improving lightweight image super-resolution network. arXiv preprint arXiv:1806.01576 (2018)
34. Zhang, L., Wei, W., Zhang, Y., Shen, C., van den Hengel, A., Shi, Q.: Cluster sparsity field: an internal hyperspectral imagery prior for reconstruction. Int. J. Comput. Vis. 126(8), 797–821 (2018)

Long Term Traffic Flow Prediction Using Residual Net and Deconvolutional Neural Network

Di Zang[1(✉)], Yang Fang[1], Dehai Wang[1], Zhihua Wei[1],
Keshuang Tang[2], and Xin Li[3]

[1] Department of Computer Science and Technology, Tongji University,
Shanghai, China
zangdi@tongji.edu.cn
[2] Department of Transportation Information and Control Engineering,
Tongji University, Shanghai, China
[3] Shanghai Lujie Electronic Technology Co., Ltd., Pudong, Shanghai, China

Abstract. Nowadays accurate and efficient traffic flow prediction is strongly needed by individual travelers and public transport management. Traffic flow prediction, especially long-term prediction, plays an important role in the application of intelligent transportation systems (ITS). In this paper, we propose a personalized design model (ResDeconvNN) based on Convolutional Neural Network (CNN) for long-term traffic flow prediction of elevated highways in Shanghai. The next whole day flow information can be predicted using the previous day flows. Taking the correlation of traffic parameters into account, we analogy flow, speed and occupancy (FSO) to the 3 channels of RGB as the 3 inputs of model. So the raw data collected from loop detectors are transformed into a spatial-temporal matrix which has 3 channels. Our model consists of two modules: Residual net and deconvolutional neural network. First, we take advantage of the residual net in deep network to extract the features of traffic. Then, we develop a deconvolutional network module and apply it to decode the flow of the next day from the comprehensive spatial and temporal traffic features. Experimental results indicate that the proposed model is robust and can achieve a better prediction accuracy compared with the other existing popular approaches.

Keywords: Traffic flow prediction · ResDeconvNN model
Intelligent transportation system

1 Introduction

With the rapid development of the society, there has been a large increase in urban traffic in recent years, resulting in many transportation problems such as congestion or accidents. ITS aims to address these problems and improve transportation intelligently. Traffic flow prediction, as an essential task of ITS, is to predict the future flow using historic flows. Traffic flow prediction is greatly helpful to make a better travel decision, alleviate traffic congestion and improve traffic operation efficiency for individual

© Springer Nature Switzerland AG 2018
J.-H. Lai et al. (Eds.): PRCV 2018, LNCS 11257, pp. 62–74, 2018.
https://doi.org/10.1007/978-3-030-03335-4_6

travelers, public transport, and transport planning. Thus accurate and efficient prediction will make great significance for ITS.

There exist a great amount of methods for traffic flow prediction, which can be divided into three main classes: data driven statistical methods, machine learning methods and deep learning methods. At the beginning, among the data driven statistical models, a majority of approaches use conventional statistical time series methods such as the Auto-Regressive Integrated Moving Average (ARIMA) model [1] and the seasonal (SARIMA) model [2]. However, a large number of studies have found that the traffic flow data are random, varied and nonlinear. The ARIMA algorithm cannot analyze the nonlinear traffic flow data because it is based on the linear relationship.

Furthermore, several machine learning approaches have also been proposed to deal with traffic flow prediction, such as SVM [3], K-nearest Neighbors (KNN), the online Support Vector Regression (SVR) [4] and so on. KNN has firstly been used in traffic flow prediction [5], Sun et al. use flow-aware WPT KNN to predict traffic parameters [6]. In [7], a spatio-temporal Bayesian multivariate adaptive-regression splines (ST-BMARS) model is developed to predict short-term freeway traffic flow. Additionally, an Artificial Neural Networks (ANN) model are used in road traffic prediction and congestion control in [8].

In recent years, deep learning has drawn growing attention from many researchers. Deep learning methods exploit much deeper and more complex architecture to extract inherent features in data from the lowest level to the highest level. So a lot of deep learning methods have been proposed and employed for traffic flow prediction, such as Stacked Auto Encoder (SAE) [9, 10], DBN [11, 12], RNN. In [13], Ma et al. combined the Restricted Boltzmann Machine (RBM) with Recurrent Neural Network (RNN) and formed a RBM-RNN model that inherits the advantages of both RBM and RNN. Zhao et al. proposed a Long Short-Term Memory (LSTM) based method for traffic flow data prediction, which uses LSTM to extract the temporal feature of traffic flow data [14]. Compared with other deep learning models, Convolutional Neural Network (CNN) has better performance in understanding and exploring the pattern characteristics of traffic data. Thus in [15], A Convolutional Neural Network based method that learns traffic as images was proposed to predict traffic speed.

In general, the short-term traffic flow prediction module has been well exploited in some deep learning models, however, there exist some defects: First, the problem of long-term prediction is still not well solved. Second, the existing models only utilize single parameter to predict and ignores the objective parameter correlation between traffic parameters. Third, most models usually adopt classic models with poor scalability and lack of personalized design for specific prediction problems. In our work, considering the advantage of deep learning, especially Convolutional Neural Network (CNN), we develop a novel CNN based model called ResDeconvNN which has 3 input channels and apply it to long-term traffic flow prediction. The spatio-temporal relations and correlation of the three traffic parameters: flow, speed and occupancy (FSO) are fully considered and applied simultaneously in traffic flow prediction problems. We combine residual net and deconvolutional neural network to form a ResDeconvNN model which can extract the spatial-temporal information of the traffic pattern features well. Experiments demonstrate that the proposed approach gets lower mean relative error, mean absolute error and root mean square error and can achieve better performance than the other existing methods.

2 Proposed Methodology

2.1 Basic Principle

Now it is generally acknowledged that CNN has shown remarkable learning ability in the pattern recognition and has a good ability to extract the input features. Compared to other deep learning models, CNN has fewer weight parameters and the raw data can be directly used as input for automatic feature-learning while avoiding the distortion of input. Based on this, in order to adapt to the transportation environment, we design a ResDeconvNN model for long-term traffic flow prediction. Since flow, speed and occupancy (FSO) are the three main elements of traffic data that have parameter correlation, which describe the traffic features in a certain time and space. So in this model, we use these correlations effectively and predict the flow of next day based on these 3 historic parameters to improve the traffic flow prediction performance.

2.2 FSO Matrix Generation

The raw flow, speed and occupancy (FSO) data are collected by a detector on the road. Generally, FSO data coming from the detector has a time interval of 5 min, and there is a certain distance between the detectors installed on highways. For each of the FSO parameters, traffic information with time and space dimensions should be considered to predict traffic flow. Thus we let x- and y-axes represent time and space dimensions of a matrix. Mathematically, denote the time-space matrix by:

$$X = \begin{bmatrix} x_{11} & x_{12} & \cdots & x_{1n} \\ x_{21} & x_{22} & \cdots & x_{2n} \\ \cdots & \cdots & \cdots & \cdots \\ x_{m1} & x_{m2} & \cdots & x_{mn} \end{bmatrix} \tag{1}$$

Matrix X can be viewed as one of the three channels of an image, where n is the length of time intervals, m is the length of road. And pixel x_{ij} is the corresponding value of FSO associated with time i and space j.

As is mentioned above, it explains the process of converting raw data to 3 matrices as 3 channels which represent the value of flow, speed and occupancy respectively in a day. For each matrix, in the time dimension, considering there is quite few traffic at night and the pattern character of traffic is simple, we choose data collected from 7 am to 10 pm. So there will be 180 time series at 5-min sampling interval, and the width of our matrix is 180. In the space dimension, we have 35 detectors and map the spatial sequence of the detector directly to the height dimension. Thus the height of our matrix is 35.

Finally, we merge the 3 channel matrices to generate a time-space FSO matrix. Considering the difference in the numerical range of each parameter. We normalized the data of each channel. Here, we adopt the maximum minimum value normalization method which is defined as:

$$x_{norm} = \frac{x - x_{min}}{x_{max} - x_{min}} \qquad (2)$$

Where x_{norm} is the normalized data of each channel, x represents the original data of each channel, x_{max} and x_{min} represent the maximum and minimum values of the original data of each channel.

2.3 The ResDeconvNN Model

The overall structure of the proposed ResDeconvNN model is shown in Fig. 1. Our method mainly incorporates two parts, where the first part is the residual net module and the second part is the deconvolutional neural network module.

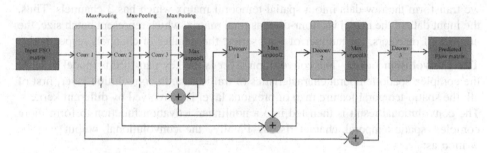

Fig. 1. The structure of the ResDeconvNN model. Where Conv denotes the convolution layer, Max-Pooling means the max pooling layer, Max unpool indicates the unpooling layer and Deconv represents the deconvolution layer.

For one thing, to make the long-term prediction of traffic flow more accurate, we draw on the ideas of residual, in this model we introduce residual structure to solve the problem of gradient disappearance when the network model is deep. Next, we designed the deconvolution neural network (DeconvNN) module to decode the traffic flow data of the next day from the integrated spatial and temporal characteristics.

The principle of the residual module is as follows.

Previous researches have shown that with the network depth increasing, accuracy gets saturated and then degrades rapidly when adding more layers to the network. Such degradation is not caused by overfitting, but because the deeper network becomes too hard to be optimized. However, when we add the identity mapping to some shallow network and change the optimization of these networks, it can greatly reduce the optimization difficulty of the whole network. Figure 2 shows a building block of residual. Assume that the input of the network is x, the expected output is H(x) = F (x) + x. By connecting the input x directly to the output, the goal of optimization is recast into residual F(x) = H(x) − x. In most cases, optimizing F(x) is much easier than optimizing H(x).

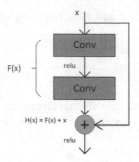

Fig. 2. Residual learning: a building block.

The Input Layer. Unlike traditional models that have only single input channel, the input layer of our designed model has 3 channels, so that we can fully exploit the parametric correlation among flow, speed and occupancy data. As mentioned in 2.2, we transform the raw data into a spatial-temporal matrix which has 3 channels. Thus, the input data of the model is a four-dimensional matrix, which represent batch size, the number of detectors, the number of time series, the number of channels respectively.

The Convolution Layer. The convolution layer is the key part of this model to learn the complex spatio-temporal characteristics of traffic data. In convolution layer, first of all, the spatio-temporal feature map of previous layer is convolved by different kernels. The convolutional result is then fed into a nonlinear activation function to form more complex spatio-temporal characteristics. Finally, the convolutional output can be written as:

$$x_j^l = \varphi\left(\sum_{i=1}^{c^{l-1}} x_i^{l-1} * k_{ij}^l + b_j^l\right) \tag{3}$$

Where * represents convolution operation, l is the index at the *lth* layer and j is the index of feature map at the *lth* layer, c^{l-1} is the number of feature maps of the previous layer. x_i^{l-1} denotes a output feature map of the $(l-1)$ layer, x_j^l, k_{ij}^l, b_j^l represent the output feature map, kernel weights and bias at the *lth* layer. φ is the rectified liner unit active function which is defined as:

$$\varphi(x) = max(0, x) \tag{4}$$

The Pooling Layer. The function of the pooling layer is to down sample the convolutional result so as to filter the redundant information of traffic characteristics. Therefore, the pooling operation reduces the size of the feature map and reduces the training parameters of the network, but also retains the significant pattern information. Common pooling operations include mean pooling, max pooling, and random pooling. In this paper, the max pooling technique is employed.

The Deconvolution Layer. The deconvolution neural network is mainly composed of deconvolution layer and unpooling layer. Deconvolution is the inverse of the convolution. In our model, we associate the forward process of deconvolution with the backward process of the convolution, and realize the deconvolution operation by referring to the reverse derivation formula of the convolution layer and we call it transpose convolution. Therefore, the output of the deconvolution layer can be defined as:

$$x_j^l = \varphi\left(\sum_{i=1}^{c^{l-1}} x_i^{l-1} * \left(x_{ij}^l\right)^R + b_j^l\right) \tag{5}$$

Where, * represents the convolution operation, R represents the transpose operation of the matrix, and φ is the activation function.

The Unpooling Layer. Pooling operation can bring the loss of information, which is an irreversible process. However, we can still realize the unpooling operation by referring to the reverse derivation process of the pooling layer. In this paper, we adopted max pooling method. Different from the formula, for the feature map j of lth pooling layer, we need to record the location of the maximum value while computing the pooling result. Then, the output of the lth unpooling layer can be defined as:

$$x_j^l = unmp\left(x_j^{l-1} argmax_j\right) \tag{6}$$

Where, unmp represents the unpooling operation, and $argmax_j$ is the index of the position where the maximum value is.

2.4 Model Optimization

In order to predict traffic flow, parameters need to be trained with training samples and we need a loss function to describe the prediction accuracy of the model. In the training phase, the loss function which is optimized by stochastic gradient descent method of our model is defined as:

$$L = L_{mse} + L_{reg} + L_{mgdl} \tag{7}$$

Where L_{mse} is mean squared error (MSE), which calculates the difference between ground truth and prediction result. L_{reg} is regularized loss which to avoid the problem of overfitting. L_{mgdl} measures the gradient loss between the predicted and real values.

3 Experiment and Results

3.1 Dataset Description

The factual FSO data associated with position and time are collected from detectors deployed on Yan'an elevated highways of shanghai in year 2011, as shown in Fig. 3, Yan'an elevated highway is marked in red, which connects the HongQiao transportation hub and the center of the city.

Fig. 3. Mark of Yan'an elevated highway in shanghai.

The process of our proposed methodology is illustrated in Fig. 4. Due to the lack of data from March 20 to March 23, there are actually only 361 days of data which are available for the experiment. In addition, there are some abnormal elements and need to be repaired. So the raw data are first preprocessed to remove abnormal elements. And then transformed to generate a spatial-temporal matrix with 3 channels. Because we need to use the previous day's flow to predict the flow of corresponding next day, thus there are 360 samples.

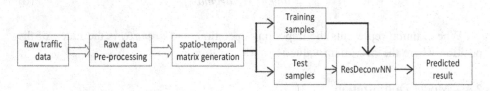

Fig. 4. The process of the proposed methodology for traffic flow prediction.

For the division of training set and test set, we first shuffle the 360 days of samples to disrupt their order. Then the traffic data for the previous day (i.e. the data for experiment) are the i th samples, and the traffic data for the next day (i.e. the labels for experiment) are the (i + 1) th samples (i = 1, 2 ... 360). As mentioned in 2.3, the 4th dimension of the input data represents the number of channels. Since the flow, speed and occupancy of the previous day are used to predict the flow of the next day, so here the 4th dimension of the data is 3, and the 4th dimension of the labels is 1. Therefore, for the training set: we select the 1st to 330th data as the training data, and the 1st to 330th label as the training labels; similarly, for the test set, we choose the 331 to 360 data as the test data, and the 331 to 360 label as the test labels. That is, our training set contains 330 samples and our test set contains 30 samples.

3.2 Learning Rate and Network Iteration

We adopt the exponential decay method to set the learning rate. Exponential decay is a more flexible method to set learning rate, which can dynamically adjust the learning rate. In our model, the initial learning rate is set to 1.0, the decay coefficient is set to 0.5, the total number of network iterations is 30000, and the learning rate are calculated every 2000 times to update the original learning rate. With the iteration of network, the learning rate would decrease exponentially, and finally the model tend to be stable and get an optimal value. In our experiment, the value of the loss function L was 0.1545 at the beginning (Where L_{mse} = 0.03827, L_{reg} = 0.00088, L_{mgdl} = 0.11535), and in the process of network iteration, the value of the loss function fluctuated slightly up and down as it decreased and converged gradually. After 30000 iterations, the loss eventually stabilized at 0.0550 (Where L_{mse} = 0.00312, L_{reg} = 0.00077, L_{mgdl} = 0.05111).

3.3 Experimental Environment and Model Configuration

The experiments are conducted on the server with i7-5820 K CPU, 48 GB memory and NVIDIA GeForce GTX1080 GPU. The proposed models and the contrastive models are implemented on TensorFlow framework of deep learning.

The configuration of our proposed model is shown in Table 1.

Table 1. Configuration of ResDeconvNN for traffic flow prediction

Layers	Name	Description
Layer1	Convolution1	64 kernels with $5 \times 5 \times 3$ size
Layer2	Max pooling1	Kernel size = 2×2, stride = 2
Layer3	Convolution2	64 kernels with $3 \times 3 \times 64$ size
Layer4	Max pooling2	Kernel size = 2×2, stride = 2
Layer5	Convolution3	128 kernels with $3 \times 3 \times 64$ size
Layer6	Max pooling3	Kernel size – 2×2, stride = 2
Layer7	Unpooling1	Kernel size = 2×2, stride = 2, output shape = output shape of Convolution3
Layer8	Deconvolution1	Kernel size = 3×3, output shape = output shape of Max-pooling2
Layer9	Unpooling2	Kernel size = 2×2, stride = 2, output shape = output shape of Convolution2
Layer10	Deconvolution2	Kernel size = 3×3, output shape = output shape of Max-pooling1
Layer11	Unpooling3	Kernel size = 2×2, stride = 2, output shape = output shape of Convolution1
Layer12	Deconvolution3	Kernel size = 5×5, output shape = output shape of input

3.4 Results and Evaluation

We compare our method to multiple existing methods including basic methods (RW), RW is to predict the current value using the last value, and classical methods (ANN) as well as some advanced deep learning methods (DBN, RNN and SAE). The prediction performance is measured by 3 criteria: Mean Relative Error (MRE), Mean Absolute Error (MAE) and Root Mean Square Error (RMSE), MAE and RMSE can evaluate absolute error between the prediction and the reality while MRE can evaluate from the perspective of the relative error. MRE, MAE and RMSE are defined as:

$$MRE = \frac{1}{N} \sum_{i=1}^{N} \frac{|y' - y|}{y} \tag{8}$$

$$MAE = \frac{1}{N} \sum_{i=1}^{N} |y' - y| \tag{9}$$

$$RMSE = \sqrt{\frac{1}{N} \sum_{i=1}^{N} (y' - y)^2} \tag{10}$$

Where y denotes the prediction, y' denotes the reality and N denotes the number of samples in test set.

The comparison results of prediction are shown in Table 2. From the table, we find that in terms of MRE, except for DBN, our mode gets the lowest error and value is nearly close to DBN. Further, in terms of the other two criteria, our method performs best when compared with other 5 methods, and we can sum up that our method can achieve better performance than the other existing methods.

Table 2. Results of Experiment

Models	MRE (%)	MAE	RMSE
ResDeconvNN	13.8	44.36	60.0
ANN	18.0	55.49	71.77
DBN	13.7	47.69	65.23
RNN	15.1	45.89	61.84
SAE	15.0	50.54	67.11
RW	16.6	51.58	76.32

Figures 5, 6, 7, 8, 9, 10, 11, 12, 13, 14, 15 and 16 show the predicted and real curves of the randomly selected detector of the Yan'an elevated highway in shanghai. Where Figs. 5, 6, 7, 8, 9 and 10 show the flow fitting curve of the 25th detector on December 12, Figs. 11, 12, 13, 14, 15 and 16 show the flow fitting curve of the 2nd detector on December 28. As shown in these figures, the predicted curves precisely fit to the ground-truth curves except where the peak of the ground-truth curve is obvious.

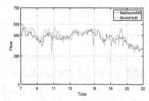

Fig. 5. Prediction results of ResDeconvNN.

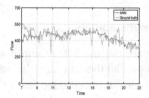

Fig. 6. Prediction results of ANN.

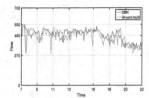

Fig. 7. Prediction results of DBN.

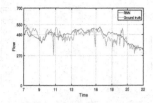

Fig. 8. Prediction results of RNN.

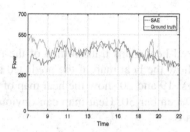

Fig. 9. Prediction results of SAE.

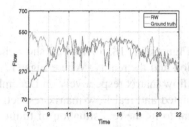

Fig. 10. Prediction results of RW.

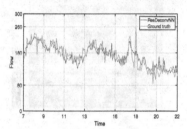

Fig. 11. Prediction results of ResDeconvNN.

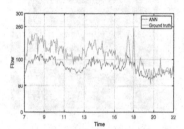

Fig. 12. Prediction results of ANN.

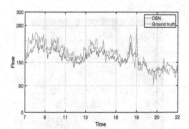

Fig. 13. Prediction results of DBN.

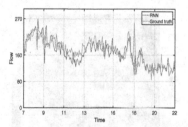

Fig. 14. Prediction results of RNN.

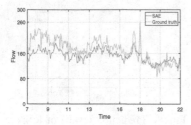

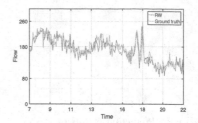

Fig. 15. Prediction results of SAE.

Fig. 16. Prediction results of RW.

Figures 17, 18, 19 and 20 show the visualized heat maps transformed of the prediction and the reality. Where Figs. 17 and 18 show the heat map of the predicted and real flow matrix respectively on December 2, Figs. 19 and 20 show the heat map of the predicted and real flow matrix respectively on December 30. Heat map can obviously reveal to us the real situation of traffic flow in a day.

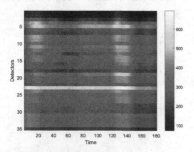

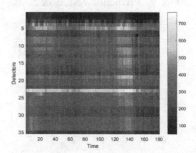

Fig. 17. Heat map visualized by the predicted flow matrix of the next day (2011/12/2).

Fig. 18. Heat map visualized by the real flow matrix of the next day (2011/12/2).

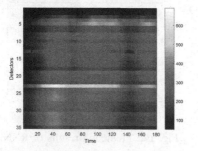

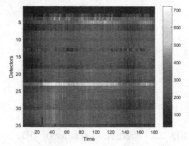

Fig. 19. Heat map visualized by the predicted flow matrix of the next day (2011/12/30).

Fig. 20. Heat map visualized by the real flow matrix of the next day (2011/12/30).

4 Conclusions

In this paper, a model using residual net and deconvolutional neural network is developed to predict long-term traffic flow accurately. The proposed method takes the advantage of residual ideal, which can successfully learn the latent nonlinear traffic flow features. Furthermore, this is also attributed to the correlation of FSO and spatio-temporal correlations of the traffic data. Finally, we apply deconvolutional neural network to decode the flow of the next day accurately. Based on experimental results, our method is robust and obtains better prediction results compared to existing methodologies.

Acknowledgment. This work is supported by National Natural Science Foundation of China (No. 61876218, No. 61573259).

References

1. Hamed, M.M., Al-Masaeid, H.R., Said, Z.M.B.: Short-term prediction of traffic volume in urban arterials. J. Transp. Eng. **121**(3), 249–254 (1995)
2. Tran, Q.T., Ma, Z., Li, H., Hao, L., Trinh, Q.K.: A multiplicative seasonal ARIMA/GARCH model in EVN traffic prediction. International Journal of Communications, Network and System Sciences **08**(04), 43–49 (2015)
3. Y. Zhang and Y. Xie, "Forecasting of short-term freeway volume with V-support vector machines," Transp. Res. Rec., J. Transp. Res. Board, vol. 2024, pp. 92–99, 2007
4. Castro-Neto, M., Jeong, Y., Jeong, M., Han, L.: Online-SVR for short-term traffic flow prediction under typical and atypical traffic conditions. Expert Syst. Appl. **36**(3), 6164–6173 (2009)
5. Davis, G.A., Nihan, N.L.: Nonparametric regression and short-term freeway traffic forecasting. J. Transp. Eng.-ASCE **117**(2), 178–188 (1991)
6. Sun, B., Cheng, W., Goswami, P., Bai, G.: Flow-aware wpt k-nearest neighbours regression for short-term traffic prediction. In: 2017 IEEE Symposium on Computers and Communications (ISCC), pp. 48–53. IEEE (2017)
7. Xu, Y., Kong, Q.-J., Klette, R., Liu, Y.: Accurate and interpretable Bayesian MARS for traffic flow prediction. IEEE Trans. Intell. Transp. Syst. **15**(6), 2457–2469 (2014)
8. More, R., Mugal, A., Rajgure, S., Adhao, R.B., Pachghare, V.K.: Road traffic prediction and congestion control using artificial neural networks. In: International Conference on Computing, Analytics and Security Trends (CAST), pp. 52–57. IEEE (2016)
9. Lv, Y., Duan, Y., Kang, W., Li, Z., Wang, F.Y.: Traffic flow prediction with big data: a deep learning approach. IEEE Trans. Intell. Transp. Syst. **16**(2), 865–873 (2015)
10. Shin, H., Orton, M.R., Collins, D., Doran, S., Leach, M.: Stacked auto encoders for unsupervised feature learning and multiple organ detection in a pilot study using 4D patient data. IEEE Trans. Pattern Anal. Mach. Intell. **35**(8), 1930–1943 (2013)
11. Tan, H., Xuan, X., Wu, K, Zhong, Y.: A comparison of traffic flow prediction methods based on DBN. In: 16th COTA International Conference of Transportation, pp. 273–283 (2016)
12. Huang, W., Song, G., Hong, H., Xie, K.: Deep architecture for traffic flow prediction: Deep belief networks with multitask learning. IEEE Trans. Intell. Transp. Syst. **15**(5), 2191–2201 (2014)

13. Ma, X., Yu, H., Wang, Y., Wang, Y.: Large-scale transportation network congestion evolution prediction using deep learning theory. PLoS ONE **10**(3), e0119044 (2015)
14. Zhao, Z., Chen, W., Wu, X., Chen, P., Liu, J.: LSTM network: a deep learning approach for short-term traffic forecast. IET Intell. Transp. Syst. **11**(2), 68–75 (2017)
15. Ma, X., Dai, Z., He, Z., Ma, J., Wang, Y., Wang, Y.: Learning traffic as images: a deep convolutional neural network for large-scale transportation network speed prediction. Sensors **17**(4), 818 (2017)

Pyramidal Combination of Separable Branches for Deep Short Connected Neural Networks

Yao Lu, Guangming Lu$^{(\boxtimes)}$, Rui Lin, and Bing Ma

Harbin Institute of Technology (ShenZhen), ShenZhen, China
yaolu_1992@126.com, luguangm@hit.edu.cn, linrui_1995@163.com,
mabing_campus@163.com

Abstract. Recent works have shown that Convolutional Neural Networks (CNNs) with deeper structure and short connections have extremely good performance in image classification tasks. However, deep short connected neural networks have been proven that they are merely ensembles of relatively shallow networks. From this point, instead of traditional simple module stacked neural networks, we propose Pyramidal Combination of Separable Branches Neural Networks (PCSB-Nets), whose basic module is deeper, more delicate and flexible with much fewer parameters. The PCSB-Nets can fuse the caught features more sufficiently, disproportionately increase the efficiency of parameters and improve the model's generalization and capacity abilities. Experiments have shown this novel architecture has improvement gains on benchmark CIFAR image classification datasets.

Keywords: Deep learning · CNNs · PCSB-Nets

1 Introduction

Deep Convolutional Neural Networks (DCNNs) have obtained a number of significant improvements in many computer vision tasks. The famous LeNet-style models [10] mark the beginning of the CNNs era. Nevertheless, AlexNet [8], possessing more convolutional layers stacked with different spatial scales, makes a big breakthrough in *ILSVRC 2012* classification competition.

1.1 Inception and Xception Module

Following this trend, some new branchy models have been emerged, for instance, the family of Google Inception-style [6,12,13] and Xception [1] models. In fundamental Inception module (see Fig. 1(a)), where all input channels are embedded into a low dimension space through "1 × 1" convolution (also called "pointwise convolution" operation). Then the embedding feature maps will be equally divided into several branches as the corresponding input of the same number convolutional operations respectively. Specially, this operation can also be called

© Springer Nature Switzerland AG 2018
J.-H. Lai et al. (Eds.): PRCV 2018, LNCS 11257, pp. 75–86, 2018.
https://doi.org/10.1007/978-3-030-03335-4_7

"grouped convolutions", which is first used in AlexNet and implemented by such as Caffe [7]. At last, output feature maps from all groups are concatenated together. An "extreme" version of Inception module is shown in Fig. 1(b). In this basic module, the first layer also adopts "point-wise convolution" operation, but at the second stage, the convolutions with the same size filters are used on per input channel (also called "depth-wise convolution" in Tensorflow) and concatenate all output feature maps. This lack communication required between different branches before being merged. Moreover, feature information from separable paths can't be sufficiently fused resulting in catching poor features.

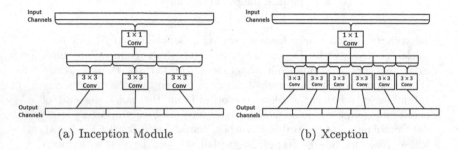

(a) Inception Module   (b) Xception

Fig. 1. Inception module and Xception module.

1.2 Short Connected Convolutional Neural Networks

With these models going deeper, it is increasingly difficult to train because of the vanishing gradient. As for this point, a novel kind of architectures with skip connections ResNets [3] have been designed, who employ identity mapping to bypass layers contributing to obtaining great gradient flow and catching better features from objects. Following up this style of architectures, DenseNets [4] are proposed, where each basic module obtains additional inputs from all preceding modules and passes on its own feature maps to all subsequent modules. Although these models seem to have more layers, they have been proven that they don't increase the depth actually but are only ensembles of relatively shallow networks [9]. Furthermore, the basic residual block is mainly composed of some traditional operation layers stacks, despite they can add more layers to the block to make it deeper, it will have much more parameters at the same time and can't deal with input message delicately.

Given the importance of these issues of above models, we introduce a novel basic module called Pyramidal Combination of Separable Branches module. And the corresponding networks, referred to PCSB-Nets, are constructed by repeating this new module multiple times. Specially, as shown in Fig. 2, we equip several layers in one PCSB module, and every layer is composed of some branches. Furthermore, the number of branches in every layer decreases exponentially from the input layer to the output layer, accordingly, the shape of these basic novel modules constructed in this way looks like an inverted pyramid. Moreover, in every branch, the corresponding input features are firstly projected into a low dimension space to reduce the model's parameters.

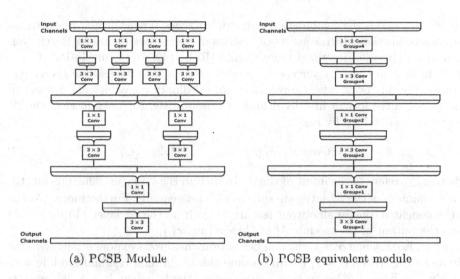

(a) PCSB Module   (b) PCSB equivalent module

Fig. 2. PCSB module.

Our architecture's superiorities are notable. It can make every module more deeper and utilizes much fewer parameters more efficiently, because of both the branchy structure and the low-dimension embedded information of every branch. Additionally, in the feed-forward phase, every small branch only needs to deal with little information at the bottom layer. Then, these small branches are combined gradually to catch a larger spatial information until they become only one branch. This structure can make the features be fused sufficiently and the global task will be assigned to different branches smoothly. Therefore, the small task can be readily fulfilled by each branch. Meanwhile, in the backward phase, the gradient information from upper layers will guide every branch to update the parameters efficiently.

2   PCSB-Nets

2.1   Pyramidal Combination of Separable Branches

The structure of the PCSB-Net's module is shown in Fig. 2(a). In the next illustration, we define a module possessing a specific number of regular operational layers, such as convolutional and nonlinearity activation layers, and it can have several same operational layers. Suppose the module M has L layers. x_0 and x_{l-1} refer to the input of M and the lth layer (or the output of the $(l-1)^{th}$

layer) respectively. The number of branches (can also be called groups) in l^{th} layer denoted by G_l is calculated as bellow:

$$G_l = \alpha^{L-l}, \quad l = (1, 2, ..., L) \tag{1}$$

where α ($\alpha \geq 1$) is the combination factor of branches. Then the non-linear transformation function which consists of a series of operations including Batch Normalization (BN) [6], Rectified Linear Units (ReLU) [2] and Convolution (Conv) of ith branch in the lth layer can be represented as $\mathscr{F}_l^i$. We assume the convolutions contain "point-wise convolution" and ordinary convolutional operations and perform the former first by default. Consequently, the output x_l of the lth layer can be obtained by Eq. 2.

$$x_l = Concat_i \, \mathscr{F}_l^i(x_{l-1}^i), \quad i = (1, 2, ..., G_l) \tag{2}$$

where x_{l-1}^i refers to the input of the ith branch in the lth layer, which means the input channels of the lth layer are split to G_l parts equally. Furthermore, $Concat$ is the concatenation of all output feature maps from the lth layer's branches. At last, the output of the module M is $Concat\{x_0, x_L\}$.

From Eq. 1, when $\alpha > 1$, the number of branches grows exponentially with the number of α. When $\alpha = 1$, it will become the traditional residual module with merely one branch in every layer. More interestingly, when $L = 1$, it degrades to bottleneck [3] architecture, which consists of a "point-wise convolution" and a regular convolutional layer.

In every layer, all the convolutional operations have the same filter size of each branch, so that they can be implemented by "grouped point-wise convolution" and "grouped convolution" operations, when the filter size is equal to 1, the former will become the special case of the latter, therefore, our module can be also equivalently represented as Fig. 2(b). Specially, the groups of residual and Xception module are equal to 1 and the number of feature map channels, respectively. However, there is a notable difference between our module and traditional module in the way of embedding input information. That is our module "grouped point-wise convolution" at every layer. While in traditional modules, they conduct "point-wise convolution" operation first for all the input feature map channels to mix information.

2.2   Network Architecture

Following DenseNet (see Fig. 3), the PCSB-Net is similar to the overall structure of it with dense connections and repeating PCSB modules multiple times. Furthermore, we have always obeyed the rule that our model's parameters are fewer than or equal to DenseNet. Since the bottom block mainly processes the detail information, there will be more layers in every module in the first dense block contributing to more branches existing at the first layer in each module (e.g., $\alpha = 2$, $L = 3$ and $G_1 = 4$), then in the second block, the number of layers will decrease (e.g., $\alpha = 2$, $L = 2$ and $G_1 = 2$) leading to fewer branches. Finally, in the last dense block, there will be only one layer with only one branch left in each module resulting in bottleneck structure, for the reason that it will catch the high-level features. Figure 4 shows the final detail structure of the PCSB-Net.

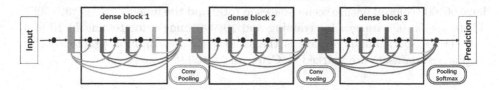

Fig. 3. DenseNets architecture.

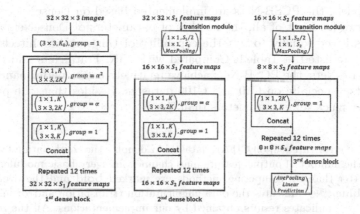

Fig. 4. PCSB-Net architecture: "1 × 1" and "3 × 3" represent the convolutional operations, every convolutional operation is followed by the number of output channels. S_1, S_2 and S_3 denote the number of accumulating output feature maps at the end of every dense block.

2.3   Implementation Details

DenseNet, and the mini-batch size is 64. Also, the number of training epochs is 300. Additionally, all the PCSB-Nets are trained by the stochastic gradient descent (SGD) method. Finally, Nesterov momentum [11] with 0 dampening is employed to optimize. The initial learning rate starts from 0.1, which is divided by 10 at 150 and 225 training epochs. The momentum is 0.9 and weight decay is $1e - 4$.

3 Experimental Results and Analysis

3.1 Datasets

CIFAR datasets includes CIFAR-10 (C10) and CIFAR-100 (C100). They both have 60,000 colored nature scene images in total and the images' size is "32×32". There are 50,000 images for training and 10,000 images for testing in 10 and 100 classes. Data augmentation is the same with the common practices. The augmented datasets are marked as C10+ and C100+, respectively.

3.2 Comparisons with State-of-the-Art Models

Performance. We place special emphasis on verifying PCSB-Nets have a better performance in spirit of utilizing fewer or same parameters than all the competing architectures. Since DenseNets have much fewer parameters than other traditional models, the PCSB-Nets are implemented based on DenseNets to make smaller networks. First of all, the number of parameters of DenseNets and the PCSB-Nets is set equally to test the capability of this novel architecture and the results are listed in Table 1. Compared with NiN, FratalNets and different versions of ResNets, the PCSB-Nets achieve relatively better performance on all the datasets, especially on C10 and C100 datasets. Besides that, the proposed models have much fewer parameters than them.

Table 1. Test error rate (%) on CIFAR datasets: α denotes the combination factor and K denotes the number of output feature map channels in every basic module. Results that are better than all competing methods are marked **bold** and the overall best results are **blue**. "+" indicates the data augmentation (translation and/or mirroring) of datasets. "*" indicates results obtained by our implementations. All the results of DenseNets are run with Dropout. The proposed models (*e.g.*, tiny PCSB-Net) achieve lower error rates while using fewer or equal parameters than DenseNet.

Method	Version and structure settings	Depth	Params	C10	C10+	C100	C100+
ResNet	[3]	110	1.7M	-	6.61	-	-
	Reported by [5]	110	1.7M	13.63	6.41	44.74	27.22
	With Stochastic Depth [5]	110	1.7M	11.66	5.23	37.80	24.58
		1202	10.2M	-	4.91	-	-
	Pre-activation (reported by [4])	164	1.7M	11.26	5.46	35.58	24.33
		1001	10.2M	10.56	4.62	33.47	22.71
	Wide ResNet [14]	16	11.0M	-	4.81	-	22.07
DenseNet	$K = 12$	40	1.0M	7.11*	5.82*	29.26*	26.96*
		58	2.2M	5.80*	5.08*	26.86*	25.46*
PCSB-Net	$\alpha = 2$, $K = 20$	150	1.0M	**5.62**	5.56	**24.73**	24.32
	$\alpha = 2$, $K = 28$	150	1.86M	**5.44**	5.08	**25.12**	22.36
	$\alpha = 3$, $K = 27$	150	1.6M	**5.08**	4.96	**24.56**	22.76
	$\alpha = 4$, $K = 32$	150	2.2M	**5.12**	3.92	**24.16**	21.80
	$\alpha = 2$, $K = 28$, with inter-active	150	1.86M	**5.32**	4.88	**22.60**	21.76
tiny PCSB-Net	-	150	**0.44M**	6.12	5.96	**26.12**	25.45

Then the PCSB-Nets are compared with DenseNets. For the models with 1.0M parameters, the PCSB-Net ($\alpha = 2$, $K = 20$) achieves relatively better performance than DenseNet (*e.g.*, the error rate is 5.62% vs 7.11% on C10, 5.56% vs 5.82% on C10+, 24.73% vs 29.26% on C100, and 24.32% vs 26.96% on C100+). Furthermore, when the number of parameters increases to 2.2M, the PCSB-Net ($\alpha = 4$, $K = 32$) has a better performance on the reduction of error rate than DenseNet (*e.g.*, the error rate is 5.12% vs 5.80% on C10, 3.92% vs 5.08% on C10+, 24.16% vs 26.86% on C100 and 21.80% vs 25.46% on C100+). Especially, the other PCSB-Nets all have obtained better results on some relevant datasets, for example, compared with DenseNet (2.2M parameters), the PCSB-Net ($\alpha = 2$, $K = 28$, 1.86M parameters), utilizing intermediate activation (we will talk about its effect later), has error rate reduction of 4.26% and 3.70% on C100 and C100+ with fewer parameters.

Parameter Efficiency. In order to test the efficiency of parameters, a tiny PCSB-Net is designed, which has a little difference from PCSB-Net ($\alpha = 2$, $K = 20$). To design a tiny model using fewer parameters and obtain a competitive result, the output channels of the last layer's bottleneck in each module is set to K/2, and the two transition module's output is respectively set to 160 and 304. This tiny network has only 0.44M parameters and obtains a comparable performance (the error rate is shown in Table 1) to that of DenseNet (with 1.0M parameters). In addition, in comparison with other architectures, although some PCSB-Nets have much fewer parameters, they all get better performance.

Since the pyramidal combination of separable branches implemented by "grouped convolution" operation is utilized in every module, fewer parameters can be used to learn the object features, so that the parameters' ability of catching information is largely improved. From these contrast experiments, the novel models have significantly improved the capability of parameters.

Computational Complexity. As shown in Fig. 5, the complexity of computations is compared between DenseNets and the PCSB-Nets. The error rates reveal that the PCSB-net can achieve generally better performance than DenseNets with likely times of flop operations ("multiply-add" step). Especially in Fig. 5(b), the PCSB-net with fewest flops obtains the lower C100 error rate than DenseNet with most Flops ($(1.8 \times 10^8$, 26.12%) vs $(5.9 \times 10^8$, 26.86%)). The less computational complexity is attributed to our branchy structure in the basic module. This branchy structure results in the input feature maps and convolutional filters are all divided into a specific number of groups. In other words, each filter only performs on much less input channels in the corresponding group, which is contributing to much fewer flop operations.

Model's Capacity and Overfitting. As the increasing of α and K, our model can achieve a better performance, which may result from more parameters. Especially, this trend can be evidently seen from the Table 1, compared with PCSB-Net ($\alpha = 2$, $K = 20$), the error rate obtained from PCSB-Net ($\alpha = 4$, $K = 32$)

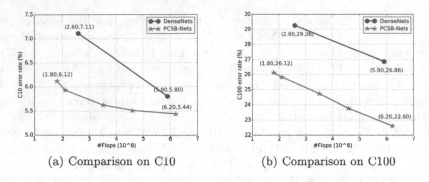

(a) Comparison on C10   (b) Comparison on C100

Fig. 5. Computational complexity comparison.

decreases by 1.64% and 2.52% on the C10+ and C100+ datasets respectively. Based on these different PCSB-Nets' results, our model can catch the features better when the model has more branches and output feature maps in every module at the first and second dense blocks.

In addition, it also suggests that the bigger networks do not get into any troubles of optimization and overfitting. Due to C100 and C100+ datasets have an abundance of object classes, who can validate the performance of models more strongly. The error rate and training loss are plotted in Fig. 6, which are obtained by DenseNets and PCSB-Nets on these two datasets in the course of the training. From Fig. 6(a) and (c), our models have lower error rate converges than DenseNets, despite the tiny PCSB-Net has only $0.44M$ parameters. And with the increase of the number of parameters, the model will have a lower error rate. However, in Fig. 6(b) and (d), the training loss obtained by PCSB-Net (with $1.0M$ parameters) converges lower than DenseNet (with $1.0M$ parameters). While to the models with $2.2M$ parameters, PCSB-Net and DenseNet have reached an almost identical training loss converges, especially, PCSB-Net converges even slightly higher than DenseNet on C100, which implies our model can avoid overfitting problem better, when the model has a bigger size without adequate training data. We argue although the bigger networks have much more parameters, they also have many branches in every module leading to distributing the parameters to these branches. Accordingly, this architecture can be regarded as an ensemble of many small networks from both horizontal and vertical aspects contributing to alleviating the trouble of overfitting well.

3.3   Affected Factors of PCSB-Nets' Optimization

In this part, we will discuss some affected factors by selecting appropriate hyperparameters and some regular techniques to optimize the PCSB-Nets.

Effect of Combination Factor. In order to explore the efficiency of the PCSB-Net's module, we observe the results of different PCSB-Nets with combination

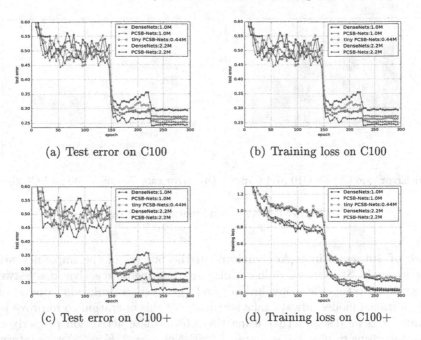

(a) Test error on C100

(b) Training loss on C100

(c) Test error on C100+

(d) Training loss on C100+

Fig. 6. Training profile on C100 and C100+: comparison of error rate and training loss in the process of training about different models with different number of parameters on C100 and C100+.

factor $\alpha = 2$, $\alpha = 3$ and $\alpha = 4$ (shown in Table 1). Because of the limitation of the implementation of "grouped convolution", the number of output channels must be the integer times of groups, hence we set $K = 28$, $K = 27$ and $K = 32$ respectively. These three PCSB-Nets are without the intermediate activation operation. Finally, in Fig. 7, we find that with the increase of combination factor α, the error rate approximately displays a decline trend, for instance, the PCSB-Net with $\alpha = 4$ achieves a much better performance on C10+, C100 and C100+. It also gets a comparable error rate on C10, most probably in that this model is the most complex one and C10 dataset merely has 10 object classes without any data augmentation. Furthermore, the model with $\alpha = 3$ is also superior to the networks with $\alpha = 2$ except on C100+. This is because these two architectures have almost the same output feature map channels of every module and the former has much more branches at the bottom layer, which results in PCSB-Net ($\alpha = 3$) has smaller parameters and obtains better performance on those less abundant datasets. However, in Fig. 7(b), C100+ is the most abundant dataset, consequently, PCSB-Net ($\alpha = 3$) has a relatively poor generalization, but it also has a competitive result (22.76% vs 22.36%). On account of the comparison of these three networks, the models with more branches will gain a better accuracy and improve the efficiency of parameters, since the networks with more branches will catch the images' information from much more perspectives and fuse the information more thoroughly and carefully.

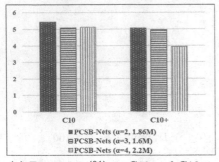
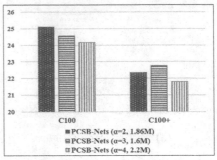

(a) Error rate (%) on C10 and C10+   (b) Error rate (%) on C100 and C100+

Fig. 7. Effects of combination factor α.

Effect of Intermediate Activation. In the process of the implementation of the above PCSB-Net, we didn't utilize any intermediate activations between the "grouped point-wise convolution" and "grouped convolution" operations. But traditional models always take advantage of this operation to improve performance and we discover that using the intermediate activation properly can obtain surprising results. For example, PCSB-Net ($\alpha = 2, K = 28$) with intermediate activation can drop the error rate to 21.76% on C100+ dataset. This model has fewer parameters and gets even slightly better performance than PCSB-Net ($\alpha = 4, K = 32$) without intermediate activation.

However, not all the models are suitable for this operation, in order to use it more reasonably, we perform four different sizes of networks with the same number of branches ($\alpha = 2$) and different output feature maps in every module on C100 dataset, and the results have been shown in Table 2. From the results, similar to traditional models, when the model has intermediate activation, the error rate will decrease as the increasing of output channels. But, when the model doesn't have intermediate activation, the error rate will decrease first and increase at the next stage as the growth of the output channels, for example, ($K = 20, error = 24.74\%$) is the turning point. Furthermore, when the number of output channels is small, the model utilizing this operation will obtain a lower accuracy than the model without this operation, however, when the number of output channels is relatively large, the model with intermediate activation will perform much better in the experiments.

Table 2. Intermediate activation effect on different sizes PCSB-models.

Model	With inter-active C100 err.	Without inter-active C100 err.
PCSB-Nets ($\alpha = 2, K = 16$)	26.08	25.84
PCSB-Nets ($\alpha = 2, K = 20$)	25.62	**24.74**
PCSB-Nets ($\alpha = 2, K = 24$)	23.76	25.08
PCSB-Nets ($\alpha = 2, K = 28$)	**22.60**	25.12

As being shown by Chollet in [1], Xception model doesn't utilize the interme-diate activation, since in shallow deep feature spaces (one channel per branch), the non-linearity may be detrimental to the final performance most probably because of the loss of information. For PCSB-Net, a very small number of out-put feature maps will lead to every branch also with fewer feature maps, which can be seen close to the Xception model, accordingly, our models have nearly same properties with it and don't need the intermediate activation. Moreover, when the number of output feature maps increases in a small range, the perfor-mance will be improved because the capacity growth of networks brings more positive impact than the negative impact from not utilizing intermediate activa-tion to the final results. On the contrary, when every branch has relative more input channels, it is best to employ this operation in the model, since every branch will have much ampler information.

4   Conclusions

A novel kind of network architecture, PCSB-Net, is introduced in this paper. This architecture can deal with bottom information from many aspects and fuse the features gradually by the exponentially pyramidal combination structures. Addi-tionally, we also explore some affected factors of the PCSB-Net's optimization, such as the combination factor and intermediate activation operation. This kind of structures are evaluated on CIFAR datasets. The experimental results show that even the tiny PCSB-Net can achieve a relatively better and competitive performance with just $0.44M$ parameters (about half of the parameters of the smallest DenseNets). In comparison with other models, all the PCSB-Nets obtain better performances with much fewer parameters. Consequently, the PCSB-Nets can largely improve the parameters' efficiency without performance penalty.

Acknowledgement. The work is supported by the NSFC fund (61332011), Shenzhen Fundamental Research fund (JCYJ20170811155442454, GRCK2017042116121208), and Medical Biometrics Perception and Analysis Engineering Laboratory, Shenzhen, China.

References

1. Chollet, F.: Deep learning with separable convolutions. arXiv preprint arXiv:1610.02357 (2016)
2. Glorot, X., Bordes, A., Bengio, Y.: Deep sparse rectifier neural networks. J. Mach. Learn. Res. **15** (2011)
3. He, K., Zhang, X., Ren, S., Sun, J.: Deep residual learning for image recognition. In: The IEEE Conference on Computer Vision and Pattern Recognition (CVPR), pp. 770–778 (2016)
4. Huang, G., Liu, Z., Weinberger, K.Q.: Densely connected convolutional networks (2016)

5. Huang, G., Sun, Y., Liu, Z., Sedra, D., Weinberger, K.Q.: Deep networks with stochastic depth. In: Leibe, B., Matas, J., Sebe, N., Welling, M. (eds.) ECCV 2016. LNCS, vol. 9908, pp. 646–661. Springer, Cham (2016). https://doi.org/10.1007/978-3-319-46493-0_39
6. Ioffe, S., Szegedy, C.: Batch normalization: accelerating deep network training by reducing internal covariate shift. Computer Science (2015)
7. Jia, Y., Shelhamer, E., Donahue, J., Karayev, S., Long, J.: Caffe: convolutional architecture for fast feature embedding. Eprint Arxiv pp. 675–678 (2014)
8. Krizhevsky, A., Sutskever, I., Hinton, G.E.: Imagenet classification with deep convolutional neural networks. Adv. Neural Inf. Process. Syst. **25**(2), 2012 (2012)
9. Larsson, G., Maire, M., Shakhnarovich, G.: FractalNet: ultra-deep neural networks without residuals (2016)
10. Lecun, Y., Bottou, L., Bengio, Y., Haffner, P.: Gradient-based learning applied to document recognition. Proc. IEEE **86**(11), 2278–2324 (1998)
11. Sutskever, I., Martens, J., Dahl, G., Hinton, G.: On the importance of initialization and momentum in deep learning. In: International Conference on Machine Learning (2013)
12. Szegedy, C., Liu, W., Jia, Y., Sermanet, P.: Going deeper with convolutions. In: Computer Vision and Pattern Recognition, pp. 1–9 (2014)
13. Szegedy, C., Vanhoucke, V., Ioffe, S., Shlens, J., Wojna, Z.: Rethinking the inception architecture for computer vision. Computer Science (2015)
14. Zagoruyko, S., Komodakis, N.: Wide residual networks. arXiv preprint arXiv:1605.07146 (2016)

Feature Visualization Based Stacked Convolutional Neural Network for Human Body Detection in a Depth Image

Xiao Liu[1,2,3]ⓘ, Ling Mei[1,2,3]ⓘ, Dakun Yang[1,2,3], Jianhuang Lai[1,2,3]ⓘ, and Xiaohua Xie[1,2,3(✉)]ⓘ

[1] Sun Yat-sen University, Guangzhou 510006, China
xiexiaoh6@mail.sysu.edu.cn
[2] Guangdong Key Laboratory of Information Security Technology, Guangzhou, China
[3] Key Laboratory of Machine Intelligence and Advanced Computing, Ministry of Education, Guangzhou, China

Abstract. Human body detection is a key technology in the fields of biometric recognition, and the detection in a depth image is rather challenging due to serious noise effects and lack of texture information. For addressing this issue, we propose the feature visualization based stacked convolutional neural network (FV-SCNN), which can be trained by a two-layer unsupervised learning. Specifically, the next CNN layer is obtained by optimizing a sparse auto-encoder (SAE) on the reconstructed visualization of the former to capture robust high-level features. Experiments on SZU Depth Pedestrian dataset verify that the proposed method can achieve favorable accuracy for body detection. The key of our method is that the CNN-based feature visualization actually pursues a data-driven processing for a depth map, and significantly alleviates the influences of noise and corruptions on body detection.

Keywords: Human detection · Depth image · Feature visualization
Sparse auto-encoder · Convolutional neural network

1 Introduction

Human body detection is a basic task in biometric recognition which can be widely applied in tracking, gait recognition and face anti-spoofing detection [1]. However, earlier detection methods used RGB camera is unavailable in some special cases such as low-lighting scenes. To address this problem, depth cameras have been considered for the human detection. Compared with RGB image, depth image containing the 3D structure of the scene is insensitive to lighting changes. Therefore human body detection in depth image has become an active and attractive research area in the computer vision community [2].

Regarding to human body detection in depth image, most of depth descriptors are similar to those in RGB or gray images [3]. For instance, Wu et al. [4]

ⓒ Springer Nature Switzerland AG 2018
J.-H. Lai et al. (Eds.): PRCV 2018, LNCS 11257, pp. 87–98, 2018.
https://doi.org/10.1007/978-3-030-03335-4_8

proposed Histogram of Depth Difference (HDD) descriptor and Spinello [5] proposed Histograms of Oriented Depths (HOD) descriptor, which were similar to HOG. Yu et al. [6] proposed a Simplified Local Ternary Patterns (SLTP) descriptor, which improved the Local Ternary Patterns (LTP) and apply to human body detection in depth imagery. However, a CNN with only one convolutional layer and one pooling layer is used in [3], which actually expresses a shallow representation of the depth image. In general, a deep representation obtained by a deep CNN is better to express an image than a shallow representation [7]. Therefore, we would like to investigate how to develop Su et al.'s method [3] to a deeper version.

Since it is unreasonable to use original image patches for training all network layers, we employ the feature visualization technology to generate layer-specific images at each network layer, then extract layer-specific image patches to train corresponding SAE. Specifically, we adopt the image representation inverting algorithm [8], which is able to use only information from image representation to reconstruct the image. Figure 1 illustrates the images reconstructed from the features at different convolution layers (conv1–conv5) for a given input image. As shown, the reconstructed images correspond to multi-level semantic abstraction but hold some invariant geometric and photometric information [9]. We call these reconstructed images as layer-specific *high-level images*.

Fig. 1. Illustration of the feature visualization for convolutional neural networks.

Overall, the feature visualization based stacked convolutional neural network (FV-SCNN) is proposed to extract features for human body detection in depth images. FV-SCNN is rather different from Stacked Sparse Autoencoders (SSAE) [10] or Stacked Denoising Autoencoders (SAE) [11]. Specially, the CNN-based feature visualization actually achieves a data-driven processing for depth map, and enables the FV-SCNN to alleviate the influences of noise and corruptions on body detection.

Moreover, sliding window approach is widely used in body detection task [12], but it is rather time-consuming. To address this problem, we follow Su et al.'s method [3] to use the histogram of depth to extract candidate depth planes. Combined with the multi-scale window strategy, our method can not only avoid the time-consuming siding window search, but also generate high-quality candidates for body detection. Compared with [3] that uses k-means algorithm to detect the candidate center, our method is more robust to the noise, corruption, and the non-body parts.

The remainder of the paper is outlined as followed. The detailed introduction of the proposed method is presented in Sect. 2. Experiments are reported in Sect. 3 and the conclusion of the paper is made in Sect. 4.

2 Technical Approach

2.1 The Overview of the FV-SCNN Body Detection Framework

We utilize the FV-SCNN to learn the candidate body centers in depth images, then develop a multi-scale body candidate windows with body centers to locate the body areas.

The proposed FV-SCNN based human body detection framework is shown in Fig. 2. As shown, the proposed model contains two CNNs with each containing one convolutional layer and one pooling layer. In the training module, a large mount of image patches are randomly extracted from original training set (depth images) and used to train a SAE network. In our experiment, the size of image patch is set to 16 by 16. The optimized weights and the bias of the SAE network are employed to construct the filter of the first CNN. After that, the sub-images with fixed aspect ratio (e.g., 120:64) extracted from original training set are resized to 120 × 64 and put into the first CNN, yielding corresponding feature maps. Based on each feature map, a high level image can be reconstructed by using the feature visualization technology [8]. Like the scheme to construct the first CNN, the randomly extracted patches from the first-layer high-level body images are used to train the weights of another SAE for forming the second CNN. After the second CNN is formed, the high-level images are input the second CNN followed by a PCA to produce the final features. The features of different labelled sub-images (body vs. non-body) are further used to train a SVM classifier. Specifically, the sub-image exactly containing a human body is labelled as a body sub-image, otherwise as non-body one.

In the application module, a set of candidate windows (sub-images) are generated for each input image. Each candidate sub-image is resized to 120 × 64 and put into the first CNN. The corresponding high level image reconstructed from the first-layer feature map is further fed into the second CNN to export the features, and further processed by PCA for a dimensionality reduction. The classifier response based on the final features will judge whether current window

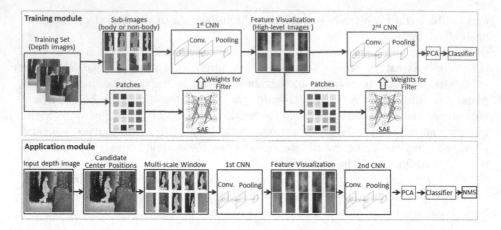

Fig. 2. Illustration of the proposed human body detection framework.

contains a human body. Finally, the non-maximal suppression (NMS) is used to merge the overlapping detected windows and get the final locations.

We demonstrate only two-layer CNNs in our model because a practicable computing cost should be considered for a body detector. Specially, the first CNN-based feature visualization tends to perform a data-driven processing for depth map, and alleviate the influences of noise, corruption, and non-body components on body detection. Actually, our model can be directly extended to more than two layers by utilizing the reconstructed high-level image of a specific CNN as the input of the following CNN. Details about our method are presented in Sect. 3.

2.2 Sparse Auto-Encoder (SAE)

Recently, deep multi-layer neural networks have many levels of non-linearities allowing them to compactly represent highly non-linear and highly-varying functions. Auto-Encoder (AE) is an unsupervised feature learning algorithm which aims to develop better feature representation of input high-dimensional data by finding the correlation among the data. For an AE network, the output vector is equal to the input vector. Training an AE can minimize reconstruction error amounts and obtain the mutual information between input and learnt representation. Intuitively, if a representation allows a good reconstruction of its input, it means that the representation has retained much of the information that was presented in the input. Specifically, the AE is a three-layers neural network with a single hidden layer forming an encoder and a decoder which proposed in [13].

Auto-Encoder (AE) can avoid the labor-intensive and handcraft feature design. When the number of hidden units in AE is less than that of the input units, a compression representation achieved. When the number of hidden units is larger, even more than that of the input units, interesting structure of input data can still be discovered by imposing a sparsity constraint on the hidden units. The Auto-Encoder with only few hidden units activated for a given input is called the Sparse Auto-Encoder (SAE). Specially, the sparsity regularization typically leads to more interpretable features for representing a visual object.

For a SAE network, let $\hat{\rho}_j$ be the mean activation probability in the jth hidden unit, namely $\hat{\rho}_j = (1/m)] \sum_{i=1}^{m} h_j$. Let ρ be the desired probability of being activated. Sparsity is imposed on the network, it is obvious that $\rho \ll 1$. Here Kullback-Leibler (KL) divergence is used to measure the similarity between the desired and actual distributions, as shown in the following equation

$$KL(\rho \parallel \hat{\rho}_j) = \rho \log \frac{\rho}{\hat{\rho}_j} + (1 - \rho) \log \frac{1 - \rho}{1 - \hat{\rho}_j}. \tag{1}$$

The SAE model can be formulated as the following optimization problem

$$\min_{W,b} \left[\sum_{i=1}^{m} (h_{W,b}(x^{(i)}) - y^{(i)})^2 + \lambda(\|W\|_2^2) + \beta \sum_{j=1}^{k} KL(\rho \| \hat{\rho}_j) \right], \tag{2}$$

where the first term is the reconstruction cost, the second term is a regularization on weight to avoid over-fitting, and the last term enforces the mapping sparsity from the input layer to hidden layer. The parameters λ and β are regularization factors used to make a tradeoff between the reconstruction cost, weight decay and sparsity penalty term. Typically, back-propagation algorithm is used to solve Eq. (2).

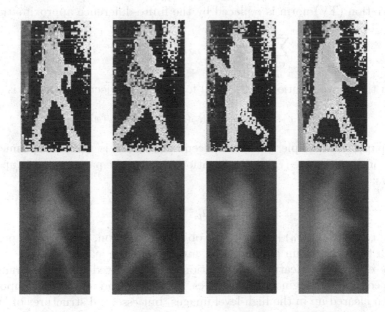

Fig. 3. Examples of feature visualization for depth images. The first row are the original images and the second row are the corresponding high level images reconstructed from CNN features.

2.3   Feature Visualization

In the proposed model, the feature maps of the first CNN are inverted and visualized to generate the high-level images as the input of the second CNN. We adapt Aravindh Mahendran's method [8] to achieve this goal. Given a representation function $\Phi : \mathbb{R}^{H \times W \times C} \to \mathbb{R}^d$ and a representation $\Phi_0 = \Phi(x_0)$ to be inverted, x_0 is the input feature image, reconstruction finds the image $x \in \mathbb{R}^{H \times W \times C}$ that minimizes the objective

$$x^* = \operatorname{argmin}_{x \in \mathbb{R}^{H \times W \times C}} \ell(\Phi(x), \Phi_0) + \lambda \Re(x), \tag{3}$$

where the loss ℓ compares the image representation $\Phi(x)$ to the target one Φ_0 and $\Re : \mathbb{R}^{H \times W \times C} \to \mathbb{R}$ is a regulariser capturing a natural image prior.

In this paper, as same as [8], we choose the Euclidean distance for the loss function ℓ as follows

$$\ell(\Phi(x), \Phi_0) = \|\Phi(x) - \Phi_0\|^2. \tag{4}$$

For the regulariser $\Re(x)$, it contains two parts which incorporate two image priors, then it can be written as

$$\Re(x) = \Re_\alpha(x) + \Re_{V^\beta}(x), \tag{5}$$

where $\Re_\alpha(x) = \|x\|_\alpha^\alpha$ is the α-norm, which encourages the range of the image to stay within a target interval instead of diverging. Since images are discrete, the total variation (TV) norm is replaced by the finite-difference approximation:

$$\Re_{V^\beta}(x) = \sum_{i,j} \left((x_{i,j+1} - x_{i,j})^2 + (x_{i+1,j} - x_{i,j})^2 \right)^{\frac{\beta}{2}}. \tag{6}$$

Through the above mentioned, the final form of the objective function is

$$\|\Phi(x) - \Phi_0\|_2^2 + \lambda_\alpha \Re_\alpha(x) + \lambda_{V^\beta} \Re_{V^\beta}(x). \tag{7}$$

In this paper, the simple gradient descent procedure is used to optimize the problem of the objective (7). In the iteration process, the parameter x is updated as follows:

$$\begin{aligned} \mu_t &= m\mu_{t-1} - \eta_{t-1} \Delta E(x) \\ x_{t+1} &= x_t + \mu_t, \end{aligned} \tag{8}$$

where $E(x) = \ell(\Phi(x), \Phi_0) + \lambda \Re(x)$ is the objective function, $m\mu_{t-1}$ is the momentum with the momentum parameter m, and η_{t-1} is the learning rate.

Some examples of feature visualization are illustrated in Fig. 3. Compared with the contents in original depth images, both noise and non-body components have been cleared up in the high-level images, but essential structures of human body are preserved.

2.4   Localization of Body Candidate

We follow Su et al.'s method [3] to compute the histogram of depth values in a depth image and further to extract a set of candidate depth planes with respect to the local peaks of the histogram. The depth map with respect to each depth plane is converted into a binary image, which indicates whether a pixel belongs to current depth plane (1 for yes and 0 for not). Such a binary image is named as a depth plane mask. For locating the human body, Su et al. [3] apply the k-means clustering on each depth plane mask and regard the clustering center as the body center of candidate. However, the accuracy of this manner could be easily affected by the noise and corruption of the depth map as well as the non-body components.

For more accurately locating the human body center, we propose using the vertical projection method to locate the X-coordinate of the body candidate. Assumes that the human center position is (x_0, y_0). We observe that the x_0-th column of depth map generally contains more points than other columns in current depth plane. Inspired by this, the current depth plane mask is vertically projected onto the horizontal axis. The positions corresponding to the maximum projection value on the horizontal axis are regarded as the X-coordinates of the candidate body centers. For each candidate X-coordinate x_p, we perform an 1 D average filtering on the x_p column of the depth plane mask. In our experiment, the filter length is set to 8. After filtering, the location with respect to the maximum response is taken as the Y-coordinates of the candidate body center. When multiple locations hold the maximum response value, the maximum coordinate and the minimum one among these locations are averaged to be the Y-coordinates of the candidate body center. The proposed candidate body center localization method is illustrated in Fig. 4. At each candidate center, we generate multi-scale windows as the candidate sub-images for the first CNN to get corresponding feature maps, and use the pre-trained classifier to judge the human body.

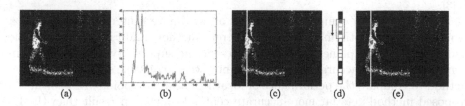

(a)   (b)   (c)   (d)   (e)

Fig. 4. Illustration of candidate body center localization scheme. For each candidate depth plane mask (a), it is vertically projected onto the X-axle (b). The column corresponds to maximum projection value is selected (c), and then is smoothed by a 1-D average filter (d). The location with respect to the maximum filtering response is taken as the candidate body center.

3   Experiments

3.1   Experimental Setting

This section presents experiments on SZU Depth Pedestrian dataset [4,14] to evaluate the proposed method for body detection. We divide the dataset as the principle in [3]. The dataset is captured by a Time-Of-Flight (TOF) camera, only depth images are used in our experiments, the resolution of them is 176×144 pixels. The number of training and testing images are 4435 and 4029 respectively. We found that both the training of the feature learning with SAE and softmax classifier need only few training examples, therefore we used 400 training images which extracted 40,000 patches randomly for training the first SAE. The number of neurons in the feature layer of SAE is set as 64. The sub-images are extracted and normalized to the size of 120×64. The size of pooling filter in each CNN is set 7×7 and the model finally outputs a 6,720 dimensional feature. The output feature is finally processed by PCA to produce a 1,000 dimensional feature vector and sent to the SVM classifier. For training the classifier, the proportion of positive and negative samples should be 1:6 [3]. We extracted 100 body sub-images and 600 non-body sub-images from the training set. These sub-images are reconstructed to train the second SAE. For body detection application, 300 positive samples (the depth images containing a pedestrian) as well as 300 negative samples are randomly opted for testing.

We first use two experiments to investigate the performance of the proposed candidate localization method, and then compare the FV-SCNN based body detection method with related methods.

3.2   Investigation on the Body Candidate Localization Method

In this experiment, we compare the proposed body candidate center localization method (in Sect. 2.4) with the k-means based method [3]. Both methods work on the same depth plane detected by the histogram analysis method mentioned in [3].

Figure 5 shows a comparison example of candidate center localization on a depth plane in a depth image by using different method, and Fig. 6 illustrates the results on all depth planes. In order to present the superiority of our method in terms of extracting accurate candidate points, we exploits the same classification method to compare the performance of locating candidate points. As shown, the proposed method gets far more accurate center localization result than the K-means method, and generates less candidates. It is notable that the k-means localization method is easily affected by the non-body objects. Further, it is a remarkable fact that k-means cost a lot of computation time. In our experiment, it takes 14.7921 s to generate all the candidate positions for each depth image while our method cost only 0.0046 s. Additionally, k-means based method is sensitive to the clustering initialization.

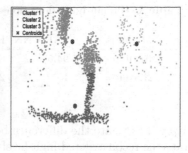

Fig. 5. Illustration of candidate center localization result on a depth plane. Left is the result of our method (shown with red cross) while the right is the result of the k-means based method (shown with black cross). (Color figure online)

Fig. 6. Illustration of the candidate center localization result on all depth planes. Left is the result of our method and the middle is the result of k-means based method. Right is the result of k-means based method by extending more eight points around each candidate position by 16 pixel step, which is also suggested in [3].

3.3 Investigation on the Feature Visualization Based Stacked Network

In this experiment, we compare the proposed FV-SCNN model with the SAE-CNN method [3] which forms a single-layer CNN by optimizing a SAE. We also implement a specially designed HOG-FV-CNN model, which first performs HOG presentation visualization [15] to obtain a HOG based high-level reconstruction image, and then use a SAE-CNN model to extract the features for classification. Simply speaking, in regard to HOG-FV-CNN, the HOG is used in place of the first CNN in the proposed FV-SCNN model.

The human body detection results by different method are shown in Table 1. In this experiment, the sub-images are directly used for testing. That is, the algorithms do not need to localize the body candidate but only return whether the input sub-image contains a body. The classification accuracy rates are reported. As shown, the performance of HOG-FV-CNN is obviously worse than the FV-SCNN model, even worse than the single-layer SAE-CNN model. The experimental results support that the deeper SAE-CNN network outperforms the single-layer one. Furthermore, the CNN features work better than the hand-designed HOG features in our framework.

Table 1. Human body detection accuracies by different methods.

Methods	SAE-CNN	HOG-FV-CNN	FV-SCNN
Accuracy rate	94.5%	86%	**96.33%**
♯Layer	1	2	2

To deeply investigate the difference between HOG-FV-CNN and FV-SCNN, we illustrate the reconstructed high-level images by these two methods in Fig. 7. As shown, the high-level image generated by FV-SCNN contains the main human structures but suppresses the noise and corruption (especially pay attention to the upper-left part of image). By contrast, the reconstructed high-level image by HOG is much rougher and the body configuration is distorted. The main reason may be that the SAE is learnt by using the patches from the body sub-images, so that the formed CNN responds more prominently on the body parts than the non-body parts. However, as a kind of hand-craft features, the HOG takes responses equally on different parts.

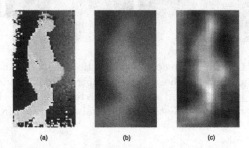

(a)   (b)   (c)

Fig. 7. Examples of high-level images reconstructed by different method. (a) is the original depth image, (b) and (c) are the high-level images reconstructed by FV-SCNN and HOG-FV-CNN, respectively.

3.4   Comparison with State-of-the-Art Methods

We also compared the proposed method with five state-of-the-art depth descriptors for pedestrian detection in depth imagery, including the Histogram of Oriented Depths (HOD) [5], Histogram of Depth Difference (HDD) [4], Relational Depth Similarity Feature (RDSF) [16], Simplified Local Ternary Patterns (SLTP) [6], and SAE-CNN [3]. For a fair comparison, we adopt the same candidate windows and the same classifier (SVM) for different methods. The body detection accuracy is evaluated using the intersection over union (IoU), which is defined as the ratio of intersection to union between the results and ground-truth bounding boxes. When the IoU is larger than 0.5, we treat current result as a correct detection.

The body detection results of different methods are shown in Fig. 8, which plots miss rate against FPPI (False Positives Per Image). Smaller miss rate at a fixed FPPI means more accuracy of the detection. As shown, the proposed FV-SCNN method outperforms all other methods, and SAE-CNN perform better than HOD, HDD, RDSF and SLTP, the superiority becomes more obvious with a higher FPPI because we add the candidate localization method to the proposed method from a systematical standpoint. The result revealing that the feature learning is better than using hand-crafted feature. The proposed FV-SCNN performs better than SAE-CNN, which verifies that a deeper network architecture is more helpful for feature learning, and the proposed feature visualization based network stacking manner is effective.

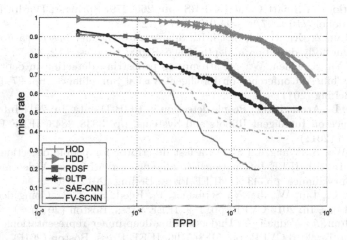

Fig. 8. Comparison of the proposed FV-SCNN with state-of-the-art methods including hand-designed descriptors (HOD, HDD, RDSF) and learning based feature (SAE-CNN).

4   Conclusion and Future Work

This paper presents a feature visualization based stacked convolutional neural network (FV-SCNN), where the feature visualization technology is used for connecting multiple CNN layers. The FV-SCNN can be learned in a layer-wise unsupervised manner by SAE. The FV-SCNN has been demonstrated for human body detection in depth images. Experiments and visualization results reveal that the proposed method significantly alleviates the influences of noise, corruption, and non-body components on body detection. The proposed method also obtains a better body candidate localization result than the traditional methods in body detection. In the future, we would like to apply the FV-SCNN to other visual recognition processing tasks with deeper architectures. We also would like to develop a fine-tuning method for the FV-SCNN, and investigate how to jointly optimize the FV-SCNN and the classifier.

Acknowledgements. This project is supported by the Natural Science Foundation of China (61573387, 61672544), Guangzhou Project (201807010070), and Fundamental Research Funds for the Central Universities (No. 161gpy41).

References

1. Mei, L., Yang, D., Feng, Z., Lai, J.: WLD-TOP based algorithm against face spoofing attacks. Biometric Recognition. LNCS, vol. 9428, pp. 135–142. Springer, Cham (2015). https://doi.org/10.1007/978-3-319-25417-3_17
2. Lee, G.-H., Kim, D.-S., Kyung, C.-M.: Advanced human detection using fused information of depth and intensity images. In: Kyung, C.-M. (ed.) Theory and Applications of Smart Cameras. KRS, pp. 265–279. Springer, Dordrecht (2016). https://doi.org/10.1007/978-94-017-9987-4_12
3. Su, S., Liu, Z., Xu, S., Li, S., Ji, R.: Sparse auto-encoder based feature learning for human body detection in depth image. Signal Process. **112**, 43–52 (2015)
4. Wu, S., Yu, S., Chen, W.: An attempt to pedestrian detection in depth images. In: 3rd Chinese Conference on Intelligent Visual Surveillance, pp. 97–100. IEEE Press, Beijing (2011)
5. Spinello, L., Arras, K.-O.: People detection in RGB-D data. In: 2011 International Conference on Intelligent Robots and Systems, pp. 3838–3843. IEEE Press, San Francisco (2011)
6. Yu, S., Wu, S., Wang, L.: SLTP: a fast descriptor for people detection in depth images. In: 9th IEEE International Conference on Advanced Video and Signal-Based Surveillance, pp. 43–47. IEEE Press, Beijing (2012)
7. Szegedy, C., Liu, W., Jia, Y., Sermanet, P., Reed, S., et al.: Going deeper with convolutions. In: 2015 CVPR, pp. 1–9. IEEE Press, Boston (2015)
8. Mahendran, A., Vedaldi, A.: Understanding deep image representations by inverting them. In: 2015 CVPR, pp. 5188–5196. IEEE Press, Boston (2015)
9. Mei, L., Chen, Z.-Y., Lai, J.-H.: Geodesic-based probability propagation for efficient optical flow. Electron. Lett. **54**(12), 758–760 (2018). https://doi.org/10.1049/el.2018.0394. Print ISSN: 0013-5194. Online ISSN: 1350-911X
10. Yang, D., Lai, J., Mei, L.: Deep representations based on sparse auto-encoder networks for face spoofing detection. In: You, Z., et al. (eds.) CCBR 2016. LNCS, vol. 9967, pp. 620–627. Springer, Cham (2016). https://doi.org/10.1007/978-3-319-46654-5_68
11. Vincent, P., Larochelle, H., Lajoie, I., Bengio, Y., Manzagol, P.-A.: Stacked denoising autoencoders: learning useful representations in a deep network with a local denoising criterion. J. Mach. Learn. Res. **11**(Dec), 3371–3408 (2010)
12. Uijlings, J., Van De Sande, K., Gevers, T., Smeulders, A.: Selective search for object recognition. Int. J. Comput. Vis. **104**(2), 154–171 (2013)
13. Hinton, G.-E., Salakhutdinov, R.-R.: Reducing the dimensionality of data with neural networks. Science **313**(5786), 504–507 (2006)
14. Li, Y.-R., Yu, S., Wu, S.: Pedestrian detection in depth images using framelet regularization. In: 2012 IEEE International Conference on Computer Science and Automation Engineering, CSAE, pp. 300–303. IEEE Press (2012)
15. Weinzaepfel, P., Jégou, H., Pérez, P.: Reconstructing an image from its local descriptors. In: 2011 CVPR, pp. 337–344. IEEE Press, Colorado Springs (2011)
16. Ikemura, S., Fujiyoshi, H.: Real-time human detection using relational depth similarity features. In: Kimmel, R., Klette, R., Sugimoto, A. (eds.) ACCV 2010. LNCS, vol. 6495, pp. 25–38. Springer, Heidelberg (2011). https://doi.org/10.1007/978-3-642-19282-1_3

Convolutional LSTM Based Video Object Detection

Xiao Wang[1,2,3], Xiaohua Xie[1,2,3(✉)], and Jianhuang Lai[1,2,3]

[1] School of Data and Computer Science, Sun Yat-sen University,
Guangzhou, China
xiexiaoh6@mail.sysu.edu.cn
[2] Guangdong Key Laboratory of Information Security Technology, Guangzhou,
China
[3] Key Laboratory of Machine Intelligence and Advanced Computing
of the Ministry of Education, Guangzhou, China

Abstract. The state-of-the-art performance for object detection has
been significantly improved over the past two years. Despite the effectiveness on still images, something stands in the way of transferring the
powerful detection networks to videos object detection. In this work, we
present a fast and accurate framework for video object detection that
incorporates temporal and contextual information using convolutional
LSTM [27]. Moreover, an Encoder-Decoder module is made up based
on the convolutional LSTM to predict the feature map. It is an end-
to-end learning framework and is general and flexible when combining
with still-image detection networks. It achieves significant improvement
on both speed and accuracy. Our method significantly improves upon
strong single-frame baselines in ImageNet VID [21], especially for more
challenging moving objects at high speed.

Keywords: Video object detection · Convolutional LSTM
Encoder-Decoder module

1 Introduction

Deep learning has achieved significant success and been widely applied to various
computer vision tasks such as image classification [7,25], object detection [1,3,4,
17], semantic segmentation [6,13], video representation [14], dense captioning [8],
etc. In the case of object detection, the performance has made a huge leap
forward with the success of deep Convolutional Neural Networks (CNN). To
make the object detection more challenging, ImageNet introduced a new task
for object detection from videos (VID), which brings object detection from still
image into the video domain. In this task, the object detection system is required
to give the position and the class of the objects in each frame. VID play an

---

X. Xie—This project is supported by the Natural Science Foundation of China
(61573387, 61672544), Guangzhou Project (201807010070).

© Springer Nature Switzerland AG 2018
J.-H. Lai et al. (Eds.): PRCV 2018, LNCS 11257, pp. 99–109, 2018.
https://doi.org/10.1007/978-3-030-03335-4_9

important helping role in a number of applications on video analysis such as video representation, video caption and object tracking.

However, existing methods focus on detecting objects in still images, and directly applying them to solve the video object detection is clumsy. Different from the ImageNet object detection (DET) challenge in still image, VID shows objects in image sequences and comes with additional challenges such as motion blur due to rapid camera or object motion, illumination variation due to scene changing or different camera angles, partial occlusion or unconventional object-to-camera poses, etc (See some examples in Fig. 1). The broad range of appearances varying in video make recognizing the class of object more difficult. Besides, video is a kind of data with high density, which raises a higher demand to object detector's speed and accuracy.

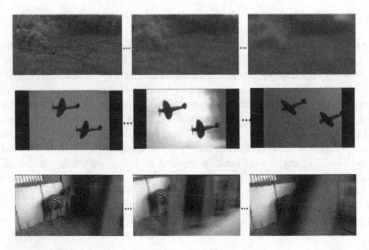

Fig. 1. Example special video images with motion blur, illumination variation and occlusion, respectively.

Although difficulties arise, videos have more rich temporal information than still image. How to exploit the relation among the image sequences become the crux of the video object detection methods. We seek to improve the video object detection quality by exploiting temporal information, in a principled way. As motivated by the success in precipitation nowcasting [27], using convolutional LSTM (ConvLSTM), we propose to improve the detection by spatiotemporal aggregation. Note that the ConvLSTM has convolutional structures in both the input-to-state and state-to-state transitions, so it can work with 2D spatial feature maps and solve the spatiotemporal sequence forecasting problem. This suggests that it may fit the video image sequences.

In this work, we propose a unified framework based on the ConvLSTM to tackle the problem of object detection in realistic video. The framework consists of three main modules: (1) firstly, a fully convolutional network, which can be some general pre-trained ImageNet models such as googlenet [25], resnet [7], to generate the feature map; (2) then a Encoder-Decoder module composed by two ConvLSTMs, one for the input feature maps of adjacent frames and another for the output feature map; (3) task module including RPN [3], the final classification subnetwork and regression subnetwork, just like the other two-stage detector. Finally, the entire architecture can be trained end-to-end.

2 Related Work

Object Detection from Still Image. State-of-the-art methods for general object detection [1,3,6,17,19,20] are mainly based on deep CNNs. In general, the detection networks are divided into two kinds according to whether the region proposals are needed. First, one-stage network that directly predict boxes for an image in one step such as YOLO [19], SSD [12] and second, two-stage network with Region Proposal Network such as Fast R-CNN [3], Faster R-CNN [20], R-FCN [1].

Our approach builds on R-FCN [1] which is a simple and efficient framework for object detection on region proposals with a fully convolutional nature. Unlike the Faster R-CNN [20], R-FCN reduces the cost for region classification by pushing the region-wise operations to the end of the network with the introduction of a position-sensitive RoI pooling layer which works on convolutional features that encode the spatially subsampled class scores of input RoIs.

Object Detection in Video. Since the object detection from video task has been introduced at the ImageNet challenge in 2015, it has drawn significant attention. Kang et al. [9,10] combined the still-image object detection with general object tracking method and proposed a tubelet proposal network to propagates predicted bounding boxes to neighboring frames and then generates tubelets by applying tracking algorithms from high-confidence bounding boxes. Seq-NMS [5] constructs sequences along nearby high-confidence bounding boxes from consecutive frames. Differing from these box-level post-processing methods, Zhu et al. [29,30] utilized a optical flow ConvNet for propagating the deep feature maps via a flow field instead of the bounding box.

Sequence Modeling. Recurrent neural networks, especially Long Short-Term Memory (LSTM), have been adopted to address many video processing tasks such as action recognition [16], video summarization [28],video representations [23] and object tracking [15]. However, limited by the fixed propagation route of existing LSTM structures where the input, cell output and states are all 1D vectors, most of these previous works can only learn some holistic information, which is impractical for image data.

Some recent approaches develop more complicated recurrent network structures. For instance, to apply the LSTM to image sequence, the ConvLSTM [27] was proposed for video prediction. In our method, we exploits spatiotemporal information by using ConvLSTM. Besides, the entire system is end-to-end trained for the task of video object detection.

3   Method

In this section, we first give an overview of object detection from video (Sect. 3.1) including the task setting and some base elements in the task. Then we give a detailed description of our framework design (Sect. 3.2). Section 3.3 describes the major component Encoder-Decoder module and introduces how to exploit the spatiotemporal information using ConvLSTM.

3.1   Overview

The ImageNet object detection from video (VID) task is similar to image object detection task (DET) in still images. There are 30 classes, which is a subset of 200 classes of the DET task. Given the input video images I_t where t is the time, the algorithms need to produce a set of annotations (r_t), which include class labels, confidence scores and bounding boxes. Therefore, a baseline approach is to apply an off-the-shelf object detector to each frame individually.

Most of the two-stage detection network include two major components: (1) a feature extraction subnetwork N_{feat} composed by a common set of convolutional layers which can generate the feature map $f_t = N_{feat}(I_t)$ on the input image; (2) a task-specific subnetwork N_{task} which executes the specific task such as classification, regression to output the result $r_t = N_{task}(f_t)$. Consecutive video frames are highly similar, likewise, their feature maps have a strong correlation. How to use the correlation information is what we present in the following sections.

3.2   Model Design

The proposed architecture takes every other frame $I_t \in R^{H_i \times W_i \times 3}$ at time t, and pushes them through a backbone N_{feat} (i.e. ResNet-101 [7]) to obtain feature maps $f_t \in R^{H_f \times W_f \times C_f}$ where H_f, W_f and C_f are the width, height and number of channels of the feature map, and then output the result r_t though the N_{task}. Our overall system builds on the R-FCN [1] object detector, specifically, the ResNet-101 models pre-trained for ImageNet classification as default. It works in two stages: first extracts candidate regions of interest (RoI) using a Region Proposal Network (RPN) [20]; and, second, performs region classification into different object categories and background by using a position-sensitive RoI pooling layer [1]. That is to say that every other frame needs to go through the whole R-FCN and get the result.

Let us now consider the other frames, which are not processed by the whole R-FCN. We extend this architecture by introducing a module named Encoder-Decoder to propagate the feature maps. It figures out how to properly fuse the features from multiple frames to get the feature map of current frame. Besides, we can control how many frames we want to fuse by defining the parameter T. Besides, to make the prediction more robust, a convolution layer follows behind the decoding ConvLSTM. Obviously, the module is much faster than the feature network. They are elaborated below (Fig. 2).

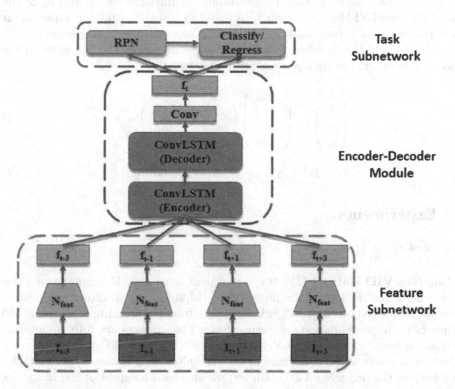

Fig. 2. Our proposed architecture based on ConvLSTM Encoder-Decoder module (see Sect. 3 for details).

3.3 Encoder-Decoder Module

The framework [24] provides a general framework for sequence-to-sequence learning problems, which include two stage: one to read the input sequence and the other to extract the output sequence, and its ability to capture long-term temporal dependencies makes it a natural choice for this application. Our spatiotemporal sequence, we use the Encoder-Decoder structure like in [24]. During the encoding step, use one ConvLSTM to read the input sequence feature maps, one timestep at a time, to compresses the whole input sequence into a hidden state tensor, and then to use another ConvLSTM to conduct the hidden state to give the prediction.

The equation of ConvLSTM are shown in Eqs. (1, 2) below, where '$*$' denotes the convolution operator. All the input-to-state kernels w_h and state-to-state kernels w_x are of size $3 \times 3 \times 512$ with the 1×1 padding. They are all randomly initialized. As we can see, the module is characterized by fewer parameters than the convolution feature network and the flow method [2,29]. Moreover, it is convenient to change the dependency scope, just adjust the parameter T.

For the start states, before the first input, we initialize the c_0 and h_0 of the encoding ConvLSTM to zero which means "no history", and the input x_t at each timestep are corresponding feature map. As well the initial state c_0 and cell output h_0 of the decoding ConvLSTM are copied from the last state of the encoding network, but its input are zeros.

$$\begin{pmatrix} i_t \\ f_t \\ o_t \\ g_t \end{pmatrix} = \begin{pmatrix} \sigma \\ \sigma \\ \sigma \\ tanh \end{pmatrix} \begin{pmatrix} w_h \\ w_x \end{pmatrix} * \begin{pmatrix} h_{t-1} \\ x_t \end{pmatrix} + b \tag{1}$$

$$c_t = f_t \cdot c_{t-1} + i_t \cdot g_t, \quad h_t = o_t \cdot tanh(c_t) \tag{2}$$

4 Experiments

4.1 Setup

ImageNet VID Dataset [21]. It is a prevalent large-scale benchmark for video object detection. Following the protocols in [10,30], model training and evaluation are performed on the 3,862 video snippets from the training set and the 555 snippets from the validation set, respectively. The snippets are fully annotated, and are at frame rates of 25 or 30 fps in general. There are 30 object categories. They are a subset of the categories in the ImageNet DET dataset. During training, besides the ImageNet VID train set, we also used a subset of the ImageNet DET train set which include the 30 categories.

Implementation Details. We use the stride-reduced ResNet-101 with dilated convolution in conv5 to reduce the effective stride and also increase its receptive field. The RPN is trained at 15 anchors corresponding to 5 scales and 3 aspect ratios, and apply non-maximum suppression (NMS) with an IoU threshold of 0.7 to select the top 300 proposals in each frame for training/testing our R-FCN detector. Then, like the Focal Loss [11] and online hard example mining method [22], we also select a certain number of hard region (with high loss) from the proposals produced by the RPN to make training more effective and efficient. By setting different weights for hard and non-hard proposals, the training can puts more focus on hard proposals. Note that, in this strategy, data forward and gradient backforward propagate through the same network.

In both training and testing, we use single scale images with shorter dimension of 400 pixels. In SGD training, 4 epochs (400K iterations) are performed on 2 GPUs, where the learning rates are 10^{-4} and 10^{-5} for the first 3 epochs and the last 1 epoch iterations, respectively.

For testing we apply NMS with IoU threshold of 0.3. For better analysis, the ground truth objects in validation set are divided into three types: slow, medium, fast according to their motion speed, just like [29] and we also report their mAP scores respectively, so we can do a more detailed analysis and in-depth understanding.

4.2 Results

Overall Results. Method R-FCN is the still-image method baseline which is trained on single-frame using ResNet-101. Note that we train the network on only two GPUs and do not add bells and whistles like multi-scale training/testing in order to facilitate comparison and draw clear conclusions. We investigate the effect of T, however, limited by the memory, we only test $T = 1, 2$ for encoding ConvLSTM. From the Table 1, the performance for single-frame testing is 73.19% mAP, but rises to 74.5% with our ConvLSTM based method. This 1.3% gain in accuracy shows that the ConvLSTM can effectively promotes the information from nearby frames in feature map lavel. Besides, when T increases (from 1 to 2), the performance also has an obvious growth (from 73.65% to 74.5%). As to runtime, the proposed ConvLSTM based method has about twice as fast, which is in accord with theory. Some example results are shown in Fig. 3.

Table 1. Performance comparison on the ImageNet VID validation set. The average precision (in %) for each class and the mean average precision over all classes is shown.

Method	airplane	antelope	bear	bicycle	bird	bus	car	cattle	dog	cat	elephant	fox
still(R-FCN)	88.11	83.26	83.33	63.55	70.29	74.40	56.81	69.64	74.15	78.98	77.06	89.64
ConvLSTM-based(T=1)	88.70	82.35	83.67	63.66	70.81	75.27	57.44	68.89	72.73	77.93	77.09	89.96
ConvLSTM-based(T=2)	89.30	83.43	84.21	64.75	71.61	76.54	58.29	69.95	73.56	78.86	77.67	90.55

Method	giant-panda	hamster	horse	lion	lizard	monkey	motor-cycle	rabbit	red-panda
still(R-FCN)	80.51	85.56	69.57	47.22	76.64	49.09	81.75	60.89	83
ConvLSTM-based(T=1)	81.2	87.0	69.36	54.64	76.94	47.99	81.72	62.78	82.72
ConvLSTM-based(T=2)	81.88	87.98	70.33	53.34	77.37	49.33	82.48	63.77	83.29

Method	sheep	snake	squirrel	tiger	train	turtle	water-craft	whale	zebra	mAP(%)	speed(fps)
still(R-FCN)	54.49	71.37	48.77	91.06	77.43	77.86	66.67	74.14	90.41	73.19	4.08
ConvLSTM-based(T=1)	56.55	71.9	48.2	91.27	78.5	78.4	67.03	74.46	90.36	73.65	7.9
ConvLSTM-based(T=2)	57.37	72.63	49.09	91.83	79.3	79.17	67.93	75.06	91.11	74.5	7.8

Table 2. Comparison of various approaches.

Method	mAP (%)
R-FCN	73.19
R-FCN + conv	73.25
ConvLSTM (T = 2)	74.5

Table 3. Detection accuracy of different motion speeds.

Method	mAP (%) slow	mAP (%) medium	mAP (%) fast
R-FCN	82.5	71.8	51.2
ConvLSTM-based (T = 1)	82.6	72.4	51.7
ConvLSTM-based (T = 1)	82.6	74.1	52.8

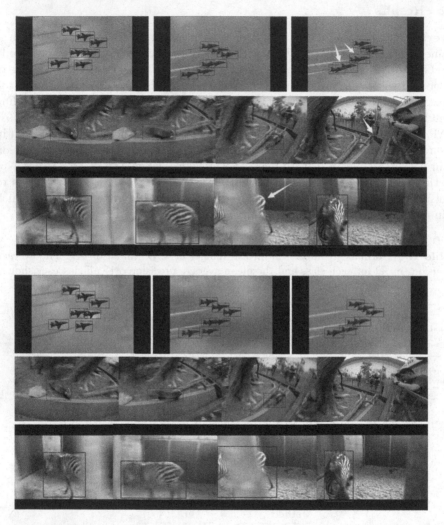

Fig. 3. Example video clips where the proposed ConvLSTM based method improves over the single-frame baseline (using ResNet-101). The first three lines are results by single-frame baseline and the last three lines are results by the proposed method.

When comparing our 74.5% mAP against the other methods, we make the following observations. The ILSVRC 2015 winner [9] combines two Faster R-CNN detectors, multi-scale training/testing, context suppression, high confidence tracking [26] and optical-flowguided propagation to achieve 73.8%. The deep feature flow [30], a recognition ConvNet (ResNet) is applied to key frames only and an optical flow FlowNet [2] is used for propagating the deep feature maps via a flow field to the rest of the frames, achieve 73.1% mAP at a higher detection speed.

Ablation Study. To take out the effect of the increased parameter size, we replace the ConvLSTM with two convolution layers, the Table 2, shows it only has a small increase in mAP. The fact is enough to prove that is ConvLSTM with gates control that aggregate the information in the image sequence.

Motion Speed. Evaluation on motion groups (Table 3) shows that detecting fast moving objects is very challenging: mAP is 82.5% for slow motion, and it drops to 51.2% for fast motion. It shows that "fast motion" is an intrinsic challenge and it is critical to consider motion in video object detection. When T changes, the medium speed objects improve the most increased by 2.3% (from 71.8% to 74.1%), while the fast have a little increment and the slow almost unchanged, that is to say T has a different influence on different speed. It is reasonable that T control the range of the dependence, when T increase, more motion information are catched.

5   Conclusion and Future Work

This work presents an accurate, end-to-end and principled learning framework for video object detection using ConvLSTM, and its main goal is to reach the accuracy-speedup tradeoff. Moreover, it would be complementary to existing box-level framework for better accuracy in video frames. More annotation data (e.g., YouTube-BoundingBoxes [18]) may be benefit to improvements. And there is still large room to be improved in fast object motion. We believe these open questions will inspire more future work.

References

1. Dai, J., Li, Y., He, K., Sun, J.: R-FCN: object detection via region-based fully convolutional networks. CoRR, abs/1605.06409 (2016)
2. Dosovitskiy, A., et al.: FlowNet: learning optical flow with convolutional networks. In: Proceedings of the IEEE International Conference on Computer Vision, pp. 2758–2766 (2015)
3. Girshick, R.: Fast R-CNN. arXiv preprint arXiv:1504.08083 (2015)
4. Girshick, R., Donahue, J., Darrell, T., Malik, J.: Rich feature hierarchies for accurate object detection and semantic segmentation. In: Proceedings of the IEEE Conference on Computer Vision and Pattern Recognition, pp. 580–587 (2014)

5. Han, W., et al.: Seq-NMS for video object detection. arXiv preprint arXiv:1602.08465 (2016)
6. He, K., Gkioxari, G., Dollár, P., Girshick, R.: Mask R-CNN. In: 2017 IEEE International Conference on Computer Vision, ICCV, pp. 2980–2988. IEEE (2017)
7. He, K., Zhang, X., Ren, S., Sun, J.: Deep residual learning for image recognition. In: Proceedings of the IEEE Conference on Computer Vision and Pattern Recognition, pp. 770–778 (2016)
8. Johnson, J., Karpathy, A., Fei-Fei, L.: DenseCap: fully convolutional localization networks for dense captioning. In: Proceedings of the IEEE Conference on Computer Vision and Pattern Recognition, pp. 4565–4574 (2016)
9. Kang, K., et al.: T-CNN: tubelets with convolutional neural networks for object detection from videos. IEEE Trans. Circ. Syst. Video Technol. (2017)
10. Kang, K., Ouyang, W., Li, H., Wang, X.: Object detection from video tubelets with convolutional neural networks. In: Proceedings of the IEEE Conference on Computer Vision and Pattern Recognition, pp. 817–825 (2016)
11. Lin, T.-Y., Goyal, P., Girshick, R., He, K., Dollár, P.: Focal loss for dense object detection. arXiv preprint arXiv:1708.02002 (2017)
12. Liu, W., et al.: SSD: single shot multibox detector. In: Leibe, B., Matas, J., Sebe, N., Welling, M. (eds.) ECCV 2016. LNCS, vol. 9905, pp. 21–37. Springer, Cham (2016). https://doi.org/10.1007/978-3-319-46448-0_2
13. Long, J., Shelhamer, E., Darrell, T.: Fully convolutional networks for semantic segmentation. In: Proceedings of the IEEE Conference on Computer Vision and Pattern Recognition, pp. 3431–3440 (2015)
14. Luo, Z., Peng, B., Huang, D.-A., Alahi, A., Fei-Fei, L.: Unsupervised learning of long-term motion dynamics for videos. arXiv preprint arXiv:1701.01821, 2 (2017)
15. Milan, A., Rezatofighi, S.H., Dick, A.R., Reid, I.D., Schindler, K.: Online multi-target tracking using recurrent neural networks. In: AAAI, pp. 4225–4232 (2017)
16. Ng, J.Y.-H., Hausknecht, M., Vijayanarasimhan, S., Vinyals, O., Monga, R., Toderici, G.: Beyond short snippets: deep networks for video classification. In: 2015 IEEE Conference on Computer Vision and Pattern Recognition, CVPR, pp. 4694–4702. IEEE (2015)
17. Ouyang, W., et al.: DeepID-Net: deformable deep convolutional neural networks for object detection. In: Proceedings of the IEEE Conference on Computer Vision and Pattern Recognition, pp. 2403–2412 (2015)
18. Real, E., Shlens, J., Mazzocchi, S., Pan, X., Vanhoucke, V.: YouTube-BoundingBoxes: a large high-precision human-annotated data set for object detection in video. In: 2017 IEEE Conference on Computer Vision and Pattern Recognition, CVPR, pp. 7464–7473. IEEE (2017)
19. Redmon, J., Divvala, S., Girshick, R., Farhadi, A.: You only look once: unified, real-time object detection. In: Proceedings of the IEEE Conference on Computer Vision and Pattern Recognition, pp. 779–788 (2016)
20. Ren, S., He, K., Girshick, R.B., Sun, J.: Faster R-CNN: towards real-time object detection with region proposal networks. CoRR, abs/1506.01497 (2015)
21. Russakovsky, O., et al.: ImageNet large scale visual recognition challenge. Int. J. Comput. Vis. 115(3), 211–252 (2015)
22. Shrivastava, A., Gupta, A., Girshick, R.: Training region-based object detectors with online hard example mining. In: Proceedings of the IEEE Conference on Computer Vision and Pattern Recognition, pp. 761–769 (2016)
23. Srivastava, N., Mansimov, E., Salakhudinov, R.: Unsupervised learning of video representations using LSTMs. In: International Conference on Machine Learning, pp. 843–852 (2015)

24. Sutskever, I., Vinyals, O., Le, Q.V.: Sequence to sequence learning with neural networks. In: Advances in Neural Information Processing Systems, pp. 3104–3112 (2014)
25. Szegedy, C., et al.: Going deeper with convolutions. In: CVPR (2015)
26. Wang, L., Ouyang, W., Wang, X., Lu, H.: Visual tracking with fully convolutional networks. In: Proceedings of the IEEE International Conference on Computer Vision, pp. 3119–3127 (2015)
27. Shi, X., Chen, Z., Wang, H., Yeung, D.-Y., Wong, W.-K., Woo, W.-C.: Convolutional LSTM network: a machine learning approach for precipitation nowcasting. In: Advances in Neural Information Processing Systems, pp. 802–810 (2015)
28. Zhang, K., Chao, W.-L., Sha, F., Grauman, K.: Video summarization with long short-term memory. In: Leibe, B., Matas, J., Sebe, N., Welling, M. (eds.) ECCV 2016. LNCS, vol. 9911, pp. 766–782. Springer, Cham (2016). https://doi.org/10.1007/978-3-319-46478-7_47
29. Zhu, X., Wang, Y., Dai, J., Yuan, L., Wei, Y.: Flow-guided feature aggregation for video object detection. arXiv preprint arXiv:1703.10025 (2017)
30. Zhu, X., Xiong, Y., Dai, J., Yuan, L., Wei, Y.: Deep feature flow for video recognition. In: Proceedings of CVPR, vol. 2, p. 7 (2017)

Agricultural Question Classification Based on CNN of Cascade Word Vectors

Lei Chen[1](✉), Jin Gao[1,2], Yuan Yuan[1], and Li Wan[1]

[1] Institute of Intelligent Machines, Chinese Academy of Sciences, Hefei, China
chenlei@iim.ac.cn
[2] University of Science and Technology of China, Hefei, China

Abstract. Compared with traditional search engines, the query method of QA system is more intelligent and applicable in non-professional scenes, e.g., agricultural information retrieval. Question classification is an important issue in QA system. Since the particularities of agricultural questions, such as words sparsity, many technical terms, and so on, some existing methods are difficult to achieve the desired result in the agricultural question classification task. Hence, it is necessary to investigate how to extract as many useful information as possible from short agricultural questions to improve the efficiency of agricultural question classification. In order to solve this problem, the paper explores effective semantic representation of agricultural question sentences and proposes a method for agricultural question classification based on CNN of cascade word vectors. Different combinations of questions, answers, and synonym information are used to learn different cascade word vectors, which are taken as the input of CNN to construct the model of question classification. The experimental results show that our method can achieve better result in the agricultural question classification task.

Keywords: Agricultural question classification
Cascade word vector · Semantic representation · CNN
Question and answering system

1 Introduction

Different from traditional search engines which use keywords as input and return some candidate answers list, question and answering (QA) system takes users' natural language questions as input and returns accurate answers [15] and has become a hot topic in the field of natural language processing [2,12]. Since the more intelligent query method, the query method of QA system is more applicable for non-professional users. For example, it is very suitable for the actual situation of agricultural information retrieval.

As an important part of QA system, question classification can reduce the space of candidate answers and formulate corresponding strategies for answer extraction, so as to improve the efficiency of whole QA system. Particularly in

© Springer Nature Switzerland AG 2018
J.-H. Lai et al. (Eds.): PRCV 2018, LNCS 11257, pp. 110–121, 2018.
https://doi.org/10.1007/978-3-030-03335-4_10

some professional fields, QA system allows users to ask questions in the specified field. So knowing the type of given question is very helpful for finding the answer of the corresponding type. Moldovan, et al. [14] discussed the influence of each module on the performance of QA system, showing that whether in open field or in professional field, question classification has an important influence on the performance of whole system. Traditional question classification methods include: experience rules based, statistics based and other machine learning models such as SVM, maximum entropy and so on [9,10]. In recent years, question classification based on deep learning has been widely studied [5,6,8]. And with the research of word vector representation, text can be effectively represented in low dimensional continuous form. Different types of word vectors for sentence classification have also been studied [7,11]. Most of the above works are focused on open field. They did not take into account the particularities of the agricultural field, such as words sparsity, many technical terms, and so on. So some existing methods are difficult to achieve the desired result in the agricultural question classification task. At present, there are some researches on information classification for agriculture [4,17,19], which depend on the agricultural ontology library or large-scale corpus. The information representation of agricultural question itself still needs further study.

The paper proposes a method which effectively obtains the semantic representation of agricultural questions based on CNN of cascade word vectors to implement classification task. First, the synonym dictionary is adopted to expand the features of agricultural questions and meanwhile the answer information is used to assist the procedure of question vectors learning. And then the cascade word vectors trained by integrating synonym information with answer information are taken as the input of CNN to construct the model of question classification.

2 Question Classification

2.1 Method Overview

The proposed agricultural question classification method consists of the cascade word vector learning module and the CNN classifier training module, described respectively as follows:

- Cascade word vector learning module: Using different combinations of questions, corresponding answers, and synonym information to learn word vectors, and cascading them to obtain different cascade word vectors.
- CNN classifier training module: Taking the cascade word vectors as the input of CNN model and using the function *softmax* to implement multi classification of agricultural questions in the output layer.

2.2 Cascade Word Vector

As the input of CNN model, the quality of word vectors directly affects the result of the final classification model. Therefore, how to learn the higher quality word vectors is very important. To achieve this goal, the paper introduces a neural network language model and proposes a cascade word vector learning model which integrates synonyms with answer information. The procedure includes the following steps:

1. Using the information of synonyms to extend the feature of question sentence and taking the expanded question, which includes synonym information, as the input of the neural network language model *word2vec* [13] to obtain the word vector of question.
2. Using the answer information to assist the process of question vectors learning, which trains the questions and answers together to learn the word vectors with more semantic information.
3. Cascading the above two word vectors to obtain the cascade word vectors.

Concretely, in the first step, the feature dimension maybe lost in the training process because the training data is limited. The classifier may ignore the synonymous expression of some missing features, and then affect the final classification result. Therefore, this paper uses synonyms information to expand the features of agricultural questions, which can alleviate the sparsity of question features, enhance the semantic representation ability of questions, and make up for the deficiency of insufficient information in agricultural questions. The synonym dictionary called HIT IR-lab Tongyici Cilin (Extended) [3] is taken as the semantic resources in this paper. In this paper, we use the fifth level synonym information of the dictionary, where the meanings of words are depicted most meticulously, to expand the features of questions. Given an agricultural question, after conducting Chinese word segmentation, the main words including nouns and verbs are concerned and extracted. And then the synonyms of each main word are searched in the synonym dictionary HIT IR-lab Tongyici Cilin (Extended). If the word appears in the dictionary, its synonym is taken out and it is directly affixing to the given question as a new feature. We can see that the extended feature of question can contain the information of all the synonyms of main words. The specific process of question feature extension is shown in the following Algorithm 1.

In the second step, the agricultural questions are usually short with less information but more terminologies, which may cause many difficulties to the classification tasks. Inspired by the work of Zhang et al. [18], the distributed representation of words will be learned by using the common context of questions and answers, which can make full use of the implied semantic information in the answer to enhance the representation ability of question vectors.

In the third step, we use many different combinations of various information, including questions, synonyms, and answers, to train a number of word vectors with different expressions, so as to investigate the effect of different training information on the quality of word vectors. Comparisons between different word vector models will be detailed in subsequent experimental section.

Given a question with n words, denoted by $q = \{w_1, w_2, \ldots, w_n\}$, when its feature extended question is taken as the input of *word2vec*, the ith word w_i will

---

Algorithm 1. Question feature extension based on synonym

Input: A question q; A synonym dictionary D_s;
Output: A feature extended question q';
  1: Conduct word segmentation of the given question q to obtain the word sequence
     $W_q = \{w_1, w_2, ..., w_n\}$;
  2: Extract main words from W_q, denoted by $W_m = \{w_i, ..., w_{i+k}\}$;
  3: Initialize the synonym sequence $W_s = \phi$;
  4: **for** each $w \in W_m$ **do**
  5:     if D_s has the synonym of w, put the synonym into W_s;
  6: **end for**
  7: $q' = W_q + W_s$;
  8: **return** q'.

---

be expressed by the vector x_{ia} of k_{ia} dimension after training. If the parallel corpus including question and answer pairs is taken as the input of *word2vec*, the word w_i will be expressed by the vector x_{ib} of k_{ib} dimension after training. Then the cascade word vector x_i can be obtained, denoted by $x_i = [x_{ai}\ x_{bi}]$, where the dimension of x_i is k_i and $k_i = k_{ia} + k_{ib}$. The cascade word vector x_i simultaneously integrates two kinds of feature information, namely synonyms and answers, so as to enhance the expression ability of question word vectors.

2.3   CNN Model

The structure of CNN model is shown in Fig. 1. The cascade word vectors are taken as the input of CNN to transform features from word granularity to sentence level. The convolution layer uses multi-granularity convolution kernel to further mining question features. The pooling layer extracts the features again and combines them to get global features. The mapping of different types of features is implemented at the full connection layer to get the final results.

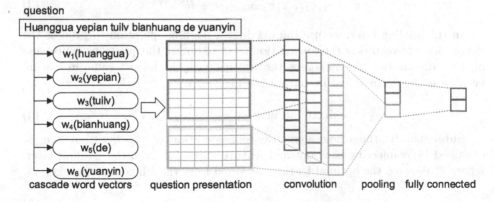

Fig. 1. The structure of CNN model

In the question presentation layer, the cascade word vectors of all words are stacked vertically to get two dimensional question feature data, that is, the feature conversion from word granularity to sentence level is conducted. Given a question $q = \{w_1, w_2, \ldots, w_n\}$, the cascade word vector of word w_i is x_i of k_i dimension and the matrix representation of question q is defined as follows:

$$x_{1:n} = x_1 \oplus x_2 \oplus \ldots \oplus x_n = \begin{bmatrix} x_{1a} & x_{1b} \\ x_{2a} & x_{2b} \\ \ldots & \ldots \\ x_{na} & x_{nb} \end{bmatrix}, \tag{1}$$

where $\oplus$ is the concatenation operator and $x_{i:m}$ is the feature matrix which consists of $x_i, x_{i+1}, \ldots, x_{i+m}$. The question presentation layer is a two-dimensional feature matrix of $n \times k$ if the maximum length of the input question is n.

In the feature convolution layer, in order to fully extract more implicit semantic features of questions, multi granularity convolution kernels are adopted to capture more contextual semantic information and extract multiple local features in the question as far as possible. Generally, the convolution kernel of $h \times k$ dimension is chosen to slide between the adjacent words of input question sentence matrix to get convolution features, where k is the dimension of the word vector and h is the size of the convolution window, namely the number of words slid across the convolution kernel, which can be changed to design the convolution kernel structure of different sizes in experiments. The h words $x_{i:i+h-1}$ in the window are performed the convolution operation to generate the following new feature output c_i:

$$c_i = f(m \cdot x_{i:i+h-1} + b) \tag{2}$$

where $m \in R^{hk}$ is a convolution kernel matrix, $b \in R$ is a bias term and f is a nonlinear activation function, using $ReLu : f(x) = max(0, x)$ in this paper to accelerate the convergence speed of training. After performing the convolution operation, the input question will be mapped into the following feature vector:

$$c = [c_1, c_2, \ldots, c_{n-h+1}], \ c \in R^{n-h+1}. \tag{3}$$

In the pooling layer, we use the maximum pooling operation to process the output feature vectors of the convolution layer to obtain the questions expression of fixed dimension, which chooses the feature with the largest value in feature vectors as the optimal feature output.

$$c^* = \max(c) = \max(c_1, c_2, \ldots, c_{n-h+1}) \tag{4}$$

Subsequently, the whole semantic representation of the question can be obtained by connecting each optimal feature extracted from the pooling layer, where c_i^* denotes the optimal feature obtained from the ith convolution kernel.

$$C = [c_1^*, c_2^*, \ldots, c_n^*] \tag{5}$$

The pooling layer implements the transformation from local features to global features. Meanwhile, both the feature matrix of the question and the number of parameters of the final classification are reduced.

The definition of the fully connected output layer is as follows:

$$y = f(w \cdot C + b), \tag{6}$$

where f is the activation function, w and b are the corresponding weight parameter and bias term when the output of the fully connected layer is y. After using the function *softmax* to normalize, the probability of question q belonging to category t can be obtained:

$$P(t|q, \theta) = \frac{\exp(y_t)}{\sum\limits_{i=1}^{m} \exp(y_i)}, \tag{7}$$

where m is the number of output categories and θ is the set of network parameters. Then the classification labels for final question prediction can be defined:

$$\hat{y} = \arg\max_{t} P(t|q, \theta). \tag{8}$$

The objective function of network training is as follows:

$$J(\theta) = -\frac{1}{m} \sum_{t=1}^{m} l_t \cdot \log(P(y_t)), \tag{9}$$

where l_t is the category label of training samples, y_t is the real label of the question q and $P(y_t)$ is the estimation probability of each category when using the *softmax* function to classify.

In addition, when training samples are few, the over-fitting phenomenon is easily to occur in the network model training process. In order to prevent this problem, we use L_2 regularization to constrain the parameters of CNN model. And the Dropout strategy [16] is introduced in the training process of the fully connected layer.

In summary, the following Algorithm 2 describes the overall flow of the proposed method.

3   Experiments

3.1   Experimental Data

Different from some open fields, this paper concerns on the research of agricultural question classification. Since there is no public data set in the field of agriculture at present, the agricultural question and answering corpus adopted in this paper is mined from Internet, including the following agricultural website:

Algorithm 2. Question classification based on CNN of cascade word vectors

---

Input: A set of questions $Q = \{q_1, q_2, ..., q_n\}$; A set of word vectors V_1 containing information of questions and synonyms; A set of word vectors V_2 containing information of questions and answers; A test set of questions T; A corresponding set of real categories L;

Output: The classification accuracy Acc of the test set of questions T;

  1: Conduct word segmentation of all questions in Q to obtain the word sequence $q = \{w_1, w_2, ..., w_k\}$;

  2: **for** each $q \in Q$ **do**

  3:      **for** each $w \in q$ **do**

  4:          Find the word vector A or B corresponding to the word w in V_1 or V_2;

  5:          Conduct cascading operation between A and B;

  6:      **end for**

  7:      Connect the cascade vector of each word in q to get the question vector v_q;

  8: **end for**

  9: Divide Q into training set S_1 and validation set S_2;

10: Train a CNN model M_1 by using S_1;

11: Conduct category prediction of S_2 by using M_1;

12: Perform iterative of the above two steps n times, and select the model with the highest accuracy of validation as the optimal classification model M^*;

13: Use M^* to do the category prediction of T to obtain the category prediction set L^* of test samples;

14: Compare L^* with L to get the number of correctly classified samples m;

15: **return** $Acc = m/|L|$.

Nongye Wenwen[1], Chinese planting technology website[2], Planting Q&A[3]. After noise cleaning and other preprocessing for the acquired data, our experimental data includes five categories: vegetable planting, fruit tree planting, flower planting, edible fungi planting and field crop planting. Each category contains 2,000 questions, where 15% (300) is used as test set and in the remaining 85%, the validation set and training set are randomly selected 10% (170) and 90% (1530) respectively. Besides, the opensource Chinese word segmentation tool jieba [1] is used to conduct word segmentation and POS tagging of questions.

3.2 Parameter Discussion

In the step of word vector training, we use the neural network language model *word2vec* to learn the distributed representation of words. Words that appear less than 3 times in corpus will be abandoned. The words that do not appear in the *word2vec* vocabulary are initialized by using the values between -1 and 1. The specific parameter settings of this model are given as follows:

– Word vector dimension: 64, 128, 192, 256;

---

[1] http://wenwen.yl01.com/index.html.
[2] http://zz.ag365.com/.
[3] http://www.my478.com/.

- Selected algorithm: Skip-gram;
- Context window: 5;
- Sampling threshold: 1e−4;
- The number of iterations: 30.

We discuss the specific values of word vector dimensions to explore the influence of the original word vector qualities on classification results. Figure 2 shows the results of verification set accuracy of different word vector dimensions. The accuracy of the validation set is increasing when the number of epochs in the network training increases, especially from 20 to 100. However, excessive epoch may lead to over fitting problem. Therefore, in this paper, the epoch value is set to 100 in all experiments.

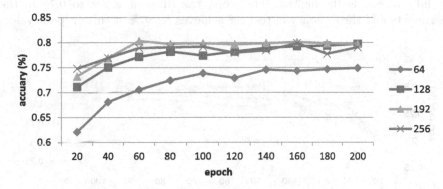

Fig. 2. Verification set accuracy of different word vector dimensions at different epochs

Table 1 gives the test set accuracy of different word vector dimensions at epoch 100. When the word vector dimension increases from 64 to 192, the accuracy of the model increases obviously. However, when the vector dimension continues to increase to 256, the accuracy rate decreases slightly. The analysis is that although the increase of the word vector dimension can contain more word statistics and semantic information, when a certain dimension is reached, more dimensions can not only improve the semantic information of word vectors, but also increase the training complexity of the whole model. Hence, the word vector dimension is set to 192 in the experiments of this paper.

Table 1. Test set accuracy of different word vector dimensions at epoch 100

Word vector dimension	64	128	192	256
Test set accuracy	75.07%	80.66%	83.43%	82.86%

In the step of question classification, we trains the CNN model with Adam update rules. Random gradient descent is performed for each batch of data. And the parameters of network are updated and optimized by back propagation in each round of training iteration. The specific parameter settings of this CNN model are given as follows:

- Convolution kernel size: 3×192, 4×192, 5×192;
- Learning rate: 1e−3;
- Batch size: 64;
- Regularization coefficient L_2: 3;
- Dropout probability: 1, 0.75, 0.5, 0.25;
- Epoch: 100.

The results of model training with different dropout values are shown in the following Fig. 3. We can see that when the dropout value is 0.75, the accuracy of validation set is the highest. Therefore, the dropout is set to 0.75 in the experiments and the accuracy of test set achieves 82.86% at this dropout value.

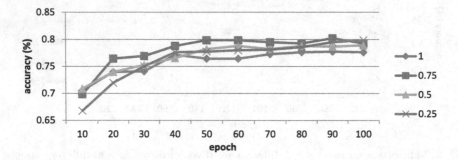

Fig. 3. Verification set accuracy of different dropout values at different epochs

3.3   Contrast Experiments

Different combinations of distributed representation of word vectors are used as the inputs of CNN model with the same structure to conduct several contrast experiments, detailed as follows:

1. CNN+Rand: Using Gauss distribution to randomly initialize all words in a question and transforming each question into a two dimensional feature matrix $n \times k$ as the input of CNN model, where n is the max size of question and k is the dimension of word vector;
2. CNN+Q: Training the word vectors by using the question set only;
3. CNN+Q_A: Training the word vectors by using the question set which is extended the feature by using the information of synonyms;
4. CNN+Q_B: Training the word vectors by using the parallel connection of the question set and the corresponding answer set;
5. CNN+Q_A_B: Training the word vectors by using the parallel connection of the extended question set with the information of synonyms and the corresponding answer set;

6. CNN+Q_A+Q_B: Using the cascade word vectors of Q_A and Q_B as the input of CNN model;
7. CNN+Q_A_B+Q_A_B: Using the cascade word vectors of Q_A_B and itself as the input of CNN model.

The experimental environment of this paper is given as follows: operating system Ubuntu 16.04, 32 GB RAM, CPU Intel Xeon E5-2687W v2 3.4 GHz, deep learning framework Tensorflow 1.4.0, programming language Python 3.5.

3.4 Experimental Results

Figure 4 shows the experimental results of each contrast model on the task of agricultural question classification.

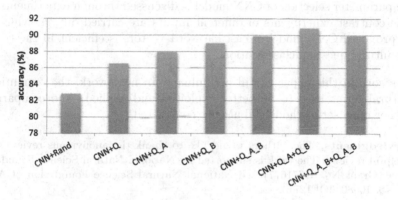

Fig. 4. Experimental results of agricultural question classification

We can see that the proposed CNN model of cascade word vectors, namely (CNN+Q_A+Q_B), can achieve the better result than other contrast methods. More concretely, comparing CNN+Rand with CNN+Q, the learned word vector can capture the contextual semantic information of sentences, and significantly improve the performance of question classification. Comparing CNN+Q with CNN+Q_A, the information of synonyms can extend the features of questions to make up for the sparsity problem, so as to capture more abundant and accurate semantic information in the process of training word vectors. Comparing CNN+Q with CNN+Q_B, using the answer information to assist the learning of question word vectors can also enhance the expression ability of word vectors. Comparing CNN+Q_A+Q_B with CNN+Q_A_B and CNN+Q_A_B+Q_A_B, although the information of synonyms and answers are also incorporated into the training of word vectors, the simple integration of multiple information may cause some information overlay and redundancy. Therefore, the result of using cascade word vectors is better than that of joint training.

4   Conclusion

This paper proposes the CNN model of cascade word vectors to deal with the question classification issue in agricultural filed. The main contributions of this work are given as follows:

- Synonymous information is introduced to expand the features of agricultural questions, so as to alleviate the problem of word sparsity, caused by many professional vocabularies and sparse distribution of words, in agricultural questions.
- The paper proposes the CNN model of cascade word vectors and discusses the influence of different information combinations on the performance of word vectors, showing that the proposed cascaded word vectors can simultaneously express more semantic features of different information.
- The parameter selection of CNN model is discussed through experiments and some contrast experiments of different inputs are carried out, showing that the proposed CNN model of cascade word vectors is efficient in the task of agricultural question classification.

The work in this paper is still preliminary. In next work, the semantics of agricultural terms need to be better exploited and applied. And comparisons with other open set methods will also be considered.

Acknowledgments. The authors would like to thank the anonymous reviewers for their helpful reviews. The work is supported by National Natural Science Foundation of China (Grant No. 31771677) and National Natural Science Foundation of Anhui (Grant No. 1608085QF127).

References

1. Chinese word segmentation component of Python: Jieba. http://www.oss.io/os/fxsjy/jieba
2. Das, R., Zaheer, M., Reddy, S., McCallum, A.: Question answering on knowledge bases and text using universal schema and memory networks. In: Proceedings of the 55th Annual Meeting of the Association for Computational Linguistics, ACL 2017, Short Papers, vol. 2, pp. 358–365 (2017)
3. HIT-SCIR: HIT IR-lab Tongyici Cilin (Extended). https://www.ltp-cloud.com/
4. Hu, D.: The research of question analysis based on ontology and architecture design for question answering system in agriculture. Ph.D. thesis. Chinese Academy of Agricultural Sciences (2013). (in Chinese)
5. Kalchbrenner, N., Grefenstette, E., Blunsom, P.: A convolutional neural network for modelling sentences. In: Proceedings of the 52nd Annual Meeting of the Association for Computational Linguistics, ACL 2014, Long Papers, vol. 1, pp. 655–665 (2014)
6. Kim, Y.: Convolutional neural networks for sentence classification. In: Proceedings of the 2014 Conference on Empirical Methods in Natural Language Processing, EMNLP 2014, A Meeting of SIGDAT, a Special Interest Group of the ACL, pp. 1746–1751 (2014)

7. Komninos, A., Manandhar, S.: Dependency based embeddings for sentence classification tasks. In: The 2016 Conference of the North American Chapter of the Association for Computational Linguistics: Human Language Technologies, NAACL
   HLT 2016, pp. 1490–1500 (2016)
8. Lai, S., Xu, L., Liu, K., Zhao, J.: Recurrent convolutional neural networks for text
   classification. In: Proceedings of the Twenty-Ninth AAAI Conference on Artificial
   Intelligence, pp. 2267–2273 (2015)
9. Le-Hong, P., Phan, X.-H., Nguyen, T.-D.: Using dependency analysis to improve
   question classification. In: Nguyen, V.-H., Le, A.-C., Huynh, V.-N. (eds.) Knowledge and Systems Engineering. AISC, vol. 326, pp. 653–665. Springer, Cham
   (2015). https://doi.org/10.1007/978-3-319-11680-8_52
10. Liu, L., Yu, Z., Guo, J., Mao, C., Hong, X.: Chinese question classification based
    on question property kernel. Int. J. Mach. Learn. Cybern. 5(5), 713–720 (2014)
11. Ma, M., Huang, L., Xiang, B., Zhou, B.: Group sparse CNNs for question clas-
    sification with answer sets. In: Proceedings of the 55th Annual Meeting of the
    Association for Computational Linguistics, ACL 2017, Short Papers, vol. 2, pp.
    335–340 (2017)
12. Mao, X., Li, X.: A survey on question and answering system. J. Front. Comput.
    Sci. Technol. 6(3), 193–207 (2012). (in Chinese)
13. Mikolov, T., Chen, K., Corrado, G., Dean, J.: Efficient estimation of word repre-
    sentations in vector space. CoRR abs/1301.3781 (2013)
14. Moldovan, D.I., Pasca, M., Harabagiu, S.M., Surdeanu, M.: Performance issues
    and error analysis in an open-domain question answering system. ACM Trans. Inf.
    Syst. 21(2), 133–154 (2003)
15. Song, H., Ren, Z., Liang, S., Li, P., Ma, J., de Rijke, M.: Summarizing answers
    in non-factoid community question-answering. In: Proceedings of the Tenth ACM
    International Conference on Web Search and Data Mining, WSDM 2017, pp. 405–
    414 (2017)
16. Srivastava, N., Hinton, G.E., Krizhevsky, A., Sutskever, I., Salakhutdinov, R.:
    Dropout: a simple way to prevent neural networks from overfitting. J. Mach. Learn.
    Res. 15(1), 1929–1958 (2014)
17. Wei, Z., Meng, F., Guo, J.: Design and implementation of agricultural information
    search engine classifier. J. Agric. Mech. Res. 2014(3), 186–189 (2014). (in Chinese)
18. Zhang, D., Li, S., Wang, J.: Semi-supervised question classification with jointly
    learning question and answer representation. J. Chin. Inf. Process. 31(1), 1–7
    (2017). (in Chinese)
19. Zhang, X.: Research on agricultural information classification method based on
    deep learning. Master's thesis. Northwest A & F University (2017). (in Chinese)

Spatial Invariant Person Search Network

Liangqi Li, Hua Yang$^{(\boxtimes)}$, and Lin Chen

Shanghai Jiao Tong University, Dongchuan Road 800, Shanghai, China
{Lewis_lee,hyang,SJChenLin}@sjtu.edu.cn

Abstract. A cascaded framework is proposed to jointly integrate the associated pedestrian detection and person re-identification in this work. The first part of the framework is a Pre-extracting Net which acts as a feature extractor to produce low-level feature maps. Then a PST (Pedestrian Space Transformer), including a Pedestrian Proposal Net to generate person candidate bounding boxes, is introduced as the second part with affine transformation and down-sampling models to help avoid the spatial variance challenges related to resolutions, viewpoints and occlusions of person re-identification. After further extracting by a convolutional net and a fully connected layer, the resulting features can be used to produce outputs for both detection and re-identification. Meanwhile, we design a directionally constrained loss function to supervise the training process. Experiments on the CUHK-SYSU dataset and the PRW dataset show that our method remarkably enhances the performance of person search.

Keywords: Person re-identification · Person search
Spatial transformation

1 Introduction

Pedestrian detection and person re-identification (Re-ID) are of great significance in real-world applications like security surveillance, crowd flow monitoring and human behavior analysis [1]. To date, they are usually regarded as two isolate problems in computer vision research. A pedestrian detection system usually ignores the identification information of pedestrian samples in the popular datasets like Caltech [2] and ETH [3], and only classifies the detected boxes as either positive or negative ones. On the other hand, Re-ID aims at matching the query person among a lot of gallery samples from video sequences or static images collected from a variety cameras. Most Re-ID benchmarks [4,5] built on the datasets, such as CUHK03 [4] and Market1501 [6], which have manually cropped bounding boxes of individual persons.

However, there are no pre-cropped individual images in real-world situations. Even though utilizing pedestrian detectors, apart from filtering false alarms like backgrounds bounding boxes, it is still tedious to assign an ID to each sample. Generally, person Re-ID is established on the basis of pedestrian detection and

© Springer Nature Switzerland AG 2018
J.-H. Lai et al. (Eds.): PRCV 2018, LNCS 11257, pp. 122–133, 2018.
https://doi.org/10.1007/978-3-030-03335-4_11

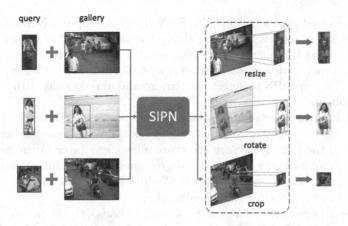

Fig. 1. Spatial transformations in our SIPN. It is difficult to straightly compare the input queries and galleries because of the giant spatial variance between them. But after implementing spatial transformations like resizing, rotating and cropping, the objective samples would be easier to identify.

the results from pedestrian detection can influence the accuracy of person Re-ID. From our observation, the two tasks can be integrated into a unified framework to improve convenience and performances, especially on the person Re-ID problem. Such cascaded task is called person search in this work.

There are only a few researchers devoting to handle this task. Pioneer works [7] and [8] just adopted simple two-stage strategies to jointly address the person search problem, and NPSM [9] coined an LSTM-based attention model to straightly search person from the image. However, all these approaches ignored the new challenges in person search task. Different from a traditional person Re-ID problem, pedestrians appear at a range of scales and orientations in person search scenes, which is much more in line with a real-world situation. Moreover, there are much more spatial variance challenges raised by multifarious resolutions, viewpoints and occlusions in person search. A lot of methods use spatial transformations like cropping, resizing and rotating for data augmentation. That is to say, vanilla Convolutional Neural Network (CNN) based models lack capabilities to cope with such spatial variance. We coin a new model named Spatial Invariant Person search Network (SIPN) to handle such challenges. As shown in Fig. 1, our SIPN can implement spatial transformations such as cropping, resizing, and rotating to make the detected samples spatially invariant. This means that, with SIPN, features extracted for identification will be much robuster. In contrast, traditional CNN, which is used as a workhorse in computer vision, can only guarantee the translation invariance of input samples.

Meanwhile, SIPN acts as a cascaded framework to implement an end-to-end pipeline. It is a CNN-based model that not only produces pedestrian candidate bounding boxes, but also goes further to extract features of these boxes to identify persons. We follow Faster R-CNN which saw heavy use in object detection area to design a network like RPN (Region Proposal Network) to generate pedestrian proposals. As stated above, the performance of person Re-ID is usually influenced by some spatial variances. We therefore combine the pedestrian proposal net with a spatial transformer to form a PST (Pedestrian Space Transformer) in our SIPN to detect pedestrians and also do away with the spatial variance problem.

To share information and propagate gradients better, the DenseNet [10] architecture is utilized. DenseNet contains densely connected layers even between the first layer and the last layer. Such structure allows any layer in the network to make use of input and may propagate the gradients from loss function directly to the initial layer to avoid gradient vanish. With DenseNet, the model can extract deeper features for detection and classification.

In general person Re-ID research, some methods [11,12] use pair-wise or triplet distance loss functions to supervise the training process. But it can be considerably complex if the dataset is of a greater scale. Xiao *et al.* [7] proposed an Online Instance Matching (OIM) loss function with which we do not need to optimize each pair of instances. The OIM loss merges instances features of the same identity offline, which makes the training of the model easier, faster and better. On the contrary, original OIM loss merges all instances which may obtain disturbing features. This work modifies OIM to only merge ground truth features thereby improving the performance of person Re-ID.

To sum up, our work provides two main contributions. First, we design a PST in our SIPN to produce pedestrian candidate bounding boxes and prevent spatial variance of person samples; Second, the improved OIM loss is proposed to learn features more effectively and conducts to robuster performance for the person search task.

2　Proposed Method

In this paper, a unified SIPN framework is proposed to process pedestrian detection and person Re-ID jointly. We adopt DenseNet [10] as a feature extractor to extract shared features for both detection and Re-ID. The PST is incorporated into our model to improve the spatial invariance of the feature maps. Finally, an improved OIM loss is applied in the model to supervise the training.

2.1　Model Structure

The cascaded SIPN model consists of three main parts. As shown in Fig. 2, the first part is the Pre-extracting Net which extracts features from a whole scene image. The second part is the PST which generates the parameters to spatially transform the feature maps and down-samples them to a fixed size. The third part of the model is a Feature Sharing Net, which further extracts features to be used for pedestrian detection as well as person Re-ID. Here are the details of our model whose structure is based on DenseNet.

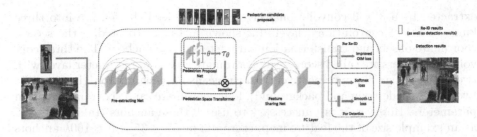

Fig. 2. Our cascaded DenseNet-based structure SIPN for processing pedestrian detection and person Re-ID jointly. Pre-extracting Net extracts low-level features which are then fed to our PST to produce pedestrian proposals and apply spatial transformations. Feature Sharing Net extracts further down-sampled features to output results for both detection and Re-ID.

There is a 7×7 convolutional layer in the front of Pre-extracting Net, followed by 3 dense blocks with 6, 12, and 24 dense layers respectively. The growth rate set in this paper is 32. We removed the initial pooling layer to make sure that input images would be pooled 4 times (by 2×2 max-pooling layer) through the Pre-extracting Net. The output will have a 1/16 resolution of the original image with 512 channels.

The Next part is our PST. It consists of a Pedestrian Proposal Net to generate pedestrian proposals and a spatial Transformer to implement transformation to these proposals. The structure of PST will be further illustrated in the next subsection.

The Features Sharing Net, a dense block with 16 dense layers and a growth rate of 32, is then built on the top of these feature maps to extract shared features. These feature maps are then pooled to 1024-dimensional vectors by an average pooling layer. And we raise 3 fully connected layers to map the vectors to 256D, 2D and 8D respectively.

At the end of the model, a Softmax classifier is used to output the classification (pedestrian or not) and a linear regressor is utilized to generate the corresponding refined localization coordinates. As for the 256 dimensional vectors, they will firstly be L2-normalized and then compared with corresponding feature vectors of target person for inference.

2.2 Pedestrian Space Transformer

In person search scenes, the performance will inevitably be influenced by the spatial variance of the samples. There are a number of reasons that can lead to increased spatial variance such as viewpoints, lights, occlusions, resolutions and so on. In an attempt to prevent spatial variances, we propose a PST to apply spatial transformations on the feature maps produced by the Pre-extracting Net.

At first, it is necessary to localize pedestrians by using the Pedestrian Proposal Net. Inspired by Faster R-CNN [13], we predict nine manually designed anchors with different scales and aspect ratios at each position of the feature map extracted by a 3×3 convolutional layer. Then we feed the feature into three kinds of 1×1 convolutional layers (as shown in Fig. 2) to predict the scores, coordinate offsets and transformation parameters of the anchors. The three convolutional layers are called score layer, coordinate layer and parameter layer with two, four and six filters respectively, which means for each anchor, there will be two scores (pedestrian and background), four coordinates and six transformation parameters. However, it is unnecessary to use all these anchors (taking 51×35 as an example size of the feature map, there will be $51 \times 35 \times 9 \approx 160k$ anchors in total) predicted from the feature map as proposals because most of them are redundant. So, we sort the anchors by their scores and implement Non-Maximum Suppression (NMS) to pick out 128 anchors as the final proposals. Coordinate offsets and transformation parameters are selected correspondingly.

Then the PST will implement spatial transformations to these proposals with transformation parameters generate before. In order to perform spatial transformation for the input feature map $U \in \mathbb{R}^{H \times W \times C}$ with width W, height H and C channels, we compute output pixels at a particular location defined by the proposals. Specifically, the output pixels are defined to lie on a regular grid $G = \{G_i\}$ of pixels $G_i = (x_i^t, y_i^t)$, forming an output feature map $V \in \mathbb{R}^{H' \times W' \times C}$, where H' and W' are the height and width of the grid. The transformation τ_θ used in this paper is a 2D affine transformation described as

$$
\begin{pmatrix} x_i^s \\ y_i^s \\ 1 \end{pmatrix} = \tau_\theta G_i = \begin{bmatrix} \theta_{11} & \theta_{12} & \theta_{13} \\ \theta_{21} & \theta_{22} & \theta_{23} \\ 0 & 0 & 1 \end{bmatrix} \begin{pmatrix} x_i^t \\ y_i^t \\ 1 \end{pmatrix}
\tag{1}
$$

where (x_i^t, y_i^t) are the target coordinates of the regular grid in the output feature map, and (x_i^s, y_i^s) are the source coordinates in the input feature map.

Such a transformation allows to apply cropping, translation, rotation, scaling and skew operations to the input feature maps, and needs only 6 parameters θ to be produced by the Pedestrian Proposal Net. To perform a spatial transformation on the input feature map, a sampler must take the set of sampling points $\tau_\theta(G)$. Meanwhile, the pedestrian proposals with a range of scales also need a sampler to resize them to an identical size. In [13], this function is finished by the ROI-pooling layer. While in our SIPN, we use a robuster sampler which can also do spatial transformation along with the input feature map U to produce the sampled output feature map V. In detail, each (x_i^s, y_i^s) coordinate in $\tau_\theta(G)$ defines the spatial location in the input where a sampling kernel is applied to get the value at a particular pixel in the output V. Just like [14], that is defined as

$$
V_i^c = \sum_n^H \sum_m^W U_{nm}^c k(x_i^s - m; \Phi_x) k(y_i^s - m; \Phi_y)
\tag{2}
$$

where $i \in [1...H'W']$, $c \in [1...C]$, Φ_x and Φ_y are the parameters of a generic sampling kernel $k()$ which defines the image interpolation, U_{nm}^c is the value at location (n, m) in channel c of the input, and V_i^c is the output value for pixel i at location (x_i^t, y_i^t) in channel c. Taking bilinear sampling kernel as an example, we can reduce Eq. 2 to

$$V_i^c = \sum_n^H \sum_m^W U_{nm}^c \max(0, 1 - |x_i^s - m|)\max(0, 1 - |y_i^s - n|) \tag{3}$$

and the partial derivatives are

$$\frac{\partial V_i^c}{\partial U_{nm}^c} = \sum_n^H \sum_m^W \max(0, 1 - |x_i^s - m|)\max(0, 1 - |y_i^s - n|) \tag{4}$$

$$\frac{\partial V_i^c}{\partial x_i^s} = \sum_n^H \sum_m^W U_{nm}^c \max(0, 1 - |y_i^s - n|) \begin{cases} 0 & \text{if } |m - x_i^s| \geq 1 \\ 1 & \text{if } m \geq x_i^s \\ -1 & \text{if } m < x_i^s \end{cases} \tag{5}$$

$$\frac{\partial V_i^c}{\partial y_i^s} = \sum_n^H \sum_m^W U_{nm}^c \max(0, 1 - |x_i^s - n|) \begin{cases} 0 & \text{if } |m - y_i^s| \geq 1 \\ 1 & \text{if } m \geq y_i^s \\ -1 & \text{if } m < y_i^s \end{cases} \tag{6}$$

This gives us a differentiable sampling mechanism that allows gradients to flow back.

As stated above, SIPN uses such PST to prevent spatial variance of detected proposals and extract robuster features for Re-ID in person search. It should be noted that there are a batch of transformation parameters matrices τ_θ (128 in our work) for an input image.

2.3 Improved OIM

Common loss functions in person Re-ID, such as verification loss or identification loss, are not suitable for the person search problem. Moreover, in person search datasets, unlabeled identities that have no target to match to are redundant for Re-ID and can not be taken into consideration.

To deal with these problems, we propose an improved OIM loss that contains directional constraints and takes advantages of the unlabeled identities features. OIM loss presented by Xiao et al. [7] makes a Look-Up Table (LUT) for labeled identities. Suppose there are L labeled identities in the dataset, and we have the LUT $V \in \mathbb{R}^{D \times L}$, where D denotes the dimension of final normalized features. Given an output normalized feature vector $x \in \mathbb{R}^D$, we can compute the similarity with all L identities by $V^T x$. During the back propagation, if the label ID of x is t, then we update the t-th column of the LUT by $v_t \leftarrow \gamma v_t + (1 - \gamma)x$, where $\gamma \in [0, 1]$, and then L2-normalize v_t. On the other hand, a circular queue is built to store features of those unlabeled identities. It is possible to customize the length of the circular queue, for example Q. Denoting the circular queue by $U \in \mathbb{R}^{D \times Q}$, it is simple to compute similarities between x and those unlabeled identities by $U^T x$. If x belongs to any unlabeled identities, we may push x into U and pop the out-of-date feature to update the circular queue. In a word, LUT is used to store representative features for the labeled identities to guide the matching process.

However, even after NMS, there are still lots of bounding boxes that are regarded as labeled identities in an image. Although these bounding boxes have different overlaps with ground-truth ones, OIM uses all their features to update the LUT. However, bounding boxes with background areas or lacking important information may corrupt the features to be merged and their features are naturally unrepresentative for those identities. Therefore, by denoting ground-truth bounding boxes as $\mathbb{G}$, we only merge features of the bounding boxes by

$$v_t \leftarrow \gamma v_t + (1 - \gamma)x, \quad \text{if } x \in \mathbb{G} \tag{7}$$

to make the LUT robust and further reduce calculations for Re-ID in this paper.

Following [7], the probability of x being recognized as the identity with class-id i is defined by a Softmax function

$$p_i = \frac{\exp(v_i^T x)}{\sum_{j=1}^{L} \exp(v_j^T x) + \sum_{k=1}^{Q} \exp(u_k^T x)}, \tag{8}$$

and the probability of being recognized as the i-th unlabeled identity in the circular queue is

$$q_i = \frac{\exp(u_i^T x)}{\sum_{j=1}^{L} \exp(v_j^T x) + \sum_{k=1}^{Q} \exp(u_k^T x)}. \tag{9}$$

The improved OIM objective is to maximize the expected log-likelihood

$$\mathcal{L} = \mathbb{E}_x[\log(p_t)]. \tag{10}$$

3   Experiments

To demonstrate the effectiveness of our method, several comprehensive experiments were conducted on two public person search datasets.

3.1   Datasets

CUHK-SYSU. CUHK-SYSU was collected by hand-held cameras and movie snapshots. It contains 18,184 images and 96,143 pedestrians bounding boxes in total. Among all the pedestrians bounding boxes, there are 8,432 labeled identities and 5,532 of them are used as training split.

Person Re-identification in the Wild. Person Re-identification in the Wild (PRW) [8] dataset was transferred from raw videos collected in Tsinghua University. A total of 6 cameras were used, among which five are 1080×1920 HD and one is 576×720 SD. PRW consists of 11,816 whole scene images including 43,110 pedestrian bounding boxes, among which 34,304 pedestrians are annotated with an ID. For the training set, we pick up 483 identities.

3.2   Evaluation Metrics

We split the two datasets both into a training subset and a test subset following the principles that there are no similar identities between two subsets. During the inference stage, given an input target person image, the aim is to find the same person from the gallery. The gallery must include all whole scene images that contain the pedestrian samples of the target person. To make the problem more challenging, we can customize the size of the gallery ranging from 50 to 4,000 for CUHK-SYSU and 1,000 to 4,000 for PRW.

Following the common person Re-ID researches, the cumulative matching characteristics (CMC top-K) metric is used in our person search problem. CMC counts a matching as there are at least one of the top-K predicted bounding boxes overlaps with the ground-truths with intersection-over-union (IoU) lager or equal to 0.5. We also adopt mean averaged precision (mAP) as used on ILSVRC object detection criterion [15] as the other metric. An averaged precision (AP) is computed for each target person image based on the precision-recall curve. Therefore, mAP is the average APs across all target person images.

3.3   Training Settings

Our experiments are carried on PyTorch [16]. Using batch size 1 like Faster R-CNN [13], we apply stochastic gradient descent (SGD) to train models for 6 epochs. The initial learning rates are set to 0.0001 for both datasets and are divided by 10 after 2 and 4 epochs gradually. As a comparison, we adopt both VGG, ResNet [17] and DenseNet [10] as our CNN-based architectures for experiments. We use Softmax loss and Smooth L1 loss to supervise the detection process during the training stage. On the other hand, an improved OIM loss is utilized to supervise the Re-ID process, for which the sizes of circular queue are set to 5000 and 500 for CUHK-SYSU and PRW respectively.

3.4   Results

We make comparisons with some priori works including separate pedestrian detection & person Re-ID methods and three unified approaches. In the separate methods, there are three main detectors, ACF, CCF and Faster R-CNN [13] (FRCN). We also use several popular Re-ID feature representations like DenseSIFT-ColorHist (DSIFT), Bag of Words (BoW) and Local Maximal Occurrence (LOMO) along with some distance metrics such as Euclidean, Cosine similarity, KISSME, and XQDA. As for the unified approaches, Xiao et al. [7] proposed an end-to-end method based on Faster R-CNN and ResNet-50. Yang et al. [18] added hand-crafted features. Liu et al. [9] used an LSTM-based attention model. Tables 1 and 2 shows the results conducted on CUHK-SYSU dataset with a gallery size of 100. We also carry experiments on the more challenging dataset - PRW with gallery size 1000. Table 3 shows the results.

From Tables 1, 2 and 3 we can see that our model outperforms separate pedestrian detection & person Re-ID methods as well as the three unified frameworks.

Table 1. CMC top-1 results comparisons between our method and priori works on CUHK-SYSU dataset.

CMC top-1 (%)	CCF	ACF	FRCN
DSIFT+Euclidean [7]	11.7	25.9	39.4
DSIFT+KISSME [7]	13.9	38.1	53.6
BoW+Cosine [7]	29.3	48.4	62.3
LOMO+XQDA [7]	46.4	63.1	74.1
OIM (Baseline) [7]	–	–	78.7
Yang et al. [18]	–	–	80.6
NPSM [9]	–	–	81.2
Ours	–	–	**86.0**

Table 2. mAP results comparisons between our method and priori works on CUHK-SYSU dataset.

mAP (%)	CCF	ACF	FRCN
DSIFT+Euclidean [7]	11.3	21.7	34.5
DSIFT+KISSME [7]	13.4	32.3	47.8
BoW+Cosine [7]	26.9	42.4	56.9
LOMO+XQDA [7]	41.2	55.5	68.9
OIM (Baseline) [7]	–	–	75.5
Yang et al. [18]	–	–	77.8
NPSM [9]	–	–	77.9
Ours	–	–	**85.3**

It demonstrates that by spatially transforming feature maps of pedestrians, the performance of person search can be improved.

3.5   Pedestrian Detection Results

We also acquire pedestrian detection results on both CUHK-SYSU and PRW datasets as shown in Table 4. It can be observed that our method does not harm the performance of pedestrian detection in person search tasks.

4   Discussion

4.1   Influence of PST

Ren et al. [13] used RPN to produce proposals that may contain objects. Sizes of the proposals are various but the network needs a fixed input size so that ROI pooling layer was proposed to pool features maps into identical sizes. In

Table 3. Comparison between baseline and our method on PRW dataset.

Method	mAP (%)	top-1 (%)
DPM-Alex+LOMO+XQDA [9]	13.0	34.1
DPM-Alex+IDE$_{det}$ [9]	20.3	47.4
DPM-Alex+IDE$_{det}$+CWS [9]	20.5	48.3
ACF-Alex+LOMO+XQDA [9]	10.3	30.6
ACF-Alex+IDE$_{det}$ [9]	17.5	43.6
ACF-Alex+IDE$_{det}$+CWS [9]	17.8	45.2
LDCF+LOMO+XQDA [9]	11.0	31.1
LDCF+IDE$_{det}$ [9]	18.3	44.6
LDCF+IDE$_{det}$+CWS [9]	18.3	45.5
OIM (baseline)	21.3	49.9
NPSM [9]	24.2	53.1
Ours	**39.5**	**59.2**

Table 4. Detection results comparison between baseline and our method on both datasets.

	CUHK-SYSU		PRW	
	Recall (%)	AP (%)	Recall (%)	AP (%)
Baseline	79.49	74.93	90.20	84.26
Ours	78.45	75.14	89.91	85.60

Table 5. Comparison between baseline and our model with PST on PRW dataset.

	mAP (%)	top-1 (%)	top-5 (%)	top-10 (%)
Baseline	21.3	49.9	72.9	81.5
Ours	**33.9**	**51.9**	**73.7**	**82.3**

our SIPN, the PST has the similar function to resize feature maps. Our PST is also able to prevent the spatial variance problem caused by different resolutions, viewpoints and occlusions. Table 5 shows that the performance of our PST is better than the model proposed by Xiao et al. [7]. When comparing the influence of PST, we maintain the same network architecture, ResNet-50, as Xiao et al.

4.2 Comparison Between Different Network Architectures

In this paper, we adopt DenseNet [10] as our CNN-based architecture to extract high-level features and compare the results between multiple structures such as VGG, ResNet and DenseNet as shown in Table 6. It can be observed that DenseNet, which connects layers densely and utilizes multiple-scale feature maps, outperforms a little bit.

Table 6. Comparisons between multiple network structures on PRW dataset. Res34, Res50 and Dense121 refer to ResNet-34, ResNet-50 and DenseNet-121 respectively.

	mAP (%)	top-1 (%)	top-5 (%)	top-10 (%)
VGG16	20.8	35.3	59.8	70.3
Res34	31.1	49.1	71.5	79.2
Res50	33.9	51.9	73.7	82.3
Dense121	**38.7**	**58.0**	**76.8**	**82.9**

4.3 Results on the Improved Loss Function

Xiao *et al.* [7] used the OIM loss to reduce calculations by merging features of the same identity. However, those features belonging to proposals produced by the model may be disturbing because they may have some redundant information such as backgrounds or lack some essential information. In this work, we suggest to just merge features of ground-truth bounding boxes. Obviously, as shown in Table 7, our improved loss function has better performance since we only use ground-truth features to update the LUT, which makes it much robuster.

Table 7. Comparisons between using OIM loss and our improved one on PRW.

	mAP (%)	top-1 (%)	top-5 (%)	top-10 (%)
OIM loss	38.7	58.0	76.8	82.9
Ours	**39.5**	**59.2**	**77.6**	**83.4**

5   Conclusion

In this paper we propose a cascaded DenseNet-based framework SPIN to process pedestrian detection and person re-identification jointly. The PST is used to generate pedestrian proposals and avoid spatial variance challenges of person search task. After comparing several different network architectures, we adopt DenseNet as our base model to extract much richer features. At last, an improved OIM loss function with directional constrains is utilized to further improve the performance of our model.

Acknowledgments. This work was supported in part by National Natural Science Foundation of China (NSFC, Grant No. 61771303 and 61671289), Science and Technology Com- mission of Shanghai Municipality (STCSM, Grant Nos. 17DZ1205602,18DZ1200102), and SJTU-Yitu/Thinkforce Joint laboratory for visual computing and application.

References

1. Zhang, S., Benenson, R., Omran, M., Hosang, J., Schiele, B.: How far are we from solving pedestrian detection? In: 2016 IEEE Conference on Computer Vision and Pattern Recognition (CVPR), pp. 1259–1267, June 2016
2. Dollar, P., Wojek, C., Schiele, B., Perona, P.: Pedestrian detection: an evaluation of the state of the art. IEEE Trans. Pattern Anal. Mach. Intell. **34**(4), 743–761 (2012)
3. Ess, A., Müller, T., Grabner, H., Van Gool, L.J.: Segmentation-based urban traffic scene understanding. In: BMVC, vol. 1, p. 2. Citeseer (2009)
4. Li, W., Zhao, R., Xiao, T., Wang, X.: DeepReID: deep filter pairing neural network for person re-identification. In: Proceedings of the IEEE Conference on Computer Vision and Pattern Recognition, pp. 152–159 (2014)
5. Felzenszwalb, P.F., Girshick, R.B., McAllester, D., Ramanan, D.: Object detection with discriminatively trained part-based models. IEEE Trans. Pattern Anal. Mach. Intell. **32**(9), 1627–1645 (2010)
6. Zheng, L., Shen, L., Tian, L., Wang, S., Wang, J., Tian, Q.: Scalable person re-identification: a benchmark. In: Proceedings of the IEEE International Conference on Computer Vision, pp. 1116–1124 (2015)
7. Xiao, T., Li, S., Wang, B., Lin, L., Wang, X.: Joint detection and identification feature learning for person search. In: 2017 IEEE Conference on Computer Vision and Pattern Recognition (CVPR), pp. 3376–3385. IEEE (2017)
8. Zheng, L., Zhang, H., Sun, S., Chandraker, M., Yang, Y., Tian, Q., et al.: Person re-identification in the wild. In: CVPR, vol. 1, p. 2 (2017)
9. Liu, H., et al.: Neural person search machines. In: ICCV, pp. 493–501 (2017)
10. Huang, G., Liu, Z., Van Der Maaten, L., Weinberger, K.Q.: Densely connected convolutional networks. In: CVPR, vol. 1, no. 2, p. 3 (2017)
11. Ahmed, E., Jones, M., Marks, T.K.: An improved deep learning architecture for person re-identification. In: Proceedings of the IEEE Conference on Computer Vision and Pattern Recognition, pp. 3908–3916 (2015)
12. Cheng, D., Gong, Y., Zhou, S., Wang, J., Zheng, N.: Person re-identification by multi-channel CNN with improved triplet loss function. In: Proceedings of the IEEE Conference on Computer Vision and Pattern Recognition, pp. 1335–1344 (2016)
13. Ren, S., He, K., Girshick, R., Sun, J.: Faster R-CNN: towards real-time object detection with region proposal networks. In: Advances in Neural Information Processing Systems, pp. 91–99 (2015)
14. Jaderberg, M., Simonyan, K., Zisserman, A., et al.: Spatial transformer networks. In: Advances in Neural Information Processing Systems, pp. 2017–2025 (2015)
15. Russakovsky, O., et al.: Imagenet large scale visual recognition challenge. Int. J. Comput. Vis. **115**, 211–252 (2015)
16. Paszke, A., et al.: Automatic differentiation in PyTorch (2017)
17. He, K., Zhang, X., Ren, S., Sun, J.: Deep residual learning for image recognition. In: Proceedings of the IEEE Conference on Computer Vision and Pattern Recognition, pp. 770–778 (2016)
18. Yang, J., Wang, M., Li, M., Zhang, J.: Enhanced deep feature representation for person search. In: Yang, J. (ed.) CCCV 2017. CCIS, vol. 773, pp. 315–327. Springer, Singapore (2017). https://doi.org/10.1007/978-981-10-7305-2_28

Image Super-Resolution Based on Dense Convolutional Network

Jie Li and Yue Zhou[✉]

Image Processing and Pattern Recognition, Shanghai Jiao Tong University,
Shanghai, China
{jaylee,zhouyue}@sjtu.edu.cn

Abstract. Recently, the performance of single image super-resolution (SISR) methods have been significantly improved with the development of the convolutional neural networks (CNN). In this paper, we propose a very deep dense convolutional network (SRDCN) for image super-resolution. Due to the dense connection, the feature maps of each preceding layer are connected and used as inputs of all subsequent layers, thus utilizing both low-level and high-level features. In addition, residual learning and dense skip connection are adopted to ease the difficulties of training very deep convolutional networks by alleviating the vanishing-gradient problem. Experimental results on four benchmark datasets demonstrate that our proposed method achieves comparable performance with other state-of-the-art methods.

Keywords: Single image super-resolution
Dense convolutional network · Residual learning

1 Introduction

In recent years, image super-resolution (SR), especially single image super-resolution (SISR) has gained increasing attention in the community of computer vision. SISR aims to restore a high-resolution (HR) image from a given low-resolution (LR) image. Therefore, it is a highly ill-posed inverse problem since the lost high-frequency information need to be reconstructed and multiple solutions exist for any given LR image additionally.

Owing to the powerful learning ability, convolutional neural networks (CNN) are widely applied to address computer vision problems such as image classification and restoration in the past five years. In SISR, as a pioneer, Dong et al. [4] has introduced a CNN model to learn a mapping from a degraded LR image to a HR image firstly. Their method, termed SRCNN, consists of only three convolutional layers while requiring no hand-crafted features and outperforms those sparsity-based methods [22,28] by a large margin. However, SRCNN does not go deeper partly due to the vanishing-gradient problem which is very challenging in training a very deep CNN model. Hence, it leads the observation that "the deeper the better" seems not suitable in SISR.

© Springer Nature Switzerland AG 2018
J.-H. Lai et al. (Eds.): PRCV 2018, LNCS 11257, pp. 134–145, 2018.
https://doi.org/10.1007/978-3-030-03335-4_12

Based on the assumption that image details recovery needs a large image region of contextual information, Kim et al. [11,12] introduce two very deep CNN models (up to 20 layers) to address the SR problem and successfully boost the performance. To accelerate the speed of convergence in training process, they use a very high learning rate (10^{-1} vs. 10^{-4} in SRCNN) and a novel residual learning strategy in [11]. Furthermore, adjustable gradient clipping is adopted to solve the vanishing-gradient problem. Despite the obvious promotion in performance, the very deep networks proposed above require lots of parameters compared with those shallow models [20,25]. In order to address this issue, Tai et al. [21] propose a deep recursive residual network (DRRN) to build a very deep yet concise model which has fewer parameters than VDSR [11] and RED30 [17]. The size of their final model (DRRN_B1U25 with 52 layers) is reduced to 29.7M. Therefore, it is expected to be used in mobile systems such as smart-phones. However, those methods are limited to only one upsample scale. Thus, multiple models need to be trained when new scales are on demand. It is obviously inefficient and impractical.

In this paper, we propose a novel dense convolutional network for single image super-resolution. By following [11], LR input images are upsampled into the same size as HR output images by linear interpolation methods. Then, images with multi-scales ($\times 2$, $\times 3$ and $\times 4$) are all used to train the network. Therefore, we only need to train a single model for all different scales. Our final model, SRDCN_D6L8, shows comparable performance with the current state-of-the-art approaches on four extensive benchmark datasets.

2   Related Work

2.1   Single Image Super-Resolution

To solve the super-resolution problem, numerous approaches have been explored with very different assumptions and evaluation criteria in recent years. Among them, interpolation based methods [1,30] such as bilinear, bicubic and Lanczos [5] are easier to implement. However, these algorithms usually generate HR pixel information by weighting neighboring LR pixel values. Thus, the results are inevitable blurry especially in a large scale factor (e.g., $\times 4$). Currently, various learning methods are widely proposed to learn a mapping from a LR image I_{LR} to the ideal HR image I_{HR}. Among them, sparse coding methods [6,28] aim to represent image patches by learning a powerful dictionary. These approaches are usually time-consuming and rely on rich image priors. In addition, other learning based methods such as neighbor embedding and random forest are also widely utilized. Nevertheless, the result images restored by these approaches are either unrealistic or blurry.

Recently, Dong et al. [3] first introduce a deep learning method into SR. After that, various CNN models have been proposed to address this ill-posed problem. Among them, Shi et al. [20] propose a novel CNN architecture with an efficient sub-pixel convolutional layer to upscale a low-resolution image into a high-resolution image at the very end of the model. By doing so, they avoid a huge computational complexity and thus their method is capable for real-time SR systems. In [15], a powerful generative adversarial network (GAN) is used to recover a photo-realistic HR image. Rather than minimizing the mean squared reconstruction error (MSE), Ledig et al. propose a perceptual loss to generate high-frequency details. The most related to our work is [24], in which, Tong et al. also adopt a dense network for feature extraction. However, they simply fuse feature maps at different levels of the network to reconstruct the HR outputs under a certain scale factor (e.g. ×4). Nevertheless, those kinds of approaches are all designed for a single upsample scale. Thus, multiple models need to be trained when new scales are on demand. It is obviously inefficient and impractical. To solve this issue, LR images are upsampled into the same size as HR images by linear interpolation methods such as bicubic in [11,21]. Then, images with multi-scales (×2, ×3, ×4) are used to train a single model. In our work, we develop a single deep SR network which also uses this simple yet effective technique for multi-scale SR tasks.

2.2   Contribution

In summary, we propose a very deep dense convolutional network (SRDCN) to solve the image super-resolution problem. Our main contributions are:

- We utilize the dense convolutional network as the backbone of our SR model. Specially, dense skip connections are adopted to combine low-level features with high-level ones at different levels. An ablation study in Sect. 4 shows a visible boost performance through this simple feature fusion strategy.
- We bridge the gap between the multi-scale task and the space-consuming problem with a single efficient model. The proposed method achieves comparable performance with state-of-the-arts on four widely used benchmark datasets under three scale factors (e.g. ×2, ×3 and ×4).

3   Proposed Method

In this section, we describe the details of our proposed model architectures. Firstly, we introduce the recently powerful dense networks [9] (DenseNets). Secondly, we give a complete description of our whole model and explain that our network is conciser with narrow layers while achieving comparable performance. Finally, we introduce the training procedure at the end of this section.

3.1   Dense Block

Hampered by the fact that the information about the input or gradient can vanish when it goes through the end of a very deep convolutional network. Most previous models are designed with shallow structures. To solve this issue, He et al. [8] successfully designed a very deep network (ResNets) by stacking residual blocks. Despite achieving record-breaking performance on many challenging

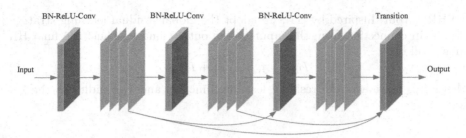

Fig. 1. Simplified structure of a dense block with three convolutional layers. Each layer generates four feature maps here.

image processing tasks, ResNets requires large number of parameters. In contrast, the layers of DenseNets are very narrow due to reuse of feature maps.

Figure 1 illustrates the simplified structure of a dense block. Different from ResNets, DenseNets concatenate all feature maps by linking all layers together rather than by directly summing features in one single unit. This technique further helps the information flow between layers and improves the efficiency of features usage in the networks. Consequently, the outputs X of one dense block will be:

$$X = H_l([X_1, X_2, \ldots, X_l]), \tag{1}$$

where l denotes the total number of convolutional layers in one dense block, $[X_1, X_2, \ldots, X_l]$ represents the concatenation of all feature maps and H_l refers to the dense block mapping function. For each layer, the number of output feature maps k is referred to as *growth rate*. Thus, one dense block generates $k \times l$ feature maps in total.

Note that, each dense block is followed by a transition layer with 1×1 kernel to reduce the number of feature maps. Unlike [24], which only use one convolutional layer (referred as a bottleneck layer) at the very end of the feature extraction networks to reduce the number of feature maps, the transition layers in proposed model avoid the redundancy of features thus make the model more compact and also improve the computational efficiency. In our experiment, the number of feature maps of a dense block is halved through the corresponding transition layer.

Owing to the benefit of reusing preceding features, in DenseNets, a tiny *growth rate* (e.g., $k = 12$) is sufficient to obtain state-of-the-art results. This advantage makes DenseNets narrower than existing networks, and therefore requires fewer parameters.

3.2   Model Architectures

As shown in Fig. 2, our model can be decomposed into three parts: The first convolutional layer (Conv) takes the input image to learn low-level feature maps, the following dense blocks (DB) for learning the mapping function from LR feature maps to HR feature maps and the last convolutional layer for generating the HR output. Inspired by [11], we adopt the global residual learning strategy via a skip connection from the input to the output image. Thus, the final HR image will be:

$$I_{HR} = f_{res}(I_{LR}) + I_{LR}, \tag{2}$$

where f_{res} represents the residual learning function and I_{LR} indicates the LR input.

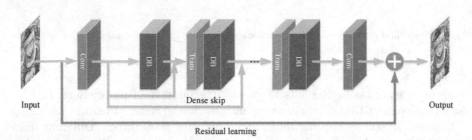

Fig. 2. The architecture of the proposed dense convolutional network (SRDCN). Note that, in our model, the input LR image is first upsampled into the same size as the origin HR image by bicubic interpolation. And then, only the luminance components are used to generate the corresponding HR images. Finally, the reconstructed intensity information is combined with other two channels to obtain the HR color image.

By following [24], we further explore the advantages of dense skip connections by linking the output features of the first convolutional layer to the inputs of all dense blocks. Tong et al. [24] claimed that this strategy provides rich information for reconstructing the high-frequency details of HR images by combining low-level features with high-level features.

For the proposed model, we use 3×3 kernel size filters for all convolutional layers except transition layers (Trans, one convolutional layer with 1×1 kernel size). Different from the origin DenseNets, we remove the pooling layer in all transition layers since pooling operation downsamples features and that is harmful to SR because of the loss of image details. In addition, for each convolutional layer with 3×3 kernel size, the inputs are zero-padded by one pixel in each side in order to keep the feature map size fixed.

In SRDCN, the number of dense blocks is denoted as D and L represents the total number of convolutional layers in one dense block. Our final model SRDCN_D6L8 includes 6 dense blocks and each stacked by 8 convolutional layers. Therefore, it's 52 layers in depth. By considering both training time and memory complexities, we use 16 filters (*growth rate* = 16) in all convolutional layers, so the total number of feature maps generated by one dense block is 128.

3.3 Training

Given a training set $\{I_{LR}^{(i)}, I_{SR}^{(i)}\}_{i=1}^N$, the goal is to train the best model to recover a HR image I_{HR} from a LR image I_{LR} and make the I_{HR} as similar with the ground truth I_{SR} as possible by minimizing the difference between them. We minimize the mean squared error(MSE) and the loss function of our model is:

$$L(\Theta) = \frac{1}{2N} \sum_{i=1}^{N} \|F(I_{LR}^{(i)}, \Theta) - I_{SR}^{(i)}\|^2, \tag{3}$$

where Θ denotes the weights and biases in the network, N is the number of training set patches. The mini-batch stochastic gradient descent (SGD) algorithm with backpropagation are used to find the optimum parameters.

We use the ReLU as the network activation function and all weights are initialized by the *MSRA* method [7]. In order to accelerate the speed of convergence, the initial learning rate is set to 0.1 and then decreased to half every 10 epochs. We stop the training process after 80 epochs when no improvement of loss is observed. To address the vanishing/exploding gradient problem, the adjustable gradient clipping method [11] is adopted to clip gradients to $[-\frac{\theta}{\gamma}, \frac{\theta}{\gamma}]$, where $\theta = 0.01$ and γ denotes the current learning rate.

4   Experiments

4.1   Datasets

We use the same benchmark as [11] for training. Specially, it includes 91 images from Yang et al. [28] and other 200 images from the Berkeley Segmentation Dataset [18]. During testing, four publicly available datasets are used for performance comparison. Among them, dataset Set5 [2] and Set14 [29] are widely used in many SR methods. Dataset BSD100 [18] contains 100 natural images. The Urban100 [10] includes 100 urban scene images which gives a big challenge to lots of methods.

4.2   Implementation Details

By following kim et al. [11], we transform the images from RGB space to YCbCr space and use the Y-channel as the inputs of our model since human vision system (HVS) is more sensitive to details in intensity than in color.

For training, 32×32 no-overlapping patches are cropped from 291 images and each of them is transformed by a special data augmentation operation. Specially, we rotate the original images every $90°$ and flip them horizontally. By data augmentation, we get other 7 augmented images. In addition, 3 different scales ($\times 2$, $\times 3$ and $\times 4$) are used to upsample the whole training sets via bicubic interpolation. The batch size of SGD is set to 16 in our final model SRDCN_D6L8. The training process takes roughly 3 days with one NVIDIA TITAN X GPU.

For testing, we adopt the data augmentation operation similarly to [16]. Thus, for a given LR image, we generate 7 additional images and then feed them all into the model to get 8 HR images $\{I_{HR}^1, I_{HR}^2, \ldots, I_{HR}^8\}$. Then, we apply inverse transformation to those output images to get the final original geometry image sets $\{\tilde{I}_{HR}^1, \tilde{I}_{HR}^2, \ldots, \tilde{I}_{HR}^8\}$. Finally, those 8 images are averaged together to get the HR image I_{HR}. In experiment, we find this simple self-ensemble strategy gives a visible boost on performance.

4.3 Ablation Study

Table 1 presents the ablation study on the effects of residual learning, dense skip connection and self-ensemble.

Table 1. Ablation study of residual learning, dense skip connection and self-ensemble. Average PSNR for the scale factor ×4 on both Set5 and Set14.

Residual	Dense-skip	Self-ensemble	Set5	Set14
	✓	✓	31.50	28.16
✓		✓	31.63	28.21
✓	✓		31.57	28.20
✓	✓	✓	**31.70**	**28.29**

Residual Learning. In order to demonstrate the effect of residual learning, we remove the residual skip connection between the input and the last convolutional layer. Thus, the model is optimized to predict the HR images directly from the given LR inputs. We observe 0.20dB and 0.13dB performance drops on Set5 [2] and Set14 [29] respectively.

Dense Skip Connection. We train a "non-dense" skip connection network by cutting all skip connections which start from the first convolutional layer and end to each dense block. This feature combination strategy simply fuse the low-level features with the high-level features thus supplement high-frequency details. This trick is widely used in high-level image processing fields such as object detection and tracking. We also show a slight increase in performance on the image SR task.

Self-ensemble. To further improve the performance of our model, we adopt an effective data augmentation method similarly to [16,23]. Specially, During test time, the input images are processed through geometric rotations and horizontal flips and the output images are obtained by averagely weighting all those augmented image results. Through this strategy, we further increase our performance by 0.13 dB and 0.09 dB respectively.

4.4 Comparison with State-of-the-Art Methods

In this section, we provide qualitative and quantitative comparisons with current state-of-the-art methods which include A+ [22], SRCNN [4], VDSR [11], DRCN [12], LapSRN [13], DRRN [21] and MS-LapSRN [14]. Note that, we keep the same experimental setting with those compared methods. Specially, by following [11,21], we also crop the borders of the HR images by six pixels, although

Table 2. Benchmark results. Average PSNR/SSIM/IFC for scale factor ×2, ×3 and ×4 on four benchmark datasets. Red indicates the best and blue indicates the second best performance.

Method	Scale	Set5	Set14	BSD100	Urban100
		PSNR/SSIM/IFC	PSNR/SSIM/IFC	PSNR/SSIM/IFC	PSNR/SSIM/IFC
Bicubic	×2	33.66/0.930/6.166	30.24/0.869/6.126	29.56/0.843/5.695	26.88/0.840/6.319
A+ [22]		36.60/0.955/8.715	32.32/0.906/8.200	31.24/0.887/7.464	29.25/0.895/8.440
SRCNN [4]		36.65/0.954/8.165	32.29/0.903/7.829	31.36/0.888/7.242	29.52/0.895/8.092
VDSR [11]		37.53/0.958/8.190	32.97/0.913/7.787	31.90/0.896/7.169	30.77/0.914/8.270
DRCN [12]		37.63/0.959/8.326	32.98/0.913/8.025	31.85/0.894/7.220	30.76/0.913/8.527
LapSRN [13]		37.52/0.959/9.010	33.08/0.913/8.505	31.80/0.895/7.715	30.41/0.910/8.907
DRRN [21]		37.74/0.959/8.671	33.23/0.914/8.320	32.05/0.897/7.613	31.23/0.919/8.917
MS-LapSRN [14]		37.78/0.960/9.305	33.28/0.915/8.748	32.05/0.898/7.927	31.15/0.919/9.406
SRDCN (Ours)		37.83/0.960/9.156	33.33/0.915/8.747	32.09/0.898/7.880	31.31/0.919/9.540
Bicubic	×3	30.39/0.868/3.580	27.55/0.774/3.473	27.21/0.739/3.168	24.46/0.735/3.620
A+ [22]		32.62/0.909/4.979	29.15/0.820/4.545	28.31/0.785/4.028	26.05/0.799/4.883
SRCNN [4]		32.75/0.909/4.658	29.30/0.822/4.338	28.41/0.786/3.879	26.24/0.799/4.584
VDSR [11]		33.66/0.921/5.221	29.77/0.831/4.730	28.82/0.798/4.070	27.14/0.828/5.194
DRCN [12]		33.82/0.923/5.202	29.76/0.831/4.686	28.80/0.796/4.070	27.15/0.828/5.187
LapSRN [13]		33.82/0.922/5.194	29.87/0.832/4.662	28.82/0.798/4.057	27.07/0.828/5.168
DRRN [21]		34.03/0.924/5.397	29.96/0.835/4.878	28.95/0.800/4.269	27.53/0.838/5.456
MS-LapSRN [14]		34.06/0.924/5.390	29.97/0.836/4.806	28.93/0.802/4.154	27.47/0.837/5.409
SRDCN (Ours)		34.04/0.925/5.640	30.03/0.836/5.090	28.98/0.801/4.433	27.58/0.837/5.788
Bicubic	×4	28.42/0.810/2.337	26.10/0.704/2.246	25.96/0.669/1.993	23.15/0.659/2.386
A+ [22]		30.32/0.860/3.260	27.34/0.751/2.961	26.83/0.711/2.565	24.34/0.721/3.218
SRCNN [4]		30.49/0.862/2.997	27.61/0.754/2.767	26.91/0.712/2.412	24.53/0.724/2.992
VDSR [11]		31.35/0.882/3.496	28.03/0.770/3.071	27.29/0.726/2.627	25.18/0.753/3.405
DRCN [12]		31.53/0.884/3.502	28.04/0.770/3.066	27.24/0.724/2.587	25.14/0.752/3.412
LapSRN [13]		31.54/0.885/3.559	28.19/0.772/3.147	27.32/0.728/2.667	25.21/0.756/3.530
DRRN [21]		31.68/0.889/3.703	28.21/0.772/3.252	27.38/0.728/2.760	25.44/0.764/3.676
MS-LapSRN [14]		31.74/0.889/3.749	28.26/0.774/3.261	27.43/0.731/2.755	25.51/0.768/3.727
SRDCN (Ours)		31.70/0.889/3.866	28.29/0.773/3.403	27.43/0.729/2.860	25.56/0.765/3.910

this is unnecessary for SRDCN. Three commonly used image quality metrics which include PSNR, SSIM [26] and IFC [19] are adopted to evaluate the SR images on Y-channels.

In Table 2, we provide average PSNR, SSIM [26] and IFC [19] values on four benchmark datasets. For PSNR and SSIM, the proposed method achieves comparable performance with state-of-the-art methods in all datasets and scale factors. Moreover, our method gets higher values under certain scale factors in each dataset. For IFC, which is shown to have good correlation with human perception of single image super-resolution [27], our method SRDCN achieves

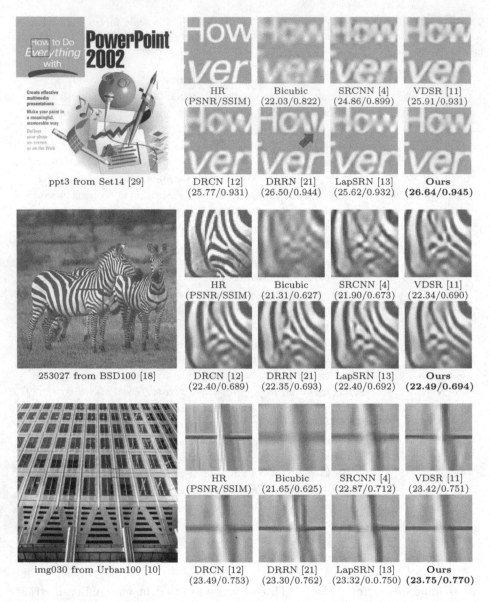

Fig. 3. Super-resolution results for "ppt3" (top figure), "253027" (middle figure), "img030" (bottom figure) with scale factor ×4.

higher values under ×3 and ×4 factors in four datasets and surpass the second best by 0.19 in average.

Figure 3 shows visual comparisons on Set14, BSD100 and Urban100 with a scale factor of ×4. For the image "ppt3" in Set14, the letters reconstructed by our method are sharper than other state-of-the-art approaches'. Interestingly, the letter "w" is incorrectly split in DRRN [21] thus giving a wrong SR result. For other two images, our method also gives a clearer SR results and obtains higher PSNR/SSIM values. In image "253027", the stripes on zebras are very hard to reconstruct precisely and all the methods are failed to give correct results compared to the HR image. However, our method still gives a slightly higher values on both PSNR and SSIM. For the image "img030", our method accurately reconstructs the straight lines and outperforms all other state-of-the-art methods. Specifically, our method surpasses the second best by 0.26dB and 0.017 on the metrics of PSNR and SSIM respectively. Moreover, the results generated by our method include fewer noticeable artifacts compared to others.

4.5 Discussions

In the proposed method, three useful tricks are adopted. Firstly, the residual learning strategy is very necessary since it decomposed the SR task into two parts in terms of frequency domain. Therefore, the network focuses on reconstructing the lost high-frequency details which are exactly lost during down-sample process. Secondly, the dense skip connections are adopted to fuse the low-level and high-level feature maps. We observe a slight boost on performance by only reusing the feature maps of the first convolutional layers. However, denser skip connections between dense blocks are proved to be useful to further boost the results in [24]. Nevertheless, it's time-consuming since feature maps are fold increased while some of them are redundant. Thus, we make a trade-off between the computation efficiency and performance. Thirdly, we further increase the experimental results during the evaluation by using the geometric self-ensemble technique. However, this simple strategy only works for symmetric downsampling methods such as the bicubic downsampling. It will be interesting to address the image SR problem under non-symmetric downsampling conditions such as motion blur, and that will be researched in our future works.

5 Conclusion

In this work, we propose a deep yet concise convolutional model (SRDCN) based on a dense convolutional structure for accurate single image super-resolution. Our model aims to reconstruct high-frequency details through several dense-connected convolutional layers. In detail, preceding feature maps are concatenated to be the inputs of the subsequent layers. With this dense connection strategy, low-level features are reused and fused with the high-level features together to generate the high frequency details of the final super resolution images. Moreover, the performance is further improved by adopting geometry self-ensemble operations. Experimental results on four public benchmark datasets show that our proposed method achieves comparable performance with the state-of-the-art SR algorithms.

References

1. Allebach, J., Wong, P.W.: Edge-directed interpolation. In: Proceedings of the International Conference on Image Processing, vol. 3, pp. 707–710. IEEE (1996)
2. Bevilacqua, M., Roumy, A., Guillemot, C., Alberi-Morel, M.L.: Low-complexity single-image super-resolution based on nonnegative neighbor embedding (2012)
3. Dong, C., Loy, C.C., He, K., Tang, X.: Learning a deep convolutional network for image super-resolution. In: Fleet, D., Pajdla, T., Schiele, B., Tuytelaars, T. (eds.) ECCV 2014. LNCS, vol. 8692, pp. 184–199. Springer, Cham (2014). https://doi.org/10.1007/978-3-319-10593-2_13
4. Dong, C., Loy, C.C., He, K., Tang, X.: Image super-resolution using deep convolutional networks. IEEE Trans. Pattern Anal. Mach. Intell. **38**(2), 295–307 (2016)
5. Duchon, C.E.: Lanczos filtering in one and two dimensions. J. Appl. Meteorol. **18**(8), 1016–1022 (1979)
6. Elad, M., Zeyde, R., Protter, M.: Single image super-resolution using sparse representation. SIAM Imaging Sci. (2010)
7. He, K., Zhang, X., Ren, S., Sun, J.: Delving deep into rectifiers: surpassing human-level performance on ImageNet classification. In: Proceedings of the IEEE International Conference on Computer Vision, pp. 1026–1034 (2015)
8. He, K., Zhang, X., Ren, S., Sun, J.: Deep residual learning for image recognition. In: Proceedings of the IEEE Conference on Computer Vision and Pattern Recognition, pp. 770–778 (2016)
9. Huang, G., Liu, Z., Weinberger, K.Q., van der Maaten, L.: Densely connected convolutional networks. In: Proceedings of the IEEE Conference on Computer Vision and Pattern Recognition, vol. 1, p. 3 (2017)
10. Huang, J.B., Singh, A., Ahuja, N.: Single image super-resolution from transformed self-exemplars. In: Proceedings of the IEEE Conference on Computer Vision and Pattern Recognition, pp. 5197–5206 (2015)
11. Kim, J., Kwon Lee, J., Lee, K.M.: Accurate image super-resolution using very deep convolutional networks. In: Proceedings of the IEEE Conference on Computer Vision and Pattern Recognition, pp. 1646–1654 (2016)
12. Kim, J., Kwon Lee, J., Lee, K.M.: Deeply-recursive convolutional network for image super-resolution. In: Proceedings of the IEEE Conference on Computer Vision and Pattern Recognition, pp. 1637–1645 (2016)
13. Lai, W.S., Huang, J.B., Ahuja, N., Yang, M.H.: Deep laplacian pyramid networks for fast and accurate super-resolution. In: Proceedings of the IEEE Conference on Computer Vision Pattern Recognition, pp. 624–632 (2017)
14. Lai, W.S., Huang, J.B., Ahuja, N., Yang, M.H.: Fast and accurate image super-resolution with deep laplacian pyramid networks. arXiv preprint arXiv:1710.01992 (2017)
15. Ledig, C., et al.: Photo-realistic single image super-resolution using a generative adversarial network. arXiv preprint arXiv:1609.04802 (2016)
16. Lim, B., Son, S., Kim, H., Nah, S., Lee, K.M.: Enhanced deep residual networks for single image super-resolution. In: The IEEE Conference on Computer Vision and Pattern Recognition (CVPR) Workshops, vol. 1, p. 3 (2017)
17. Mao, X., Shen, C., Yang, Y.B.: Image restoration using very deep convolutional encoder-decoder networks with symmetric skip connections. In: Advances in Neural Information Processing Systems, pp. 2802–2810 (2016)

18. Martin, D., Fowlkes, C., Tal, D., Malik, J.: A database of human segmented natural images and its application to evaluating segmentation algorithms and measuring ecological statistics. In: Proceedings of the Eighth IEEE International Conference on Computer Vision, ICCV 2001, vol. 2, pp. 416–423. IEEE (2001)
19. Sheikh, H.R., Bovik, A.C., De Veciana, G.: An information fidelity criterion for image quality assessment using natural scene statistics. IEEE Trans. image process. **14**(12), 2117–2128 (2005)
20. Shi, W., et al.: Real-time single image and video super-resolution using an efficient sub-pixel convolutional neural network. In: Proceedings of the IEEE Conference on Computer Vision and Pattern Recognition, pp. 1874–1883 (2016)
21. Tai, Y., Yang, J., Liu, X.: Image super-resolution via deep recursive residual network. In: Proceedings of the IEEE Conference on Computer Vision and Pattern Recognition (2017)
22. Timofte, R., De Smet, V., Van Gool, L.: A+: adjusted anchored neighborhood regression for fast super-resolution. In: Cremers, D., Reid, I., Saito, H., Yang, M.-H. (eds.) ACCV 2014. LNCS, vol. 9006, pp. 111–126. Springer, Cham (2015). https://doi.org/10.1007/978-3-319-16817-3_8
23. Timofte, R., Rothe, R., Van Gool, L.: Seven ways to improve example-based single image super resolution. In: 2016 IEEE Conference on Computer Vision and Pattern Recognition (CVPR), pp. 1865–1873. IEEE (2016)
24. Tong, T., Li, G., Liu, X., Gao, Q.: Image super-resolution using dense skip connections. In: 2017 IEEE International Conference on Computer Vision (ICCV), pp. 4809–4817. IEEE (2017)
25. Wang, Z., Liu, D., Yang, J., Han, W., Huang, T.: Deep networks for image super-resolution with sparse prior. In: Proceedings of the IEEE International Conference on Computer Vision, pp. 370–378 (2015)
26. Wang, Z., Bovik, A.C., Sheikh, H.R., Simoncelli, E.P.: Image quality assessment: from error visibility to structural similarity. IEEE Trans. Image Process. **13**(4), 600–612 (2004)
27. Yang, C.-Y., Ma, C., Yang, M.-H.: Single-image super-resolution: a benchmark. In: Fleet, D., Pajdla, T., Schiele, B., Tuytelaars, T. (eds.) ECCV 2014. LNCS, vol. 8692, pp. 372–386. Springer, Cham (2014). https://doi.org/10.1007/978-3-319-10593-2_25
28. Yang, J., Wright, J., Huang, T.S., Ma, Y.: Image super-resolution via sparse representation. IEEE Trans. Image Process. **19**(11), 2861–2873 (2010)
29. Zeyde, R., Elad, M., Protter, M.: On single image scale-up using sparse-representations. In: Boissonnat, J.-D., et al. (eds.) Curves and Surfaces 2010. LNCS, vol. 6920, pp. 711–730. Springer, Heidelberg (2012). https://doi.org/10.1007/978-3-642-27413-8_47
30. Zhang, L., Wu, X.: An edge-guided image interpolation algorithm via directional filtering and data fusion. IEEE Trans. Image Process. **15**(8), 2226–2238 (2006)

A Regression Approach for Robust Gait Periodicity Detection with Deep Convolutional Networks

Kejun Wang$^{(\boxtimes)}$, Liangliang Liu, Xinnan Ding, Yibo Xu,
and Haolin Wang

College of Automation, Harbin Engineering University, Harbin, China
{wangkejun, liuliangliang,
dingxinnan, xuyibo}@hrbeu.edu.cn, WHLhrbeu@163.com

Abstract. This paper presents a regression approach to gait periodicity detection via fitting gait sequence to a sine function by deep convolutional neural networks. The key idea is to model the gait fluctuation as a sinusoidal function because of similar periodic regularity. Each frame of the gait video corresponds to a function value that can represent its periodic features. Convolutional network serves to learn and locate a frame in a gait cycle. To the best of our knowledge, it is the first work based on deep neural networks for gait period detection in the literature. An extensive empirical evaluation is provided on the CASIA-B dataset in terms of different views and network architectures with comparison to the existing works. The results show the good accuracy and robustness of the proposed method for gait periodicity detection.

Keywords: Gait period detection · Deep convolutional neural networks
Gait recognition · Biometrics technology

1 Introduction

As one of the biometric identification methods, gait recognition is particularly suitable for human identification at a long distance [1]. It requires no contact or explicit cooperation by subjects, compared with other biometric features such as face and fingerprint. Therefore, gait recognition has good prospects for application in many fields such as safety monitoring, human-computer interaction and entrance guard. In recent years, it has attracted wide attention of researchers and many effective algorithms have been proposed.

Periodicity detection is an essential step for vision-based gait recognition. Unlike other biometric techniques, it is not suitable to use a single image of the silhouette for gait recognition because of the wobble of the body in walking. Thus, the input of gait recognition is a video sequence rather than a gait silhouette. Gait period detection is the process of making the suitable length of the input video. A gait cycle can include complete gait features with the least frames. The shorter detected gait periods may miss the effective gait features while the longer ones may contain redundant data and need

© Springer Nature Switzerland AG 2018
J.-H. Lai et al. (Eds.): PRCV 2018, LNCS 11257, pp. 146–156, 2018.
https://doi.org/10.1007/978-3-030-03335-4_13

more computation. The gait recognition, based on silhouette sequences or class energy images, is directly affected by the accuracy of the periodic detection [2, 3].

Many of the previous researches on gait period detection are based on the width and height of the human body [4, 5], which is usually easy and straightforward. These methods achieve high accuracy near the side view of 90°. But they are not robust to the different condition such as various views and clothes. Recently, the convolutional neural network (CNN) [6] has become the common workhorse for feature learning from images [7]. For the gait period detection task, CNN can extract periodic features of gait silhouette sequences automatically instead of a single artificial feature by the traditional methods. A CNN-based gait periodicity detection approach can be workable to get better effectiveness and robustness.

In this paper, we make the following contributions:

- We propose a regression approach based on a fitting method for gait periodicity detection. The gait sequences are modeled as the sinusoidal function due to the similar periodicity. The function value represents the periodic features of the corresponding frame.
- A CNN-based method is presented to gait period detection. The networks will learn the periodic features of silhouette sequences and locate their position in the period automatically. To the best of our knowledge, it is the first to use deep CNNs for gait periodicity detection in the literature.
- We conduct an extensive evaluation in terms of different views and network architectures. The proposed method shows high accuracy in various views, compared with the existing works.

In the remaining part of this paper, Sect. 2 presents more related works on gait periodicity detection and CNNs. And then Sect. 3 describes the proposed method in detail. An experimental evaluation is conducted on the CASIA-B gait database and results are shown in Sect. 4. Finally, conclusions are drawn in Sect. 5.

2 Related Work

2.1 Gait Periodicity Detection

The existing gait period detection methods mainly base on height and width of body, because the height and the size of footstep change periodically in walking. Collins et al. [4] proposed a method by using the width and height of the body for the period detection, but it is greatly affected by the change of the distance between the person and the camera; Lee et al. [8] utilized the width of silhouettes to detect gait period after the normalization of the pedestrians solving the problem of the changing distance; Wang et al. [5] considered silhouettes changing in size from different views and proposed a method based on the ratio of height to width, leaving out the process of normalization; Wang et al. [9] chose the average width of the legs as a feature to detect periodicity avoid the influence of bags and clothes. Moreover, the area of the body is effective to represent periodic features. Sarkar et al. [10] used the area of the legs as the feature to detect period.

Besides, model fitting is also an effective algorithm. Ben et al. [11] proposed a dual-ellipse fitting approach. Two regions of the whole silhouette divided by the centroid are fitted into two ellipses and the gait fluctuation is constructed as a periodic function depending on the eccentricities of two halves of the silhouette over time.

2.2   Deep Convolutional Neural Networks

CNN has shown many advantages in feature learning since it was submitted. The Lenet-5 model is first network designed by CNN [7]. And CNN composes the kernel parts of all the outstanding algorithms in the ImageNet large scale visual recognition challenge since 2012, when Krizhevsky et al. won the championship with the AlexNet [12]. VGG is one of the networks that have achieved excellent results in the ImageNet competition after Alexnet [13]. It has inherited and deepened some of the frameworks of Lenet and Alexnet. And the following year, the deep GoogLeNet won the first with 22 trainable layers and has reduced the top-5 classification error rate down to 6.67% [14]. These successful applications of CNNs motive us to develop gait periodicity detection methods based on CNN.

3   Method

3.1   Overview

We present a novel method to determine a gait cycle via fitting gait sequence to a sine function by deep CNNs. As shown in Fig. 1, the gait silhouette sequence is sent to the deep CNN to extract periodic features after normalization. Then the output is filtered to find the key frame of the gait period, and the frames between two peaks or troughs contribute a periodicity of gait.

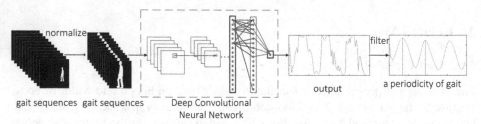

Fig. 1. Process flow of the proposed method. After normalization, deep CNN extracts periodic features of the gait sequence and outputs a waveform. (The horizontal axis shows the number of frames, and the vertical axis shows the value of output). A gait periodicity can be found through locating peaks or troughs after filtering.

The aim of normalization is to make the size of all silhouettes equal to avoid the influence of the change of distance and angle between person and camera. Each frame of the gait sequences should be cropped and resized. We locate the top and bottom pixels of the silhouettes to pick up the areas of pedestrians, and then compute their gravity center. With the gravity center, the height of silhouettes and the aspect ratio (11/16), the frames are cropped off and rescaled into 88×128.

After normalization, the gait silhouette is input into a trained network in sequence, and output of each frame is a value that can represent its periodic features through learning of CNN. And a waveform similar to the sinusoidal function consists of the output values of a gait sequence.

Finally, filtering is an important step. The mean filtering is applied in this work. Because of the errors, the output value corresponding to a frame is an approximation of the actual value. As long as the most output of frames are relatively accurate values, the rest of fluctuation can be avoided by filtering.

3.2   Modeling as a Sinusoidal Function

The purpose of modeling is to quantify the gait periodic features of each frame into a numerical value. A sinusoidal function as a low dimensional signal is used to represent the periodic fluctuation of the gait sequence. Because the sine function is continuous and periodic with a peak and a trough within one cycle, fitting the characteristics of a gait period with maximum footsteps twice. And it is not difficult to locate the peaks and troughs, which is helpful to find the key frames to determine a gait cycle.

Table 1. The values corresponding to the periodic features of gait

Gait silhouette								
The value corresponding to the periodic feature	0	0.270	0.520	0.731	0.888	0.979	0.998	0.942
Gait silhouette								
The value corresponding to the periodic feature	0.816	0.630	0.397	0.134	-0.136	-0.400	-0.633	-0.818
Gait silhouette								
The value corresponding to the periodic feature	-0.943	-0.998	-0.979	-0.887	-0.729	-0.517	-0.267	0

We choose the sinusoidal function with a period and an amplitude of 1 to be fitted. In order to keep the consistency of evaluation periodic features, we define a standard that corresponds to the output value and the periodic feature of gait. In a silhouette sequence, we set the value of the image where the legs are closed together and the right foot is forward as 0, i.e. the beginning. The period terminates when the legs are closed and the right foot has a forward trend once more. It is the end of the last period and the beginning of the next period. After locating the beginning and the end, the interval is the period (i.e. 1) divided by the number of frames between them. The values are obtained by accumulative and sinusoidal calculation. For example as the periodicity and the corresponding values shown in Table 1, this gait cycle contains 24 frames, so the interval is 1/24 (1 divided by the number of frames), and the position of the each frame of the period is 0, 1/24, 2/24, 3/24,..., 1 respectively. Then the values can be produced easily by sin(0), sin(1/24), sin(2/24), sin(3/24),..., sin(1). In this way, the gait fluctuation is modeled as a sinusoidal function.

3.3   Network Architectures

Deep CNN is the tool to fit the gait frames to a sinusoidal function. And it is used to learn the periodic feature of a frame and locate it in a gait cycle. Thus the input of the network is a silhouette in a frame ($128 \times 88 \times 1$), and the output is a regression value. We present 3 networks architectures for gait periodicity detection with different depths and widths. Thanks to good performance of Alexnet, VGG and GoogLeNet in images classification, similar structures are adopted at bottom layers for feature extraction. The mean squared error (MSE) is applied as their loss functions in this paper.

Basic Network for Gait Periodicity Detection. Table 2 shows the structure of the network in detail. Conv7 represents the convolution layer with 7×7 kernels. Similarly, Conv5 is with 5×5 kernels, and Conv3 is with 3×3 kernels. Larger convolution kernels are used to extract periodic features preliminarily. The number of neurons in the last layer is 1 because the output should be a regression value. And all of the activation functions are Relu.

Table 2.   Detailed architecture of basic network

Layer	Output shape
Conv7-Relu-Batch_norm	30,20,48
Maxpool	15,10,48
Conv5-Relu-Batch_norm	11,6,128
Maxpool	5,3,128
Conv3-Relu	5,3,192
Conv3-Relu	5,3,192
Conv3-Relu	5,3,128
Maxpool	2,1,128
FC-Relu	1024
FC-Relu	512
FC-Relu	1

Deep Network for Gait Periodicity Detection. Is has a deeper network structure than the previous, and its structure that we use is shown in Table 3 where Conv3 is also the convolution layer with 3×3 kernels. And the output layer is the same, a neuron with Relu activation function. The difference is that smaller convolutional kernels are adopted totally. A convolutional sequence can simulate the larger receptive fields to reduce computation.

Table 3. Detailed architecture of deep network

Layer	Output shape
Conv3-Relu	128,88,64
Conv3-Relu	128,88,64
Maxpool	64,44,64
Conv3-Relu	64,44,128
Conv3-Relu	64,44,128
Maxpool	32,22,128
Conv3-Relu	32,22,256
Conv3-Relu	33,22,256
Conv3-Relu	32,22,256
Maxpool	16,11,256
Conv3-Relu	16,11,512
Conv3-Relu	16,11,512
Conv3-Relu	16,11,512
Maxpool	8,5,512
Dropout-FC-Relu	1000
Dropout-FC-Relu	250
FC-Relu	1

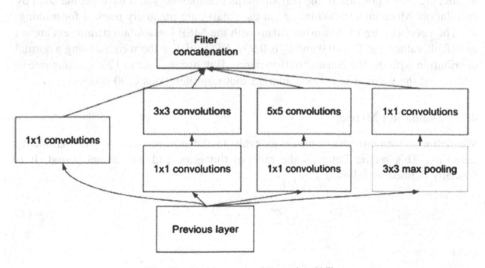

Fig. 2. Architecture of Inception [15]

Wide Network for Gait Periodicity Detection. The unique feature of GoogleNet network model,i.e. Inception, is applied in third network architecture. Inception expands the network by improving the width of the network instead of the depth alone as shown in Fig. 2 [14, 15]. Table 4 is the schematic diagram of the third network architecture used in this paper. As in the same way, the output layer transforms the extracted gait periodic features into a regression value.

Table 4. Network architecture based on Inception

Layer	Output shape
9 × Inception	1000
FC-Relu	250
FC-Relu	1

4 Experiments

An empirical evaluation with different network architectures is provided on CASIA-B dataset. There are 124 subjects and 11 views (0, 18, …, 180°) and 10 sequences per subject for each view in the CASIA-B gait dataset [16]. And we evaluate our method with comparison to alternative approaches in terms of different views and network architectures.

4.1 Training

Deep CNN needs to learn from a large number of labeled data. Thus, it is necessary to mark the periodic features of each frame as their labels for training. The function value of each frame represents its periodic features as its label in the training set. We have located the initial position of the periodic sequence manually and have got the label by calculation. More than 96000 images in the dataset are manually marked for training.

The networks are trained using Adam with the MSE loss. Adam parameters are set as default values, i.e. β_1 is 0.9 and β_2 is 0.999. We initialize the weights using a normal distribution with the 0 mean and 0.01 variance. Batch size is set to 128, learning rate to 0.001, and the training is stopped after 75 thousand iterations (100 epochs).

4.2 Evaluation Metric

We define a straightforward metric to evaluate the performance of gait periodicity detection. This metric indicates the ratio of the error and the factual period. It is formally defined as follows:

$$C = \frac{|T - T_s|}{T} \tag{1}$$

where T is the number of the frames in an actual periodicity and T_s is the detected number. The smaller the value of C, the smaller the error is, and the higher accuracy the method gets. Conversely, the larger C value means the worse performance.

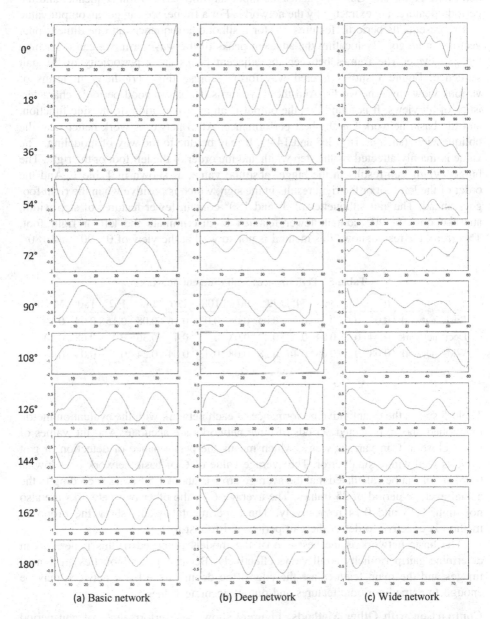

(a) Basic network   (b) Deep network   (c) Wide network

Fig. 3. Output waveforms of different networks and views. Column (a)–(c): The output waveforms in terms of 0°, 18° ..., 180° of the basic network, deep network and the network based on Inception respectively. The number of the input frame is shown on the horizontal axis, and the output value is shown on the vertical axis.

4.3 Comparison

Different Network Architectures. After training, the networks can be used to determine gait cycle. Gait silhouettes are input into the networks in sequence, and the periodic features are extracted by the networks. For a frame, we can get an output value that represents its periodic features. So for a silhouette sequence, an one-dimensional vector can be got. By locating the adjacent peaks of the waveform, we can determine the gait cycle. The frames between the adjacent peaks are a periodicity of the gait sequence. Figure 3 shows filtered waveforms representing periodicity in terms of various views by 3 networks. And the waveforms can show good periodic characteristics of all views. It is found that the output is an approximation of the sine function, and the basic network has the best performance. All 3 networks work better near the oblique view (such as 18°, 36° and 144°). It may be due to the way of modeling. The value is mainly affected by the step width and the order of the left foot or the right. The bigger width step results in the bigger absolute value, as shown in Table 1. And the order of the left foot or the right results in the sign, which is positive when the right foot goes ahead. The gait silhouettes of 0° and 180° contain fewer features of step width, and the ones of 90° contain fewer features to discriminate the left or right foot. Therefore, the result shows this method is not so well at the view of 0°, 90° and 180°.

Table 5. Performances with different networks

	0°	18°	36°	54°	72°	90°	108°	126°	144°	162°	180°	Mean
Basic network	0.04	0	0	0	0.04	0.08	0.08	0.16	0.08	0.15	0.04	0.06
Deep network	0.04	0	0.04	0	0.42	0.08	0	0.4	0.36	0	0.08	0.13
Wide network	0.08	0	0.08	0.46	0.38	0.08	0.48	0.04	0.24	0	0.04	0.14

Table 5 shows the quantitative performance of each network with the evaluation metric mentioned above. Detected periods of three networks are accurate. And the values of C are close to 0 in various views, which means the performance of detection of gait cycle is well with a small error. The average value of C of basic network is as low as 0.06, and it can be calculated that the average error is about 1.5 frames according to the actual average period of 25 frames. The average C of the other two networks are also not high, 0.13 and 0.14 respectively. The experimental results show the proposed method is effective to detect the gait period and robust to various views.

The basic network is the best one of the models proposed in this paper. It can determine gait periodicity at all views effectively. Because gait silhouettes are binary images and the main features are the edges, the depth of the basic network may be enough to extract periodic features and output accurate values.

Comparison with Other Methods. Figure 4 shows the performances of gait period detection with different approaches. We choose several previous methods that can work in all views to compare (mentioned in Sect. 2). The lines warped on both sides belong to the traditional methods. That means errors of the existing works are nearly a periodicity of gait at the views near 0° and 180°. By comparison, the proposed method based on the deep CNN can have relatively good effect on the front and back views. At the view near 90°, the errors of our method are larger than the traditional slightly. But the largest C in all views of our method is 0.16. That is to say the error is about 3 to 4 frames. They are acceptable relative to a gait cycle containing about 25 frames. In general, gait periodicity detection by convolutional neural network is feasible in terms of various views, making up for the low accuracy of the previous methods in the front and back view. Besides, the error is reasonable at the side view. Therefore, it is an effective method and robust to various views.

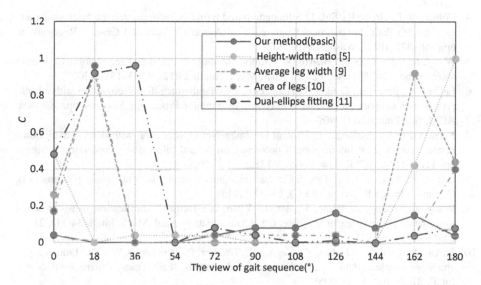

Fig. 4. Comparison with other existent methods. Our approach is shown with the basic nework. And it is compared with the methods of Wang et al. [5], Wang et al. [9], Sarkar et al. [10] and Ben et al. [11].

5   Conclusion

We present a novel approach for robust gait periodicity detection based on regression method by deep CNNs. The networks can learn the periodic features of the gait sequences and output a value that can represent the features of each frame. Experimental results confirm the effectiveness and robustness of the proposed method for gait periodicity detection in terms of various views, compared with the existing works.

References

1. Phillips, P.J.: Human identification technical challenges. In: 2002 International Conference on Image Processing, pp. 49–52. IEEE, Rochester (2002)
2. Makihara, Y., Sagawa, R., Mukaigawa, Y., Echigo, T., Yagi, Y.: Gait recognition using a view transformation model in the frequency domain. In: Leonardis, A., Bischof, H., Pinz, A. (eds.) ECCV 2006. LNCS, vol. 3953, pp. 151–163. Springer, Heidelberg (2006). https://doi.org/10.1007/11744078_12
3. Li, C., Min, X., Sun, S., Lin, W., Tang, Z.: Deepgait: a learning deep convolutional representation for view-invariant gait recognition using joint Bayesian. Appl. Sci. **7**(3), 210 (2017)
4. Collins, R.T., Gross, R., Shi. J.: Silhouette-based human identification from body shape and gait. In: 5th IEEE International Conference on Automatic Face and Gesture Recognition, pp. 366–372. IEEE, Washington (2002)
5. Wang, L., Tan, T., Ning, H., Hu, W.: Silhouette analysis-based gait recognition for human identification. IEEE Trans. Pattern Anal. Mach. Intell. **25**(12), 1505–1518 (2003)
6. LeCun, Y., Boser, B., Denker, J., Henderson, D.: Handwritten digit recognition with a back-propagation network. In: Advances in Neural Information Processing Systems, pp. 396–404. ACM, San Francisco (1990)
7. Krizhevsky, A., Sutskever, I., Hinton, G.: ImageNet classification with deep convolutional neural networks. In: International Conference on Neural Information Processing Systems, pp. 1106–1114. ACM, New York (2012)
8. Lee, C.P., Tan, A.W.C., Tan, S.C.: Gait recognition with transient binary patterns. Vis. Commun. Image Represent. **33**(C), 69–77 (2015)
9. Wang, C., Zhang, J., Wang, L., Pu, J., Yuan, X.: Human identification using temporal information preserving gait template. IEEE Trans. Pattern Anal. Mach. Intell. **34**(11), 2164–2176 (2012)
10. Sarkar, S., Phillips, P.J., Liu, Z., Vega, I.R., Grother, P., Bowyer, K.W.: The humanid gait challenge problem: data sets, performance, and analysis. IEEE Trans. Pattern Anal. Mach. Intell. **27**(2), 162–177 (2005)
11. Ben, X., Meng, W., Yan, R.: Dual-ellipse fitting approach for robust gait periodicity detection. Neurocomputing. **79**(3), 173–178 (2012)
12. Lecun, Y., Bottou, L., Bengio, Y., Haffner, P.: Gradient-based learning applied to document recognition. Proc. IEEE **86**(11), 2278–2324 (1998)
13. Simonyan, K., Zisserman, A..: Very deep convolutional networks for large-scale image recognition. CoRR (2014). https://arxiv.org/abs/1409.1556
14. Szegedy, C., Liu, W., Jia, Y., Sermanet, P., Reed, S., Anguelov, D., et al.: Going deeper with convolutions. In: 2015 IEEE Conference on Computer Vision and Pattern Recognition, pp. 1–9. IEEE, Boston (2015)
15. Szegedy, C., Ioffe, S., Vanhoucke, V., Alemi, A.: Inception-v4, Inception-ResNet and the impact of residual connections on learning. CoRR (2016). https://arxiv.org/pdf/1602.07261
16. Yu, S., Tan, D., Tan, T.: A framework for evaluating the effect of view angle, clothing and carrying condition on gait recognition. In: 18th International Conference on Pattern Recognition, pp. 441–444. IEEE, Hong Kong (2006)

Predicting Epileptic Seizures from Intracranial EEG Using LSTM-Based Multi-task Learning

Xuelin Ma[1,3], Shuang Qiu[1], Yuxing Zhang[2], Xiaoqin Lian[2],
and Huiguang He[1,3,4(✉)]

[1] Research Center for Brain-inspired Intelligence
and National Laboratory of Pattern Recognition, Institute of Automation,
Chinese Academy of Sciences, Beijing, China
{maxuelin2015,shuang.qiu,huiguang.he}@ia.ac.cn
[2] School of Computer and Information Engineering,
Beijing Technology and Business University, Beijing, China
zhang.y.x0325@foxmail.com, lianxq@263.net
[3] University of Chinese Academy of Sciences, Beijing, China
[4] Center for Excellence in Brain Science and Intelligence Technology,
Chinese Academy of Sciences, Beijing, China

Abstract. Epilepsy afflicts nearly 1% of the world's population, and is characterized by the occurrence of spontaneous seizures. It's important to make prediction before seizures, so that epileptic can prevent seizures taking place on some specific occasions to avoid suffering from great damage. The previous work in seizure prediction paid less attention to the time-series information and their performances may also restricted to the small training data. In this study, we proposed a Long Short-Term Memory (LSTM)-based multi-task learning (MTL) framework for seizure prediction. The LSTM unit was used to process the sequential data and the MTL framework was applied to perform prediction and latency regression simultaneously. We evaluated the proposed method in the American Epilepsy Society Seizure Prediction Challenge dataset and obtained an average prediction accuracy of 89.36%, which was 3.41% higher than the reported state-of-the-art. In addition, the input data and output of middle layers were visualized. The visual and experiment results demonstrated the superior performance of our proposed LSTM-MTL method for seizure prediction.

Keywords: Seizure prediction · LSTM · Multi-task learning
Intracranial EEG

1 Introduction

Epilepsy is a common brain disorder characterized by intermittent abnormal neuronal firing in the brain which can lead to seizures [15]. Seizure forecasting

© Springer Nature Switzerland AG 2018
J.-H. Lai et al. (Eds.): PRCV 2018, LNCS 11257, pp. 157–167, 2018.
https://doi.org/10.1007/978-3-030-03335-4_14

systems have the potential to help epileptic to lead a more normal lives [20,22]. With these systems, epileptic could avoid to do dangerous activities like driving or swimming and medications could be administered before impending seizures. Therefore, predicting epilepsy before seizure it's very important for building the seizure forecasting systems [15].

Intracranial EEG (iEEG) is a chronological electrophysiological record of epileptic. Seizure prediction from iEEG has been extensively studied in the previous work. Most work to date relies on spectral information and pays attention to traditional machine learning methods like k-nearest neighbors algorithm (KNN), SVM, Random Forest and XGBoost [4], etc. On the other hand, iEEG also contains a lot of timing information except spectral information. Most of the previous work doesn't utilize the sequential information of iEEG data [16].

Inspired by the success of deep recurrent neural networks (RNNs) for speech feature learning and time series prediction [8,9], we intend to build an effective seizure prediction model based on deep Long Short-Term Memory (LSTM) network. The applications of LSTM remain a challenge in neuroimaging domain. One of the reasons is the limited number of samples, which makes it difficult for training large-scale networks with millions of parameters [1]. This problem can be alleviated by applying sliding window approach over the raw data, which would increase the amount of training samples hundreds of times [7,11,19].

Actually, most of the seizure datasets focus on the classification between preictal state (prior to seizure) and interictal state (between seizures, or baseline) [12,13]. The preictal data are recorded with the latency before seizure, which can be utilized as additional information for seizure prediction. Multitask learning (MTL) [3] aims to improve generalization performance of multiple tasks by appropriately sharing relevant information across them. Some studies showed that the MTL method performed better than methods based on individual learning [5,17,21]. Therefore, the additional latency information can be integrated by multi-task learning.

In this paper, we proposed a novel Long Short-Term Memory based multi-task learning framework (refer to LSTM-MTL) for seizure prediction. The LSTM network can inherently process the sequential data, and the multi-task learning framework performs prediction and latency regression simultaneously to improve the prediction performance. We evaluated our proposal on public seizure dataset and showed that the LSTM-MTL framework outperformed the KNN and XGBoost methods. The LSTM-MTL model showed the prediction AUC up to 89.36%, which is 3.41% higher than the reported state-of-the-art and 2.5% higher than the LSTM model without MTL. The results demonstrated the effectiveness of our proposed LSTM based multi-task learning framework.

In addition, the input data and the output of middle layers of the multi-task LSTM network are visualized for intuitive perception. The visual results demonstrated that the representation learning ability of the network is remarkable. The linearly inseparable original data become linearly separable gradually through layer-by-layer process.

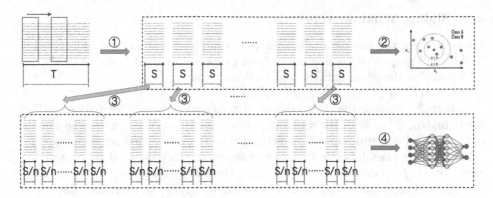

Fig. 1. The overall preprocessing flowchart. Step 1: Sliding Window Approach with window length of S and 50% overlapping. Step 2: Feature extraction (see Sect. 2.1) over each sample for traditional classifier input. Step 3: Sliding Window Approach with window length of S/n and no overlapping. Step 4: Feature extraction (see Sect. 2.1) over the sequential subsamples for LSTM networks.

The rest of this paper is organized as follows: Sect. 2 introduces the method we adopted and the framework we proposed. Section 3 describes the experiments in detail. Section 4 shows the experiment result and some discussion about it. Section 5 is the conclusion of this work.

2   The Proposed Method

In this section, we introduce the feature extraction, sliding window approach, training and testing strategies and the proposed LSTM based multi-task learning architecture.

2.1   Feature Extraction

Typically, given an iEEG record segment $r \in \mathbb{R}^{C \times S}$, where C denotes the numbers of channels, S denotes the time steps, the feature vector $x \in \mathbb{R}^{1 \times (C^2 + 8*C)}$ are extracted with following components:

One part of the features are the average spectral power in six frequency bands of each channel and the standard deviation of this six powers, resulting a vector with length of $C * 7$. The six frequency bands are delta (0.1–4 Hz), theta (4–8 Hz), alpha (8–12 Hz), beta (12–30 Hz), low gamma (30–70 Hz) and high gamma (70–180 Hz).

Another part of the features are the correlation in time domain and frequency domain (upper triangle values of correlation matrices) with their eigenvalues, resulting a vector with length of $C * (C + 1)$. Therefore, the length of feature vector x is $C^2 + 8 * C$.

2.2 Sliding Window Approach

We preprocess the raw data to obtain more samples for training deep networks. The overall preprocessing flowchart of our proposed method is shown in Fig. 1.

Typically, the given datasets can be denoted as

$D^i = \{(E^1, y^1, L^1), ..., (E^{N_i}, y^{N_i}, L^{N_i})\},$

where N_i denotes the total number of recorded segments for patient i. The input matrix $E^j \in \mathbb{R}^{C \times T}$ of segment j, where $1 \leq j \leq N_i$, contains the signals of C recorded electrodes and T discretized time steps recorded per segment. The corresponding class label and latency of segment j are denoted by y^j and L^j, respectively. L^j is defined as the beginning timesteps of the sequential segment.

The sliding window approach is applied to divide the segment data into individual samples, which are used for later processing. Each sample has a fixed length S, with 50% overlapping between continuous neighbors.

For traditional classifier, a sample can be denoted as follow:

$$r_k^j \in \mathbb{R}^{C \times S}, \tag{1}$$

$$y_k^j = y^j \tag{2}$$

where $1 \leq j \leq N_i$ and $1 \leq k \leq [\frac{T}{(S/2)}] - 1$.

By feature extraction, r_k^j is converted into $x_k^j \in \mathbb{R}^{1 \times (C^2 + 8*C)}$, which can be used as the input to traditional classifiers.

For sequential deep learning models, a sample r_k^j is clipped into n non-overlapping sequential records and can be denoted as follow:

$$rs_k^j \in \mathbb{R}^{n \times C \times \frac{S}{n}}, \tag{3}$$

$$y_k^j = y^j, \tag{4}$$

$$l_k^j = \begin{cases} L^j + \frac{S/2}{T}, & \text{if } y_k^j = 1 \\ 0, & \text{if } y_k^j = 0 \end{cases} \tag{5}$$

where $1 \leq j \leq N_i$ and $1 \leq k \leq [\frac{T}{(S/2)}] - 1$.

In the same way, rs_k^j is converted into $xs_k^j \in \mathbb{R}^{n \times 1 \times (C^2 + 8*C)}$, which can be used as the input to sequential deep learning models.

2.3 Training and Testing Input

In training, using samples $\{(r_1^1, y_1^1), ..., (r_k^1, y_k^1), ..., (r_1^{N_i}, y_1^{N_i}), ..., (r_k^{N_i}, y_k^{N_i})\}$ and $\{(rs_1^1, y_1^1), ..., (rs_k^1, y_k^1), ..., (rs_1^{N_i}, y_1^{N_i}), ..., (rs_k^{N_i}, y_k^{N_i})\}$ as input to traditional classifiers and LSTM-based models, respectively.

In testing, we evaluated the models with sample data r_k^j or rs_k^j, used the mean rule to fuse k predicted sample label probabilities $pred\_p_k^j$ into predicted segment label probability $pred\_p^j$ and computed the segment-wise Area Under Curve (AUC).

2.4   Long Short-Term Memory Network

RNN is a class of neural network that maintains internal hidden states to model the dynamic temporal behaviour of sequences through directed cyclic connections between its units. LSTM extends RNN by adding three gates to an RNN neuron, which enable LSTM to learn long-term dependency in a sequence, and make it easier to optimize [10]. There is sequential information containing in the iEEG data and LSTM is an excellent model for encoding sequential iEEG data.

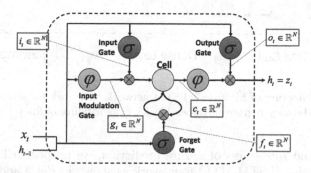

Fig. 2. A block diagram of the LSTM unit (there are minor differences in comparison to [6], with *phi* symbol after *cell* element and some annotation about the dimension of each state inside the red box). (Color figure online)

A block diagram of the LSTM unit is shown in Fig. 2, and the recurrence equations is as follows:

$$i_t = \sigma\left(W_{xi}x_t + W_{hi}h_{t-1} + b_i\right), \tag{6}$$

$$f_t = \sigma\left(W_{xf}x_t + W_{hf}h_{t-1} + b_f\right), \tag{7}$$

$$o_t = \sigma\left(W_{xo}x_t + W_{ho}h_{t-1} + b_o\right), \tag{8}$$

$$g_t = \phi\left(W_{xc}x_t + W_{hc}h_{t-1} + b_c\right), \tag{9}$$

$$c_t = f_t \odot c_{t-1} + i_t \odot g_t, \tag{10}$$

$$h_t = o_t \odot \phi\left(c_t\right). \tag{11}$$

A LSTM unit contains an input gate i_t, a forget gate f_t, a cell c_t, an output gate o_t and an output response h_t. The input gate and the forget gate govern the information flow. The output gate controls how much information from the cell is passed to the output h_t. The memory cell has a self-connected recurrent edge of weight 1, ensuring that the gradient is able to pass across many time steps without vanishing or exploding. Units are connected recurrently to each other, replacing the usual hidden units of ordinary recurrent networks.

2.5   LSTM Based Multi-task Learning

While class label y_k^j only provides hard and limited information, the latency l_k^j can show much softer and more plentiful details about the seizure. To improve

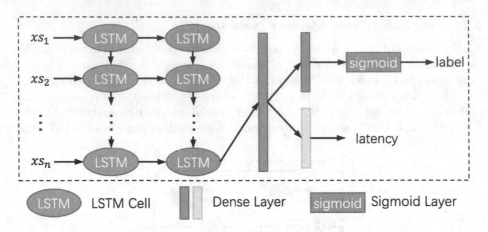

Fig. 3. The architecture of Multi-task LSTM network. One task for seizure prediction and another for latency regression (green block). (Color figure online)

the accuracy and robustness of seizure prediction, we propose a LSTM based multi-task learning (LSTM-MTL) framework as shown in Fig. 3 and describe in detail as follow.

The LSTM-MTL model takes sequential data xs_k^j as input. Two LSTM layers are cascaded to encoding the sequential information of input. The last timestep output of the second LSTM layer is followed by a dense layer for learning representation further. For prediction task, the dense layer is followed by another dense layer with two nodes, which used a sigmoid activate function to generate the final prediction. Simultaneously, for latency regression task, a dense layer with one node is utilized to regress urgency degree from the output of first dense layer.

The loss function of prediction task L_{pred} is sigmoid cross-entropy and the loss function of latency regression L_{reg} is mean square error. For multi-task learning, we define a loss function to combine above loss functions as follow:

$$L = \alpha L_{pred} + (1 - \alpha)L_{reg}, \tag{12}$$

where α is a hyper-parameter between 0 and 1.

3 Experiments

This section first describes the dataset used for evaluation, and then describes the experimental setup of the proposed method. Then, we briefly describe the details and parameter settings of the comparison models.

3.1 Dataset

We validated the effectiveness of our method on a public seizure prediction competition dataset [12]. Seizure forecasting focuses on identifying a *preictal (prior to seizure)* state that can be differentiated from the interictal (between seizures, or baseline), ictal (seizure), and postictal (after seizures) states, especially the interictal state. The goal of the dataset is to demonstrate the existence and accurate classification of the *preictal* brain state in humans with epilepsy. It's a binary classification. The dataset contains 2 patients (263 and 210 samples, respectively). Every 10 min of the data is intercepted as a sample. For detailed information, please refer to the website of Kaggle [12].

3.2   Implementation Details

The whole neural networks were implemented with the Keras framework and trained on a Nvidia 1080Ti GPU from scratch in a fully-supervised manner. The Adam algorithm was used to optimize the loss function with a learning rate of $0.5 * 10^{-4}$. The dropout probability was 0.5. The hidden states number of the LSTM cell was 32. There were 128 nodes in the first dense layer. The hyperparameter α in loss function was tuned to balance the magnitude of two types of loss.

3.3   Comparison Models

Then, we compared our approach with two baseline methods k-nearest neighbors algorithm (KNN) and the eXtreme Gradient Boosting (XGBoost) algorithm which were widely used, as well as the LSTM network without multi-task learning for component evaluation. Here we briefly describe some of the details and parameter settings used in these methods.

KNN. The k-nearest neighbors algorithm (KNN) is one of the simplest and most common classification methods based on supervised learning which is classified as a simple and lazy classifier due to its lack of complexity. In this algorithm, k is the number of neighbors, which may largely affects the classification performance. k was selected by cross-validation on training set $(k = 1, 2, 3, ..., 18, 19, 20, 25, 30, 35, 40)$.

XGBoost. The eXtreme Gradient Boosting (XGBoost) algorithm is a well-designed Gradient Boosted Decision Tree (GBDT) algorithm, which demonstrates its state-of-the-art advantages in the scientific research of machine learning and data mining problem.

Two hyperparameters of XGBoost for preventing overfitting was adjusted through cross-validation on training set$(max\_depth = 3, 4, 5, ..., 8, 9, 10$ and $subsample = 0.5, 0.6, 0.7, 0.8)$.

LSTM Network with Single-Task Learning. To evaluate the performance of LSTM-MTL framework strictly, LSTM network with single-task learning

(LSTM-STL) is used in the experiment. The LSTM-STL performs seizure prediction without latency regression task, as shown in Fig. 3 with blue blocks. That is to say, the hyperparameter α of LSTM-MTL framework is equal to 1. For comparison purpose, we kept all the hyper-parameters of LSTM-STL the same with LSTM-MTL.

4   Results and Discussion

In this section, the prediction AUC of different models were showed in Table 1. In addiction, we give some visualization figures to explore into the model and have some discussions about the results.

Table 1. Prediction AUC of different models

	Patient_1	Patient_2	Average
KNN	41.14	52.78	46.96
XGB	85.93	66.49	76.21
LSTM-STL	89.66	84.06	86.86
LSTM-MTL	**92.37**	**86.34**	**89.36**

4.1   Compared with Baseline Performance

Overall, our proposed LSTM-MTL method significantly outperformed the KNN and XGBoost algorithms.

KNN algorithm performed badly, showing an average AUC score even below 50%. This algorithm is very sensitive to local distribution of features and may not work well. In general, no determinate comment can be made about the performance of the KNN classifier in EEG-related problems [18].

XGBoost performed relatively better with an AUC of 76.21%, but there was a gap between its performance and the state-of-the-art 85.95% [2]. Actually, the reported state-of-the-art was achieved by an ensemble of different features and different classical classifiers. Using only XGBoost algorithm is hard to get a comparable performance.

LSTM networks utilized the same types of features with KNN and XGBoost algorithms but achieved comparable or better performance against state-of-the-art, which illustrated that the LSTM networks can learn useful information from sequential iEEG features.

4.2   Compared with LSTM-STL

LSTM-STL network achieved an average AUC of 86.86%, which was comparable with the state-of-the-art. LSTM-MTL outperformed LSTM-STL with AUC

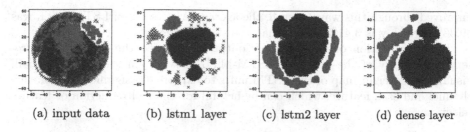

(a) input data   (b) lstm1 layer   (c) lstm2 layer   (d) dense layer

Fig. 4. The T-SNE feature visualizations of input data and output of middle layers. (a) The visualization of input data. (b) The visualization of the output feature of the first lstm layer. (c) The visualization of the output feature of the first lstm layer. (d) The visualization of the dense layer output. The figure is best viewed under the electronic edition.

improvement of 2.5%. This results demonstrated the necessity of adding latency regression as an additional task.

The latency of segments can provide urgency degree information about the seizure. Through combining the latency information, the LSTM network can take full advantage of limited data and performed better in prediction task. LSTM-MTL can not only improve the prediction accuracy but also report an urgency degree about seizure, which is important for patients to take nichetargeting action.

4.3 Visualization

Finally, we visualized the input data as well as the output of LSTM layers and the dense layer of LSTM-MTL by t-distributed Stochastic Neighbor Embedding (T-SNE) [14]. T-SNE is a tool to visualize high-dimensional data, converting similarities between data points to joint probabilities and tries to minimize the Kullback-Leibler divergence between the joint probabilities of the low-dimensional embedding and the high-dimensional data. The visual results showed that the data became increasingly linearly detachable along with the layer-by-layer process. An visualization example of Patient 1 is shown in Fig. 4. Two classes of the input data are aliasing. Through the first LSTM layer, the data clustered and one cluster contained nearly only one class of data. Through the second LSTM layer, two classes of data could be separated by a simple quadratic function in two-dimension space. Through the dense layer, the data became more linearly detachable.

5 Conclusion and Future Work

In this paper we presented a novel LSTM based multi-task learning framework for seizure prediction. The proposed multi-task framework performed prediction and latency regression simultaneously and the prediction performance was improved through this way. Overall, the average AUC score of LSTM-MTL was 89.36%, which was 3.41% higher than the state-of-the-art.

The visualization of middle layers output illustrated the sequential representation ability of the proposed LSTM-MTL network. In the future, we will visualize the weight map of the LSTM units to explore the significations of each channel and each feature, which can be helpful for channel reduction or feature selection.

Acknowledgments. This work was supported by National Natural Science Foundation of China (91520202, 81701785), Youth Innovation Promotion Association CAS, the CAS Scientific Research Equipment Development Project (YJKYYQ20170050) and the Beijing Municipal Science&Technology Commission (Z181100008918010).

References

1. Bashivan, P., Rish, I., Yeasin, M., Codella, N.: Learning representations from EEG with deep recurrent-convolutional neural networks. arXiv preprint arXiv:1511.06448 (2015)
2. Brinkmann, B.H., et al.: Crowdsourcing reproducible seizure forecasting in human and canine epilepsy. Brain **139**(6), 1713–1722 (2016)
3. Caruana, R.: Multitask learning. Mach. Learn. **28**(1), 41–75 (1997)
4. Chen, T., Guestrin, C.: XGBoost: a scalable tree boosting system. In: Proceedings of the 22nd ACM SIGKDD International Conference on Knowledge Discovery and Data Mining, pp. 785–794. ACM (2016)
5. Doersch, C., Zisserman, A.: Multi-task self-supervised visual learning. In: The IEEE International Conference on Computer Vision (ICCV) (2017)
6. Donahue, J., et al.: Long-term recurrent convolutional networks for visual recognition and description. In: Proceedings of the IEEE Conference on Computer Vision and Pattern Recognition, pp. 2625–2634 (2015)
7. Golmohammadi, M., et al.: Deep architectures for automated seizure detection in scalp EEGs. arXiv preprint arXiv:1712.09776 (2017)
8. Graves, A., Liwicki, M., Bunke, H., Schmidhuber, J., Fernández, S.: Unconstrained on-line handwriting recognition with recurrent neural networks. In: Advances in neural information processing systems, pp. 577–584 (2008)
9. Graves, A., Mohamed, A.-R., Hinton, G.: Speech recognition with deep recurrent neural networks. In: 2013 IEEE International Conference on Acoustics Speech and Signal Processing (ICASSP), pp. 6645–6649. IEEE (2013)
10. Hochreiter, S., Schmidhuber, J.: Long short-term memory. Neural Comput. **9**(8), 1735–1780 (1997)
11. Jaffe, A.S.: Long short-term memory recurrent neural networks for classification of acute hypotensive episodes. Ph.D. thesis, Massachusetts Institute of Technology (2017)
12. kaggle: American epilepsy society seizure prediction challenge. https://www.kaggle.com/c/seizure-prediction/data
13. kaggle: Melbourne university aes/mathworks/nih seizure prediction. https://www.kaggle.com/c/melbourne-university-seizure-prediction/data
14. van der Maaten, L., Hinton, G.: Visualizing data using t-SNE. J. Mach. Learn. Res. **9**(Nov), 2579–2605 (2008)

15. Mormann, F., Andrzejak, R.G., Elger, C.E., Lehnertz, K.: Seizure prediction: the long and winding road. Brain **130**(2), 314–333 (2006)
16. O'Regan, S., Faul, S., Marnane, W.: Automatic detection of EEG artefacts arising from head movements using EEG and gyroscope signals. Med. Eng. Phys. **35**(7), 867–874 (2013)
17. Ranjan, R., Patel, V.M., Chellappa, R.: Hyperface: a deep multi-task learning framework for face detection, landmark localization, pose estimation, and gender recognition. IEEE Trans. Pattern Anal. Mach. Intell. (2017)
18. Tahernezhad-Javazm, F., Azimirad, V., Shoaran, M.: A review and experimental study on the application of classifiers and evolutionary algorithms in EEG-based brain-machine interface systems. J. Neural Eng. **15**(2), 021007 (2018)
19. Thodoroff, P., Pineau, J., Lim, A.: Learning robust features using deep learning for automatic seizure detection. In: Machine Learning for Healthcare Conference, pp. 178–190 (2016)
20. Tzallas, A.T., Tsipouras, M.G., Fotiadis, D.I.: Epileptic seizure detection in EEGs using time-frequency analysis. IEEE Trans. Inf. Technol. Biomed. **13**(5), 703–710 (2009)
21. Van Esbroeck, A., Smith, L., Syed, Z., Singh, S., Karam, Z.: Multi-task seizure detection: addressing intra-patient variation in seizure morphologies. Mach. Learn. **102**(3), 309–321 (2016)
22. Wang, Y., et al.: A cauchy-based state-space model for seizure detection in EEG monitoring systems. IEEE Intell. Syst. **30**(1), 6–12 (2015)

Multi-flow Sub-network and Multiple Connections for Single Shot Detection

Ye Li[1], Huicheng Zheng[1,2,3(✉)], and Lvran Chen[1]

[1] School of Data and Computer Science, Sun Yat-sen University,
Guangzhou, China
`zhenghch@mail.sysu.edu.cn`
[2] Key Laboratory of Machine Intelligence and Advanced Computing,
Ministry of Education, Guangzhou, China
[3] Guangdong Key Laboratory of Information Security Technology,
Guangzhou, China

Abstract. One-stage object detection methods are usually more computationally efficient than two-stage methods, which makes it more likely to be applied in practice. However, one-stage methods often suffer from lower detection accuracies, especially when the objects to be detected are small. In this paper, we propose a multi-flow sub-network and multiple connections for single shot detection (MSSD), which is built upon a one-stage strategy to inherit the computational efficiency and improve the detection accuracy. The multi-flow sub-network in MSSD aims to extract high quality feature maps with high spatial resolution, sufficient non-linear transformation, and multiple receptive fields, which facilitates detection of small objects in particular. In addition, MSSD uses multiple connections, including up-sampling, down-sampling, and resolution-invariant connections, to combine feature maps of different layers, which helps the model capture fine-grained details and improve feature representation. Extensive experiments on PASCAL VOC and MS COCO demonstrate that MSSD achieves competitive detection accuracy with high computational efficiency compared to state-of-the-art methods. MSSD with input size of 320×320 achieves 80.6% mAP on VOC2007 at 45 FPS and 29.7% mAP on COCO, both with a Nvidia Titan X GPU.

Keywords: Object detection · Single shot detection
Feature representation enhancement

1 Introduction

In recent years, many outstanding object detection methods based on deep learning have been proposed. They are mainly divided into two categories: two-stage methods and one-stage methods. The two-stage methods usually achieve better detection performance, while the one-stage methods are usually more computationally efficient. However, when an object detection method is to be applied in

© Springer Nature Switzerland AG 2018
J.-H. Lai et al. (Eds.): PRCV 2018, LNCS 11257, pp. 168–179, 2018.
https://doi.org/10.1007/978-3-030-03335-4_15

practice, the detection accuracy and computational efficiency must be considered together.

It is a feasible idea to design an advanced one-stage method which has good accuracy while maintain the advantage of in computationally efficiency. Some advanced one-stage methods, such as DSSD [5], RetinaNet [6], and BPN [7] sacrifice computational efficiency when improving the accuracy. In order to improve the accuracy while maintaining the computational efficiency, this paper analyzes the deficiencies of the one-stage methods. Many experimental results show that one-stage methods are weak in small object detection and feature representation. To address these issues, we propose a single shot detector with multi-flow sub-network and multiple connections (MSSD). The main motivations and corresponding operations of MSSD are as follows.

First, this paper tries to solve the difficulty in small object detection. Since low-level features are important for small object detection, as mentioned in [9], this paper proposes a multi-flow sub-network module to optimize the low-level feature representation by obtaining deeply non-linear transformation and different receptive fields. Then, this paper tries to enhance the feature representation of the model. A common method is to employ a complex backbone network such as ResNet101 [10], but this will lead to low computational efficiency. This paper enhances feature representation by reusing different feature maps through multiple connections, which has little affect on computational efficiency. Thanks to the multi-flow sub-network and multiple connections, MSSD achieves state-of-art results with a lightweight backbone network, such as ResNet18 [10], while maintaining the real-time computational speed. Different from SSD, we introduce shortcut connections to the extra feature layers to strengthen feature propagation and further reduce the number of detected feature maps to improve the generalization of the network.

The contributions of this paper can be summarized as follows:

1. A multi-flow sub-network module is proposed to obtain high quality feature maps with high spatial resolution, sufficient non-linear transformation, and multiple receptive fields, which is beneficial for object detection, especially for small instances.
2. A multiple connection module is proposed to enhance feature representation by encouraging feature reuse rather than using complex backbone networks.
3. The extra feature layers are modified to strengthen feature propagation and improve the network generalization.
4. MSSD achieves the state-of-the-art results on PASCAL VOC 2007, 2012 [1] and MS COCO [2].

2   Related Work

Object Detection. Early object detection methods like those based on DPM [11] and HOG [12] employ hand-crafted features, and the detection system consist of three modules: region selection, feature extraction, and classification. With the development of deep convolutional networks, deep learning based methods have attracted great attention. These methods can be roughly divided into two categories, two-stage methods and one-stage methods.

Two-stage methods, such as RCNN [13], Fast RCNN [14], and Faster RCNN [15], consist of two parts, where the first one generates candidate object proposals, and the second one classifies the candidate regions and determines its accurate location using convolutional neural networks. Such methods are superior in accuracy, but difficult to achieve real-time performance. Methods like Mask-RCNN [3], R-FCN [24], and CoupleNet [4] achieve state-of-the-art accuracies with complex backbone networks. However, the resulting huge computational cost restricts their applications in practice.

One-stage methods, represented by YOLO [16] and SSD [8], convert the object detection problem into a regression problem. Such methods implement end-to-end training and detection, and do not require the generation of candidate regions, which ensures their high computational efficiency. However, the accuracy of one-stage methods trails that of two-stage methods. Some methods like DSSD [5] and RetinaNet [6] use complex backbone network to achieve high accuracy comparable to two-stage methods but sacrifice computational speed.

Receptive Fields. There are several methods to improve feature representation by constructing feature map with different receptive fields. [20] uses a multi-scale input layer to construct an image pyramid to achieve multiple levels of receptive field sizes. GoogLeNet [21] uses filters of different sizes to obtain feature map with different receptive fields. The deformable-net [22] replaces the original fixed position sample with the offset sample, so that the sample point position can change with the image content. In addition, DICSSD [18] and RBFnet [19] use dilated convolution [17] to obtain feature map with different receptive fields. The multi-flow sub-network of MSSD also employ dilated convolution. However, compared with DICSSD which only uses dilated convolution directly on all detected feature maps, MSSD combines dilated convolution, group convolution and bottle-net into a sub-network module and performs much better. Unlike RBFnet whose module is complicated and motivated by biological vision, the multi-flow sub-network of MSSD has simple structure (each branch is the same in topology) and is proposed to solve the difficulty of small object detection.

Short-Path Methods. Among the various connection methods currently used, some methods only use resolution-invariant connections such as DenseNet [23]; some methods only use up-sampling and resolution-invariant connections, such as DSSD; and some methods only use down-sampling connections, such as ResNet [8]. In contrast to them, the multiple connections of MSSD includes up-sampling, down-sampling, and resolution-invariant connections. To the best of our knowledge, in the one-stage object detection methods, MSSD is the first one to combine such multiple connections.

3   MSSD

The pipeline of the MSSD proposed in this paper is shown in Fig. 1, which consists of five parts. The first is a backbone network. The second is the extra feature layers (conv8_1–conv10_1) with shortcut connections marked in yellow. The third part is two dilated convolutional layers (conv6, conv7), used to connect the backbone network and the extra feature layers. The fourth is a multiple connection module that makes full use of the five detected feature maps. The fifth is the multi-flow sub-network module proposed for addressing the problem of small object detection.

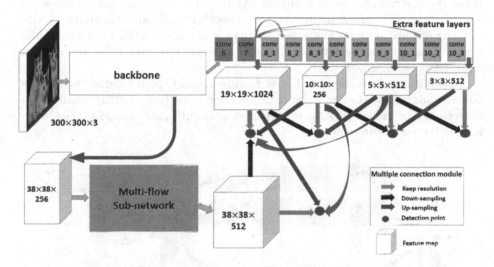

Fig. 1. The network structure of MSSD. The backbone is a pre-trained ResNet18 whose average pooling layer and fc layer are removed. B1 to B4 are layers of ResNet18 and the size of the feature map after B3 is $38 \times 38 \times 256$. The yellow connections between different extra feature layers are three convolutional layers which are used to connect different feature maps. (Color figure online)

3.1   The Multi-flow Sub-network Module

The multi-flow sub-network module aims to solve the problem in small object detection. The poor performance of small object detection is mainly due to the fact that the spatial resolutions of the high-level feature maps are too low and the receptive fields are too large.

In high-level feature maps, the model tends to focus on large objects, ignoring small objects. Although the low-level feature maps have high spatial resolution, they have insufficient nonlinear transformation due to a limited number of convolutional layers and nonlinear active layers they passed. Therefore, it is also difficult to detect small objects. In addition, each feature map used for detection has a fixed receptive field size, which is undoubtedly not the best choice for detecting objects with different sizes and shapes.

The multi-flow sub-network module is shown in Fig. 2. The module consists of multiple branches, each with four convolutional layers (each convolutional layer followed by a batch normalization layer and ReLU layer). The conv1 of each branch is a dilated convolutional layer [17] with different parameters, so that different branches can obtain feature maps of different receptive fields. This paper refers to the bottleneck architecture in GoogLeNet [21], so conv2 and conv4 are designed as convolutional layers with 1×1 kernel sizes. In addition, conv3 uses group convolution. These two operations allow MSSD to obtain feature maps with good feature representations without much increase in computation. Each of the branches is the same except for conv1, but the parameters between these same structures are not shared. At the end of the module, the feature maps extracted from the multi-flow sub-network module are concatenated with the original feature map and a feature map with high spatial resolution, sufficiently complex nonlinear transformation, multiple receptive fields and context information is obtained.

In addition, since the lowest-level feature maps (which produce more than 70% default boxes) are significant to objects detection (especially to small object detection), the multi-flow sub-network module is only used to process the lowest-level detected feature map.

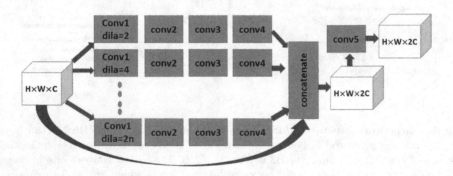

Fig. 2. Structure of the multi-flow sub-network

3.2   The Multiple Connection Module

Many methods like CoupleNet [4], R-FCN [24], and DSSD [5] enhance feature representation by using complex backbone networks, but sacrifice computational efficiency. In this paper, in order to enhance feature representation, five feature maps extracted from the model are reused by multiple connections such as up-sampling convolution, down-sampling convolution, and resolution-invariant convolution. Without sacrificing computational speed, 5 high quality feature maps were extracted for detecting. The specific operation of the multiple connection module is shown in Fig. 3.

Each detection point may obtain different number of feature maps obtained through different connection methods. These different feature maps are complementary. In this paper, the feature maps obtained from up-sampling convolution

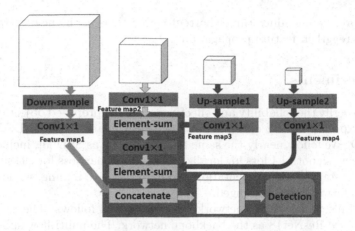

Fig. 3. Detection point

and resolution-invariant convolution are combined together through element-sum operation. The new feature map will be concatenated with the feature map obtained through down-sampling convolution. Then, the high quality feature maps are obtained. For example, if the detection point get *Feature map1*, *Feature map2* and *Feature map3*, *Feature map2* and *Feature map3* are firstly combined together through element-sum operation. Then the new feature map will be concatenated with *Feature map1* to get the final feature map. If the detection point only get *Feature map1* and *Feature map2*, *Feature map2* will be concatenated with *Feature map1* to get the final feature map. This kind of well-designed structure makes the information of the feature maps fully utilized, and helps the model to capture more fine-grained details. Finally, these 5 high quality feature maps are used to calculate the final detection results by following SSD, more details of which can be found in [8].

3.3   The New Extra Feature Layers Module

The original SSD method is very classic, which employs 6 layers to produce 6 detected feature maps. More specifically SSD divides the target objects in the image into six parts according to their sizes. Each part corresponds to a size range, and then the network extract six feature maps that are responsible for different sizes of objects. However, such kind of design is not very generalized. When different data sets are trained and tested, it is necessary to repartition the six detection ranges, often resulting in some inconveniences.

Therefore, when designing the new extra feature layers of MSSD, this paper removes the original con11_1 and conv11_2 that generate the 1×1 feature map, which reduces the number of detected feature maps and enhances the generalization. In addition, in order to improve the expression ability of the model, conv8_3, conv9_3, and conv10_3 are introduced in the new extra feature layers.

What's more, we introduce three shortcut connections in the new extra feature layers to strengthen feature propagation.

4   Experiments

In order to verify the reliability and effectiveness of the proposed object detection method, experiments are conducted on two benchmarks: PASCAL VOC and MS COCO. We follow nearly the same training policy as SSD [8], including loss function (e.g., smooth L1 loss for localization and softmax loss for classification), matching strategy, data augmentation and hard negative mining, while learning rate scheduling is slightly changed.

The details of the MSSD network structure are as follows: The MSSD uses the pre-trained ResNet18 as the backbone network. The multi-flow sub-network module uses four branches. The conv1 of each branch network uses dilated convolution and the corresponding dilation parameters are $\{2, 4, 6, 8\}$, respectively. The group parameter of the group convolution layer for each branch is 4. In addition, all experiments are carried out on one Nvidia Titan X GPU.

4.1   PASCAL VOC

There are two types of experiments conducted on PASCAL VOC, one is trained on the union set of 2007 *trainval* and 2012 *trainval*, tested on 2007 *test* set. The other one is trained on union set of 2007 *trainval* and 2012 *trainval* and 2007 *test*, tested on the 2012 *test* set. In the experiments of PASCAL VOC, the training setting of MSSD is basically the same as that of SSD [8]. We use the SGD algorithm to train the network. The initial learning rate is 10^{-3}, the momentum is 0.9, the weight decay is 0.0005, and the batch size is 32. Due to resource limitations, batch size is 16 when training MSSD512. The number of MSSD training iterations is 120k. When the number of iterations are 80k, 90k, 100k, and 110k, the learning rates are reduced to 5×10^{-4}, 1×10^{-4}, 5×10^{-5}, and 1×10^{-5}, respectively. The results of two types of experiments are shown in Table 1 and 2, respectively.

Compared with all the one-stage methods and two-stage methods in Table 1, MSSD512 achieves the best detection accuracy while maintaining the real-time computational speed. MSSD achieves better performance than the baseline SSD in detection accuracy and computational speed. MSSD300_v and MSSD512_v achieve comparable performance with MSSD300 and MSSD512, respectively, which further verifies the effectiveness of the contributions we proposed.

In order to ensure the reliability and stability of MSSD, this paper also shows the test results of MSSD in PASCAL VOC2012. From Table 2, we can see that MSSD still achieved excellent performance. MSSD300 exceeds SSD300 2.5% in detection accuracy and achieves better performance than OHME++ which employs a larger input size.

Table 1. PASCAL VOC 2007 detection results. All methods are trained on VOC 2007 *trainval* sets and VOC 2012 *trainval* sets, and tested on VOC 2007 *test* set with a Nvidia Titan X GPU. Only the batch size of MSSD512 is 16 during training.

Method	Backbone	Input size	mAP	FPS
Faster RCNN [15]	VGG16	~1000 × 600	73.2	7
R-FCN [24]	ResNet101	~1000 × 600	80.5	9
CoupleNet [4]	ResNet101	~1000 × 600	81.7	8.7
SSD300 [8]	VGG16	300 × 300	77.2	46
SSD512 [8]	VGG16	512 × 300	79.8	19
RSSD300 [25]	VGG16	300 × 300	78.5	35
YOLOv2 [26]	Darknet-19	544 × 544	78.6	40
FSSD300 [27]	VGG16	300 × 300	78.8	–
DSOD300 [28]	DS/64-192-48-1	300 × 300	77.7	–
DSSD321 [5]	ResNet101	321 × 321	78.6	9.5
DICSSD300 [18]	VGG16	300 × 300	78.1	40.8
RefineDet320 [29]	VGG16	320 × 320	80.0	40.3
RefineDet512 [29]	VGG16	512 × 512	81.8	24.1
BPN320 [7]	VGG16	320 × 320	80.3	32.4
BPN512 [7]	VGG16	512 × 512	**81.9**	18.9
MSSD300_v	VGG16	300 × 300	80.0	43.0
MSSD512_v	VGG16	512 × 512	81.6	20.0
MSSD300	ResNet18	300 × 300	80.3	**55.7**
MSSD320	ResNet18	320 × 320	80.6	45.4
MSSD512	ResNet18	512 × 512	**81.9**	21.4

Table 2. PASCAL VOC 2012 detection results. All methods are trained on union set of PASCAL VOC 2007 *trainval* and PASCAL VOC 2012 *trainval* and PASCAL VOC2007 *test*, and tested on PASCAL VOC 2012 *test* set. For more details about our results, please see http://host.robots.ox.ac.uk:8080/anonymous/5BMTAL.html

Method	Backbone	Input size	mAP
Faster RCNN [15]	VGG16	~1000 × 600	70.4
R-FCN [24]	ResNet101	~1000 × 600	77.6
SSD300 [8]	VGG16	300 × 300	75.8
DSSD321 [5]	ResNet101	321 × 321	76.3
RefineDet320 [29]	VGG16	320 × 320	78.1
MSSD300	ResNet18	300 × 300	**78.3**

4.2 MS COCO

In order to further verify the effectiveness of MSSD, especially to assess the performance of MSSD in small object detection, this paper also conducted experiments on MS COCO. MSSD is trained on *trainval35k* (2014 *train* + 2014 *val35k*) and the training policy of MSSD is also almost the same as that of SSD [8]. We train the network using SGD with momentum 0.9, weight decay 0.0005 and batch size 32. The number of MSSD training epochs is 120. In the top 5 epochs, we apply the "warmup" technique to gradually increase learning rate from 1×10^{-6} to 1×10^{-3}. When the number of epochs are 80 and 100, the learning rate are reduced to 1×10^{-4} and 1×10^{-5}, respectively.

Table 3. MS COCO 2017 test-dev detection results. Our MSSD are trained on *trainval35k*.

Method	Backbone	Data	AP	AP_{50}	AP_{75}	AP_S	AP_M	AP_L
Faster RCNN [15]	VGG16	trainval	21.9	42.7	–	–	–	–
OHME++ [30]	VGG16	trainval	25.5	45.9	26.1	7.4	27.7	40.3
YOLOv2 [26]	DarkNet-19	trainval35k	21.6	44.0	19.2	5.0	22.4	35.5
SSD300 [8]	VGG16	trainval35k	25.1	43.1	25.8	6.6	25.9	41.4
DSSD321 [5]	ResNet101	trainval35k	28.0	46.1	29.2	7.4	28.1	**47.6**
RefineDet320 [29]	VGG16	trainval35k	29.4	49.2	**31.3**	10.0	32.0	44.4
MSSD300	ResNet18	trainval35k	29.1	49.6	30.1	11.2	31.2	43.4
MSSD320	ResNet18	trainval35k	**29.7**	**50.4**	30.8	**12.8**	**32.1**	42.8

Table 3 shows that MSSD300 exceeds SSD300 3.9% in AP. MSSD320 achieves state-of-the-art detection accuracy. In the small object detection, all the methods in Table 3 are exceeded by MSSD320. This fully proves that the multi-flow network module for small object detection is very effective. Compared to most of other state-of-the-art one-stage methods (such as RefineDet) and two-stage methods (such as OHME++), MSSD achieves higher detection accuracy in the same condition.

4.3 Ablation Study

In order to verify the role of the three innovations of MSSD, a series of confirmatory experiments were also conducted in this paper. All confirmatory experiments were trained on the union set of PASCAL VOC 2007 *trainval* and 2012 *trainval*, and tested on the 2007 *test* set. The input image size for all experiments was 300×300. The experimental results are shown in Table 4.

The primitive model v1 is SSD with a ResNet18 backbone network. At this time, the mAP is 76.9. If the multi-flow sub-network module is added to the model v1, the model v2 is obtained, and the mAP of v2 is 78.6. The multiple

Table 4. Results of the confirmatory experiments.

Component	MSSD300			
	v1	v2	v3	v4
Multi-flow sub-network		√	√	√
Multiple connection module			√	√
New extra feature layers				√
mAP	76.9	78.6	79.8	80.3

connection module is introduced into the model v2, and the model v3 is obtained. The mAP of v3 is 79.8. Finally, we remove the conv11_1 and conv11_2 of the extra feature layers of v3 and introduce shortcut connections and three convolution layers to obtain new extra feature layers. At this point the model is v4, and the mAP becomes 80.3.

Table 4 shows that each key component in this paper can bring about improvements in the detection performance. In addition, as the number of key components increases, the model performs better, which further confirms the reliability and effectiveness of MSSD.

4.4 Visualization

In order to understand the detection effect of MSSD more intuitively, this section presents some of the results of MSSD testing on PASCAL VOC 2007, as shown in Fig. 4.

Fig. 4. Detection examples on PASCAL VOC 2007 *test* set with MSSD512 model.

5   Conclusion

This paper analyzes deficiencies of the existing object detection methods and proposes a multi-flow sub-network and multiple connections for single shot detection

(MSSD). MSSD maintains real-time computational speed and achieves better detection accuracy than state-of-the-art methods. Compared with the existing object detection method, MSSD achieved the state-of-the-art detection accuracy with a smaller input size and a higher computational speed. MSSD has successfully achieved the original intention of this paper. It helps object detection method to be applied in practice better, and also contributes to the solution of the difficulty in small object detection and weak feature representation, which are commonly found in one-stage methods. MSSD has achieved good performance on PASCAL VOC and MS COCO. In the future, we may consider combining relevant knowledge in the field of transfer learning and further migrate more information.

Acknowledgements. This work was supported by National Natural Science Foundation of China (U1611461), Special Program for Applied Research on Super Computation of the NSFC-Guangdong Joint Fund (the second phase, No. U1501501), and Science and Technology Program of Guangzhou (No. 201803030029).

References

1. Everingham, M., Gool, L.V., Williams, C.K., Winn, J., Zisserman, A.: The PASCAL visual object classes (VOC) challenge. Int. J. Comput. Vis. **88**(2), 303–338 (2010)
2. Lin, T.-Y., et al.: Microsoft COCO: common objects in context. In: Fleet, D., Pajdla, T., Schiele, B., Tuytelaars, T. (eds.) ECCV 2014. LNCS, vol. 8693, pp. 740–755. Springer, Cham (2014). https://doi.org/10.1007/978-3-319-10602-1_48
3. He, K., Gkioxari, G., Dollár, P., Girshick, R.: Mask R-CNN. In: International Conference on Computer Vision, pp. 2980–2988. IEEE, Venice (2017)
4. Zhu, Y., Zhao, C., Wang, J., Zhao, X., Wu, Y., Lu, H.: CoupleNet: coupling global structure with local parts for object detection. In: International Conference on Computer Vision, pp. 4146–4154. IEEE, Venice (2017)
5. Fu, C.Y., Liu, W., Ranga, A., Tyagi, A., Berg, A.C.: DSSD: deconvolutional single shot detector. arXiv preprint arXiv:1701.06659 (2017)
6. Lin, T.Y., Goyal, P., Girshick, R., He, K., Dollár, P.: Focal loss for dense object detection. In: International Conference on Computer Vision, Venice, pp. 2999–3007. IEEE (2017)
7. Wu, X., Zhang, D., Zhu, J., Steven C.H.: Single-shot bidirectional pyramid networks for high-quality object detection. arXiv preprint arXiv:1803.08208 (2018)
8. Liu, W., et al.: SSD: single shot MultiBox detector. In: Leibe, B., Matas, J., Sebe, N., Welling, M. (eds.) ECCV 2016. LNCS, vol. 9905, pp. 21–37. Springer, Cham (2016). https://doi.org/10.1007/978-3-319-46448-0_2
9. Hu, P., Ramanan, D.: Finding tiny faces. In: IEEE Conference on Computer Vision and Pattern Recognition, Hawaii, pp. 1522–1530. IEEE (2017)
10. He, K., Zhang, X., Ren, S., Sun, J.: Deep residual learning for image recognition. In: IEEE Conference on Computer Vision and Pattern Recognition, Las Vegas, pp. 770–778. IEEE (2016)
11. Felzenszwalb, P., McAllester, D., Ramanan, D.: A discriminatively trained, multiscale, deformable part model. In: IEEE Conference on Computer Vision and Pattern Recognition, Anchorage, pp. 1–8. IEEE (2008)

12. Dalal, N., Triggs, B.: Histograms of oriented gradients for human detection. In: IEEE Conference on Computer Vision and Pattern Recognition, San Diego, pp. 886–893. IEEE (2005)
13. Girshick, R., Donahue, J., Darrell, T., Malik, J.: Rich feature hierarchies for accurate object detection and semantic segmentation. In: IEEE Conference on Computer Vision and Pattern Recognition, Columbus, pp. 580–587. IEEE (2014)
14. Girshick, R.: Fast R-CNN. In: International Conference on Computer Vision, Santiago, pp. 1440–1448. IEEE (2015)
15. Ren, S., He, K., Girshick, R., Sun, J.: Faster R-CNN: towards real-time object detection with region proposal networks. In: International Conference on Neural Information Processing Systems, Montreal, pp. 91–99. MIT (2015)
16. Redmon, J., Divvala, S., Girshick, R., Farhadi, A.: You only look once: unified, real-time object detection. In: IEEE Conference on Computer Vision and Pattern Recognition, Las Vegas, pp. 779–788. IEEE (2016)
17. Chen, L.C., Papandreou, G., Schroff, F., Adam, H.: Rethinking atrous convolution for semantic image segmentation. arXiv preprint arXiv:1706.05587 (2017)
18. Xiang, W., Zhang, D.Q., Athitsos, V., Yu, H.: Context-aware single-shot detector. arXiv preprint arXiv:1707.08682 (2017)
19. Liu, S., Huang, D., Wang, Y.: Receptive field block net for accurate and fast object detection. arXiv preprint arXiv:1711.07767 (2017)
20. Fu, H., Cheng, J., Xu, Y., Wong, D.W.K., Liu, J., Cao, X.: Joint optic disc and cup segmentation based on multi-label deep network and polar transformation. IEEE Trans. Med. Imaging **37**(7), 1597–1605 (2018)
21. Szegedy, C., et al.: Going deeper with convolutions. In: IEEE Conference on Computer Vision and Pattern Recognition, Boston, pp. 1–9. IEEE (2015)
22. Dai, J., et al.: Deformable convolutional networks. In: IEEE International Conference on Computer Vision, Venice, pp. 764–773. IEEE (2017)
23. Huang, G., Liu, Z., Maaten, L.V.D., Weinberger, K.Q.: Densely connected convolutional networks. In: IEEE Conference on Computer Vision and Pattern Recognition, Hawaii, pp. 2261–2269. IEEE (2017)
24. Dai, J., Li, Y., He, K., Sun, J., et al.: R-FCN: object detection via region-based fully convolutional networks. In: International Conference on Neural Information Processing Systems, Barcelona, pp. 379–387. MIT (2016)
25. Jeong, J., Park, H., Kwak, N.: Enhancement of SSD by concatenating feature maps for object detection. arXiv preprint arXiv:1705.09587 (2017)
26. Redmon, J., Farhadi, A.: YOLO9000: better, faster, stronger. In: IEEE Conference on Computer Vision and Pattern Recognition, Las Vegas, pp. 6517–6525. IEEE (2016)
27. Li, Z., Zhou, F.: FSSD: feature fusion single shot multibox detector. arXiv preprint arXiv:1712.00960 (2017)
28. Shen, Z., Liu, Z., Li, J., Jiang, Y.G., Chen, Y., Xue, X.: DSOD: learning deeply supervised object detectors from scratch. In: IEEE International Conference on Computer Vision, Venice, pp. 1937–1945. IEEE (2017)
29. Zhang, S., Wen, L., Bian, X., Lei, Z., Li, S.: Single-shot refinement neural network for object detection. arXiv preprint arXiv:1711.06897 (2017)
30. Shrivastava, A., Gupta, A., Girshick, R.: Training region-based object detectors with online hard example mining. In: IEEE Conference on Computer Vision and Pattern Recognition, Las Vegas, pp. 761–769. IEEE (2016)

Consistent Online Multi-object Tracking with Part-Based Deep Network

Chuanzhi Xu and Yue Zhou[✉]

Institute of Image Processing and Pattern Recognition,
Shanghai Jiao Tong University, Shanghai, China
{ChuanzhiXu,zhouyue}@sjtu.edu.cn

Abstract. Multi-object tracking is still a challenge problem in complex and crowded scenarios. Mismatches will always happen when objects have similar appearance or are occluded with each other. In this paper, we appeal for more attention to the consistency of the trajectories and propose a part-based deep network which employs ROI pooling method to extract full and part-based features for the objects. An occlusion detector is proposed to predict the occlusion degree and guide the procedure of part-based feature fusion and appearance model update. In this way, the feature extraction speed of our tracker is faster, and the objects can be associated correctly even if they are partly occluded. Besides, we train the network based on siamese architecture to learn a dissimilarity metric between pairs of identities. Extensive experiments with multiple evaluation metrics show that our tracker can associate the objects consistently and gain a significant improvement in tracking accuracy.

Keywords: Multi-object tracking · Part-based model
Occlusion detector · Consistent trajectories

1 Introduction

Multi-object tracking (MOT) is an important computer vision task and has a wide application in surveillance, robotics, and human-computer interaction. With recent development of object detectors, MOT has been formulated as tracking by detection framework. Most multi-object tracking benchmarks such as MOT16 [16] provide the tracking video sequences and detection results with public detectors. The key issue of the multi-object tracker is to associate tracklets and corresponding detection responses into long trajectories. Tracklets denote the trajectory set which is established up to current frame.

Recent tracking-by-detection methods could be categorized into batch and online methods. The batch methods process video sequences in a batch mode and take into consideration the frames from the future time steps. These methods always solve the association problem by optimization methods. For example, [17] formulates the MOT problem as minimization of a continuous energy. [5]

© Springer Nature Switzerland AG 2018
J.-H. Lai et al. (Eds.): PRCV 2018, LNCS 11257, pp. 180–192, 2018.
https://doi.org/10.1007/978-3-030-03335-4_16

models the MOT problem as the min-cost network flow and finds the optimization solution with convex relaxation. Such systems may obtain a nearly global optimal solution but are not suitable for practical application. The online MOT methods only consider the observations up to current frame and associate the tracklets and detection responses frame by frame. The baseline of these online trackers is to build different models to measure the affinities between tracklets and detection responses. Then an online association algorithm is applied to get global optimum. Motion model, appearance model and interaction model are most frequently adopted to build affinity matrix. In [13], integral channel features are adopted to build a robust appearance model. [6] proposes a nonlinear motion model to get reliable motion affinity. [20] establishes an LSTM interaction model to explore the group behavior and compute the matching likelihoods.

In complex and crowded scenarios, many objects are presented with similar appearance and may be occluded with each other. Mismatches always occur in such scenarios. The result is that the tracker can not associate objects consistently. However, the consistency of the trajectories plays an important role in the follow up works such as trajectory prediction and analysis. Spatial constraints and motion model can not handle such problems. To address this problem, a robust appearance model must be established. Appearance model could improve the tracker's ability to associate objects consistently and reduce the mismatch rate. Some online trackers [12] adopt raw pixels or histogram as appearance model. These trackers may get a rapid speed but could not distinguish objects with similar appearance. Recent development on convolutional neural network has drove people to train a deep network to extract deep appearance feature. [1,26] measure appearance similarity with a person re-identification network. However, all these trackers need to crop the objects from images first, then put them into the network in a batch mode. Pre-processing procedure and frequent forward propagations make these trackers time consuming.

The MOTA [2] metric is the widely accepted metric for multi-object tracking evaluation, but it is not capable of evaluating the consistency of the trajectories, and the reasons are explained in Sect. 3.1. In this paper, we adopt ID switch rate and IDF_1 score to evaluate the consistency of the trajectories, which is initially proposed for evaluating the ID consistency for cross camera multi-object tracking.

In this paper, we propose a part-based deep network combined with a confidence-based association metric to address above problems. The main contributions are summarized as below: (i) We propose a part-based deep network which employs ROI pooling method [10] to extract part-based deep appearance feature for all objects by just one forward propagation. The network is trained based on the siamese architecture [7], and this makes our tracker gain the ability to associate correctly even if the objects are partly occluded; (ii) we propose an occlusion detector which could predict the occlusion degree and guide the procedure of part-based similarity fusion and appearance model update; (iii)we appeal for more attention to the consistency of the trajectories and conduct extensive experiments with multiple evaluation metrics introduced in [19] and

[2] on MOT benchmark. The results demonstrate our tracker can associate the objects consistently and gains a significant improvement in tracking accuracy.

2   MOT Framework

The baseline of our tracker is confidence-based association metric. Appearance, motion and shape models are established to measure the affinities between tracklets and object detections. In Sect. 2.1, the structure of fast part-based deep network is described in detail. Section 2.2 introduces the network training procedure. Section 2.3 describes the confidence-based association metric.

2.1   Fast Part-Based Deep Network

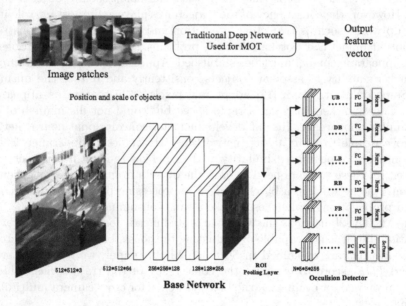

Fig. 1. The feature extraction pipeline of traditional deep network and our part-based deep network

Network Structure. Traditional deep appearance network in MOT field usually takes as input the object regions cropped from the original image in a batch mode. But it is time consuming and needs to do some pre-processing work. The more objects one frame contains, the more times for forward propagation.

The main structure of our part-based deep network is shown in Fig. 1. The network takes as input the entire image and a set of detection responses. The whole image is first processed by several convolutional layers and max pooling layers to generate a shared feature map. Then the ROI pooling method is adopted to generate five feature maps for each detection: the left body (LB), right body (RB), upper body (UB), down body (DB) and full body (FB). Five types of features are fed into the fully-connected layers separately, and the follow up normalization layers normalize the output to obtain the final feature vectors. In this way, our network could extract deep features for all objects by just one forward propagation. Beyond that, an occlusion detector based on the shared feature map is adopted to detect occlusion degree in current detection response, and then guide the procedure of part-based similarity fusion and appearance model update.

The detailed processing steps about ROI pooling are as below: At first, the ROI pooling layer maps the position and scale of the object from original image to the shared feature map, and gets the corresponding ROI window. Then divides the $h*w$ ROI window into an $H*W$ grid of sub-window of approximate size $h/H*w/W$ and maxpools the values in each sub-window into corresponding output grid cell [10]. By adopting ROI pooling layer, the speed for feature extraction gains an improvement compared with other trackers based on deep appearance model.

Part-Based Model. For MOT task, occlusion is still a challenge problem waited to be solved. This can easily cause fragmented trajectories and ID switches especially for online trackers. Mismatches have a great damage to the consistency of the trajectories. We adopt a part-based appearance network combined with a simple occlusion detector to address this problem. It is easy to implement based on the ROI pooling method with almost no speed loss. Persons detected by high position cameras would be easy to be occluded up and down, but they are more likely to be occluded left and right when detected by low position cameras. In this place, we do not design elaborate part detector for the sake of high feature extraction speed and rely more on the representative ability of deep feature. The detected persons are simply divided into UB, DB, LB and RB to overcome multi-view occlusion. During forward propagation, the ROI pooling layer extract features for FB and four divided parts, then a slice layer is added to separate features generated from different parts. So when the object is partly occluded, part-based feature is still reliable for appearance similarity computation. At the same time, the part feature is extracted from the shared convolutional feature map, and there is almost no speed loss for the added part modular.

Occlusion Detector. We propose a novel occlusion detector to detect whether there exist occlusion in current detection and guide the procedure of part-based similarity fusion and appearance model update. At first, the width and height of the detected bounding boxes are enlarged to 1.2 times of original to get more context information. Then the ROI pooling layer is employed to extract corresponding features from the shared feature maps. Follow up classifier takes the features as inputs and outputs the occlusion label, which is composed of three fully-connected layers followed by one softmax layer. The occlusion detector could classify the detections into three types: severe-occluded, part-occluded and non-occluded. For severe-occluded detections, appearance similarity is no more reliable and would not be adopted for final similarity computation. For part-occluded detections, the part-based appearance feature is still reliable would be adopted to measure appearance similarity. For non-occluded detections, FB feature vectors would be employed.

2.2   Network Training

The training procedure is divided into two stages, at first, the part-based deep network is trained based on siamese architecture, then the occlusion detector is trained based on the pretrained base network.

Siamese Architecture Training. To make the deep network gain the ability to distinguish different persons, we select part ALOV300++ sequences [22] which take person as tracking object and MOT training sequences [16] as base training dataset. Then generate positive and negative pairs by randomly sampling same and different identities from video sequences. The part-based deep appearance network is trained based on siamese architecture to learn a dissimilarity metric between pairs of identities. As shown in Fig. 2, we design a siamese network composed of two branches sharing with same structure and filter weights. Each branch has the same architecture with part-based deep network. Two branches are connected with five loss layers for network training. We employ the margin contrastive loss, and the calculation formula is below:

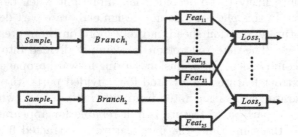

Fig. 2. The structure of siamese training.

$$L\left(x_i, x_j, y_{ij}\right) = \frac{1}{2} * y_{ij} * D + \frac{1}{2}(1 - y_{ij})max(0, \varepsilon - D) \qquad (1)$$

Where $D = ||x_i, x_j||^2$ is the Euclidean distance of two normalized feature vector: x_i and x_j, y_{ij} indicates whether the object pairs are same identities, ε is the minimum distance margin that different pairs of objects should satisfy. We set ε to 1 during experiment. The final training loss is the sum of five kinds of losses. After training the siamese architecture network with margin contrastive loss, the part-based deep network could generate good feature representations that are close by enough for positive pairs, whereas they are far away at least by a minimum for negative pairs, and a simple cosine distance metric could measure the appearance similarity.

Occlusion Detector Training. The MOT16 dataset provides the visibility ratio for each annotated bounding box, and we divide these bounding boxes into three types. Bounding boxes with visibility ratio lower than 0.9 and higher than 0.4 is regarded as part-occluded detections, otherwise would be regarded as non-occluded and severe-occluded detections respectively.

After training the part-based network with siamese architecture, the weights of base network are frozen, and the occlusion detector is added after the base network and is trained with softmax loss. To improve the generalization ability of the occlusion detector, the data augmentation metric is adopted during network training. We flap and crop the object, change the brightness, contrast, sharpness and saturation of the images with a certain probability. Finally two components are integrated together to get the final model.

2.3   Association Procedure

The association between tracklets and object detections could be formulated as an assignment problem, We adopt a modified version of confidence-based association metric [1] to solve this problem.

Affinity Computation. The representation of tracklet T_i^t and detection D_j^t at frame t is defined as below:

$$T_i^t = \{P_i^{t-d:t}(x, y, w, h), A_i^q(FB, UB, DB, LB, RB), conf_i, K_i(m, p)\} \qquad (2)$$

$$D_j^t = \{x, y, w, h, F_j(FB, UB, DB, LB, RB), Olabel\} \qquad (3)$$

where $P_i^{t-d:t}(x, y, w, h)$ is the positions and shapes of the objects from frame $t - d$ to frame t. $K(m, p)$ is a kalman motion model and m, p denote the mean and covariance matrix respectively. At frame $t+1$, $K_i(m, p)$ predicts the object's position $P_i^{t+1}(x, y, w, h)$ and calculates the motion and shape affinity as Eqs. 4 and 5, where D_j^{t+1} is the j-th object in frame $t+1$. Once the tracklet is associated with new detections, the detected bounding box is employed to update $K(m, p)$. Besides, $K(m, p)$ is also adopted to estimate positions for missed objects.

$$sim_{mot}\left(T_i^{t+1}, D_j^{t+1}\right) = e^{-w_1\left(\left(\frac{P_i^{t+1}(x) - D_j^{t+1}(x)}{D_j^{t+1}(w)}\right)^2 + \left(\frac{P_i^{t+1}(y) - D_j^{t+1}(y)}{D_j^{t+1}(h)}\right)^2\right)} \qquad (4)$$

$$sim_{shp}\left(T_i^{t+1}, D_j^{t+1}\right) = e^{-w_2\left(\frac{|P_i^{t+1}(h) - D_j^{t+1}(h)|}{P_i^{t+1}(h) + D_j^{t+1}(h)} + \frac{|P_i^{t+1}(w) - D_j^{t+1}(w)|}{P_i^{t+1}(w) + D_j^{t+1}(w)}\right)} \qquad (5)$$

$A_i^q(FB, UB, DB, LB, RB)$ is a queue which stores part-based deep appearance feature vectors in q frames. $F_j(FB, UB, DB, LB, RB)$ is the appearance feature vectors of detection D_j, *Olabel* is the occlusion label. The largest cosine distance between corresponding feature vectors in F_j and A_i^q queue is regarded as appearance similarity. When D_j is non-occluded, FB feature vector is employed for similarity computation and A_i^q would be updated by five types of feature vectors. When D_j is part-occluded, the maximum similarity of four divided parts would be employed. The corresponding feature vector which is employed for similarity computation would be adopted to update A_i^q, and when D_j is severe-occluded, the appearance similarity would not be adopted and A_i^q would not be updated. During experiment, parameter q and d are set to 6 as most occlusions in MOT dataset last for less than 6 frames. Two linear SVMs are trained to fuse two or three types of affinities in severe-occlusion and other occasions, and yield the final affinity in range of $[0,1]$.

Association Procedure. A simple Hungarian algorithm is employed to obtain the global optimum based on affinity matrix. An affinity threshold τ_1 is set to filter unreliable associations whose affinity score is lower. During association, the tracklets with long length and high association affinities in previous frames should be more reliable and associated first. So each tracklet is modeled with a confidence score $conf_i$ which is calculated as Eq. 6, where sim_k is the association score in previous steps. A confidence threshold τ_2 is set to divide the tracklets into high confidence tracklets and low confidence tracklets. The association procedure is performed on them hierarchically and is summarized in Algorithm 1.

$$conf_i = \frac{\sum_{k=2}^{length(T_i)} sim_k}{length(T_i) - 1}(1 - e^{-w_3*length(T_i)}) \tag{6}$$

Algorithm 1. The Association Procedure

Input:

The set of object detections in the current frame $D = \{1, ..., N\}$; The set of trajectories associated up to current frame $T = \{1, ..., M\}$;

1: Divide the tracklets into high confidence tracklets T^h and low confidence tracklets T^l according to the confidence threshold τ_2;
2: Calculate the affinity matrix between D and T^h, associate them with hungarian algorithm, remove unreliable association whose score is below τ_1
3: Use the same procedure as step 2 to associate T^l and unassociated detections.
4: Update the tracklet confidence using Equ.6, update the kalman filter and the appearance queue, remove the tracklets which have been unassociated for more than T_{max} frames;
5: Calculate the IOU affinity matrix between unassociated detections in consecutive frames and generate new tracklets if three detections in successive frames are associated;

---

3   Experiment

3.1   Evaluation Metrics

A good tracker should find correct numbers of objects and associate them with correct tracklets when a new frame arrives. At the same time, a good tracker should also track each object consistently and overcome the mismatch phenomenon. Based on the above criteria, most trackers adopt MOTA as main metric to evaluate their trackers' performance, which is calculated as below:

$$MOTA = 1 - \frac{\sum_t (FN_t + FP_t + IDSW_t)}{\sum_t GT_t} \qquad (7)$$

In above formula, FN indicates the number of missed objects, FP indicates the number of false positives, IDSW indicates the number of mismatches. However, in most cases, the number of FN is one order higher than FP and two order higher than IDSW. This means the reduction of IDSW is of little significance for the improvement of MOTA. In addition, a mismatch should not be treated equal with a FP. With recent development of the precision of detectors, the number of FP and FN has dropped a lot, so we appeal for more attention to the consistency of trajectories. The score of MOTA is a good indicator of the tracking accuracy, but not capable of evaluating the consistency, so we adopt ID switch rate, ID precision, ID recall and IDF_1 introduced in [19] to evaluate the consistency of the trajectories. IDF_1 is calculated by matching trajectories to the ground-truth so as to minimize the sum of discrepancies between corresponding pairs. Unlike MOTA, it penalizes ID switches over the whole trajectory fragments with wrong ID, and can evaluate how well computed identities conform to true identities [19].

Besides above evaluation metrics, following common metrics are also adopted to evaluate our tracker comprehensively:

MT: Mostly tracked targets [2]. The ratio of ground-truth trajectories that are covered by a track hypothesis for at least 80% of their respective life span.

ML: Mostly lost targets [2]. The ratio of ground-truth trajectories that are covered by a track hypothesis for at most 20% of their respective life span.

MOTP: Multiple Object Tracking Precision [2]. The misalignment between the annotated and the predicted bounding boxes.

3.2   Thresholds Selection

To obtain robust affinity threshold τ_1 and confidence threshold τ_2, we test our tracker with grid search method on MOT16 train dataset. The relationship between MOTA and two thresholds is shown in Fig. 3. We set τ_1 to 0.4 and set τ_2 to 0.3 for the rest experiments. The Fig. 3 also demonstrates that adopting confidence-based association metric could improve tracking accuracy.

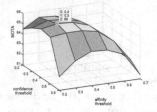

Fig. 3. Thresholds selection on MOT16 train dataset

3.3 Runtime

To investigate the feature extraction speed of our part-based deep appearance network comprehensively, we test our network and other trackers which adopt deep appearance model and take image patches as inputs on the same platform. The feature extraction speed is tested on a Quadro M4000 GPU and Intel E5V3 CPU and shown in Table 1. Dan and Pdan denote our full-part and part-based deep appearance network respectively. Compared with other trackers, our deep model gets faster speed with smaller batch size, and there is just a minor speed loss for the added part model. The speed for confidence-based association is not very fast and is about 5.16 fps, which is mostly owning to the large number of objects, but our part-based deep appearance network could be transplanted to other association metric conveniently.

Table 1. The speed and consumption for feature extraction

App model	Lmp [23]	AMIR [20]	DeepSort [24]	Dan	Pdan
Batch size	16 patches	16 patches	16 patches	1 frame	1 frame
Speed(fps)	2.47	2.42	16.19	20.75	19.10

3.4 Experiment Result

Table 2 shows the tracking results on MOT16 test dataset, Hist means histogram appearance model, and Dan-OD denotes full-part deep network without the guidance of occlusion detector for appearance model update. Trackers marked with * adopt same detections supplied in [26]. The results show that adopting part-based deep appearance network and occlusion detector could improve tracking accuracy and consistency obviously. Compared with histogram appearance model, the ID switches reduce from 1014 to 762, both ID precision and ID recall have a certain improvement. The reduction of mismatches also increases the rate of MT, this means our tracker is more capable of getting consistent and long trajectories.

Table 2. Tracking results on MOT16 test Dataset with private detector

Trackers		MOTA↑	IDSW↓	IDF₁ ↑	IDP↑	IDR↑	MOTP↑	MT↑	ML↓
KDNT* [26]	Batch	**68.2**	**933**	60.0	66.9	**54.4**	79.4	41.0%	19.0%
MCMOT-HDM [15]	Batch	62.4	1394	51.6	60.7	44.9	78.3	31.5%	24.2%
IOU [4]	Batch	57.1	2167	46.9	59.8	38.6	77.1	23.6%	32.9%
DeepSort* [24]	Online	61.4	781	62.2	72.1	54.7	79.1	32.8%	**18.2%**
Sort* [3]	Online	59.8	1423	53.8	65.2	45.7	**79.6**	25.4%	22.7%
EAMTT-16 [21]	Online	52.5	910	53.3	**72.7**	42.1	78.8	19.0%	34.9%
COMOT+Hist*	Online	58.7	1014	59.9	62.7	**57.3**	77.8	30.2%	18.3%
COMOT+Dan-OD*	Online	60.3	957	61.0	66.5	56.3	78.0	33.1%	18.4%
COMOT+Dan+OD*	Online	61.1	873	61.4	68.4	56.0	78.3	32.9%	18.7%
COMOT+Pdan*	Online	**62.8**	**762**	62.6	71.5	55.7	78.3	**34.9%**	18.3%

Table 3. Overall performance on MOT17 test dataset with public detections

Tracker		MOTA↑	IDSW↓	IDF₁↑	IDP↑	IDR↑	MT↑	ML↓
FWT-17 [11]	Batch	**51.3**	2648	**47.6**	63.2	**38.1**	**21.4%**	35.2%
MHT-DAM [14]	Batch	50.7	**2314**	47.2	**63.4**	37.6	20.8%	36.9%
IOU17 [4]	Batch	45.5	5988	39.4	56.4	30.3	15.7%	40.5%
EAMTT-17 [21]	Online	42.6	4488	41.8	59.3	32.2	12.7%	42.7%
GM-PHD [8]	Online	36.4	4607	33.9	54.2	24.7	4.1%	57.3%
COMOT(ours)	Online	**46.8**	**2,121**	49.2	**68.7**	**38.3**	15.3%	**39.1%**

Table 4. Tracking results on MOT17 test dataset based on different public detections

Trackers		DPM [9]		FRCNN [18]		SDP [25]	
		MOTA↑	IDSW↓	MOTA↑	IDSW↓	MOTA↑	IDSW↓
FWT-17 [11]	Batch	**46.4**	833	**48.2**	780	59.4	1035
MHT-DAM [14]	Batch	44.6	**593**	46.9	**742**	**60.6**	**979**
IOU17 [4]	Batch	35.2	1272	44.9	1509	56.3	3207
EAMTT-17 [21]	Online	32.0	1244	42.3	1569	53.6	1675
GM-PHD [8]	Online	24.5	2155	39.3	920	45.2	1532
COMOT(ours)	Online	**36.0**	**756**	**45.3**	**618**	**59.1**	**747**

Tables 3 and 4 demonstrate the overall performance and the separated results based on different detectors on MOT17 benchmark respectively. The MOT17 benchmark provides three detection results: the DPM [9], FasterRCNN [18] and SDP detector [25]. As most trakers in MOT ranking list are anonymous submissions, we select trackers with explicit source for comparison. As demonstrated in Table 3, our tracker achieves competitive performance compared with other online trackers, both the consistency and accuracy gain a significant improvement. Compared with the FWT-17 [11] tracker, our tracker yields higher IDF₁ score and lower ID switch rate, this demonstrates our trajectories are more consistent. The overall accuracy of our tracker is lower than FWT-17, this is mostly due to our poor performance on DPM weak detections, and it is the inherent inferiority between online association and batch association. The batch methods take into consideration the frames in future time steps. Some sampled trajectories are shown in Fig. 4, and the numbers following '#' denote the frame numbers.

(a) Pedestrian street #240   (b) Moving bus #650

Fig. 4. Sampled trajectories in MOT17 benchmark.

4   Conclusion

In this paper, we propose a part-based deep network which employs ROI pooling method to extract part-based appearance feature to overcome the part-occlusion problem. An occlusion detector is proposed to predict the occlusion degree and guide the procedure of similarity fusion and appearance update. Extensive experiments show our tracker is more capable of getting consistent and long trajectories. Both the consistency and accuracy are competitive on MOT benchmark.

References

1. Bae, S.H., Yoon, K.J.: Confidence-based data association and discriminative deep appearance learning for robust online multi-object tracking. IEEE Trans. Pattern Anal. Mach. Intell. **PP**(99), 1 (2017)
2. Bernardin, K., Stiefelhagen, R.: Evaluating multiple object tracking performance: the CLEAR MOT metrics. Eurasip J. Image Video Process. **2008**(1), 246309 (2008)
3. Bewley, A., Ge, Z., Ott, L., Ramos, F., Upcroft, B.: Simple online and realtime tracking. In: IEEE International Conference on Image Processing, pp. 3464–3468 (2016)
4. Bochinski, E., Eiselein, V., Sikora, T.: High-speed tracking-by-detection without using image information. In: IEEE International Conference on Advanced Video and Signal Based Surveillance (2017)
5. Chari, V., Lacoste-Julien, S., Laptev, I., Sivic, J.: On pairwise cost for multi-object network flow tracking. CoRR, abs/1408.3304 (2014)
6. Chen, X., Qin, Z., An, L., Bhanu, B.: Multiperson tracking by online learned grouping model with nonlinear motion context. IEEE Trans. Circuits Syst. Video Technol. **26**(12), 2226–2239 (2016)

7. Chopra, S., Hadsell, R., Lecun, Y.: Learning a similarity metric discriminatively, with application to face verification. In: IEEE Computer Society Conference on Computer Vision and Pattern Recognition, pp. 539–546 (2005)
8. Eiselein, V., Arp, D., Ptzold, M., Sikora, T.: Real-time multi-human tracking using a probability hypothesis density filter and multiple detectors. In: IEEE Ninth International Conference on Advanced Video and Signal-Based Surveillance, pp. 325–330 (2012)
9. Felzenszwalb, P., McAllester, D., Ramanan, D.: A discriminatively trained, multiscale, deformable part model. In: 2008 IEEE Conference on Computer Vision and Pattern Recognition, pp. 1–8. IEEE (2008)
10. Girshick, R.: Fast R-CNN. In: IEEE International Conference on Computer Vision, pp. 1440–1448 (2015)
11. Henschel, R., Lealtaix, L., Cremers, D., Rosenhahn, B.: A novel multi-detector fusion framework for multi-object tracking. Eprint arXiv:1705.08314 (2017)
12. Huang, C., Wu, B., Nevatia, R.: Robust object tracking by hierarchical association of detection responses. In: Forsyth, D., Torr, P., Zisserman, A. (eds.) ECCV 2008. LNCS, vol. 5303, pp. 788–801. Springer, Heidelberg (2008). https://doi.org/10.1007/978-3-540-88688-4_58
13. Kieritz, H., Becker, S., Hubner, W., Arens, M.: Online multi-person tracking using integral channel features. In: IEEE International Conference on Advanced Video and Signal Based Surveillance, pp. 122–130 (2016)
14. Kim, C., Li, F., Ciptadi, A., Rehg, J.M.: Multiple hypothesis tracking revisited. In: IEEE International Conference on Computer Vision, pp. 4696–4704 (2015)
15. Lee, B., Erdenee, E., Jin, S., Nam, M.Y., Jung, Y.G., Rhee, P.K.: Multi-class multi-object tracking using changing point detection. In: Hua, G., Jégou, H. (eds.) ECCV 2016. LNCS, vol. 9914, pp. 68–83. Springer, Cham (2016). https://doi.org/10.1007/978-3-319-48881-3_6
16. Milan, A., Leal-Taixe, L., Reid, I., Roth, S., Schindler, K.: MOT16: a benchmark for multi-object tracking. Eprint arXiv:1603.00831 (2016)
17. Milan, A., Roth, S., Schindler, K.: Continuous energy minimization for multitarget tracking. IEEE Trans. Pattern Anal. Mach. Intell. 36(1), 58–72 (2013)
18. Ren, S., Girshick, R., Girshick, R., Sun, J.: Faster R-CNN: towards real-time object detection with region proposal networks. IEEE Trans. Pattern Anal. Mach. Intell. 39(6), 1137 (2017)
19. Ristani, E., Solera, F., Zou, R., Cucchiara, R., Tomasi, C.: Performance measures and a data set for multi-target, multi-camera tracking. In: Hua, G., Jégou, H. (eds.) ECCV 2016. LNCS, vol. 9914, pp. 17–35. Springer, Cham (2016). https://doi.org/10.1007/978-3-319-48881-3_2
20. Sadeghian, A., Alahi, A., Savarese, S.: Tracking the untrackable: learning to track multiple cues with long-term dependencies. Eprint arXiv:1701.01909 (2017)
21. Sanchez-Matilla, R., Poiesi, F., Cavallaro, A.: Online multi-target tracking with strong and weak detections. In: Hua, G., Jégou, H. (eds.) ECCV 2016. LNCS, vol. 9914, pp. 84–99. Springer, Cham (2016). https://doi.org/10.1007/978-3-319-48881-3_7
22. Smeulders, A.W., Chu, D.M., Cucchiara, R., Calderara, S., Dehghan, A., Shah, M.: Visual tracking: an experimental survey. IEEE Trans. Pattern Anal. Mach. Intell. 36(7), 1442–68 (2014)
23. Tang, S., Andriluka, M., Andres, B., Schiele, B.: Multiple people tracking by lifted multicut and person re-identification. In: Proceedings of the IEEE Conference on Computer Vision and Pattern Recognition, pp. 3539–3548 (2017)

24. Wojke, N., Bewley, A., Paulus, D.: Simple online and realtime tracking with a deep association metric. In: IEEE International Conference on Image Processing, pp. 3645–3649 (2017)
25. Yang, F., Choi, W., Lin, Y.: Exploit all the layers: fast and accurate CNN object detector with scale dependent pooling and cascaded rejection classifiers. In: Computer Vision and Pattern Recognition, pp. 2129–2137 (2016)
26. Yu, F., Li, W., Li, Q., Liu, Y., Shi, X., Yan, J.: POI: multiple object tracking with high performance detection and appearance feature. In: Hua, G., Jégou, H. (eds.) ECCV 2016. LNCS, vol. 9914, pp. 36–42. Springer, Cham (2016). https://doi.org/10.1007/978-3-319-48881-3_3

Deep Supervised Auto-encoder Hashing for Image Retrieval

Sanli Tang, Haoyuan Chi, Jie Yang[✉], Xiaolin Huang,
and Masoumeh Zareapoor

Institution of Image Processing and Pattern Recognition,
Shanghai Jiao Tong University, Shanghai, China
jieyang@sjtu.edu.cn

Abstract. Image hashing approaches map high dimensional images to compact binary codes that preserve similarities among images. Although the image label is important information for supervised image hashing methods to generate hashing codes, the retrieval performance will be limited according to the performance of the classifier. Therefore, an effective supervised auto-encoder hashing method (SAEH) is proposed to generate low dimensional binary codes in a point-wise manner through deep convolutional neural network. The auto-encoder structure in SAEH is designed to simultaneously learn image features and generate hashing codes. Moreover, some extra relaxations for generating binary hash codes are added to the objective function. The extensive experiments on several large scale image datasets validate that the auto-encoder structure can indeed increase the performance for supervised hashing and SAEH can achieve the best image retrieval results among other prominent supervised hashing methods.

Keywords: Image retrieval · Image hashing · Supervised learning
Deep neural network · Convolutional auto-encoder

1 Introduction

With the growing number of image data on the Internet, fast image retrieval is becoming an increasingly important topic. Image hashing attempts to map higher dimension images to lower dimension binary codes, and thus, the similarity between two sequences can be easily and quickly calculated. Hashing technique, which is the most powerful and important technique in image retrieval, achieves a great success, due to its effectiveness to reduce the cost in term of storage and time.

In previous years, many prominent hashing methods have been proposed [2,15,17,23], including many learning based hashing approches, see, e.g. [25]. Hashing methods based on handcrafted features (e.g. GIST [20] and HOG [5]) have firstly been studied. Iterative Quantization (ITQ) [13] applies a random

© Springer Nature Switzerland AG 2018
J.-H. Lai et al. (Eds.): PRCV 2018, LNCS 11257, pp. 193–205, 2018.
https://doi.org/10.1007/978-3-030-03335-4_17

orthogonal transformation to the PCA-projected data and then refines the former orthogonal transformation to minimize quantization error. Kernel-Based Supervised Hashing (KSH) [3] employs a kernel trick to accommodate with the data which are linearly inseparable. [15] proposes to encode the relative order of features rather than quantize the values in ranking subspaces, which can effectively handle prevalent noises in real-world dataset.

In addition, convolution neural networks act as end-to-end methods to extract the features and then to be applied in various tasks. Recently, notable success of deep neural network models [9, 11] in a wide range of areas such as: object detection, image classification, and object recognition, has aroused the researchers' interest to develop hashing methods through deep neural networks. CNNH+ [26] is developed for image hashing and comprises of two efficient stages. In the first stage, it decomposes the similarity matrix into a product of matrix of target hash codes. In the second stage, it builds a convolution network to learn hashing codes from labelled data (if it is on supervised scenario). Later, Deep Supervised Hashing (DSH) [16] prudently combines these two aforementioned stages in CNNH+ into a single network, in which it takes a pair of images with their labels as inputs and attempts to maximize the discriminability of the output space. As a point-wise method which takes single image as the input of network for training, Supervised Semantics-preserving Deep Hashing (SSDH) [27] uses a deep convolution network based on AlexNet [11] to obtain hash codes and directly uses these codes to minimize the classification error. Deep Quantization Network (DQN) [2] proposes a product quantization loss for controlling hashing quality and the quantizability of bottleneck representation.

In the most recent, CNN-based auto-encoder methods [6, 24] emerge as a powerful technique to extract highly abstract features from image data. These extracted features can capture the semantic information of images, which can be used for image hashing in the retrieval task. Several hashing methods based on convolution auto-encoders (CAE) have also been proposed. For example, [21] is one of the most recent method which presents a new hashing method by using variational auto-encoder [7] on unsupervised scenario.

Although many efficient deep supervised hashing methods [2, 15, 16, 27] have been proposed in the last few years, which achieved exciting performance, the studies on supervised auto-encoder structure in image hashing task are limited. En [8] proves the effectiveness of the auto-encoder structure for unsupervised hashing, which encourages the study in this paper on the supervised image hashing by incorporating an auto-encoder structure into a supervised hashing network. The effectiveness of the auto-encoder structure has been proved in image classification [22] and generation [12, 18] tasks, while in this paper, we validate its effectiveness for supervised image hashing method in image retrieval task.

Since the supervised information from image labels is a strong regularization term which drives the images with the same label to be encoded into the same hashing codes, the performance of supervised hashing methods might be limited by the classification accuracy of the supervisory network. However, considering misclassified images by the supervisory network, the auto-encoder structure is able to restrict those with similar patterns to be encoded with similar hashing codes, which is proved to be effective in unsupervised image hashing task [8,21] and consequently improves the retrieval results on supervised scenario.

The motivation of this work is straightforward, since the auto-encoder structure has the ability to keep the semantic feature between images. In our work, in order to improve the generalization ability and remedy the overly dependent on the performance of the supervisory network for deep supervised hashing method, we propose a framework based on a supervised auto-encoder hashing (SAEH) model to generate binary hash codes while still keeping their semantic similarities. The auto-encoder structure is also designed to assist the supervisory network to learn more semantic features, which therefore, will increase the semantic information represented by each hashing bit. Following previous works [11,12], supervised information is incorporated in the deep hashing architecture to associate the hashing bits with the given label, where the mean-square error of original and recovered images and the classification error are simultaneously minimized. In order to convert these codes to binary, some additional relaxations are also incorporated into the objective function. In summary, there are three main contributions of this paper: (1) A framework is proposed to incorporate auto-encoder into supervisory hashing model, which will increase the semantic-keeping and generalization ability. (2) Several typical methods for combining auto-encoder structure with supervised hashing network are inspected to validate their effectiveness in supervised image hashing task. (3) The proposed framework can achieve the best image retrieval results among other prominent supervised hashing methods on several large-scale datasets.

The practicalness and effectiveness of SAEH model are validated through various experiments on MNIST, CIFAR-10, SVHN and UT-Zap50K datasets. In order to statistically compare the performance of the proposed SAEH model and the deep supervised hashing model without the auto-encoder structure, the decoder network with the recovery loss is removed from our hashing model to identify that the effectiveness of auto-encoder. Multiple comparison experiments are also carried out to show the effectiveness of SAEH with other state of art image retrieval methods.

The rest of the paper is organized as follows. Section 2 describes our framework based on the supervised auto-encoder hashing model in detail. Section 3 presents experiments on four large datasets to evaluate the capability of SAEH to generate binary hashing bits. Section 4 gives conclusions of this paper.

2 Supervised Auto-encoder Hashing

Let $\mathcal{X} = \{x_n\}_{n=1}^N$ be N images belonging to labels $\mathcal{Y} = \{y_n \in \{0,1\}^C\}_{n=1}^N$, where C is the number of classes. For example, if x_n belongs to class $c_n \in \{1, 2, \cdots, C\}$, we assign its label vector y_n as $(y_n)_j = 1$ if $j = c_n$ and 0 otherwise. Then we use $h_n \in [0,1]^K$ to denote the codes generated from x_n through a encoder function with the code length K. Similarly, we denote the binary hashing codes as $b_n \in \{0,1\}^K$ by setting a threshold to h_n. In order to obtain hashing

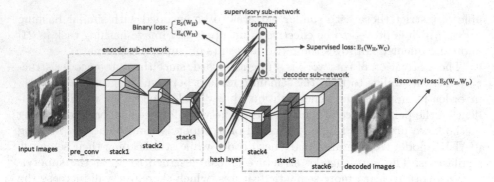

Fig. 1. The architecture of SAEH (The source codes of this paper will be public in the future) proposed in this paper, which includes three parts: encoder sub-network, decoder sub-network, and supervisory sub-network. The encoder sub-network is based on ResNet50 [9] where we remove the last two layers and add a fully connected layer to generate hash codes. The $stackn(n = 1, 2, \cdots, 6)$ denotes a group of cascaded residual units as building blocks in [9].

codes from highly abstract features of images, we design a supervised auto-encoder architecture as illustrated in Fig. 1, including: the encoder sub-network, the supervisory sub-network and the decoder sub-network.

2.1   Architecture of SAEH

The encoder sub-network is designed to map the normalized input image x_n into hashing codes h_n in the latent space of SAEH model. We define the parameters in the encoder sub-network as W_H and the mapping function is signified as $\mathcal{H} : x_n \mapsto h_n$. Hereafter, in this paper, the output layer of the encoder sub-network is named as hash layer. As the most importance information contained by an image, image labels are used to regularize the latent variables through a supervisory sub-network. The supervisory sub-network takes the latent variables as input, which is generated by the encoder and contains a softmax function: $\text{softmax}(x)_i = e^{w_i x_i} / \sum_{c=1}^{C} e^{x_c w_c}$. It is used to predict the label $\hat{y}_n$ of input x_n based on its hashing codes h_n during training process. And it can be formulated as $\mathcal{C} : h_n \mapsto \hat{y}_n$, which is parameterized by W_C. Supervisory sub-network aims to minimize the classification error with the given label y, where we calculate the categorical cross-entropy error:

$$l(y_n, \hat{y}_n) = -\sum_{c=1}^{C} y_{nc} \log(\hat{y}_{nc}). \tag{1}$$

And similarly, the loss of the supervisory sub-network among the whole training set can be calculated as follows:

$$E_1(W_H, W_C) = \frac{1}{N} \sum_{n=1}^{N} l(\boldsymbol{y}_n, \hat{\boldsymbol{y}}_n)$$

$$= \frac{1}{N} \sum_{n=1}^{N} l(\boldsymbol{y}_n, \mathcal{C}(\mathcal{H}(\boldsymbol{x}_n; W_H); W_C). \tag{2}$$

At the same time, the content of an image is important for image hashing, which can be used to improve the generalization ability of the supervised hashing methods and get rid of the heavy dependence on the classification performance. Thus, a decoder sub-network is designed to recover the input image from its hashing codes in the latent space. It can be signified as $\mathcal{D} : \boldsymbol{h}_n \mapsto \hat{\boldsymbol{x}}_n$, where $\hat{\boldsymbol{x}}_n$ is the recovered image and the parameters are represented in term of W_D. Here, we use mean square error (MSE) between the input images and the decoded images in pixel-wise manner to measure this recovery error as Eq. (3).

$$E_2(W_H, W_D) = \frac{1}{N} \sum_{n-1}^{N} ||\boldsymbol{x}_n - \hat{\boldsymbol{x}}_n||_2^2$$

$$= \frac{1}{N} \sum_{n=1}^{N} ||\boldsymbol{x}_n - \mathcal{D}(\mathcal{H}(\boldsymbol{x}_n; W_H); W_D)||_2^2 \tag{3}$$

2.2 Binary Hashing Codes

Considering that the codes generated by encoder $\mathcal{H}$ are distributed in continuous space, in order to obtain the binary hashing codes, some relaxations should be added to the hash layer. Since we use a sigmoid function: $\text{sigmoid}(x) = 1/(1 + \exp(-x))$ to activate the output nodes of the hash layer, the output of the hash layer is restricted between 0 and 1.

Following the previous works by [8,27], we then attempt to convert these activation values into binary values as 0 or 1, which also means to be far from their midpoint. So the relaxation term to get binary hashing codes can be given as following:

$$E_3(W_H) = -\frac{1}{N} \sum_{n=1}^{N} ||\boldsymbol{h}_n - 0.5\boldsymbol{e}||_2^2, \tag{4}$$

where $\boldsymbol{e}$ is a vector with all elements equal to 1.

Moreover, inspired by [27], in order to increase the gap of Hamming distance between the hash codes of the input belonging to different classes, an additional relaxation is added to make sure that hashing codes are as uniformly distributed as possible. Since the latent variables are restricted into $[0, 1]$ through a sigmoid function, we can regularize the mean of the elements in a sequence of hash codes closer to 0.5 as the mean of the even distribution between $[0, 1]$.

$$E_4(W_H) = \sum_{k=1}^{K} \Big(\frac{1}{N} \big(\sum_{n=1}^{N} h_{nk} \big) - 0.5 \Big)^2 \tag{5}$$

The final binary hashing code b_n is easily obtained by setting a threshold θ ($\theta = 0.5$ in our work) to h_n as Eq. (6), where the quantization error is quite less because the relaxation term in Eq. (4) is incorporated into the objective function for training SAEH model.

$$b_{ni} = \begin{cases} 1 & h_{ni} > \theta \\ 0 & otherwise \end{cases} \tag{6}$$

2.3 Different Ways for Incorporating Autoencoder Structure

Usually, there are three main ways for incorporating an auto-encoder structure into supervised classification tasks: pre-training a supervised classifier network through an auto-encoder structure, simultaneously training classifier with an auto-encoder, and training an auto-encoder model as warm-up for a classifier. The pre-training and warm-up training methods are usually designed to initialize the parameters in the supervised classification networks for fast convergence and improving the performance. Specifically, the pre-training method trains the feature extraction network in the classifier as an encoder with an extra decoder through a few iterations, and then directly removes such decoder network with the recovery error in the objectives and only trains the classifier continuously. Simultaneously training an auto-encoder with a classifier means to train those networks for the whole time during the training process. Training an auto-encoder as warm-up for a classifier attempts to gradually reduce the weight of the decoder with the recovery error during the training process and eventually remove it after some iterations. In this paper, we also investigate the above methods for incorporating auto-encoder structure in supervised hashing model. More formally, those methods for updating the weight γ of the recovery loss term can be summarized as following:

$$\gamma_t = \begin{cases} u(t < t_{\mathrm{pre}}) * \gamma_{\mathrm{init}} & \text{pre-train} \\ \gamma_{\mathrm{init}} & \text{simultaneous train} \\ \min\{\gamma_{\mathrm{max}}, \max\{\gamma_{t-1} - t \cdot k, 0\}\} & \text{warm-up} \end{cases} \tag{7}$$

In Eq. (7), $u(\text{condition})$ is an indicator function, which is 1 if the condition is true and 0 otherwise. t_{pre} is the iteration times, when the auto-encoder is pre-trained for initialization. γ_{init} is the initial value of the weight of the recovery loss. k controls the decreasing speed of the recovery error weight in the warm-up method with γ_0 to be γ_{init}, where the linear decreasing strategy is chosen in our framework and the weight γ_t is clipped into $[0, \gamma_{\mathrm{max}}]$ after each update.

2.4 Objective Function and Implementation

Before going to further discussion, we first formulate the objective function. The final objective function will be obtained by summing all the loss terms, including the classification loss, the recovery loss, and the relaxations with their corresponding weights and formulated as:

$$E(W_H, W_D, W_C) = E_1(W_H, W_C) + \gamma E_2(W_H, W_D)$$
$$+ \alpha E_3(W_H) + \beta E_4(W_H)$$
$$+ \eta \left(||W_H||_2^2 + ||W_D||_2^2 + ||W_C||_2^2 \right), \tag{8}$$

where an l_2 regularization term for all of the parameters in SAEH is added during training to reduce the overfitting issue.

SAEH is implemented in Keras [4] with Tensorflow [1] on an NVIDIA GTX 1080 GPU. As shown in Fig. 1, the encoder sub-network is based on ResNet [9], in which we remove the last two layers and add a fully connected layer (hash layer) to generate hashing codes. The supervisory sub-network is connected after the encoder, of which the output layer with C nodes is directly connected from the hash layer. The decoder network is a inverted architecture of the encoder network, where the bilinear interpolation approach, as the inverted operation of max pooling in the encoder sub-network, is designed to increase the size of the feature maps as up-sampling layer. In addition, We apply the stochastic gradient descend (SGD) method in order to address the problem in Eq. (8) and we set the momentum to 0.9. The learning rate is initialized by 0.1 and reduces 80% every 30 epochs. To validate the effectiveness of auto-encoder structure for supervised hashing, we mainly discuss the influence of recovery weight γ in the following experiments, while other parameters such as α, β and η are fixed to be: 0.1, 0.1 and 0.0005 respectively based on some preliminary experiments.

3   Experiments

In this section, we carry out various experiments to evaluate the performance of the proposed image hashing framework based on supervised auto-encoder hashing model on several publicly available image datasets. Notice that after the SAEH model being well trained, the supervisory and decoder sub-networks can be simply removed from the framework since only the encoder sub-network is required to generate hashing codes on the test scenario. Thus, our framework is as efficient as other deep supervised hashing models except some extra efforts for training.

3.1   Datasets

- MNIST [14] contains 70k 28×28 handwritten images from 0 to 9 in grayscale. Following common splits, we select 6k images per class (60k in total) as training set and the rest as testing set.
- CIFAR-10 [10] consists of 60k 32×32 color images of ten common objects. In our experiments, we have divided the images into training set with 5k images per class and the remain for testing set.

- SVHN [19] is a color house number dataset obtained from Google Street View images including 73,257 samples for training and 26,032 for testing.
- UT-Zap50K [28] is a large shoe dataset involving 50,025 images belonging to 4 categories respectively. We randomly select 46,025 samples for training and the rest 4,000 samples for testing.

Table 1. mAP@1000(%) and precision rate (with Hamming radius to be 2) on CIFAR-10 dataset w.r.t different γ ($\alpha = \beta = 0.1$)

γ	0	0.01	0.1	1.0	10
mAP@1000	84.56	87.30	**87.35**	87.00	86.13
Precision	88.16	88.77	88.90	91.93	**95.59**

Table 2. mAP@1000(%), precision rate(%) (with Hamming radius to be 2), and the classification accuracy (as a reference) on CIFAR-10 and UT-Zap50K datasets with 32 bits w.r.t different methods to incorporate auto-encoder structure into supervised hashing model. Notice that the evaluation result by accuracy is the classification accuracy of the supervisory sub-network.

Method	CIFAR-10			UT-Zap50K		
	mAP@1000	Precision	Accuracy	mAP@1000	Precision	Accuracy
SAEH	**87.35**	88.90	0.8868	**85.74**	**88.35**	**0.8135**
SAEH$^-$	84.56	88.16	**0.9110**	80.70	75.59	0.8080
SAEH^{pre}	86.52	**89.3**	0.8873	83.78	79.94	0.7970
SAEH^{wu}	86.59	88.61	0.8938	83.65	79.56	0.7959

3.2   Ablation Study for Auto-encoder Structure

To evaluate the effectiveness of the decoder structure in SAEH model, where we simultaneously train an auto-encoder with a classifier, for alleviating the dependence on the classification accuracy, we apply SAEH and contrastive method (denoted as SAEH$^-$, where we remove the decoder structure from SAEH by setting the weight of recovery error γ to 0 in the Eq. (8)) on the MNIST, CIFAR-10 and SVHN datasets respectively. The retrieval results of SAEH and SAEH$^-$ measured by mAP@1000 are shown in the last two rows in Table 3. Comparing to SAEH$^-$ model, where the decoder sub-network with the recovery loss is ignored during training, SAEH increases the mAP around 0.6%–3.64% on different datasets with the help of decoder structure. Moreover, the weight on the decoder loss γ is inspected to evaluate influences of the decoder network on the performance in supervised image retrieval tasks. The retrieval results on CIFAR-10 dataset of 32 bits with various γ are illustrated in Table 1, where

SAEH achieves best retrieval result under the measurement of mAP@1000 when $\gamma = 0.1$ and the precision rate with Hamming distance lower than 2 when $\gamma = 10.0$. Besides, the model with $\gamma = 0$ by removing the auto-encoder structure has the worst behaviour among the models with weight $\gamma > 0$, which also validates the advantage of the auto-encoder structure in supervised image hashing task. As a trade off, we assign γ to 1 in the following experiments.

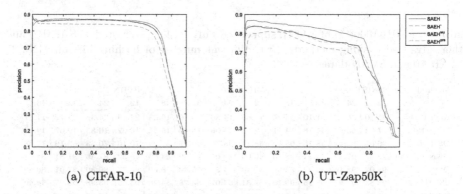

(a) CIFAR-10   (b) UT-Zap50K

Fig. 2. Precision-recall (PR) curves of the four methods for incorporating auto encoder structure into supervised hashing model on (a) CIFAR-10 and (b) UT-Zap50K datasets, with hashing bit length to be 32.

3.3 Ablation Study for Incorporating Auto-encoder Methods

We carry out some experiments to evaluate the effectiveness of the three different methods in Eq. (7) for incorporating auto-encoder structure in supervised hashing model. We initialize the hyperparameters γ_{init}, t_{pre} and k as 0.1, 2k, 0.0001 respectively while other parameters in the objective function remains the same. We denote the three methods in Eq. (7): pre-training, simultaneously training and warm-up training as SAEH^{pre}, SAEH (corresponding with the notation in other experiments), and SAEH^{wu} respectively. We compare those methods on the CIFAR-10 and UP-Zap50K datasets with bit length to be 32. The experiment results measured by mAP@1000 and precision rate with Hamming radius to be 2 are in Table 2. For comparison, we also add the result without the auto-encoder structure as SAEH^- in the table. The classification accuracy by the supervisory sub-network is also appended as the reference.

From Table 2, we can find that the auto-encoder structure indeed increases the effective of supervised hashing methods. Although the SAEH^- with out the auto-encoder structure achieves the excellent results under the evaluation of the classification accuracy, comparing to the other three variants with auto-encoder structure, it has the worst behaviour for supervised image hashing under the measurement of both the mAP@1000 and precision rate with Hamming radius to be 2, which verifies that the auto-encoder structure can alleviate the overly dependant on the classification accuracy in supervised hashing methods.

The experiments results in Table 2 also shows the advantage of simultaneously training auto-encoder with a classifier, which achieves the best results on both CIFAR-10 and UT-Zap50K datasets according to criterion of mAP@1000. In other words, when the recall rate decreases, the precision rate of the simultaneously training method increases faster than other incorporating methods as well as the supervised-only SAEH⁻, which is illustrated in Fig. 2 as the precision recall curves on CIFAR-10 and UT-Zap50K datasets, respectively.

Table 3. mAP@1000(%) of SAEH, supervised-only hashing (denoted as SAEH⁻) and other advanced hashing methods w.r.t. different number of hashing bits on MNIST, CIFAR-10 and SVHN datasets.

Method	MNIST				CIFAR-10				SVHN			
	12	24	32	48	12	24	32	48	12	24	32	48
KSH [3]	24.30	36.63	31.10	33.25	17.65	14.80	15.50	16.63	24.18	24.36	24.72	21.87
ITQ [13]	37.63	53.87	51.76	54.11	12.93	14.06	13.40	15.11	16.22	16.85	19.67	19.89
DSH [16]	96.05	97.35	98.10	98.13	38.17	38.70	40.19	37.29	73.16	70.33	82.16	77.33
CNNH+ [26]	97.57	97.89	98.04	98.33	40.00	42.00	44.89	44.55	78.32	81.46	81.81	84.00
DQN [2]	98.02	98.16	98.22	98.06	55.40	55.80	56.40	58.00	86.77	86.80	87.01	86.89
SSDH* [27]	98.83	98.97	98.96	99.15	82.31	84.07	83.78	84.28	93.19	93.98	93.95	94.46
SAEH⁻	99.30	99.38	99.38	99.41	84.30	85.71	84.56	82.69	94.91	95.55	95.86	96.14
SAEH	99.50	99.44	99.53	99.54	85.85	87.38	87.00	86.33	95.48	96.28	95.95	96.45

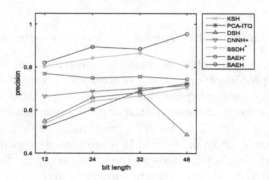

Fig. 3. Precision rate (with Hamming distance r = 2) of different hashing methods on UT-Zap50K dataset w.r.t different length of hash bits.

3.4   Evaluation on SAEH and Other Methods

In this experiment, we compare our proposed framework based on a supervised auto-encoder hashing model with other prominent hashing methods to verify the effectiveness and competitiveness of our framework in supervised image hashing task. We adopt the simultaneously training auto-encoder with a supervisory sub-network mentioned above as our SAEH model. For KSH and ITQ methods based on handcraft features, we first calculate the 512 GIST features of each image for training. In the second stage of CNNH+ [26], we follow the authors' scheme to carefully design a convolution network for generating hashing codes based on image label information. So far as we know, SSDH [27] is the most prominent supervised hashing method. For fair comparison, we also re-implement SSDH by using ResNet50 [9] as its inference model, denoted as SSDH*. For convincing evaluation, we repeat the experiments for each hashing method mentioned above for 5 times and illustrate the average results. The retrieval results of mAP@1000 on MNIST, CIFAR-10 and SVHN datasets are shown in Table 3 and the precision rate with Hamming distance $r = 2$ on UT-Zap50K dataset is shown in Fig. 3. From Table 3, comparing to the results from other competitive hashing methods, SAEH increases the mAP@1000 from 0.39% to 3.54%, while it also increases the precision rate with Hanming radius to be 2 from 1.7% to 15.1% on UT-Zap50K dataset in Fig. 3, which validates of the effectiveness and practicalness of the proposed supervised hashing framework based on the auto-encoder structure.

4   Conclusion

The performance of supervised hashing methods are always limited by the classification accuracy of the classifier in the model. Consider that the semantic information in the image can be captured efficiently through an auto-encoder structure, which is able to improve the performance of the supervised hashing methods by alleviating the dependence on the accuracy of classification sub-network. Therefore, in this paper, we propose a hashing framework based on a supervised auto-encoder model, which learns semantic preserving hashing codes of images. Moreover, some extra relaxations are introduced that turn the output of hash layer into binary codes and increase the gap of the Hamming distance between classes. Experiment results prove that SAEH takes both the advantage of supervisory and auto-encoder networks and performs better than the contrastive model without the decoder structure. The equilibrium of the recovery loss and supervisory loss is also inspected in this paper. The extended experiments on three main methods to incorporate auto-encoder structure into supervised hashing show the superior effectiveness of simultaneously training an auto-encoder and a supervisory sub-network. Moreover, comparing to other state-of-art methods in supervised image retrieval task, the proposed framework SAEH achieves superior retrieval performance and provides a promising architecture for deep supervised image hashing.

References

1. Abadi, M., Agarwal, A., Barham, P., et al.: TensorFlow: large-scale machine learning on heterogeneous distributed systems (2016)
2. Cao, Y., Long, M., Wang, J., Zhu, H., Wen, Q.: Deep quantization network for efficient image retrieval. In: Thirtieth AAAI Conference on Artificial Intelligence, pp. 3457–3463 (2016)

3. Chang, S.F., Jiang, Y.G., Ji, R., Wang, J., Liu, W.: Supervised hashing with kernels. In: IEEE Conference on Computer Vision and Pattern Recognition, pp. 2074–2081 (2012)
4. Chollet, F.: Keras (2015). https://github.com/fchollet/keras
5. Dalal, N., Triggs, B.: Histograms of oriented gradients for human detection. In: 2005 IEEE Computer Society Conference on Computer Vision and Pattern Recognition. CVPR 2005, pp. 886–893 (2005)
6. Dilokthanakul, N., et al.: Deep unsupervised clustering with gaussian mixture variational autoencoders (2016)
7. Doersch, C.: Tutorial on variational autoencoders. arXiv preprint arXiv:1606.05908 (2016)
8. En, S., Crémilleux, B., Jurie, F.: Unsupervised deep hashing with stacked convolutional autoencoders. Working paper or preprint, May 2017. https://hal.archives-ouvertes.fr/hal-01528097
9. He, K., Zhang, X., Ren, S.: Deep residual learning for image recognition. In: Computer Vision and Pattern Recognition, pp. 770–778 (2016)
10. Krizhevsky, A.: Learning multiple layers of features from tiny images (2009)
11. Krizhevsky, A., Sutskever, I., Hinton, G.E.: Imagenet classification with deep convolutional neural networks. In: International Conference on Neural Information Processing Systems, pp. 1097–1105 (2012)
12. Larsen, A.B.L., Snderby, S.K.: Larochelle: autoencoding beyond pixels using a learned similarity metric, pp. 1558–1566 (2015)
13. Lazebnik, S.: Iterative quantization: a procrustean approach to learning binary codes. In: IEEE Conference on Computer Vision and Pattern Recognition, pp. 817–824 (2011)
14. Lcun, Y., Bottou, L., Bengio, Y., Haffner, P.: Gradient-based learning applied to document recognition. Proc. IEEE **86**(11), 2278–2324 (1998)
15. Li, K., Qi, G.J., Ye, J., Yusuph, T., Hua, K.A.: Semantic image retrieval with feature space rankings. Int. J. Semant. Comput. **11**(2), 171–192 (2017)
16. Liu, H., Wang, R., Shan, S., Chen, X.: Deep supervised hashing for fast image retrieval. In: Computer Vision and Pattern Recognition, pp. 2064–2072 (2016)
17. Liu, W., Wang, J., Kumar, S., Chang, S.F.: Hashing with graphs. In: International Conference on Machine Learning, ICML 2011, Bellevue, Washington, USA, 28 June–July, pp. 1–8 (2011)
18. Makhzani, A., Shlens, J., Jaitly, N., Goodfellow, I.: Adversarial autoencoders. Computer Science (2015)
19. Netzer, Y., Wang, T., Coates, A., Bissacco, A., Wu, B., Ng, A.Y.: Reading digits in natural images with unsupervised feature learning. In: Nips Workshop on Deep Learning and Unsupervised Feature Learning (2011)
20. Oliva, A., Torralba, A.: Modeling the shape of the scene: a holistic representation of the spatial envelope. Int. J. Comput. Vis. **42**(3), 145–175 (2001)
21. Pu, Y., Gan, Z., Henao, R.: Variational autoencoder for deep learning of images, labels and captions (2016)
22. Rasmus, A., Berglund, M., Honkala, M., Valpola, H., Raiko, T.: Semi-supervised learning with ladder networks. In: Cortes, C., Lawrence, N.D., Lee, D.D., Sugiyama, M., Garnett, R. (eds.) Advances in Neural Information Processing Systems 28, pp. 3546–3554. Curran Associates, Inc. (2015). http://papers.nips.cc/paper/5947-semi-supervised-learning-with-ladder-networks.pdf
23. Shao, J., Wu, F., Ouyang, C., Zhang, X.: Sparse spectral hashing. Pattern Recognit. Lett. **33**(3), 271–277 (2012)

24. Vincent, P., Larochelle, H., Lajoie, I., et al.: Stacked denoising autoencoders: learning useful representations in a deep network with a local denoising criterion. J. Mach. Learn. Res. **11**(12), 3371–3408 (2010)
25. Wang, J., Zhang, T.: A survey on learning to hash. IEEE Trans. Pattern Anal. Mach. Intell. **PP**(99), 1 (2016)
26. Xia, R., Pan, Y., Lai, H., Liu, C.: Supervised hashing for image retrieval via image representation learning. In: AAAI, vol. 1, p. 2 (2014)
27. Yang, H.F., Lin, K., Chen, C.S.: Supervised learning of semantics-preserving hash via deep convolutional neural networks. IEEE Trans. Pattern Anal. Mach. Intell. **PP**(99), 1 (2015)
28. Yu, A., Grauman, K.: Fine-grained visual comparisons with local learning. In: Computer Vision and Pattern Recognition, pp. 192–199 (2014)

Accurate Spectral Super-Resolution from Single RGB Image Using Multi-scale CNN

Yiqi Yan[1], Lei Zhang[2], Jun Li[4], Wei Wei[2,3(✉)], and Yanning Zhang[2,3]

[1] School of Electronics and Information,
Northwestern Polytechnical University, Xi'an, China
`yanyiqinwpu@gmail.com`
[2] School of Computer Science, Northwestern Polytechnical University,
Xi'an, China
`zhanglei211@mail.nwpu.edu.cn`, `{weiweinwpu,ynzhang}@nwpu.edu.cn`
[3] National Engineering Laboratory for Integrated Aero-Space-Ground-Ocean
Big Data Application Technology, Xi'an, China
[4] Guangdong Provincial Key Laboratory of Urbanization and Geo-simulation,
School of Geography and Planning, Sun Yat-Sen University, Guangzhou, China
`lijun48@mail.sysu.edu.cn`

Abstract. Different from traditional hyperspectral super-resolution approaches that focus on improving the spatial resolution, spectral super-resolution aims at producing a high-resolution hyperspectral image from the RGB observation with super-resolution in spectral domain. However, it is challenging to accurately reconstruct a high-dimensional continuous spectrum from three discrete intensity values at each pixel, since too much information is lost during the procedure where the latent hyperspectral image is downsampled (e.g., with ×10 scaling factor) in spectral domain to produce an RGB observation. To address this problem, we present a multi-scale deep convolutional neural network (CNN) to explicitly map the input RGB image into a hyperspectral image. Through symmetrically downsampling and upsampling the intermediate feature maps in a cascading paradigm, the local and non-local image information can be jointly encoded for spectral representation, ultimately improving the spectral reconstruction accuracy. Extensive experiments on a large hyperspectral dataset demonstrate the effectiveness of the proposed method.

Keywords: Hyperspectral imaging · Spectral super-resolution
Multi-scale analysis · Convolutional neural networks

1 Introduction

Hyperspectral imaging encodes the reflectance of the scene from hundreds or thousands of bands with a narrow wavelength interval (e.g., 10 nm) into a hyperspectral image. Different from conventional images, each pixel in the hyperspectral image contains a continuous spectrum, thus allowing the acquisition of

© Springer Nature Switzerland AG 2018
J.-H. Lai et al. (Eds.): PRCV 2018, LNCS 11257, pp. 206–217, 2018.
https://doi.org/10.1007/978-3-030-03335-4_18

abundant spectral information. Such information has proven to be quite useful for distinguishing different materials. Therefore, hyperspectral images have been widely exploited to facilitate various applications in computer vision community, such as visual tracking [20], image segmentation [18], face recognition [14], scene classification [5], and anomaly detection [10].

The acquisition of spectral information, however, comes at the cost of decreasing the spatial resolution of hyperspectral images. This is because a fewer number of photons are captured by each detector due to the narrower width of the spectral bands. In order to maintain a reasonable signal-to-noise ratio (SNR), the instantaneous field of view (IFOV) needs to be increased, which renders it difficult to produce hyperspectral images with high spatial resolution. To address this problem, many efforts have been made for the hyperspectral imagery super-resolution.

Most of the existing methods mainly focus on enhancing the spatial resolution of the observed hyperspectral image. According to the input images, they can be divided into two categories: (1) fusion based methods where a high-resolution conventional image (e.g., RGB image) and a low-resolution hyperspectral image are fused together to produce a high-resolution hyperspectral image [11, 22] (2) single image super-resolution which directly increases the spatial resolution of a hyperspectral image [12, 24, 25, 27]. Although these methods have shown effective performance, the acquisition of the input hyperspectral image often requires specialized hyperspectral sensors as well as extensive imaging cost. To mitigate this problem, some recent literature [2, 4, 7, 13] turn to investigate a novel hyperspectral imagery super-resolution scheme, termed spectral super-resolution, which aims at improving the spectral resolution of a given RGB image. Since the input image can be easily captured by conventional RGB sensors, imaging cost can be greatly reduced.

However, it is challenging to accurately reconstruct a hyperspectral image from a single RGB observation, since mapping three discrete intensity values to a continuous spectrum is a highly ill-posed linear inverse problem. To address this problem, we propose to learn a complicated non-linear mapping function for spectral super-resolution with deep convolutional neural networks (CNN). It has been shown that the 3-dimensional color vector for a specific pixel can be viewed as the downsampled observation of the corresponding spectrum. Moreover, for a candidate pixel, there often exist abundant locally and no-locally similar pixels (i.e. exhibiting similar spectra) in the spatial domain. As a result, the color vectors corresponding to those similar pixels can be viewed as a group of downsampled observations of the latent spectra for the candidate pixel. Therefore, accurate spectral reconstruction requires to explicitly consider both the local and non-local information from the input RGB image. To this end, we develop a novel multi-scale CNN. Our method jointly encodes the local and non-local image information through symmetrically downsampling and upsampling the intermediate feature maps in a cascading paradigm, thus enhancing the spectral reconstruction accuracy. We experimentally show that the proposed method can be easily trained in an end-to-end scheme and beat several state-of-the-art methods on a large hyperspectral image dataset with respect to various evaluation metrics.

Our contributions are twofold:

- We design a novel CNN architecture that is able to encode both local and non-local information for spectral reconstruction.
- We perform extensive experiments on a large hyperspectral dataset and obtain the state-of-the-art performance.

2   Related Work

This section gives a brief review of the existing spectral super-resolution methods, which can be divided into the following two categories.

Statistic Based Methods. This line of research mainly focus on exploiting the inherent statistical distribution of the latent hyperspectral image as priors to guide the super-resolution [21, 26]. Most of these methods involve building overcomplete dictionaries and learning sparse coding coefficients to linearly combine the dictionary atoms. For example, in [4], Arad *et al.* leveraged image priors to build a dictionary using K-SVD [3]. At test time, orthogonal matching pursuit [15] was used to compute a sparse representation of the input RGB image. [2] proposed a new method inspired by A+ [19], where sparse coefficients are computed by explicitly solving a sparse least square problem. These methods directly exploit the whole image to build image prior, ignoring local and non-local structure information. What's more, since the image prior is often handcrafted or heuristically designed with shallow structure, these methods fail to generalize well in practice.

Learning Based Methods. These methods directly learn a certain mapping function from the RGB image to a corresponding hyperspectral image. For example, [13] proposed a training based method using a radial basis function network. The input data was pre-processed with a white balancing function to alleviate the influence of different illumination. The total reconstruction accuracy is affected by the performance of this pre-processing stage. Recently, witnessing the great success of deep learning in many other ill-posed inverse problems such as image denoising [23] and single image super-resolution [6], it is natural to consider using deep networks (especially convolutional neural networks) for spectral super-resolution. In [7], Galliani *et al.* exploited a variant of fully convolutional DenseNets (FC-DenseNets [9]) for spectral super-resolution. However, this method is sensitive to the hyper-parameters and its performance can still be further improved.

3   Proposed Method

In this section, we will introduce the proposed multi-scale convolution neural network in details. Firstly, we introduce some building blocks which will be utilized in our network. Then, we will illustrate the architecture of the proposed network.

Table 1. Basic building blocks of our network

Double Conv	Downsample
3 × 3 convolution	2 × 2 max-pooling
Batch normalization	
Leaky ReLU	
2D Dropout	
3 × 3 convolution	Upsample
Batch normalization	Pixel shuffle
Leaky ReLU	
2D Dropout	

3.1 Building Blocks

There are three basic building blocks in our network. Their structures are shown in Table 1.

Double convolution (Double Conv) block consists of two 3 × 3 convolutions. Each of them is followed by batch normalization, leaky ReLU and dropout. We exploit batch normalization and dropout to deal with overfitting.

Downsample block contains a regular max-pooling layer. It reduces the spatial size of the feature map and enlarges the receptive field of the network.

Upsample block is utilized to upsample the feature map in the spatial domain. To this end, much previous literature often adopts the transposed convolution. However, it is prone to generate checkboard artifacts. To address this problem, we use the pixel shuffle operation [17]. It has been shown that pixel shuffle alleviates the checkboard artifacts. In addition, due to not introducing any learnable parameters, pixel shuffle also helps improve the robustness against over-fitting.

3.2 Network Architecture

Our method is inspired by the well known U-Net architecture for image segmentation [16]. The overall architecture of the proposed multi-scale convolution neural network is depicted in Fig. 1. The network follows the encoder-decoder pattern. For the **encoder** part, each downsampling step consists of a "Double Conv" with a downsample block. The spatial size is progressively reduced, and the number of features is doubled at each step. The **decoder** is symmetric to the encoder path. Every step in the decoder path consists of an upsampling operation followed by a "Double Conv" block. The spatial size of the features is recovered, while the number of features is halved every step. Finally, a 1 × 1 convolution maps the output features to the reconstructed 31-channel hyperspectral image. In addition to the feedforward path, skip connections are used to concatenate the corresponding feature maps of the encoder and decoder.

Our method naturally fits the task of spectral reconstruction. The encoder can be interpreted as extracting features from RGB images. Through downsampling in a cascade way, the receptive field of the network is constantly increased,

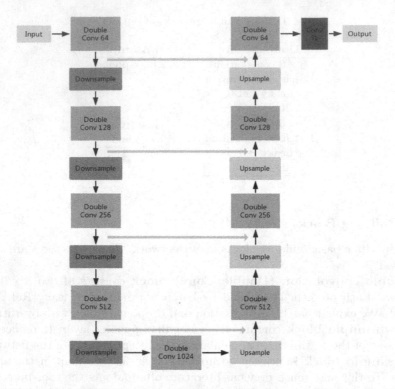

Fig. 1. Diagram of the proposed method. "Conv m" represents convolutional layers with an output of m feature maps. We use 3×3 convolution in green blocks and 1×1 convolution in the red block. Gray arrows represent feature concatenation (Color figure online).

which allows the network to "see" more pixels in an increasingly larger field of view. By doing so, both the local and non-local information can be encoded to better represent the latent spectra. The symmetric decoder procedure is employed to reconstruct the latent hyperspectral images based on these deep and compact features. The skip connections with concatenations are essential for introducing multi-scale information and yielding better estimation of the spectra.

4   Experiments

4.1   Datasets

In this study, all experiments are performed on the NTIRE2018 dataset [1]. This dataset is extended from the ICVL dataset [4]. The ICVL dataset includes 203 images captured using Specim PS Kappa DX4 hyperspectral camera. Each image is of size 1392×1300 in spatial resolution and contains 519 spectral bands in the range of 400–1000 nm. In experiments, 31 successive bands ranging from

Table 2. Quantitative results on each test image.

$RMSE_1$

	BGU_00257	BGU_00259	BGU_00261	BGU_00263	BGU_00265	Average
Interpolation	1.8622	1.7198	2.8419	1.3657	1.9376	1.9454
Arad et al.	1.7930	1.4700	1.6592	1.8987	1.2559	1.6154
A+	1.3054	1.3572	1.3659	1.4884	0.9769	1.2988
Galliani et al.	0.7330	0.7922	0.8606	0.5786	**0.8276**	0.7584
Our	**0.6172**	**0.6865**	0.9425	**0.5049**	0.8375	**0.7177**

$RMSE_2$

	BGU_00257	BGU_00259	BGU_00261	BGU_00263	BGU_00265	Average
Interpolation	3.0774	2.9878	4.1453	2.0874	3.9522	3.2500
Arad et al.	3.4618	2.3534	2.6236	2.5750	2.0169	2.6061
A+	2.1911	1.9572	1.9364	2.0488	1.3344	1.8936
Galliani et al.	1.2381	**1.2077**	**1.2577**	0.8381	**1.6810**	**1.2445**
Ours	**0.9768**	1.3417	1.6035	**0.7396**	1.7879	1.2899

$rRMSE_1$

	BGU_00257	BGU_00259	BGU_00261	BGU_00263	BGU_00265	Average
Interpolation	0.0658	0.0518	0.0732	0.0530	0.0612	0.0610
Arad et al.	0.0807	0.0627	0.0624	0.0662	0.0560	0.0656
A+	0.0580	0.0589	0.0612	0.0614	0.0457	0.0570
Galliani et al.	0.0261	0.0268	0.0254	0.0237	0.0289	0.0262
Ours	**0.0235**	**0.0216**	**0.0230**	**0.0205**	**0.0278**	**0.0233**

$rRMSE_2$

	BGU_00257	BGU_00259	BGU_00261	BGU_00263	BGU_00265	Average
Interpolation	0.1058	0.0933	0.1103	0.0759	0.1338	0.1038
Arad et al.	0.1172	0.0809	0.0819	0.0685	0.0733	0.0844
A+	0.0580	0.0589	0.0612	0.0614	0.0457	0.0610
Galliani et al.	0.0453	**0.0372**	**0.0331**	0.0317	**0.0562**	**0.0407**
Ours	**0.0357**	0.0413	0.0422	**0.0280**	0.0598	0.0414

SAM (degree)

	BGU_00257	BGU_00259	BGU_00261	BGU_00263	BGU_00265	Average
Interpolation	3.9620	3.0304	4.2962	3.1900	3.9281	3.6813
Arad et al.	4.2667	3.7279	3.4726	3.3912	3.3699	3.6457
A+	3.2952	3.5812	3.2952	3.0256	3.2952	3.2985
Galliani et al.	1.4725	1.5013	**1.4802**	1.4844	**1.8229**	1.5523
Ours	**1.3305**	**1.2458**	1.7197	**1.1360**	1.9046	**1.4673**

400–700 nm with 10 nm interval are extracted from each image for evaluation. In the NTIRE2018 challenge, this dataset is further extended by supplementing 53 extra images of the same spatial and spectral resolution. As a result, 256 high-resolution hyperspectral images are collected as the training data. In addition, another 5 hyperspectral images are further introduced as the test set. In the NTIRE2018 dataset, the corresponding RGB rendition is also provided for each image. In the following, we will employ the RGB-hyperspectral image pairs to evaluate the proposed method.

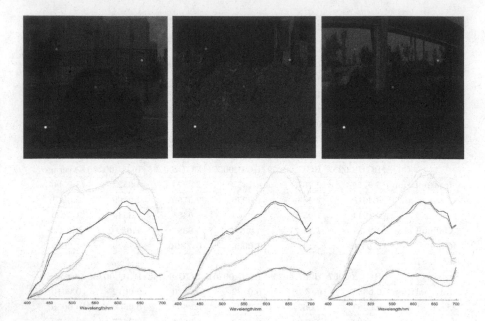

Fig. 2. Sample results of spectral reconstruction by our method. Top line: RGB rendition. Bottom line: groundtruth (solid) and reconstructed (dashed) spectral response of four pixels identified by the dots in RGB images.

4.2   Comparison Methods and Implementation Details

To demonstrate the effectiveness of the proposed method, we compare it with four spectral super-resolution methods, including spline interpolation, the sparse recovery method in [4] (Arad *et al.*), A+ [2], and the deep learning method in [7] (Galliani *et al.*). [2,4] are implemented by the codes released by the authors. Since there is no code released for [7], we reimplement it in this study. In the following, we will give the implementation details of each method.

Spline Interpolation. The interpolation algorithm serves as the most primitive baseline in this study. Specifically, for each RGB pixel $p_l = (r, g, b)$, we use spline interpolation to upsample it and obtain a 31-dimensional spectrum (p_h). According to the visible spectrum[1], the r, g, b values of an RGB pixel are assigned to 700 nm, 550 nm, and 450 nm, respectively.

Arad *et al.* and A+. The low spectral resolution image is assumed to be a directly downsampled version of the corresponding hyperspectral image using some specific linear projection matrix. In [2,4] this matrix is required to be perfectly known. In our experiments, we fit the projection matrix using training data with conventional linear regression.

---

[1] http://www.gamonline.com/catalog/colortheory/visible.php.

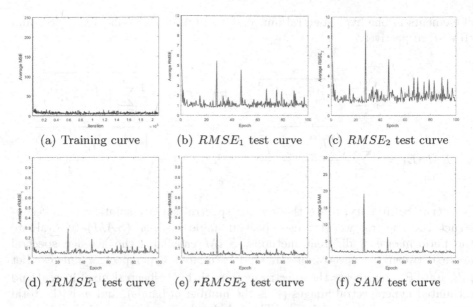

(a) Training curve   (b) $RMSE_1$ test curve   (c) $RMSE_2$ test curve

(d) $rRMSE_1$ test curve   (e) $rRMSE_2$ test curve   (f) SAM test curve

Fig. 3. Training and test curves.

Galliani *et al*. and Our Method. We experimentally find the optimal set of hyper-parameters for both methods. 50% dropout is applied to Galliani *et al*., while our method utilizes 20% dropout rate. All the leaky ReLU activation functions are applied with a negative slope of 0.2. We train the networks for 100 epochs using Adam optimizer with 10^{-6} regularization. Weight initialization and learning rate vary for different methods. For Galliani *et al*., the weights are initialized via HeUniform [8], and the learning rate is set to 2×10^{-3} for the first 50 epochs, decayed to 2×10^{-4} for the next 50 epochs. As for our method, we use HeNormal initialization [8]. The initial learning rate is 5×10^{-5} and is multiplied by 0.93 every 10 epochs. We perform data augmentation by extracting patches of size 64×64 with a stride of 40 pixels from training data. The total amount of training samples is over $267,000$. At the test phase, we directly feed the whole image to the network and get the estimated hyperspectral image in one single forward pass.

4.3 Evaluation Metrics

To quantitatively evaluate the performance of the proposed method, we adopt the following two categories of evaluation metrics.

Pixel-Level Reconstruction Error. We follow [2] to use absolute and relative root-mean-square error (RMSE and rRMSE) as quantitative measurements for reconstruction accuracy. Let $I_h^{(i)}$ and $I_e^{(i)}$ denote the ith element of the real and estimated hyperspectral images, $\bar{I}_h$ is the average of I_h, and n is the total number of elements in one hyperspectral image. There are two formulas for RMSE and rRMSE respectively.

$$RMSE_1 = \frac{1}{n}\sum_{i=1}^{n}\sqrt{\left(I_h^{(i)} - I_e^{(i)}\right)^2} \qquad RMSE_2 = \sqrt{\frac{1}{n}\sum_{i=1}^{n}\left(I_h^{(i)} - I_e^{(i)}\right)^2}$$

$$rRMSE_1 = \frac{1}{n}\sum_{i=1}^{n}\frac{\sqrt{\left(I_h^{(i)} - I_e^{(i)}\right)^2}}{I_h^{(i)}} \qquad rRMSE_2 = \sqrt{\frac{1}{n}\sum_{i=1}^{n}\frac{\left(I_h^{(i)} - I_e^{(i)}\right)^2}{\bar{I}_h^2}}$$

Spectral Similarity. Since the key for spectral super-resolution is to reconstruct the spectra, we also use spectral angle mapper (SAM) to evaluate the performance of different methods. SAM calculates the average spectral angle between the spectra of real and estimated hyperspectral images. Let $p_h^{(j)}, p_e^{(j)} \epsilon \mathbb{R}^C$ represents the spectra of the jth hyperspectral pixel in real and estimated hyperspectral images (C is the number of bands), and m is the total number of pixels within an image. The SAM value can be computed as follows.

$$SAM = \frac{1}{m}cos^{-1}\left(\sum_{j=1}^{m}\frac{(p_h^{(j)})^T \cdot p_e^{(j)}}{\left\|p_h^{(j)}\right\|_2 \cdot \left\|p_e^{(j)}\right\|_2}\right)$$

4.4   Experimental Results

Convergence Analysis. We plot the curve of MSE loss on the training set and the curves of five evaluation metrics computed on the test set in Fig. 3. It can be seen that both the training loss and the value of metrics gradually decrease and ultimately converge with the proceeding of the training. This demonstrates that the proposed multi-scale convolution neural network converges well.

Quantitative Results. Table 2 provides the quantitative results of our method and all baseline methods. It can be seen that our model outperforms all competitors with regards to $RMSE_1$ and $rRMSE_1$, and produces comparable results to Galliani *et al.* on $RMSE_2$ and $rRMSE_2$. More importantly, our method surpasses all the others with respect to spectral angle mapper. This clearly proves that our model reconstructs spectra more accurately than other competitors. It is worth pointing out that reconstruction error (absolute and relative $RMSE$) is not necessarily positively correlated with spectral angle mapper (SAM). For example, when the pixels of an image are shuffled, $RMSE$ and $rRMSE$ will remain the same, while SAM will change completely. According to the results in Table 2, we can find that our finely designed network enhances spectral super-resolution from both aspects, *viz.*, yielding better results on both average root-mean-square error and spectral angle similarity.

Fig. 4. Visualization of absolute reconstruction error. From left to right: RGB rendition, A+, Galliani *et al.*, and our method

Visual Results. To further clarify the superiority in reconstruction accuracy. We show the absolute reconstruction error of test images in Fig. 4. The error is summarized over all bands of the hyperspectral image. Since A+ outperforms Arad *et al.* in terms of any evaluation metric, we use A+ to represent the sparse coding methods. It can be seen that our method yields smoother reconstructed images as well as lower reconstruction error than other competitors.

In addition, we randomly choose three test images and plot the real and reconstructed spectra for four pixels in Fig. 2 to further demonstrate the effectiveness of the proposed method in spectrum reconstruction. It can be seen that only slight difference exists between the reconstructed spectra and the ground truth.

According to these results above, we can conclude that the proposed method is effective in spectral super-resolution and outperforms several state-of-the-art competitors.

5 Conclusion

In this study, we show that leveraging both the local and non-local information of input images is essential for the accurate spectral reconstruction. Following this idea, we design a novel multi-scale convolutional neural network, which employs a symmetrically cascaded downsampling-upsampling architecture to jointly encode the local and non-local image information for spectral reconstruction. With extensive experiments on a large hyperspectral images dataset, the proposed method clearly outperforms several state-of-the-art methods in terms of reconstruction accuracy and spectral similarity.

Acknowledgement. This work was supported in part by the National Natural Science Foundation of China (No. 61671385, 61571354), Natural Science Basis Research Plan in Shaanxi Province of China (No. 2017JM6021, 2017JM6001) and China Postdoctoral Science Foundation under Grant (No. 158201).

References

1. NTIRE 2018 challenge on spectral reconstruction from RGB images. http://www.vision.ee.ethz.ch/ntire18/
2. Aeschbacher, J., Wu, J., Timofte, R.: In defense of shallow learned spectral reconstruction from RGB images. In: Proceedings of the IEEE Conference on Computer Vision and Pattern Recognition, pp. 471–479 (2017)
3. Aharon, M., Elad, M., Bruckstein, A.: rmk-SVD: an algorithm for designing overcomplete dictionaries for sparse representation. IEEE Trans. Signal Process. **54**(11), 4311–4322 (2006)
4. Arad, B., Ben-Shahar, O.: Sparse recovery of hyperspectral signal from natural RGB images. In: Leibe, B., Matas, J., Sebe, N., Welling, M. (eds.) ECCV 2016. LNCS, vol. 9911, pp. 19–34. Springer, Cham (2016). https://doi.org/10.1007/978-3-319-46478-7_2
5. Cheng, G., Yang, C., Yao, X., Guo, L., Han, J.: When deep learning meets metric learning: remote sensing image scene classification via learning discriminative CNNs. IEEE Trans. Geosci. Remote. Sens. **56**, 2811–2821 (2018)
6. Dong, C., Loy, C.C., He, K., Tang, X.: Image super-resolution using deep convolutional networks. IEEE Trans. Pattern Anal. Mach. Intell. **38**(2), 295–307 (2016)
7. Galliani, S., Lanaras, C., Marmanis, D., Baltsavias, E., Schindler, K.: Learned spectral super-resolution. CoRR abs/1703.09470 (2017). http://arxiv.org/abs/1703.09470
8. He, K., Zhang, X., Ren, S., Sun, J.: Delving deep into rectifiers: surpassing human-level performance on imagenet classification. In: Proceedings of the IEEE International Conference on Computer Vision, pp. 1026–1034 (2015)
9. Jégou, S., Drozdzal, M., Vazquez, D., Romero, A., Bengio, Y.: The one hundred layers tiramisu: fully convolutional densenets for semantic segmentation. In: 2017 IEEE Conference on Computer Vision and Pattern Recognition Workshops (CVPRW), pp. 1175–1183. IEEE (2017)
10. Kang, X., Zhang, X., Li, S., Li, K., Li, J., Benediktsson, J.A.: Hyperspectral anomaly detection with attribute and edge-preserving filters. IEEE Trans. Geosci. Remote. Sens. **55**(10), 5600–5611 (2017)
11. Loncan, L., et al.: Hyperspectral pansharpening: a review. IEEE Geosci. Remote. Sens. Mag. **3**(3), 27–46 (2015)
12. Mei, S., Yuan, X., Ji, J., Zhang, Y., Wan, S., Du, Q.: Hyperspectral image spatial super-resolution via 3D full convolutional neural network. Remote Sens. **9**(11), 1139 (2017)

13. Nguyen, R.M.H., Prasad, D.K., Brown, M.S.: Training-based spectral reconstruction from a single RGB image. In: Fleet, D., Pajdla, T., Schiele, B., Tuytelaars, T. (eds.) ECCV 2014. LNCS, vol. 8695, pp. 186–201. Springer, Cham (2014). https://doi.org/10.1007/978-3-319-10584-0_13

14. Pan, Z., Healey, G., Prasad, M., Tromberg, B.: Face recognition in hyperspectral images. IEEE Trans. Pattern Anal. Mach. Intell. 25(12), 1552–1560 (2003)

15. Pati, Y.C., Rezaiifar, R., Krishnaprasad, P.S.: Orthogonal matching pursuit: recursive function approximation with applications to wavelet decomposition. In: 1993 Conference Record of The Twenty-Seventh Asilomar Conference on Signals, Systems and Computers, pp. 40–44. IEEE (1993)

16. Ronneberger, O., Fischer, P., Brox, T.: U-Net: convolutional networks for biomedical image segmentation. In: Navab, N., Hornegger, J., Wells, W.M., Frangi, A.F. (eds.) MICCAI 2015. LNCS, vol. 9351, pp. 234–241. Springer, Cham (2015). https://doi.org/10.1007/978-3-319-24574-4_28

17. Shi, W., et al.: Real-time single image and video super-resolution using an efficient sub-pixel convolutional neural network. In: Proceedings of the IEEE Conference on Computer Vision and Pattern Recognition, pp. 1874–1883 (2016)

18. Tarabalka, Y., Chanussot, J., Benediktsson, J.A.: Segmentation and classification of hyperspectral images using watershed transformation. Pattern Recogn. 43(7), 2367–2379 (2010)

19. Timofte, R., De Smet, V., Van Gool, L.: A+: adjusted anchored neighborhood regression for fast super-resolution. In: Cremers, D., Reid, I., Saito, H., Yang, M.-H. (eds.) ACCV 2014. LNCS, vol. 9006, pp. 111–126. Springer, Cham (2015). https://doi.org/10.1007/978-3-319-16817-3_8

20. Van Nguyen, H., Banerjee, A., Chellappa, R.: Tracking via object reflectance using a hyperspectral video camera. In: 2010 IEEE Computer Society Conference on Computer Vision and Pattern Recognition Workshops (CVPRW), pp. 44–51. IEEE (2010)

21. Yan, Q., Sun, J., Li, H., Zhu, Y., Zhang, Y.: High dynamic range imaging by sparse representation. Neurocomputing 269, 160–169 (2017)

22. Yokoya, N., Grohnfeldt, C., Chanussot, J.: Hyperspectral and multispectral data fusion: a comparative review of the recent literature. IEEE Geosci. Remote. Sens. Mag. 5(2), 29–56 (2017)

23. Zhang, K., Zuo, W., Chen, Y., Meng, D., Zhang, L.: Beyond a Gaussian denoiser: residual learning of deep CNN for image denoising. IEEE Trans. Image Process. 26(7), 3142–3155 (2017)

24. Zhang, L., et al.: Adaptive importance learning for improving lightweight image super-resolution network. arXiv preprint arXiv:1806.01576 (2018)

25. Zhang, L., Wei, W., Bai, C., Gao, Y., Zhang, Y.: Exploiting clustering manifold structure for hyperspectral imagery super-resolution. IEEE Trans. Image Process. 27, 5969–5982 (2018)

26. Zhang, L., Wei, W., Shi, Q., Shen, C., Hengel, A.v.d., Zhang, Y.: Beyond low rank: a data-adaptive tensor completion method. arXiv preprint arXiv:1708.01008 (2017)

27. Zhang, L., Wei, W., Zhang, Y., Shen, C., van den Hengel, A., Shi, Q.: Cluster sparsity field: an internal hyperspectral imagery prior for reconstruction. Int. J. Comput. Vis. 1–25 (2018)

Dynamic Facial Expression Recognition Based on Trained Convolutional Neural Networks

Ming Li[1,2,3] and Zengfu Wang[1,2,3]($\boxtimes$)

[1] Institute of Intelligent Machines, Chinese Academy of Sciences, Hefei, Anhui, China
[2] University of Science and Technology of China, Hefei, Anhui, China
lm910415@mail.ustc.edu.cn, zfwang@ustc.edu.cn
[3] National Engineering Laboratory for Speech and Language Information Processing, Hefei, China

Abstract. Recently, dynamic facial expression recognition in videos receives more and more attention. In this paper, we propose a method based on trained convolutional neural networks for dynamic facial expression recognition. In our system, we improve Deep Dense Face Detector (DDFD) developed by Yahoo to reduce training parameters. The LBP feature maps of facial expression images are selected as the inputs of the designed network architecture which is fine-tuned on FER2013 dataset. The trained network model is considered as a feature extractor to extract the features of inputs. In an image sequence, the mean, variance, maximun and minimum of feature vectors over all frames are calculated according to its dimensions and combined into a vector as the feature. Finally, Support Vector Machine is used for classification. Our method achieves a recognition accuracy of 53.27% on the AFEW 6.0 validation set, surpassing the baseline of 38.81% with a significant gain of 14.46%. The experimental results verify the effectiveness of our method.

Keywords: Dynamic facial expression recognition · Face detection
Convolutional neural networks · Local Binary Patterns
Support Vector Machine

1 Introduction

With the rapid development of the biometric identification technology, facial expression recognition has attracted much attention. Automatic facial expression recognition has been an active research topic in computer vision and pattern recognition. It has enormous potential for development and can be used in intelligent human-computer interaction, mass entertainment, safe driving, medical assistance, online education, etc. Facial expression recognition aims to classify a given facial image or video into six prototypical categories (angry, disgust, fear, happy, sad and surprise). Automatic, accurate and real-time dynamic facial

© Springer Nature Switzerland AG 2018
J.-H. Lai et al. (Eds.): PRCV 2018, LNCS 11257, pp. 218–226, 2018.
https://doi.org/10.1007/978-3-030-03335-4_19

expression recognition is still a challenge due to the complexity and variation of facial expressions.

Traditional facial expression recognition methods are mostly based on hand-crafted features. It takes a lot of time to design features. There are three main streams in the current research on facial expression recognition: geometry-based, texture-based and hybrid-based. The appearance of deep learning introduces facial expression recognition to a new stage. Specifically, convolutional neural networks have made breakthroughs in object detection, image recognition and many other computer vision tasks. It has become the prevalent entry solutions in recent facial expression recognition.

However, most of facial expression recognition methods have been performed on laboratory controlled data, which pooly represents the environment and conditions faced in real-world situations. To promote the development of emotion recognition under uncontrolled conditions, the Emotion Recognition in the Wild (EmotiW) challenge [3–7] has been held from 2013 by ACM. The goal of EmotiW challenge is to provide a common platform for evaluation of emotion recognition methods in real-world conditions. In the past five years, a large number of methods have been proposed for dynamic facial expression recognition. Yao [19] analyzed spontaneously expressed emotions from the perspective of making a deep exploration of expression-specific AU-aware features and their latent relations. [9] proposed a hybrid network that combines recurrent neural network and 3D convolutional neural networks in a late-fusion fashion. HoloNet combined CReLU, residual structure and inception-residual structure to produce a deep yet computational efficient convolutional neural network for emotion recognition in the wild [18]. Hu presented a new learning method named Supervised Scoring Ensemble (SSE) [12] for advancing EmotiW challenge with deep convolutional neural networks.

In this paper, we propose a novel dynamic facial expression recognition method based on trained convolutional neural networks. The primary contributions of this work can be summarized as follows: 1. Based on the multi-view face detection algorithm developed by Yahoo [10], we improve the performance and reduce the training parameters by changing its network architecture and establishing a more appropriate face database. 2. The Local Binary Patterns (LBP) [15] feature maps are selected as the inputs of the designed network architecture. We try to explore the performance of network using different types of input. 3. The trained convolutional neural network model is considered as a feature extractor to capture the features of the inputs. Then, in an image sequence, the mean, variance, maximum and minimum of feature vectors over all frames are calculated according to its dimensions and combined into a vector as the feature. Finally, Support Vector Machine (SVM) [2] is utilized for classification. Our method only uses a single network model and achieves a recognition accuracy of 53.27% on the AFEW 6.0 validation set, surpassing the baseline of 38.81% with a significant gain of 14.46%.

The rest of this paper is organized as follows. Section 2 describes the proposed method, including preprocessing, network architecture, fine-tune training,

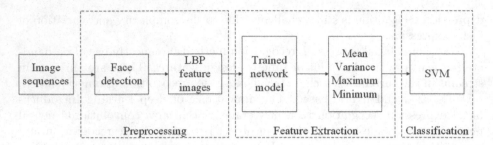

Fig. 1. Framework of the proposed dynamic facial expression recognition method.

feature extraction and facial expression classification. In Sect. 3, we evaluate our scheme and compare it with other methods. Finally, conclusions are presented in Sect. 4.

2   The Proposed Method

The framework of the proposed method is shown in Fig. 1. It consists of three parts: preprocessing, feature extraction and classification. In what follows, we will give the detailed descriptions for each part.

2.1   Preprocessing

The preprocessing procedure consists of three steps. First, we use a improved DDFD multi-view face detector to locate target faces from all frames in a facial expression sequence. And the frames without faces are directly discarded. Second, the detected facial images are resized to match the input size of our designed network architecture. Third, the facial images are converted to its corresponding LBP feature maps, which are feed to the network.

Traditional face detection algorithms only detect frontal or close-to-frontal faces. However, humans have various head posture changes in the wild, which requires multi-view face detector. So we adopt DDFD face detection algorithm and make some improvements. The original DDFD algorithm only uses a single model based on deep convolutional neural networks. And it has minimal complexity and does not require additional components for segmentation, bounding-box regression, or SVM classifiers.

The network architecture of DDFD algorithm is similar to AlexNet, which contains relatively large convolution kernels, such as 5×5, 11×11. They bring more weight parameters. Therefore, we change the network architecture to reduce the amount of parameters. Specifically, we replace a 5×5 kernel with two concatenated 3×3 kernels, and replace a 11×11 kernel with five concatenated 3×3 kernels (see Fig. 2). At the same time, 1×1 kernel can decrease the feature maps and achieves cross-channel information integration. This design can reduce the parameters and improve the nonlinearity of the network. Compared

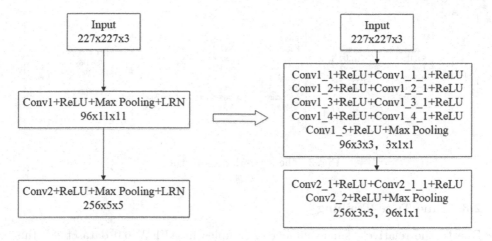

Fig. 2. The improved network architecture in relatively large convolution kernels.

with original network, the parameters of the first and second convolutional layer are reduced by 59% and 24%, respectively. Moreover, it increases the depth of the network and contributes to learn features.

In addition, the number of positive and negative samples used by DDFD algorithm is quite different. And the positive samples are randomly sampled sub-windows of the images if they have more than a 50% IOU (intersection over union) with the ground truth, which is insufficient to express faces. So we build a new face detection dataset. It contains 91067 face images and 96555 non-face images. The face images are cropped by IOU>= 0.65 from AFLW [13] dataset. And the non-face images are sampled and selected from the PASCAL VOC2012 dataset.

2.2 Network Architecture

In our work, we only train a single network architecture: VGG-Face [16]. It is a network model based on convolutional neural network proposed by the Institute of Visual Studies at Oxford University for face recognition. Figure 3 gives the details of the network architecture that contains 13 convolutional layers and 3 fully connected layers. Each convolutional layer is followed by ReLU activation function and a max-pooling layer, which adds nonlinearity to the network and reduces the dimension of feature maps. And all the convolutional kernels are 3×3. Besides, we use dropout in the first two fully connected layers to reduce over-fitting of the network. The input to the network is a LBP feature map of size 224×224 with the average face image (computed from the training set) subtracted.

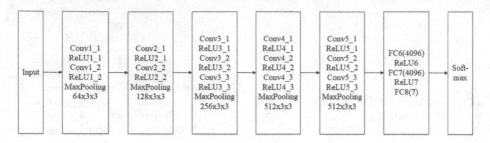

Fig. 3. The network architecture.

2.3 Fine-Tune Training

Due to the relatively small number of samples in AFEW 6.0 dataset [8], the network is fine-tuned on FER2013 dataset [11]. The trained VGG-Face model is regarded as pre-training model, whose weight parameters are used to initialize the network. And the initial learning rate of the network should not be set too large. The learning rate is initially set to 10^{-4} and decreased by factor of 10. Optimisation is by stochastic gradient descent using mini-batches of 64 samples and momentum coefficient of 0.9. The coefficient of weight decay is set to 5×10^{-4}, and dropout is applied with a rate of 0.5.

2.4 Feature Extraction

Different from traditional feature extraction methods, the features are extracted based on trained convolutional neural network (see Fig. 4). For an image sequence, the LBP feature map of each frame is feed to the trained network model for extracting features. Then, we choose the feature maps of fully connected layer 6 (fc6) from the network as the feature vector of the input image. The dimension of the feature vector is 4096.

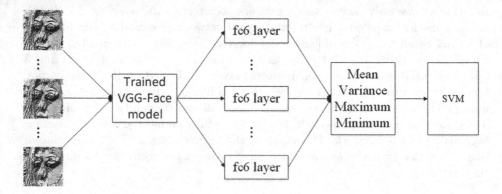

Fig. 4. The process of feature extraction.

After the above process, the set of feature vectors from all frames can be obtained. Then, we attempt to make use of these frame-level feature vectors to represent the image sequences. In an image sequence, the mean, variance, maximum and minimum of feature vectors over all frames are calculated according to its dimensions and combined into a vector. Its dimension is $16384(4096 \times 4)$. Finally, the vectors are normalized as the feature representation.

2.5   Facial Expression Classification

After extracting features, we train a Support Vector Machine (SVM) to give each sequence one of the seven emotion classes. Facial expression recognition is a multi-class problem, so we use LIBSVM with the Radial Basis Function (RBF) kernel for classification. To evaluate the performance of our method, we use 5-fold cross-validation, 10-fold cross-validation, 15-fold cross-validation and leave-one-out cross-validation schemes in our work.

3   Experiments

3.1   Datasets

In order to train the network model and evaluate the performance of the proposed method, we adopt two datasets: FER2013 dataset and AFEW 6.0 dataset.

FER2013 dataset. It's a large and publicly available facial expression dataset. The dataset contains 28709 training images, 3589 validation images and 3589 test images. All images are grayscale and have a resolution of 48×48 pixels. Each image is labeled with one of seven expressions: anger, disgust, fear, happy, sad, surprise or neutral. In our experiments, the dataset is used to fine-tune the network model.

AFEW 6.0 dataset. The Acted Facial Expressions in the Wild (AFEW) 6.0 Dataset is the official dataset provided by the EmotiW 2016. It consists of 1749 video clips, which are split into three parts: 773 samples for training, 383 samples for validation and 593 samples for test. All video clips are collected from Hollywood real movie records and reality TV clips. Therefore, there are numerous variations in head pose movements, lighting, background, occlusion, etc. Only samples for training and validation have emotional labels, which are categorized into seven classes: anger, disgust, fear, happy, sad, surprise and neutral. Due to the lack of emotional labels in test set, we conduct our experiments on the training and validation sets.

3.2   Experimental Results

The experiments consist of two parts: fine-tuning training experiment and dynamic expression recognition experiment. Then, we analyze the experimental results of the two parts.

Fine-Tuning Training Experiment. Table 1 shows the recognition accuracy fine-tuned on FER2013 dataset. Compared with other methods, our experimental result is also acceptable. We achieve a recognition accuracy of 71.28% on FER2013 test set. The humans accuracy on this dataset is around 65.5%, and our method exceeds 5.78% of it.

Table 1. Recognition accuracy fine-tuned on FER2013 dataset

Method	Recognition accuracy (%)
Tang [17]	71.20
Yu [20]	72.03
Mollahosseini [14]	66.4 ± 0.6
Ours	71.28

Dynamic Facial Expression Experiment. We combine the training set and validation set of AFEW 6.0 dataset. Then, we use 5-fold cross-validation (5-fold-CV), 10-fold cross-validation (10-fold-CV), 15-fold cross-validation (15-fold-CV) and leave-one-out cross-validation (LOO-CV) schemes to conduct experiments, respectively. Table 2 presents the recognition accuracy using different schemes. As shown in Table 2, when 15-fold-CV is adopted, the recognition accuracy is highest.

Table 2. The recognition accuracy using different schemes.

Schemes	Recognition accuracy (%)
5-fold-CV	52.17
10-fold-CV	52.83
15-fold-CV	53.75
LOO-CV	52.76

In order to compare with other methods, we use SVM to train facial expression classifier on AFEW 6.0 training set. Then, the classifier is utilized to test the samples from AFEW 6.0 validation set. We get a recognition accuracy of 53.27% which surpasses the baseline of 38.81% with a significant gain of 14.46%. The experimental results compared with other method are shown in Table 3. The recognition accuracy of our method is better than the first and second place in EmotiW 2016 challenge, but we still have a certain gap from [1]. The reason may be that they trained a better network model using additional dataset. In addition, we use original expressional images as the inputs of the network, and obtain a recognition accuracy of 51.57%. It means that the LBP feature maps are helpful for facial expression recognition, which also explains the impact of different inputs on network performance.

Table 3. Comparisons with different approaches on AFEW 6.0 validation set.

Method	Recognition accuracy (%)
Baseline	38.81
Fan [9]	51.96
Yao [18]	51.96
Bargal [1]	59.42
Ours	53.27

4   Conclusions

In this paper, we propose a novel method for dynamic facial expression recognition in the wild. The original DDFD face detection algorithm is improved in network architecture to reduce the parameters and increase the nonlinearity of the network. We use the LBP feature maps of expressional images as the inputs of the network architecture which is fine-tuned on FER2013 dataset. Then, the trained network model is used to extract feature of one sequence. The experimental results verify the effectiveness of our method. In the feature, we will select other network models to extract different features to enhance the representation of the facial expressions. Besides, we will integrate audio information, language information and behavioral information to help facial expression recognition.

Acknowledgement. This work is supported by National Natural Science Foundation of China (No: 61472393).

References

1. Bargal, S.A., Barsoum, E., Ferrer, C.C., Zhang, C.: Emotion recognition in the wild from videos using images. In: Proceedings of the 18th ACM International Conference on Multimodal Interaction, pp. 433–436. ACM (2016)
2. Chang, C.C., Lin, C.J.: LIBSVM: a library for support vector machines. ACM Trans. Intell. Syst. Technol. (TIST) **2**(3), 27 (2011)
3. Dhall, A., Goecke, R., Ghosh, S., Joshi, J., Hoey, J., Gedeon, T.: From individual to group-level emotion recognition: EmotiW 5.0. In: Proceedings of the 19th ACM International Conference on Multimodal Interaction, pp. 524–528. ACM (2017)
4. Dhall, A., Goecke, R., Joshi, J., Hoey, J., Gedeon, T.: EmotiW 2016: video and group-level emotion recognition challenges. In: Proceedings of the 18th ACM International Conference on Multimodal Interaction, pp. 427–432. ACM (2016)
5. Dhall, A., Goecke, R., Joshi, J., Sikka, K., Gedeon, T.: Emotion recognition in the wild challenge 2014: baseline, data and protocol. In: Proceedings of the 16th International Conference on Multimodal Interaction, pp. 461–466. ACM (2014)
6. Dhall, A., Goecke, R., Joshi, J., Wagner, M., Gedeon, T.: Emotion recognition in the wild challenge 2013. In: Proceedings of the 15th ACM on International Conference on Multimodal Interaction, pp. 509–516. ACM (2013)

7. Dhall, A., Ramana Murthy, O., Goecke, R., Joshi, J., Gedeon, T.: Video and image based emotion recognition challenges in the wild: EmotiW 2015. In: Proceedings of the 2015 ACM on International Conference on Multimodal Interaction, pp. 423–426. ACM (2015)
8. Dhall, A., et al.: Collecting large, richly annotated facial-expression databases from movies (2012)
9. Fan, Y., Lu, X., Li, D., Liu, Y.: Video-based emotion recognition using CNN-RNN and C3D hybrid networks. In: Proceedings of the 18th ACM International Conference on Multimodal Interaction, pp. 445–450. ACM (2016)
10. Farfade, S.S., Saberian, M.J., Li, L.J.: Multi-view face detection using deep convolutional neural networks. In: Proceedings of the 5th ACM on International Conference on Multimedia Retrieval, pp. 643–650. ACM (2015)
11. Goodfellow, I.J., et al.: Challenges in representation learning: a report on three machine learning contests. In: Lee, M., Hirose, A., Hou, Z.-G., Kil, R.M. (eds.) ICONIP 2013. LNCS, vol. 8228, pp. 117–124. Springer, Heidelberg (2013). https://doi.org/10.1007/978-3-642-42051-1_16
12. Hu, P., Cai, D., Wang, S., Yao, A., Chen, Y.: Learning supervised scoring ensemble for emotion recognition in the wild. In: Proceedings of the 19th ACM International Conference on Multimodal Interaction, pp. 553–560. ACM (2017)
13. Koestinger, M., Wohlhart, P., Roth, P.M., Bischof, H.: Annotated facial landmarks in the wild: a large-scale, real-world database for facial landmark localization. In: 2011 IEEE International Conference on Computer Vision Workshops (ICCV Workshops), pp. 2144–2151. IEEE (2011)
14. Mollahosseini, A., Chan, D., Mahoor, M.H.: Going deeper in facial expression recognition using deep neural networks. In: 2016 IEEE Winter Conference on Applications of Computer Vision (WACV), pp. 1–10. IEEE (2016)
15. Ojala, T., Pietikainen, M., Maenpaa, T.: Multiresolution gray-scale and rotation invariant texture classification with local binary patterns. IEEE Trans. Pattern Anal. Mach. Intell. **24**(7), 971–987 (2002)
16. Parkhi, O.M., Vedaldi, A., Zisserman, A., et al.: Deep face recognition. In: BMVC. vol. 1, p. 6 (2015)
17. Tang, Y.: Deep learning using linear support vector machines. arXiv preprint arXiv:1306.0239 (2013)
18. Yao, A., Cai, D., Hu, P., Wang, S., Sha, L., Chen, Y.: HoloNet: towards robust emotion recognition in the wild. In: Proceedings of the 18th ACM International Conference on Multimodal Interaction, pp. 472–478. ACM (2016)
19. Yao, A., Shao, J., Ma, N., Chen, Y.: Capturing au-aware facial features and their latent relations for emotion recognition in the wild. In: Proceedings of the 2015 ACM on International Conference on Multimodal Interaction, pp. 451–458. ACM (2015)
20. Yu, Z., Zhang, C.: Image based static facial expression recognition with multiple deep network learning. In: Proceedings of the 2015 ACM on International Conference on Multimodal Interaction, pp. 435–442. ACM (2015)

Nuclei Classification Using Dual View CNNs with Multi-crop Module in Histology Images

Xiang Li, Wei Li$^{(\boxtimes)}$, and Mengmeng Zhang

College of Information Science and Technology,
Beijing University of Chemical Technology, Beijing 100029, China
liwei089@ieee.org

Abstract. Histopathology image diagnostic technique is a quite common requirement; however, cell nuclei classification is still one of key challenge due to complex tissue structure and diversity of nuclear morphology. Cell nuclei categories are often defined by contextual information, including central nucleus and surrounding background. In this paper, we propose a Dual-View Convolutional Neural Networks (DV-CNNs) that captures contextual contents from different views. The DV-CNNs are composed of two independent pathways, one for global region and another for center local region. Noted that each pathway with "multi-crop module" can extract five different feature regions. Common networks do not fully utilize the local information, but the designed cropping module catches information for more complete features. In experiments, two pipelines are complementary to each other in score fusion. To verify the performance in proposed framework, it is evaluated on a colorectal adenocarcinoma image database with more than 20,000 nuclei. Compared with existing methods, our proposed DV-CNNs with multi-crop module demonstrate better performance.

Keywords: Histopathology image analysis
Convolutional neural network · Cell nuclei classification

1 Introduction

Histopathology is the most commonly used microscopic research for the diagnosis of cancer diseases. The cancer tissues are sampled from the body and then prepared for observing under the microscope. Stained with the standard hematoxylin and eosin (H&E) stain [1] can mark nuclei in histopathology images of cancer tissues, and pathologists need to identify the type of nuclei. The recognition of cell nuclei in histopathology images become one of the core challenge

This work was supported by the National Natural Science Foundation of China under Grant No. NSFC-61571033, Beijing Natural Science Foundation (4172043), Beijing Nova Program (Z171100001117050), and partly by the Fundamental Research Funds for the Central Universities (BUCTRC201615).

© Springer Nature Switzerland AG 2018
J.-H. Lai et al. (Eds.): PRCV 2018, LNCS 11257, pp. 227–236, 2018.
https://doi.org/10.1007/978-3-030-03335-4_20

for qualitative and quantitative analysis at cell levels [5]. A single histopathology image may contain about thousands of nuclei, and pathologists are incapable of identifying all nuclei precisely. Traditional approach requires experienced pathologists to manually identify the cell, which is extremely laborious. Consequently, developing an automatic and reliable method [8] for classification tasks becomes an attractive research topic and automated images classification will allow pathologists to quickly obtain the specific information which can increase objectivity and less burden on observers.

Most of the existing automated attribute classification techniques for cells in histology images include two aspects, i.e., traditional machine learning methods and convolutional neural network (CNNs) [13]. Kumar et al. proposed a k-nearest neighbor based method for microscopic biopsy images, and the efficacy of other classifiers such as SVM, random forest, and fuzzy k-means was examined [12]. Recently, deep convolutional neural networks appear to be attracting considerable attention due to its excellent performance on visual recognition task. Different from traditional approaches, CNNs act more dynamically to provide multilevel hierarchies of features, have been extensively employed for histopathology image classification. Malon et al. [9] combined manually designed nuclear features with the learned features extracted by CNN which handled the variety of appearances of mitotic figures and decreased sensitivity to the manually crafted features and thresholds [16].

Different from usual scene classification, cell nuclei classification belongs to fine-grained image categorization which aims to classify sub-categories, such as different species of dogs. Therefore, variability in the appearance of the same type of nuclei is a critical factor that makes classification of individual nucleus equivalently difficult. Pathologists analyze the cell nuclei of the histopathological images, looking for detailed texture around nucleus and the shape of the nucleus [15,17]. So in cell nuclei recognition, nuclei categories are often defined by local nuclei and global background around nuclei. But existing classification approaches are limited in considering different region of cell nuclei. In this paper, we present a Dual View convolutional neural networks by employing a dual network strategy to classify nuclei in routine H&E stained histopathology images of colon cancer. To be specific, CNNs at global way are able to capture cell background information, while CNNs at local way are capable of describing local details of center nucleus. Meanwhile, multi-crop module is added to the two subnets, which can catch diverse feature regions. DV-CNNs with multi-crop module integrate complementary diagnostic criteria of different hierarchy concepts, allowing them to explore the intrinsic connection between cellular background and nucleus.

We design different experiments to ensure a fair comparison. And the experimental results demonstrate that multiple feature regions around nuclei and different image views are important for cell nuclei classification in histopathology images and show superior performance to current methods on the HistoPhenotypes datasets.

2   Nuclei Classification Framework

Cell nuclei classification always couples global background with local part in a diagnosis. We need to consider this contextual information of histopathology images during building models. In order to address these challenges, we utilize the CNNs to propose an effective architecture that dual views of images are first conducted and then send to two branches for attaining multiple feature regions. In this section, we first describe the framework of DV-CNNs and then discuss multi-crop module.

2.1   Dual View Convolutional Neural Networks

To derive an efficient classifier in cell nuclei images, we need to overcome the challenge posed by variability in the appearance of the same type of nuclei [10]. Pathologists analyze the cell nuclei by looking for detailed texture around nucleus and the shape of the nucleus and then determine the possible nuclei type. Following the pathologist's experiences [11], we propose DV-CNNs as illustrated in Fig. 1.

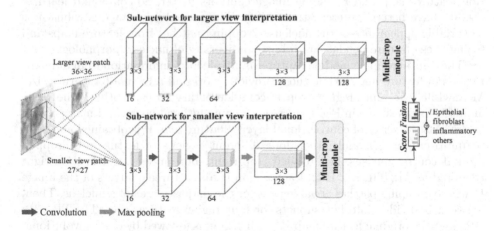

Fig. 1. The overall flowchart of the proposed Dual View CNNs.

The proposed model offers a dual view of images, with one pathway considering information from the larger area around the nucleus and another pathway focusing on local, nucleus level information. We observe contexts in the cell nuclei imagery, where nucleus is relatively small and it is easy to include larger region as input. If we focus only on larger region, the specific attributes of the nucleus will be ignored, and vice versa. The proposed approach is based on multiple cues extracted from a dual view of images such as the background and the center nuclei features, and then, they provide each other with complementary features to avoid missing important diagnostic information.

In this framework, two pathways process images in parallel. Then, two individual networks are concatenated to combine extracted features. As illustrated in Fig. 1, they are designed to describe cell nuclei at different views for contextual understanding. We feed larger view patches 36×36 and smaller view patches 27×27 to two sub-network to extract different features, respectively. For two sub-networks, each 3×3 convolution layer is followed with the Rectified Linear Unit activation layer and Batch Normalization layer [4]. A 2×2 max pooling operation with stride 2 for reducing half. Multi-cropping modules are added to two pathways, and next section will have detailed introduction about this module. Finally, the prediction results of our models are complementary to each other by fusing scores.

2.2   Multi-cropping Module

After feature extraction in both larger region and center local region, multi-crop module is discussed as shown in Fig. 2. There are two reasons by utilizing multi-crop module. The first reason is uncertainty of the central location of the nucleus. Input images with the same size but of different central location of the nucleus display different feature representations. Combinations of different location features help understanding image contents better. So compound features usually have better representation ability. The second advantage is robustness to variable appearance of the nucleus. Cropping patches from feature maps and fusing these feature patches are robust to diversity of nuclear morphology.

The multi-cropping module captures multiple local information from different regions in feature maps, while those previous works all rely on a fix feature size. Meanwhile, the multi-region crop is complementary to each other. The basic architecture as shown in Fig. 1 starts with convolutional layers and max pooling layers. After a series of convolutional layers, feature map P is obtained and send to multi-cropping module, then four different regions of feature are cropped around central nucleus, i.e., top-left, top-right, bottom-left, and bottom-right (denoted as TL, TR, BL, BR). Each region is about three quarters of the image P, where cropping patches are able to cover the majority area of a nucleus. Then, network is divided into five subnets for four region features (i.e., TL, TR, BL, BR) and the original feature map P. Each region is followed by one convolutional layer and a global average pooling layer. Batch Normalization layer is applied to the activations of convolutional layers, following by the ReLU layer for non-linearity. Those five networks produce five output as F_{TL}, F_{TR}, F_{BL}, F_{BR}, F_P, respectively. Finally, those five outputs are concatenated as,

$$Z = F_{TL} \oplus F_{TR} \oplus F_{BL} \oplus F_{BR} \oplus F_P, \tag{1}$$

where Z combines comprehensive information derived from different regions. Suppose the number of categories is N, then z is expanded to $N \times 1$ vector, named as $\tilde{z}$. The probability of each category is calculated as follows,

$$\sigma(\tilde{z})_j = \frac{e^{\tilde{z}_j}}{\sum_{k=1}^{N} e^{\tilde{z}_k}}, \tag{2}$$

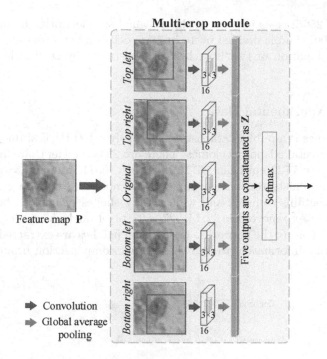

Fig. 2. Multi-cropping module in detail.

where $\tilde{z}_j$ is the j th value of $N \times 1$ vector. After a softmax layer, $\sigma(\tilde{z}_{global})_j$ and $\sigma(\tilde{z}_{local})_j$ are obtained. Finally, the prediction results of $\sigma(\tilde{z}_{global})_j$ and $\sigma(\tilde{z}_{local})_j$ are complementary to each other by fusing them. And the losses between outputs and label is computed through categorical cross entropy loss function. In the nuclei classification framework, the proposed DV-CNNs model is based on multiple cues extracted from dual views of images, plus multi-region features of the branch networks. As illustrated in Figs. 1 and 2, they are designed to describe cell nuclei at different regions for contextual understanding. At this final level, it is expected that the nuclear interaction with its background reaches the purpose to avoid missing important diagnostic information. It also leverages the idea of multi-region locations in features that effect the recognition of nuclei, making it suitable for building cell nuclei recognition networks.

3 Experiment Results and Analysis

The proposed CNNs are implemented in Keras, on Tensorflow backend. The training data are augmented by rotating and flipping all the images. In order to achieve effective fusion, two networks are trained to the best performance, respectively, and then dual CNNs are trained on this basis. We update parameters with Adam strategy [6]. All network models are trained for 80 epochs. A batch size of 256 images is used. In the designed sub-network, the initial learning rate is 0.001, and is divided by 10 at 50 epochs. In the proposed Dual-View network, combination of two branches are fine-tuned by setting learning rate 0.00001.

3.1 The Experimental Data

HistoPhenotypes is a public database which involves 100 H&E stained histology images of colorectal adenocarcinomas. There are 22444 nuclei that classified into four class labels: 7722 epithelial, 5712 fibroblast, 6971 inflammatory and 2039 others. Figure 3 illustrates some examples of the nuclei in the dataset. Note that the dataset contains complex and wide variety shapes of nuclei where overlap is also present. As reported in [2,14], 27×27 pixel nucleus-center patches are cropped to feed one of the networks. 36×36 pixel patches are extracted, including more contextual information to feed the another compensation branch.

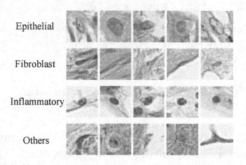

Fig. 3. Example patches of different types of nuclei found in the dataset. Each row corresponds to a cell nuclei class.

3.2 Classification Performance

Experiment One. First of all, experiments are conducted to compare with results in [14], where four classes are considered, i.e., epithelial, fibroblast, inflammatory and others. We employ 2-fold cross-validation the same as [14] for parameter tuning. And then, we calculate the F1 average score for all the classes, an area under the receiver operating characteristic curve for multiclass classification (multiclass AUC) [3] and overall accuracy.

Classification performance of the proposed DV-CNNs with or without multi-crop module is provided as listed in Table 1. $\times$ represents the sub-network without multi-crop module(denoted as MC.module) and vice versa. From comparison of "without multi-crop module" and "with multi-crop module", it is observed that network with this module trained from different images patches (27×27 or 36×36) both yield better performance than "without multi-crop module" networks. Thus, multi-crop module actually contains more local details and richer

Table 1. Comparative results about DV-CNNs with or without multi-crop module for four-classes classification.

Input	+MC.module	Average F1 score	Multiclass AUC	Overall accuracy
36 × 36	×	0.827	0.939	82.63%
	√	**0.835**	**0.945**	**83.75%**
27 × 27	×	0.798	0.930	80.48%
	√	**0.815**	**0.936**	**81.86%**

Table 2. Comparative results about DV-CNNs and other classification approaches for four-classes classification.

Model		Average F1 score	Multiclass AUC
Softmax CNN+SSPP		0.748	0.893
Softmax CNN+NEP		0.784	0.917
Superpixel descriptor		0.687	0.853
CRImage		0.488	0.684
Dual-View CNNs	36 × 36 branch + MC.module	0.835	0.945
	27 × 27 branch + MC.module	0.815	0.936
	Score fusion	**0.843**	**0.947**

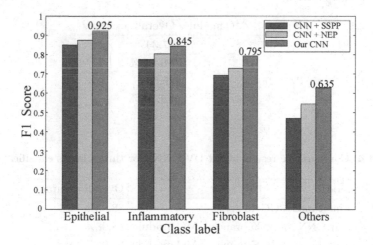

Fig. 4. Comparative results for nucleus four-classes classification stratified with respect to class label.

information of multi-region feature content. After verifying effectiveness of this extra module, an experiment is performed to investigate the proposed DV-CNNs.

Experimental results are listed in Table 2, where also includes the strategies of Standard Single-Patch Predictor (SSPP), Neighboring Ensemble Predictor (NEP), superpixel descriptor and CRImage proposed in [14]. From the results, it is obvious that the existing methods are both lower than any single branch of the proposed CNNs. Furthermore, the larger input branch learned on whole images yields better results than the smaller input branch (i.e., 0.835 vs. 0.815 overall accuracy) by comparing the performance of CNNs at different views. This phenomenon indicates that the global branch has more discriminative information which may compensate for the lack of local branch. Finally, we fuse prediction scores of dual networks, and obtain the final performance with weighted F1 average score of 0.843 and multiclass AUC of 0.947. We obtain an improvement of 6% F1 scores over the CNN + NEP. Figure 4 further illustrates the class specific accuracy for the proposed method compared with existing methods. Generally, the proposed one produces higher accuracy for each class.

Experiment Two. Experiments are also designed to compare with results in [2], where only three classes are considered, i.e., epithelial, fibroblast and inflammatory. Others category consists of mixed cell nuclei; therefore, authors in [2] have excluded it from their study. The split of the training and testing set is the same; that is, there are 17004 training images and 3401 testing images.

Table 3. Comparative results about DV-CNNs with or without multi-crop module for three-classes classification.

Input	+MC.module	Overall accuracy
36×36	×	87.34%
	√	**88.98%**
27×27	×	86.34%
	√	**88.06%**

Table 4. Comparative results about DV-CNNs for three-classes classification.

Model		Overall accuracy
Fine-tuned VGG-16[2]		88.03%
Our CNN	36×36 branch + MC.module	88.98%
	27×27 branch + MC.module	88.06%
	Score fusion	**90.40%**

Classification performance of DV-CNNs with or without cropping module is provided as listed in Table 3. It is also proved that network with multi-crop module trained from different images patches (27×27 or 36×36) both yield better performance than "without module networks". In [2], authors employed very deep architectures like GoogleNet, AlexNet [7] and VGG-16 trained with transfer learning, which applied a pre-trained model to fine-tune on this dataset.

It achieved the best result with the VGG-16 architecture with an overall accuracy of 88.03%. After fusing prediction scores of dual networks, we obtain the final performance with overall accuracy of 90.40% as listed in Table 4. From another point of view, DV-CNNs have much less parameter than the deep network VGG-16, but it can also reach the accuracy of the very deep network.

Through the above experiments, they demonstrate the efficiency of our methods in two aspects:

- Multi-crop module actually contains more local details and richer information of multi-region feature content. It is obvious that the multi-crop operation for training data has a direct influence for classification task; for example, evaluation metrics achieved with multi-crop module are higher than those without cropping module.
- As mentioned in Sect. 2, existing methods for histopathology images do not consider the global and local context. For the proposed DV-CNNs, we realize the best results compared with state-of-the-art work using four or three classes experimental data. These excellent results in Tables 1 and 2 demonstrate the effectiveness of the proposed method for cell nuclei recognition which allows us to hypothesize that joint global and local information is more beneficial to variability in the appearance of nuclei.

4   Conclusion

In this paper, we proposed an interesting Dual View CNNs with multi-crop module which are able to capture contextual information from different regions for nucleus classification in routine stained histology images of colorectal adenocarcinomas. The extracted features integrate complementary diagnostic criteria of different hierarchy concepts, allowing them to explore the intrinsic connection between cellular background and nucleus. We conducted experiments on a large dataset with more than 20000 annotated nuclei. The encouraging results compared with other approaches on cell nuclei classification demonstrated its effectiveness of the proposed method.

References

1. Adur, J., et al.: Colon adenocarcinoma diagnosis in human samples by multicontrast nonlinear optical microscopy of hematoxylin and eosin stained histological sections. J. Cancer Therapy **5**(13), 1259–1269 (2014)
2. Bayramoglu, N., Hcikkilä, J.: Transfer learning for cell nuclei classification in histopathology images. In: Hua, G., Jégou, H. (eds.) ECCV 2016 Part III. LNCS, vol. 9915, pp. 532–539. Springer, Cham (2016). https://doi.org/10.1007/978-3-319-49409-8_46
3. Hand, D.J., Till, R.J.: A simple generalisation of the area under the roc curve for multiple class classification problems. Mach. Learn. **45**(2), 171–186 (2001)
4. Ioffe, S., Szegedy, C.: Batch normalization: accelerating deep network training by reducing internal covariate shift. In: International Conference on International Conference on Machine Learning, pp. 448–456 (2015)

5. Irshad, H., Veillard, A., Roux, L., Racoceanu, D.: Methods for nuclei detection, segmentation, and classification in digital histopathology: a review-current status and future potential. IEEE Rev. Biomed. Eng. **7**(1–5), 97–114 (2014)
6. Kingma, D., Ba, J.: Adam: a method for stochastic optimization. In: International Conference on Learning Representations (2014)
7. Krizhevsky, A., Sutskever, I., Hinton, G.E.: Imagenet classification with deep convolutional neural networks. In: International Conference on Neural Information Processing Systems, pp. 1097–1105 (2012)
8. Madabhushi, A., Lee, G.: Image analysis and machine learning in digital pathology: challenges and opportunities. Med. Image Anal. **33**, 170–175 (2016)
9. Malon, C.D., Cosatto, E.: Classification of mitotic figures with convolutional neural networks and seeded blob features. J. Pathol. Inform. **4**(1), 9 (2013)
10. Murthy, V., Hou, L., Samaras, D., Kurc, T.M., Saltz, J.H.: Center-focusing multi-task CNN with injected features for classification of Glioma nuclear images. In: Applications of Computer Vision, pp. 834–841. IEEE (2016)
11. Nguyen, K., Bredno, J., Knowles, D.A.: Using contextual information to classify nuclei in histology images. In: IEEE International Symposium on Biomedical Imaging, pp. 995–998 (2015)
12. Rajesh, K., Rajeev, S., Subodh, S.: Detection and classification of cancer from microscopic biopsy images using clinically significant and biologically interpretable features. J. Med. Eng. **2015**, 457906 (2015)
13. Schmidhuber, J.: Deep learning in neural networks: an overview. Neural Netw. Off. J. Int. Neural Netw. Soc. **61**, 85 (2014)
14. Sirinukunwattana, K., Shan, E.A.R., Tsang, Y.W., Snead, D.R.J., Cree, I.A., Rajpoot, N.M.: Locality sensitive deep learning for detection and classification of nuclei in routine colon cancer histology images. IEEE Trans. Med. Imaging **35**(5), 1196–1206 (2016)
15. Veta, M., Pluim, J.P.W., Diest, P.J.V., Viergever, M.A.: Breast cancer histopathology image analysis: a review. IEEE Trans. Bio-Med. Eng. **61**(5), 1400–1411 (2014)
16. Wang, H., Cruzroa, A., Gilmore, H., Feldman, M., Tomaszewski, J., Madabhushi, A.: Cascaded ensemble of convolutional neural networks and handcrafted features for mitosis detection. In: SPIE Medical Imaging, pp. 90410B–90410B-10 (2015)
17. Yu, Y., Lin, H., Meng, J., Wei, X., Guo, H., Zhao, Z.: Deep transfer learning for modality classification of medical images. Information **8**(3), 91 (2017)

Multi-level Three-Stream Convolutional Networks for Video-Based Action Recognition

Yijing Lv[1,2,3], Huicheng Zheng[1,2,3](✉), and Wei Zhang[1,2,3]

[1] School of Data and Computer Science, Sun Yat-sen University, Guangzhou, China
zhenghch@mail.sysu.edu.cn
[2] Key Laboratory of Machine Intelligence and Advanced Computing,
Ministry of Education, Guangzhou, China
[3] Guangdong Key Laboratory of Information Security Technology,
135 West Xingang Road, Guangzhou 510275, China

Abstract. Deep convolutional neural networks (ConvNets) have shown remarkable capability for visual feature learning and representation. In the field of video-based action recognition, much progress has been made with the development of ConvNets. However, main-stream ConvNets used for video-based action recognition, such as two-stream ConvNets and 3D ConvNets, still lack the ability to represent fine-grained features. In this paper, we propose a novel architecture named multi-level three-stream convolutional network (MLTSN), which contains three streams, i.e., the spatial stream, the temporal stream, and the multi-level correlation stream (MLCS). The MLCS contains several correlation modules, which fuse appearance and motion features at the same levels and obtain spatial-temporal correlation maps. The correlation maps will further be fed in several convolution layers to get refined features. The whole network is trained in a multi-step modality. Extensive experimental results show that the performance of the proposed network is competitive to state-of-the-art methods on HMDB51 and UCF101.

Keywords: Action recognition · Convolutional networks
Multi-level correlation mechanism

1 Introduction

Video-based action recognition is an important task in the field of computer vision, due to its wide range of applications, such as content-based video retrieval, human computer interaction, and group activity understanding. In recent years, convolutional neural networks (ConvNets) have achieved great success in image-based tasks, such as face recognition [1], image classification [2], etc., owing to its powerful representation and learning ability. However, their applications in action recognition have not gained such satisfactory results as in image-based tasks. To form a complete understanding of an action in a video, one needs not

© Springer Nature Switzerland AG 2018
J.-H. Lai et al. (Eds.): PRCV 2018, LNCS 11257, pp. 237–249, 2018.
https://doi.org/10.1007/978-3-030-03335-4_21

only to grasp its spatial appearance information, but also to combine its motion information in the time dimension. Therefore, it is critical to take full advantage of temporal information for action classification.

Fig. 1. Some samples from HMDB51 of confusing actions. These actions are similar in terms of temporal motion or global spatial appearance features, so more subtle features need to be captured to classify them correctly. For example, as for actions of eat and drink, the subtle difference are the objects hold in hands and the local facial motion, both of which are subtle features.

Recently, some methods based on ConvNets have been proposed to capture temporal features, which can be divided into two major directions essentially: (1) methods based on two-stream ConvNets [3], which employ single frame and stacked optical flow fields as input; (2) methods based on 3D ConvNets [8], which carry out 3D convolution on stacked continuous frames. As for the former, the temporal features are learned from the pre-computed optical flow, which represent motion information in the time dimension. Some fusion methods [4–7] based on two-stream ConvNets are proposed to learn spatial-temporal relationship. As for the latter, the temporal features are learned from stacked continuous frames by 3D convolution. There are also some methods [9,10] proposed to improve the efficiency and accuracy of 3D convolution. In addition, there are some other frameworks [11–14] proposed for the sake of modeling long-term temporal information.

To sum up, current main-stream methods focus on either extracting appearance and motion or on modeling long-term temporal information. However, these methods have not paid much attention to fine-grained representations that are crucial for distinguishing confusing actions. As shown in Fig. 1, the actions of eat and drink, laugh and smile, throw and somersault are confusing from the perspective of global appearance and motion. Specifically, to classify actions of eat and drink, more attention should be paid to the local appearance, such as the objects hold in hands, and to the facial motion. Both of these features are fine-grained and if not given special treatment, they may be weakened by other features.

Based on above analysis, we propose a novel architecture named multi-level three-stream convolutional network (MLTSN), as shown in Fig. 2. The MLTSN utilizes spatiotemporal correlation to represent fine-grained local features which are crucial for distinguishing confusing actions. Specifically, the MLTSN consists of three streams, i.e., spatial stream, temporal stream, and multi-level correlation stream (MLCS), each of which generates different semantic features for classification. Similar to two-stream ConvNets [3], the spatial stream takes single frame as input to generate appearance features, while the temporal stream takes stacked optical flow fields as input to capture motion information. And both of their high-level features are used for classification. As for MLTSN, these two streams are not only responsible for generating their own classification scores, but also for generating multi-level features for MLCS as input.

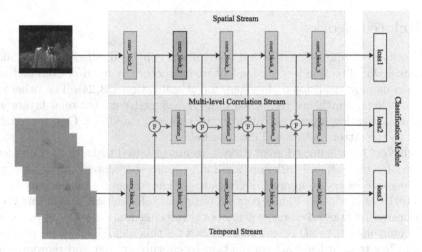

Fig. 2. The overview of the multi-level three-stream netwrok (MLTSN). The MLTSN consists of three streams, i.e., spatial stream, temporal stream, and multi-level correlation stream (MLCS), each of which can generate high-level features for classification. The conv_block_n ($n = 1, 2, 3, 4$) generate feature maps at different levels with different sizes, which will be fed in correlation modules to learn fine-grained features.

The MLCS consists of several correlation modules, which take appearance and motion features at the same levels instead of the raw images as input. Then the correlation modules fuse these features to obtain correlation maps, which will further be fed in several convolution layers to get refined features. The temporal stream responds more to the regions with significant motion than the insignificant regions. If we do not take into account the impact of camera movement, the areas with significant motion are generally the ones in space that need to be paid special attention to. From this point of view, motion features can be used as a mask for spatial features, so as to suppress some interference information and enlarge the effective information at the same time. We employ multiplication to fuse the spatial and temporal features in all correlation modules. In order to better train the MLCS and make the three streams mutually promote each other, we propose a multi-step training method.

In general, our contributions can be summarized as three points. Firstly, we propose a novel network named MLTSN, which preserves the spatial and temporal information maximally, while simultaneously makes full use of their correlation. Secondly, the proposed MLCS can focus on fine-grained features by fusing several levels of spatial and temporal features. Thirdly, the MLTSN is competitive to state-of-the-art methods on HMDB51 and UCF101, which verifies its effectiveness.

The rest of the paper is organized as follows. In Sect. 2, we briefly introduce the related work. The principles of the proposed MLTSN are explained in Sect. 3. Section 4 introduces the experimental details and gives the results on HMDB51 and UCF101. Finally, we summarize the paper in Sect. 5.

2   Related Work

The methods of video-based action recognition can be divided into two main directions. One direction is to design feature extractors by hand-crafted methods and then employ traditional classifiers for classification [23,24]. The other one uses ConvNets, which are composed of well-designed convolutional layers and nonlinear activation layers, as feature extractors and classifiers. Our approach is related to the latter and we will discusse below.

ConvNets have achieved great success in image-based tasks [1,2]. The methods used for video-based tasks are similar to image-based tasks in some ways. Some researchers try to apply ConvNets to action recognition according to the characteristics of videos. Videos contain temporal information, which images do not contain. To take advantage of temporal information, one way is to extend the 2D convolution to 3D convolution. Based on this idea, Ji et al. [8] proposed 3D ConvNet that utilized 3D convolution to capture spatial and temporal features. Tran et al. [9] proposed a common video descriptor named C3D based on 3D ConvNet. However, 3D convolution kernels are hard to train well on some relatively small datasets, such as HMDB51 [21] and UCF101 [22]. In order to alleviate the problem, Sun et al. [10] suggested to factorize 3D convolution kernel learning as 2D spatial kernel learning in the lower layers and 1D temporal kernel learning in the upper layers, which made training 3D ConvNets more effectively.

At the same time, another research direction realized the importance of optical flow fields in describing motion. Simonyan et al. [3] proposed two-stream ConvNet, which consisted of two independent networks. They took single frame and stacked optical flow fields as input to capture appearance and motion features independently. For the sake of finding the relationship between appearance and motion, some fusion methods based on two-stream ConvNets [4,5,7,15] were discussed. Karpathy et al. [15] compared several fusion methods, such as early fusion, late fusion, and slow fusion. Feichtenhofer et al. [4] suggested to fuse two streams at the middle layers and demonstrated that fusing at the last convolution layer can obtain the best results. Feichtenhofer et al. [5] introduced residual connections in a two-stream ConvNet model to find spatiotemporal relationship. In order to make spatial and temporal stream promote each other, Wang et al. [7] proposed a spatiotemporal pyramid architecture.

Two-stream ConvNets can model short-term temporal information from continuous optical flow fields. But it lacks the ability to model long-term temporal information. Some researches [11–14] noticed that some actions may be confused in one short snippet, so the long-term temporal information is important for correctly distinguishing actions. Wang et al. [11] proposed to divide a video into several segments at equal interval, and use average pooling to fuse their features after fully connected layers. Chen et al. [13] believed the average pooling operation may result in loss of temporal information, so they proposed a new architecture named SSN to aggregate these features and got better performance.

The most related work to ours is the spatiotemporal pyramid architecture [7]. However, they only embedded spatiotemporal fusion module at the last level, which is the high-level semantic information that may have lost corresponding location information of appearance and motion. Instead, our MLCS aggregates spatial and temporal features at several levels from bottom to top, which can fully mine their correlation. Besides, we adopt a multi-step training strategy, which maximally retains the original information of appearance and motion.

3   Action Recognition with Multi-level Three-Stream Convolutional Networks

The architecture of our MLTSN is shown in Fig. 2. In this section, we firstly introduce the MLTSN in detail. Next we describe how to train the MLTSN in a multi-step strategy and explain some testing details.

3.1   Network Architecture

Network Architecture Overview. Figure 2 shows the overall architecture of the MLTSN. The MLTSN contains one classification module and three streams, i.e., spatial stream, temporal stream, multi-level correlation stream. Similar to common two-stream ConvNet [3], the spatial stream takes single frame as input to capture appearance features, while the temporal stream takes stacked optical flow fields as input to capture motion features. In particular, both of streams are responsible for generating features at several levels for MLCS as input. The purposes of the MLCS are to capture fine-grained features by utilizing the correlation between spatial and temporal features and further facilitate their learning. The three streams generate three types of high-level features, which will be sent to the classification module to predict action labels. Next, we will discuss these three streams and classification module in detail.

Spatial and Temporal Streams. Deep ConvNets contain well-designed convolution layers and nonlinear activation layers, which are deep enough to implement very complex functions. Therefore, deep ConvNets, such as VGG-16 [16], ResNet-50 [17], and BN-Inception [18] have outperformed hand-crafted methods in terms of feature extraction in image-based tasks. In our experiments, we employ BN-Inception as the backbone of spatial and temporal streams and use the method of TSN [11] to construct the MLTSN. In TSN, inputs of spatial and temporal streams have no correspondence in time series. To help the MLCS build spatial-temporal correlation more reasonably, we align them in time.

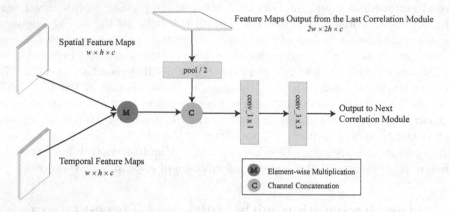

Fig. 3. Detailed architecture of one correlation module. We utilize the element-wise multiplication to fuse spatial and temporal features at the same level. The concatenation is used to concat features computed from the last correlation block and features at current level.

Multi-level Correlation Stream. The MLCS consists of several correlation modules at different levels, the inputs of which are features of different sizes output from spatial and temporal streams in several specific layers. Figure 3 shows the details of one correlation module and others have the same structure except for the channels and sizes of feature maps. We utilize element-wise multiplication to build the correlation between spatial and temporal features, which can be represented as:

$$F_{cor}(w, h, c) = F_{spa}(w, h, c) \odot F_{tem}(w, h, c), \qquad (1)$$

where $F_{spa}(w, h, c)$ and $F_{tem}(w, h, c)$ represent the feature maps output from spatial and temporal streams, respectively. They have the same width w, height h, and channels c. The $F_{cor}(w, h, c)$ denotes correlation maps that have the same dimension with $F_{spa}(w, h, c)$. Then the previous level of feature maps F_{pre} will concatenate with $F_{cor}(w, h, c)$ to form $F'_{cor}(w, h, c)$, which will be fed in two stacked convolution layers to get refined features. The process can be represented as:

$$F_{ref}(w, h, c) = f(concat(F_{cor}(w, h, c), f_{pool}(F_{pre}(2w, 2h, c)))) \qquad (2)$$

where $f_{pool}(\cdot)$ means the max pooling operation that makes the size of feature maps half of the original and $concat(\cdot, \cdot)$ means concatenating two feature maps along the dimension of channels. In this way, the information from the last level can be used in current level for refinement. The $f(\cdot, \cdot)$ represents the convolution operation followed with the ReLU activation function [19], while we do not use batch normalization after convolutional layers. Besides, the 1×1 convolutional layer is designed for dimension reduction. It is worth noting that the parameters of the MLCS are less than the other two streams.

Classification Module. The MLTSN consists of three streams, which means that three types of high-level features can be generated and fed in the classification module to get the classification scores independently. Specifically, one dropout layer is used for each stream before the fully connected layer to reduce the impact of over-fitting. We will employ the cross-entropy function to compute loss of three streams after the fully connected layer during training. During testing, we use values output from three fully connected layers as the classification scores.

3.2   Learning Multi-level Correlation Three-Stream Network

Training Strategy. We employ three steps to train the proposed MLTSN. In the first step, the spatial and temporal streams will be trained independently using the existing methods in TSN [11]. Specifically, they will be pre-trained on ImageNet [2] firstly and then fine-tuned on HMDB51 or UCF101 with data augmentation techniques proposed in [20]. In the second step, the parameters of these two streams are loaded to initialize the MLTSN. Next, the MLCS is trained from scratch on HMDB51 or UCF101. It is worth mentioning that the weights of spatial and temporal streams are fixed except for their first batch normalization layer. In the third step, the whole MLTSN is further fine-tuned with a unified loss. The parameters of batch normalization layers are still fixed except for the first one of spatial and temporal streams, which has been proved to be effective in [11]. Besides, the stochastic gradient descent algorithm is used during the whole procedure. And the loss L_{MLTSN} used in the second and third steps can be represented as: $L_{MLTSN} = \alpha L_{spa} + \beta L_{tem} + \gamma L_{MLCS}$. In the second step, α, β, and γ are set to 0, 0, 1, respectively. In the third step, they are set to 1.

Testing Details. The MLTSN consists of three streams, each of which can generate one classification score. In our experiments, we will use the values after fully connected layers as the classification scores, which have not been processed by softmax operation. Specifically, at first, we sample 25 frames at equal time intervals and corresponding optical flow fields for each test video. Next, they are fed in spatial and temporal streams to not only get the classification scores, but also generate multi-level features for MLCS as input. Finally, the 25 classification scores of each stream are averaged to get the final scores. As there are three classification scores, the final fusion score is represented as: $S_{MLTSN} = aS_{spa} + bS_{tem} + cS_{MLCS}$, where a, b, c are set to 1, 2, 0.5, respectively.

4 Experiments

In this section, we firstly describe the datasets that we use to evaluate the MLTSN. Then implementation details are discussed. Next, the performance of MLTSN on HMDB51 and UCF101 are displayed. Finally, we compare our model with state-of-the-art methods.

4.1 Evaluation Datasets and Implementation Details

Evaluation Datasets. We evaluate the methods presented in this paper on two challenging public datasets named HMDB51 [21] and UCF101 [22], which are widely used in video-based action recognition recently. HMDB51 contains 51 action classes with a total of 6766 video clips. These action categories cover a wide range, such as facial actions, general body actions, human-to-human interactions, and human-to-object interactions. UCF101 contains 101 action classes with a total of 13320 videos, which are divided into 5 groups: people-to-things interactions, human actions, human-to-human interactions, performing musical instruments, and sports. Both are challenging because the video samples suffer from changes in posture, camera movement, etc. However, as for HMDB51, the number of samples is still not enough to effectively train a deep network, which is one of the reasons for its worse classification performance than UCF101. For fair comparison, the following experiments will use the standard test protocols recommended by the authors of datasets.

Implementation Details. In order to help others to reproduce the experiments in this paper, more technical details are elaborated below. We employ the TSN [11] as the basic framework of spatial and temporal streams, which divided each video into three segments and selected one frame or stacked optical flow fields from each segment randomly when training. As for MLCS, there are four levels of feature fusion. The corresponding sizes of feature maps for fusion are $64 \times 56 \times 56$, $256 \times 28 \times 28$, $576 \times 14 \times 14$, and $1024 \times 7 \times 7$ in the form of *channels* $\times$ *width* $\times$ *height*. After four levels of correlation modules, the feature maps with sizes of $1024 \times 7 \times 7$ are generated. The feature maps are sent to a global pooling layer and a fully connected layer to generate the classification scores. We employ cross entropy to compute losses for backward propagation finally.

We train the MLTSN following the illustrations in Sect. 3.2. In the first step, the hyper-parameters are the same as [11]. In the second step, the MLCS is trained by stochastic gradient descent algorithm and the batch size is set to 64. Besides, the weight decay and momentum are set to 0.0005 and 0.9, respectively. We use multi-step policy to change the learning rate, which is initialized as 0.02 and divided by 10 when accuracy of validation set does not change. We will stop training when the accuracy of validation set no longer improves. We reduce the learning rate two times on both HMDB51 and UCF101. In the third step, the whole network is fine-tuned with the same hyper-parameters as the second step, except for the initial learning rate, which is set to 0.00002. After these three steps, we obtain the final model, which will be employed for testing.

4.2 Evaluation of MLTSN

In this part, extensive experimental results are displayed to verify the effectiveness of the MLTSN. The testing details follow the illustrations in Sect. 3.2. Table 1 shows the comparison of the baseline TSN [11] and the MLTSN on HMDB51 and UCF101. The accuracy of TSN is computed using the codes provided in [11]. In Table 1, the $s + t$ means a weighted sum of classification scores of spatial and temporal streams and MLTSN represents a weighted sum of three streams. From Table 1 we see that MLTSN gets better results. Specifically, the average accuracies of the MLTSN reach 69.8% and 94.4% on HMDB51 and UCF101, respectively, which increase by 1.3% and 0.7%, respectively, compared with TSN. When compared to the performance of $s + t$ of TSN, the $s + t$ of MLTSN also improves accuracies by 0.8% on HMDB51, which shows the MLCS further promotes the learning of spatial and temporal streams. Besides, Fig. 4 displays some confusing samples on HMDB51 split1, which are classified correctly by our MLTSN, while misclassified by TSN. This shows our MLTSN can learn fine-grained features to distinguish confusing actions.

Table 1. The accuracy of the TSN and MLTSN on HMDB51 and UCF101 (In %)

Dataset		Method	Spatial	Temporal	MLCS	$s + t$	MLTSN
HMDB51	split1	TSN	54.4	62.4	-	69.5	-
		MLTSN	55.0	62.2	68.0	70.1	**71.1**
	split2	TSN	50.0	63.3	-	67.4	-
		MLTSN	50.5	63.2	65.4	68.3	**68.7**
	split3	TSN	49.2	63.9	-	68.5	-
		MLTSN	50.3	64.3	64.6	69.4	**69.5**
	Average	TSN	51.0	63.2	-	68.5	-
		MLTSN	51.9	63.2	65.9	69.3	**69.8**
UCF101	split1	TSN	86.0	87.6	-	93.7	-
		MLTSN	85.9	87.8	89.8	93.9	**93.9**
	split2	TSN	85.0	90.2	-	94.0	-
		MLTSN	85.1	91.0	91.9	94.3	**94.6**
	split3	TSN	84.5	91.3	-	93.5	-
		MLTSN	85.0	91.2	92.3	94.6	**94.8**
	Average	TSN	85.2	89.7	-	93.7	-
		MLTSN	85.3	90.0	91.3	94.3	**94.4**

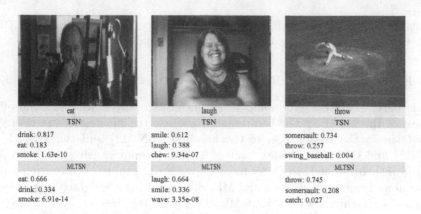

Fig. 4. The comparison of top-3 prediction scores between the TSN and MLTSN. The text in yellow and green bars denote the ground truth labels and classification methods, respectively. The text and number below represent the predicted labels and corresponding scores by TSN or MLTSN. (Color figure online)

Table 2. The accuracy of the MSTIN and MLTSN* on HMDB51 and UCF101 (In %)

Dataset	Method	Spatial	Temporal	MLCS	$s + t$	MLTSN*
HMDB51 (average)	MSTIN [28]	57.2	59.7	-	70.8	-
	MLTSN*	57.3	59.4	65.2	70.8	**71.3**
UCF101 (average)	MSTIN [28]	87.3	90.9	-	95.3	-
	MLTSN*	87.4	90.1	90.1	95.4	**95.8**

4.3 Comparison with State-of-the-Art Approaches

To compare our methods with recent state-of-the-art methods on HMDB51 and UCF101, we employ another framework named MSTIN [28] to construct the spatial and temporal streams of our MLTSN and rename it to MLTSN*. MSTIN [28] is a deep multi-scale temporal inception convolutional network and it performs better than TSN. The MSTIN introduced two methods named max pooling and rank pooling to build the multi-scale temporal inception modules. In our experiment, we use the max pooling method to build the three streams of MLTSN*. The training and testing details are the same with those mentioned above. The comparisons of the MSTIN and MLTSN* are shown in Table 2. From Table 2, we see that the average accuracy of MLTSN reaches 71.3% on HMDB51 and 95.8% on UCF101, which increases by 0.5% on both datasets.

We show the comparison of MLTSN* and state-of-the-art methods in Table 3. The right column of Table 3 shows recent methods based on two-stream ConvNets and the left column shows other methods, such as traditional methods [23,24], 3D ConvNets based methods [9,27]. From Table 3 we see that the MLTSN* performs slightly better than recent state-of-the-art methods, which further ensures the effectiveness of MLTSN.

Table 3. The comparison of our MLTSN with state-of-the-art methods on HMDB51 and UCF101 (In %)

Method	HMDB51	UCF101	Method	HMDB51	UCF101
IDT [23]	61.7	86.4	TSC [3]	59.4	88.0
IDT+MIFS [24]	65.1	89.1	TSF [4]	65.4	92.5
C3D+IDT [9]	-	90.4	STRN [5]	66.4	93.4
TDD+IDT [26]	65.9	91.5	STMN [6]	68.9	94.2
DIN+IDT [25]	65.2	89.1	STPN [7]	68.9	94.6
I3D [27]	66.4	93.4	MLTSN (ours)	69.8	94.4
TSN [11]	68.4	94.0	MLTSN* (ours)	**71.3**	**95.8**

5 Conclusion

We propose a new architecture named multi-level three-stream network (MLTSN), which maximally preserves spatial and temporal features, while makes full use of their correlation at the same time. The MLCS, consisting of multi-level correlation modules, learns fine-grained features with information provided by spatial and temporal streams. The three streams of MLTSN can be fine-tuned together and they can promote the learning of each other to generate more complementary features. To verify the effectiveness of our ideas, we embed the MLCS to two frameworks, i.e. TSN and MSTIN to construct our MLTSN and MLTSN*, respectively. Experimental results show they both behave better than the baseline, which shows that the proposed MLTSN is competitive to state-of-the-art methods.

Acknowledgments. This work was supported by National Natural Science Foundation of China (U1611461), Special Program for Applied Research on Super Computation of the NSFC-Guangdong Joint Fund (the second phase, No. U1501501), and Science and Technology Program of Guangzhou (No. 201803030029).

References

1. Parkhi, O.M., Vedaldi, A., Zisserman, A.: Deep face recognition. In: British Machine Vision Conference, pp. 41.1–41.12 (2015)
2. Krizhevsky, A., Sutskever, I., Hinton, G.E: Imagenet classification with deep convolutional neural networks. In: International Conference on Neural Information Processing Systems, pp. 1097–1105 (2012)
3. Simonyan, K., Zisserman, A.: Two-stream convolutional networks for action recognition in videos. In: International Conference on Neural Information Processing Systems, pp. 568–576 (2014)
4. Feichtenhofer, C., Pinz, A., Zisserman, A.: Convolutional two-stream network fusion for video action recognition. In: IEEE Conference on Computer Vision and Pattern Recognition, pp. 1933–1941 (2016)

5. Feichtenhofer, C., Pinz, A., Wildes, R.: Spatiotemporal residual networks for video action recognition. In: International Conference on Neural Information Processing Systems, pp. 3468–3476 (2016)
6. Feichtenhofer, C., Pinz, A., Wildes, R.: Spatiotemporal multiplier networks for video action recognition. In: IEEE Conference on Computer Vision and Pattern Recognition, pp. 7445–7454 (2017)
7. Wang, Y., Long, M., Wang, J.: Spatiotemporal pyramid network for video action recognition. In: IEEE Conference on Computer Vision and Pattern Recognition, pp. 097–2106 (2017)
8. Ji, S., Xu, W., Yang, M.: 3D convolutional neural networks for human action recognition. IEEE Trans. Pattern Anal. Mach. Intell. **35**(1), 221–231 (2013)
9. Tran, D., Bourdev, L., Fergus, R.: Learning spatiotemporal features with 3D convolutional networks. In: IEEE International Conference on Computer Vision, pp. 4489–4497 (2015)
10. Sun, L., Jia, K., Yeung, D., Shi, B.: Human action recognition using factorized spatio-temporal convolutional networks. In: IEEE International Conference on Computer Vision, pp. 4597–4605 (2015)
11. Wang, L., et al.: Temporal segment networks: towards good practices for deep action recognition. In: Leibe, B., Matas, J., Sebe, N., Welling, M. (eds.) ECCV 2016 Part VIII. LNCS, vol. 9912, pp. 20–36. Springer, Cham (2016). https://doi.org/10.1007/978-3-319-46484-8_2
12. Donahue, J., Hendricks, L., Guadarrama, S., Rohrbach, M., Venugopalan, S.: Long-term recurrent convolutional networks for visual recognition and description. In: IEEE Conference on Computer Vision and Pattern Recognition, pp. 2625–2634 (2015)
13. Chen, Q., Zhang, Y.: Sequential segment networks for action recognition. Sig. Process. Lett. **24**(5), 712–716 (2017)
14. Varol, G., Laptev, I., Schmid, C.: Long-term temporal convolutions for action recognition. arXiv preprint arXiv:1604.04494 (2016)
15. Karpathy, A., Toderici, G., Shetty, S.: Large-scale video classification with convolutional neural networks. In: IEEE Conference on Computer Vision and Pattern Recognition, pp. 1725–1732 (2014)
16. Simonyan, K., Zisserman, A.: Very deep networks for large-scale image recognition. arXiv preprint arXiv:1409.1556 (2014)
17. He, K., Zhang, X., Ren, S., Sun, J.: Deep residual learning for image recognition. In: IEEE Conference on Computer Vision and Pattern Recognition, pp. 770–778 (2016)
18. Ioffe, S., Szegedy, C.: Batch normalization: accelerating deep network training by reducing internal covariate shift. In: International Conference on Machine Learning, pp. 448–456 (2015)
19. Glorot, X., Bordes, A., Bengio, Y.: Deep sparse rectifier neural networks. In: Internaional Conference on Artificial Intelligence Statistics, pp. 315–323 (2011)
20. Wang, L., Xiong, Y., Wang, Z.: Towards good practices for very deep two-stream convnets. arXiv preprint arXiv:1507.02159 (2015)
21. Kuehne, H., Jhuang, H., Garrote, E., Poggio, T., Serre, T.: HMDB: a large video database for human motion recognition. In: International Conference on Computer Vision, pp. 2556–2563 (2011)
22. Soomro, K., Zamir, A.R., Shah, M.: UCF101: a dataset of 101 human actions classes from videos in the wild. arXiv preprint arXiv:1212.0402 (2012)
23. Wang, H., Schmid, C.: Action recognition with improved trajectories. In: International Conference on Computer Vision, pp. 3551–3558 (2013)

24. Lan, Z., Lin, M., Li, X.: Beyond Gaussian pyramid: multi-skip feature stacking for action recognition. In: IEEE Conference on Computer Vision and Pattern Recognition, pp. 204–212 (2015)
25. Bilen, H., Fernando, B., Gavves, E.: Dynamic image networks for action recognition. In: IEEE Conference on Computer Vision and Pattern Recognition, pp. 3034–3042 (2016)
26. Wang, L., Qiao, Y., Tang, X.: Action recognition with trajectory-pooled deep-convolutional descriptors. In: IEEE Conference on Computer Vision and Pattern Recognition, pp. 4305–4314 (2015)
27. Carreira, J., Zisserman, A.: Quo vadis, action recognition? A new model and the kinetics dataset. In: IEEE Conference on Computer Vision and Pattern Recognition, pp. 4724–4733 (2017)
28. Cen, J.: Robust action recognition. Sun Yat-sen University, Guangdong, Guangzhou, China (2017)

Deep Classification and Segmentation Model for Vessel Extraction in Retinal Images

Yicheng Wu[1], Yong Xia[1,2](✉), and Yanning Zhang[1]

[1] National Engineering Laboratory for Integrated Aero-Space-Ground-Ocean Big Data Application Technology, School of Computer Science and Engineering, Northwestern Polytechnical University, Xi'an 710072, China
yxia@nwpu.edu.cn
[2] Centre for Multidisciplinary Convergence Computing (CMCC), School of Computer Science and Engineering, Northwestern Polytechnical University, Xi'an 710072, China

Abstract. The shape of retinal blood vessels is critical in the early diagnosis of diabetes and diabetic retinopathy. Segmentation of retinal vessels, particularly the capillaries, remains a significant challenge. To address this challenge, in this paper, we adopt the "divide-and-conquer" strategy, and thus propose a deep neural network-based classification and segmentation (CAS) model to extract blood vessels in color retinal images. We first use the network in network (NIN) to divide the retinal patches extracted from preprocessed fundus retinal images into wide-vessel, middle-vessel and capillary patches. Then we train three U-Nets to segment three classes of vessels, respectively. Finally, this algorithm has been evaluated on the digital retinal images for vessel extraction (DRIVE) database against seven existing algorithms and achieved the highest AUC of 97.93% and top three accuracy, sensitivity and specificity. Our comparison results indicate that the proposed algorithm is able to segment blood vessels in retinal images with better performance.

Keywords: Retinal vessels segmentation · Deep learning
Classification and segmentation

1 Introduction

Diabetic retinopathy (DR) is one of the most serious and common complications, the leading cause of visual impairment in many countries. Early diagnosis of diabetes and DR, in which vessels segmentation in color images of the retina plays a pivotal role, is critical for best patient care.

A number of automated retinal vessels segmentation algorithms have been published in the literature, which can be roughly categorized into three groups. First, vessels segmentation algorithms can be guided by the prior domain knowledge. Staal et al. [1] introduced the vessels location and others heuristics to the

© Springer Nature Switzerland AG 2018
J.-H. Lai et al. (Eds.): PRCV 2018, LNCS 11257, pp. 250–258, 2018.
https://doi.org/10.1007/978-3-030-03335-4_22

vessels segmentation process. Second, Lupascu et al. [2] jointly employed filters with different scales and directions to extract 41-dimensional visual features and applied the AdaBoosted decision trees to those features for vessels segmentation. Next, recent years have witnessed the success of deep learning techniques in retinal vessels segmentation. Liskowski et al. [3] trained a deep network with the augmented blood vessels data at variable scales to facilitate segmentation. Li et al. [4] adopted an auto-encoder to initialize the neural network for vessel segmentation and avoided the preprocessing of retinal images. Ronneberger et al. [5] proposed a fully convolutional network called U-Net for retinal vessels segmentation. Fu et al. [6] applied deep neural network and fully connected conditional random field (FC-CRF) to improve the performance. Despite their success, deep learning-based algorithms still suffer from mis-segmentation, particularly in capillary regions.

Comparing to major arteries and veins, capillaries have smaller diameter, extremely lower contrast and very different appearance in retinal images. Therefore, we suggest that applying different methods to segment retinal vessels with different widths. In this paper, we adopt the "divide and conque" strategy and propose a deep neural network-based classification and segmentation (CAS) model to extract blood vessels in color retinal images. We first extract patches from preprocessed retinal images, and then classify these patches into three categories: wide-vessel, middle-vessel and capillary patches. Next, we construct three U-Nets to segment three categories of patches. Finally, we use those segmented patches to reconstruct the completed retinal vessels. We have evaluated the proposed algorithm against seven existing retinal vessels segmentation algorithms on the benchmark digital retinal images vessel extraction (DRIVE) database [1].

2 Dataset

The DRIVE database used for this study comes from a diabetic retinopathy screening program initiated in Netherlands. It consists of 20 training and 20 testing fundus retinal color images of size 584×565. These images were taken by optical camera from 400 diabetic subjects, whose ages are 25–90 years. Among them, 33 images do not have any pathological manifestations and the rest have very small signs of diabetes. Each original image is equipped with the ground truth from two experts' manual segmentation and the corresponding mask.

3 Method

The proposed CAS model consists of retinal images preprocessing, retinal patches extraction, classification and segmentation and retinal vessels reconstruction. A diagram that summarizes this algorithm is shown in Fig. 1.

3.1 Retinal Image Preprocessing

To avoid the impact of hue and saturation, we calculate the intensity at each pixel, and thus convert each color retinal image into a gray-level image. Then, we apply the contrast limited adaptive histogram equalization (CLAHE) algorithm [7] and gamma adjusting algorithm to each gray-level image to improve its contrast and suppress its noise.

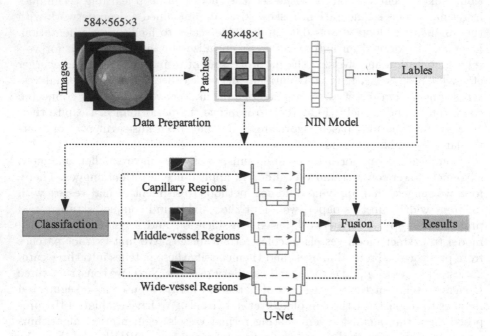

Fig. 1. Diagram of the proposed CAS model (color figure online)

3.2 Training a Patch Classification Network

A fundus retinal image contains a dark macular area, a bright optic disc region, high contrast major vessels and low contrast capillaries (see Fig. 2). To address the difficulties caused by such variety, we extract partly overlapped patches in each image, classify them into three groups, and design a deep neural network to segment each group of patches.

We randomly extract 9,500 patches of size 48 × 48 in each training image, and thus have totally 190,000 patches for training. In each training patch, we firstly calculate the distance between each vessel pixel and the background pixel nearest to it. The maximum distance along each line that is perpendicular to the direction of the vessel is defined as the radius of the vessel at that point. A vessel segment with a radius larger than T_1 is defined as wide vessel, a vessel segment with a radius smaller than T_2 is defined as capillary, and other vessel segments are defined as middle vessels. For this study, the threshold T_1 and T_2 are empirically set to five and three, respectively. Three types of retinal vessels in two training images are illustrated in Fig. 3.

Accordingly, each training patch can be assigned to one of three classes based on the majority type of vessels within it. Then, we use those annotated patches

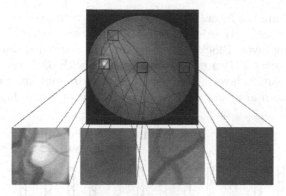

Fig. 2. A fundus retinal image: the optic disc region (1st column), macular area (2nd column), high contrast patch (3rd column) and low contrast patch (4th column) (color figure online)

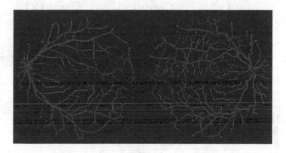

Fig. 3. Three types of vessels, including (blue) the wide-vessel, (red) middle-vessel, and (green) capillary, in two training images (Color figure online)

to train a patch classifier. Since the number of training patches is too small to train a very deep neural network, we use a network in network (NIN) model [8] as the patch classifier, which contains nine convolutional layers, including two layers with 5×5 kernels, one layer with 3×3 kernels and six layers with 1×1 kernels (see Fig. 4). To train this NIN, we fix the maximum iteration number to 120, choose the min-batch stochastic gradient decent with a batch size of 100, use the learning rate from 0.01 to 0.0004, and set the weight decay as 0.0005.

3.3 Training Patch Segmentation Networks

We use each class of patches to train a U-Net, which predicts each pixel in a patch belonging to either blood vessels or background. The U-Net consists of an input layer that accepts 48×48 patches, a Softmax output layer and five blocks in the middle (see Fig. 5). Block-1 has two convolutional layers, each consisting of 32 kernels of size 3×3, and a 2×2 max-pooling layer. Block-2 is identical to Block-1 except for using 64 kernels in each convolution layer. In Block-3, the number of kernels in each convolutional layer increases to 128, and there is an extra 2×2 up-sampling layer. Block-4 accepts the combined output of Block-3 and Block-2. The rest part is identical to Block-2 except that the last layer is a 2×2 up-sampling layer. Block-5, that accepts the combined output of Block-4 and Block-1, consists of two convolutional layers with 32 kernels of size 3×3 and a 1×1 convolution layer. Moreover, there is a dropout layer with a dropout rate of 20% between any two adjacent identical convolutional layers.

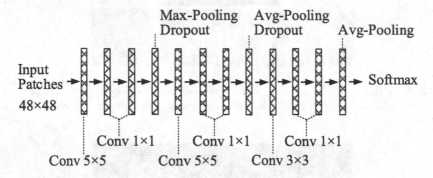

Fig. 4. Architecture of the NIN [8] model used in our algorithm

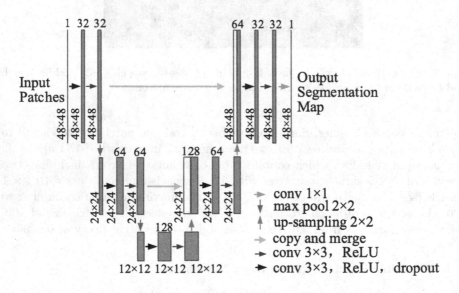

Fig. 5. Architecture of the U-Net [5] used in our algorithm

To train each U-Net, we fix the maximum iteration number to 150 and set the batch size as 32. Considering the small dataset, we first use all training patches to pre-train a U-Net, and then use three classes of patches to fine-tune this pre-trained U-Net, respectively.

Retinal Images   Pre-processed
                      Images   Ground-truth   Results

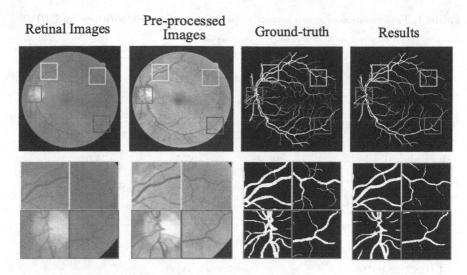

Fig. 6. An example test image (1st column), pre-processed image (2nd column), ground-truth (3rd column) and segmentation result (4th column) (color figure online)

3.4 Testing: Retinal Vessels Segmentation

Applying the proposed CAS model to retinal vessels segmentation consists of four steps. First, partly overlapped patches of size 48×48 are extracted in each retinal image, which has been preprocessed in the same way, with a stride of 5 along both horizontal and vertical directions. Second, each patch is inputted to the trained NIN model for a class label. Third, wide-vessel patches and capillary patches are segmented by the U-Net fine-tuned on the corresponding class of training patches, whereas each middle-vessel patch is segmented by three U-Nets and labelled by binarizing the average of three probabilistic outputs with the threshold 0.5. Fourth, since patches are heavily overlapped, each pixel may appear in multiple patches. Hence, we use the majority voting to determine the class label of each pixel in the final segmentation result.

4 Results

Figure 6 shows an example test image, its preprocessed version, segmentation result and ground-truth. To highlight the accurate segmentation obtained by our algorithm, we randomly selected four areas in the image, enlarged them, and displayed them in the bottom row of Fig. 6. It shows that our algorithm is able to detect most of retinal vessels, including low contrast capillaries.

Table 1 gives the average accuracy, specificity, sensitivity and area under curve (AUC) of our algorithm and seven existing retinal vessels segmentation algorithms. It reveals that our algorithm achieved the highest AUC and the top three performance when measured in terms of accuracy, specificity and sensitivity.

Table 1. Performance of seven retinal vessels segmentation algorithms on DRIVE

Algorithm	AUC (%)	Accuracy (%)	Specificity (%)	Sensitivity (%)
Lupascu et al. [2]	95.61	95.97	98.74	67.28
Fraz et al. [9]	97.47	94.80	98.07	74.06
Fu et al. [6]	94.70	N.A	N.A	72.94
Lahiri et al. [10]	N.A	95.33	N.A	N.A
Liskowski et al. [3]	97.90	95.35	98.07	78.11
Fu et al. [11]	N.A	95.23	N.A	76.03
Dasgupta et al. [12]	97.44	95.33	98.01	76.91
Orlando et al. [13]	95.07	N.A	96.84	78.97
CAS model	*97.93*	*95.62*	*98.30*	*77.21*

5   Discussions

5.1   Computational Complexity

Due to the use of deep neural networks, the proposed CAS model has a very high computation complexity. It takes more than 32 h to perform training (Intel Xeon CPU, NVIDIA Titan Xp GPU, 128 GB Memory, 120 GB SSD and Keras 1.1.0). However, applying this algorithm to segmentation is relatively fast, as it takes less than 20 s to segment a 584×565 color retinal image on average.

Table 2. Performance of our algorithm when using one to four patch classes

# Patch classes	1 (%)	2 (%)	3 (%)	4 (%)
AUC	97.90	97.86	*97.93*	95.99
Accuracy	95.58	95.48	*95.62*	93.28
Specificity	98.03	97.71	*98.30*	94.82
Sensitivity	78.79	80.14	*77.21*	**82.78**

5.2   Number of Patch Classes

To deal with the variety of retinal patches, we divided them into three classes and employed different U-Nets to segment them. We also tried to categorize those patches into one to four classes, and displayed the corresponding performance in Table 2. It shows that (a) using three classes of patches performed best, (b) increasing the number of patch classes to four resulted in worst performance, and (c) separating patches into two or four classes performed worse even than not separating patches at all.

6   Conclusion

In this paper, we propose the CAS model to extract blood vessels in color images of the retina. The intra- and inter-image variety can be largely addressed by separating retinal patches into wide-vessel, middle-vessel and capillary patches and by using three U-Nets to segment them, respectively. Our results on the DRIVE database indicates that the proposed algorithm is able to segment retinal vessels more accurately than seven existing segmentation algorithms.

Ackonwledge. This work was supported in part by the National Natural Science Foundation of China under Grants 61471297 and 61771397, and in part by the China Postdoctoral Science Foundation under Grant 2017M623245, and in part by the Fundamental Research Funds for the Central Universities under Grant 3102018zy031. We also appreciate the efforts devoted to collect and share the DRIVE database for comparing algorithms of vessels segmentation in color images of the retina.

References

1. Staal, J.J., Abramoff, M.D., Niemeijer, M., Viergever, M.A., Van Ginneken, B.: Ridge-based vessel segmentation in color images of the retina. IEEE TMI **23**(4), 501–509 (2004)
2. Lupascu, C.A., Tegolo, D., Trucco, E.: FABC: retinal vessel segmentation using AdaBoost. IEEE TITB **14**(5), 1267–1274 (2010)
3. Liskowski, P., Krawiec, K.: Segmenting retinal blood vessels with deep neural network. IEEE TMI **35**(11), 2369–2380 (2016)
4. Li, Q., Feng, B., Xie, L.P., Liang, P., Zhang, H., Wang, T.: A cross-modality learning approach for vessel segmentation in retinal images. IEEE TMI **35**(1), 109–118 (2016)
5. Ronneberger, O., Fischer, P., Brox, T.: U-Net: convolutional networks for biomedical image segmentation. In: Navab, N., Hornegger, J., Wells, W.M., Frangi, A.F. (eds.) MICCAI 2015. LNCS, vol. 9351, pp. 234–241. Springer, Cham (2015). https://doi.org/10.1007/978-3-319-24574-4_28
6. Fu, H., Xu, Y., Wong, D.W.K., Liu, J.: Retinal vessel segmentation via deep learning net-work and fully-connected conditional random fields. In: ISBI, pp. 698–701. IEEE, Prague (2016)
7. Setiawan, A.W., Mengko, T.R., Santoso, O.S., Suksmono, A.B.: Color retinal image enhancement using CLAHE. In: ICISS, pp. 1–3. IEEE, Jakarta (2013)
8. Lin, M., Chen, Q., Yan, S.: Network in network. In: ICLR. IEEE, Banff (2014)
9. Fraz, M.M., Remagnino, P., Hoppe, A., Uyyanonvara, B., Rudnicka, A.R., Owen, C.G.: An ensemble classification-based approach applied to retinal blood vessel segmentation. IEEE TBE **59**(9), 2538–2548 (2012)
10. Lahiri, A., Roy, A.G., Sheet, D., Biswas, P.K.: Deep neural ensemble for retinal vessel segmentation in fundus images towards achieving label-free angiography. In: EMBC, pp. 1340–1343. IEEE, Orlando (2016)
11. Fu, H., Xu, Y., Lin, S., Kee Wong, D.W., Liu, J.: DeepVessel: retinal vessel segmentation via deep learning and conditional random field. In: Ourselin, S., Joskowicz, L., Sabuncu, M.R., Unal, G., Wells, W. (eds.) MICCAI 2016. LNCS, vol. 9901, pp. 132–139. Springer, Cham (2016). https://doi.org/10.1007/978-3-319-46723-8_16

12. Dasgupta, A., Singh, S.: A fully convolutional neural network based structured prediction approach towards the retinal vessel segmentation. In: ISBI, pp. 248–251. IEEE, Melbourne (2017)
13. Orlando, J., Prokofyeva, E., Blaschko, M.: A discriminatively trained fully connected conditional random field model for blood vessel segmentation in fundus images. IEEE TBE **64**(1), 16–27 (2017)

APNet: Semantic Segmentation for Pelvic MR Image

Ting-Ting Liang[1](ID), Mengyan Sun[2](ID), Liangcai Gao[1](✉), Jing-Jing Lu[2](✉)(ID), and Satoshi Tsutsui[3]

[1] ICST, Peking University, Beijing, China
glc@pku.edu.cn
[2] Peking Union Medical College Hospital, Beijing, China
cjr.lujingjing@vip.163.com
[3] Indiana University Bloomington, Bloomington, IN, USA

Abstract. One of the time-consuming routine work for a radiologist is to discern anatomical structures from tomographic images. For assisting radiologists, this paper develops an automatic segmentation method for pelvic magnetic resonance (MR) images. The task has three major challenges (1) A pelvic organ can have various sizes and shapes depending on the axial image, which requires local contexts to segment correctly. (2) Different organs often have quite similar appearance in MR images, which requires global context to segment. (3) The number of available annotated images are very small to use the latest segmentation algorithms. To address the challenges, we propose a novel convolutional neural network called Attention-Pyramid network (APNet) that effectively exploits both local and global contexts, in addition to a data-augmentation technique that is particularly effective for MR images. In order to evaluate our method, we construct fine-grained (50 pelvic organs) MR image segmentation dataset, and experimentally confirm the superior performance of our techniques over the state-of-the-art image segmentation methods.

Keywords: Medical image · Semantic segmentation Convolutional neural networks · Pyramid pooling Attention mechanism

1 Introduction

Medical doctors routinely identify the anatomical structure of human body from tomographic images, which is extremely time-consuming. In order to assist these doctors to understand tomographic images efficiently, it is one of the key research in medical imaging to develop a method to automatically segment tomographic images into anatomical categories [6,9,11,15]. Among various tomography techniques, magnetic resonance (MR) imaging is often preferred for the purpose of radiotherapy planning due to the better soft-tissue contrast for organs involved in radiation therapy.

© Springer Nature Switzerland AG 2018
J.-H. Lai et al. (Eds.): PRCV 2018, LNCS 11257, pp. 259–272, 2018.
https://doi.org/10.1007/978-3-030-03335-4_23

In this paper, we are particularly interested in automatically segmenting pelvic MR images into 50 anatomical categories, which is much larger than previous work. The fine-grained segmentation results can greatly help radiologists to quickly identify pelvic structures, and be used for high-quality anatomical 3D reconstruction. In addition, the precise segmentation can help the doctors with follow-up diagnosis of relevant diseases such as sarcopenia. These are the primary motivations that we want to develop a system that automatically segment pelvic structures.

Our method is based on convolutional neural networks (CNNs), which is the backbone of state-of-the-art methods for image segmentation. However, segmenting pelvic MR images is more challenging than standard image segmentation due to its own characteristics. In fact, it is often not an easy task, even for experienced doctors, to correctly segmenting pelvic MR images, especially when the images have unusual anatomical structures. The task requires a thorough comprehension of the pelvic anatomy, knowledge in the pelvic diseases that cause the unusual structure, and the ability to recognize patterns in the scanned images. We collaborate with doctors in radiology department who actually segment pelvic MR images, and identify the three challenges for training CNNs. To address the challenges, we propose a novel CNN architecture called Attention-Pyramid network (APNet) and train it with a domain specific data augmentation. The challenges and our strategies are discussed in the following paragraphs.

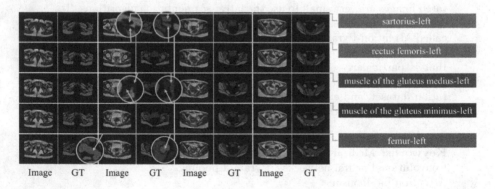

Fig. 1. An exemplar series pelvic MR images belongs to one patient, each image presenting separate scanning sessions of different axial. Taking an image and its ground truth (GT) as a pair, the correct reading order is from top to bottom, from left to right. To stress our challenge, the magnified part of the image shows the characteristics of MR images.

The first challenge is that a pelvic structure varies greatly in size and shape on different axial images, often with blurry boundaries caused by patient's belly movement when breathing. For example, Fig. 1 shows a series of MRI from a patient, where *femur-left* has two different shapes in the second and fourth columns of the last row. Moreover, there is no clear boundary between *muscle of the gluteus medius-left* and *muscle of the gluteus minimus-left* in the middle row. For these cases, doctors often rely on multiple local contexts about the position of organ (e.g. a particular organ should have two neighboring organs at bottom and right). In order for CNNs to effectively use these local contexts as doctors do, we adapt a layer that is particularly designed for multiple-level contexts aggregation, which is called a spatial pyramid pooling (see Sect. 3.1).

The second challenge is that different pelvic organs have similar appearances in MR images. For example, in Fig. 1, *sartorius-left* and *rectus femoris-left* look very similar, the key to distinguish them is their positions: one on top and one on bottom. For these cases, doctors usually depend on global contexts such as absolute positions of structures (e.g. a particular organ should be always at the bottom-right of the image). To equip the similar ability for CNNs, we adopt an mechanism that is designed to gather global level context, which is called attention mechanism (see Sect. 3.2).

Third, the number of annotated images is limited. The annotation cost for the segmentation is much higher than other typical computer vision tasks such as image classification (i.e., tag annotation) or object detection (i.e., bounding box annotation). Furthermore, unlike the natural images where we can use crowdsourcing for annotation, the medical task demands professional knowledge, which is not easily accessible. Our dataset is composed of only 320 MR images from 14 patients. To address this problem, we apply elastic deformation to the annotated images, which is a type of data augmentation. This is an effective way especially for MR image segmentation, because image deformation often occurs in real MR images and thus realistic deformations can be simulated easily (see Fig. 4).

Our extensive experiments show that each technique (pyramid module, attention mechanism, and data augmentation) contributes to the better performance for pelvic MR image segmentation (see Sect. 4).

Overall, the main contributions of our work are:

- We propose an automatic pelvic MR image segmentation method, which is the first one that completes pixel-level segmentation for a large number of structures (50 bones and muscles) on pelvic MR images.
- We equip the network with a spatial pyramid pooling layer for aggregating the multiple level of local contexts.
- We build an attention-mechanism that effectively gathers global level of contexts.
- We adopt a data augmentation strategy with image deformation to increase realistic training images.
- We conduct extensive experiments to show the effectiveness of our proposed method.

The rest of the paper is organized as follows. Section 2 reviews relevant literature. Section 3 introduces the proposed model. Section 4 presents the experimental results, and Sect. 5 concludes the paper.

2 Related Work

Pelvic Segmentation. Various methods for medical image segmentation have been developed over the past few years. Dowling et al. [6] use an atlas-based prior method to detect the edges of hip-bone, prostate, bladder and rectum, and the Mean Dice Similarity Coefficient (DSC) of the four organs reached 0.7. Ma et al. [15] use a shape-guided Chan-Vese model, exploit the difference between pelvic organs' intensity distribution and simultaneously detect the edges of four organs. In [9], MRI is used together with CT images to identify muscle structures, and the CycleGAN [23] is extended by adding a gradient consistency loss to improve the accuracy of boundary. Kazemifar et al. [11] use an encoder-decoder network called U-Net to segment male pelvic images, and it achieved 0.9 in Mean DSC. However, they segment sparsely distributed organs into four categories only. To the best of our knowledge, our work is the first that classify each pixel in pelvic MR images into the fine-grained categories (50 bones and muscles) that are densely distributed, which is more challenging than previous work that typically segments sparsely distributed organs into a few categories.

Semantic Segmentation in Deep Learning. Semantic segmentation is a task to classify every pixel in an image. Fully convolutional network [14] is the model that modifies image classification CNNs into semantic segmentation, and is a de facto backbone model for the state-of-the-art image segmentation. A problem in adopting CNN for segmentation is the existence of pooling layers. The pooling layer increases the receptive field by discarding the position information, but semantic segmentation requires pixel-wise classification, the position information needs to be preserved.

Researchers proposed two forms of methods to address this problem. The first is an encoder-decoder architecture such as U-Net [17] or SegNet [2]. The encoder uses the pooling layer to gradually reduce spatial dimensions of input data, and the decoder gradually recovers the details of target and the corresponding spatial dimensions through a network layer such as a deconvolution layer. It usually has a direct connection to pass information from encoder to decoder for better recovery of the position information.

Another method is multi-scaling, which is the idea to use multiple sizes of input images (i.e., sharing network), convolutional filters (i.e., dilated convolution), or pooling layers (i.e., spatial pyramid pooling). The sharing network [5,16] adjusts the size of input image to several proportions and passes them through a shared deep network. Then the final prediction result is from the fusion of the resulting multi-scale features. Dilated convolution [3,20,21] uses filters with multiple dilation (or atrous) factors, which can increase the receptive field without changing the size of feature map. Spatial pyramid pooling (SPP) [8,13,22] divides input image into subregions, aggregates the characteristics of each subregion, and finally concatenates features of all subregions to form a complete feature. This is an effective way to gather multiple levels of local contexts so we adapt it in our network.

Attention Mechanism. Attention mechanism has been widely used in image processing. Xu et al. [19] introduce spatial visual attention mechanisms which extracts image features from the middle CNN layer. Jing et.al [10] propose an attention mechanism that learns the weights of both visual and semantic features, to define abnormal locations in medical images and generate relevant description sentences. While these methods apply attention mechanism in two-dimensional space or time dimension, we apply an attention mechanism for the scaling factors. Inspired from [10], we propose an attention mechanism of joint learning, which combines predictions from multi-scale features when predicting the semantic label of a pixel. The final output of our model is generated by the maximum response of all scale predictions. We show that the proposed attention model effectively uses features at different locations and scales, which is crucial for identifying pelvic anatomical structures from global contexts.

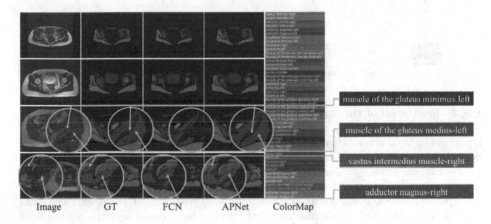

Image   GT   FCN   APNet   ColorMap

Fig. 2. Pelvic parsing issues we observe on our testset. FCN can only describe the structures roughly.

3   Model

This section describes our Attention-Pyramid Network (APNet) as illustrated in Fig. 3, which is designed to capture both local and global contexts. Our architecture engineering started from observing the segmentation results from FCN, which is a basic CNN for segmentation. In Fig. 2, we show samples from FCN and our APNet that we propose in this section. We can see that FCN fails to segment the boundary of *muscle of the gluteus minimus-left* and *muscle of the gluteus medius-left*. To segment this correctly, we need to care the local contexts of the two organs' boundaries. To equip this ability to CNN, we introduce spatial pyramid pooling that can capture multiple level of local contexts (See Sect. 3.1). Moreover, we can also see FCN fails to distinguish *vastus intermedius muscle-right* and *adductor magnus-right*, which is due to the lack of the global context

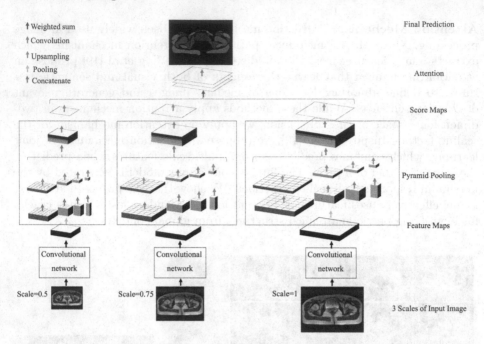

Fig. 3. Illustration of the proposed APNet. First we resize input image into 3 scales with portion of $\{1, 0.75, 0.5\}$, and use CNN separately to get feature maps of 3 sizes from last convolutional layer. Then a pyramid pooling layer, each for a feature map, forms pooled representation with bin sizes of $1 \times 1, 2 \times 2, 3 \times 3, 6 \times 6$ respectively. Followed by convolution, upsampling and concatenation, the four sub-region representations are concatenated with original feature map into a score map. Then score maps of 3 scales are upsampled to the maximum size, and the weighted sum of them gets the final score map. Finally, the representation is fed into a convolutional layer to get the final pixel-level prediction.

that *vastus intermedius muscle-right* should be at lower place on this axial image. To recognize global context effectively, we introduce attention mechanism (see Sect. 3.2). After technically describe the pyramid module and attention module, we finally describe the whole APNet architecture.

3.1 Pyramid Pooling Layer

Spatial Pyramid Pooling (SPP) [8] is to gather multiple levels of local contexts by pooling with multiple kernel sizes. Zhao et al. [22] apply the SPP for FCN based segmentation to aggregate information across subregions of different scales (i.e., different level of local contexts). We adopt this SPP module for our pyramid pooling layer. The layer firstly separates feature map into different sub-regions and forms pooled representation for different positions. Assuming that a pyramid pooling layer has L levels, in each spatial bin, it pools the responses of each filter of input feature map under L level scales from course to fine. Assuming the input feature map has the size of $n \times n$, for one pyramid level of $l \times l$ bins, we implement this pooling level as a sliding window pooling, where the window kernel size $= [1, n/l, n/l, 1]$, stride $= [1, n/l, n/l, 1]$, where $[\cdot]$ denotes ceiling operations. Each level reduces the dimension of feature map size to $1/l$ of the original one with level bin size of $l \times l$. Then we apply bilinear interpolation to upsample the low dimension features to the same size as the original feature map, and concatenate these features from multiple local contexts to form the final output of the pyramid pooling layer (See Sect. 3.3).

3.2 Attention

Our attention mechanism is to capture the global contexts efficiently, and help the network to find the optimal weighting scheme for multiple input image sizes. We apply the attention mechanism for the output of pyramid pooling layer. Assuming we use S scales (i.e., input image sizes), for ecah scale, the input image is resized and fed into a shared CNN that outputs a score map. The score maps from multiple scales are upsampled to the same size of the largest score map by bilinear interpolation. The final output is the weighted sum of score maps from all scales, where the weight reflects the importance of feature for each scale. The weighting scheme is initialized equally but, is updated by back-propagation in the training phase, so that it captures the global contexts effectively.

Furthermore, to better merge discriminative features for the final convolutional layer output, we add extra supervision [12] for each scale in this attention mechanism. Lee et al. [12] point out that distinguished classifiers trained with distinguished features demonstrate better performance in classification tasks. Particularly, the loss function for attention contains $1 + S$ cross entropy loss functions(one for final output and the other for each scale):

$$F = \sum_{i=1}^{S} \lambda_i \cdot F_i \tag{1}$$

$$\lambda_i = exp(F_i) / \sum_{t=1}^{S} exp(F_t) \tag{2}$$

$$Loss = min(H(F, gt)) + \sum_{i=1}^{S} min(H(F_i, gt_i)) \tag{3}$$

where F denotes the final output, gt denotes the original ground truth. F_i is the score map of scale s_i and gt_i is the corresponding ground truth. The ground truths are downsampled accurately to the same size of corresponding outputs during training. λ_i is the weight of scale s_i. H is cross entropy formula.

3.3 Attention-Pyramid Network Architecture

With the attention mechanism on top of the pyramid pooling module, we propose our Attention-Pyramid network (APNet), as shown in Fig. 3. We use the three scales $\{0.5, 0.75, 1\}$, resize the input image for each scale, and feed the resized images to a shared CNN. We specifically use the ImageNet pre-trained ResNet [7] with dilated network strategy [20] to extract a feature map from conv5 layer, which is $1/8$ of the input image in size. We feed the feature map into the pyramid pooling layer to gather multiple local contexts. The pooling window sizes are the whole, half, $1/3$, and $1/6$ of the feature map. Then we upsample the four pooled feature maps to the same size of original feature map, and concatenate them all. The pyramid pooling layer is followed by a convolutional layer to generate a score map for each scale. The weighted sum of three score maps will be the final segmentation results, where the weights are learned by the attention mechanism.

APNet effectively exploits both local and global contexts for pixel-level pelvic segmentation. The pyramid pooling layer can collect local information and is more representative than the *global coordinator* [13]. It learns local features and can adapt to the deformation of a structure on different axial images, but it sometimes confuses the categories (i.e., *category confusion* [22]) due to the lack of global contexts. This naturally calls for the attention mechanism that provides global contexts. The attention mechanism makes the model adaptively find the optimal weight for multiple scaled (or resized) images. Resizing does not change the relative size and position of organs, but smaller images helps CNNs to capture global contexts more easily than the high resolution images. Therefore, jointly training the attention mechanism and the spatial pooling layer is an effective way to gather both local contexts (by spatial pooling layer) and global contexts (by attention mechanism).

We note that the global contexts include the absolute position of pelvic structures (left-right symmetry, up-and-down order) in the image. In other words, some organ categories are determined by the (global) position in the MR image. For example, a hint to recognize *sartorius-right* is to check if it is on the left side of the image or not, which is exactly what radiologists do.

4   Experiments

4.1   Datasets

We prepare 320 MR images from 14 female patients, and professional doctors annotated them. The dataset covers image sizes of 611×610, 641×640, and 807×582. Images belong to one patient is called a series. Each series has 24 or 20 images of same size presenting separate scanning sessions of different axes. We use 240 MR images from 10 patients for training, 60 images from 3 patients for validation, and 20 MR images from a patient as test set.

4.2   Data Augmentation

For data augmentation, we originally tried random mirror, random resize, random rotation, and Gaussian Blur, which are effectively used in the state-of-the-art methods for natural scene parsing [3, 22], but these conventional methods did

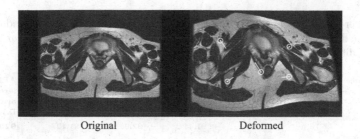

Original   Deformed

Fig. 4. Example of image deformation. Blue circles are control points. (Color figure online)

not perform well. We call it common data augmentation (CDA) in the experiment section. In our work, we adopt image deformation using moving least squares [18]. This is much more effective than the conventional methods, and can simulate one of the most common variation in MR images, because image deformation often occurs in real MR images. An example of data augmentation is shown in Fig. 4. We perform random deformation multiple times on the dataset to get a training set with 30k MR images, a validation set with 2k MR images. We make sure that images from a patient are not in multiple sets.

4.3 Evaluation Metrics

Following [14], we use the pixel wise accuracy and region intersection over union (IoU) between the segmentation results and ground truth to evaluate performance. Let TP_i (true positive) be the number of pixels of class i predicted to belong to class i, FP_i (false positive) be the number of pixels of any other classes but i predicted to be class i, FN_i (false negative) be the number of pixels of class i predicted to belong to any other classes but i. Then we compute IoU_i for class i and *mean IoU* for all classes:

- $IoU_i = TP_i/(TP_i + FP_i + FN_i)$
- $Mean\,IoU = \sum_{i=1}^{n}(TP_i/(TP_i + FP_i + FN_i))$
- $Pixel\,Accuracy = \sum_{i=1}^{n} TP_i/(TP_i + FN_i)$

4.4 Implementation Details

We use the Resnet-101 network pre-trained on Imagenet that is adapted for semantic segmentation as described in Sect. 3.2. To improve model speed, we reduce kernel size of resent101 conv5 from 7×7 to 3×3. Following [3], we implement dilated convolution with atrous sampling rate 12. For training, we adapt the *poly* learning rate policy [3] where current learning rate is multiplied by $(1 - \frac{iter}{max_{iter}})^{power}$. We set initial learning rate of 2.5×10^{-5}, power to 0.9 respectively. With iteration number of 110K in max, momentum and weight decay are set to 0.9 and 0.0005 respectively. We use Tensorflow [1] for implementation.

Table 1. Per-class IoU(%) on test set. *CDA* refers to common data augmendation. *DA* refers to the deformation data augmentation we performed, *levels of attention* indicates how many different sizes we adjust for the input image.

No.	Class name	FCN + DA	DeepLab- v2 + DA	PSPNet + DA	PSPNet + CDA	APNet (2 levels of attention) + DA	APNet (3 levels of attention) + DA
1	vastus lateralis-right	56.73	90.31	91.44	82.04	91.12	**92.68**
2	vastus lateralis-left	16.06	74.75	72.66	57.27	75.71	**77.81**
3	adductor brevis-right	61.71	**88.01**	85.94	70.07	87.46	87.85
4	adductor brevis-left	45.22	82.35	84.87	74.76	**88.51**	87.26
5	adductor magnus-right	69.21	87.72	87.30	73.70	**89.48**	**89.48**
6	adductor magnus-left	53.39	88.55	87.71	79.94	**91.23**	90.99
7	quadrauts femoris-right	50.78	74.77	76.60	60.17	77.77	**81.85**
8	quadrauts femoris-left	23.40	69.65	70.32	52.37	72.85	**73.75**
9	pectineus- right	69.05	80.29	81.10	62.90	84.30	**85.99**
10	pectineus-left	52.95	77.62	75.88	62.13	**79.98**	79.28
11	muscle of the tensor fasciae latae-right	70.74	91.47	91.18	77.45	**94.68**	94.30
12	muscle of the tensor fasciae latae-left	31.96	72.28	71.73	56.84	**76.05**	74.08
13	rectus femoris-Right	58.38	91.34	92.02	80.44	**94.86**	94.77
14	rectus femoris-left	35.62	76.76	77.33	62.59	79.25	**80.18**
15	obturator externus-right	69.18	88.16	87.11	71.61	87.16	**88.34**
16	obturator externus-left	65.64	88.86	87.71	74.13	89.68	**90.56**
17	urinary bladder	92.15	96.30	95.26	87.97	96.36	**96.52**
18	muscle of the obturator internus-right	56.49	74.51	72.89	53.95	73.68	**75.66**
19	muscle of the obturator internus-left	51.02	65.15	61.87	47.45	65.70	**66.62**
20	piriformis- right	71.52	88.19	87.30	74.10	89.01	**89.10**
21	piriformis-left	72.00	72.13	67.69	52.45	71.63	**74.27**
22	sartorius- right	51.58	81.98	86.69	73.75	**89.59**	89.40
23	sartorius-left	27.23	68.60	69.33	53.45	**72.97**	72.89
24	muscle of the gluteus minimus-right	55.44	87.44	89.62	79.94	91.97	**92.82**

(continued)

Table 1. (*continued*)

No.	Class name	FCN + DA	DeepLab-v2 + DA	PSPNet + DA	PSPNet + CDA	APNet (2 levels of attention) + DA	APNet (3 levels of attention) + DA
25	muscle of the gluteus minimus-left	29.01	53.50	53.19	39.59	58.28	**58.3**
26	muscle of the gluteus medius-right	74.86	93.20	93.88	85.31	94.94	**95.28**
27	muscle of the gluteus medius-left	48.44	76.29	74.55	59.10	77.59	**77.84**
28	muscle of the gluteus maximus-right	86.61	91.19	91.25	78.87	91.76	**93.65**
29	muscle of the gluteus maximus-left	81.25	84.06	82.12	65.75	84.02	**84.70**
30	erector spinae-right	69.41	77.64	76.07	56.49	77.43	**83.24**
31	erector spinae-left	62.81	71.16	69.88	50.68	72.35	**73.26**
32	rectus abdominis-right	80.10	81.52	81.07	68.65	**88.45**	86.69
33	rectus abdominis-left	77.56	84.69	81.63	68.76	**87.89**	87.55
34	iliacus-right	67.93	90.30	92.20	80.61	**93.61**	93.23
35	iliacus-left	48.71	69.02	64.92	52.40	69.34	**71.25**
36	psoas major-right	66.03	87.22	84.47	72.77	88.90	**88.9**
37	psoas major-left	48.53	66.97	64.74	49.70	69.72	**69.72**
38	femur-right	80.97	91.95	91.70	79.35	92.51	**93.99**
39	femur-left	72.57	84.85	83.72	68.90	85.10	**86.35**
40	hip bone-right	73.26	87.67	86.92	73.59	88.67	**89.70**
41	hip bone-left	62.82	68.51	64.85	48.57	68.52	**70.13**
42	sacrum	73.07	79.82	82.38	72.16	84.60	**84.73**
43	semiten-dinosus-right	21.18	65.73	64.80	49.30	63.22	**70.94**
44	semiten-dinosus-left	24.17	56.17	52.36	44.85	61.87	**63.25**
45	gracilis-right	6.37	46.88	43.58	29.04	57.89	**63.04**
46	gracilis-left	6.40	43.25	38.82	30.77	50.13	**50.18**
47	vastus intermedius muscle-right	9.82	80.23	79.06	70.98	85.42	**86.46**
48	vastus intermedius muscle-left	3.08	63.02	64.77	55.44	67.53	**70.22**
49	adductor longus-right	50.87	81.07	83.32	69.88	**89.58**	89.18
50	adductor longus-left	48.44	78.53	82.20	72.67	**87.90**	87.19

4.5   Baselines and Experimental Setup

We compare APNet with three existing neural network architectures: FCN [14], Deeplab-v2 [3], and PSPNet [22]. FCN is based on VGG architecture while others including ours are based on Dilated [21] Resnet-101 [5]. PSPNet is the state-of-the-art in natural image segmentation. Both APNet and PSPNet have spatial pyramid pooling [8] with the level of 4 [22]. For APNet, we use two different levels of attention: $\{1, 0.75, 0.5\}$ and $\{1, 0.75\}$ where each number is a scaling factor for input image resizing. We intentionally use the factor more than 0.5 because it is known that scale portion less than 0.5 leads to unsatisfactory results [4]. The experiments with more levels of scaling factors are future work.

All methods are trained with data augmentation strategies, as we describe in Sect. 4.2. To demonstrate the effectiveness of our data augmentation strategy, we also train PSPNet with common data augmentation (CDA) such as random mirror, random resize, and random rotation, and call it *PSPNet + CDA*.

4.6   Results and Discussions

We show our experimental results on test set in Table 1. APNet performs the best among FCN, DeepLab-v2, and PSPNet. Of the two variants of APNet, 3 levels ($\{1, 0.75, 0.5\}$) yields the best performance. With attention mechanism, our network has the highest score of 80.27% mIOU and 87.12% mean pixel accuracy. We can also see the benefit of our data augmentation (DA) strategy over the common data augmentation (CDA). When we train PSPNet with CDA, it only has 64.72% mIOU and 74.39% mean pixel accuracy but with DA, it has 76.08% mIOU and 84.10%, which is 10% better results (Table 2).

Table 2. Test mIOU and mean pixel accuracy for each method. DA refers to deformation data augmentation based on image deformation. CDA refers to the common data augmentation.

	mIoU(%)	Pixel Acc(%)
FCN + DA	52.58	72.03
DeepLab-v2 + DA	76.70	84.90
PSPNet + DA	76.08	84.10
PSPNet + CDA	64.72	74.39
APNet (2 levels of attention) + DA	79.38	86.20
APNet (3 levels of attention) + DA	**80.27**	**87.12**

We also show sample images from the test set in Fig. 5. APNet is designed to capture both local contexts and global contexts. The samples tell that DeepLab often fails to capture local contexts, and PSPNet does not perform satisfactorily in capturing global context, but APNet captures both. For example, in the first

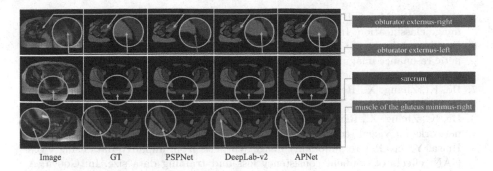

Fig. 5. Improvements on test set. APNet captures more global context than PSPNet, and more local context than DeepLab-v2.

row, PSPNet misclassified a little part of *obturator externus-left* to *obturator externus-right*. APNet is able to fix the error due to the global context captured by attention mechanism. For another example, in the second row, we see that DeepLab-v2 failed to segment *sarcrum* precisely while APNet captured local context to describe its contour. Similarly in the third row, DeepLab-v2 failed to capture the local context when segmenting the connected area of *muscle of the gluteus minimus-right* while APNet can segment it precisely.

5 Conclusion

In this paper, we automatically segment MR pelvic images, with the goal to help medical professionals discern anatomical structures more efficiently. Our proposed methods address the three major challenges: high variation of organs' sizes and shapes often with the ambiguous boundaries, similar appearances of different organs, and small number of annotated MR images. To cope with these challenges, we propose Attention-Pyramid network and adopt a data augmentation strategy with image deformation. We experimentally demonstrate the effectiveness of our proposed methods over the baselines.

References

1. Abadi, M., Barham, P., Chen, J., Chen, Z., et al.: TensorFlow: a system for large-scale machine learning. In: 12th USENIX Symposium on Operating Systems Design and Implementation (OSDI) (2016)
2. Badrinarayanan, V., Kendall, A., Cipolla, R.: SegNet: a deep convolutional encoder-decoder architecture for image segmentation. arXiv:1511.00561 (2015)
3. Chen, L.C., Papandreou, G., Kokkinos, I., Murphy, K., Yuille, A.L.: DeepLab: semantic image segmentation with deep convolutional nets, atrous convolution, and fully connected CRFs. TPAMI (2016)
4. Chen, L.C., Yang, Y., Wang, J., Xu, W., Yuille, A.L.: Attention to scale: scale-aware semantic image segmentation. In: CVPR (2016)

5. Ciresan, D., Meier, U., Schmidhuber, J.: Multi-column deep neural networks for image classification. In: CVPR (2012)
6. Dowling, J.A., et al.: An atlas-based electron density mapping method for magnetic resonance imaging (MRI)-alone treatment planning and adaptive MRI-based prostate radiation therapy. Int. J. Radiat. Oncol. **83**(1), e5–e11 (2011)
7. He, K., Zhang, X., Ren, S., Sun, J.: Deep residual learning for image recognition. In: CVPR (2016)
8. He, K., Zhang, X., Ren, S., Sun, J.: Spatial pyramid pooling in deep convolutional networks for visual recognition. TPAMI (2015)
9. Hiasa, Y., et al.: Cross-modality image synthesis from unpaired data using Cycle-GAN: effects of gradient consistency loss and training data size. In: Gooya, A., Goksel, O., Oguz, I., Burgos, N. (eds.) SASHIMI 2018. LNCS, vol. 11037, pp. 31–41. Springer, Cham (2018). https://doi.org/10.1007/978-3-030-00536-8_4
10. Jing, B., Xie, P., Xing, E.: On the automatic generation of medical imaging reports. In: CVPR (2018)
11. Kazemifar, S., et al.: Segmentation of the prostate and organs at risk in male pelvic CT images using deep learning. arXiv:1802.09587 (2018)
12. Lee, C.Y., Xie, S., Gallagher, P., Zhang, Z., Tu, Z.: Deeply-supervised nets. In: AISTATS (2015)
13. Liu, W., Rabinovich, A., Berg, A.C.: ParseNet: looking wider to see better. In: ICLR (2016)
14. Long, J., Shelhamer, E., Darrell, T.: Fully convolutional networks for semantic segmentation. In: CVPR (2015)
15. Ma, Z., Jorge, R.N.M., Mascarenhas, T., Tavares, J.M.R.S.: Segmentation of female pelvic cavity in axial T2-weighted MR images towards the 3D reconstruction. Int. J. Numer. Method Biomed. Eng. **28**(6–7), 714–726 (2012). https://doi.org/10.1002/cnm.2463
16. Felzenszwalb, P.F., Girshick, R.B., McAllester, D., Ramanan, D.: Object detection with discriminatively trained part-based models. TPAMI (2010)
17. Ronneberger, O., Fischer, P., Brox, T.: U-Net: convolutional networks for biomedical image segmentation. In: Navab, N., Hornegger, J., Wells, W.M., Frangi, A.F. (eds.) MICCAI 2015. LNCS, vol. 9351, pp. 234–241. Springer, Cham (2015). https://doi.org/10.1007/978-3-319-24574-4_28
18. Schaefer, S., McPhail, T., Warren, J.: Image deformation using moving least squares. ACM Trans. Graph. (TOG) **25**(3), 533–540 (2006). Proceedings of ACM SIGGRAPH
19. Xu, K., et al.: Show, attend and tell: neural image caption generation with visual attention. In: ICML (2015)
20. Yu, F., Koltun, V.: Multi-scale context aggregation by dilated convolutions. arXiv:1511.07122 (2015)
21. Yu, F., Koltun, V., Funkhouser, T.: Dilated residual networks. In: CVPR (2017)
22. Zhao, H., Shi, J., Qi, X., Wang, X., Jia, J.: Pyramid scene parsing network. In: CVPR (2017)
23. Zhu, J.Y., et al.: Unpaired image-to-image translation using cycle-consistent adversarial networks. In: CVPR (2017)

LSTN: Latent Subspace Transfer Network for Unsupervised Domain Adaptation

Shanshan Wang and Lei Zhang[✉]

College of Communication Engineering, Chongqing University,
No. 174 Shazheng Street, Shapingba District, Chongqing 400044, China
{wangshanshan,leizhang}@cqu.edu.cn

Abstract. For handling cross-domain distribution mismatch, a specially designed subspace and reconstruction transfer functions bridging multiple domains for heterogeneous knowledge sharing are wanted. In this paper, we propose a novel reconstruction-based transfer learning method called Latent Subspace Transfer Network (LSTN). We embed features/pixels of source and target into reproducing kernel Hilbert space (RKHS), in which the high dimensional features are mapped to nonlinear latent subspace by feeding them into MLP network. This approach is very simple but effective by combining both advantages of subspace learning and neural network. The adaptation behaviors can be achieved in the method of joint learning a set of hierarchical nonlinear subspace representation and optimal reconstruction matrix simultaneously. Notably, as the latent subspace model is a MLP Network, the layers in it can be optimized directly to avoid a pre-trained model which needs large-scale data. Experiments demonstrate that our approach outperforms existing non-deep adaptation methods and exhibits classification performance comparable with that of modern deep adaptation methods.

Keywords: Domain adaptation · Latent subspace · MLP

1 Introduction

In computer vision, the dilemma of insufficient labeled data is common in visual big data, one of the prevailing problems in the practical application, is that when training data (source domain) exhibit a different distribution to test data (target domain), the task-specific classifier usually does not work well on related but distribution mismatched tasks.

Domain adaptation (DA) [5,15,31] techniques that are capable of easing such domain shift problem have received significant attention from engineering recently. It is thus of great practical importance to explore DA methods. These models allow machine learning methods to be self-adapted among multiple knowledge domains, that is, the trained model parameters from one data domain can be adapted to another domain. The assumption underlying DA is that, although the domains differ, there is sufficient commonality to support such adaptation.

© Springer Nature Switzerland AG 2018
J.-H. Lai et al. (Eds.): PRCV 2018, LNCS 11257, pp. 273–284, 2018.
https://doi.org/10.1007/978-3-030-03335-4_24

A substantial number of approaches to domain adaptation have been proposed in the context of both shallow learning and deep learning, which bridge the source and target domains by learning domain-invariant feature representations without using target labels, such that the classifier learned from the source domain can also be applied to the target domain.

Visual representations learned by deep CNNs are fairly domain-invariant. Relatively high accuracy is always reported over a lot of visual tasks using off the-shelf CNN representations [4,26]. However, on one hand, deep neural networks which learn abstract feature representations can only reduce, but not remove, the cross-domain discrepancy. On the other, training a deep model relies on massive amounts of labeled data. Compared with deep method, shallow domain adaptation methods which are more suitable for small-scale data usually fail to reach the high accuracy as deep learning.

Our work is primarily motivated by [21] which investigates a provocative question that domain adaptation is necessary even if CNN-based features are powerful. We thus proposed a non-deep method which combines both advantages of subspace learning and neural networks inspired by [12]. Although this LSTN method is simple, it can achieve competitive results compared with deep methods. The main contribution and novelty of this work are threefold:

- In order to achieve the domain alignment, we propose a simple but effective net called Latent Subspace Transfer Network (LSTN). In order to get an optimal subspace representation, a joint learning mechanism is adopted for pursuing the latent subspace and reconstruction matrix simultaneously.
- The optimal latent subspace to map the source and target samples in LSTN is achieved by MLP network, which has a simple network structure but is effective. The model is a non-linear neural network and can be optimized directly to avoid a pre-trained model which needs large-scale data.
- In this simple network, we embed features/pixels of source and target into reproducing kernel Hilbert spaces (RKHS) as preprocessing before putting them into the optimization procedure. In this way, the dimension of input and the cost of running time are both reduced.

2   Related Works

2.1   Shallow Domain Adaptation

A number of shallow learning methods have been proposed to tackle DA problems. Generally, these shallow domain adaptation methods comprise of three categories: Classifier based approaches, feature augmentation/transformation based approaches and feature reconstruction based approaches. [5] proposed an adaptive multiple kernel learning (AMKL) for web-consumer video event recognition. [35] proposed a robust domain classifier adaptation method (EDA) with manifold regularization for visual recognition. [19] also proposed a Transfer Joint Matching (TJM) which tends to learn a non-linear transformation across domains by minimizing the MMD based distribution discrepancy. [36] proposed a Latent Sparse Domain Transfer (LSDT) method by jointly learning a subspace projection and sparse reconstruction across domains. Similarly, Shao et al. [25] proposed a LTSL method by pre-learning a subspace using PCA or LDA. Jhuo et al. [13] proposed a RDALR method, in which the source data is reconstructed by the target data using low-rank model. Recently, [21] proposed a LDADA method which can achieve the effect of DA without explicit adaptation by a LDA-inspired approach.

2.2 Deep Domain Adaptation

As deep CNNs become a mainstream technique, deep learning has witnessed a great achievements [22, 29, 32] in unsupervised DA. Very recently, [27] explored the performance improvements by combining the deep learning and DA methods.

Donahue et al. [4] proposed a deep transfer strategy for small-scale object recognition, by training a CNN network (AlexNet) on ImageNet. Tzeng et al. [29] proposed a CNN based DDC method which achieved successful knowledge transfer between domains and tasks. Long et al. [17] proposed a deep adaptation network (DAN) by imposing MMD loss on the high-level features across domains. Additionally, Long et al. [20] also proposed a residual transfer network (RTN) which tends to learn a residual classifier based on softmax loss. Hu et al. [12] proposed a non-CNN based deep transfer metric learning (DTML) method to learn a set of hierarchical nonlinear transformations for cross-domain visual recognition. Recently, GANs inspired adversarial domain adaptation methods have been preliminarily studied. Tzeng et al. proposed a novel ADDA method [30] for adversarial domain adaptation, in which CNN is used for adversarial discriminative feature learning. The work has shown the potential of adversarial learning in domain adaptation. In [11], Hoffman et al. proposed a CyCADA method which adapts representations at both the pixel-level and feature-level, enforcing cycle-consistency by leveraging a task loss.

However, most deep DA methods need large-scale data to train the model in advance, the insufficient data task involved is just used to fine tune the model. In contrast to these ideas, we show that one can achieve fairly good classification performance without pre-trained.

3   The Proposed Latent Subspace Transfer Network

3.1   Notation

In this paper, the source and target domain are defined by subscript "S" and "T". The training set of source and target domain are defined as $X_S \in \mathbb{R}^{d \times n_S}$ and $X_T \in \mathbb{R}^{d \times n_T}$, where d denotes dimension of input, n_S and n_T denote the number of samples in source and target domain, respectively. Let C represents the number of classes, $Z \in \mathbb{R}^{n_S \times n_T}$ represents the reconstruction coefficient matrix. $\| \cdot \|_F$ and $\| \cdot \|_*$ denotes Frobenius norm and nuclear norm, respectively.

Notably, in order to reduce the feature dimension of input, we first embed the features in source and target domain into reproducing kernel Hilbert spaces

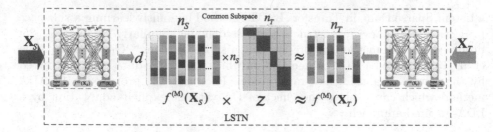

Fig. 1. The basic idea of the LSTN method is shown in Fig. 1. For each sample in the training sets from the source domain and the target domain, we pass it to the MLP network. We enforce the reconstruction constraint on the outputs of all training samples at the top of the network, in this way, the adaptation behaviors can be achieved by joint learning a set of hierarchical nonlinear subspace representation and optimal reconstruction matrix simultaneously. The network architecture of the MLP used in our methods is also shown in Fig. 1. The X is the data points in the input space, $f^{(1)}(X)$ is the output in the hidden layer and $f^{(2)}(X)$ is the resulting representation of X in the common subspace. In our experiments, the number of layers is set as $M = 2$.

(RKHSs) as preprocessing to get X_S and X_T, then feed them to nonlinear neural network latent subspace. The kernel embedding represents a probability distribution $\mathbf{P}$ by an element in RKHS endowed by a kernel $k(\cdot)$ where the distribution is mapped to the expected feature map.

In our experiments, we consider a closer to reality case where no labeled training set is obtained from the target domain in unsupervised setting.

3.2 Model Formulation

As is shown is Fig. 1, unlike most previous transfer learning methods which usually seek a single linear subspace to map samples into a common latent subspace, we construct a multilayer perceptron network to compute the representations of each sample x by passing it to multiple layers of nonlinear transformations. By using such a network, besides the nonlinear mapping function can be explicitly obtained, the network structure is much simpler than deep methods which can avoid a pre-trained model.

Assume there are $M + 1$ layers in the designed network. The output X at the mth layer is computed as:

$$f^{(m)}(\mathbf{X}) = \mathbf{h}^{(m)} = \varphi(\mathbf{Z}^{(m)}) = \varphi(\mathbf{W}^{(m)}\mathbf{h}^{(m-1)} + \mathbf{b}^{(m)}) \tag{1}$$

where $m = 1, 2, \ldots, M$ and $p^{(m)}$ units in the mth layer. $\mathbf{W}^{(m)} \in \mathbb{R}^{p^{(m)} \times p^{(m-1)}}$ and $\boldsymbol{b}^{(m)} \in \mathbb{R}^{p^{(m)}}$ are the parameters of weight matrix and bias in this layer, the $\mathbf{Z}^{(m)} = \mathbf{W}^{(m)}\mathbf{h}^{(m-1)} + \mathbf{b}^{(m)}$ and $\varphi(\cdot)$ is a nonlinear activation function which operates component-wisely, such as widely used tanh or sigmoid functions. The nonlinear mapping $f^{(m)} : \mathbb{R}^{p^{(m-1)}} \to \mathbb{R}^{p^{(m)}}$ is a function in the mth layer parameterized by $\{\mathbf{W}^{(i)}\}_{i=1}^m$ and $\{\mathbf{b}^{(i)}\}_{i=1}^m$. For the first layer, we assume $\mathbf{h}^{(0)} = \mathbf{X}$ ($\boldsymbol{X}_S$ or $\boldsymbol{X}_T$) and $p^{(0)} = d$.

For both source data $\boldsymbol{X}_S$ and target data $\boldsymbol{X}_T$, their probability distributions are different in the original feature space. In order to reduce the distribution difference, it is desirable to map the probability distribution of the source domain and that of the target domain into the common transformed subspace. The two domains are finally represented as $f^{(m)}(\boldsymbol{X}_S)$ and $f^{(m)}(\boldsymbol{X}_T)$ at the mth layer of our designed network respectively, and their reconstruction error can be expressed by computing the squared Euclidean distance between the representations $f^{(M)}(\boldsymbol{X}_S)$ and $f^{(M)}(\boldsymbol{X}_T)$ at the last layer as:

$$D_{st}(\mathbf{X}_S, \mathbf{X}_T) = ||f^{(M)}(\mathbf{X}_S)\boldsymbol{Z} - f^{(M)}(\mathbf{X}_T)||_F^2 \tag{2}$$

The low-rank representation is advantageous in getting the block diagonal solution for subspace segmentation, so that the global structure can be preserved. In constructing the reconstruction matrix $\boldsymbol{Z}$ in this paper, the low-rank regularizer is used to better account for the global characteristics. By combining the reconstruction loss and the regularizer item together, the general objective function of the proposed LSTN model can be formulated as follows.

$$\begin{aligned} \min_{f^{(m)}, \boldsymbol{Z}} J &= D_{st}(\mathbf{X}_S, \mathbf{X}_T) + \lambda ||\boldsymbol{Z}||_* + \gamma \sum_{m=1}^M (||\mathbf{W}^{(m)}||_F^2 + ||\mathbf{h}^{(m)}||_2^2) \\ &= ||f^{(M)}(\mathbf{X}_S)\boldsymbol{Z} - f^{(M)}(\mathbf{X}_T)||_F^2 + \lambda ||\boldsymbol{Z}||_* + \gamma \sum_{m=1}^M (||\mathbf{W}^{(m)}||_F^2 + ||\mathbf{b}^{(m)}||_2^2) \end{aligned} \tag{3}$$

where $\lambda(\lambda > 0)$ and $\gamma(\gamma > 0)$ are the tunable positive regularization parameters.

3.3   Optimization

To solve the optimization problem in Eq. (3), a variable alternating optimization strategy is considered, i.e., one variable is solved while frozen the other one. In addition, the inexact augmented Lagrangian multiplier (IALM) and alternating direction method of multipliers (ADMM) are used in solving each variable, respectively. We just set reconstruction matrix ($\boldsymbol{Z}$) and subspace representation ($f^{(m)}(\mathbf{X})$) as two variables. For solving the $\boldsymbol{Z}$, auxiliary variable J is added. To obtain the parameters $\mathbf{W}^{(m)}$ and $\mathbf{b}^{(m)}$, stochastic sub-gradient descent method is employed. With the two updating steps for $f^{(m)}(\mathbf{X})$ and $\boldsymbol{Z}$, the iterative optimization procedure of the proposed LSTN is summarized in Algorithm 1.

3.4   Classification

In this paper, the superiority of the proposed method is shown through the cross-domain or cross-place classification performance on the source data and target data in subspace, which can be represented as $\boldsymbol{\mathcal{X}}_S = f^{(M)}(\mathbf{X}_S)$ and $\boldsymbol{\mathcal{X}}_T = f^{(M)}(\mathbf{X}_T)$, respectively. Then, the general classifiers can be used for training on the source data $\boldsymbol{\mathcal{X}}_S$ with label $\boldsymbol{\mathcal{Y}}_S$ in unsupervised mode. Finally, the recognition performance is verified and compared based on the target data $\boldsymbol{\mathcal{X}}_T$ and target label $\boldsymbol{\mathcal{Y}}_T$.

Algorithm 1. The Proposed LSTN

Input: X_S, X_T, λ, γ.

Procedure:

1. Initialize: Add auxiliary variable J, where $\mathcal{Z} = J$.

              Add Lag-multipliers R_1 and penalty parameter μ.

2. **While** not converge **do**

  2.1 **Step1**: Do forward propagation to all data points;

  2.2 **Step2**: Compute objective function;

  2.3 **Step3**: Fix J and $\mathcal{Z}$, and update $\mathbf{W}^{(m)}$ and $\mathbf{b}^{(m)}$ in $f^{(m)}$;

      For $m = M, M-1, ..., 1$ do

         Compute $\nabla(\mathbf{W}^{(m)})$ and $\nabla(\mathbf{b}^{(m)})$ by back-propagation operator using

         $\nabla(\mathbf{W}^{(m)}) = 2\mathbf{L}s^{(m)}(\mathbf{h}_S^{(m-1)})^T - 2\mathbf{L}_T{}^{(m)}(\mathbf{h}_T^{(m-1)})^T + 2\gamma\mathbf{W}^{(m)a}$ and

         $\nabla(\mathbf{b}^{(m)}) = 2\mathbf{L}s^{(m)} - 2\mathbf{L}_T{}^{(m)} + 2\gamma\mathbf{b}^{(m)a}$;

      end

      For $m = 1, 2, ..., M$ do

         Update $\mathbf{W}^{(m)}$ and $\mathbf{b}^{(m)}$ according to Gradient descent operator[24];

      end

  2.4 **Step4**: Fix $\mathbf{W}^{(m)}$ and $\mathbf{b}^{(m)}$, and update $\mathcal{Z}$ using ADMM;

      Fix $\mathcal{Z}$, and update J by using the SVT operator;

      Fix J, and compute $\nabla(\mathcal{Z})$ by back-propagation operator using

         $\nabla(\mathcal{Z}) = 2(\mathbf{h}_S^{(M)})^T(\mathbf{h}_S^{(M)}\mathcal{Z} - \mathbf{h}_T^{(M)}) + R_1 + \mu(\mathcal{Z} - J)$;

      Update $\mathcal{Z}$ according to Gradient descent operator[24];

  2.5 Update the multiplier R_1 by $R_1 = R_1 + \mu(\mathcal{Z} - J)$

  2.6 Update the parameter μ by $\mu = min(\mu \times 1.01, max_\mu)$

  2.7 Check convergence

end while

Output: $\mathbf{W}^{(m)}$, $\mathbf{b}^{(m)}$ and $\mathcal{Z}$.

$$\mathbf{L}s^{(M)} = (\mathbf{h}_S^{(M)}\mathcal{Z} - \mathbf{h}_T^{(M)})\mathcal{Z}^T \odot \varphi'(Z_S^{(M)})$$
$$\mathbf{L}s^{(m)} = (\mathbf{W}^{(m+1)})^T\mathbf{L}s^{(m+1)} \odot \varphi'(Z_S^{(m)})$$
$$\mathbf{L}_T{}^{(M)} = (\mathbf{h}_S^{(M)}\mathcal{Z} - \mathbf{h}_T^{(M)}) \odot \varphi'(Z_T^{(M)})$$
$$\mathbf{L}_T{}^{(m)} = (\mathbf{W}^{(m+1)})^T\mathbf{L}_T{}^{(m+1)} \odot \varphi'(Z_T^{(m)})$$

4   Experiments

In this section, the experiments on several benchmark datasets [7,9,16] have been exploited for evaluating the proposed LSTN method, including: cross-domain 4DA office data and cross-place Satellite-Scene5 (SS5) dataset [21]. Several related transfer learning methods based on feature transformation and reconstruction, such as GFK [8], SA [6], DIP [2], TJM [19], LSSA [1], CORAL [28], JDA [18], JGSA [34], ILS [10], even the latest LDADA [21] have been compared and discussed. As the LSTN model we proposed can be regarded as a shallow domain adaptation approach, therefore, the shallow feature (4DA SURF features) and deep feature (4DA-VGG-M features) can be fed into the model. The deep transfer learning methods are also used to compare with our method (Fig. 2).

Fig. 2. Some samples from 4DA datasets

Results on 4DA Office Dataset (Amazon, DSLR, Webcam and Caltech 256) [8]

This dataset is a standard cross-domain object recognition dataset. Four domains such as Amazon (A), DSLR (D), Webcam (W), and Caltech 256 (C) are included in 4DA dataset, which contains 10 object classes. With the domain adaptation setting, 12 cross-domain tasks are tested, e.g. $A \to D$, $C \to D$. In our experiment, the configuration is followed in [17] by full protocol. We compare the classification performance of LSTN using the conventional 800-bin SURF features [8]. The recognition accuracies are reported in Table 1, from which we observe that the performance of our method is higher than state-of-the-art method and 3.6% higher than the latest LDADA method in average cross-domain recognition performance.

CNN features (FC7 of VGG-M) of 4DA datasets are also used to verify the classification performance. This allows us to compare against several recently reported results. We have chosen the first nine tasks to exploit the performance in our method. Average multi-class accuracy is used as the performance measure. We have highlighted the best results in Table 2, from which we can observe that the proposed LSTN (92.2%) is better than LDADA (92.0%), and shows a superior performance over other related methods.

The compared methods above are shallow transfer learning. It is interesting to compare with deep transfer learning methods, such as AlexNet [14], DDC [29], DAN [17] and RTN [20]. The first nine tasks are used to verify the classification performance. The comparison is described in Table 3, from which we can observe that our proposed method ranks the second in average performance (92.2%), which is inferior to the residual transfer network (RTN), but still better than other deep transfer learning models. The comparison shows that the proposed LSTN, as a shallow transfer learning method, has a good competitiveness.

Notably, the 4DA and CNN features in 4DA tasks are challenging benchmarks, which attract many competitive approaches for evaluation and comparison. Therefore, excellent baselines have been achieved.

Results on SS5 (Satellite-Scene5) (Banja Luka (B), UC Merced Land Use (U), and Remote Sensing (R))

To validate that LSTN is general and can be applied to other images with different characteristics and particularly to the categories which are not included

Table 1. Recognition accuracy (%) in 4DA-SURF features and time cost (s) in LSTN

4DA tasks	NA	GFK	DIP	SA	JDA	TJM	LSSA	CORAL	ILS	JGSA	LDADA	Ours
$A \rightarrow D$	36.3	39.9	47.8	37.7	44.2	45.6	39.2	38.5	37.3	**49.4**	39.1	46.5 (2.75 s)
$C \rightarrow D$	37.6	42.9	46.9	40.9	44.1	38.4	46.3	31.8	38.3	46.0	41.5	**52.2 (3.65 s)**
$W \rightarrow D$	73.6	78.7	79.6	70.3	86.3	83.6	57.4	80.9	80.1	78.5	74.6	**86.6 (0.51 s)**
$A \rightarrow C$	37.3	44.3	41.4	44.8	**44.9**	42.4	40.9	37.1	35.4	40.8	38.4	44.6 (24.42 s)
$W \rightarrow C$	23.7	32.0	30.0	32.3	29.8	33.3	29.7	32.5	33.1	29.7	31.7	**36.8 (7.37 s)**
$D \rightarrow C$	25.5	30.8	29.3	31.1	34.4	32.3	31.2	27.8	**36.8**	30.2	29.9	36.2 (5.06 s)
$D \rightarrow A$	28.4	40.4	31.6	40.8	**44.6**	37.1	32.9	31.9	41.9	39.0	40.6	40.3 (3.86 s)
$W \rightarrow A$	28.7	38.3	33.8	**43.3**	42.0	39.5	38.5	39.4	38.0	34.6	35.1	40.4 (5.67 s)
$C \rightarrow A$	46.4	56.6	56.4	54.4	**59.8**	54.4	51.5	45.9	28.5	55.1	54.8	53.7 (23.87 s)
$C \rightarrow W$	39.0	48.1	51.2	45.8	50.1	44.0	43.9	37.8	28.4	49.7	**60.2**	47.5 (5.53 s)
$D \rightarrow W$	61.6	80.3	67.5	74.4	83.3	83.7	42.6	69.4	81.5	75.1	74.7	**86.1 (0.63 s)**
$A \rightarrow W$	34.4	42.7	44.8	44.1	47.0	39.5	40.2	37.9	40.0	**59.0**	49.3	42.7 (4.33 s)
Average	39.4	47.9	46.7	46.7	50.9	47.8	41.2	42.6	43.3	48.9	47.5	**51.1**

in the ImageNet dataset, we conduct evaluations on a cross-place satellite scene dataset. Three publicly available datasets as Banja Luka (B) [23], UC Merced Land Use (U) [33], and Remote Sensing (R) [3] datasets are selected specifically. In experiment, for cross-place classification, 5 common semantic classes: farmland/field, trees/forest, industry, residential, and river have been explored, respectively. There are 6 DA problem settings on this dataset. Several example images are shown in Fig. 3.

We follow the full protocol explained in LDADA [21], which allows us to compare against several recently reported results on the SS5 dataset. Results are shown in Table 4. We observe that LSTN (76.4%) which equals to the recent ILS [10] and LDADA [21], still outperforms other competitors and consistently improves the cross-place accuracy in DA tasks. The result suggests that LSTN should also be applicable to other general visual recognition problems.

(a) Banja Luka   (b) UC Merced Land Use   (c) Remote Sensing

Fig. 3. Some samples from Satellite-Scene5 datasets

Table 2. Recognition accuracy (%) in 4DA-VGG-M model with shallow methods

4DAVGG	A→D	C→D	W→D	A→C	W→C	D→C	D→A	W→A	C→A	Average
NA	77.2	89.9	99.0	81.7	77.3	75.0	83.6	85.5	91.5	84.5
GFK	85.5	91.0	98.0	85.3	81.3	82.3	90.8	90.2	93.6	88.7
DIP	83.4	91.4	98.0	86.0	81.2	81.0	90.0	88.4	93.3	88.1
SA	89.6	**95.0**	98.0	77.1	77.9	78.6	83.8	87.3	93.2	86.7
JDA	91.3	93.2	96.1	**90.1**	86.7	84.8	91.7	93.8	93.7	91.3
TJM	89.9	90.8	97.6	86.4	81.4	81.8	91.4	91.1	93.9	89.4
LSSA	86.2	91.8	95.3	88.0	82.8	81.7	91.2	91.8	93.8	89.2
CORAL	76.2	87.6	98.0	80.1	77.6	73.1	84.5	90.7	91.6	84.4
ILS	83.7	87.7	96.9	86.2	87.0	85.7	91.2	93.6	93.1	89.5
JGSA	**94.1**	94.4	96.1	87.2	82.3	85.2	93.8	**94.9**	94.2	91.4
LDADA	90.0	93.2	99.6	88.7	**88.3**	84.8	**94.2**	94.3	**95.1**	92.0
Ours	91.1	93.0	**100.0**	89.6	88.1	**87.8**	93.4	92.9	94.1	**92.2**

Table 3. Recognition accuracy (%) in 4DA-VGG-M model with deep methods

4DAVGG	A→D	C→D	W→D	A→C	W→C	D→C	D→A	W→A	C→A	Average
AlexNet	88.3	89.1	100.0	84.0	77.9	81.0	89.0	83.1	91.3	87.1
DDC	89.0	88.1	100.0	85.0	78.0	81.1	89.5	84.9	91.9	87.5
DAN	92.4	90.5	100.0	85.1	84.3	82.4	92.0	92.1	92.0	90.1
RTN	**94.6**	92.9	100.0	88.5	**88.4**	84.3	**95.5**	**93.1**	**94.4**	**92.4**
Ours	91.1	**93.0**	100.0	**89.6**	88.1	**87.8**	93.4	92.9	94.1	92.2

Table 4. Recognition accuracy (%) in SS5 setting and time cost (s) in LSTN

SS5 tasks	NA	GFK	DIP	SA	JDA	TJM	LSSA	CORAL	ILS	JGSA	LDADA	Ours
$B→R$	46.4	56.9	35.9	46.3	37.0	46.1	44.9	59.2	**75.3**	51.4	51.8	59.8 (2.01 s)
$R→B$	39.4	48.5	41.9	46.9	65.6	52.1	60.7	27.3	56.1	25.1	58.9	**66.3 (2.43 s)**
$B→U$	60.8	66.2	56.8	57.2	61.0	56.4	64.8	57.6	78.9	59.4	**81.6**	76.8 (4.48 s)
$U→B$	69.9	64.4	61.4	62.8	74.5	63.4	57.5	66.6	66.2	**77.3**	70.5	75.8 (4.53 s)
$R→U$	72.2	88.6	76.2	79.6	91.6	85.0	89.6	80.4	95.4	94.6	**97.2**	90.8 (2.02 s)
$U→R$	75.2	80.7	69.9	72.3	95.1	79.6	83.5	71.2	86.7	97.4	**98.1**	89.1 (1.63 s)
Average	60.7	67.6	57.0	60.9	70.8	63.8	66.8	60.4	**76.4**	67.5	**76.4**	76.4

5 Discussion

5.1 Parameter Setting

In our method, two trade-off coefficients γ and λ are involved. γ and λ are fixed as 0.01 and 1 in experiments, respectively. The number of iterations $T = 10$ is enough in the experiments. The Gaussian kernel function $k(\mathbf{x}_i, \mathbf{x}_j) = exp(-\|\mathbf{x}_i - \mathbf{x}_j\|^2/2\sigma^2)$ is used, where σ can be set as $\sigma = 1.4$ in the tasks. The least square classifier is used in DA experiments. In the MLP network, the number of layers is set as $M = 2$. The dimension of output in the latent space is the same as input. Tanh activation function $\varphi(\cdot)$ is adopted in MLP network. The parameters of the weights and bias are auto updated by gradient descent based on back-propagation algorithm.

5.2 Computational Complexity

In this section, the computational complexity of the Algorithm 1 is presented. The algorithm includes three basic steps: update $\mathcal{Z}$, update J, and update $f^{(m)}$. The computation of $f^{(m)}$ involves $\mathbf{W}^{(m)}$ and $\mathbf{b}^{(m)}$, and the complexity is $O(2MN^2)$. The computation of updating J and $\mathcal{Z}$ is $O(N^2)$. Suppose that the number of iterations is T, then the total computational complexity of LSTN can be expressed as $O(T \times 2MN^2) + O(TN^2)$.

In LSTN model, CPU is enough for model optimization, without using GPU. The time cost is much lower as shown in the last column of Tables 1 and 4. All experiments are implemented on the computer with Intel i7-4790K CPU, 4.00 GHz, and 16 GB RAM. The time cost is calculated under this setting. It is noteworthy that the time of data preprocessing and classification is excluded.

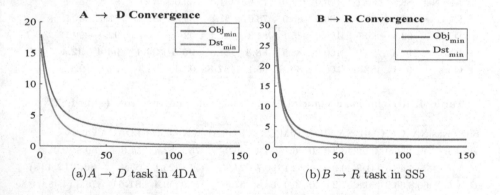

(a)$A \rightarrow D$ task in 4DA   (b)$B \rightarrow R$ task in SS5

Fig. 4. Convergence analysis on different tasks of LSTN model

5.3 Convergence

In this section, the convergence will be discussed. We have conducted the experiments on 4DA ($A \rightarrow D$) and SS5 ($B \rightarrow R$), respectively. The convergence of our LSTN method is explored by observing the variation of the objective function. In the experiments, the number of iterations is set to be 150 for verification the convergence better. The variation of the objective function (Obj_{min}) and reconstruction loss function (Dst_{min}) are described in Fig. 4. It is clear that the objective function and reconstruction loss function decrease to a constant value after several iterations. By running the algorithm, on 4DA and SS5 tasks, respectively, we can observe the good convergence of LSTN.

6   Conclusion

In this paper, we show that one can achieve the effect of DA by combining both advantages of subspace learning and neural network. Specifically, a reconstruction-based transfer learning approach called LSTN is proposed. It offers a simple but effective solution for DA with ample scope for improvement. In the method, we embed features/pixels of source and target into reproducing kernel Hilbert space (RKHS), in which the high dimensional features are mapped to nonlinear latent subspace by feeding them into MLP network. Leveraging the simple MLP, not only the layers can be optimized directly to avoid a pre-trained model which needs large-scale data, but also the adaptation behaviors can be achieved by joint learning a set of hierarchical nonlinear subspace representation and optimal reconstruction matrix simultaneously. Extensive experiments are conducted to justify our proposition in both effectiveness and efficiency. Results demonstrate that LSTN is applicable to small sample sizes, outperforms existing non-deep DA approaches, exhibits comparable accuracy against recent deep DA alternatives.

References

1. Aljundi, R., Emonet, R., Muselet, D., Sebban, M.: Landmarks-based kernelized subspace alignment for unsupervised domain adaptation. In: CVPR (2015)
2. Baktashmotlagh, M., Harandi, M.T., Lovell, B.C., Salzmann, M.: Unsupervised domain adaptation by domain invariant projection. In: ICCV, pp. 769–776 (2013)
3. Dai, D., Yang, W.: Satellite image classification via two-layer sparse coding with biased image representation. IEEE Geosci. Remote Sens. Lett. **8**(1), 173–176 (2011)
4. Donahue, J., et al.: DeCAF: a deep convolutional activation feature for generic visual recognition. In: PMLR, pp. 647–655 (2014)
5. Duan, L., Xu, D., Tsang, I.W., Luo, J.: Visual event recognition in videos by learning from web data. In: CVPR, pp. 1959–1966 (2010)
6. Fernando, B., Habrard, A., Sebban, M., Tuytelaars, T.: Unsupervised visual domain adaptation using subspace alignment. In: ICCV, pp. 2960–2967 (2014)
7. Gaidon, A., Zen, G., Rodriguez-Serrano, J.A.: Self-learning camera: autonomous adaptation of object detectors to unlabeled video streams. arXiv (2014)
8. Gong, B., Shi, Y., Sha, F., Grauman, K.: Geodesic flow kernel for unsupervised domain adaptation. In: CVPR, pp. 2066–2073 (2012)
9. Gong, B., Grauman, K., Sha, F.: Learning kernels for unsupervised domain adaptation with applications to visual object recognition. IJCV **109**(1–2), 3–27 (2014)
10. Herath, S., Harandi, M., Porikli, F.: Learning an invariant hilbert space for domain adaptation. In: CVPR, pp. 3956–3965 (2017)
11. Hoffman, J., et al.: CyCADA: cycle-consistent adversarial domain adaptation. arXiv preprint arXiv:1711.03213 (2017)
12. Hu, J., Lu, J., Tan, Y.P.: Deep transfer metric learning. In: CVPR, pp. 325–333 (2015)
13. Jhuo, I.H., Liu, D., Lee, D., Chang, S.F.: Robust visual domain adaptation with low-rank reconstruction. In: CVPR, pp. 2168–2175 (2012)
14. Krizhevsky, A., Sutskever, I., Hinton, G.E.: Imagenet classification with deep convolutional neural networks. In: NIPS, vol. 25, no. 2, pp. 1097–1105 (2012)

15. Kulis, B., Saenko, K., Darrell, T.: What you saw is not what you get: domain adaptation using asymmetric kernel transforms. In: CVPR, pp. 1785–1792 (2011)
16. Liu, D., Hua, G., Chen, T.: A hierarchical visual model for video object summarization. IEEE Trans. PAMI **32**(12), 2178–2190 (2010)
17. Long, M., Cao, Y., Wang, J., Jordan, M.: Learning transferable features with deep adaptation networks. In: ICML, pp. 97–105 (2015)
18. Long, M., Wang, J., Ding, G., Sun, J., Yu, P.S.: Transfer feature learning with joint distribution adaptation. In: ICCV, pp. 2200–2207 (2014)
19. Long, M., Wang, J., Ding, G., Sun, J., Yu, P.S.: Transfer joint matching for unsupervised domain adaptation. In: CVPR, pp. 1410–1417 (2014)
20. Long, M., Zhu, H., Wang, J., Jordan, M.I.: Unsupervised domain adaptation with residual transfer networks. In: NIPS, pp. 136–144 (2016)
21. Lu, H., Shen, C., Cao, Z., Xiao, Y., van den Hengel, A.: An embarrassingly simple approach to visual domain adaptation. IEEE Trans. Image Process. **PP**(99), 1 (2018)
22. Oquab, M., Bottou, L., Laptev, I., Sivic, J.: Learning and transferring mid-level image representations using convolutional neural networks. In: CVPR, pp. 1717–1724 (2014)
23. Risojevic, V., Babic, Z.: Aerial image classification using structural texture similarity, vol. 19, no. 5, pp. 190–195 (2011)
24. Rosasco, L., Verri, A., Santoro, M., Mosci, S., Villa, S.: Iterative projection methods for structured sparsity regularization. Computation (2009)
25. Shao, M., Kit, D., Fu, Y.: Generalized transfer subspace learning through low-rank constraint. IJCV **109**(1–2), 74–93 (2014)
26. Sharif Razavian, A., Azizpour, H., Sullivan, J., Carlsson, S.: CNN features off-the-shelf: an astounding baseline for recognition. In: CVPR, pp. 806–813 (2014)
27. Simon, K., Jonathon, S., Le, Q.V.: Do better imagenet models transfer better? arXiv preprint arXiv:1805.08974v1 (2018)
28. Sun, B., Feng, J., Saenko, K.: Return of frustratingly easy domain adaptation. In: AAAI, vol. 6, p. 8 (2016)
29. Tzeng, E., Hoffman, J., Darrell, T., Saenko, K.: Simultaneous deep transfer across domains and tasks. In: ICCV, pp. 4068–4076 (2015)
30. Tzeng, E., Hoffman, J., Saenko, K., Darrell, T.: Adversarial discriminative domain adaptation. In: CVPR (2017)
31. Wang, S., Zhang, L., Zuo, W.: Class-specific reconstruction transfer learning via sparse low-rank constraint. In: ICCVW, pp. 949–957 (2017)
32. Xie, M., Jean, N., Burke, M., Lobell, D., Ermon, S.: Transfer learning from deep features for remote sensing and poverty mapping. arXiv (2015)
33. Yang, Y., Newsam, S.: Bag-of-visual-words and spatial extensions for land-use classification. In: SIGSPATIAL International Conference on Advances in Geographic Information Systems, pp. 270–279 (2010)
34. Zhang, J., Li, W., Ogunbona, P.: Joint geometrical and statistical alignment for visual domain adaptation. In: CVPR, pp. 5150–5158 (2017)
35. Zhang, L., Zhang, D.: Robust visual knowledge transfer via extreme learning machine-based domain adpatation. IEEE Trans. Image Process. **25**(3), 4959–4973 (2016)
36. Zhang, L., Zuo, W., Zhang, D.: LSDT: latent sparse domain transfer learning for visual adaptation. IEEE Trans. Image Process. **25**(3), 1177–1191 (2016)

Image Registration Based on Patch Matching Using a Novel Convolutional Descriptor

Wang Xie, Hongxia Gao$^{(\boxtimes)}$, and Zhanhong Chen

School of Automation Science and Engineering, South China University
of Technology, Guangzhou 510640, Guangdong, People's Republic of China
hxgao@scut.edu.cn

Abstract. In this paper we introduce a novel feature descriptor based on deep learning that trains a model to match the patches of images on scenes captured under different viewpoints and lighting conditions. The patch matching of images capturing the same scene in varied circumstances and diverse manners is challenging. Our approach is influenced by recent success of CNNs in classification tasks. We develop a model which maps the raw image patch to a low dimensional feature vector. As our experiments show, the proposed approach is much better than state-of-the-art descriptors and can be considered as a direct replacement of SURF. The results confirm that these techniques further improve the performance of the proposed descriptor. Then we propose an improved Random Sample Consensus algorithm for removing false matching points. Finally, we show that our neural network based image descriptor for image patch matching outperforms state-of-the-art methods on a number of benchmark datasets and can be used for image registration with high quality.

Keywords: Feature descriptor · Deep learning · Patch matching

1 Introduction

Finding correspondences between image patches is one of the most widely studied issues in computer vision. Many of the most widely used approaches, like SIFT [1] or SURF [2] descriptors which have made a critical and wide impact in various computer vision tasks, are based on hand-crafted features and have limited ability to deal with negative factors such as noise which makes a search of similar patches more difficult. Recently, a variety of methods based on supervised machine learning have been successfully applied for learning patch descriptors which are always low dimensional feature vectors [3–5]. These methods are significantly superior to the hand-crafted approaches and promote our research in learned feature descriptors.

The discussion about comparison between learned feature descriptors and traditional handcrafted feature descriptors never stops. The deep feature has achieved the superior performance for many classification tasks, even fine-grained object recognition. While the performance improvements with CNN based descriptors come at the cost of extensive training time. Another issue in the area of matching patches is the limited benchmark data. The handcrafted local feature has been a subject of study in computer vision for almost twenty years, the recent progress in deep neural network

© Springer Nature Switzerland AG 2018
J.-H. Lai et al. (Eds.): PRCV 2018, LNCS 11257, pp. 285–296, 2018.
https://doi.org/10.1007/978-3-030-03335-4_25

has led to a particular interest-learnable local feature descriptor. Specially, the features from the trained model of a convolutional network on ImageNet [12] can improve over SIFT in [9]. [10, 11] train a siamese deep network with hinge loss which have created great improvements in image patch matching (Fig. 1).

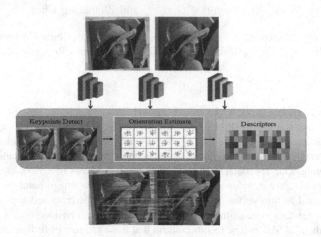

Fig. 1. We propose a new method for jointly learning key-point detection and patch-based representations in depth images towards the key-point matching objective.

The strategies of our novel feature descriptor learning are as follows: Our descriptor include feature point detector, orientation estimation and descriptor three parts, During the training phase, we use the image patches centroids and orientations of the key-points used by the Structure-from-Motion algorithm that we ran on images of a scene captured under distinct viewpoints and brightness to produce image patches. Siamese architecture is utilized to minimize a loss function with the similarity metric to be small for positive image patchpairs but large for negative image patchpairs. Then we conduct images registration with different viewpoints and illumination using our trained novel convolutional descriptor. We measure the key-point similarities by correlation of descriptors and we perform the final transformation by a new variant of Random-Sample-Consensus (RANSAC). As our experiments show, this new approach produces accurate registration results on images with different viewpoints and illumination settings.

In this paper we propose a descriptor based on CNN whose convolutional filters are learned to robustly detect feature points in spite of lighting and viewpoint changes. More over, we also use deep learning-based approach to predict stable orientations. Lastly, the model extract features directly from raw image patches with CNNs trained on large volumes of data. Those improve the performance of traditional hand-crafted method and has reduced matching error and increased registration accuracy.

The rest of the paper is organized as follows. In Sect. 2, we present related work focusing on patch matching problem and image registration. Section 3 describes the proposed method. In Sect. 4, we discuss implementation details and our experimental results, respectively. We provide conclusions in Sect. 5.

2 Related Work

Image registration via patch matching always revolves about matching the selecting feature descriptor and removing mismatched points via a Random-Sample Consensus algorithm to calculate the transform model. In this section, we will therefore discuss these two elements separately.

2.1 Feature Descriptors

Feature descriptors which are robust to transformations such as viewpoint or illumination changes have been widely applied for finding similar and dissimilar image patches in computer vision tasks. The feature descriptors are carefully designed from general measurement methods such as moment invariants, histograms of gradients in the past few years. SIFT [1] is computed from local histograms of gradient orientations and is distinguishable. However, the matching procedure is time-consuming owing to that the dimension of feature vector is high. Therefore, SURF [2] uses a low-dimensional vector representations to speed up the computation.

Nowadays, the trend has alternated from manually-designed methods to learned descriptors. Specially, end-to-end learning of patch descriptors using CNN has been developed in several works [9–11] and are far well compared to the state-of-the-art descriptors. It was demonstrated in [9] that the features from the trained model of a convolutional network on ImageNet [12] can improve over SIFT. Additionally, training a siamese deep network with hinge loss in [10, 11] based on positive and negative patch pairs, create vital improvements in matching achievement.

2.2 Image Registration

Image registration is useful in studying computer vision tasks such as getting the ultimate information from a combination of a great deal of divergent origins catching the same information in diverse circumstances and various manners and there are a great number of related literatures. Image registration methods [13, 14] perform an important part in scores of applications like image fusion. Early methods solve registration based on the gradients of the image such as [15]. Developed methods are using key-points [16, 17] and invariant descriptors to capture the geometric alignment.

According to the style of image acquisition, the utilization of Image registration can be divided into the following categories.

Multi-view Analysis. Capture images of similar object or scenes from multiple viewpoints to gain a better representation of the scanned object or scene. Examples include mosaicing of images and shape recovery from the stereo.

Multi-temporal Analysis. Images of the same scene are captured at different times usually under various conditions to notice alternations in the spectacle which emerge between the consecutive images acquisitions. Examples include motion tracking.

Multi-modal Analysis. Acquiring the images of the same spectacle via different sensors to merge the information obtained from a variety of sources to gain the minutiae of the spectacle.

An Image Registration task includes key-point detection, patch matching, conversion model assessment, image transformation determined.

3   Method

In this section, we first develop the complete feature descriptor. Then, So as to get the global transformation between the feature points, we introduce an approach which is an iterative RANSAC method to remove error matching from the same information in varied circumstances or diverse viewpoints after matching feature points.

3.1   Our Network Architecture

We select Faster R-CNN [8] with shared weights as the foundation for our network architecture due to that it is trained for the work of target detection and can offer us block representations and a trainable methods for choosing those patches. Then, image patches are linked to our ORI-EST network to predict stable orientations. After the image blocks has been rotated, image patches of both branches are connected to a fully connected layer to extract the feature vectors (Fig. 2).

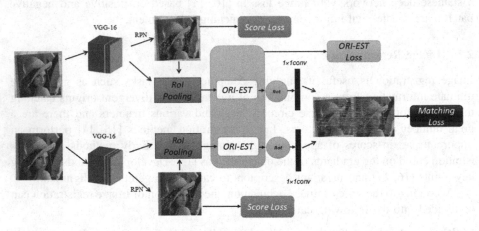

Fig. 2. Overview of our siamese architecture. Each branch uses VGG-16 as the base representation network. Features from conv5_3 are fed into both the Region Proposal network (RPN) and the region of interest (RoI) pooling layer, while their RoIs are fed to the RoI pooling layer, ORI-EST network and a fully connected layer to extract the feature vectors.

3.2 Descriptor

The descriptor can be formalized simply as

$$d = h_\rho(\boldsymbol{p}_\theta), \tag{1}$$

where $h(.)$ denotes the descriptor convolutional neural network, ρ its parameters, and $\boldsymbol{p}_\theta$ is the rotated patch from the Orientation Estimator. During the training phase, we use the image patches centroids and orientations of the key-points used by the Structure-from-Motion (SfM) algorithm to produce image patches $\boldsymbol{p}_\theta$.

To optimize the proposed network, we have to use a loss function which is able to discriminate positive and negative image patch pairs. More specifically, we train the weights of the network by using a loss function which prompts similar examples to be close, and dissimilar pairs to have Euclidean distance larger or equal to a margin m from each other.

$$L_{MatchLoss}(P_1, P_2, l) = \frac{1}{2N_{pos}}\sum\nolimits_{i=1}^{N} lD^2 + \frac{1}{2N_{neg}}\sum\nolimits_{i=1}^{N}(1-l)\{\max(0, m-D)\}^2, \tag{2}$$

where N_{pos} is the number of positive and negative pairs are represented by N_{neg} ($N = N_{pos} + N_{neg}$), l is a binary label is a positive ($l = 1$) or negative ($l - 0$) for choosing whether the input pair consisting of patch P_1 and P_2, $m > 0$ is the margin for negative pairs and $D = \|h(P_1) - h(P_2)\|$ is the Euclidean Distance between feature vectors $h(P_1)$ and $h(P_2)$ of input images P_1 and P_2.

3.3 Orientation Estimation

SIFT determines the main orientation based on the histograms of gradient direction. SURF uses Haar-wavelet responses of sample points to extract the dominant orientation in the neighborhood of feature points.

We give a new orientation estimation approach for image patches. First, we introduce our convolutional neural networks then show details of our model. Given a patch $\boldsymbol{p}$ from the region computed by the detector, the Orientation Estimator estimates an orientation

$$\theta = f_w(\boldsymbol{p}), \tag{3}$$

where f denotes the Orientation Estimator CNN, and w its parameters.

We minimize a loss function $\sum_i L_i$ over the parameters w of a CNN, with

$$L_{ORI-ESTLoss}(\mathbf{p}_i) = \left\| h_\rho\left(\boldsymbol{p}_i^1, f_w\left(\boldsymbol{p}_i^1\right)\right) - h_\rho\left(\boldsymbol{p}_i^2, f_w\left(\boldsymbol{p}_i^2\right)\right) \right\|_2^2, \tag{4}$$

where the pairs $\boldsymbol{p}_i = \{\boldsymbol{p}_i^1, \boldsymbol{p}_i^2\}$ are pairs of image patches from the training dataset, $f_w(\boldsymbol{p}_i^*)$ means the orientation computed for image patch $\boldsymbol{p}_i^*$ using a CNN with parameters w, and $h(\boldsymbol{p}_i^*, \theta_i^*)$ is the descriptor for patch $\boldsymbol{p}_i^*$ and orientation θ_i^*.

3.4   Feature Point Detectors

Each Faster R-CNN branch has a novel score loss for training the key-point detection stage, which is an uncomplicated but valid mean to recognize possibly stable key-points in training images. The score loss fine-tunes the parameters of the Region Proposal Network (RPN) of the Faster R-CNN [8] to obtain high-scoring proposals in regions of the image maps. We then use them to generate a score map whose values are local maxima at these positions. The region S proposed by the detector for patch P is computed as:

$$S = g_\mu(p), \tag{5}$$

where $g_\mu(p)$ denotes the detector itself with parameters μ

$$L_s(s,l) = \frac{1}{1+N_{pos}} - \frac{\gamma \sum_{i=1}^{N} l_i \log s_i}{1+N_{pos}}, \tag{6}$$

where l_i is the label for the ith key-point from image I whose value depends whether the key-point belongs to a positive or negative pair, S is the score of the key-point and γ is a regularization parameter.

$$L_{ScoreLoss}(\mathbf{p}_i) = \left\| h_\rho\left(p_i^1, f_w\left(g_\mu\left(p_i^1\right)\right)\right) - h_\rho\left(p_i^2, f_w\left(g_\mu\left(p_i^2\right)\right)\right) \right\|_2^2 + \lambda L_S(s,l), \tag{7}$$

λ is a regularization parameter.

3.5   Image Registration

Image registration is the procedure of aligning two or more images of the same scene which are captured from various sensors at different times or at multiple view-points. Image registration is significant in getting a better map of any alteration of a scene or object over a long time.

It is unavailable to use the group of all matches M to compute the final global transformation T between the images I_0 and I_1 in that a majority of matches in M are outliers. Therefore, it is necessary to apply RANSAC [18] for rejecting outliers before compute the transformation T. Moreover, In order to improve the accuracy of the transformation, we form the transformation T by our iterative RANSAC outliers rejection approach (Fig. 3).

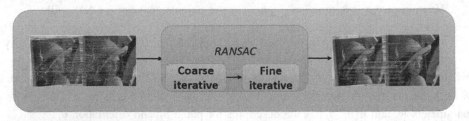

Fig. 3. Overview of RANSAC process, we propose a new RANSAC method for removing error key-point matching which is consisted of coarse and fine iterative.

The methods of iterative RANSAC are consisted of coarse iteration and fine iteration. The coarse iteration use RANSAC in a conventional way. We get a group of matches M_c by computing for each key-point $p \in I_0$ its best match $q^* \in I_1$. Obviously, this group includes inlier and outlier matches. The RANSAC outliers rejection approach is as follows, we sample subgroups of matches $m_1, ..., m_l, ... \in M_c$ and compute via least square the transformation T_l that most adapts these matches to each subgroup m_l. Therefore if our transformation T is characterized by n parameters, then we have $|m_l| = \lceil \frac{n}{2} \rceil$ since each match induces two linear constraints.

Ultimately, we choose T^* derived from the best group of matches m^* as the best transformation which has the greatest agreement in other matches. The number of other matches is formalized as $M_c - m^*$. A match agrees with a transformation if

$$\left\| T_{2\times3} \begin{pmatrix} x_p \\ y_p \\ 1 \end{pmatrix} - \begin{pmatrix} x_{q^*} \\ y_{q^*} \\ 1 \end{pmatrix} \right\|_2 \leq RansacDistance, \tag{8}$$

the Ransac Distance in the first iteration is $r\, d_c$. T_c is expressed as the transformation that is found by RANSAC in the coarse iteration.

In the fine iteration we duplicate the same procedure as the coarse iteration, but use this initial guess T_c to limit the group of all matches in fine iteration M_f. More precisely, $p \in I_0$ can be matched to $q^* \in I_1$ only if their distance under T_c (like Eq. (8)), is less than MatchDistance. In fine iteration, MatchDistance $= md_f$ and RansacDistance $= rd_c$. We denote by T_f the transformation found by our fine iteration.

The parameters of the mapping function are computed with the established feature correspondence obtained from the previous step. Then, the mapping functions are applied for aligning the sensed image with the reference image.

4 Experimental Validation

In this section, we first present the datasets we used. We then present qualitative results, followed by a thorough quantitative comparison against a number of state-of-the-art baselines. The experiment was running on a machine with Ubuntu, Tensorflow, NVIDIA GeForce GTX 1080, Intel (R) Core (TM) i7-6700K CPU @ 4.00 GHz, 16 GB RAM. It took about one day to train our model. Our Input image size is about 2000×1000 and the runtime of testing process is about 12.5 s per image.

4.1 Dataset

We use the following two datasets to evaluate our method under illumination changes and multiple viewpoints, the *Webcam* dataset [6], which includes 710 images of 6 scenes with apparent illumination alternations but captured from the same viewpoint. The *Strecha* dataset [7], which involves 19 images of two scenes captured from manifest different viewpoints.

4.2   Qualitative Examples

We compare our method to the following combination of feature point detectors and descriptors, as reported by the authors of the corresponding papers: SIFT, SURF, ORB [19], PN-Net [20] with SIFT detector, and MatchNet [11] with SIFT detector.

A qualitative evaluation of the key-points shown in Fig. 4 reveals the tendency of the other methods to generate more key-points than ours. This demonstrates that our method is much less susceptible to the image noise, and validates our claim for learning the key-point generation process jointly with the representation.

Fig. 4. Qualitative local feature matching examples of left: SURF and right: ours. Matches recovered by each method are shown in green color circles. SURF returns more key-points than ours. (Color figure online)

We compute the transformation T by RANSAC [18] rejection method. Figure 5 shows image key-points correct matching results, for both SURF and Ours. As expected, ours returns more correct correspondences.

These results show that our method outperforms traditional methods in matching correct key-points. Additionally, our method is much more reliable to the image under different conditions, and correct the mistakes of the original detectors.

4.3   Iterative RANSAC and Image Registration

The transformation T for every sample of matches from M is computed by least-squares. In order to ensure the accuracy of the transformation, we compute the transformation T by our iterative RANSAC outliers rejection method. Figure 6 shows image key-points correct matching results, for both RANSAC and our iterative RANSAC. As expected, ours returns more correct correspondences.

These results demonstrate that our method compares favorably with traditional RANSAC method in removing outliers.

Fig. 5. The figure shows the matching results after the traditional RANSAC. Feature matching examples of left: SURF and right: ours. Correct matches recovered by each method are shown in red color lines and the green color circles. Ours matches more key-points than SURF. (Color figure online)

Fig. 6. The figure shows the matching results after the traditional RANSAC and our iterative RANSAC. Local feature matching examples of left: RANSAC and right: our iterative RANSAC. Matches recovered by each method are shown in red color lines and the descriptor support regions with green color circles. RANSAC matches less key-points than our iterative RANSAC matches. (Color figure online)

We use the *Webcam* dataset and the *Strecha* dataset to evaluate our method under illumination changes and multiple viewpoints. As our experiment show, most of the scenes are out door and with static objects but not include moving objects with a large obvious change in position. Our future work will focus on the registration for video frames under the scenes which are indoor and with some moving objects.

4.4   Quantitative Evaluation

In this section, we first present qualitative results, followed by a thorough quantitative comparison against a number of state-of-the-art feature descriptor baselines, which we consistently outperform. We then present our iterative RANSAC qualitative results, followed by traditional RANSAC (Fig. 7), (Tables 1 and 2).

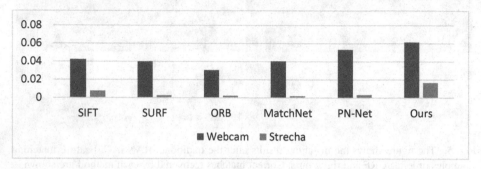

Fig. 7. Average matching score for all baselines.

Table 1. Average correct matching ratio for all baselines.

	SIFT	SURF	ORB	MatchNet	PN-Net	Ours
Webcam	.0422	.0398	.0304	.0402	.0531	.0613
Strecha	.0076	.0025	.0022	.0018	.0033	.0166

Table 2. Average correct matching ratio for different RANSAC.

	RANSAC	Our iterative RANSAC
Webcam	.0588	.0613
Strecha	.0157	.0166

5   Conclusions

We introduce a novel deep network architecture that combines the three components training a novel feature descriptor model to match the patches of images of a scene captured under different viewpoints and lighting conditions. The unified framework simultaneously learns a key-point detector, orientation estimator and view-invariant descriptor for key-point matching. Furthermore, we introduced a new score loss objective that maximizes the number of positive matches between images from two viewpoints. To remove false matching points, we propose an improved Random Sample Consensus algorithm.

Our experimental results demonstrate that our integrated method outperforms the state-of-the-art. A future performance improvement could be to study better structures of the orientation estimator network which could make the local feature descriptor even more robust to rotation transformations.

Acknowledgements. This work was supported by Natural Science Foundation of China under Grant 61603105, Fundamental Research Funds for the Central Universities under Grant 2015ZM128 and Science and Technology Program of Guangzhou, China under Grant (201707010054, 201704030072).

References

1. Lowe, D.: Distinctive image features from scale-invariant key-points. IJCV **60**(2), 91–110 (2004)
2. Bay, H., Ess, A., Tuytelaars, T., Van Gool, L.: SURF: speeded up robust features. CVIU **110**(3), 346–359 (2008)
3. Hua, G., Brown, M., Winder, S.: Discriminant learning of local image descriptors. IEEE Trans. Pattern Anal. Mach. Intell. (2010)
4. Trzcinski, T., Christoudias, C., Lepetit, V., Fua, P.: Learning image descriptors with the boosting-trick. In: NIPS, pp. 278–286 (2012)
5. Trzcinski, T., Christoudias, M., Fua, P., Lepetit, V.: Boosting binary key-point descriptors. In: Proceedings of the 2013 IEEE Conference on Computer Vision and Pattern Recognition, CVPR 2013, Washington, DC, USA, pp. 2874–2881. IEEE Computer Society (2013)
6. Verdie, Y., Yi, K., Fua, P., Lepetit, V.: TILDE: a temporally invariant learned detector. In: CVPR (2015)
7. Strecha, C., Hansen, W., Van Gool, L., Fua, P., Thoennessen, U.: On benchmarking camera calibration and multi-view stereo for high resolution imagery. In: CVPR (2008)
8. Ren, S., He, K., Girshick, R., Sun, J.: Faster R-CNN: towards real-time object detection with region proposal networks. In: Advances in Neural Information Processing Systems, vol. 28, pp. 91–99 (2015)
9. Fischer, P., Dosovitskiy, A., Brox, T.: Descriptor matching with convolutional neural networks: a comparison to sift. Arxiv (2014)
10. Simo-Serra, E., Trulls, E., Ferraz, L., Kokkinos, I., Fua, P., Moreno-Noguer, F.: Discriminative learning of deep convolutional feature point descriptors. In: ICCV (2015)
11. Han, X., Leung, T., Jia, Y., Sukthankar, R., Berg, A.: MatchNet: unifying feature and metric learning for patch-based matching. In: CVPR (2015)
12. Russakovsky, O., et al.: ImageNet large scale visual recognition challenge. IJCV 1–42 (2015)
13. Brown, L.: A survey of image registration techniques. ACM Comput. Surv. (CSUR) **24**(4), 325–376 (1992)
14. Zitova, B., Flusser, J.: Image registration methods: a survey. Image Vis. Comput. **21**(11), 977–1000 (2003)
15. Lucas, B., Kanade, T.: An iterative image registration technique with an application to stereo vision (1981)
16. Harris, C., Stephens, M.: A combined corner and edge detector. In: Alvey Vision Conference, Manchester, UK, vol. 15 (1988). https://doi.org/10.5244/c.2.23
17. Lowe, D.: Distinctive image features from scale-invariant key-points. Int. J. Comput. Vis. **60**, 91–110 (2004)

18. Fischler, M., Bolles, R.: Random sample consensus: a paradigm for model fitting with applications to image analysis and automated cartography. Commun. ACM **24**(6), 381–395 (1981)
19. Rublee, E., Rabaud, V., Konolidge, K., Bradski, G.: ORB: an efficient alternative to SIFT or SURF. In: ICCV (2011)
20. Balntas, V., Johns, E., Tang, L., Mikolajczyk, K.: PN-Net: conjoined triple deep network for learning local image descriptors. arXiv Preprint (2016)

CAFN: The Combination of Atrous and Fractionally Strided Convolutional Neural Networks for Understanding the Densely Crowded Scenes

Lvyuan Fan, Minglei Tong[✉], and Min Li

Shanghai University of Electric Power, Shanghai 200082,
People's Republic of China
tongminglei@gmail.com

Abstract. The task to estimate crowd count in highly clustered scenes is extremely challenged on account of variable scales with non-uniformity. This paper aims to develop a simple but valid method that concentrates on predicting the density map accurately. We proposed a combination of atrous and fractionally strided convolutional neural network (CAFN), which is merely constituted by two components: an atrous convolutional neural network as the front-end for 2D features extraction which utilizes dilated kernels to deliver larger receptive fields and to lessen the network parameters, a fractionally strided convolutional neural network for the back-end to lower the loss of details during down-sampling. CAFN is an easy-trained model because of its unadulterated convolutional structure. We demonstrated CAFN on three datasets (Shanghai Tech dataset A and B, UCF_CC_50) and deliver satisfactory performance. Additionally, CAFN achieves lower Mean Absolute Error (MAE) on Shanghai Tech A (MAE = 100.8), UCF_CC_50 (MAE = 305.3) while the experiment results reveal that the proposed model can effectively lower estimation errors when compared with previous methods.

Keywords: CAFN · Crowd density estimation · Atrous convolutions
Fractionally strided convolutions

1 Introduction

The automatic estimation of crowd density as a method of crowd control and management is a decisive research area in current video surveillance. The existing methods perform density estimation by extracting complex features, however, it is difficult to meet the requirements in practical applications because of crowd mutual occlusion and perplexed environments. Convolutional neural networks have marked capabilities in feature learning, for instance, automatically and reliably obtaining the number of people in monitoring or population density can not only alert and alarm certain abnormalities of the crowd, but also can be used for crowd simulation, crowd behavior and crowd psychology research.

© Springer Nature Switzerland AG 2018
J.-H. Lai et al. (Eds.): PRCV 2018, LNCS 11257, pp. 297–307, 2018.
https://doi.org/10.1007/978-3-030-03335-4_26

Many methods have been developed that coalesce scale information into the learning process. Some of the early methods relied on people detection to estimate the instantaneous count of pedestrians crossing a line of interest in a video sequence which catered merely to low density crowded scenes [1]. These methods are hampered in dense crowds and the performance is far from expected. Inspired by the success of Convolutional Neural Networks (CNNs) for various computer vision tasks, many types of CNN-based methods have been developed, some new methods related to visual understanding [2, 3] while some techniques devoted to overcoming the difficulties of crowd counting [4, 5]. In terms of receptive field and the loss of details issues, the algorithms that can achieve better accuracy still have some limited capabilities, certain CNN-based methods specifically meet the issue of utilizing features at different scales via multi-column or recover spatial resolution via transposed convolutions in CNN-based cascaded multi-task learning (Cascaded-MTL) network [6, 7]. Though these methods demonstrated robustness to corresponding issues, they are still restricted to the scales that are used during training and hence are limited in their capacity to learn well-generalized models.

This paper has been devoted to the generalization of the predigestion of model in an attempt to fetch as much prolific features as possible and minimize network parameters to our best knowledge. The global features is learned along with density map estimation via a dilated convolutional neural network. Results of the proposed method on a sample image and corresponding density map are shown in Fig. 1(a)–(b). Note that it differs from the latest works, such as the deep CNN applied for appurtenance, we focus on designing an easy-trained CNN-based density map manager. Our model uses pure convolutional layers as the hard core to support input images with flexible resolutions. We deploy dilated convolution layers as the front-end to enlarge receptive fields and fractionally strided convolution layers as the back-end to restore its spatial resolution. By making use of such simply equipped structure, we lower the number of network parameters which makes CAFN be trained easily. In addition, we outperform previous crowd counting solution lower MAE in Shanghai Tech Part A and Part B datasets respectively.

(a)   (b)

Fig. 1. Results of the proposed method. Left one is input image (from the Shanghai tech dataset [6]) with ground truth number (819). Right one is corresponding density map generated by the proposed method with estimated count (834).

The rest of the paper is structured as follows. Section 2 presents the previous works for crowd counting and density map generation. Section 3 introduces the fabric and configuration of our model while Sect. 4 presents the experimental results on several datasets. In Sect. 5, we conclude the paper.

2 Related Work

Traditional approaches for crowd counting from images relied on hand-crafted representations to extract low level features. These features were then mapped for counting or generating density maps via various regression techniques. Detection-based methods typically employ sliding window-based detection algorithms to count people in an image [8]. These methods are disadvantageously influenced by the existence of high density crowd and background disturbance. To overcome these obstacles, researchers attempted to count by regression where they learn a mapping to their counts via features extracted from local image patches to their counts [9].

Unlike counting by detection, estimating crowd counts without recognizing the location of each person via regression, preparatory works employ edge and texture features such as HOG and LBP to learn the mapping from image patterns to corresponding crowd counts [10–12]. Multi-source information is utilized [13] to regress the crowd counts in extreme dense crowd images. An end-to-end CNN model adopted from AlexNet [14] is constructed recently for counting in extremely crowded scenes. Later, instead of regressing the count directly, the spatial information of crowds are taken into consideration by regressing the CNN feature maps as crowd density maps. Similar frameworks are also developed in [15], where a Hydra-CNN architecture is designed to estimate crowd densities in a variety of scenes. Better performance can be obtained by further exploiting switching structures or contextual correlations using LSTM [16–18]. Though counting by regression is reliable in crowded settings, without information of object location, their predictions for low density crowds tend to be overestimated. The firmness of such kind of methods depends upon the stability of statistical data, while in such scenarios the instance number is too small to help explore the its intrinsic statistical philosophy. Detection and regression methods ignore key spatial information present in the images as they regress on the global count. Hence, Lempitsky et al. [10] proposed a new approach of learning a linear mapping between local patch features and corresponding object density maps so as to incorporate spatial information present in the images.

Most recently, Sam et al. [17] propose the Switch-CNN using a density level classifier to choose different regressors for particular input patches. Sindagi et al. [18] present a Contextual Pyramid CNN, which uses CNN networks to estimate context at various levels for achieving lower count error and better quality density maps. These two solutions achieve the state-of-the-art performance, and both of them used multi-column based architecture (MCNN) and density level classifier. However, we observe several disadvantages in these approaches: Multi-column CNNs are hard to train according to the training method described in work [6]. Such inflated network structure requires more time to train. Both solutions require density level classifier before sending pictures in the MCNN. However, the granularity of density level is hard to define in real-time congested scene analysis since the number of objects keeps varying in a large scale. Also, using a classifier means more columns need to be implemented which makes the design more complicated and causes more overabundance. These works spend a large portion of parameters for density level classification to label the input regions instead of feeding parameters into the final density map generation. Since the branch structure in MCNN is not efficient, the lack of parameters for generating density map is unfavorable to the final accuracy. Taking all above drawbacks into consideration, we propose a novel approach to concentrate on encoding the wider and deeper features in clustered scenes and generating high quality density map. Our CAFN increases the receptive fields through atrous convolution, while reducing the number of convolutional networks, and finally the loss of details will be restored by transposed convolutional layers as much as possible.

3   Proposed Method

The fundamental idea of the proposed design is to deploy a double-column dilated CNN for capturing high-level features with larger receptive fields and generating high-quality density maps without brutally expanding network complexity. In this section, we firstly introduce the architecture, a network whose input is the image and the output is a density map of the crowd (say how many people per square meter), and then obtain the head count by integration, then we present the corresponding training method.

3.1   CAFN Architecture

The front-end VGG-16 [19] of the model named CSRNet in [20] outputs a picture, which is 1/8 size of the original input. As discussed in CSRNet, the output size will be further shrunken if proceeding to stack more convolution layers and pooling layers (basic components in VGG-16), additionally, it is difficult to generate high-quality density maps, so the back-end employs dilated convolutions used to extract deeper salient information and improve output resolution. Inspired by the idea of CSRNet, we utilized dilated convolutions as the front-end of CAFN because of its greater receptive fields, unlike adopting dilated convolution to capture more features when the resolution has been dropped off to a very low level in CSRNet. Atrous convolutions are primarily made use of in this paper, which intent to gain more image information from original image, then the transposed convolutional layer is for the purpose of enlarging the size of image and upsampling the previous layer's output to supplement the loss of details.

In this paper, for attaining the training dataset, we crop 9 patches from each image at different locations with 1/4 size of the original image. The first four patches contain four quarters of the image without overlapping while the other five patches are randomly cropped from the input image. Based on three branches of MCNN, we add dilation rate to filters to enlarge its receptive fields. For the purpose of reducing net parameters, we consider 4 types of double-column association as experimental objects, which will be discussed in details on Sect. 4. After extracting features from filters with different scales, we try to deploy transposed convolutional layers as the back-end for maintaining the output resolution. We choose a relatively better model, taking into account the stability of the model, of which MAE is not the lowest (but MSE is the lowest) by comparing different groups.

The overall structure of our network is illustrated in Fig. 2. It contains double parallel columns whose filters are with different dilation rates and local receptive fields of different sizes. Double convolutional columns are merged for fusing features from different scales, here we use the function (torch.cat) to concatenate matrices (feature maps) output from double columns respectively on the first dimension. For simplification, we use the same network structures for all columns (i.e. conv–pooling–conv–pooling) except for the sizes and numbers of filters. Max pooling is applied for each 2×2 region, and Parametric Rectified linear unit (PReLU) is adopted as the activation function because of its favourable performance for CNNs. To diminish the computational complexity (the number of parameters to be optimized), we apply less number of filters for convolutional layer with larger filters. We stack the output feature maps of all convolutional layers and map them to a density map. To map the feature maps to the density map, we adopt filters whose sizes are 1×1. Configuration of our network is shown below in details (See Table 1).

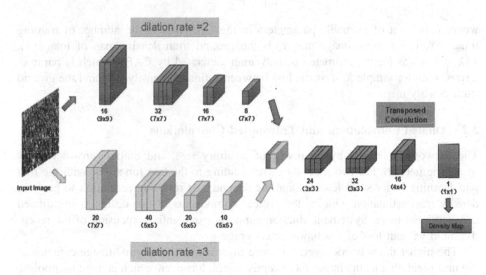

Fig. 2. The structure of the proposed double-column convolutional neural network for crowd density map estimation.

All convolutional layers use padding to maintain the previous size. The convolutional layers' parameters are denoted as "conv(kernel size) @ (number of filters)", max-pooling layers are conducted over a 2×2 pixel window with stride 2, The fractionally strided convolutional layer is denoted as "ConvTransposed (kernel size) @ (number of filters)", PReLU is used as non-linear activation layer.

Table 1. Configuration of CAFN

Front-end (double-column)		Back-end
Dilation rate = 2	Dilation rate = 3	No dilation
Conv9×9 @ 16	Conv7×7 @ 20	Conv3×3 @ 24
Max-pooling	Max-pooling	Conv3×3 @ 32
Conv7×7 @ 32	Conv5×5 @ 40	ConvTranspose4×4@16
Max-pooling	Max-pooling	PReLU
Conv7×7 @ 16	Conv5×5 @ 20	Conv1×1 @ 1
Conv7×7 @ 8	Conv5×5 @ 10	Max-pooling

Then Euclidean distance is used to measure the difference between the estimated density map and ground truth. The loss function is defined as follows:

$$L(\theta) = \frac{1}{2N} \sum_{i=1}^{N} \left\| Y(X_i; \theta) - Y_i^{GT} \right\|_2^2 \tag{1}$$

where θ is a set of learnable parameters in the CAFN. N is the number of training image. X_i is the input image and Y_i is the ground truth density map of image X_i. $Y(X_i; \theta)$ stands for the estimated density map generated by CAFN which is parameterized with for sample X_i. L is the loss between estimated density map and the ground truth density map.

3.2 Dilated Convolutions and Transposed Convolutions

The network is fetched by an image of arbitrary size, and outputs crowd density map. The network has two sections corresponding to the two functions, with the first part learning larger scale features and the second part restoring resolution to preform density map estimation. One of the critical components of our design is the dilated convolutional layer. Systematic dilation supports exponential expansion of the receptive field without loss of resolution or coverage.

The higher the network layer, the more information the original image contains in the unit pixel, that is, the larger the receptive field, however, which is done by pooling and takes the reduction of the resolution and the loss of the information in the original image as a cost. Due to the existence of the pooling layer, the size of the feature map in the back layer will be smaller and smaller. Dilated convolution is a kind of convolution idea that the down sampling will reduce the image resolution and the loss of information for image semantic segmentation. This character enlarges the receptive field without increasing the number of parameters or the amount of computation. Examples can be found in Fig. 3(c) where normal convolution (dilation = 1) is 3×3 receptive field and the dilated convolutions (dilation rate = 2) deliver 5×5 receptive fields.

The second component consists of a transposed convolutional layer for upsampling the previous layer's output to account for the loss of details due to earlier pooling layers, and we add a 1×1 convolutional layer as output layer.

Convolution arithmetic are shown in Fig. 3

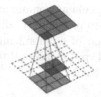

(a) Convolution   (b) Transposed Convolution   (c) Dilated Convolution

Fig. 3. Different convolution methods in this paper. Blue maps are inputs, and cyan maps are outputs. (a) Half padding, no strides. (b) No padding, no strides, transposed. (c) No padding, no stride, dilation. (Color figure online)

We use a simple method in order to ensure that the improvements achieved are due to the proposed method and are not dependent on the sophisticated methods for calculating the ground truth density maps. Ground truth density map D_i corresponding to the i th training patch is calculated by summing a 2D Gaussian kernel centered at every person's location as defined below:

$$D_i(x) = \sum_{x_g \in P} G(x - x_g, \delta) \tag{2}$$

where σ is the scale parameter of the 2D Gaussian kernel and P is the set of all points at which people are located. The training and evaluation was performed on NVIDIA TITAN-X GPU using Torch framework [21]. Adam optimization with a learning rate of 0.00001 and momentum of 0.9 was used to train the model.

4 Experiments

In this section, we present the experimental details and evaluation results on three publicly available datasets: Shanghai Tech Part_A, Part_B and UCF_CC_50 [13]. For the purpose of evaluation, the standard metrics used by many existing methods for crowd counting were used. These metrics are defined as follows:

$$MAE = \frac{1}{N} \sum_{i=1}^{N} (y_i - \hat{y}_i) \tag{3}$$

$$MSE = \sqrt{\frac{1}{N} \sum_{1}^{N} (|y_i - \hat{y}_i|)^2} \tag{4}$$

where MAE is mean absolute error, MSE is mean squared error, N is number of test samples, is ground truth count and y_i is estimated count corresponding to the i th image. Roughly speaking, MAE indicates the accuracy of the estimates, and MSE indicates the robustness of the estimates.

We compare four types of different column combinations (see Fig. 4) with different dilation rates. Type1 is the combination of column1 (dilation rate = 2) with column2 (dilation rate = 3). Type2 is the fusion of column2 and colum3 (dilation rate = 4). Type3 combines the column1 and 3. Type4 merges all the columns. The experimental results are shown as the following Table 2.

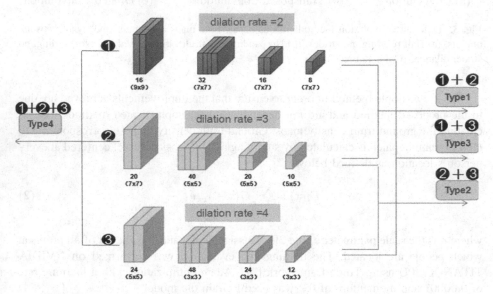

Fig. 4. Four types of combinations

4.1 Shanghai Tech Dataset

Shanghai tech dataset contains 1198 annotated images, in which a total of 330,165 people with centers of their heads annotated. As far as we know, this dataset is the largest one in terms of the number of annotated people. This dataset consists of two parts: there are 482 images in Part A which are randomly crawled from the Internet, and 716 images in Part B which are taken from the busy streets of metropolitan areas in Shanghai. The crowd density varies significantly between the two subsets, making accurate estimation of the crowd more challenging than most existing datasets. Both Part A and Part B are divided into training and testing: 300 images of Part A are used for training and the remaining 182 images for testing; and 400 images of Part B are for training and 316 for testing.

First we design an experiment to demonstrate that the MCNN does not perform better compared to a regular network in Table 3.

Then, to demonstrate that MCNN may not be the best choice, we design a deeper, double-column network with fewer parameters compared to MCNN. Results show that the double-column version achieves higher performance on Shanghai Tech Part A dataset with the lowest MAE. As shown in Table 4.

Table 2. Comparison of experiments results on Shanghai tech dataset

Type	Part_A		Part_B	
	MAE	MSE	MAE	MSE
Type1	100.87	152.31	21.55	38.07
Type2	103.01	161.98	24.82	45.81
Type3	99.66	155.0	28.35	48.78
Type4	101.19	160.53	24.15	45.76

Table 3. Comparison to MCNN

Method	Parameters	MAE
Col. 1 of MCNN	57.75 K	206.8
Col. 2 of MCNN	45.99 K	239.0
Col. 3 of MCNN	25.14 K	230.2
MCNN total	127.68 K	185.9
CAFN	122.75 K	100.87

Table 4. Estimation errors on Shanghai tech dataset.

Method	Part_A MAE	MSE	Part_B MAE	MSE
Zhang et al. [4]	181.8	277.7	32.0	49.8
Marsden et al. [22]	126.5	173.5	23.8	33.1
MCNN [6]	110.2	173.2	26.4	41.3
Switching-CNN [17]	90.4	135.0	21.6	33.4
Cascaded-MTL [7]	101.3	152.4	20.0	31.1
CAFN(ours)	100.8	152.3	21.5	33.4

4.2 UCF_CC_50 Dataset

UCF_CC_50 dataset includes 50 images with different perspective and resolutions. With arriving at an average number of 1280, the number of persons annotated per image varies from 94 to 4543.5-fold cross-validation is performed following the standard setting in [13]. Result comparisons of MAE and MSE are listed in Table 5.

Table 5. Estimation errors on UCF_CC_50 dataset

Method	MAE	MSE
Zhang et al.	467.0	498.5
MCNN	377.6	509.1
Marsden et al.	338.6	424.5
Cascaded-MTL	322.8	397.9
Switching-CNN	318.1	439.2
CAFN(ours)	305.3	429.4

5 Conclusions

In this paper, we presented a CAFN network for jointly adopting dilated convolutions and fractionally strided convolutions. Atrous convolutions are devoted to enlarging receptive fields which is beneficial to incorporate abundant characteristics into the network, which enables the model to learn glob ally relevant discriminative features thereby accounting for large count variations in the dataset. Additionally, we employed fractionally strided convolutional layers as the back-end so as to restore the loss of details due to max-pooling layers in the earlier stages, therefore allowing us to regress on full resolution density maps. The model structure has moderate complexity and strong generalization ability, which possess presentable density estimation performance in densely crowded scenes via the experiments on multiple datasets.

Acknowledgement. Sponsored by Natural Science Foundation of Shanghai (16ZR1413300).

References

1. Ma, Z., Chan, A.B.: Crossing the line: crowd counting by integer programming with local features. In: 31st IEEE International Conference on Computer Vision and Pattern Recognition, pp. 2539–2546. IEEE, Portland (2013)
2. Li, Z., Tang, J.: Weakly supervised deep matrix factorization for social image understanding. IEEE Trans. Image Process. 26(1), 276–288 (2017)
3. Li, Z., Tang, J., Mei, T.: Deep collaborative embedding for social image understanding. IEEE Trans. Pattern Anal. Mach. Intell. **PP**(99), 1 (2018)
4. Zhang, C., Li, H., Wang, X., et al.: Cross-scene crowd counting via deep convolutional neural networks. In: 33rd IEEE International Conference on Computer Vision and Pattern Recognition, pp. 833–841. IEEE, Boston (2015)
5. Boominathan, L., Kruthiventi, S.S., Babu, R.V.: CrowdNet: a deep convolutional network for dense crowd counting. In: 24th Proceedings of the ACM on Multimedia Conference, pp. 640–644. Springer, Amsterdam (2016)
6. Zhang, Y., Zhou, D., Chen, S., Gao, S., Ma, Y.: Single-image crowd counting via multi-column convolutional neural network. In: 34th IEEE International Conference on Computer Vision and Pattern Recognition, pp. 589–597. IEEE, Las Vegas (2016)
7. Sindagi, V.A., Patel, V.M.: CNN-based cascaded multi-task learning of high-level prior and density estimation for crowd counting. In: 14th IEEE International Conference on Advanced Video and Signal Based Surveillance, pp. 1–6. IEEE, Lecce (2017)
8. Topkaya, I.S., Erdogan, H., Porikli, F.: Counting people by clustering person detector outputs. In: 11th IEEE International Conference on Advanced Video and Signal-Based Surveillance, pp. 313–318. IEEE, Seoul (2014)
9. Chen, K., Loy, C.C., Gong, S., Xiang, T.: Feature mining for localised crowd counting. In: 23rd British Machine Vision Conference, Guildford (2012)
10. Lempitsky, V., Zisserman, A.: Learning to count objects in images. In: 24th Neural Information Processing Systems, pp. 1324–1332, Curran Associates Inc., Vancouver (2010)
11. Pham, V., Kozakaya, T., Yamaguchi, O., Okada, R.: COUNT Forest: co-voting uncertain number of targets using random forest for crowd density estimation. In: 17th IEEE International Conference on Computer Vision (ICCV), pp. 3253–3261. IEEE, Santiago (2015)

12. Xu, B., Qiu, G.: Crowd density estimation based on rich features and random projection forest. In: 21th IEEE Winter Conference on Applications of Computer Vision (WACV), Lake Placid, NY, pp. 1–8 (2016)
13. Idrees, H., Saleemi, I., Seibert, C., Shah, M.: Multi-source multi-scale counting in extremely dense crowd images. In: 31st IEEE International Conference on Computer Vision and Pattern Recognition, pp. 2547–2554. IEEE, Portland (2013)
14. Wang, C., Zhang, H., Yang, L., et al.: Deep people counting in extremely dense crowds. In: 23rd International Conference ACM on Multimedia, pp. 1299–1302. ACM, Brisbane (2015)
15. Oñoro-Rubio, D., López-Sastre, R.J.: Towards perspective-free object counting with deep learning. In: Leibe, B., Matas, J., Sebe, N., Welling, M. (eds.) ECCV 2016. LNCS, vol. 9911, pp. 615–629. Springer, Cham (2016). https://doi.org/10.1007/978-3-319-46478-7_38
16. Shang, C., Ai, H., Bai, B.: End-to-end crowd counting via joint learning local and global count. In: 23rd IEEE International Conference on Image Processing (ICIP), pp. 1215–1219. IEEE, Phoenix (2016)
17. Sam, D.B., Surya, S., Babu, R.V.: Switching convolutional neural network for crowd counting. In: 35th IEEE International Conference on Computer Vision and Pattern Recognition, Hawaii, pp. 5744–5752 (2017)
18. Sindagi, V.A., Patel, V.M.: Generating high-quality crowd density maps using contextual pyramid CNNs. In: 19th IEEE International Conference on Computer Vision (ICCV), pp. 1879–1888. IEEE, Venice (2017)
19. Simonyan, K., Zisserman, A.: Very deep convolutional networks for large-scale image recognition. In: 6th International Conference on Learning Representations, San Diego (2015)
20. Li, Y., Zhang, X., Chen, D.: CSRNet: dilated convolutional neural networks for understanding the highly congested scenes. In: 36th IEEE International Conference on Computer Vision and Pattern Recognition. IEEE, Utah (2018)
21. Collobert, R., Kavukcuoglu, K., Farabet, C.: Torch7: a matlab-like environment for machine learning. In: 26th Annual Conference on Neural Information Processing Systems (NIPS), Biglcain, Nips Workshop, Lake Tahoe (2012)
22. Marsden, M., Mcguinness, K., Little, S., et al.: Fully convolutional crowd counting on highly congested scene, pp. 27–33 (2016)

Video Saliency Detection Using Deep Convolutional Neural Networks

Xiaofei Zhou[1,2,3], Zhi Liu[2,3(✉)], Chen Gong[4], Gongyang Li[2,3],
and Mengke Huang[2,3]

[1] Institute of Information and Control, Hangzhou Dianzi University,
Hangzhou, China
zxforchid@outlook.com
[2] Shanghai Institute for Advanced Communication and Data Science,
Shanghai University, Shanghai, China
liuzhisjtu@163.com, lllgongyang@gmail.com, mengkehuang@gmail.com
[3] School of Communication and Information Engineering,
Shanghai University, Shanghai, China
[4] Key Laboratory of Intelligent Perception and Systems for High-Dimensional
Information of Ministry of Education, School of Computer Science and Engineering,
Nanjing University of Science and Technology, Nanjing, China
chen.gong@njust.edu.cn

Abstract. Numerous deep learning based efforts have been done for image saliency detection, and thus, it is a natural idea that we can construct video saliency model on basis of these image saliency models in an effective way. Besides, as for the limited number of training videos, existing video saliency model is trained with large-scale synthetic video data. In this paper, we construct video saliency model based on existing image saliency model and perform training on the limited video data. Concretely, our video saliency model consists of three steps including feature extraction, feature aggregation and spatial refinement. Firstly, the concatenation of current frame and its optical flow image is fed into the feature extraction network, yielding feature maps. Then, a tensor, which consists of the generated feature maps and the original information including the current frame and the optical flow image, is passed to the aggregation network, in which the original information can provide complementary information for aggregation. Finally, in order to obtain a high-quality saliency map with well-defined boundaries, the output of aggregation network and the current frame are used to perform spatial refinement, yielding the final saliency map for the current frame. The extensive qualitative and quantitative experiments on two challenging video datasets show that the proposed model consistently outperforms the state-of-the-art saliency models for detecting salient objects in videos.

This work was supported by the National Natural Science Foundation of China under Grants 61771301 and 61602246, the Natural Science Foundation of Jiangsu Province under Grant BK20171430, the Fundamental Research Funds for the Central Universities under Grant 30918011319 and the Summit of the Six Top Talents Program under Grant DZXX-027.

J.-H. Lai et al. (Eds.): PRCV 2018, LNCS 11257, pp. 308–319, 2018.
https://doi.org/10.1007/978-3-030-03335-4_27

Keywords: Video saliency · Convolutional neural networks
Feature aggregation

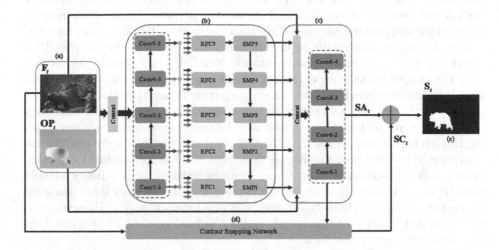

Fig. 1. The main flowchart of the proposed video saliency model. Given (a) the current frame $\mathbf{F}_t$ and its optical flow image $\mathbf{OP}_t$, we obtain five feature maps $\{\mathbf{SMP}_i, i = 1, \ldots, 5\}$ via (b) the feature extraction network. Then these feature maps and the original information including $\mathbf{F}_t$ and $\mathbf{OP}_t$ are concatenated and passed to (c) the aggregation network. Besides, the current frame $\mathbf{F}_t$ and the output of aggregation network $\mathbf{SA}_t$ are passed to (d) the contour snapping network, to perform spatial refinement. (e) Shows the saliency map $\mathbf{S}_t$ of current frame, which is the summation of the outputs of aggregation network and contour snapping network, *i.e.* $\mathbf{SA}_t$ and $\mathbf{SC}_t$.

1 Introduction

Saliency detection aims to identify the salient object regions in images or videos, which plays an important role as a preprocessing step in many computer vision applications such as object detection and segmentation [7,11,21,29,33], content-aware image/video retargeting [8,28], and content-based image/video compression [12,13]. According the input of the visual system, saliency detection can be categorized into two classes including image saliency models and video saliency models. Up to now, numerous efforts have been devoted to the saliency detection for still images, but the research on video saliency has received relatively few attention. In this paper, we focus on the video saliency detection.

Video saliency detection is different from image saliency detection, since it takes into account both spatial and temporal information of the video sequences simultaneously. In order to deal with both cues in videos and pop-out the prominent objects from videos, many priors efforts have been done from various aspects such as the center-surround scheme [15,22], information theory [18], machine learning [16,25], information fusion [5,9], and regional saliency assessment [19,20,26,32]. The above saliency models can obtain satisfactory results to some degree, however their performances degrade in dealing with complicated motion and complex scenes such as fast motion, dynamic background, nonlinear deformation, and occlusion, etc. Fortunately, convolutional neural networks (CNNs) have been successfully applied to many areas in computer vision such as object detection and semantic segmentation [6,10]. Further, it also pushes forward the progress of saliency detection in still images such as the multi-context deep learning framework [31] and the aggregation of multi-level convolutional feature framework [30]. Obviously, it is a natural idea that we can construct video saliency model based on existing deep learning based image saliency models. Unfortunately, we can see that the temporal information over frames is not incorporated by these deep saliency models, thus, it is not appropriate to conduct video saliency detection on each frame by using existing deep saliency models directly. Recently, deep learning is also applied in video saliency detection such as the two cascade modules based deep saliency network in [27]. However, due to the limited number of annotated training videos, this model is trained on large-scale synthetic video data.

Motivated by this, we propose a video saliency model based on existing image saliency model and train it with limited video data only. Concretely, our model consists of three steps including feature extraction, feature aggregation and spatial refinement. The current frame and its optical flow image are first concatenated and fed into the feature extraction network, generating the corresponding feature maps. Notably, we employ an off-the-shelf convolutional neural networks (CNNs) based image saliency model [30] as our feature extraction network. Then, the obtained feature maps, the current frame and its optical image are combined and passed to the aggregation network, which is used to perform feature integration. Finally, a contour snapping network based spatial refinement network is deployed to the output of aggregation network and generates the final saliency map.

The advantages of our model are threefold. Firstly, the input of the feature extraction network is the concatenation of the current frame and its optical flow image, which gives a strong prior for the salient objects in videos. Secondly, the aggregation network not only incorporates the feature maps generated by the feature extraction network, but also aggregates the original information including the current frame and the optical flow image. The original information can provide complementary information for the aggregation of feature maps. Thirdly, a contour snapping based spatial refinement is introduced to improve the quality of spatiotemporal saliency maps, which not only highlight salient objects effectively, but also be with well-defined boundaries. Overall, our main contributions are summarized as follows:

1. Based on existing image saliency models, we propose a deep convolutional neural network based video saliency model, which consists of three steps

including feature extraction, feature aggregation and spatial refinement. Specifically, the three steps correspond to three sub-networks including feature extraction network, feature aggregation network and contour snapping network.

2. In order to obtain complementary information for the aggregation of feature maps, we incorporated the original information including the current frame and its optical flow image into the aggregation network. Concretely, a tensor that consists of feature maps and original information is fed into the aggregation network.

3. We compare our model with several state-of-the-art saliency models on two public video datasets, and the experimental results firmly demonstrate the effectiveness and superiority of the proposed model.

2 Our Approach

Figure 1 shows an overview of the proposed video saliency model. Concretely, in the first step, i.e. feature extraction, the input is the concatenation of the current frame $\mathbf{F}_t$ and its corresponding optical flow image $\mathbf{OP}_t$. Then, we obtain the feature maps originated from different layers, as shown in Fig. 1(b) and denoted as $\{\mathbf{SMP}_i, i - 1, 2, 3, 4, 5\}$. Successively, these feature maps and the original information including $\mathbf{F}_t$ and $\mathbf{OP}_t$ are concatenated and passed to the aggregation network as shown in Fig. 1(c). Further, a contour snapping network [4] based spatial refinement shown in Fig. 1(d), is deployed in our model. The contour snapping network incorporates the current frame $\mathbf{F}_t$ and the output of aggregation network $\mathbf{SA}_t$ together. Finally, the saliency map $\mathbf{S}_t$, as shown in Fig. 1(e), is computed as the summation of the output of the aggregation network and the contour snapping network, i.e. $\mathbf{SA}_t$ and $\mathbf{SC}_t$.

2.1 Feature Extraction

In order to obtain an appropriate representation for salient objects in videos, we employ the feature extraction network in [30], which achieves a superiority performance in saliency detection for still images, to extract feature maps. We should note that one of the difference between our model and [30] is the input. Specifically, the input of feature extraction in our model is the concatenation of the current frame and its corresponding optical flow image, which is a strong prior for salient objects in videos. Differently, [30] focus on image saliency, thus, its input is the static image only.

As aforementioned, the input of feature extraction is the concatenation of the current frame $\mathbf{F}_t$ and its corresponding optical flow image $\mathbf{OP}_t$, which is generated using the method of large displacement optical flow (LDOF) [3] and then converted to a 3-channel (RGB) color coded optical flow image [2]. Besides, we should note that we concatenate $\{\mathbf{F}_t, \mathbf{OP}_t\}$ in the channel direction, thus generating a tensor with the size of $h \times w \times 6$, in which h and w refer to the height and width of the scaled current frame/optical flow image, respectively.

Here, we set h and w as 256. Then, the generated tensor is fed into the feature extraction network shown in Fig. 1(b), in which $\{\mathbf{RFC}_i, i = 1, 2, 3, 4, 5\}$ refer to the resolution-based feature combination structure as detailed in [30]. The output of feature extraction, namely $\{\mathbf{SMP}_1, \mathbf{SMP}_2, \mathbf{SMP}_3, \mathbf{SMP}_4, \mathbf{SMP}_5\}$ are all with the size of $256 \times 256 \times 2$, which are two channel feature maps consistent with [30].

2.2 Feature Aggregation

With the output of the feature extraction network, namely feature maps $\{\mathbf{SMP}_i, i = 1, 2, 3, 4, 5\}$, we design an aggregation network to effectively aggregate these feature maps and generate the coarse result of video saliency detection, *i.e.* $\mathbf{SA}_t$. To provide complementary information for convolutional features originated from feature maps, the original information including the current frame $\mathbf{F}_t$ and its optical flow image $\mathbf{OP}_t$ is also incorporated to the aggregation operation.

Specifically, we first concatenate these feature maps, the current frame $\mathbf{F}_t$ and its optical flow image $\mathbf{OP}_t$ in the channel direction, yielding a tensor with the size of $256 \times 256 \times 16$. Secondly, the generated tensor is fed into a series of convolutional layers including $\{Conv6 - 1, Conv6 - 2, Conv6 - 3\}$, each of them is a convolutional layer with 3×3 kernel size. Successively, there is a layer denoted as $Conv6 - 4$, which is a 1×1 convolutional filter. Finally, the output of aggregation network, *i.e.* $\mathbf{SA}_t$, is generated via a softmax layer. Besides, a batch normalization layer [1] and a ReLU layer are deployed between $Conv6 - 1$ and $Conv6 - 2$, as well as between $Conv6 - 2$ and $Conv6 - 3$.

In our model, the feature extraction network and the aggregation network are jointly trained in an end-to-end manner. Given the training dataset $\mathbf{D}_{train} = \{(\mathbf{F}_n, \mathbf{OP}_n, \mathbf{Y}_n)\}_{n=1}^N$ with N training samples, in which $\mathbf{F}_n = \{\mathbf{F}_n^j, j = 1, ..., N_p\}$, $\mathbf{OP}_n = \{\mathbf{OP}_n^j, j = 1, ..., N_p\}$ and $\mathbf{Y}_n = \{\mathbf{Y}_n^j, j = 1, ..., N_p\}$ denote the input current frame, its optical flow image and the binary ground-truth with N_p pixels, respectively. Besides, $\mathbf{Y}_n^j = 1$ indicates the salient object pixel and $\mathbf{Y}_n^j = 0$ represents the background pixel. For simplicity, we drop the subscript n and consider $\{\mathbf{F}, \mathbf{OP}\}$ for each frame independently. Thus, the loss function can be defined as:

$$\mathcal{L}(\mathbf{W}, \boldsymbol{b}) = -\beta \sum_{j \in \mathbf{Y}_+} \log P\left(\mathbf{Y}^j = 1 | \mathbf{F}, \mathbf{OP}; \mathbf{W}, \boldsymbol{b}\right)$$
$$- (1 - \beta) \sum_{j \in \mathbf{Y}_-} \log P\left(\mathbf{Y}^j = 0 | \mathbf{F}, \mathbf{OP}; \mathbf{W}, \boldsymbol{b}\right), \tag{1}$$

where $\mathbf{W}$ and $\boldsymbol{b}$ are denoted as kernel weights and bias of convolutional layers, and $\mathbf{Y}_+$ and $\mathbf{Y}_-$ indicate the label sets for salient objects and background, respectively. β refers to the ratio of salient objects pixels in the ground truth $\mathbf{G}$, *i.e.* $\beta = |\mathbf{Y}_+|/|\mathbf{Y}_-|$. $P\left(\mathbf{Y}^j = 1 | \mathbf{F}, \mathbf{OP}; \mathbf{W}, \boldsymbol{b}\right)$ denotes the probability of the pixel belonging to salient objects. Besides, the loss function is also the difference between our model and [30]. Concretely, the loss function in [30] consists of the fusion loss and the layer loss of other five layers. Differently, the loss function in our model is the aggregation loss.

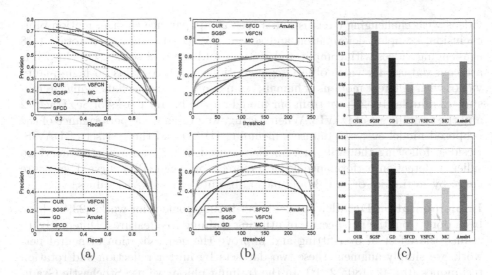

Fig. 2. (better viewed in color) Quantitative evaluation of different saliency models: (a) presents PR curves, (b) presents F-measure curves, and (c) presents MAE. From top to down, each row shows the results on the UVSD dataset and the DAVIS dataset, respectively.

2.3 Spatial Refinement

To further improve the detection accuracy, we introduce a contour snapping network into our method to perform spatial refinement. The contour snapping network [4] is trained offline and used to detect object contours. Here, we exploit the contour snapping network without training or fine-tuning. In our implementation, we first train the aforementioned networks including feature extraction network and aggregation network shown in Fig. 1(a, b, c) in an end-to-end manner. Then, in the test phase, we add a second branch, *i.e.* the contour snapping network, into our model. Concretely, the current frame $\mathbf{F}_t$ and the output of aggregation network $\mathbf{SA}_t$ are first passed to the contour snapping network shown in Fig. 1(d), and the output is denoted as $\mathbf{SC}_t$. Then, the outputs of contour snapping network and aggregation network are combined via linear summation. Finally, we obtain the final saliency map $\mathbf{S}_t$ for the current frame:

$$\mathbf{S}_t = \mathrm{Norm}\left[\mathbf{SA}_t + \mathbf{SC}_t\right], \qquad (2)$$

where the operation Norm normalizes the saliency map into the range of $[0, 1]$.

3   Experimental Results

3.1   Experimental Setup

Datasets and Metrics: The datasets in training and test phases consist of three public challenging datasets. Concretely, SegTrackV2 [17] consists of 14 videos with challenging circumstances such as appearance change, motion blur, occlusion, complex deformation and so on. UVSD [19] contains a total of 18 challenging videos with complicated motions and complex scenes. DAVIS [24] is a recent dataset for video object segmentation, which contains 50 high-quality videos with different motions of human, animal and vehicle in challenging circumstances. Similar to [27], we train our model on the binary masks of SegTrackV2 and the training set of DAVIS. When testing, we evaluate the performance of the proposed model over two datasets including UVSD and the test set of DAVIS. Besides, following the evaluation measures used in [27], we evaluate the video saliency detection performance using the precision-recall (PR) curve, F-measure curve by setting its β^2 to 0.3, and mean absolute error (MAE) values.

Implementation Details: To avoid over-fitting, some prior works [23,34] have been done from the perspective of utilizing training-free features. Differently, to reduce the effect of over-fitting and improve the generalization of neural network, we simply augment these two datasets by mirror reflection and rotation techniques $(0°, 90°, 180°, 270°)$. In the training phase, we use Stochastic Gradient Descent (SGD) with momentum 0.9 for 22000 iterations with base learning rate 10^{-8}, mini-batch size 32 and a weight decay 0.0001. Besides, the parameters of multi-level feature extraction layers are initialized from the model [30]. For other convolutional layers, we initialize the weights by the "msra" method [14].

3.2 Performance Comparison with State-of-the-art

We compare our model with state-of-the-art saliency models including SGSP [19], GD [26], SFCD [5], VSFCN [27], MC [31] and Amulet [30]. The former three models aim at video saliency while the latter two are deep learning based image saliency models. Besides, our model is denoted as "OUR". In the following, quantitative and qualitative comparisons are performed successively.

A quantitative comparison among OUR, SGSP, GD, SFCD, VSFCN, MC and Amulet is shown in Fig. 2. We can see that our model achieves the best performance in terms of PR curves, F-measure curves and MAE values on UVSD and DAVIS datasets. It clearly demonstrates the effectiveness of our model. Figures 3 and 4 provide the qualitative evaluation for our model and the state-of-the-art saliency models on UVSD and DAVIS, respectively. All these videos exhibits various challenges such as shape complexity, occlusion and non-rigid deformation and motion blur and so on. Thus, it is a challenging task for video saliency detection. Compared with other models, we can see that our model achieves the best performance with completely highlighted salient objects and effectively suppressed background regions, as shown in Figs. 3(c) and 4(c). For the results of MC and Amulet shown in Figs. 3(h, i) and 4(h, i), some background regions are also highlighted due to the lack of temporal information in these two models. For other three models including SGSP, GD and SFCD, their results can pop-out the main parts of salient objects and also highlight some background regions around salient objects. The reason behind this lies in that the features in these models are not discriminative enough. Thus, it is incapable of differentiating the salient objects and background regions effectively. From the results of VSFCN, as shown in Figs. 3(g) and 4(g), we can see that some background regions are also popped out for videos with fast motion and non-rigid deformation.

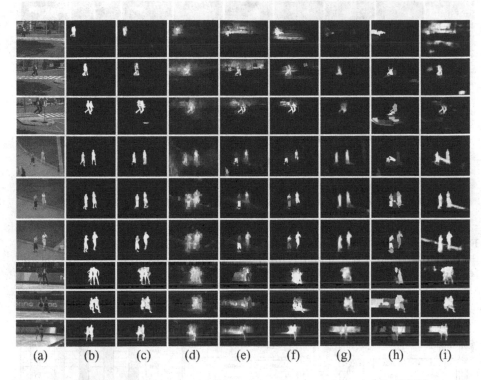

(a)   (b)   (c)   (d)   (e)   (f)   (g)   (h)   (i)

Fig. 3. Examples of spatiotemporal saliency maps for some videos in the UVSD dataset. (a): Input video frames, (b): binary ground truths, (c): OUR, (d): SGSP, (e): GD, (f): SFCD, (g): VSFCN, (h): MC, (i): Amulet.

3.3 Analysis of the Proposed Model

To investigate the effectiveness of feature aggregation and spatial refinement, we conduct ablation experiments on UVSD dataset, and the results are shown in Fig. 5. In these experiments, our model without contour snapping is denoted as "woCS", and on the basis of "woCS", the input of aggregation network without current frame, optical flow image and the previous two are denoted as "woRGB", "woOP" and "woRGBOP", respectively. Concretely, firstly, "woCS" achieves the second best performance, and with the help of contour snapping, "OUR" performs best compared to variants of the proposed model. It clearly demonstrates the effectiveness of spatial refinement. Secondly, the performance of "woRGB", "woOP" and "woRGBOP" is worse than "woCS", it demonstrates

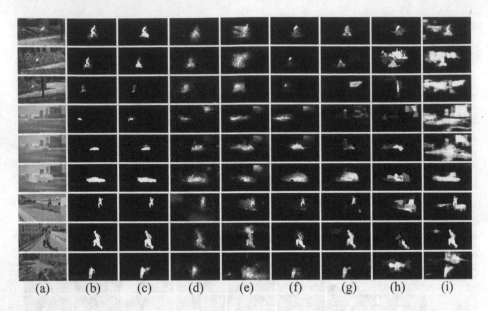

Fig. 4. Examples of spatiotemporal saliency maps for some videos in the DAVIS dataset. (a): Input video frames, (b): binary ground truths, (c): OUR, (d): SGSP, (e): GD, (f): SFCD, (g): VSFCN, (h): MC, (i): Amulet.

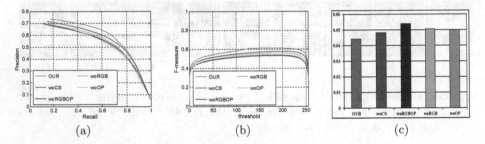

Fig. 5. (better viewed in color) Quantitative-evaluation for the model analysis: (a) presents PR curves, (b) presents F-measure curves, and (c) presents MAE.

the effectiveness and rationality of feature aggregation, which needs the complementary information originated from current frame and optical flow image. Lastly, from the perspective of PR curves, F-measure curves and MAE values, we can see that "woRGB" and "woOP" perform better than "woRGBOP", and it indicates that the complementary information originated from current frame and optical flow image is crucial for aggregation network. Generally speaking, the ablation study shown in Fig. 5 demonstrates the effectiveness and rationality of feature aggregation and spatial refinement in the proposed model.

4   Conclusion

Based on the existing image saliency model, we propose a novel video saliency model, in which feature extraction, feature aggregation and spatial refinement are integrated in a unified architecture. Firstly, the concatenation of the current frame and its optical flow image is fed into the feature extraction network, which defines an appropriate representation for salient objects in videos. Then, the aggregation network is used to aggregate the generated feature maps and the original information. The novelty lies in the introduction of the original information, which provides complementary information for the aggregation of feature maps. Finally, the contour snapping network is introduced to perform spatial refinement, yielding a high-quality saliency map with well-defined boundaries. The experimental results on two public datasets show the effectiveness of the proposed model.

References

1. Badrinarayanan, V., Kendall, A., Cipolla, R.: SegNet: a deep convolutional encoder-decoder architecture for image segmentation. IEEE Trans. Pattern Anal. Mach. Intell **39**, 2481–2495 (2017)
2. Baker, S., Scharstein, D., Lewis, J.P., Roth, S., Black, M.J., Szeliski, R.: A database and evaluation methodology for optical flow. Int. J. Comput. Vis. **92**(1), 1–31 (2011)
3. Brox, T., Malik, J.: Large displacement optical flow: descriptor matching in variational motion estimation. IEEE Trans. Pattern Anal. Mach. Intell. **33**(3), 500–513 (2011)
4. Caelles, S., Maninis, K., Ponttuset, J., Lealtaixe, L., Cremers, D., Van Gool, L.: One-shot video object segmentation, pp. 221–230, June 2016
5. Chen, C., Li, S., Wang, Y., Qin, H., Hao, A.: Video saliency detection via spatial-temporal fusion and low-rank coherency diffusion. IEEE Trans. Image Process. **26**(7), 3156–3170 (2017)
6. Chen, L.C., Papandreou, G., Kokkinos, I., Murphy, K., Yuille, A.L.: DeepLab: semantic image segmentation with deep convolutional nets, atrous convolution, and fully connected CRFs. IEEE Trans. Pattern Anal. Mach. Intell. **40**(4), 834–848 (2018)
7. Chen, L., Shen, J., Wang, W., Ni, B.: Video object segmentation via dense trajectories. IEEE Trans. Multimed. **17**(12), 2225–2234 (2015)
8. Du, H., Liu, Z., Jiang, J., Shen, L.: Stretchability-aware block scaling for image retargeting. J. Vis. Commun. Image Represent. **24**(4), 499–508 (2013)
9. Fang, Y., Wang, Z., Lin, W., Fang, Z.: Video saliency incorporating spatiotemporal cues and uncertainty weighting. IEEE Trans. Image Process. **23**(9), 3910–3921 (2014)
10. Girshick, R.: Fast R-CNN. In: IEEE International Conference on Computer Vision (ICCV), pp. 1440–1448. IEEE (2015)
11. Gong, C., et al.: Saliency propagation from simple to difficult. In: The IEEE Conference on Computer Vision and Pattern Recognition (CVPR), pp. 2531–2539. IEEE, June 2015

12. Guo, C., Zhang, L.: A novel multiresolution spatiotemporal saliency detection model and its applications in image and video compression. IEEE Trans. Image Process. **19**(1), 185–198 (2010)
13. Guo, J., Song, B., Du, X.: Significance evaluation of video data over media cloud based on compressed sensing. IEEE Trans. Multimed. **18**(7), 1297–1304 (2016)
14. He, K., Zhang, X., Ren, S., Sun, J.: Delving deep into rectifiers: Surpassing human-level performance on imageNet classification. In: The IEEE International Conference on Computer Vision (ICCV), pp. 1026–1034. IEEE (2015)
15. Itti, L., Koch, C., Niebur, E.: A model of saliency-based visual attention for rapid scene analysis. IEEE Trans. Pattern Anal. Mach. Intell. **20**(11), 1254–1259 (1998)
16. Lee, W.F., Huang, T.H., Yeh, S.L., Chen, H.H.: Learning-based prediction of visual attention for video signals. IEEE Trans. Image Process. **20**(11), 3028–3038 (2011)
17. Li, F., Kim, T., Humayun, A., Tsai, D., Rehg, J.M.: Video segmentation by tracking many figure-ground segments. In: IEEE International Conference on Computer Vision (ICCV), pp. 2192–2199. IEEE (2013)
18. Liu, C., Yuen, P.C., Qiu, G.: Object motion detection using information theoretic spatio-temporal saliency. Pattern Recognit. **42**(11), 2897–2906 (2009)
19. Liu, Z., Li, J., Ye, L., Sun, G., Shen, L.: Saliency detection for unconstrained videos using superpixel-level graph and spatiotemporal propagation. IEEE Trans. Circuits Syst. Video Technol. **27**(12), 2527–2542 (2017)
20. Liu, Z., Zhang, X., Luo, S., Le Meur, O.: Superpixel-based spatiotemporal saliency detection. IEEE Trans. Circuits Syst. Video Technol. **24**(9), 1522–1540 (2014)
21. Liu, Z., Zou, W., Le Meur, O.: Saliency tree: a novel saliency detection framework. IEEE Trans. Image Process. **23**(5), 1937–1952 (2014)
22. Mahadevan, V., Vasconcelos, N.: Spatiotemporal saliency in dynamic scenes. IEEE Trans. Pattern Anal. Mach. Intell. **32**(1), 171–177 (2010)
23. Mahapatra, D., Winkler, S., Yen, S.C.: Motion saliency outweighs other low-level features while watching videos. In: Human Vision and Electronic Imaging XIII, vol. 6806, p. 68060P. International Society for Optics and Photonics (2008)
24. Perazzi, F., Pont-Tuset, J., McWilliams, B., Van Gool, L., Gross, M., Sorkine-Hornung, A.: A benchmark dataset and evaluation methodology for video object segmentation. In: The IEEE Conference on Computer Vision and Pattern Recognition (CVPR), pp. 724–732. IEEE (2016)
25. Vig, E., Dorr, M., Martinetz, T., Barth, E.: Intrinsic dimensionality predicts the saliency of natural dynamic scenes. IEEE Trans. Pattern Anal. Mach. Intell. **34**(6), 1080–1091 (2012)
26. Wang, W., Shen, J., Porikli, F.: Saliency-aware geodesic video object segmentation. In: The IEEE Conference on Computer Vision and Pattern Recognition (CVPR), pp. 3395–3402. IEEE (2015)
27. Wang, W., Shen, J., Shao, L.: Video salient object detection via fully convolutional networks. IEEE Trans. Image Process. **27**(1), 38–49 (2018)
28. Yan, B., Yuan, B., Yang, B.: Effective video retargeting with jittery assessment. IEEE Trans. Multimed. **16**(1), 272–277 (2014)
29. Ye, L., Liu, Z., Li, L., Shen, L., Bai, C., Wang, Y.: Salient object segmentation via effective integration of saliency and objectness. IEEE Trans. Multimed. **19**(8), 1742–1756 (2017)
30. Zhang, P., Wang, D., Lu, H., Wang, H., Ruan, X.: Amulet: aggregating multi-level convolutional features for salient object detection. In: The IEEE International Conference on Computer Vision (ICCV), pp. 202–211. IEEE, October 2017

31. Zhao, R., Ouyang, W., Li, H., Wang, X.: Saliency detection by multi-context deep learning. In: The IEEE Conference on Computer Vision and Pattern Recognition (CVPR), pp. 1265–1274. IEEE, June 2015

32. Zhou, X., Liu, Z., Gong, C., Liu, W.: Improving video saliency detection via localized estimation and spatiotemporal refinement. IEEE Trans. Multimed. (2018). https://doi.org/10.1109/TMM.2018.2829605

33. Zhou, X., Liu, Z., Sun, G., Ye, L., Wang, X.: Improving saliency detection via multiple kernel boosting and adaptive fusion. IEEE Signal Process. Lett. **23**(4), 517–521 (2016)

34. Zhu, Z., et al.: An adaptive hybrid pattern for noise-robust texture analysis. Pattern Recognit. **48**(8), 2592–2608 (2015)

Seagrass Detection in Coastal Water
Through Deep Capsule Networks

Kazi Aminul Islam[1]([⊠]) (iD), Daniel Pérez[2] (iD), Victoria Hill[3] (iD), Blake Schaeffer[4] (iD),
Richard Zimmerman[3] (iD), and Jiang Li[1] (iD)

[1] Department of Electrical and Computer Engineering, Old Dominion University,
Norfolk, VA 23529, USA
{kisla001,JLi}@odu.edu
[2] Department of Modeling, Simulation and Visualization Engineering,
Old Dominion University, Norfolk, VA 23529, USA
dpere013@odu.edu
[3] Department of Ocean, Earth and Atmospheric Sciences, Old Dominion University,
Norfolk, VA 23529, USA
{VHill,RZimmerm}@odu.edu
[4] Office of Research and Development, U.S. Environmental Protection Agency,
Durham, NC, USA
Schaeffer.Blake@epa.gov

Abstract. Seagrass is an important factor to balance marine ecological
systems, and there is a great interest in monitoring its distribution in different parts of the world. This paper presents a deep capsule network for
classification of seagrass in high-resolution multispectral satellite images.
We tested our method on three satellite images of the coastal areas in
Florida and obtained better performances than those achieved by the
traditional deep convolutional neural network (CNN) model. We also
propose a few-shot deep learning strategy to transfer knowledge learned
by the capsule network from one location to another for seagrass detection, in which the capsule network's reconstruction capability is utilized
to generate new artificial data for fine-tuning the model at new locations.
Our experimental results show that the proposed model achieves superb
performances in cross-validation on three satellite images collected in
Florida as compared to support vector machine (SVM) and CNN.

Keywords: Seagrass detection · Convolutional neural network
Capsule network · Deep learning · Remote sensing · Transfer learning

1 Introduction

Seagrass is an important component in coastal ecosystems. It provides food and
shelter for fish and marine organisms, protects ecological systems, stabilizes sea

This work was realized by a student. This work is supported by NASA under Grant
NNX17AH01G and the support of NVIDIA Corporation for the donation of the TESLA
K40 GPU used in this research is gratefully acknowledged.

J.-H. Lai et al. (Eds.): PRCV 2018, LNCS 11257, pp. 320–331, 2018.
https://doi.org/10.1007/978-3-030-03335-4_28

bottom, keeps the desired level of water quality and helps local economy [1,2, 18,33]. Coastal areas have been significantly impacted over the last decades by activities of nearby inhabitants and coastal visitors. Due to the growing of human population and industrial evolution, the release of waste and polluted water has also increased significantly in the coastal area [1,2,18,33]. These are causing the deterioration of water quality and a decrease in seagrass distribution. Seagrass distribution is also damaged by natural calamities such as typhoons, strong wind, rainfall, aquaculture and human with propeller current [1,2,18,33]. Florida has lost 50% of seagrass between 1880s and 1950s [18]. Therefore, improving water quality to restore seagrass has been a priority during the last few decades.

In this paper, we develop a deep capsule network to detect seagrass in Florida coastal areas based on multispectral satellite images. To generalize a trained seagrass detection model to new locations, we utilize the capsule network as a data augmentation method to generate new artificial data for fine-tuning the model. The main contributions of this paper are:

1. A capsule network was developed for seagrass detection in multispectral satellite images.
2. A few-shot deep learning strategy was implemented for seagrass detection and it may be applicable to other applications.

The paper is structured as follows: Sect. 2 discusses the relevant literature. Section 3 describes the proposed method. Sections 4 and 5 present results and discussions, respectively, and Sect. 6 summarizes the paper.

2   Related Work

2.1   CNN and Transfer Learning

Deep CNN models use multiple processing layers to learn new representations for better recognition and achieved state-of-the-art in many applications including image classification [12,13], medical imaging [10,14,15,17], speech recognition [8], cybersecurity [5,20], biomedical signal processing [16] and remote sensing [24]. Transfer learning tries to train a predictive model through adaptation by utilizing common knowledge between source and target data domains [31]. Oquab et al. have used transfer learning with CNN for small data set visual recognition task [22]. Transfer learning has been explored also in computer-aided detection [27], post-traumatic stress disorder diagnosis [4] and face representation [29].

2.2   Capsule Network

Sabour et al. recently proposed the capsule network for image classification [26]. It is more robust to affine transformation and it has been considered a better method than CNN for identifying overlapping digits in MNIST [26]. In 2018, the same group improved the capsule network with matrix capsules and the expectation maximization algorithm was used for dynamic routing [9]. The improved model achieved state-of-the-art performance on the smallNORB data set [9]. Capsule network has also been used in breast cancer detection [11], brain tumor type classification [3]. For highly complex data sets such as CIFAR10, capsule network has not achieved good performances [32].

2.3 Seagrass Detection

WorldView-2 multispectral images have been used for shallow-water Benthic identification [19]. Pasqualinia *et al.* have found the overall accuracies between 73% and 96% for identifying four classes: sand, photo-philous algae on rock, patchy seagrass beds and continuous seagrass beds, with two spatial resolutions of 2.5 m and 10 m [23]. Vela *et al.* used fused image of SPOT-5 and IKONOS in southern Tunisia near the Libyan border to detect four classes including low seagrass cover, high seagrass cover, superficial mobile sediments and deep mobile sediments [30]. For the lagoon environment mapping, they have obtained 83.25% accuracy over the entire area and 85.91% accuracy over the testing area with SPOT-5 images, and 73.41% accuracy over the testing area with IKONOS images [30]. Dahdough-Guebas *et al.* combined red, green, blue of visible bands with near infra-red band for seagrass and algae detection [6]. Oguslu *et al.* used sparse coding method for sea-grass's propeller scar detection in WorldView-2 satellite images [21].

3   Methods

3.1   Datasets

We collected three multispectral satellite images captured by the WorldView-2 (WV-2) satellite. These images have a wavelength between 400–1100 nm and spatial resolution of 2 m in the 8 visible and near infrared (VNIR) bands. In this study, an experienced operator selected several regions in each of the three images with highest confidence of the labeling. These regions have been identified as blue, cyan, green and yellow boxes, corresponding to sea, sand, seagrass and land respectively (Fig. 1). At Saint Joseph Bay, intertidal class was added and it is represented as white in Fig. 1(a).

3.2   Capsule Network

We develop a capsule network for seagrass detection by following the design in [26]. The model has two convolutional layers and 32 convolutional kernels with a size of 2×2 for extracting high level features. The extracted features are then fed into the capsule layers, in which a weight matrix of 8×16 is used to find the most similar capsule in the next layer. The last capsule layer, Feature-caps, stores a capsule per class, and each capsule has a total of 16 features. The length of each capsule represents posterior probability for a class. Additionally, the features in Feature-caps are used to reconstruct original images. The reconstruction architecture has 3 fully connected layers with a sigmoid activation function and sizes

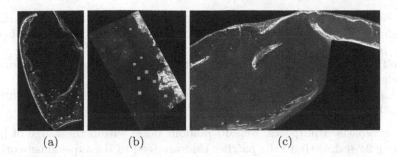

Fig. 1. Satellite images taken from Saint Joseph Bay (a), Keeton Beach (b) and Saint George Sound (c). The blue, cyan, green, yellow and white boxes correspond to the selected regions belonging to sea, sand, seagrass, land and intertide respectively. (Color figure online)

of the layers are 256, 512 and 200, respectively. Output size of the reconstruction structure is the same as that of input patch ($5 \times 5 \times 8$).

3.3 Transfer Learning

The ultimate goal of this study is to develop a deep learning model that is able to detect seagrass at any location in the world. However, there exists a significantly amount of variations in seagrass representation from different satellite images. To resolve this issue, we propose a transfer learning approach such that only a small number of samples are needed to adapt a trained deep model for predicting seagrass at a new location:

1. Train a capsule network using all the selected data from Saint Joseph Bay.
2. Feed the trained model with few labeled samples from Keeton Beach and extract features from the Feature-caps as new representations for the data.
3. Utilize the new representations to classify the entire Keeton Beach image based on the 1-nearest neighbor (1-NN) rule.
4. Repeat the procedures for the image from Saint George Sound bay.

3.4 Capsule Network as a Generative Model for Data Augmentation

The capsule network has the capability of reconstructing input data from features in Feature-caps. We generate artificial labeled data at new locations to improve model adaptation as follows,

1. Train a capsule network with the selected patches at Saint Joseph Bay and fine-tune the model with a limited number of samples from Keeton Beach.
2. For each of the patches used for fine-tuning the model, extract the 16 corresponding features in the Feature-caps and compute mean (μ_C) and standard deviation (σ_C) for each of the 16 features.

3. For each patch from Keeton Beach, generate a total of 176 new artificial patches by varying each of the features 11 times within the range of $[\mu_C - 2\sigma_C, \mu_C + 2\sigma_C]$.
4. Fine-tune the trained capsule network with these artificial and original patches.
5. Repeat this procedure for 20 iterations and repeat the same procedure for Saint George Sound.

For comparison purposes, we add random noise within the range of $[\mu_C - 2\sigma_C, \mu_C + 2\sigma_C]$ directly to the patches that are feed to the capsule network and then we extract their features to classify all the patches from Keeton Beach and Saint George Sound using the 1-NN rule.

3.5   Convolutional Neural Network

A similar method is implemented on CNN for comparison purposes. The CNN model has two convolutional layers with a ReLU activation function and 16 2 × 2 and 64 4 × 4 convolutional kernels, respectively. The convolutional layers are followed by one fully connected layer with 16 hidden units and a soft-max layer to perform classification. We utilize the dropout technique with a probability of 0.1 to reduce over-fitting [28].

4   Results

4.1   Model Structure Determination

We have selected Saint Joseph Bay as the primary location to train deep models with the selected regions. To have a fair comparison of the performances between capsule network and CNN, we keep the same number of parameters, 9k, in convolutional layers for both models. In the capsule network, there are 46k parameters for routing and 254k parameters for reconstruction. We train 10 epochs for CNN and 50 epochs for capsule network to roughly keep the same amount of training for both models.

4.2   Cross-Validation Results in Selected Regions

To validate our model, we perform 3-fold cross-validation (CV) in the selected regions for the three locations separately. Table 1 shows the classification accuracies for each satellite image using SVM, CNN and capsule network. Additionally, each model is trained with all the patches from the selected regions and then applied to the corresponding whole image as shown in Fig. 2.

4.3   Transfer Learning

Table 2 shows the classification accuracies in the selected regions by transfer learning with different number of labeled samples (shots) from new locations. Zero shot transfer learning means applying the deep learning model trained at Saint Joseph Bay directly to Keeton Beach and Saint George Sound. It is observed that CNN has better performances in transfer learning.

Table 1. Three-fold CV results of Saint (St) Joseph Bay, Keeton Beach and Saint (St) George Sound.

Location	SVM	CNN	Capsule network
St Joseph Bay	90.20%	**99.99%**	99.94%
Keeton Beach	81.13%	97.20%	**99.97%**
St George Sound	76.27%	80.20%	**99.40%**
Mean	82.53%	92.46%	**99.77%**

Table 2. Transfer learning using CNN and capsule network for Keeton Beach and Saint George Sound.

Method	Location	0 shot	1 shot	10 shots	50 shots	100 shots
CNN	Keeton Beach	**47.23%**	**56.90%**	**99.56%**	**99.63%**	**99.75%**
	St George Sound	**22.08%**	**75.26%**	**95.92%**	**98.66%**	**98.76%**
Capsule network	Keeton Beach	38.74%	54.85%	94.45%	96.13%	97.27%
	St George Sound	21.88%	47.58%	89.36%	94.00%	92.96%

4.4 Capsule Network as a Generative Model for Data Augmentation

We use the capsule network as a generative model to obtain new training data for model adaptation as described in Sect. 3.4. For comparison purposes, we have identified the following cases:

- Regular fine-tuning: We fine-tune the capsule network with a small number of labeled samples (shots) from the new locations. After fine-tuning, we use the transfer learning procedures to classify the rest of the patches.
- Random noise: We add some random noises into the labeled patches to generate artificial patches for transfer learning.
- Generative fine-tuning: We fine-tune the capsule network with a small number of labeled samples (shots) from the new locations. After fine-tuning, we generated artificial patches as described in Sect. 3.4 and use the transfer learning procedures to classify the rest of the patches.

Table 3 shows the classification accuracies for each of these cases with different number of fine-tuning shots. It can be observed that the best accuracies are obtained using generative fine-tuning for most of the cases.

The results displayed in Table 3 shows the accuracies for only one iteration in generative fine-tuning. To investigate the effect of the number of iteration on the performances, we run the generative fine-tuning method with different number of iterations in 100 shots deep learning and show the results in Table 4, where the accuracies obtained in Keeton Beach and Saint George Sound either with generated data only or combined with the original patches. Additionally, we show the classification maps of each method in Fig. 3. The Figure shows classification maps of one shot and 100 shots by each of the methods previously discussed. In the case of generative fine-tuning, we show the results after 20 iterations with the combination of generated and original data.

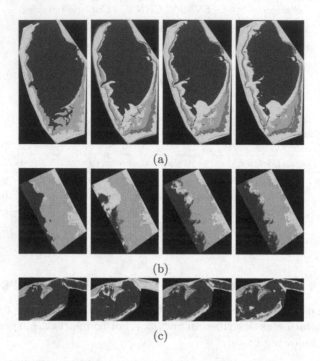

(a)

(b)

(c)

Fig. 2. Three-fold CV results. From left to right, the classification map by the physics model [7], SVM, CNN and capsule network on Saint Joseph Bay (a), Keeton Beach (b) and Saint George Sound (c). The colors blue, cyan, green, yellow and magenta represent sea, sand, seagrass, land and intertide, respectively. (Color figure online)

4.5 Changes in Feature Orientation

We investigated the feature orientation changes in the Feature-caps layer of the capsule network while using each of the fine tuning methods. Figure 4 shows the average values of the features in Feature-caps after each fine-tuning method. The plots in Fig. 4 are generated through the following steps:

1. For each class in the data set, collect all image patches and extract the feature matrix computed by the Feature-caps layer in the capsule network, which contains 5 capsules (where 5 is the number of classes), each of them with a size of 16 features.
2. Reshape each feature matrix into an 1-dimensional vector in which the first 16 numbers are the features corresponding to the first class, the next 16 are the ones corresponding to the second class and so on. This feature vector has a total size of $5 * 16$.

Table 3. Transfer Learning results with regular fine-tuning, random noise and generative fine-tuning for Keeton Beach and Saint (St) George Sound locations.

Method	Location	1 shot	10 shots	50 shots	100 shots
Regular fine-tuning	Keeton Beach	69.66%	94.00%	96.79%	98.35%
	St George Sound	77.58%	87.39%	99.32%	99.37%
Random noise	Keeton Beach	54.88%	94.52%	96.10%	97.22%
	St George Sound	47.58%	89.36%	94.00%	92.96%
Generative fine-tuning (1 iteration)	Keeton Beach	53.11%	89.43%	98.70%	98.85%
	St George Sound	78.20%	95.13%	99.15%	99.42%

Table 4. Classification results with different number of iterations by the generative fine-tuning method in 100 shots learning.

Iteration	Keeton Beach		Saint George Sound	
	Generated data only	Generated and original data	Generated data only	Generated and original data
5	87.15%	98.82%	86.56%	99.47%
10	85.69%	98.86%	**93.34%**	**99.73%**
15	91.88%	99.09%	78.00%	98.20%
20	**93.00%**	**99.16%**	89.57%	99.67%

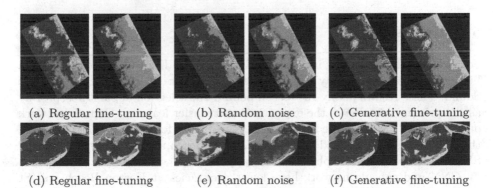

(a) Regular fine-tuning   (b) Random noise   (c) Generative fine-tuning

(d) Regular fine-tuning   (e) Random noise   (f) Generative fine-tuning

Fig. 3. Classification maps by the generative fine-tuning method after 20 iterations at Keeton Beach (a, b, c) and Saint George Sound (d, e, f) with 0 shot (left) and 100 shots (right). The colors blue, cyan, green and yellow represent the patches classified as sea, sand, seagrass and land, respectively. (Color figure online)

3. Average all the feature vectors belonging to each class and plot them in a 2D graph. Since the probability of an entity belonging to a class is measured by the length of its instantiation parameters (or features), the absolute value of the features belonging to a class should be significantly larger than the rest of the features.

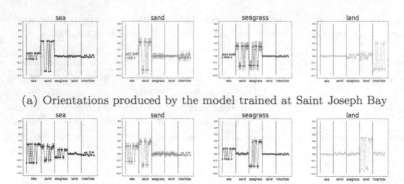

(a) Orientations produced by the model trained at Saint Joseph Bay

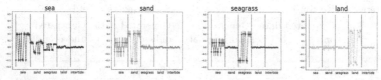

(b) Orientations after fine-tuning the model trained at Saint Joseph Bay with 100 shots from Saint George Sound

(c) Orientations after using Capsule Network as a Generative Model (for 20 iterations)

Fig. 4. Features orientation in feature-caps at Saint George Sound.

5 Discussion

For cross validation results in Table 1, SVM, CNN and capsule network perform better at Saint Joseph Bay location than at Keeton Beach and Saint George Sound. These results justify the reason behind the selection of Saint Joseph Bay as the primary location in the experiment of transfer learning. Capsule network outperforms SVM at all the three locations and CNN for two locations. In Fig. 2, the sea class is misclassified as sand in Keeton Beach and ST George Sound by SVM as compared to the physics based approach.

CNN and capsule network have lower accuracies at Keeton Beach and St George Sound in zero shot and one shot learning. Model trained at Saint Joseph Bay performed poorly at other two locations because of the variations of class orientation as shown in Fig. 4. One shot transfer learning is not enough to represent the entire orientation changes at different locations. However, with the increase of number of samples/shots, the classification accuracies were significantly improved (Table 2). In Table 3 and Fig. 3, we have compared the generative fine-tuning approach with regular fine-tuning and random noise approaches. Random noises may not be related to original data and its performances were worse than the generative fine-tuning approach.

In Fig. 4, we have evaluated how the capsule's features are changing in different steps. In ideal situation if one of the classes is used as input, the capsule representing that class should have higher feature values. For example, in Fig. 4(a), the first 16 features should be large because sea patches were used as input. However, the second 16 features are large because of the location variations between Saint Joseph Bay and Saint George Sound as shown in Fig. 4(a). Because Saint George Sound's sea sample (the first 16 features) is similar to sand sample (the second 16 features) at Saint Joseph Bay. Likewise, seagrass class and Land class of Saint George Sound are similar to sand and inter-tide class of Saint Joseph Bay respectively. Sand class samples are similar at both locations. The capsule feature's orientations also explain the poor zero shot results using capsule-network. After fine-tuning the network with generative fine-tuning approach for 20 iterations, we can see that this capsule features are representing correct classes (Fig. 4(c)).

We have achieved the best accuracy of 99.16% and 99.67% in Keeton Beach and Saint George Sound location after 20 iterations in generative fine-tuning. Comparing Table 4 with Table 2, the accuracy is either comparable (99.16% vs. 99.75%) or better (99.67% vs. 98.76%) at both locations in transfer learning by CNN. Using generated data only for 1-NN rule, the best accuracy we have achieved are 93.00% and 93.34% in Keeton Beach and Saint George Sound. If we compare the end to end classification map in Figs. 2 and 3, generative fine-tuning approach has produced the best results for both locations. In our companion paper [25], we studied seagrass quantification after identification.

6 Conclusion

To the best of our knowledge, this study represents the first work of designing a capsule network for seagrass detection. We have achieved better classification accuracy than the baseline models (CNN and SVM) in 3-fold CV. Transfer learning proved to be a good technique to address the problem of model adaptation. In addition, our generative model is able to increase the classifier performance by iteratively generating new data from the capsule's features. Using this method, we obtained accuracies of 99.16% and 99.67% at Keeton Beach and Saint George Sound, respectively. When we only used the generated data, we achieved accuracies of 93.00% and 93.34% at the two new locations, respectively, proving the similarity between the original samples and generated samples.

We also demonstrated the effectiveness of our method through a set of 2D plots that are able to display the capsule features. Since magnitudes of the capsule features determine probabilities of classes, the plots are able to visually assess performance of a trained capsule network in a significantly simple manner. To the best of our knowledge, we are the first to offer this visualization tool for the evaluation of capsule network's performance.

References

1. Floridadep: Florida coastal office. https://floridadep.gov/fco. Accessed 20 Oct 2017
2. MyFWC: Florida fish and wildlife conservation commission. http://myfwc.com/research/habitat/seagrasses/information/importance/. Accessed 20 Oct 2017

3. Afshar, P., Mohammadi, A., Plataniotis, K.N.: Brain tumor type classification via capsule networks. arXiv preprint arXiv:1802.10200 (2018)
4. Banerjee, D., et al.: A deep transfer learning approach for improved post-traumatic stress disorder diagnosis. In: 2017 IEEE International Conference on Data Mining (ICDM), pp. 11–20. IEEE (2017)
5. Chowdhury, M.M.U., Hammond, F., Konowicz, G., Xin, C., Wu, H., Li, J.: A few-shot deep learning approach for improved intrusion detection. In: IEEE 8th Annual Ubiquitous Computing, Electronics and Mobile Communication Conference (UEMCON), 2017, pp. 456–462. IEEE (2017)
6. Dahdouh-Guebas, F., Coppejans, E., Van Speybroeck, D.: Remote sensing and zonation of seagrasses and algae along the Kenyan coast. Hydrobiologia 400, 63–73 (1999)
7. Hill, V.J., Zimmerman, R.C., Bissett, W.P., Dierssen, H., Kohler, D.D.: Evaluating light availability, seagrass biomass, and productivity using hyperspectral airborne remote sensing in Saint Josephs Bay, Florida. Estuaries Coasts 37(6), 1467–1489 (2014)
8. Hinton, G., et al.: Deep neural networks for acoustic modeling in speech recognition: the shared views of four research groups. IEEE Signal Process. Mag. 29(6), 82–97 (2012)
9. Hinton, G., Frosst, N., Sabour, S.: Matrix capsules with EM routing (2018)
10. Ibanez, D.P., Li, J., Shen, Y., Dayanghirang, J., Wang, S., Zheng, Z.: Deep learning for pulmonary nodule CT image retrievalâan online assistance system for novice radiologists. In: 2017 IEEE International Conference on Data Mining Workshops (ICDMW), pp. 1112–1121. IEEE (2017)
11. Iesmantas, T., Alzbutas, R.: Convolutional capsule network for classification of breast cancer histology images. arXiv preprint arXiv:1804.08376 (2018)
12. Krizhevsky, A., Sutskever, I., Hinton, G.E.: ImageNet classification with deep convolutional neural networks. In: Advances in Neural Information Processing Systems, pp. 1097–1105 (2012)
13. LeCun, Y., Bengio, Y., Hinton, G.: Deep learning. Nature 521(7553), 436 (2015)
14. Li, F., Tran, L., Thung, K.-H., Ji, S., Shen, D., Li, J.: Robust deep learning for improved classification of AD/MCI patients. In: Wu, G., Zhang, D., Zhou, L. (eds.) MLMI 2014. LNCS, vol. 8679, pp. 240–247. Springer, Cham (2014). https://doi.org/10.1007/978-3-319-10581-9_30
15. Li, F., Tran, L., Thung, K.H., Ji, S., Shen, D., Li, J.: A robust deep model for improved classification of AD/MCI patients. IEEE J. Biomed. Health Inform. 19(5), 1610–1616 (2015)
16. Li, F., et al.: Deep models for engagement assessment with scarce label information. IEEE Trans. Hum.-Mach. Syst. 47(4), 598–605 (2017)
17. Li, R., et al.: Deep learning based imaging data completion for improved brain disease diagnosis. In: Golland, P., Hata, N., Barillot, C., Hornegger, J., Howe, R. (eds.) MICCAI 2014. LNCS, vol. 8675, pp. 305–312. Springer, Cham (2014). https://doi.org/10.1007/978-3-319-10443-0_39
18. Li, R., Liu, J.K., Sukcharoenpong, A., Yuan, J., Zhu, H., Zhang, S.: A systematic approach toward detection of seagrass patches from hyperspectral imagery. Mar. Geodesy 35(3), 271–286 (2012)
19. Manessa, M.D.M., Kanno, A., Sekine, M., Ampou, E.E., Widagti, N., As-syakur, A.R.: Shallow-water benthic identification using multispectral satellite imagery: investigation on the effects of improving noise correction method and spectral cover. Remote Sens. 6(5), 4454–4472 (2014)

20. Ning, R., Wang, C., Xin, C., Li, J., Wu, H.: DeepMag: sniffing mobile apps in magnetic field through deep convolutional neural networks. In: 2018 IEEE International Conference on Pervasive Computing and Communications (PerCom), pp. 1–10. IEEE (2018)

21. Oguslu, E., et al.: Detection of seagrass scars using sparse coding and morphological filter. Remote Sens. Environ. **213**, 92–103 (2018)

22. Oquab, M., Bottou, L., Laptev, I., Sivic, J.: Learning and transferring mid-level image representations using convolutional neural networks. In: 2014 IEEE Conference on Computer Vision and Pattern Recognition (CVPR), pp. 1717–1724. IEEE (2014)

23. Pasqualini, V., et al.: Use of spot 5 for mapping seagrasses: an application to posidonia oceanica. Remote Sens. Environ. **94**(1), 39–45 (2005)

24. Perez, D., et al.: Deep learning for effective detection of excavated soil related to illegal tunnel activities. In: 2017 IEEE 8th Annual Ubiquitous Computing, Electronics and Mobile Communication Conference (UEMCON), pp. 626–632. IEEE (2017)

25. Perez, D., Islam, K.A., Schaeffer, B., Zimmerman, R., Hill, V., Li, J.: Deepcoast: Quantifying seagrass distribution in coastal water through deep capsule networks. In: Lai, J.-H., et al. (eds.) The First Chinese Conference on Pattern Recognition and Computer Vision, PRCV 2018. LNCS, vol. 11257, pp. 404–416. Springer, Heidelberg (2018)

26. Sabour, S., Frosst, N., Hinton, G.E.: Dynamic routing between capsules, pp. 3859–3869 (2017)

27. Shin, H.C., et al.: Deep convolutional neural networks for computer-aided detection: CNN architectures, dataset characteristics and transfer learning. IEEE Trans. Med. Imaging **35**(5), 1285–1298 (2016)

28. Srivastava, N., Hinton, G., Krizhevsky, A., Sutskever, I., Salakhutdinov, R.: Dropout: a simple way to prevent neural networks from overfitting. J. Mach. Learn. Res. **15**(1), 1929–1958 (2014)

29. Sun, Y., Wang, X., Tang, X.: Deep learning face representation from predicting 10,000 classes. In: Proceedings of the IEEE Conference on Computer Vision and Pattern Recognition, pp. 1891–1898 (2014)

30. Vela, A., et al.: Use of spot 5 and ikonos satellites for mapping biocenoses in a tunisian lagoon (2005)

31. Weiss, K.R., Khoshgoftaar, T.M.: An investigation of transfer learning and traditional machine learning algorithms. In: 2016 IEEE 28th International Conference on Tools with Artificial Intelligence (ICTAI), pp. 283–290. IEEE (2016)

32. Xi, E., Bing, S., Jin, Y.: Capsule network performance on complex data. arXiv preprint arXiv:1712.03480 (2017)

33. Yang, D., Yang, C.: Detection of seagrass distribution changes from 1991 to 2006 in xincun bay, hainan, with satellite remote sensing. Sensors **9**(2), 830–844 (2009)

Deep Gabor Scattering Network
for Image Classification

Li-Na Wang, Benxiu Liu, Haizhen Wang, Guoqiang Zhong[✉],
and Junyu Dong[✉]

Department of Computer Science and Technology,
Ocean University of China, Qingdao, China
{gqzhong,dongjunyu}@ouc.edu.cn

Abstract. Deep learning models obtain exponential ascension in the field of image classification in recent years, and have become the most active research branch in AI research. The success of deep learning prompts us to make greater achievements in image classification. How to obtain effective feature representation becomes particularly important. In this paper, we combine the wavelet transformation and the idea of deep learning to build a new deep learning model, called Deep Gabor Scattering Network (DGSN). Concretely, in DGSN, we use the Gabor wavelet transformation to extract the invariant information of the images, partial least square regression (PLSR) for feature selection, and support vector machine (SVM) for classification. A key benefit of DGSN is that Gabor wavelet transformation can extract rich invariant features from the images. We show that DGSN is computationally simpler and delivers higher classification accuracy than related methods.

Keywords: Deep learning · Gabor filter · Invariant information
Deep Gabor scattering network (DGSN)

1 Introduction

In recent years, with the deepening of deep learning research, variety of deep learning models have been proposed and their application fields have been rapidly expanded. Nowadays, deep learning becomes to the most active branch of the artificial intelligence research. But the history of deep learning is not long. LeCun et al. [11] published the foreword exploration of the convolutional neural network in 1998, but it experienced years of deposition before deep learning really broke out. Since in 2006 Hinton and Salakhutdinov [8] proposed the concept of deep learning, researchers have gradually started the study of deep learning, constructed a variety of different deep learning models, and achieved a series of breakthrough research results. The rise of deep learning models has greatly improved the accuracy of object recognition and even surpassed the human level in some recognition tasks. However, in the actual image classification problems, deep learning models still face many challenges. How to construct an effective

© Springer Nature Switzerland AG 2018
J.-H. Lai et al. (Eds.): PRCV 2018, LNCS 11257, pp. 332–343, 2018.
https://doi.org/10.1007/978-3-030-03335-4_29

deep network model and apply it to image classification is an important issue that needs to be solved urgently.

The challenge of image classification is mainly manifested in: lighting, shooting angle, deformation and other factors may cause image diversity. In image classification research, wavelet transform can solve this problem to a certain extent. It can recover images from unsuitable lighting and deformation situations and can better extract the invariant information in images.

In 1985, Meyer proved the existence of the wavelet function in the one-dimensional case and made a deep study in theory [14]. Based on the idea of multi-resolution analysis, Mallat proposed the Mallat algorithm, which plays an important role in the application of wavelet [19]. Its position in wavelet analysis is equivalent to CNN in deep learning. In image processing, the Gabor function is a linear filter for edge extraction. Its working principles are similar to the human visual system. Some existing study found that Gabor filter is very suitable for texture expression and separation. In the spatial domain, a two-dimensional Gabor filter is a Gaussian kernel function modulated by a sinusoidal plane wave. Mehrotra, Namuduri and Ranganathan [13] designed a computational model based on Gabor filters and the model was successfully used for edge detection, texture classification, etc. Chen, Cheng and Mallat [4] introduced a Haar scattering transform which computes invariant signal descriptors. Based on these, several researchers have demonstrated the utility of wavelet network for image analysis.

In this paper, we combine the wavelet transformation and the machine learning algorithms, in which we employ Gabor wavelet transformation to extract the invariant information of the images and use the partial least square regression (PLSR) [16,18] for feature selection and SVM for classification. We name the designed architecture as Deep Gabor Scattering Network (DGSN). Similar to LeNet-5 [11] and its variants [10], the structure of DGSN can be deeper by adding some convolutional and fully connected layers. However, to demonstrate the effectiveness of DGSN, we only use its prototype model here. The remaining part of this paper is composed of four sections. The deep learning methods based on wavelet are reviewed in Sect. 2. The architecture of our DGSN model is introduced in Sect. 3. Section 4 reports the experimental results with comparison to related work. Finally, Sect. 5 concludes this paper.

The main contributions of this paper are as follows:

(1) We propose a new network structure called Deep Gabor Scattering Network (DGSN) for image classification.
(2) A key benefit of DGSN is that based on the Gabor wavelet transformation, DGSN can extract rich invariant information of the images.
(3) We show that DGSN is computationally simpler and delivers a better classification accuracy than compared approaches [4].

2   Related Work

In 2006, Hinton and Salakhutdinov [8] proposed the concept of deep learning which had gradually become more and more popular. Especially, in the field of image recognition, the rise of convolutional neural networks (CNNs) had greatly improved the recognition accuracy and even in some tasks that had exceeded the recognition of human eyes, such as on object recognition [9,12] and image classification [5]. With the development of the neural network, people tend to construct a deep network and believe that this deep network structure can learn more abstract features and have high learning ability.

As the application of deep network more and more extensive, many scholars have proposed a variety of deep network models to deal with different tasks. Among others, Krizhevsky et al. [10] put forward the AlexNet network structure to win the 2012 ImageNet Large Scale Visual Recognition Challenge (ILSVRC 2012). AlexNet contains eight layers, including five convolutional and three fully connected layers, and uses the "Dropout" technology. The model also performed well when migrating to other image classification tasks and became a commonly used model. In the ILSVRC 2014, researchers of Google proposed a deep network structure named GoogLeNet, which has 22 layers. This "deeper" network structure can learn more abstract features from images and achieved better classification results than AlexNet.

In practice, the problems of image diversity can be caused by lighting, shooting angle and deformation. To alleviate these problems, Bruna and Mallat [1] proposed the Invariant Scattering Convolution Networks (ISCN), which introduced the wavelet transformation into the deep learning area, and achieved fairly good classification results. Moreover, Guo and Mousavi [7] designed a deep CNN named Deep Wavelet Super-Resolution (DWSR) to predict the "missing details" of wavelet coefficients of the low-resolution images to obtain the Super-Resolution (SR) results. Said et al. [15] proposed a novel approach for image classification using wavelet networks and deep learning methods, which was called Deep Wavelet Network. The work of [4] introduced a Haar scattering transformation, which computes the invariant signal descriptors. It is implemented with a deep cascade of additions, subtractions and absolute values, iteratively computing the orthogonal Haar wavelet transformation. In this paper, we exploit the Gabor transformation for image feature learning.

In this paper, we aim to combining the Gabor wavelets with machine learning techniques for image classification. We propose a novel deep architecture called Deep Gabor Scattering Network (DGSN), which can effectively extract the invariant information of the images and categorize them.

3   Deep Gabor Scattering Network (DGSN)

In this section, we introduce the proposed new model, DGSN. We begin with a brief overview of the network architecture, followed by specific details. In order to classify the images, a deep CNN generally uses convolutional operations to extract the features of images. However, there are some difficulties to extract invariant information of the images with the convolutional operation, due to lighting, shooting angle and deformation, which may cause the image diversity problem. In order to overcome this problem, we use the Gabor wavelet transformation to replace the convolutional operation for the images' feature extraction, followed by PLSR for feature selection and SVM for classification. To the end, we obtain a deep Gabor scattering network, which can effectively learn the representations of the images and classify them.

3.1   The Structure of DGSN

DGSN is constructed by combining the Gabor wavelet transformation, PLSR and SVM classifier. It is constituted of five layers. The structure of DGSN is illustrated in Fig. 1, which follows the work of Deep Haar Scattering Network (HaarScat) [4]. Suppose the input images are of size $n \times n$. The Gabor layer consists of 32 Gabor filters corresponding to 4 scales and 8 orientations for image feature extraction, the PLSR layer is used for feature selection and dimensionality reduction, and the SVM layer for images classification. The main difference between DGSN and HaarScat is on the image feature learning. DGSN uses Gabor wavelet transformation, while the latter uses Haar wavelet transformation to extract the image features. Compared to HaarScat, DGSN can greatly reduce the training time and improve the classification performance under the condition of ensuring the classification accuracy.

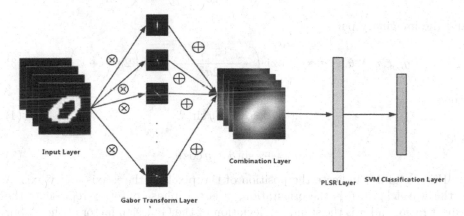

Fig. 1. The structure of DGSN.

3.2   Gabor Filters

In image processing, the Gabor wavelet transformation is an effective feature extraction algorithm. The working principles of the Gabor wavelet transformation are similar to the human visual system. Gabor wavelet transformation has good scale and direction selection characteristics. It is sensitive to the edge information of the image and able to adapt to the situation of light changes. Many pieces of work have found that Gabor wavelet transformation is very suitable for texture expression and separation. Compared with other methods in feature extraction, Gabor wavelet transformation in general needs less training data and can meet the real-time requirements of some practical systems. Furthermore, it can tolerate to a certain degree of image rotation and deformation.

A Gabor kernel can obtain the response of the image in the frequency domain, and the result of the response can be regarded as a feature of the image. Then, if we use multiple Gabor kernels with different frequencies to obtain the response of the images, we can finally construct the representations of the images in the frequency domain.

In the space domain, a two-dimensional Gabor filter is a Gaussian kernel function with sine wave modulation. The filter consists of a real part and an imaginary part, which are orthogonal to each other. The mathematical expression of the Gabor function is as follows [6]:

$$g(x, y; \lambda, \theta, \psi, \sigma, \gamma) = exp\left(-\frac{x'^2 + \gamma^2 y'^2}{2\sigma^2}\right) exp\left(i\left(2\pi\frac{x'}{\lambda} + \psi\right)\right), \qquad (1)$$

with the real part:

$$g_r(x, y; \lambda, \theta, \psi, \sigma, \gamma) = exp\left(-\frac{x'^2 + \gamma^2 y'^2}{2\sigma^2}\right) cos\left(2\pi\frac{x'}{\lambda} + \psi\right), \qquad (2)$$

and the imaginary part:

$$g_i(x, y; \lambda, \theta, \psi, \sigma, \gamma) = exp\left(-\frac{x'^2 + \gamma^2 y'^2}{2\sigma^2}\right) sin\left(2\pi\frac{x'}{\lambda} + \psi\right), \qquad (3)$$

where

$$x' = x\cos\theta + y\sin\theta, \qquad (4)$$

and

$$y' = -x\sin\theta + y\cos\theta. \qquad (5)$$

Here, x and y indicate the position of the pixel on the x-axis and y-axis, λ is the wavelength, θ is the orientation, ψ is the phase offset, γ represents the aspect ratio, and σ is the standard deviation of the Gaussian factor of the Gabor function.

Gabor filters are self-similar. All Gabor filters can be generated from a mother wavelet after expansion and rotation. In many applications, when an image is given to a Gabor filter, the Gabor filter extracts the invariant feature of the image and produces different features with different scales and frequencies. Finally, all feature images are superimposed as a tensor, which is then normalized as the input of the next layer in DGSN.

3.3 PLSR and Classification

In DGSN, the Gabor transform layer is followed by PLSR for Gabor feature selection and the Gaussian kernel SVM for classification.

PLSR is a statistical method, and to some extent related to the principal components analysis (PCA). It can find a linear regression model through projecting the predicted and observed variables into a new space, rather than looking for the hypherplanes of maximum variance between independent variables and the response variables. PLSR can solve many problems which cannot be solved by ordinary multiple variable regression, and it can also realize the comprehensive application of various data analysis methods. Here, we use PLSR to select Gabor features and reduce the feature's dimensionality simultaneously.

Support vector machine (SVM) is one of the most commonly used classifiers and one of the most effective classifiers. It has excellent generalization ability and its own optimization goal is to achieve the least structural risk. In the classification layer, we use the SVM model in LibSVM [3], which is an easy, fast and effective SVM pattern recognition and regression package. The LibSVM Toolkit provides the default parameters. In most cases, researchers can use these default parameters to achieve a good classification effect and greatly reduce the time used to adjust the parameters. Even if the researcher wants to adjust the parameters, the toolkit provides a very convenient method of parameter selection. In the LibSVM toolkit, researchers can choose the type of SVM, kernel functions, and their parameters based on specific problems.

4   Experiments and Results

4.1   Data Sets

We train and evaluate our network on three standard data sets: MNIST, Yale [2] and Fashion-MNIST [17].

(1) MNIST is a database which contains a training set of 60,000 handwritten digits images and a test set of 10,000 handwritten digits images with the resolution of 28 * 28 pixels.
(2) Yale is a face database which contains 165 grayscale images in GIF format of 15 individuals. There are 11 images per individuals, one per different facial expression or configuration: center-light, w/glasses, happy, left-light, w/no glasses, normal, right-light, sad, sleepy, surprised, and wink. The resolution of each image is 32 * 32 pixels.
(3) Fashion-MNIST is a database of 70,000 positive images of 10 different products. The size, format, and the division of training set and test set of Fashion-MNIST are fully aligned with the original MNIST. It also contains a training set of 60,000 products images and a test set of 10,000 products images with the resolution of 28 * 28 pixels. It contains 10 classes, some example images are shown in Fig. 2.

Over the past decades, classical MNIST dataset is often used as a benchmark for testing algorithms in the field of machine learning, machine vision, artificial intelligence and deep learning. MNIST is too simple and many algorithms have achieved 99% performance on the test set. Fashion-MNIST is an image data set that replaces the handwritten digits set of MNIST. Therefore, in addition to train and test our DGSN on the MNIST data set, we also train and test DGSN on the Fashion-MNIST data set. For Fashion-MNIST, we don't need to modify any algorithm and can adopt the dataset directly. Furthermore, we have tested our DGSN on a data set, Yale, for face recognition.

4.2 Experimental Settings

During the training process, the size of the input images is fixed to 32 * 32. In the Gabor transform layer, we use 32 Gabor filters with 4 scales and 8 orientations to extract the frequency information of the images. The parameters of the wave lengthes, bandwidths, aspect ratios and angles are set to $\{2, 4, 6, 8\}$, 1, 0.5, $\{0, \pi/2\}$, and $\{0, \pi\}$, respectively. The orientation is set to $\{0, \pi/8, 2\pi/8, 3\pi/8, 4\pi/8, 5\pi/8, 6\pi/8, 7\pi/8\}$. To show the effect of the wave length, we illustrate the classification accuracy against different values of λ in Fig. 3. We can see that the classification accuracy increases with the increment of the value of the wave length λ. In order to extract rich invariant feature from the images, we select 4 values for the Gabor filters.

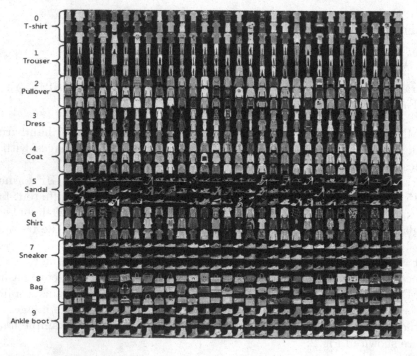

Fig. 2. Some example images in the Fashion-MNIST data set (each category takes up three lines).

In Gabor transform layer of DGSN, 32 Gabor filters are used as shown in Fig. 4. The image information extracted by each Gabor filter is shown in Fig. 5. Then, we combine them into one image as illustrated in Fig. 6.

4.3   Experimental Results

In this section, we mainly compare DGSN with the work of [4]. [4] used Haar wavelet transformation to extract invariant information of the images. Compared with this model, we use Gabor wavelet transformation to compute the invariant representations of the images. Classification results on the MNIST data set are shown in Table 1.

Table 1. Classification results on the MNIST data set.

Model	100	200	300	400	500	All
HaarScat [4]	91.20%	94.80%	95.47%	95.80%	96.18%	—
DGSN (ours)	94.70%	95.20%	95.93%	96.55%	96.86%	98.99%

Due to out of memory, we didn't obtain the results of [4] on the total MNIST data set (as well as on the Fashion-MNIST data set). Therefore, we select some images from each class in the MNIST data set to construct small training set. The $100, 200, \ldots, 500$ in Table 1 represent the numbers of images from each class. We can see that DGSN performs much better than HaarScat [4].

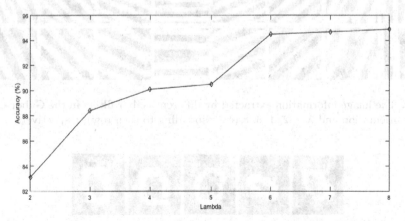

Fig. 3. The effect of the wave length λ with respect to the classification accuracy. The results are obtained on a subset of MNIST with 100 images in each class.

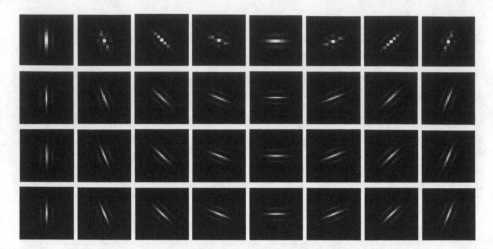

Fig. 4. The Gabor filters in the Gabor Layer with 8 orientation and $\lambda = 2, 4, 6, 8$ (corresponding to each row), respectively.

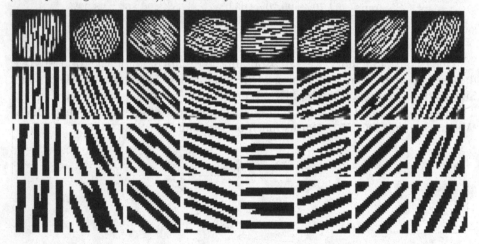

Fig. 5. The image information extracted by different Gabor filters in the Gabor Layer with 8 orientation and $\lambda = 2, 4, 6, 8$ (corresponding to each row), respectively.

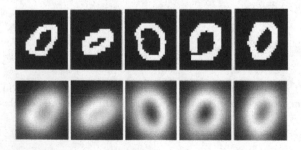

Fig. 6. The Gabor features. Top: the input images to the Gabor layer. Bottom: The Gabor features extracted by the Gabor filters.

Next, we apply our model to the Yale faces. The results obtained on the Yale faces is shown in Table 2. The "$(4, 5, 6, 7, 8)$ Train" is a random subset of the images per individual, which is taken with labels to form the training set and the rest of the database was considered to be the test set. For each given setting, there are 50 randomly splits [4]. We can see that DGSN outperforms HaarNet [4] with a large margin.

Table 2. Results obtained on the Yale faces.

Model	4 Train	5 Train	6 Train	7 Train	8 Train
HaarScat [4]	36.19%	55.56%	60.00%	55.00%	62.22%
DGSN(ours)	49.52%	57.78%	65.33%	61.67%	68.89%

The training time of DGSN and HaarScat on the MNIST and Yale data sets is shown in Table 3. The training time on the MNIST data set is on the entire data set, and the training time on the Yale data set is the average training time on the 50 splits.

Table 3. Comparison of the training time on the MNIST and Yale data sets.

Model	MNIST	Yale
HaarScat [4]	—	773 s
DGSN(ours)	8172 s	18 s

According to the results shown in Tables 2 and 3, we can see that DGSN has a better performance than HaarScat on both the MNIST and the Yale data sets. More importantly, the training time of DGSN is much less than HaarScat, and DGSN can achieve high classification accuracy without large memory, which demonstrates the advantage of DGSN over HaarScat.

Finally, we apply DGSN to the Fashion-MNIST data set. The accuracy obtained by DGSN is 90.60%. We compare its classification results with that obtained by previous methods on this data set [17]. The results are shown in Fig. 7. From the histogram, we can see that DGSN delivers higher accuracy than the compared methods.

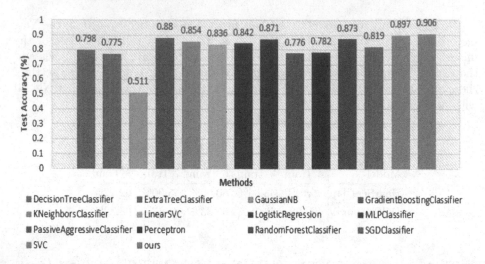

Fig. 7. Results obtained on the Fashion-MNIST data set.

5   Conclusion

We propose a new deep architecture called Deep Gabor Scattering Network (DGSN) for image classification. DGSN combines the wavelet transformation and the idea of deep learning. It uses Gabor wavelet transformation to extract the invariant information of the images, PLSR for feature selection, and SVM for classification. A key benefit of DGSN is that rich invariant features of the images can be extracted by the Gabor wavelet transformation. With extensive experiments, we show that DGSN is computationally simpler and delivers higher classification accuracy than compared methods. For future work, we plan to combine the Gabor wavelet transformation with deep convolutional neural networks (CNNs), so that we can replace the convolutional operation with Gabor transformation on account of the invariant feature extraction from images.

Acknowledgments. This work was supported by the Science and Technology Program of Qingdao under Grant No. 17-3-3-20-nsh, the CERNET Innovation Project under Grant No. NGII20170416 and the Fundamental Research Funds for the Central Universities of China.

References

1. Bruna, J., Mallat, S.: Invariant scattering convolution networks. IEEE Trans. Pattern Anal. Mach. Intell. **35**(8), 1872–1886 (2013)
2. Cai, D., He, X., Hu, Y., Han, J., Huang, T.S.: Learning a spatially smooth subspace for face recognition. In: CVPR (2007)
3. Chang, C., Lin, C.: LIBSVM: a library for support vector machines. ACM Trans. Intell. Syst. Technol. **2**(3), 1–27 (2011)

4. Chen, X., Cheng, X., Mallat, S.: Unsupervised deep haar scattering on graphs. In: NIPS, pp. 1709–1717 (2014)
5. Ciresan, D., Meier, U., Masci, J., Gambardella, L., Schmidhuber, J.: Flexible, high performance convolutional neural networks for image classification. In: IJCAI, pp. 1237–1242 (2011)
6. Grigorescu, C., Petkov, N., Westenberg, M.A.: Contour detection based on non-classical receptive field inhibition. IEEE Trans. Image Process. **12**(7), 729–739 (2003)
7. Guo, T., Mousavi, H., Vu, T., Monga, V.: Deep wavelet prediction for image super-resolution. In: CVPR Workshops, pp. 1100–1109. IEEE Computer Society (2017)
8. Hinton, G.E., Salakhutdinov, R.R.: Reducing the dimensionality of data with neural networks. Science **313**, 504–507 (2006)
9. Jarrett, K., Kavukcuoglu, K., Ranzato, M., LeCun, Y.: What is the best multi-stage architecture for object recognition? In: ICCV, pp. 2146–2153. IEEE Computer Society (2009)
10. Krizhevsky, A., Sutskever, I., Hinton, G.: ImageNet classification with deep convolutional neural networks. In: NIPS, pp. 1106–1114 (2012)
11. LeCun, Y., Bottou, L., Bengio, Y., Haffner, P.: Gradient-based learning applied to document recognition. Proc. IEEE **86**(11), 2278–2324 (1998)
12. LeCun, Y., Huang, F.J., Bottou, L.: Learning methods for generic object recognition with invariance to pose and lighting. In: CVPR, pp. 97–104 (2004)
13. Mehrotra, R., Namuduri, K., Ranganathan, N.: Gabor filter-based edge detection. Pattern Recognit. **25**(12), 1479–1494 (1992)
14. Meyer, Y.: Principe D"Incertitude, Bases Hilbertiennes Et Algebres D"Operateurs. Seminaire Bourbaki **662**(145–146), 1985–1986 (1985)
15. Said, S., Jemai, O., Hassairi, S., Ejbali, R., Zaied, M., Amar, C.B.: Deep wavelet network for image classification. In: SMC, pp. 922–927 (2016)
16. Schwartz, W.R., Kembhavi, A., Harwood, D., Davis, L.S.: Human detection using partial least squares analysis. In: ICCV, pp. 24–31 (2009)
17. Xiao, H., Rasul, K., Vollgraf, R.: Fashion-MNIST: A Novel Image Dataset for Benchmarking Machine Learning Algorithms. CoRR abs/1708.07747 (2017)
18. Zhang, H., Kiranyaz, S., Gabbouj, M.: Cardinal sparse partial least square feature selection and its application in face recognition. In: EUSIPCO, pp. 785–789 (2014)
19. Zhou, K., Wu, D.: Research of Mallat algorithm based on multi-resolution analysis. Softw. Guide **10**, 54–55 (2008)

Deep Local Descriptors with Domain Adaptation

Shuwen Qiu and Weihong Deng[✉]

School of Information and Communication Engineering, Beijing University of Posts
and Telecommunications, Beijing 100876, China
whdeng@bupt.edu.cn

Abstract. Due to the different distributions of training and testing
datasets, the performance of the trained model based on the training
set can rarely achieve the most optimal. Inspired by the successful application of domain adaptation in the object recognition area, we apply
domain adaptation methods to CNN based local feature descriptors
based on their own traits. Different from previous domain adaptation
methods that focus only on the fully connected layer, we apply maximum mean discrepancy (MMD) criterion to both the fully connected
layer and the convolutional layer, which makes the primary local filters
of CNN adaptive to the target dataset in an unsupervised manner. Extensive experiments on Photo Tour and HPatches dataset show that domain
adaption is effective to local feature descriptors, and, more importantly,
the convolutional layer adaption can further improve the performance of
traditional domain adaptation.

Keywords: Local feature descriptor · Domain adaptation
Maximum Mean Discrepancy

1 Introduction

One of the most extensively studied problems in computer vision area is to
find correspondences between images according to local feature descriptors that
embed local features into vectors. Compared with global features, local feature
represents only part of the image so that it is more robust to illuminations.
Recently, local descriptors based on CNN architectures have been proved to significantly outperform handcrafted local descriptors [4,21,23], meanwhile large
datasets are available for training [20,22]. However, due to the distribution discrepancies of different datasets, trained models based on patches from training
sets may not generalize the most optimal results in the testing sets, which is
mainly caused by potential variations between domains. For example, patches
of the training sets are extracted from images of buildings while patches from
testing sets are mainly from decorations indoors or natural scenery. Therefore,
it is a natural adoption of domain adaptation methods to explore the domain-
invariant structure between the source domain (labeled training set) and the
target domain (unlabeled testing set).

© Springer Nature Switzerland AG 2018
J.-H. Lai et al. (Eds.): PRCV 2018, LNCS 11257, pp. 344–355, 2018.
https://doi.org/10.1007/978-3-030-03335-4_30

Recent studies have demonstrated that the deep neural networks can learn transferable features to establish knowledge transfer by exploring the invariant factors between different datasets so as to make features robust to noise [13]. However, most of the studies focus on object recognition and a systematic study of the application of domain adaptation in local descriptors is yet to be done. Therefore, in this work, we will investigate the application of domain adaptation in local descriptors. Our contributions include: (1) we investigate the performance of different CNN based local descriptors, combining maximum mean discrepancy (MMD) criterion. Extensive experiments on Photo Tour and HPatches dataset show that domain adaption is effective to local feature descriptors; (2) Different from previous domain adaptation methods that focus only on the fully connected layer, we jointly calculate MMD from both the fully connected layer and the Convolutional layer of the network considering local descriptors' own traits, which can further improve the performance of traditional domain adaptation.

2 Related Work

2.1 Local Descriptors

End-to-end learning local descriptors based on CNN architectures have been investigated in many studies, and the improvement has been shown over state of art descriptors [4,21,23]. In [21], feature layers and metric layers are learnt in the same network. Therefore, the final hinge-based loss can be optimized using the last abstract metric layer of the network. MatchNet [24] also includes both feature extracting layers and metric layers while using entropy loss to update the network.

On the contrary, [4,23] directly use the last feature layer as the feature descriptor of the input patch without training of the metric layer so that it can be judged by traditional evaluation criterion. Based on Siamese network, Deepdesc [4] trains the network using L2 distance meanwhile adopting a mining strategy to select training samples. However, it requires large quantity of samples to guarantee its performance. TFeat [23] uses Triplet network to decrease the distance between matching pairs and increase the distance between non-matching pairs. Based on triplet loss, L2-Net [26] also proposes a progressive sampling method with consideration of the intermediate layers.

Another important observation is that multi-scale network architectures can achieve better results compared with single-scale network architectures.

2.2 Domain Adaptation

Transfer learning [19] aims to build a learning model that can follow different probability distributions according to different domains [3,8,10,16,19]. Recent studies of deep domain adaptation embed an adaptive layer into the deep network to enhance the transfer ability [5–7,13,14,25]. The deep domain confusion network (DDC) by Tzeng et al. [5] uses two CNNs with shared weights, according to the source and target domain respectively. The network of the source domain is updated by the originally defined loss function when the difference between the two domains is calculated by the MMD metric of the adaptive layer. DDC only adjusts a single layer of the network, which may limit the transfer ability of the multi-layer network. Therefore, Long et al. [13] proposed the deep adaptation network (DAN) combining multi-layer adaptation using multi-kernel MMD metric to match the shift of different domains. In order to avoid mutual influence of layers, a joint adaptation network (JAN) [12] based on a joint maximum mean discrepancy (JMMD) criterion was proposed to align the shift of the joint distribution of multiple layers in the network. Besides, there are several extensions of DAN aimed at aligning the distributions of both the classifier and the feature layer. In this work, we only investigate domain adaptation methods based on feature layers.

3   Model

3.1   Maximum Mean Discrepancy (MMD)

In standard CNN architecture, the features of the last layer tend to transfer from general to specific because it is tailored for the source data at the expense of degraded performance on the target task [13]. Hence, in order to get the most optimal performance, after pre-training on the training set, we require the distributions of the features of the fully connected layer from the source and the target domain to be similar. This can be achieved by adding an MMD metric to the original loss function, which can limit the target error by the source error plus a discrepancy metric between the source and the target [18].

MMD is an efficient metric that can compare the distributions of two datasets using a kernel two-sample test [11]. Given two distributions S and T, MMD is defined as:

$$MMD(X_S, X_T) = \left\| \frac{1}{|X_S|} \sum_{x_s \in X_S} \Phi(x_s) - \frac{1}{|X_T|} \sum_{x_t \in X_T} \Phi(x_t) \right\| \tag{1}$$

where Φ is a kernel function that maps the original data to a reproducing kernel Hilbert space (RKHS) and $\|\Phi\|_H \leq 1$ defines a set of functions in the unit ball of RKHS. This MMD metric considers the distribution of each domain to reduce the mismatch in a latent space. Subsequently, Tzeng et al. [5] and Long et al. [13] extended the MMD metric to a multi-kernel MMD metric. Multi-kernel MMD enhances the two-sample test power meanwhile minimizes the Type II error, i.e., the failure of rejecting a false null hypothesis [13]. Its final result is calculated by a weighted summation of several single kernel tests:

$$K \triangleq \left\{ k = \sum_{u=1}^{m} \beta_u k_u : \sum_{u=1}^{m} \beta_u = 1, \beta_u \geq 0, \forall u \right\} \tag{2}$$

where k_u stands for one single MMD test and the $\{\beta_u\}$ is limited in the way to make each kernel more representative. The multi-kernel MMD improves the testing power of MMD and leads to a more optimal result.

3.2 Adaptative Networks

Based on the idea of domain adaptation, we first combine MMD metric with TFeat [23] to exploit data from both the source and the target domain. Figure 1 gives an illustration of the proposed combined model. TFeat (Fig. 1-left) is a typical CNN based local descriptor. It is comprised of 2 Convolutional layers and one fully connected layer. For each layer, it is followed by an activation $f^l = tanh(x)$. The objective function of TFeat is:

$$\lambda(\delta^+, \delta^-) = max(0, \mu + \delta^+ - \delta^-) \tag{3}$$

where $\delta^+ = \|Net(x^+) - Net(x)\|_2$ is the L2 distance between the matching pairs (x^+, x), and $\delta^- = \|Net(x^-) - Net(x)\|_2$ is the L2 distance between the non-matching pairs (x^-, x), and μ is a constant. The objective function aims to make $\delta^- > \mu + \delta^+$, so the distance between non-matching pairs will be longer and between matching pairs will be shorter.

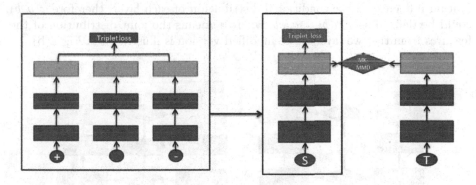

Fig. 1. Left is the original TFeat Network. It is comprised of 2 Convolutional layers(blue) and one fully connected layer(green). Right shows the modified adaptive model. (Color figure online)

In previous studies, deep networks are pre-trained on ImageNet [17], but our network is rather shallow so we only pre-train TFeat on the original training sets. Then we fix the Convolutional layers and update the fully connected layer using the new loss function,

$$L = L_C + \lambda MMD(X_S, X_T) \tag{4}$$

where L_C is the original loss function $\lambda(\delta^+, \delta^-)$. MMD is used for calculating the discrepancy between the training set and the testing set. $\lambda > 0$ is a penalty parameter that can control the balance between the task specification and the discrepancy between two domains. As pointed out by Gretton et al. [1], kernel choice is important for the testing power of MMD because different kernel will map the probability distribution into different RKHS. Therefore, we choose the performance of multi-kernel MMD on the local descriptor learning.

3.3 Joint Adaptation of the Fully Connected Layer and the Convolutional Layer

In [21], it has been pointed out that it is important to jointly use information from the first layer of the network. Therefore, we consider the modification of the MMD loss calculation to fit features from the first layer into the MMD metrics,

$$L = L_C + \lambda\varphi(MMD_{fc}(X_S, X_T), MMD_{cov}(X_S, X_T)) \tag{5}$$

where $\varphi(a, b)$ is a way to combine the MMD loss from both fully connected layer and the first Convolutional layer.

To train the network with multi-layer MMD, there are two ways. On the one hand, we could define $\varphi(a, b) = a + b$, which means we directly add up two MMD results from two separate layers, as Fig. 2(a) illustrates. On the other hand, As [12] points out, separate adaptation of different layers will exert a mutual influence on the conditional distribution of each layer, therefore $\varphi(a, b)$ could be defined as $\varphi(a, b) = a * b$, where $*$ means the joint distribution of the features from the two layers. The modified version is illustrated in Fig. 2(b).

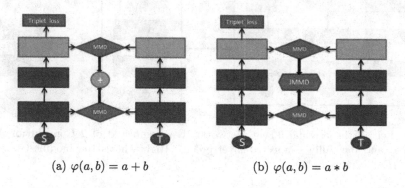

(a) $\varphi(a, b) = a + b$ (b) $\varphi(a, b) = a * b$

Fig. 2. Two architectures to apply MMD loss

3.4 Dimension Reduction

In [1], it is proved that high dimension will decrease the power of MMD to calculate the discrepancies between different distributions. Allowing for the high dimensions of the Convolutional feature maps, we need to reduce the dimension before calculating the MMD metrics. For convenience, we consider simple ways of average pooling. As the dataset (Fig. 3) shows, location information in patches are less important for domain adaptation since different subsets contains completely different scenes. Therefore, when considering dimension reduction, we could adopt average pooling to get a smoother distribution of pixel tensity in the patch.

4   Experiment

We combine the CNN based local descriptors with MMD metric, focusing on the improvement of the performance that domain adaptation can offer.

4.1   Photo Tour Dataset

Photo Tour dataset [20] is a standard benchmark for patch training and testing. It consists of around 1M patches from each distinct scene: Notredame(N, grand building), Liberty(L, statue), Yosemite(Y, natural park), which we could think as three subsets. Each subset consists of three components: two patches and their label that shows whether they are matching pair(label = 1) or non-matching pair(label = 0). Figure 3 gives an illustration of the structure of the dataset, which mainly shows pairs of patches and their labels from three different subsets. For each learning task, we take one subset as training set and another as testing set so that there are 6 ways of subset combination. We evaluate the domain adaptation performance on the 6 learning tasks, $N \rightarrow L$, $N \rightarrow Y$, $L \rightarrow N$, $L \rightarrow Y$, $Y \rightarrow N$, $Y \rightarrow L$(training set$\rightarrow$testing set).

We use FPR95 to calculate the error rate when the matching accuracy achieves 95%.

(a) Notredame(N)   (b) Liberty(L)   (c) Yosemite(Y)

Fig. 3. Photo tour dataset examples

4.2   HPatches Dataset

HPatches dataset [22] is a standard benchmark for patch testing. It consists of around 2M patches from 116 scenes. This dataset evaluates the local descriptors on three tasks: patch verification, image matching and patch retrieval. We evaluate the domain adaptation by training the networks on Photo Tour dataset and testing on Hpatches.

4.3   Evaluation Protocol

For evaluation on Photo Tour dataset, we mainly evaluate the performance following the protocol below.

TFeat Network. We first extract 5M triplets from the training set and find the best results in certain epochs as the pre-trained model following the original procedure in [23]. Then we use 5M labeled triplets from the training set and 5M random selected unlabeled triplets from the testing set to update the fully connected layer of the pre-trained network using new loss function and fix the Convolutional layer, and evaluate the descriptors' performance using FPR95. As for joint adaptation of both fully connected layer and Convolutional layer, we update the whole network after pre-training.

Siamese Network. Siamese Network [21] (as Fig. 4 shows) is another typical CNN based local descriptors. It consists of 3 Convolutional layers(blue), two maxpooling layers(red) and two fully connected layers(green) while the output of the last layer is a number representing whether these two patches are matching or not. Compared with TFeat, Siamese Network is trained with matching and non-matching pairs instead of triplets. Its objective function adopts a hinge-based loss. For adaptation, it follows the above protocol.

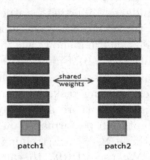

Fig. 4.   Siamese network (Color figure online)

4.4   Parameters

When using multi-kernel MMD and considering a family of m Gaussian kernels $\{k_u\}_{u=1}^{m}$, we mainly follow the procedure in [13] to set the varying bandwidth γ_u. We use stochastic gradient descent (SGD) with 0.9 momentum and the learning rate is set to 0.1 at the beginning and is gradually decreased.

5   Results

5.1   Performance Changes on λ Variation

On TFeat Network, we first investigate the effect of the parameter λ. Table 1 illustrates the variation of the error rate with $\lambda \in \{0.005, 0.008, 0.01, 0.02\}$ on tasks N → and the number of MMD kernel is set to 3. We can see from the variation that when λ varies, the error rate first decreases and then increases forming a notching curve. It shows that it is important to find the balance between learning more specific deep features and adapting to target domain.

Table 1. Performance changes on λ variation.

λ	0	0.005	0.008	0.01	0.02
Error rate	7.3	6.14	5.95	5.87	5.88

5.2 Domain Adaptation on Photo Tour Dataset with Fully Connected Layer

For the convenience of implementation, we set λ to 0.01 for all tasks, which means results that Table 2 below shows can be decreased in an effective way even though the performance is not the most optimal. It demonstrates that MMD can effectively transfer features across domains and further boost the performance of our networks.

Table 2. Results of six learning tasks combining local descriptors with domain adaptation. The first row shows the original results and the second row shows results after domain adaptation.

Method	N → L	N → Y	L → Y	L → N	Y → N	Y → L
TFeat	7.30	7.34	8.52	3.10	3.10	9.09
TFeat-fc	5.87	6.56	6.95	2.70	2.79	8.10
Decrease(%)↓	19.60	10.60	18.40	12.90	10.0	10.90
Siamese	13.17	12.07	18.42	6.48	8.22	16.90
Siamese-fc	11.58	11.07	17.24	5.93	7.28	13.89
Decrease(%)↓	12.07	8.29	6.41	8.49	11.44	17.81

5.3 Domain Adaptation on HPatches Dataset with Fully Connected Layer

In [22], experiments show that TFeat Network has achieved higher results. Therefore, we tested TFeat Network on HPatches after domain adaptation. We could see from Fig. 5 that all of the three tasks have gained 2% increase, which proves the effectiveness of domain adaptation.Also, verification tasks between same sequence and matching tasks between illumination changes could gain bigger increase. Also, domain adaptation influences more on tough tasks.

5.4 Multi-layer Adaptation

In previous work, domain adaptation only considers fully connected layers. Given local descriptors' own traits, which implies that the first Convolutional layer contains important information, we add Convolutional layer to layer adaptation. Table 3 shows the comparison of different ways of layer combination. First of all,

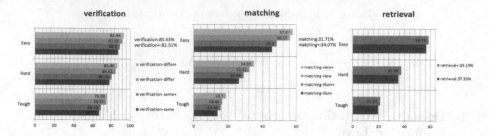

Fig. 5. HPatches evaluation:for each task, '+' represents results after domain adaptation. The mean values of the results before and after domain adaptation are put on the right, which shows that all the mean values get 2% increase. 'differ' and 'same' stand for different and same sequences verification. 'view' and 'illum' show matching under changes of view or illumination.

we adopt the traditional way to only update the fully connected layer. Then, we simply sum the MMD losses from the fully connected layer and the first Convolutional layer respectively. We can see from the results that error rate can be reduced because of the extra information the first layer offers. However, as [12] points out that the update of the former layers will change the distribution of the following layers so the joint MMD losses are also calculated following [12]. We can see from the results that improvement can be further achieved.

Table 3. Error rates with different ways of combining MMD losses from fully connected and Convolutional layers

Method	TFeat-fc	TFeat-(fc+cov)	TFeat-(fc*cov)
FPR95(%)	5.87	5.51	**5.45**

5.5 Performance with Respect to Dimension Reduction

First we run several experiments of average pooling to find the variation tendency of the performance with different scale of pooling size. We can see from the figure that the error rate first decreases and then increases which means there is a balance between reducing the dimension and keeping enough feature information (Table 4).

Table 4. Error rates with different average pooling size. The first row shows the final dimension of the first layer after pooling.

Dimension	5408	1152	800	512	128
Error rate	5.76	5.71	5.77	5.8	6.02

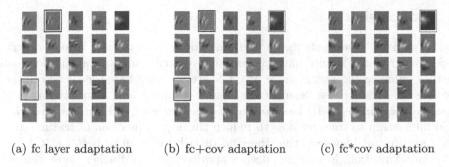

(a) fc layer adaptation   (b) fc+cov adaptation   (c) fc*cov adaptation

Fig. 6. The changes of feature maps with three ways of adaption

6 Discussion

6.1 First Layer Filter Visualization

For one original patch on the right, Fig. 6 shows
the changes of feature maps with three ways of
adaptation(TFeat-fc, TFeat-(fc+cov), TFeat-(fc*cov)).
From the first layer filter visualization, we could see
the color of features from fc adaptation to fc+cov adaptation change more strongly while there are still little
changes from fc+cov adaptation to fc*cov adaptation,
which shows different ways of domain adaptation indeed
influence the features of the first Convolutional layer.

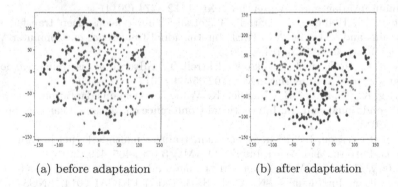

(a) before adaptation   (b) after adaptation

Fig. 7. t-SNE visualization of deep features before and after domain adaption

6.2 t-SNE Visualization

Seeing from t-SNE visualization [15] (Fig. 7), features from the source(blue) and
the target(red) become more collective and mixed with each other after adaptation while most of the original features of the source lie outside the target
features.

7   Conclusion

In this work, we investigate the application of domain adaptation in local descriptors. Experiments results have proven that domain adaptation methods can further enhance the performance of CNN architecture based local descriptors. Besides, the results also demonstrate that it is important to jointly use information to calculate MMD loss from both the first layer and the last layer. It is also interesting to consider how to reduce the high dimension of features from the Convolutional layers so that the joint distribution can be better learnt from domain adaptation. Meanwhile, deeper architecture will further boost the performance.

References

1. Gretton, A., Sejdinovic, D., Strathmann, H., et al.: Optimal kernel choice for large-scale two-sample tests. In: Advances in Neural Information Processing Systems, pp. 1205–1213 (2012)
2. Ramdas, A., Reddi, S.J., Poczos, B., et al.: On the high-dimensional power of linear-time kernel two-sample testing under mean-difference alternatives. arXiv preprint arXiv:1411.6314 (2014)
3. Gong, B., Grauman, K., Sha, F.: Connecting the dots with landmarks: discriminatively learning domain-invariant features for unsupervised domain adaptation. In: International Conference on Machine Learning, pp. 222–230 (2013)
4. Simo-Serra, E., Trulls, E., Ferraz, L., et al.: Discriminative learning of deep convolutional feature point descriptors. In: 2015 IEEE International Conference on Computer Vision (ICCV), pp. 118–126. IEEE (2015)
5. Tzeng, E., Hoffman, J., Zhang, N., et al.: Deep domain confusion: maximizing for domain invariance. arXiv preprint arXiv:1412.3474 (2014)
6. Tzeng, E., Hoffman, J., Darrell, T., et al.: Simultaneous deep transfer across domains and tasks. In: 2015 IEEE International Conference on Computer Vision (ICCV), pp. 4068–4076. IEEE (2015)
7. Tzeng, E., Hoffman, J., Saenko, K., Darrell, T.: Adversarial discriminative domain adaptation. arXiv preprint arXiv:1702.05464 (2017)
8. Zhang, K., ScholKopf, B., Muandet, K., Wang, Z.: Domain adaptation under target and conditional shift. In: International Conference on Machine Learning, pp. 819–827 (2013)
9. Duan, L., Tsang, I.W., Xu, D.: Domain transfer multiple kernel learning. IEEE Trans. Pattern Anal. Mach. Intell. (TPAMI) 34(3), 465–479 (2012)
10. Ghifary, M., Kleijn, W.B., Zhang, M.: Domain adaptive neural networks for object recognition. In: Pham, D.-N., Park, S.-B. (eds.) PRICAI 2014. LNCS (LNAI), vol. 8862, pp. 898–904. Springer, Cham (2014). https://doi.org/10.1007/978-3-319-13560-1_76
11. Borgwardt, K.M., Gretton, A., Rasch, M.J., Kriegel, H.P., Smola, A.J.: Integrating structured biological data by kernel maximum mean discrepancy. Bioinformatics 22(14), e49–e57 (2006)
12. Long, M., Zhu, H., Wang, J., et al.: Deep transfer learning with joint adaptation networks. arXiv preprint arXiv:1605.06636 (2016)
13. Long, M., Cao, Y., Wang, J., et al.: Learning transferable features with deep adaptation networks. arXiv preprint arXiv:1502.02791 (2015)

14. Long, M., Zhu, H., Wang, J., Jordan, M.I.: Unsupervised domain adaptation with residual transfer networks. In: Advances in Neural Information Processing Systems (NIPS), pp. 136–144 (2016)
15. van der Maaten, L.J.P., Hinton, G.E.: Visualizing high-dimensional data using t-SNE. Mach. Learn. Res. **9**, 2579–2605 (2008)
16. Sugiyama, M., Nakajima, S., Kashima, H., et al.: Direct importance estimation with model selection and its application to covariate shift adaptation. In: Advances in Neural Information Processing Systems, pp. 1433–1440 (2008)
17. Russakovsky, O., et al.: ImageNet Large Scale Visual Recognition Challenge. Technical report. arXiv:1409.0575 (2014)
18. Ben-David, S., Blitzer, J., Crammer, K., Kulesza, A., Pereira, F., Vaughan, J.W.: A theory of learning from different domains. Mach. Learn. **79**(1–2), 151–175 (2010)
19. Pan, S.J., Yang, Q.: A survey on transfer learning. IEEE Trans. Knowl. Data Eng. **22**(10), 13451359 (2010)
20. Winder, S., Hua, G., Brown, M.: Picking the best daisy. In: IEEE Conference on Computer Vision and Pattern Recognition, CVPR 2009, pp. 178–185. IEEE (2009)
21. Zagoruyko, S., Komodakis, N.: Learning to compare image patches via convolutional neural networks. In: 2015 IEEE Conference on Computer Vision and Pattern Recognition (CVPR), pp. 4353–4361. IEEE (2015)
22. Balntas, V., Lenc, K., Vedaldi, A., et al.: HPatches: a benchmark and evaluation of handcrafted and learned local descriptors. In: Computer Vision and Pattern Recognition (CVPR), vol. 4, no. 5, p. 6 (2017)
23. Balntas, V., Riba, E., Ponsa, D.: Learning local feature descriptors with triplets and shallow convolutional neural networks. BMVC **1**(2), 3 (2016)
24. Han, X., Leung, T., Jia, Y., Sukthankar, R., Berg, A.C.: MatchNet: unifying feature and metric learning for patch-based matching. In: Computer Vision and Pattern Recognition, pp. 3279–3286. IEEE (2015)
25. Ganin, Y., Lempitsky, V.: Unsupervised domain adaptation by backpropagation. arXiv preprint arXiv:1409.7495 (2014)
26. Tian, Y., Fan, B., Wu, F.: L2-Net: deep learning of discriminative patch descriptor in euclidean space. In: Conference on Computer Vision and Pattern Recognition, pp. 6128–6136. IEEE Computer Society (2017)

Deep Convolutional Neural Network with Mixup for Environmental Sound Classification

Zhichao Zhang, Shugong Xu[⊠], Shan Cao, and Shunqing Zhang

Shanghai Institute for Advanced Communication and Data Science,
Shanghai University, Shanghai 200444, China
{zhichaozhang,shugong,cshan,shunqing}@shu.edu.cn

Abstract. Environmental sound classification (ESC) is an important and challenging problem. In contrast to speech, sound events have noise-like nature and may be produced by a wide variety of sources. In this paper, we propose to use a novel deep convolutional neural network for ESC tasks. Our network architecture uses stacked convolutional and pooling layers to extract high-level feature representations from spectrogram-like features. Furthermore, we apply mixup to ESC tasks and explore its impacts on classification performance and feature distribution. Experiments were conducted on UrbanSound8K, ESC-50 and ESC-10 datasets. Our experimental results demonstrated that our ESC system has achieved the state-of-the-art performance (83.7%) on UrbanSound8K and competitive performance on ESC-50 and ESC-10.

Keywords: Environmental sound classification
Convolutional neural network · Mixup

1 Introduction

Sound recognition is a front and center topic in today's pattern recognition theories, which covers a rich variety of fields. Some of sound recognition topics have made remarkable research progress, such as automatic speech recognition (ASR) [9,10] and music information retrieval (MIR) [4,31]. Environmental sound classification (ESC) is an another important branch of sound recognition and is widely applied in surveillance [21], home automation [33], scene analysis [3] and machine hearing [14]. However, unlike speech and music, sound events are more diverse with a wide range of frequencies and often less well defined, which make ESC tasks more difficult than ASR and MIR. Hence, ESC still faces critical design issues in performance and accuracy improvement.

Traditional ASR techniques such as MFCC, LPC, PLP are applied directly to ESC fields in previous works [7,13,16,28]. However, state-of-the-art performance has been achieved when using more discriminative representations such as Mel filterbank features [5], Gammatone features [34] and wavelet-based features [8].

© Springer Nature Switzerland AG 2018
J.-H. Lai et al. (Eds.): PRCV 2018, LNCS 11257, pp. 356–367, 2018.
https://doi.org/10.1007/978-3-030-03335-4_31

These features were modeled with some typical machine learning algorithms such as SVM [32], GMM [17] and KNN [20] for ESC tasks. However, the performance gain introduced by these approaches is still unsatisfying. One main reason is that traditional classifiers do not have feature extraction ability.

Over the past few years, deep neural networks (DNNs) have made great success in ASR and MIR [10,25]. For audio signals, DNNs have ability to extract features from raw data or hand-draft feature. Therefore, some DNN-based ESC systems [12,15] were proposed and performed much better than SVM-based ESC system. However, deep fully-connected architecture of DNNs is not robust for transformative features [22]. Some new researchs find convolutional neural networks (CNNs) have strong abilities to explore inherit and hidden patterns through huge amount of training data. Several attempts that apply CNN to ESC have received performance boosts by learning spectrogram-like features from environment sounds [19,23,35]. However, the existing networks for ESC mostly use shallow architecture, such as 2 convolutional layers [19,35] and 3 convolutional layers [23]. Getting a more discriminative and powerful information usually requests a deeper model. Therefore in this paper, we propose an enhanced CNN architecture with a deeper network based on VGG Net [26]. The main contributions of this paper includes

- We propose a novel CNN network based on VGG Net. We find that simply using stacked convolutional layers with 3×3 convolution filters is unsatisfying in our tasks. So we redesign a novel CNN architecture in our ESC system. Instead of 3×3 convolution filters, We use 1-D convolution filters to learn local patterns across frequency and time, respectively. And our method performs better than CNN using 3×3 convolution filters with same depth of network.
- Mixup is applied in our ESC system for ESC tasks. Every training sample is created by mixing two examples randomly selected from original training dataset when using mixup. And the training target is also changed to the mix ratio. The effectiveness of mixup on classification performance and feature distribution is then explored further.
- Experiments were conducted on UrbanSound8K, ESC-50 and ESC-10 datasets, the result of which demonstrated that our ESC system has achieved the state-of-the-art performance (83.7%) on UrbanSound8K and competitive performance on ESC-50 and ESC-10.

The rest of this paper is organized as follows. Recent related works of ESC are introduced in Sect. 2. Section 3 provides detailed introduction of our methods. Section 4 presents the experiments settings on ESC-10, ESC-50 and Urban-Sound8K datasets, and Sect. 5 gives both experimental results and detailed discussions of our results. Finally, Sect. 6 concludes the paper.

2   Related Work

In this section, we introduce the recent deep learning methods for environmental sound classification. Piczak [20] proposed to apply CNNs to the log mel spectrogram which is calculated for each frame of audio and represents the squared magnitude of each frequency area. Piczak created a two-channel feature by applying log mel spectrogram and its delta information as the input of his CNN model and gave a 20.5% improvement over Random Forest method on ESC-50 dataset. Takahashi et al. [27] also used log mel spectrogram and their delta and delta-delta information as a three-channel input in a manner similar to the RGB inputs of the image. Agrawal et al. [1] used gammatone spectrogram and a similar CNN architecture as Piczak [19] and claimed that they achieved 79.1% and 85.34% accuracy on ESC-50 and UrbanSound8K dataset, respectively. However, since their results were not reproducible, we contacted with the author and realized that the results achieved by them didn't follow the official cross validation methods, which means they used different training data and validation data than main published papers and not comparable. So we will not compare our results with the results from [1].

Some researchers also proposed to train model directly from raw waveforms. Dai et al. [6] proposed a deep CNN architecture (up to 34 layers) with 1-D convolutional layers using 1-D raw data as input and they showed competitive accuracy with CNN using log mel spectrogram inputs [20]. Tokozume et al. [29] proposed a end-to-end network named EnvNet using raw data as inputs and reported EnvNet could extract a discriminative feature that complements the log mel features. In [30], they constructed a deeper recognition network based on EnvNet, referred as EnvNet-v2, and achieved better performance.

In addition, some researchers proposed to use external data for sound recognition. Mun et al. [18] proposed a DNN based transfer learning method for ESC. They first trained a DNN model using merged different web accessible environmental sound datasets. Then, they transferred the parameters of the pre-trained model and adapted the sound recognition system for target domain task using additional layers. Aytar et al. [2] proposed to learn rich sound representations from large amounts of unlabeled sound and videos dataset. They transferred the knowledge of pre-trained visual recognition network into the sound recognition network. Then, they used a linear-SVM classifier to classify the feature which is the output of the hidden layer of the sound recognition network to the target task.

3 Methods

3.1 Convolutional Neural Network

CNN is a stack of multi-layer neural networks including a group of convolutional layers, pooling layers and a limited number of fully connected layers. In this section, we propose a novel CNN as our ESC system model inspired by VGG Net [26], the architecture of which is presented in Table 1. The proposed CNN architecture is comprised of eight convolutional layers and two fully connected layers. We first use 2 convolutional layers with large filter kernals as a basic feature extractor. Then, we learn local patterns across frequency and time using 3×1 and 1×5 convolution filters, respectively. Next, we use small convolution filters (3×3) to learn joint time-frequency patterns. Batch normalization [11] is applied to the output of convolutional layers to speed up training. We use the Rectified Linear Units (ReLU) to model the non-linearly for the output of each layer. After every two convolutional layers, a pooling layer is used to reduce the dimensions of the convolutional features maps, where maximum pooling is chosen in our network. To reduce the risks of overfitting, the dropout technique is applied after the first fully connected layers, with the probability of 0.5. L2-regularization is applied to the weights of each layer with the coefficient 0.0001. In the output layer, softmax function is used as the activation function which outputs probabilities of all classes.

Table 1. Configuration of proposed CNN. Out shape represents the dimension in (frequency, time, channel). Batch normalization is applied for each convolutional layer.

Layer	Ksize	Stride	Nums of filters	Out shape
Input	-	-	-	(128, 128, 2)
Conv1	(3, 7)	(1, 1)	32	(128, 128, 32)
Conv2	(3, 5)	(1, 1)	32	(128, 128, 32)
Pool1	(4, 3)	(4, 3)	-	(32, 43, 32)
Conv3	(3, 1)	(1, 1)	64	(32, 43, 64)
Conv4	(3, 1)	(1, 1)	64	(32, 43, 64)
Pool2	(4, 1)	(4, 1)	-	(8, 43, 64)
Conv5	(1, 5)	(1, 1)	128	(8, 43, 128)
Conv6	(1, 5)	(1, 1)	128	(8, 43, 128)
Pool3	(1, 3)	(1, 3)	-	(8, 15, 128)
Conv7	(3, 3)	(1, 1)	256	(8, 15, 256)
Conv8	(3, 3)	(1, 1)	256	(8, 15, 256)
Pool4	(2, 2)	(2, 2)	-	(4, 8, 256)
FC1	-	-	512	(512,)
FC2	-	-	Nums of classes	(Nums of classes,)

3.2 Mixup

Mixup is an simple but effective method to generate training data [36]. Figure 1 shows the pipeline of mixup. Different from traditional augmentation approaches, mixup constructs virtual training samples by mixing training samples. Normally, a model is optimized by using a mini-batch optimization method, such as mini-batch SGD, and each mini-batch data is selected from the whole original training data. In mixup, however, each data and label of a mini-batch is generated by mixing two training samples, which are determined by

$$\begin{cases} \hat{\mathbf{x}} = \lambda x_i + (1 - \lambda)x_j \\ \hat{\mathbf{y}} = \lambda y_i + (1 - \lambda)y_j \end{cases} \tag{1}$$

where x_i and x_j are two samples randomly selected from training data, and y_i and y_j are their one-hot labels. The mix factor λ is decided by a hyper-parameter α and $\lambda \sim \mathrm{Beta}(\alpha, \alpha)$. Therefore, mixup extends the training data distribution by mixing various training data within or without the same class by a linear way, leading to a linear interpolation of the associated targets. Note that we do not use mixup for testing phase.

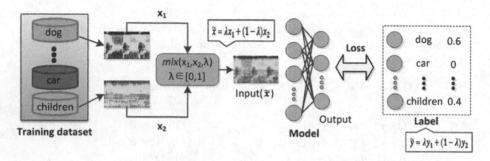

Fig. 1. Pipeline of mixup. Every training sample is created by mixing two examples randomly selected from original training dataset. We use the mixed sound to train the model and the train target is the mixing ratio.

4   Experiments

4.1   Dataset

Three publicly available datasets are used for model training and performance evaluation of the proposed approach, including ESC-10, ESC-50 [20] and Urban-Sound8K [24], the detailed information of which is shown in Table 2.

The ESC-50 dataset consists of 2000 short environmental records which are divided into 50 classes in 5 major categories, including *animals, natural soundscapes and water sounds, human non-speech sounds, interior/domestic sounds,* and *exterior/urban noises*. All audio samples are 5 seconds with 44.1 kHz sampling frequency.

The ESC-10 dataset is a subset of 10 classes (400 samples) selected from the ESC-50 dataset (*dog bark, rain, sea waves, baby cry, clock tick, person sneeze, helicopter, chainsaw, rooster, fire crackling*).

The UrbanSound8K dataset is a collection of 8732 short (up to 4 s) audio clips of urban sound areas. And the audio clips are prearranged into 10 folds. The dataset is divided into 10 classes: *air conditioner, car horn, children playing, dog bark, drilling, engine idling, gun shot, jackhammer, siren,* and *street music*.

Table 2. Information of datasets.

Datasets	Classes	Nums of samples	Duration
UrbanSound8K	10	8732	9.7 h
ESC-50	50	2000	2.8 h
ESC-10	10	400	33 min

4.2 Preprocessing

We use a 44.1 kHz sampling rate for ESC-10, ESC-50, UrbanSound8K datasets. All audio samples are normalized into a range from −1 to 1. In order to avoid overfitting and to effectively utilize the limited data, we use Time Stretch [23] and Pitch Shift [23] deformation methods to generate new audio samples. We use two spectrogram-like representations, log mel spectrogram (Mels) and gammatone spectrogram (GTs). Both features are extracted from all recordings with hamming window size of 1024, hop length of 512 and 128 bands. Then, the resulting spectrograms are converted into logarithmic scale. In our experiments, we use a simple energy-based silence drop algorithm to drop silence regions. Finally, the spectrograms are split into 128 frames (approximately 1.5 s) length with 50% overlap. The delta information of the original spectrogram is calculated, which is the first temporal derivative of the spectrogram feature. Then, we use the segments with their deltas as a two-channel input to the network.

4.3 Training Settings

All models are trained using mini-batch stochastic gradient descent (SGD) with Nesterov momentum of 0.9. We used a learning rate decrease schedule with a initial learning rate of 0.1, and then divided the learning rate by 10 every 80 epoch for UrbanSound8K and 100 epoch for ESC-10 and ESC-50. Every batch consists of 200 samples randomly selected from training set without repetition. The models are trained for 200 epochs for UrbanSound8K and 300 epochs for ESC-50 and ESC-10. We initialize all the weights to zero mean Gaussian noise with a standard deviation of 0.05. We use cross entropy as the loss function, which is typically used for multi classification task.

In the test stage, feature extraction and audio cropping patterns are the same as those used in the training stage. Prediction probability of a test audio sample is the average of predicted class probability of each segment. The predicted label of the test audio sample is the class with the highest posterior possibility. The classification performance of the methods is evaluated by the K-fold cross-validation. For the ESC-50 and ESC-10 dataset, K is set to 5, while for the UrbanSound8K dataset, K is set to 10.

All models are trained using Keras library with TensorFlow backend on an Nvidia P100 GPU with a 12 GB memory.

5   Results and Analysis

The classification accuracy of the proposed method compared with recent related works is shown in Table 3. It can be observed that our method achieved the state-of-the-art performance (83.7%) on UrbanSound8K dataset and competitive performance (91.7%, 83.9%) on ESC-10 and ESC-50. The average classification accuracy of our methods with Mels outperformed PiczakCNN [19] (baseline) by 10.8%, 17.6%, 9.9% on ESC-10, ESC-50 and UrbanSound8K datasets, respectively. Data augmentation is an important technique for increasing performance for limited dataset, which gave an improvement of 1.1%, 3.3% and 5.3% on ESC-10, ESC-50 and UrbanSound8K, respectively. In addition, GTs improved by 0.4%, 1.4% and 1.1% over Mels on ESC-10, ESC-50 and UrbanSound8K, respectively. We can see that classification accuracy with GTs is always better than accuracy with Mels on ESC-10, ESC-50 and UrbanSound8K datasets, which indicates that feature representation is a critical factor for classification performance. What's more, mixup is a powerful way to improve performance which can always perform better results than that without mixup. In our experiments, Mixup gave an improvement of 1.5%, 2.4% and 2.6% with Mels on ESC-10, ESC-50, UrbanSound8k datasets, respectively. As mentioned in Sect. 3, mixup trains a network using a linear combination of training examples and their labels and leads to a regularization for neural network and generalization for unseen data. For the effect of mixup, we do a further exploration in the following parts.

Table 3. Classification accuracy (%) of different ESC systems. In our ESC system, we compare two different features with augmentation and without augmentation. 'aug' stands for augmentation, including Pitch Shift, Time Stretch. Note that we will not compare with the results of Agrawal [1] which was discussed in Sect. 2.

Model	Acc (%)			
	Feature	ESC10	ESC50	UrbanSound8K
PiczakCNN [19]	Mels	80.5	64.9	72.7
D-CNN [37]	Mels	-	68.1	81.9
SoundNet [2]	-	**92.1**	74.2	-
Envnet-v2 [29]	Raw data	91.4	**84.9**	78.3
proposedCNN	Mels	88.7	76.8	74.7
	GTs	89.2	78.9	77.4
proposedCNN + mixup	Mels	90.2	79.2	77.3
	GTs	90.7	80.7	79.8
proposedCNN + aug + mixup	Mels	91.3	82.5	82.6
	GTs	**91.7**	83.9	**83.7**
Human performance	-	95.7	81.3	-
Agrawal [1]	GTs	-	79.10	85.34

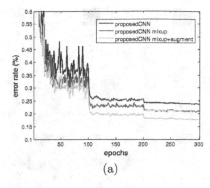 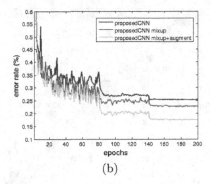

(a)   (b)

Fig. 2. Training curves of our proposed CNN on (a) ESC-50 and (b) UrbanSound8K datasets.

5.1   Comparison of Network Architecture

We compare our proposed CNN with a VGG network architecture with same depth of network. This VGG network has same network parameters with our proposed CNN except for replacing to use 3×3 convolution filters and 2×2 stride pooling and we refer to this architecture as VGG10. In Table 4, we provide classification accuracy of proposedCNN and VGG10 on ESC-10, ESC-50 and UrbanSound8K datasets. The results shows that our proposed CNN always performs better than VGG10 on three datasets.

Table 4. Comparison between proposed CNN and VGG10 Net (%).

Model	ESC-10	ESC-50	UrbanSound8K
proposedCNN	88.7	76.8	74.7
VGG10	87.5	73.3	73.2

5.2   Effects of Mixup

Analysis. The confusion matrix by the proposed CNN with Mels and mixup for the UrbanSound8K dataset is given in Fig. 3(a). We can observe that the most misrecognition happened between two noise-like classes, such as *jackhammer* and *drilling*, *engine idling* and *jackhammer*, and *air conditioner* and *engine idling*. In Fig. 3(b), we provide the difference of the confusion for the proposed CNN method with and without mixup. We see that mixup gives an improvement for most classes, especially for *air conditioner, drilling, jackhammer* and *siren*. However, mixup also has a slightly harmful effect on the accuracy for some classes and increases confusion between some specific pairs classes. For example,

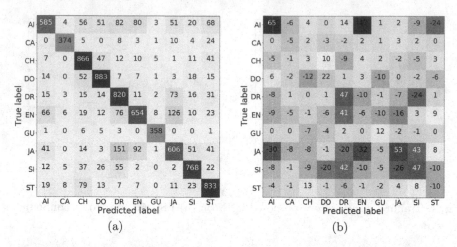

Fig. 3. (a) Confusion matrix for UrbanSound8K dataset using the proposed CNN model applying to Mels with mixup augmentation methods. (b) Different between the confusion matrix for UrbanSound8K dataset using the proposed CNN and Mels with mixup and without mixup: the negative values (brown) mean the confusion is decreased with mixup, the positive (blue) values mean the confusion is increased with mixup. Classes are air conditioner (AI), car horn (CA), children playing (CH), dog barking (DO), drilling (DR), engine idling (EN), gun shot (GU), jackhammer (JA), siren (SI) and street music (ST). (Color figure online)

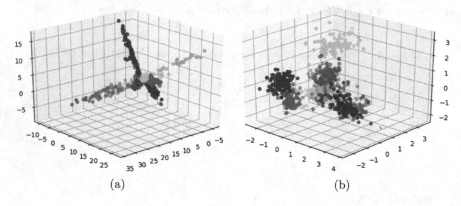

Fig. 4. Visualization of the feature distribution at the output of FC1 using PCA (a) without mixup and (b) with mixup.

although mixup reduces the confusion between *jackhammer* and *engine idling*, it increases the confusion between *jackhammer* and *siren*.

To gain further insights to the effect of mixup, we visualized the feature distributions for UrbanSound8K with mixup and without mixup using PCA in Fig. 4. The feature dots represent the high-level feature vectors obtained at the output of the first fully connected layer (FC1). We can observe that it is quite different between feature distributions with and without mixup. Figure 4(a) shows the feature distributions of different classes with mixup. Some classes have a large within-class variance of the feature distribution, while some have a small within-class variance. In addition, the between-class distances of different pairs of classes are also varied, which may make models more sensitive to some classes. However, features of most classes distribute within a small space with a relative smaller within-class variance and the boundary of most classes is clear as shown in Fig. 4(b).

Hyper-parameter α Selected. In order to achieve a better performance for our system on ESC, the effect of mixup hyper-parameter α is further explored. Figure 5 shows the change of accuracy with different α ranging from $[0.1, 0.5]$. We see that when $\alpha = 0.2$, the best accuracy is achieved on all three datasets.

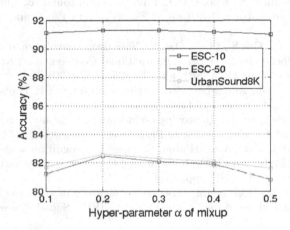

Fig. 5. Curves of an accuracy with different α for ESC-10, ESC-50, UrbanSound8K

6   Conclusion

In this paper, we proposed a novel deep convolutional neural network architecture for environmental sound classification. We compared our proposed CNN with VGG10 and results showed that our proposed CNN always performed better. To further improve the classification accuracy, mixup was applied in our ESC system. As a result, the proposed ESC system achieved state-of-the-art performance on UrbanSound8K dataset and competitive performance on ESC-10 and ESC-50 dataset. Furthermore, we explored the impacts of mixup on the classification accuracy and feature space distribution of different classes on UrbanSound8K dataset. The results showed that mixup is a powerful method to improves classification accuracy. Our future work will focus on the network design and exploration for using mixup method for specific classes.

References

1. Agrawal, D.M., Sailor, H.B., Soni, M.H., Patil, H.A.: Novel teo-based gammatone features for environmental sound classification. In: 2017 25th European Signal Processing Conference (EUSIPCO), pp. 1809–1813. IEEE (2017)
2. Aytar, Y., Vondrick, C., Torralba, A.: Soundnet: learning sound representations from unlabeled video. In: Advances in Neural Information Processing Systems, pp. 892–900 (2016)
3. Barchiesi, D., Giannoulis, D., Dan, S., Plumbley, M.D.: Acoustic scene classification: classifying environments from the sounds they produce. IEEE Signal Process. Mag. **32**(3), 16–34 (2015)
4. Casey, M.A., Veltkamp, R., Goto, M., Leman, M., Rhodes, C., Slaney, M.: Content-based music information retrieval: current directions and future challenges. Proc. IEEE **96**(4), 668–696 (2008)
5. Chu, S., Narayanan, S., Kuo, C.C.J.: Environmental sound recognition with time-frequency audio features. Institute of Electrical and Electronics Engineers Inc., (2009)
6. Dai, W., Dai, C., Qu, S., Li, J., Das, S.: Very deep convolutional neural networks for raw waveforms. In: 2017 IEEE International Conference on Acoustics, Speech and Signal Processing (ICASSP), pp. 421–425. IEEE (2017)
7. Eronen, A.J., et al.: Audio-based context recognition. IEEE Trans. Audio Speech Lang. Process. **14**(1), 321–329 (2006)
8. Geiger, J.T., Helwani, K.: Improving event detection for audio surveillance using gabor filterbank features. In: Signal Processing Conference, pp. 714–718 (2015)
9. Graves, A., Mohamed, A.R., Hinton, G.: Speech recognition with deep recurrent neural networks. In: 2013 IEEE International Conference on Acoustics, Speech and Signal Processing (ICASSP), pp. 6645–6649. IEEE (2013)
10. Hinton, G., et al.: Deep neural networks for acoustic modeling in speech recognition: the shared views of four research groups. IEEE Signal Process. Mag. **29**(6), 82–97 (2012)
11. Ioffe, S., Szegedy, C.: Batch normalization: accelerating deep network training by reducing internal covariate shift, pp. 448–456 (2015)
12. Kons, Z., Toledo-Ronen, O.: Audio event classification using deep neural networks. In: Interspeech, pp. 1482–1486 (2013)
13. Lee, K., Ellis, D.P.: Audio-based semantic concept classification for consumer video. IEEE Trans. Audio Speech Lang. Process. **18**(6), 1406–1416 (2010)
14. Lyon, R.F.: Machine hearing: an emerging field [exploratory dsp]. Signal Process. Mag. IEEE **27**(5), 131–139 (2010)
15. McLoughlin, I., Zhang, H., Xie, Z., Song, Y., Xiao, W.: Robust sound event classification using deep neural networks. IEEE/ACM Trans. Audio Speech Lang. Process. **23**(3), 540–552 (2015)
16. McLoughlin, I.V.: Line spectral pairs. Signal Process. **88**(3), 448–467 (2008)
17. Mesaros, A., et al.: Detection and classification of acoustic scenes and events: outcome of the dcase 2016 challenge. IEEE/ACM Trans. Audio Speech Lang. Process. **26**(2), 379–393 (2018)
18. Mun, S., Shon, S., Kim, W., Han, D.K., Ko, H.: Deep neural network based learning and transferring mid-level audio features for acoustic scene classification. In: 2017 IEEE International Conference on Acoustics, Speech and Signal Processing (ICASSP), pp. 796–800. IEEE (2017)

19. Piczak, K.J.: Environmental sound classification with convolutional neural networks. In: IEEE International Workshop on Machine Learning for Signal Processing, pp. 1–6 (2015)
20. Piczak, K.J.: ESC: dataset for environmental sound classification. In: ACM International Conference on Multimedia, pp. 1015–1018 (2015)
21. Radhakrishnan, R., Divakaran, A., Smaragdis, P.: Audio analysis for surveillance applications. In: IEEE Workshop on Applications of Signal Processing to Audio and Acoustics, pp. 158–161 (2005)
22. Sainath, T.N., Mohamed, A.R., Kingsbury, B., Ramabhadran, B.: Deep convolutional neural networks for LVCSR. In: 2013 IEEE International Conference on Acoustics, Speech and Signal Processing (ICASSP), pp. 8614–8618. IEEE (2013)
23. Salamon, J., Bello, J.: Deep convolutional neural networks and data augmentation for environmental sound classification. IEEE Signal Process. Lett. **PP**(99), 1 (2016)
24. Salamon, J., Jacoby, C., Bello, J.P.: A dataset and taxonomy for urban sound research. In: Proceedings of the 22nd ACM International Conference on Multimedia, pp. 1041–1044. ACM (2014)
25. Schedl, M., Gómez, E., Urbano, J., et al.: Music information retrieval: recent developments and applications. Found. Trends® Inf. Retr. **8**(2–3), 127–261 (2014)
26. Simonyan, K., Zisserman, A.: Very deep convolutional networks for large-scale image recognition. arXiv preprint arXiv:1409.1556 (2014)
27. Takahashi, N., Gygli, M., Pfister, B., Van Gool, L.: Deep convolutional neural networks and data augmentation for acoustic event detection. arXiv preprint arXiv:1604.07160 (2016)
28. Temko, A., Monte, E., Nadeu, C.: Comparison of sequence discriminant support vector machines for acoustic event classification. In: 2006 IEEE International Conference on Acoustics, Speech and Signal Processing, 2006. ICASSP 2006 Proceedings, vol. 5, p. V. IEEE (2006)
29. Tokozume, Y., Harada, T.: Learning environmental sounds with end-to-end convolutional neural network. In: 2017 IEEE International Conference on Acoustics, Speech and Signal Processing (ICASSP), pp. 2721–2725. IEEE (2017)
30. Tokozume, Y., Ushiku, Y., Harada, T.: Learning from between-class examples for deep sound recognition. arXiv preprint arXiv:1711.10282 (2018)
31. Typke, R., Wiering, F., Veltkamp, R.C.: A survey of music information retrieval systems. In: Proceedings of the 6th International Conference on Music Information Retrieval, pp. 153–160. Queen Mary, University of London (2005)
32. Uzkent, B., Barkana, B.D., Cevikalp, H.: Non-speech environmental sound classification using svms with a new set of features. Int. J. Innov. Comput. Inf. Control **8**(5), 3511–3524 (2012)
33. Vacher, M., Serignat, J.F., Chaillol, S.: Sound classification in a smart room environment: an approach using gmm and hmm methods. In: SpeD, vol. 1 (2014)
34. Valero, X., Alias, F.: Gammatone cepstral coefficients: biologically inspired features for non-speech audio classification. IEEE Trans. Multimedia **14**(6), 1684–1689 (2012)
35. Zhang, H., Mcloughlin, I., Song, Y.: Robust sound event recognition using convolutional neural networks. In: IEEE International Conference on Acoustics, Speech and Signal Processing, pp. 559–563 (2015)
36. Zhang, H., Cisse, M., Dauphin, Y.N., Lopez-Paz, D.: Mixup: beyond empirical risk minimization. arXiv preprint arXiv:1710.09412 (2017)
37. Zhang, X., Zou, Y., Shi, W.: Dilated convolution neural network with LeakyReLU for environmental sound classification. In: 2017 22nd International Conference on Digital Signal Processing (DSP), pp. 1–5. IEEE (2017)

Focal Loss for Region Proposal Network

Chengpeng Chen[1,2], Xinhang Song[1,2], and Shuqiang Jiang[1,2(✉)]

[1] Key Laboratory of Intelligent Information Processing, Institute of Computing
Technology, Chinese Academy of Sciences, Beijing, China
{chengpeng.chen,xinhang.song}@vipl.ict.ac.cn,sqjiang@ict.ac.cn
[2] University of Chinese Academy of Scienses, Beijing, China

Abstract. Currently, most state-of-the-art object detection models are
based on a two-stage scheme pioneered by R-CNN and integrated with
region proposal network (RPN), which is served as proposal generation.
During the training of RPN, only a fixed number of samples with a fixed
object/not-object ratio are sampled to avoid class imbalance problem. In
contrast to the sampling strategies, *focal loss* is utilized to solve the class
imbalance problem by down-weighting the losses of vast number of easy
samples, which is encountered in one-stage detection methods. Inspired
by this, we investigate the adaptation of focal loss to RPN in this paper,
which allow us to train RPN free of the sampling process. Based on
Faster R-CNN, we adapt focal loss to RPN and the experimental results
on PASCAL VOC 2007 and COCO datasets outperform the baseline,
which shows the efficiency of the proposed method and implies that focal
loss can be applied to RPN directly.

Keywords: Object detection · Region proposal network · Focal loss

1 Introduction

In this era of deep learning, most object detection models with state-of-the-art
performance are based on a two-stage scheme [1,5,7,8,25,26], where a sparse
set of proposals are generated at the first stage, followed by regional object
classification and coordinate regression at the second stage. The process of generating proposals has developed from off-line methods, such as Selective Search
[15] and objectness [16], to integrated learning ones [1,18,19], in which Region
Proposal Network (RPN) has become a standard component of these state-of-
the-art two-stage methods. During the training of RPN, candidate proposals are
first sampled among pre-located dense anchors, and then fed to the classifier of
object/not-object and regressor. Within those dense anchors, the samples with
class *object/not-object* are very imbalanced, particularly, the samples of *not-
object* are much more than the ones of *object*, which make it difficult to train a
classifier with regular policies. Thus, as a usual strategy, only a fixed number of
anchors with a fixed *object/not-object* ratio, *e.g.,* 256 and 1:1 [1], are sampled for
training. Although such constraint in sampling progress can balance the samples, it also results in losing the diversity of proposals. Instead of constraining

© Springer Nature Switzerland AG 2018
J.-H. Lai et al. (Eds.): PRCV 2018, LNCS 11257, pp. 368–380, 2018.
https://doi.org/10.1007/978-3-030-03335-4_32

the sampling progress, we investigate this imbalance problem from the aspect of designing desired loss function during training.

The class imbalance problem is also encountered in one-stage detection models [3,11–13], in which different types of example sampling strategies [11,14,23] are proposed to address this problem. However, Lin *et al.* [3] claims that it is the vast number of easy samples that overwhelms the detectors. Thus, they propose to take all pre-located dense anchors for training with a dynamically cross entropy loss, called *focal loss*, which prevents these easy samples from overwhelming the training process by down-weighting the losses of easy samples.

In this paper, we investigate the adaptation of focal loss to RPN (see Sect. 3.3), such that much more samples can be included for training while free of the training problems caused by class imbalance. By replacing standard cross entropy loss in RPN with focal loss, RPN can be trained directly with no need for specially designed sampling strategies. Besides, due to the full convolutional implementation of RPN, no extra computation cost is required. We take Faster R-CNN [1,2] as our baseline model and conduct the experiments on PASCAL VOC 2007 [24] and COCO [10] detection benchmarks. The experimental results show the efficiency of the proposed method, implying that this sampling free strategy can be directly applied to RPN, so as to all the state-of-the-art two-stage detectors.

2   Related Work

Two-Stage Detectors. With the fast development of deep leaning [9] over past few years, two-stage object detectors [1,4–8,25,26] have become one of the fashion of object detection methods. In the two-stage methods, a sparse set of candidate proposals with high probabilities of containing objects are first generated [1,15,18,19], followed by a second stage of object classification and coordinate regression. Empowered with deep neural networks [9,20–22] and a series of improvements in both speed and accuracy [1,4,6,7], the whole detection system is integrated into a single network, *i.e.*, the widely-used Faster R-CNN [1] framework. Many works to extend this framework have been conducted [5, 8,25,26]. We also utilize Faster R-CNN as our base model to investigate the adaptation of focal loss to RPN in this paper.

Region Proposal Methods. As the first stage in the two-stage scheme, region proposal methods have been developed from pioneering off-line methods, such as Selective Search [15] and objectness [16], to integrated learning ones [1,18,19], in which RPN integrated this proposal process into the base networks by sharing their convolutional layers. During training, dense anchors are pre-located first, to which RPN applies *object/not-object* classification and class-agnostic regression, while for inference, it generates a sparse set of proposals for the second stage by applying coordinate refinements and non-maximum suppression (NMS) to the dense anchors. RPN enables the end-to-end training of the two-stage detectors, and has become one of their components.

It is worth to note that not all the pre-located anchors are employed for training due to its class imbalance problem, that is, majority of the dense anchors are easy samples with class *not-object*. And if all these anchors are taken into account, they would overwhelm the detector during training. In this paper, we focus on this class imbalance problem in RPN.

Class Imbalance. As same as RPN in two-stage detectors, one-stage detectors also encounter class imbalance during training [3,11–13], and some types of example sampling strategies are often the employed solutions [11,14,23]. In contrast, Lin *et al.* [3] propose a novel type of loss function, called focal loss, to down-weight the losses of easy samples, so as to include all samples for training and handle the class imbalance. Inspired by this work, we try to adapt focal loss to RPN such that we can also avoid the sampling process during the training of RPN.

Loss Function Design. There are two tasks, classification *(cls)* and bounding box regression *(reg)*, in both first and second stage of these two-stage methods, which classifies the anchors/proposals to a specific class and regresses the bouncing boxes, respectively. The *cls* loss is taken as standard cross entropy loss, while for binary *cls*, it is shown as:

$$CE\left(p,y\right) = \frac{1}{N_{cls}} \sum_i CE\left(p_i, y_i\right)$$

$$= \frac{1}{N_{cls}} \sum_i y_i \log(p_i) + (1 - y_i) \log\left(1 - p_i\right) \qquad (1)$$

where y_i is the label, p_i is the estimated probability for each sample, and N_{cls} is the number of samples and taken as a normalization term. For multi-class *cls* task, the cross entropy loss can be extended straightforwardly.

For the *reg* task, smoothed L_1 loss [7] is applied as:

$$smooth_{L_1}\left(x\right) = \begin{cases} 0.5x^2 & if \; |x| \le 1 \\ |x| - 0.5 \; otherwise \end{cases} \qquad (2)$$

where x is the difference between anchors/proposals and bounding boxes of ground true.

We note that the *cls* task is *object/not-object* binary classification in the first stage, *i.e.*, RPN, while in the second stage, it is taken as multi-class ones to classify foreground classes/background. For the *reg* tasks in both stages, the smooth L_1 loss is only computed on anchors/proposals belong to *object*/foreground classes.

We follow the literature and use these losses in our model except that we use focal loss in *cls* task of RPN instead of cross entropy loss, such that we can include much more anchors for training.

3   Focal Loss for RPN

As a Region Proposal Network (RPN) based detection model, Faster R-CNN [1] is taken as our base model for evaluating the adaption of focal loss to RPN. In the following of this section, we will briefly review RPN in Faster R-CNN (Sect. 3.1), focal loss [3] applied in detection models (Sect. 3.2), and finally introduce our focal loss equipped RPN (Sect. 3.3).

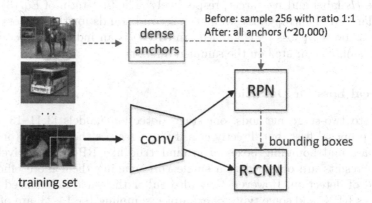

Fig. 1. The training process of Faster RCNN with focal loss. The blue/dashed lines indicate the generation/feeding of anchors or bounding boxes. (Color figure online)

3.1   RPN in Faster R-CNN

Faster R-CNN is a widely-used two-stage detection model which integrates RPN to generate proposal regions, enabling an end-to-end detection model. Based on RPN, the two-stage detection approaches develop fast and achieve good performance in recent years [1,5,8,25,26].

As Fig. 1 shown, RPN shares convolutional (conv) layers with base detection network, *e.g.,* first 5 conv layers in Zeiler and Fergus model (ZF net) [20], 13 in VGG16 [21] and first 4 blocks in ResNet [22]. On the top of these shared conv layers, RPN is included as external branch for *cls* and *reg*, consisting of an $3 * 3$ conv layer followed by two sibling fully-connected layers (or $1 * 1$ conv layers) for *cls* and *reg*, respectively. Note that, RPN only classifies *object/not-object* for each anchor, where we also apply sigmoid (1 for *object* and 0 for *not-object*) and softmax (as usual in two-stage detectors) for our focal loss adaptation, which will be introduced in Sect. 3.3. Besides, RPN regresses bounding boxes via refining pre-fixed anchors, which are centered at each position of the top shared conv layer. k anchors at each position are taken according to different scales and aspect ratios, *e.g.,* 3 scales and 3 aspect ratios result in $k = 9$ anchors in [1]. Therefore, with a typical image scale $\sim 600 * 1000$ and feature stride 16 of the shared conv layers [20–22], $\sim 20,000$ anchors are obtained in total, in which the numbers of *object/not-object* are very imbalanced, *e.g.*, $\sim 1 : 1000$. However, only fixed number of anchors are sampled for training to ensure a relative balanced samples (in [1], 256 anchors with ratio 1 : 1). The loss function of RPN is formulated as:

$$L_{RPN} = \frac{1}{N_{cls}} \sum_i CE\left(p_i, p_i^t\right) + \frac{1}{N_{reg}} \sum_i I\left(t_i^t\right) L_{reg}\left(t_i, t_i^t\right) \tag{3}$$

where N_{cls} and N_{reg} are the normalization terms, *e.g.*, 256 in [1], and p_i^t and t_i^t are the *cls* label and *reg* target, respectively. The first term of Eq. (3) stands for standard cross entropy loss, while the second stands for the *reg* loss, where standard smooth L_1 loss [7] is applied, and $I\left(t_i^t\right)$ is an indicator function. The loss here is only computed on the sampled anchors.

3.2   Focal Loss for Detection

Different to two-stage methods, one-stage detection models [3,11–13] do not generate proposal first, but directly classify and regress the anchors (or priors) to the class and bounding boxes of ground true like RPN, respectively. The detection results are obtained in a single run, making them more efficient in the speed of detection. However, they also suffer the same imbalanced sample problem as RPN, and some types of examples sampling [11,14,23] are often the applied solutions. In [3], all pre-located anchors are used for training instead of a relative small number of sampled ones. The authors claim the affects of the imbalanced problem is that the accumulated loss from the vast number of easy samples overwhelms the detector [3]. Therefore, in order to address with this imbalanced problem, it proposed focal loss to down-weight the loss of the easy samples. Focal loss is a dynamically scaled cross entropy loss, which can be formulated as:

$$FL(p_t) = -\alpha_t(1 - p_t)^\gamma \log(p_t) \tag{4}$$

where for binary classification, $p_t \epsilon [0, 1]$ is the probability for the ground true class, $\alpha_t \epsilon [0, 1]$ the re-weighting factor to balance positive and negative samples, and $\gamma \geq 0$ a hyper-parameter. Note that, when $\alpha_t = 0.5, \gamma = 0$, focal loss deforms to standard cross entropy loss.

As in Eq. (4), for those easy samples (p_t close to 1), the scale term $(1 - p_t)^\gamma$ down-weights the loss greatly; thus, it leads the model to focus more on hard samples. Through this dynamically scaled loss, the model can avoid the problem of the model being overwhelmed by much more easy samples, so as to include all the anchors for training.

3.3   Focal Loss for RPN

To investigate the application of focal loss to RPN, we re-formulate the loss of RPN with focal loss as:

$$L_{RPN-FL} = \frac{\lambda_{fl}}{N'_{cls}} \sum_i FL\left(p_i^t\right) + \frac{1}{N'_{reg}} \sum_i I\left(t_i^t\right) L_{reg}\left(t_i, t_i^t\right) \qquad (5)$$

where we simply the replace the cross entropy loss with focal loss and use all anchors ($\sim 20,000$ per image) for training instead of those sampled. λ_{fl} is served as a balancing weight. Note that, in the first term of Eq. (5), we set $N'_{cls} = |p_i^t \epsilon\, object|$, which means the *cls* loss is normalized with number of *object* samples in this dense anchor scenario, while in the second term, we set $N'_{reg} = 2 * |p_i^t \epsilon\, object|$.

Figure 1 illustrates our adaptation of focal loss in RPN. In contrast to only training with a part of anchors as previous works [1,8,25,26], all the generated dense anchors are taken for training with our adaptive focal loss. The focal loss equipped RPN is integrated into Faster R-CNN framework [1,2] in the following form:

$$L = L_{RPN-FL} + L_{RCNN} \qquad (6)$$

where L_{RCNN} includes multi-class *cls* loss and class-aware *reg* loss, and we do not modify it so as to verify the effect of focal loss applied in RPN on the whole detection system.

To get the probability p_t in Eq. (4), we utilize two output functions, softmax and sigmoid. For output with softmax, we get two scores $[p_p, p_n]$ implying *object* and *not-object*, respectively, and get $p_t = p_p$ if the anchor matches with *object* label, while $p_t = p_n$ if the anchor matches with *not-object* label. For output with sigmoid, only one score p_s is got and $p_t = p_s$ for *object* label, while for *not-object* label $p_t = 1 - p_s$. These two output function will be compared in the following experiments.

Implement Details. This work is based on the public TensorFlow implementation of Faster R-CNN[1][2], and we follow most of the parameter settings from the original implementation. We use stochastic gradient descent (SGD) for optimization and set momentum as 0.9 and weight decay as 0.0001. The model is trained with one image per iteration following [2], and the only data augmentation strategy is to randomly flip the training images. ImageNet [9] pre-trained VGG16 [21] is used as our base network, and the conv1 and conv2 layers are fixed.

We set the base learning rate as 0.001 for first 50k/350k iteration and decrease by 10 for next 20k/140k for PASCAL VOC 2007/COCO datasets. For the hyperparameters, we set $\alpha_t = 0.25, \gamma = 2$ and $\lambda_{fl} = 0.1$ by default, and they will be evaluated in the following experiments.

---

[1] https://github.com/endernewton/tf-faster-rcnn.

4   Experiments

We evaluate our model on PASCAL VOC 2007 [24] and COCO [10] detection benchmarks and follow the standard data splits. Average precision (AP) is reported following the literature. An image scale of 600 pixels is applied for both training and test [1,2]. Note that, for fair comparison, we only modify the loss function and do not include any additional parameters in all our experiments, except the model of sigmoid output contains less parameters, where we reduce the output from two to one.

PASCAL VOC 2007. PASCAL VOC [24] has been a classical dataset for computer vision tasks, *e.g.,* classification and detection and segmentation. In the following experiments, we also utilize this dataset for evaluating our model. It contains 20 object categories for detection, and there are 2.47 objects in each image in average. We use the trainval split for training, and test split for evaluation. which consist of 5,011 and 4,952 images, respectively. Average precision (AP) is reported with the IOU threshold set as 0.5.

COCO 2014. As a more complicate dataset, COCO [10] has been a challenging benchmarks of object detection, and is most widely-used for evaluating various detection models. It contains 80 object categories for detection, and there are 7.58 objects in each image in average. We use COCO 2014 in our experiments, which contains of 82,783 images for training, 40,504 for validation and 40,775 for test. Due to the unavailable of the ground true of test split, we follow the literature [2,10] to re-split the dataset to train+valminumsminival and minival. During test, COCO employs a more strict metric, where average precision (AP) is computed with different IOU thresholds, *i.e.*, [0.5 : 0.95] and report their average. Besides, the performances for different scales, *i.e.*, small/middle/large, are also reported.

Table 1. Parameters evaluation Detection average precision (%). All use faster R-CNN on VGG16. For each column, we only change the corresponding parameter and keep others as default. The missing values mean that the model failed in those settings.

	γ			α			λ_{fl}		
	1.0	2.0	3.0	0.25	0.5	0.75	0.1	0.2	0.3
FL-sigmoid	**70.8**	70.7	70.7	70.7	70.5	70.5	70.7	70.5	70.5
FL-softmax	-	**71.2**	71.1	**71.2**	70.9	70.7	**71.2**	-	-

4.1   Parameters Evaluation

We evaluate the hyper-parameters in Table 1. FL-softmax and FL-sigmoid stand for Faster R-CNN with focal loss equipped RPN which output with softmax and sigmoid, respectively, as introduced in Sect. 3.3. As the table shown, FL-softmax always gain a higher performance than FL-sigmoid, while the latter performs much more stable under different parameter settings. We assume that it is the saturation of sigmoid function that leads the model less sensitive to the hyper-parameters and also stuck the optimization process, which result in inferior performances. For those several failed scenarios in FL-softmax, the large scale of focal loss computed on all anchors may be the cause, $e.g.$, small exponent $\gamma \leq 1$ or large loss scale $\lambda_{fl} \geq 0.2$ could result in the exposure of loss and further hurt the optimization process. Thus, for FL-softmax, we should design the hyper-parameters more carefully to make the computed focal loss in a reasonable scale, so as to train the model correctly.

Table 2. VOC 2007 test Detection average precision (%). These models use the default hyper-parameters except that $\gamma = 1$ in FL-sigmoid. In baseline+FL, we combine focal loss with the original RPN. *Baseline we trained using the public implementation.

	mAP	Aero	Bike	Bird	Boat	Bottle	Bus	Car	Cat	Chair	Cow
Baseline*	70.9	71.0	78.8	69.5	55.5	56.0	79.5	84.9	81.3	50.2	79.8
FL-sigmoid	70.8	71.4	78.0	68.7	55.6	56.7	**80.5**	85.8	84.4	47.9	77.9
FL-softmax	**71.2**	72.1	**79.4**	**72.4**	55.1	**57.7**	78.0	84.5	**85.4**	48.5	**80.6**
Baseline+FL	**71.2**	69.6	78.7	72.0	**56.4**	57.4	79.7	**85.1**	84.8	**51.2**	77.5
	Table	Dog	Horse	mbike	Person	Plant	Sheep	Sofa	Train	Tv	
Baseline*	**65.9**	80.6	**84.0**	74.6	77.3	44.2	73.0	65.7	72.7	**73.4**	
FL-sigmoid	64.8	**81.3**	83.7	**77.3**	76.9	41.8	72.3	65.4	73.8	71.3	
FL-softmax	63.0	**81.3**	83.0	74.4	77.5	**44.3**	**74.0**	63.5	**76.4**	73.2	
Baseline+FL	63.5	81.2	83.3	75.8	**77.7**	43.6	72.1	**67.0**	75.1	73.2	

4.2 Performance Comparison

Table 2 shows the detection results of baseline and our models which are adapted with focal loss. The performances are comparable to the baseline, implying that focal loss can be modified to apply in RPN directly to replace the sampling mechanism, but only with a mirror impact on the performance.

As Table 2 shown, however, when slightly changing the mAP metric (0.1% lower in FL-sigmoid and 0.3% higher in FL-softmax), the performance of each class changes obviously, $e.g.$, obtaining 2.9% lower for 'table' class and 4.1% higher for 'cat' class in FL-softmax, which may indicate that focal loss is complementary to standard cross entropy loss. Inspired by this, we simply add focal loss to the original RPN, denoted as baseline+FL in Table 2, which obtains the same performance as FL-softmax and also mirror improvements over baseline. Specifically, in baseline+FL, focal loss is computed on all anchors as before while cross entropy loss is computed on sampled anchors, and these two losses are directly combined by average. Figure 3 displays some examples on PASCAL VOC 2007 detected by model baseline+FL, where we get the satisfactory results with a wide range of scales and aspect ratios.

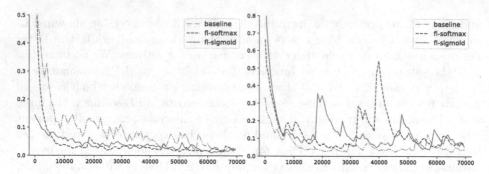

Fig. 2. Loss curves of RPN. **Left:** *cls* loss. **Right:** *reg* loss. The loss curves in baseline+FL display similar to baseline, so we omit them for simplicity.

4.3   Training Process in RPN

To further analyze the influence of focal loss on RPN, we plot the *cls* and *reg* losses during training in Fig. 2. In the *cls* loss curve, the two focal loss equipped RPNs converge much faster and more stable than baseline. This effect is benefited from the intrinsic characteristic of focal loss that it is capable of training with much more anchors. For the *reg* loss curve, however, these two models perform worse than baseline; they are much unstable and have large scale. This may be the reason why focal loss can not boost RPN (and Faster R-CNN) greatly like one-stage detection model [3], *e.g.*, after we get the satisfied scores for all the anchors, these anchors can not be refined well to produce satisfied proposals for R-CNN, which may affect the performance of the whole detection system. This may implies that the training signals produced by focal loss is conflict to those from bounding box regression in some terms.

Besides, it is worth to note that, RetinaNet [3], the network first applied focal loss to detection, decouples the *cls* and *reg* tasks into two sub-networks, and thus avoids this conflict signals problem. In this work, we only follow the original design of RPN where these two tasks share the same networks except the task specific layers. Thus, decoupling *cls* and *reg* tasks like RetinaNet in our focal loss equipped RPN may further improves the model performance. Other ways to make focal loss more compatible with bounding box regression can also be taken into consideration, and this will be our future work.

Table 3. COCO 2014 minival object detection average precision (%). Legend same as Table 2. *Baseline we trained using the public implementation.

	AP	AP-.5	AP-.75	AP-S	AP-M	AP-L
Baseline*	26.5	46.7	27.2	11.8	30.4	37.5
FL-softmax	26.6	46.7	27.4	**12.0**	**30.9**	37.3
Baseline+FL	**27.0**	**47.5**	**27.7**	**12.0**	30.8	**37.9**

Fig. 3. Examples on PASCAL VOC 2007 detected by baseline+FL. The score threshold for display is set as 0.5

4.4   More Results on COCO

We also conduct experiments of the focal loss equipped RPN in COCO 2014 dataset [10], where we use train+valminumsminival and minival split following [2,10]. As Table 3 shown, FL-softmax performs comparable to baseline, while baseline+FL is superior in all the metrics. In terms of the performance difference of baseline+FL in these two datasets, we assume that it is the difference between the statistics of each dataset that counts; COCO contains much more objects in each image than PASCAL VOC 2007 (7.58 vs 2.47 in average), which may results in differences in the training process, *i.e.*, the anchors for computing focal loss in COCO is not such imbalanced like PASCAL VOC 2007. That is, in dataset with dense objects, such as COCO, focal loss combined with standard cross entropy loss may work better than either of them alone.

In other aspects, the original implementation [2] claims that the performance on COCO could continue to improve if we train with more iterations, *e.g.*, 900k/1190k; thus the reason why baseline+FL performs better than baseline and FL-softmax may be its fast convergence characteristic. So, whether the statistic difference or convergence characteristic contribute to performance difference is further to be explored.

We note that the training processes also display the same trends as in Sect. 4.3. And these experimental results show that focal loss is also adaptable to more complicate datasets.

5   Conclusion

In this work, we investigate how to adapt focal loss to train RPN without applying the sampling strategy. By down-weighting the losses of those vast numbers of easy samples, focal loss can intrinsically handle the class imbalance problem and prevent their losses from overwhelming the detector. Using focal loss is capable of including much more samples for training. Thus, RPN can also take all anchors into account for training via replacing standard cross entropy loss with focal loss or simply combining them. As the experiments conducted on PASCAL VOC 2007 and COCO shown, it is feasible to train RPN without particularly designed sampling. We also discuss the compatibility between focal loss and bounding box regression in RPN, and this is left as future work.

Acknowledge. This work was supported in part by the National Natural Science Foundation of China under Grant 61532018, in part by the Lenovo Outstanding Young Scientists Program, in part by National Program for Special Support of Eminent Professionals and National Program for Support of Top-notch Young Professionals, in part by the National Postdoctoral Program for Innovative Talents under Grant BX201700255.

References

1. Ren, S., He, K., Girshick, R., Sun, J.: FasterR-CNN: towards real-time object detection with region proposal networks. In: NIPS (2016)
2. Chen, X., Gupta, A.: An implementation of faster R-CNN with study for region sampling. arXiv:1702.02138 (2017)
3. Lin, T.-Y., Goyal, P., Girshick, R., He, K., Dollàr, P.: Focal loss for dense object detection. In: ICCV (2017)
4. He, K., Zhang, X., Ren, S., Sun, J.: Spatial pyramid pooling in deep convolutional networks for visual recognition. In: Fleet, D., Pajdla, T., Schiele, B., Tuytelaars, T. (eds.) ECCV 2014. LNCS, vol. 8691, pp. 346–361. Springer, Cham (2014). https://doi.org/10.1007/978-3-319-10578-9_23
5. Dai, J., Li, Y., He, K., Sun, J.: R-FCN: object detection via region-based fully convolutional networks. In: NIPS (2016)
6. Girshick, R., Donahue, J., Darrell, T. Malik, J.: Rich feature hierarchies for accurate object detection and semantic segmentation. In: CVPR (2014)
7. Girshick, R.: Fast R-CNN. In: ICCV (2015)
8. He, K., Gkioxari, G., Dollàr, P., Girshick, R.: Mask R-CNN. In: ICCV (2017)
9. Krizhevsky, A., Sutskever, I., Hinton, G.: ImageNet classification with deep convolutional neural networks. In: NIPS (2012)
10. Lin, T.-Y., et al.: Microsoft COCO: common objects in context. In: Fleet, D., Pajdla, T., Schiele, B., Tuytelaars, T. (eds.) ECCV 2014. LNCS, vol. 8693, pp. 740–755. Springer, Cham (2014). https://doi.org/10.1007/978-3-319-10602-1_48
11. Liu, W., et al.: SSD: Single shot MultiBox detector. In: Leibe, B., Matas, J., Sebe, N., Welling, M. (eds.) ECCV 2016. LNCS, vol. 9905, pp. 21–37. Springer, Cham (2016). https://doi.org/10.1007/978-3-319-46448-0_2
12. Redmon, J., Divvala, S., Girshick, R., Farhadi, A.: You only look once: unified, real-time object detection. In: CVPR (2016)
13. Redmon, J., Farhadi, A.: YOLO9000: better, faster, stronger. In: CVPR (2017)
14. Shrivastava, A., Gupta, A., Girshick, R.: Training region based object detectors with online hard example mining. In: CVPR (2016)
15. Uijlings, J.R., Van de Sande, K.E., Gevers, T., Smeulders, A.W.: Selective search for object recognition. IJCV **104**, 154–171 (2013)
16. Alexe, B., Deselaers, T., Ferrari, V.: Measuring the objectness of image windows. IEEE TPAMI **34**(11), 2189–2202 (2012)
17. Zitnick, C.L., Dollár, P.: Edge boxes: locating object proposals from edges. In: Fleet, D., Pajdla, T., Schiele, B., Tuytelaars, T. (eds.) ECCV 2014. LNCS, vol. 8693, pp. 391–405. Springer, Cham (2014). https://doi.org/10.1007/978-3-319-10602-1_26
18. Szegedy, C., Reed, S., Erhan, D., Anguelov, D.: Scalable, high-quality object detection. arXiv preprint arXiv:1412.1441v2 (2014)
19. Erhan, D., Szegedy, C., Toshev, A., Anguelov, D.: Scalable object detection using deep neural networks. In: CVPR (2014)
20. Zeiler, M.D., Fergus, R.: Visualizing and understanding convolutional networks. In: Fleet, D., Pajdla, T., Schiele, B., Tuytelaars, T. (eds.) ECCV 2014. LNCS, vol. 8689, pp. 818–833. Springer, Cham (2014). https://doi.org/10.1007/978-3-319-10590-1_53
21. Simonyan, K., Zisserman, A.: Very deep convolutional networks for large-scale image recognition. In: ICLR (2015)

22. He, K., Zhang, X., Ren, S., Sun, J.: Deep residual learning for image recognition. In: CVPR (2016)
23. Sung, K.-K., Poggio, T.: Learning and example selection for object and pattern detection. In: MIT A.I. Memo No. 1521 (1994)
24. Everingham, M., Van Gool, L., Williams, C.K., Winn, J., Zisserman, A.: The pascal visual object classes (VOC) challenge. IJCV **88**(2), 303–338 (2010)
25. Singh, B., Davis, L. S.: An analysis of scale invariance in object detection - SNIP. In: CVPR (2018)
26. Hu, H., Gu, J., Zhang, Z., Dai, J., Wei, Y.: Relation networks for object detection. In: CVPR (2018)

A Shallow ResNet with Layer Enhancement for Image-Based Particle Pollution Estimation

Wenwen Yang, Jun Feng$^{(\boxtimes)}$, Qirong Bo$^{(\boxtimes)}$, Yixuan Yang,
and Bo Jiang

Northwest University, Xian 710127, China
{fengjun, boqirong}@nwu.edu.cn

Abstract. Airborne particle pollution especially matter with a diameter less than 2.5 μm (PM2.5) has become an increasingly serious problem and caused grave public health concerns. An easily and reliable accessible method to monitor the particles can greatly help raise public awareness and reduce harmful exposures. In this paper, we proposed a shallow ResNet with layer enhancement for PM2.5 Index Estimation, called PMIE. An inter-layer weights discrimination of convolutional neural networks method is proposed, providing a meaningful reference for CNN's design. In addition, a new method for enhancing the effect of the convolution layer was first introduced and was applied under the guidance of the CNN inter-layer weights discrimination method we proposed. This shallow ResNet consists of seven residual blocks with last two layer enhancements. We assessed our method on two datasets collected from Shanghai City and Beijing City in China, and compared with the state-of-the-art. For Shanghai dataset, PMIE reduced RMSE by 11.8% and increased R-squared by 4.8%. For Beijing dataset, RMSE is reduced by 14.4% and R-squared is increased by 23.6%. The results demonstrated that the proposed method PMIE outperforming the state-of-the-art for PM2.5 estimation.

Keywords: Particulate matter · Image enhancement · Shallow ReNet
Layer enhancement

1 Introduction

Air pollution has become a serious issue globally and threaten public health. Many studies [1, 2] have shown that these pollutants especially fine particles with diameters less than 2.5 μm (PM2.5) has very complicated and harmful effect on human body more susceptible to respiratory diseases (such as asthma, emphysema, pneumonia, etc.), and also likely to increase cardiovascular and cerebrovascular diseases (such as ischemic heart disease, coronary heart disease, myocardial infarction, high blood pressure and cerebral infarction, etc.). Thus, how to measure and reduce the air pollution effectively becomes an important and practical problem.

Nowadays, smart phones and camera surveillances are widely available to obtain images, which together with the ever-increasing computational power for sophisticated image processing, provide a great opportunity to quality and analyze airborne particle

J.-H. Lai et al. (Eds.): PRCV 2018, LNCS 11257, pp. 381–391, 2018.
https://doi.org/10.1007/978-3-030-03335-4_33

based images. The studies that have been reported in the literature can be divided into two categories: image-feature based approaches and deep learning approaches.

In image feature-base methods, Li *et al.* [3] proposed a method to estimate haze levels from images in image feature-base methods. They get two features, depth map and transmission matrix from haze images. And they use two features to estimate haze levels by statistical methods. Mao *et al.* [4] proposed a method by detecting numerical haze image by using the statics of various images and the atmospheric scattering model. And this method can estimate the haze factor from a single image. Liu *et al.* [5] first extracts 6 image features for each image, transmittance, overall and local image contrast, sky color and smoothness, and entropy, and two non-image features, solar zenith angle and humidity, and then applies principal components analysis (PCA) and Sequential Backward Feature Selection (SBFS) to optimize the feature set. Finally, creating a SVR model to predict PM2.5 indices.

Recently, deep learning has become the state-of-the-art solution for solving typical computer vision problems. In CNN based methods, Zhang *et al.* [6] built a CNN and classify images. The CNN has 9 convolution layers, 2 pooling layers, and 2 dropout layers. And they solve vanishing gradient problem by using a modified rectified liner unit as the activation function. In order to adapt to air pollution problem, they also have to use a negative log-log ordinal classifier to replace softmax classifier. Chakma *et al.* [7] proposed method applies a VGG-16 CNN model for image-based PM2.5 level analysis. The images are classified into three classes according to their PM2.5 concentration levels based on two major transfer learning strategies, CNN fine-tuning and CNN features-based random forest. Bo *et al.* [8] first uses a Residual convolutional neural network (ResNet50) to predict the PM2.5 index based on image information, and achieved the-state-of-the-art performance.

Compared with traditional image feature-based PM2.5 analysis, deep learning-based approaches tends to achieve better results due to the simple preprocess and complete feature extraction. The existing networks such as VGG [9], Inception [10], ResNet50 [11] achieved great performance on the ImageNet Large Scale Visual Recognition Challenge (ILSVRC). However, the existing networks were designed for object recognition, the complexity of these networks make it more difficult to optimize and easy to get over-fitting for PM2.5 estimation task.

In this paper, we explore the way for how to design a CNN model for air particle pollution estimation. A deep network with fewer layers is presented in this paper for PM2.5 Index Estimation (PMIE). Our contributions are: (1) An inter-layer weights discrimination of convolutional neural networks method is proposed, providing a meaningful reference for CNN's design. (2) A shallow ResNet with layer enhancement is proposed, which not only improve the convergence speed in the training, but also improve the over-fitting performance. Meanwhile, the training time is greatly reduced due to the shallow network in the case of the same training epochs. (3) The proposed method PMIE achieves a good performance on the dataset [5, 8]. For Shanghai dataset, PMIE reduced RMSE by 11.8% and increased R-squared by 4.8%. For Beijing dataset, our method PMIE outperformed [8], which is reported based on ResNet50. RMSE is reduced by 14.4% and R-squared is increased by 23.6%.

2 Methodology

The complexity of these existing deep networks designed for object recognition made it more difficult to optimize and easy to get over-fitting in our task. Therefore, we proposed a shallow convolutional neural network with layer enhancement for PM Index Estimation, called PMIE. First, we proposed a network consist seven residual block, which is shallow compared to the Residual networks such as ResNet50, ResNet101. In addition, a new method for enhancing the effect of the convolution layer was first introduced and was applied behind the convolution layer that has obvious effect on the output. In our task, we add the layer enhancement following block six and seven. The flowchart was illustrated in the Fig. 1.

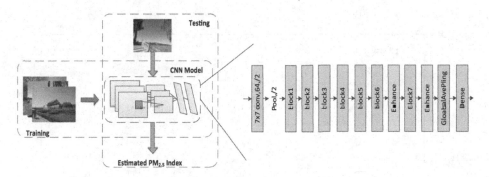

Fig. 1. Flowchart of the proposed method

2.1 Layer Weight Distribution Discrimination Method

In the machine translation mechanism [12] of text deep learning, the weight of each word in the process of translation is not same, and more attention is paid to the core words. Similarly, the weight distribution of each layer is also different in a convolutional neural network. According to this consideration, we propose a CNN inter-layer weight distribution discriminant method. For a convolutional network, we assign a random weight K_{ij} to the output of each residual block and train K_{ij} by the back-propagation algorithm which is showed at Fig. 2. The specific approach is as follows: (1) Training basic convolutional neural networks; (2) Fixing the weight of the basic network, and assign a random weight K_{ij} to the output layer of each residual block, i represents the ith residual block, and j represents the jth feature map of this residual block; (3) Training the random weights; (4) Outputting the weight of each layer and seeing the distribution.

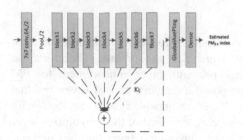 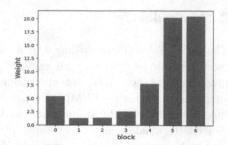

Fig. 2. Inter-layer weight distribution discrimination method

Fig. 3. Weight distribution results in Shanghai dataset.

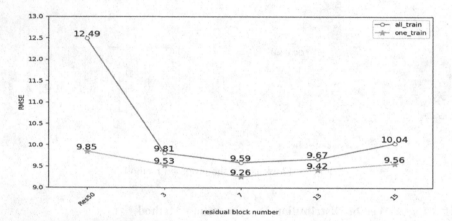

Fig. 4. Different residual block number and train method results in Shanghai dataset

2.2 Shallow ResNet

Applying deep learning methods to images based PM2.5 index Estimation is a challenging task. The existing CNN models are suitable for object recognition tasks, but our task is to explore whether the edge of the object is clear and whether the image texture is clear. The existing deep and large networks are difficult to train and easy to get over-fitting for PM2.5 index estimation task. Therefore, we proposed a shallow ResNet with fewer layers compared to existing architecture. This architecture is presented in Fig. 1, which takes a square 224 * 224 pixels RGB image as input and composed of one convolutional layers, one pooling layers, and seven residual blocks selected from ResNet-50 [11], the select of residual blocks number is from experience, the result is shown in Fig. 4.

Shallow architecture tends to learn low level features such as edges, lines, texture and colors. As the number of model layers deepens, the edges extracted by layers tend to be semantic and gradually change to the shape of objects. In our PM2.5 estimation

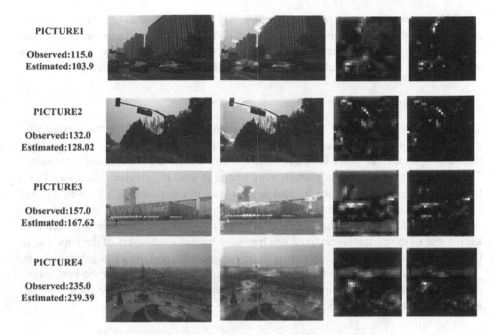

PICTURE1

Observed:115.0
Estimated:103.9

PICTURE2

Observed:132.0
Estimated:128.02

PICTURE3

Observed:157.0
Estimated:167.62

PICTURE4

Observed:235.0
Estimated:239.39

Fig. 5. Layer enhancement samples

task, the focus is not to identify the object itself, but to identify whether the edges or lines of the object is clear, the shallow architecture is more suitable for our task.

2.3 Layer Enhancement

The Attention mechanism [13] was previously used in the task of text classification, and recently was widely used in object detection of images. In the object detection task, the initially selected ROI (region of interest) is given a higher weight value for more attention. Inspired by this, we proposed an enhance method, multiplying each weighted probability value learned by the convolutional layer by itself, so that the effects of activation and suppression are doubled, it also means image enhancement. At a convolution layer, the previous layer's feature maps are convolved with learnable kernels and put through the activation function to form the output feature map. Based on Sect. 2.1 weight distribution results shown in Fig. 3, we add enhancements after residual block six and block seven. That is, each output map may combine convolutions with multiple input maps except that the output after residual block six and seven combine input map multiple with itself. In general, we have that

$$x_j^l = \begin{cases} f\left(\sum_{j\in M_j} x_i^{l-1} * k_{ij}^l + b_j^l\right), & l = others \\ x_{ij}^{l-1} * x_{ij}^{l-1}, & l = 7,9 \end{cases} \qquad (1)$$

Where x^l represents the pixel of lth block, M_j represents a selection of input maps. According to these observations, the proposed PMIE with enhancement suppresses the features that have little bit relationship with the output and strengthens those features with greater concern. Several examples of the enhancement are depicted in Fig. 5.

2.4   Training and Testing

The PMIE-model is trained by the back-propagation algorithm with batch stochastic gradient descend such that the mean squared error loss is minimized. RGB images from the training dataset are resized to 224 * 224 * 3 and fed to the PMIE-model for training. The observed PM2.5 index of each training image is used to calculate MSE loss. Fine-tuning was adopted due to the limited dataset was not large enough to train the full CNNs. There are two possible approaches of performing fine-tuning in a pretrained network: The first one is to fine-tune all the layers of the CNNs, the other approach is to keep some of the earlier layers fixed and fine-tune higher level layers of the network. In this paper, we fine-tuned all layers using the parameters learned from ImageNet datasets.

Training is done per epoch, the CNN parameters updated based on the best results on the validation set. After training, the testing dataset were fed to the trained model and get the predicted PM2.5 index.

3   Experiments

3.1   Dataset

We present the PM2.5 prediction task on two images datasets: Shanghai dataset and Beijing dataset. (1) Shanghai dataset is a single-scene dataset [6]. This dataset contains 1885 pictures captured at the Oriental Pearl Tower in Shanghai city, China, and contains different capture times from May to December of 2014. (2) Beijing dataset is a non-single scene dataset that contains 1514 pictures collect from Beijing tourist website by ourselves [14]. These pictures were captured at diverse locations in Beijing City, China.

The U.S. consulate in Beijing and a Shanghai provided PM2.5 indices hourly, we used these to retrieve the PM2.5 indices of two datasets. Figure 6 shows the histogram distribution of the PM2.5 index of two datasets.

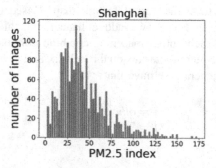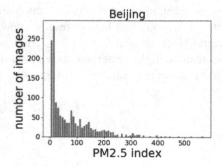

Fig. 6. The histograms of PM2.5 of Shanghai dataset and Beijing dataset.

3.2 Evaluation Protocols

We use mean squared error (RSME) and R-squared to evaluate the error of prediction. RSME is defined as:

$$RMSE = \sqrt{\frac{1}{N}\sum_{i=1}^{N}(y_i - y_i')^2},\qquad(2)$$

Where y_i' is the ith forecast value, and y_i is the ith observed value, $i = 1, 2.... N$. And R-squared is defined as:

$$R^2 = 1 - \frac{\sum_{i=1}^{N}(y_i - y_i')^2}{\sum_{i=1}^{N}(y_i - avg(y))^2},\qquad(3)$$

Where y_i' is the ith forecast value, $avg(y)$ is the average forecast value, and y_i is the ith observed value, $i = 1, 2...$, R-squared increases with the agreement between the observed value and the forecast value with a maximum value of 1, which indicates the best match.

3.3 Experiment Setting

In order to train and evaluate our PMIE network, we randomly select 80% images as training set and tune the CNN, 10% images as validation set, and 10% are used for testing. To fine-tune the model, we loaded the first convolutional and the earlier seven residual block weights from ResNet-50. After loading the pretrained weights, we adjusted all the parameters in PMIE networks to fit our goal.

For the PMIE network training parameters, we ran the code for 500 iterations and set the learning rate to a very small variations of 0.001. The batch size is 64 and the momentum is assigned to 0.9. The program was implemented using keras 2.05 in Ubuntu 16.04.

3.4 Experiments Result

In this study, we measure the performance of the proposed method using evaluation protocol described in Sect. 3.2. Table 1 presents the results of PMIE on two datasets with the RSME and R-squared values with comparison results in [6, 8]. In order to better compare our experiments, we also joined the VGG16 network as a comparison.

It is clear that the deep learning method such as ResNet and VGGnet achieved better result than traditional image feature extraction method like literate [6]. Since our network is improved on ResNet50, our focus is on comparing our PMIE methods with ResNet50 reported literate [8]. We can see that our method performed better in the same dataset of Beijing and Shanghai.

For Shanghai dataset, the RMSE of our PMIE method is reduced by 11.86% and R-squared increased by 4.59% in Shanghai dataset with ResNet50 from literate [8]. For Beijing dataset, the RMSE and R-squared values of PMIE are 50.64 and 0.68, reduced by 14.38% and increase by 23.63% respectively. Besides, compared with the traditional resnet50 network, the training time of PMIE is greatly reduced.

Figure 7 shows the correlations between the estimated PM2.5 indices and observed PM2.5 indices of Shanghai dataset and Beijing dataset.

Figure 8 shows the training and validation loss of our PMIE and ResNet50 on two data sets. We can see that the method we proposed overall performs better on validation sets and better to overcome overfitting challenges. In addition, in non-single scene Beijing datasets, our method converges faster during training, and it performs steadier during training and validating.

Table 1. PMIE performance vs other networks

Dataset	Method	RMSE	R-squared	Run time
Shanghai	[6]	19.23	0.57	–
	VGG16	11.26	0.84	3 h 2 m 20 s
	ResNet50 [8]	10.11	0.87	3 h 8 m 50 s
	PMIE	**8.91**	**0.91**	**2 h 7 m 56 s**
Beijing	VGG16	60.67	0.52	2 h 28 m 23 s
	ResNet50 [8]	59.15	0.55	2 h 31 m 30 s
	PMIE	**50.64**	**0.68**	**1 h 40 m 7 s**

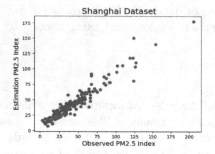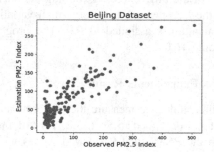

Fig. 7. The correlation of estimated and observed PM2.5 index.

Figure 9 shows images with their observed and estimated PM2.5 indices. The first two rows pictures are from Shanghai dataset and the last two rows are from Beijing dataset. The first row and the third row are pictures with accurate prediction, the second

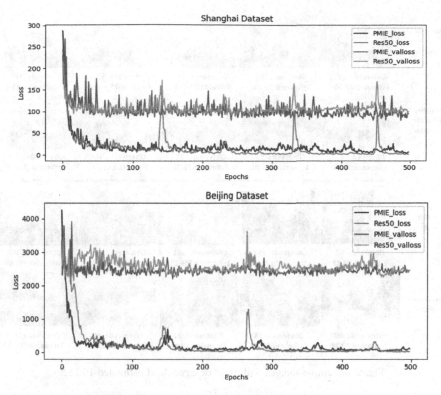

Fig. 8. Train loss and validation loss of proposed PMIE and ResNe50 for Shanghai and Beijing datasets

row and the last row are pictures with inaccurate prediction. By analyzing the dataset, we find there are some reasons for inaccurate prediction. We can see the images from second and last looks different between human visual observation and image labels. For example, the 1st image in last row looks very clear but its actual PM2.5 index is 80, the 3rd picture in the last row has larger estimated index than observed index because of its gray hue. In addition, lack of high PM2.5 images in dataset also resulted in the inaccurate prediction on high PM2.5 images. One the other hand, it shows that our algorithm is more accurate for most image predictions except these pictures does not match subjective visual bringing lager errors.

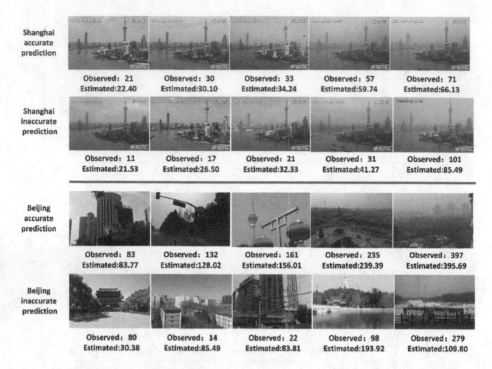

Fig. 9. Example images with their observed and estimated PM2.5

4   Conclusion

In this paper, we proposed a PMIE network that using residual block stacking with enhancement to estimate PM2.5 from images. Our main findings are that shallow CNN model and convolutional layer with enhancement provide better performance than typical deep CNN architecture. We also studied the performance for training and validating loss. The results on single scene Shanghai dataset and Non-single scene Beijing dataset outperforming the state-of-the-art.

Acknowledgement. The work in this paper is support by National Natural Science Foundation of China (No. 41601353), Shaanxi Provincial Natural Science Research Project (2017KW-010) and Shaanxi Provincial Department of Education Science Research Project (15JK1689).

References

1. Chow, J., et al.: Health effects of fine particulate air pollution: lines that connect. Air Repair **56**(6), 709 (2006)
2. Mcginnis, J.M., Foege, W.H.: Actual causes of death in the United States. JAMA, J. Am. Med. Assoc. **291**(10), 1238–1245 (1993)

3. Li, Y., Huang, J., Luo, J.: Using user generated online photos to estimate and monitor air pollution in major cities. In: International Conference on Internet Multimedia Computing and Service (2015)
4. Mao, J.: Detecting foggy images and estimating the haze degree factor. J. Comput. Sci. Syst. Biol. **7**(6), 1 (2014)
5. Liu, C., et al.: Particle pollution estimation based on image analysis. PLoS ONE **11**(2), e0145955 (2016)
6. Zhang, C., et al.: On estimating air pollution from photos using convolutional neural network. In: ACM on Multimedia Conference (2016)
7. Chakma, A., Vizena, B., Cao, T., Lin, J., Zhang, J.: Image-based air quality analysis using deep convolutional neural network. In: IEEE International Conference on Image Processing (2017)
8. Bo, Q., Yang, W., Rijal, N., Xie, Y., Feng, J., Zhang, J.: Particle pollution estimation from images using convolutional neural network and weather feature. In: IEEE International Conference on Image Processing (2018)
9. Shelhamer, E., Long, J., Darrell, T.: Fully convolutional networks for semantic segmentation. IEEE Trans. Pattern Anal. Mach. Intell. **39**(4), 640–651 (2014)
10. Szegedy, C., et al.: Rethinking the inception architecture for computer vision, pp. 2818–2826 (2015). Computer Science
11. He, K., et al.: Deep residual learning for image recognition, pp. 770–778 (2015)
12. Andrychowicz, M., Kurach, K.: Learning efficient algorithms with hierarchical attentive memory (2016)
13. Vaswani, A., et al.: Attention is all you need (2017)
14. https://goo.gl/F1tkM4

Fully CapsNet for Semantic Segmentation

Su Li, Xiangyu Ren, and Lu Yang[✉]

School of Automation Engineering,
University of Electronic Science and Technology of China, Chengdu 611731, China
yanglu@uestc.edu.cn

Abstract. Fully convolutional networks (FCNs) are powerful models for semantic segmentation. But convolutional networks fail to perform well in recognizing and parsing images with spatial variation. In this paper, a novel Capsule network called Fully CapsNet is proposed. We introduce Capsule to FCN and improve Equivariance of the neural network in image segmentation. Compared with traditional FCN based networks, a trained Fully CapsNet shows robustness in recognizing image pixels with more or less spatial variation. Each capsule layer is connected by dynamic routing algorithm. The effectiveness of the proposed model is verified through PASCAL VOC. Results show that Fully CapsNet outperforms the FCN in understanding both original images and rotated images.

Keywords: Fully convolutional network · Semantic segmentation
Capsule network · PASCAL VOC

1 Introduction

Image segmentation is one of the main research field in image processing. Semantic segmentation can understand images at pixel level. Image semantic segmentation can be regarded as the gist of image understanding which plays an important role in many applications. For example, street view recognition in robot guiding system [17], determination of landing site of UAV [6] and wearable device application [9] etc.

The idea of semantic segmentation has been raised before deep learning is popularized. Many semantic algorithms such as Thresholding methods [7], Clustering-based segmentation methods [16] and Graph partitioning segmentation methods [11,14] have been proposed in computer vision. The work of semantic segmentation at that time was to segment the image according to low-level visual cues. For instance, abstracting images to the form of graphs and then achieve semantic segmentation on the basis of Graph theory. Other methods require supporting information such as bounding box and scribbled lines. These algorithms perform poorly when applied to complex images without enough supporting information. Semantic segmentation algorithms attracted growing research interests as deep learning popularized. Fully convolutional networks (FCN) [10,13] and deep convolutional Nets [2–4] for semantic segmentation are

© Springer Nature Switzerland AG 2018
J.-H. Lai et al. (Eds.): PRCV 2018, LNCS 11257, pp. 392–403, 2018.
https://doi.org/10.1007/978-3-030-03335-4_34

widely employed by deep learning based approaches. Key observation of FCN is that the fully connected layers in classification networks can be viewed as convolutions with kernels that cover their entire input regions. Feature maps still need to be upsampled because of pooling operations in CNNs. Instead of using simple bilinear interpolation, deconvolutional layers can learn the interpolation by themselves. However, information of images losses because of pooling layers. Therefore, skip connections are introduced to address this problem from higher resolution feature maps [13].

One of the main drawbacks of convolutional networks is their lacking in 'comprehension' to images. Human vision builds up coordinate frames when recognizing images. Coordinate frames effect the way human observe images through comprehension to space. However, coordinate frame does not exist in convolutional networks. A novel neuron structure called 'Capsule' proposed by Hinton in [12] manages to solve this problem. Hinton et al. believes that the relationship between objects and observers (e.g. pose of objects) should be described by a set of neurons instead of a single neuron. Priori knowledge of coordinate frames can then be expressed effectively. This set of neuron in general is called 'Capsule'. Furthermore, Capsule network offers equivariant mapping, which means that both location information and pose information of objects can be reserved. Routing tree in Capsule networks maps the partial hierarchy of the target, therefore each part is assigned to a whole. In summary, Capsule network is robust to rotation, translation and other forms of transformations.

In this paper, we managed to leverage both FCN and Capsule network and proposed a novel neural network called Fully CapsNet. To our best knowledge, this is the first work to modify neural structure in FCN with Capsule for semantic segmentation. Fully CapsNet introduces the principle of capsule to Fully convolutional network. It adds several capsule layers and linked each layer by *dynamic routing algorithm* [12]. Fully CapsNet improves the robustness of convolutional network to pose transformation of objects as well as accuracy in semantic segmentation.

The rest of this paper is organized as follows: Related literatures for the construction of our model are introduced in Sect. 2. In Sect. 3, details of the proposed work is demonstrated and reviewed. The network structure of Fully CapsNet is presented in Sect. 4. Comparison experiments are demonstrated and discussed in Sect. 5. Segmentation results are evaluated on PASCAL VOC where Fully CapsNet will show the significant outperformance compared to the original FCN.

2   Related Work

2.1   Deconvolutional Network

Deconvolutional network is first proposed by Zeiler et al. in [18], which is a framework that permits the unsupervised construction of hierarchical image representations. Compared with CNN, which obtain feature map from input images convoluted by feature filter, deconvolutional network restores input images through feature map convoluting feature filter. For each input image x, there are several feature z to represent its latent features, and feature filters F can be obtained through learning the given images $X = \{x^1, x^2, \ldots, x^N\}$. The trained filters can be then used to infer the feature map when a new image is given.

The input of the first layer of deconvolutional network is the original image and the output is the feature map z^1 extracted from the input image. The rest of the layers has an input of the previous layer's output feature map z^{L-1} and an output of feature map z^L. Several cost functions are introduced to optimize the parameters F and z. To learn the parameters in filters, deconvolutional network alternately minimizes cost functions over the feature maps while keeping the filters fixed (i.e. perform inference). The trained filters can be then used to infer the feature map when a new image is given.

Deconvolutional network is a powerful tool for mid and high level feature learning. Visualization and understanding of each feature map obtained from convolutional layers can be achieved through deconvolution.

2.2 VGG

VGG is a convolutional neural network model proposed by Simonyan et al. in [15]. VGG is made up a concise structure. There are 5 convolutional layers, 3 fully connected layers and a softmax output layer. Each layer is separated by a max-pooling layer and the activation unit of the hidden layer adopts ReLu function. In this paper a VGG-16 structure is adopted. VGG-16 contains 16 layers in the framework in total. Small-scale kernel function is one of the main feature of VGG. Convolutional layers in VGG consist of several small-scale kernel functions (3×3), where kernel functions in other structure such as AlexNet [8] are bigger in size (7×7). On the one hand, the amount of parameters can be reduced by bringing down the size of kernel functions. On the other hand, more nonlinear mapping can be carried out, which can increase the fitting and expressing ability of the network.

Our work is similar to [5] in the sense that an architectural change to layers is proposed. The authors propose to modify several layers in VGG.16 to formulating them as CapsNets, creating a new class of FCN, called Fully CapsNet. The idea can be extended to other forms of FCNs.

3   Preliminaries

3.1 Fully Convolutional Network

FCN is proposed by Long et al. in [13]. It replaces the fully connected layers with several convolutional layers. A net with only layers of convolutional layers computes a nonlinear filter is called fully convolutional network. Each layer of data in a convolutional network is a three-dimensional array of size $h \times w \times d$, where h and w are spatial dimensions, and d is the feature or channel dimension. The first layer is the input image, with pixel size $h \times w$, and d color channels.

Locations in higher layers correspond to the locations in the image they are
path-connected to, which are called their receptive fields. Writing x_{ij} for the
data vector at location (i, j) in a particular layer, and y_{ij} for the following layer,
these functions compute outputs y_{ij} by

$$y_{ij} = f_{ks}(\{x_{si+\delta}\}) \tag{1}$$

where k is called the kernel size, s is the stride, and f_{ks} determines the layer
type. This functional form is maintained under composition, with kernel size and
stride obeying the transformation rule:

$$f_{ks} \cdot g_{k's'} = (f \cdot g)_{k'+(k-1)s', ss'} \tag{2}$$

A real-valued loss function composed with an FCN defines a task. If the loss func-
tion is a sum over the spatial dimensions of the final layer, $l(x; \theta) = \Sigma_{ij} l'(x_{ij}; \theta)$,
its gradient will be a sum over the gradients of each of its spatial components.
Thus stochastic gradient descent on l computed on whole images will be the
same as stochastic gradient descent on l', taking all of the final layer receptive
fields as a minibatch. In order to obtain the original size of image, an upsampling layer or deconvolutional layer is applied in FCN. It simply reverses the
forward and backward passes of convolution. However, upsampling produces
coarse segmentation maps because of loss of information during pooling. Thus,
skip architecture is introduced to FCN. A skip architecture is learned end-to-
end to refine the semantics and spatial precision of the output. In addition, FCN
ignores spatial regularization procedure which is normally used in pixel-level
segmentation. Researches have been done regarding to these problems, such as
RFCN [5], ResNet, GoogLeNets [1] etc.

3.2   Capsule Networks

Capsules are locally invariant groups of neurons that learn to recognize the
presence of visual entities and encode their properties into vector outputs, with
the vector length (limited to $[0, 1]$) representing the presence of the entity. To
achieve the limitation of the vector length, a squashing function (Eq. 3) is used.

$$v_j = \frac{||s_j||^2}{1 + ||s_j||^2} \frac{s_j}{||s_j||} \tag{3}$$

where v_j is the vector output of capsule j and s_j is its total input.

Each capsule can learn to identify certain objects or object-parts in images.
Within the framework of neural networks, several capsules can be grouped
together to form a capsule-layer where each unit produces a vector output instead
of a scalar activation.

Sabour et al. introduced a routing-by-agreement mechanism in [12] for the
interaction of capsules within deep neural networks with several capsule-layers,
which works by pairwise determination of the passage of information between
capsules in successive layers. For each capsule h_i^l in layer l and each capsule

$h_j^{(l+1)}$ in the layer above, a coupling coefficient c_{ij} is adjusted iteratively based on the agreement (cosine similarity) between h_i's prediction of the output of h_j and its actual output given the product of c_{ij} and h_i's activation:

$$S_j = \sum_i c_{ij}\hat{u}_{j|i}, \quad \hat{u}_{j|i} = W_{ij}u_i \tag{4}$$

where $\hat{u}_{ij}$ is the prediction vector of all the capsule below, u_i is the output of one capsule and W_{ij} is a weight matrix.

The coupling coefficients c_{ij} inherently decide how information flows between pairs of capsules. Sabour et al. proposed a *routing softmax* which enables the coupling coefficients between capsules in layer i and above sum up to 1. The initial logits b_{ij} of coupling coefficients are the log prior probabilities that capsule i should be coupled to capsule j:

$$c_{ij} = \frac{\exp(b_{ij})}{\sum_k \exp(b_{ik})} \tag{5}$$

For a classification task involving K classes, the final layer of the CapsNet can be designed to have K capsules, each representing one class. Since the length of a capsule's vector output represents the presence of a visual entity, the length of each capsule in the final layer can then be viewed as the probability of the image belonging to a particular class. The algorithm is shown in Procedure 1 [12].

Procedure 1. ROUTING ALGORITHM

1: Routing $(\hat{u}_{j|i}, r, l)$
2: for all capsule i in layer l and capsule j in layer $l+1$: $b_{ij} \leftarrow 0$
3: **for** r iterations **do**
4:     for all capsule i in layer l: $c_i \leftarrow \text{softmax}(b_i)$
5:     for all capsule j in layer $l+1$: $s_j \leftarrow \sum_i c_{ij}\hat{u}_{j|i}$
6:     for all capsule j in layer $l+1$: $v_j \leftarrow \text{squash}(s_j)$
7:     for all capsule i in layer l and capsule j in layer $l+1$: $b_{ij} \leftarrow b_{ij} + \hat{u}_{j|i} \times v_j$
8:     **return**
9: **end for**

---

4   Fully CapsNet

Capsule network is essentially parallel attention network. Each capsule layer focuses on linking to the capsules in next layer, which are more active to the information extracted in the previous capsule layer and then ignore those inactive capsules. The idea of capsule is more close to that how human react to information processing: information processing between neurons are vector instead of scale. For example, CNNs have the ability to recognize a human face with all facial features, even they are not in their correct position. This is because the pooling layers in CNNs simply learn each of these features separately abandoning the spatial connection among them. Capsule, however, builds a feature group containing both features and their spatial connections. Thus, CapsNet would not recognize it a human face if the facial features are not in the correct order. The transition of information between capsules is conducted by *dynamic routing*. On the basis of discussion above, the idea of Capsule Network and its routing algorithm (*dynamic routing*) is applied in our model.

4.1   Construction of Fully CapsNet

Fully CapsNet is similar in structure to the FCN model in general. A traditional FCN structure *VGG-16* is selected as the feature extractor of Fully CapsNet. *VGG-16* is a mature and widely used Convolutional Neural Network structure and the original FCN is proposed based on it. Then we modified the output layer of *VGG-16*. Instead of upsampling directly with the output of last convolutional layer, several capsule layers are added after them. Firstly, the feature map from conv.6 is transformed into the form of a vector. Information of the map is extracted by dynamic routing method and capsules in each layer are activated according to Margin Loss function. Finally, upsampling (or deconvolution) method is used. Deconvolution helps to restore the size of initial image. The *Skip* structure in FCN is also applied in Fully CapsNet in order to fine-tune the output results. It learns to combine coarse, high layer information with fine, low layer information. A demonstration for the architecture of Fully CapsNet is shown in Fig. 1.

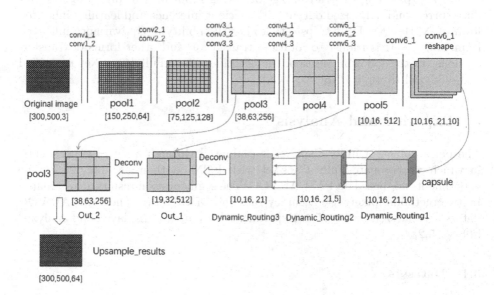

Fig. 1. Framework of fully CapsNet

The whole process can be simplified to several progress: Feature extraction $\rightarrow$ dynamic routing $\rightarrow$ upsampling, or Encoder $\rightarrow$ Decoder process.

It is noticeable in Fig. 1 that the size of the featured map in the $con6_1$ *reshape* stage increased by one dimension. The purpose of reshaping the size is aimed at preparing for the introduction of Capsule structure.

4.2   Modification on Routing Algorithm

The Dynamic routing algorithm is fully connected in every pixel. In other word, it requires adequate storage in computers to store data and powerful abilities for calculation, which is hardly achievable for general users. Thus, we modified the routing algorithm through a *partial connection method*. For example, given a image with the size 20×30, the original dynamic routing algorithm requires a $20 \times 30 \times 20 \times 30$ (360000 in total) space to store the weighting value between each pixel, which can be space consuming when the size of input images increase. As for partial connection method, which splits the original image into 150 (10×15) small images of size 2×2. Therefore, the space required is reduced to $10 \times 15 \times 2 \times 2 \times 2 \times 2$ (2400 in total). What's more, in order to reduce the storage space for calculations required by Capsule Network the dynamic routing algorithm is applied only on image data in higher layers, such as data in con6 layers. The data in higher layers are the feature maps extracted from lower layers, which contain essential information that represent the nature of the input images. In this way, the adjusted routing algorithm largely cuts down the usage of storage and calculation complexity.

Fully CapsNet has the advantage of taking input of arbitrary size and produce correspondingly-sized output with efficient inference and learning inherited form FCN. Besides, Fully CapsNet also has the ability of equivariance inherited from Capsule. It is robust to rotation, translation and other forms of transformations. In the following section, the effectiveness of Fully CapsNet is verified and analyzed through PASCAL VOC.

5   Experimental Analysis

The performance of Fully CapsNet is evaluated through a set of experiments, in which we compare Fully CapsNet with FCN on their accuracy rate. The experiments are based on PASCAL VOC. The segmentation results are evaluated by two methods: pixel-wise accuracy rate and MAP value. The PASCAL VOC dataset is analyzed in Sect. 5.1. Experimental results are displayed and analyzed in Sect. 5.2.

5.1   Datasets

A major part in computer vision is about object recognition, detection and classification, which are fundamental functions in application field. Therefore, the correctness and efficiency of an algorithm is verified through whether or not these three functions can be completed. Large quantities of images are then collected by researchers to be applied to their algorithms. PASCAL VOC Challenge is a platform where algorithms are contrasted based on the same data set. PASCAL VOC provides adequate standardized image data sets for pixel-wise scene understanding as well as a common set of tools for accessing the data sets and annotations. There are twenty object classes in PASCAL VOC and are divided into four categories: Person, Animal, Vehicle and Indoor objects. In this paper PASCAL VOC 2012 is selected for semantic segmentation. Figures 2 and 3 shows the original images and their groundtruth segmentation results obtained from PASCAL VOC 2012.

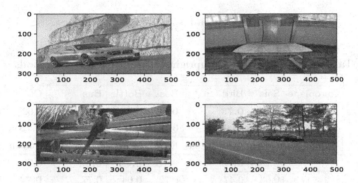

Fig. 2. Original images

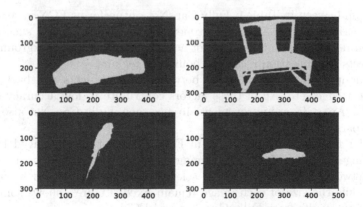

Fig. 3. Groundtruth

5.2 Segmentation Results and Analysis

The authors qualitatively compare images generated randomly using both Fully Convolutional Network and Fully CapsNet. Figure 4 shows segmentation results of a image by the two algorithms, where the first column is the groundtruth and the second and third column are segmentation results generated by Fully

CapsNet and Fully Convolutional Network respectively. Obviously, Fully CapsNet's segmentation results outperforms initial Fully Convolutional Network's. The accuracy rate of the segmentation results of other objects are shown in Table 1.

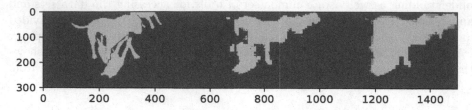

Fig. 4. Segmentation results of original images

Table 1. Accuracy rate of upright images by the two methods

Object	Aeroplane	Sofa	Bird	Boat	Bottle	Bus	Car	Cat
Fully caps	**0.88**	**0.62**	**0.73**	**0.68**	0.48	**0.91**	0.62	**0.86**
FCN	0.77	0.37	0.69	0.49	**0.60**	0.75	**0.75**	0.78

Object	Chair	Cow	Diningtable	Dog	Horse	Motorbike	Person	Sheep
Fully caps	0.35	**0.94**	**0.55**	**0.79**	**0.79**	**0.80**	0.70	**0.88**
FCN	0.21	0.63	0.47	0.72	0.64	0.77	**0.74**	0.72

As it can be seen in Table 1, Fully CapsNet outperforms FCN in segmenting normal position images. Although segmentation of some objects such as chair (colored in red) and dining table is not accurate because the background of the image effects segmentation results in boundary regions.

For example, similar color exists between target objects and backgrounds, fuzzy object edges etc. All of these factors contribute to low accuracy segmentation rate. Apart from improvements in accuracy, Fully CapsNet also has the ability in parsing rotated images.

In order to show 'Equivariance' in Fully CapsNet, we managed to rotate several images obtained from the training set and then set them as input of the trained network. The objects in the selected images are rotated by 5, 10, 15 and 20° while the size of each image remain fixed. Figure 5 shows some of the segmentation results from Fully CapsNet and FCN.

In Fig. 5, the first column of each image shows the ground truth, the second column shows segmentation results from Fully CapsNet and the third column shows segmentation results from FCN. It is obvious that Fully CapsNet shows better equivariance compared with FCN when the pose of objects varies to a small extent. Take Fig. 5(a) as an example, Fully CapsNet can segment the edge of the target object while FCN performs badly in segmenting the edges as well as classifying the target objects. Experiments with more degree of rotation of the objects are carried out and the results are shown in Table 2.

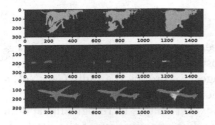

(a) Results with 5 degree rotation

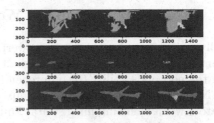

(b) Results with 10 degree rotation

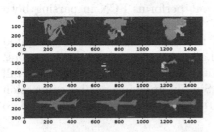

(c) Results with 15 degree rotation

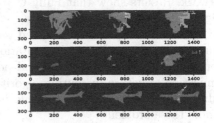

(d) Results with 20 degree rotation

Fig. 5. Results with different rotation degree

Table 2. Segmentation results of rotated objects

Fully CapsNet	Aeroplane	Bicycle	Bird	Boat	Bottle	Bus	Car	Cat
5	0.85	0.37	0.71	0.66	0.44	0.89	0.60	0.86
10	0.84	0.34	0.71	0.62	0.43	0.88	0.56	0.85
15	0.83	0.34	0.69	0.61	0.42	0.87	0.57	0.85
20	0.80	0.34	0.67	0.59	0.43	0.83	0.54	0.85
FCN	Aeroplane	Bicycle	Bird	Boat	Bottle	Bus	Car	Cat
5	0.75	0.24	0.62	0.59	0.39	0.84	0.53	0.76
10	0.73	0.24	0.60	0.57	0.38	0.82	0.53	0.77
15	0.73	0.23	0.60	0.53	0.34	0.79	0.51	0.75
20	0.70	0.22	0.60	0.48	0.33	0.76	0.48	0.74
Fully CapsNet	Cow	Diningtable	Dog	Horse	Motorbike	Person	Train	Sheep
5	0.94	0.54	0.78	0.78	0.79	0.67	0.90	0.87
10	0.90	0.51	0.79	0.78	0.78	0.66	0.88	0.84
15	0.90	0.48	0.77	0.74	0.77	0.64	0.85	0.85
20	0.86	0.49	0.75	0.73	0.75	0.62	0.80	0.83
FCN	Cow	Diningtable	Dog	Horse	Motorbike	Person	Train	Sheep
5	0.80	0.50	0.82	0.75	0.73	0.63	0.82	0.77
10	0.80	0.47	0.79	0.73	0.72	0.61	0.80	0.73
15	0.78	0.42	0.77	0.72	0.71	0.58	0.79	0.76
20	0.76	0.40	0.74	0.70	0.68	0.55	0.75	0.73

6   Discussion and Future Work

Fully convolutional networks are powerful deep learning models for semantic segmentation. Motivated by the success of Capsule network over CNNs at improving the network's ability to comprehend images, we proposed a Fully CapsNet, a FCN framework but incorporates Capsule network instead of CNNs as discriminators when modeling image data. Fully CapsNet adapts to recognizing spatial transformation of objects in trained images. The effectiveness of the model is verified through PASCAL VOC and compared with original Fully convolutional network. Results show that Fully CapsNet out performs FCN in parsing both original images and rotated images.

However, the proposed method shows robustness in recognizing rotated images only to a small extent of rotation. In addition, Capsule network requires tremendous space to store data and powerful calculating ability due to its full connection structure in routing algorithm. Simply applying partial connection reduces the performance of Capsule network. Further research works need to handle these problems.

Acknowledgement. This research was supported by NSFC (No. 61871074) and Fundamental Research Funds for the Central Universities (ZYGX2018J064).

References

1. Ballester, P., Araujo, R.M.: On the performance of GoogLeNet and AlexNet applied to sketches. In: Thirtieth AAAI Conference on Artificial Intelligence, pp. 1124–1128 (2016)
2. Branson, S., Horn, G.V., Belongie, S., Perona, P.: Bird species categorization using pose normalized deep convolutional nets. eprint Arxiv (2014)
3. Chatfield, K., Simonyan, K., Vedaldi, A., Zisserman, A.: Return of the devil in the details: delving deep into convolutional nets. Computer Science (2014)
4. Chen, L.C., Papandreou, G., Kokkinos, I., Murphy, K., Yuille, A.L.: DeepLab: semantic image segmentation with deep convolutional nets, atrous convolution, and fully connected CRFs. IEEE Trans. Pattern Anal. Mach. Intell. **40**(4), 834–848 (2018)
5. Dai, J., Li, Y., He, K., Sun, J.: R-FCN: object detection via region-based fully convolutional networks. In: Advances in Neural Information Processing Systems, pp. 379–387 (2016)
6. Fitzgerald, D.L.: Landing site selection for UAV forced landings using machine vision. Unmanned Arial Vehicle (2007)
7. Han, S.Q., Wang, L.: A survey of thresholding methods for image segmentation. Syst. Eng. Electron. **41**, 233–260 (2002)
8. Krizhevsky, A., Sutskever, I., Hinton, G.E.: ImageNet classification with deep convolutional neural networks. In: International Conference on Neural Information Processing Systems, pp. 1097–1105 (2012)
9. Lee, C.M., Schroder, K.E., Seibel, E.J.: Efficient image segmentation of walking hazards using IR illumination in wearable low vision. In: International Symposium on Wearable Computers, pp. 127–128 (2002)

10. Li, H., Qian, X., Li, W.: Image semantic segmentation based on fully convolutional neural network and CRF. In: Yuan, H., Geng, J., Bian, F. (eds.) GRMSE 2016. CCIS, vol. 698, pp. 245–250. Springer, Singapore (2017). https://doi.org/10.1007/978-981-10-3966-9_27
11. Rother, C., Kolmogorov, V., Blake, A.: "GrabCut": interactive foreground extraction using iterated graph cuts. In: ACM SIGGRAPH, pp. 309–314 (2004)
12. Sabour, S., Frosst, N., Hinton, G.E.: Dynamic routing between capsules. In: Advances in Neural Information Processing Systems, pp. 3859–3869 (2017)
13. Shelhamer, E., Long, J., Darrell, T.: Fully convolutional networks for semantic segmentation. IEEE Trans. Pattern Anal. Mach. Intell. **39**(4), 640–651 (2014)
14. Shi, J., Malik, J.: Normalized Cuts and Image Segmentation. IEEE Computer Society (2000)
15. Simonyan, K., Zisserman, A.: Very deep convolutional networks for large-scale image recognition. Computer Science (2014)
16. Wang, S.L., Cao, A.J., Chen, C., Wang, R.Y.: A comparative study on fuzzy-clustering-based lip region segmentation methods. Commun. Comput. Inf. Sci. **234**, 376–381 (2011)
17. Wong, Y.W., Tang, L., Bailey, D.: Vision system for a robot guide system. In: Fourth International Conference on Computational Intelligence, Robotics and Autonomous Systems, pp. 337–341 (2007)
18. Zeiler, M.D., Krishnan, D., Taylor, G.W., Fergus, R.: Deconvolutional networks. In: Computer Vision and Pattern Recognition, pp. 2528–2535 (2010)

DeepCoast: Quantifying Seagrass Distribution in Coastal Water Through Deep Capsule Networks

Daniel Pérez[1]([✉]) [iD], Kazi Islam[2] [iD], Victoria Hill[3] [iD], Richard Zimmerman[3] [iD], Blake Schaeffer[4] [iD], and Jiang Li[2] [iD]

[1] Department of Modeling, Simulation and Visualization Engineering, Old Dominion University, Norfolk, VA 23508, USA
dpere013@odu.edu

[2] Department of Electrical and Computer Engineering, Old Dominion University, Norfolk, VA 23508, USA
{kisla001,jli}@odu.edu

[3] Department of Earth and Atmospheric Sciences, Old Dominion University, Norfolk, VA 23508, USA
{vhill,rzimmerm}@odu.edu

[4] Office of Research and Development, U.S. Environmental Protection Agency, Corvallis, USA
schaeffer.blake@epa.gov

Abstract. Seagrass is a highly valuable component of coastal ecosystems ecologically and economically, yet reliable mapping of seagrass density is not available due to the high cost of data processing and spatial mapping. This paper presents a deep learning approach for quantification of leaf area index (LAI) levels of seagrass in coastal water using high resolution multispectral satellite images. Specifically, a deep capsule network (DCN) is developed for simultaneous classification and quantification of seagrass based on the multispectral images. The DCN is jointly optimized for classification and regression, and is capable of performing end-to-end seagrass quantification. We separately validated the proposed method on three images taken in Florida coastal area and achieved better results with DCN when compared against a deep convolutional neural network (CNN) model and a linear regression model. In addition, transfer learning strategies are developed to transfer knowledge in a DCN trained at one location for seagrass quantification to different locations with minimum field observations, which saves a significant amount of time and resources in the mapping of seagrass LAI. Our experimental results show that the developed capsule network achieved superb performances

This work was realized by a student and supported by NASA under Grant NNX17AH01G. Subjected to review by the National Exposure Research Laboratory and approved for publication. Mention of trade names or commercial products does not constitute endorsement or recommendation for use by the U.S. Government. The views expressed in this article are those of the authors and do not necessarily reflect the views or policies of the U.S. Environmental Protection Agency.

© Springer Nature Switzerland AG 2018
J.-H. Lai et al. (Eds.): PRCV 2018, LNCS 11257, pp. 404–416, 2018.
https://doi.org/10.1007/978-3-030-03335-4_35

in few-shot transfer learning as compared to direct linear regression and traditional CNN models.

Keywords: Seagrass quantification · Deep learning
Convolutional neural networks · Capsule networks · Transfer learning

1   Introduction

Seagrass is an important ecological, economic and social well-being component of coastal ecosystems [5,19]. Ecologically, seagrass provides multiple benefits such as pollution filtering, sediment trapping or organic fertilization. Economically, seagrass ecosystems are considered 23 and 33 times more valuable than terrestrial and oceanic ecosystems respectively [19]. However, reliable information about the distribution of seagrass is not tracked in most parts of the world due to the high cost of comprehensive mapping [19]. In this paper, we propose a deep learning model for the detection of seagrass in a given area based on multispectral images taken from operational satellite remote sensing platforms. The developed method can quantify the leaf area index (LAI) for each valid pixel within a scene. LAI is defined as leaf area per square area [2], and it is considered one of the most important biophysical components of seagrass [19].

The goal of this project is to develop a model that is able to quantify LAI from high resolution satellite imagery with limited field observations that may be ubiquitously applied to other localities. To achieve this goal, the following two questions need to be answered: (1) Do the satellite multispectral images contain enough information for a machine learning model to learn and quantify LAI in the same region? (2) Can a machine learning model trained at one location be generalized to other locations for LAI mapping?

To answer the first question, we utilize high resolution multispectral images taken by the Worldview-2 (WV-2) satellite with a resolution of 1.24 m in the 8 visible and near infrared (VNIR) bands to train a deep capsule network (DCN) for LAI quantification. Historically, an experienced operator labeled the image as four different classes (sea, sand, seagrass and land) and applied a physics model [6] in the seagrass region to map LAI. The physics model has a known error rate of 10% [6], so not all the labeled regions are suitable to train machine learning models. Therefore, an experienced operator selected the most confident regions in the images to train the DCN. To answer the second question, we train a DCN at one location using the multispectral images and develop transfer learning strategies to adapt the trained model to new locations for LAI quantification. The key contributions of this paper are: (1) an innovative deep capsule network that performs classification and regression simultaneously to achieve end-to-end seagrass quantification, and (2) the first attempt to apply transfer learning to DCN for satellite derived seagrass quantification at different locations.

The deep capsule network is jointly optimized for classification and regression so that it is capable of performing end-to-end seagrass quantification. In addition, transfer learning strategies are developed to adapt a deep capsule network trained at one location for seagrass quantification at different locations. To the best of our knowledge, we are among the first to apply capsule network for seagrass mapping in the remote sensing community. The remainder of the paper reviews the literature in Sect. 2, describes the proposed methods in Sect. 3, presents (in Sect. 4) and discusses (in Sect. 5) the experimental results, and finally concludes the paper in Sect. 6.

2 Related Work

2.1 Deep Learning

Deep learning has been successful in numerous fields such as image classification [10], speech recognition [7], medical imaging [15], cybersecurity [3,11] and remote sensing [12,14]. Among different deep learning models, deep Convolutional Neural Networks (CNNs) are currently popular for various applications. A CNN consists of a set of convolutional layers followed by several fully connected layers. The convolutional layers learn effective representations for the raw data and the fully connected layers perform classification or regression based on the learned representations. Many CNN based image classification systems can perform an end-to-end learning in which feature extraction (representation learning) is jointly optimized with classification, and it is believed that this automatic feature learning process plays a critical role to achieve the superb performances of CNNs.

2.2 Capsule Networks

Capsule networks are a promising deep learning method recently introduced by Sabour *et al.* [17]. A capsule is a group of neurons that represents the instantiation parameters of an entity in the input image, while the length of the capsule represents the posterior probability that the entity exists in the input image. The capsule network obtained a 99.75% accuracy on the MNIST dataset, which, at the time of writing, represents state-of-the-art. Additionally, the network has shown promising results on the classification of overlapping images. An improved version of the capsule network was just released by the same research group that achieved the state-of-the-art result on the smallNORB benchmark dataset [8].

An interesting characteristic of the capsule network is that it can reconstruct an input image by using the outputs of the capsule vectors. The last layer of the capsule network consists of a set of capsule vectors, each of them corresponding to one class in the dataset. During training, the capsule vector corresponding to the training label of the image is used to reconstruct the input image as a regularization for the optimization. The error between the reconstructed image and the input image is then used to optimize both the reconstruction weights and the weights in the capsule network through back propagation. It has been shown that the reconstruction part is a significant contributor to the overall excellent performance on the MNIST dataset.

There are a few recent works on the capsule network in the literature. Xi *et al.* [20] investigated the application of capsule networks on the classification of the CIFAR-10 dataset. The best accuracy they obtained was 71.55%, which is far from the state-of-the-art (96.53%). In addition, it was demonstrated that the reconstruction network did not perform well when applied to a high-dimensional image. In our companion paper [9], a capsule network was designed as a generative model to adapt a trained capsule model to new locations for seagrass identification. To the best of our knowledge, we are the first to design a capsule network for seagrass quantification.

2.3 Seagrass LAI Mapping

The majority of the studies of seagrass mapping focus on assessing the accuracy of manually mapping methods [16,18]. Yang *et al.* [21] manually computed the distribution of seagrass from satellite images using a remote sensing method. They obtained an accuracy slightly better than 80%. However, their approach only determined whether seagrass was found in a region instead of quantifying the LAI index. An automatic algorithm for seagrass LAI mapping was implemented by Wicaksono *et al.* [19]. In this case, they provided regression results and obtained a best standard error of estimates of 0.72.

2.4 Transfer Learning

Transfer learning is a technique that consists of using a model that has gained knowledge from one domain to solve problems in different but similar domains where training data is limited [13]. One of the first successful attempts to use transfer learning in deep learning was reported in DeCaf [4], in which Donahouse *et al.* investigated the problem of generalizing a CNN trained on ImageNet [10] for other problem domains. Their transfered model outperformed the state-of-the-art by extracting features directly from the trained CNN and training a simple classifier on the features for classification. A different approach was carried out by Yosinki *et al.* [22]. In the study, they tested whether or not the features learned by a 8-layer CNN with one dataset could be applied to another dataset. To achieve this goal, they froze the first few layers in the model and retrained the remaining layers on the new database. Their experiments demonstrated that fine-tuning the whole network obtained the best accuracy. Banerjee *et al.* [1] showed how transfer learning with deep belief network (DBN) can be utilized to improve diagnosis of post-traumatic stress disorder (PTSD).

3 Methodology

3.1 Datasets

We collected three different multispectral images captured by the Worldview-2 (WV-2) satellite in Florida coastal areas. For each image, pixels were classified into four classes (sea, land, seagrass and sand) and LAI mappings for seagrass pixels were computed by the physics model [6].

3.2   Data Labeling

In the original physics model, not all pixels were validated with field observations for LAI quantification. Comparison of coincident field observations and satellite pixels demonstrated there was a 10% error rate in the LAI mapping [6]. Therefore, the LAI mapping was not treated as ground truth for model training. However, there were certain regions in the satellite images where the mappings were more reliable.

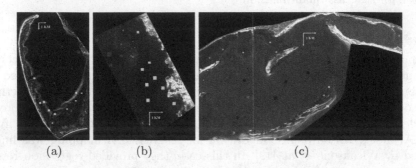

(a)   (b)   (c)

Fig. 1. Satellite images taken from Saint Joseph Bay on 11/10/2010 (a), Keeton Beach on 05/20/2010 (b) and Saint George Sound on 04/27/2012 (c). The blue, cyan, green and red boxes correspond to the selected regions for training belonging to sea, sand, seagrass and land, respectively. (Color figure online)

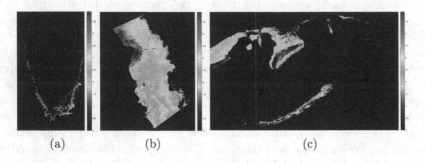

(a)   (b)   (c)

Fig. 2. LAI mappings of satellite images by the physics model [6] taken from Saint Joseph Bay on 11/10/2010 (a), Keeton Beach on 05/20/2010 (b) and Saint George Sound on 04/27/2012 (c). (Color figure online)

In this study, an experienced operator (a co-author of the physics model in [6]) selected several regions in each of the three images with highest confidence of the labeling and the LAI mapping. These regions have been identified as blue, cyan, green and red boxes, corresponding to sea, sand, seagrass and land respectively (Fig. 1). The LAI mapping is represented as a continuous color rainbow scale where blue is the minimum LAI index (0) and red is the maximum (Fig. 2). To ensure the reliability of quantification results, we trained our models only on those selected regions. We noticed that the datasets extracted from the selected regions were highly unbalanced, specially those obtained from Keeton Beach and St. George Sound. We balanced the datasets for training by upsampling or downsampling the classes in the data.

3.3 Joint Optimization of Classification and Regression in Capsule Networks

Figure 3 shows the structure of the capsule network that is designed for seagrass LAI mapping. The model needs to handle multispectral image patches with a size of $5 \times 5 \times 8$. The first convolutional layer in the capsule network has 32 kernels with a size of $2 \times 2 \times 8$ and a stride of 1. The *PrimaryCaps* layer has 8 blocks of $3 \times 3 \times 8$ capsules produced by 64 kernels of size $2 \times 2 \times 32$ in the second convolutional layer.

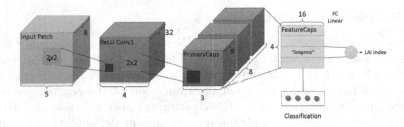

Fig. 3. Structure of the proposed capsule network for classification and regression of LAI.

The reconstruction block in the original capsule network [17] is redesigned as a linear regression model for LAI quantification based on the seagrass vector in the *FeatureCaps* layer. The LAI index of a patch is defined as the LAI index of the center pixel in the input patch. The structure in Fig. 3 enables us to jointly optimize classification and LAI regression. The *FeatureCaps* layer performs classification of the four classes (sea, land, seagrass and sand) with a separate margin loss as in [17].

When a seagrass patch is inputted during training, we mask out all but the seagrass vector in the *FeatureCaps* to regress its LAI. The mapping error is then back propagated to optimize all weights in the network, thus jointly optimizing classification and regression. For all other types of patches during training, the regression part is ignored. The number of routings in the DCN is set to 3.

3.4 Transfer Learning with Capsule Networks

The ultimate goal of this project is to develop a model that is able to quantify LAI from high resolution satellite imagery with limited field observations that may be ubiquitously applied to other locations, but the distribution of seagrass LAI at different locations shows a wide range of variation. It is difficult to collect enough ground truth data from each of the locations and train a machine learning model specific to the location. We propose a transfer learning approach using the features from the *FeatureCaps* layer to generalize the trained capsule network models to different locations with minimum information from the new locations. First, we train a capsule network with all the patches from the selected regions at St. Joseph Bay. Then, we select a few labeled patches from one of the other 2 images (Keeton Beach or St. George Sound), and pass those samples through the trained capsule network to retrieve all the 64 features from *FeatureCaps* as new representations for the patches. These labeled representations are then used to classify all other patches from Keeton Beach based on *1*-nearest neighbor (*1-NN*) rule. Separately, we extract the seagrass vector in the *FeatureCaps* (16 features) corresponding to the selected labeled seagrass patches and train a linear regression model to predict LAI. Finally, we predict LAI using the linear model for all patches that are classified as seagrass by the *1-NN* rule and set LAI as '0' for non seagrass patches.

3.5   Models for Comparison

For comparison purposes, we design a CNN with a similar complexity to the capsule network in representation learning. The CNN has 2 convolutional layers with $32 \ 2 \times 2$ and $16 \ 4 \times 4$ convolutional kernels, respectively. The fully connected layer has 16 hidden units to match the dimension of the seagrass vector in *FeatureCaps*. The last layer of the CNN performs linear regression to quantify LAI. We also implement a simple linear regression model applied to the image patch directly as the baseline method for comparison.

4   Experiments and Results

4.1   Model Structure Determination

We utilize the selected labeled regions in St. Joseph to determine parameters of the models. After cross-validation (CV) with different choices for the models, the patch size is set as $5 \times 5 \times 8$, the capsule network has two convolutional layers and contains 32 and 64 kernels, respectively. We make sure that the number of parameters for representation learning in both CNN and capsule network are roughly the same, having around 9k parameters and 17 parameters for linear LAI mapping in the last layer including the bias term.

It is worth to note that the capsule network has about 38k parameters in the capsule layers for routing, making the total number of parameters as 46k, which is approximately 5 times as that in CNN. Therefore, we decide to train the CNN for 5 times less than the capsule network. Specifically, we train the CNN for 10 epochs and the capsule network for 50 epochs.

4.2   Cross-Validation in Selected Regions

For each image, we perform a *3*-fold cross-validation (CV) in the selected regions where the classification and LAI mapping are more reliable. We compute the root mean squared errors (RMSEs) for comparison among different models. Table 1 shows that the capsule network produces the best results at the majority of the locations.

Table 1. *3*-fold CV results (RMSEs) on selected regions.

Image	Linear regression	CNN	Capsule network
St. Joseph Bay	0.58	0.48	**0.46**
Keeton Beach	0.16	0.11	**0.07**
St. George Sound	0.12	**0.11**	**0.11**
Mean	0.29	0.23	**0.21**

4.3 End-to-End LAI Mapping

We use all patches from the selected regions to train the capsule network for LAI mapping. During training, the capsule model first classifies a patch (with a size of $5 \times 5 \times 8$) as one of the four classes. It then maps seagrass patches to LAI index and non seagrass patches set to '0'. Therefore, the model performs end-to-end mapping by jointly optimizing classification and regression. The trained models are then applied to the whole images to produce LAI mappings.

To illustrate the effect of the end-to-end learning, we train the linear model and CNN with seagrass patches and non-seagrass patches (with LAI − 0) in the selected regions and show the full LAI mappings (Figs. 4, 5 and 6). Note that these Figures are shown here for visualization only because the physics model mapping should not be considered as ground truth. Only the accuracies computed in the selected regions (Table 1) should be used as performance metrics for model comparison.

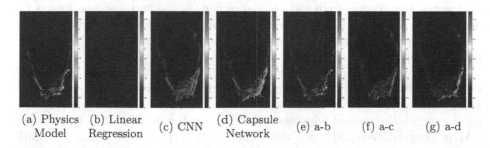

(a) Physics Model   (b) Linear Regression   (c) CNN   (d) Capsule Network   (e) a-b   (f) a-c   (g) a-d

Fig. 4. Mapping of LAI at St. Joseph Bay using a model trained on the patches from the selected regions.

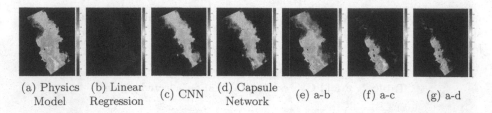

(a) Physics   (b) Linear   (c) CNN   (d) Capsule   (e) a-b   (f) a-c   (g) a-d
Model   Regression   Network

Fig. 5. Mapping of LAI at Keeton Beach using a model trained on the patches from the selected regions.

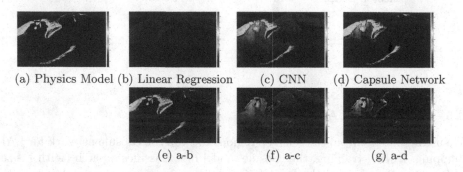

(a) Physics Model (b) Linear Regression   (c) CNN   (d) Capsule Network

(e) a-b   (f) a-c   (g) a-d

Fig. 6. Mapping of LAI at St. George Sound using a model trained on the patches from the selected regions.

4.4   Transfer Learning with Capsule Network

We train models using all patches in the selected regions at St. Joseph Bay and apply transfer learning at Keeton Beach and St. George Sound for LAI quantification. In transfer learning, the trained models are used as a feature extractor to convert all patches at the two locations as new representations (outputs of the layer just before the regression layer in capsule network or CNN). Then, we randomly sample 50, 100, 500 and 1,000 patches (roughly balanced among the four classes) from the selected regions at the two new locations, and use the sampled seagrass patches to train a linear model for LAI mapping using their new representations. We also fine-tune the whole model using the sampled patches to optimize the representation at new locations.

To apply the transferred models to the whole images at the two new locations, we first use the randomly sampled patches to classify a given patch to one of the four classes by the 1-nearest neighbor (1-NN) rule. If it is identified as a seagrass patch, we use the trained regression model to predict its LAI. Otherwise, a '0' LAI is assigned. We performed this experiment 5 times. Mean and standard deviation of accuracies of classification and LAI mapping in the selected regions are reported in Tables 2 and 3 respectively.

The classification results of capsule network are always superior to those by CNN in all the scenarios (Table 2). For LAI mapping, capsule network is always superior to CNN at Keeton Beach, it is either much better or comparable to CNN after fine-tuning at St. George Sound (Table 3).

Table 2. Classification accuracies by transfer learning with different number of samples from new locations. For each subsampling size, 5 experiments are conducted. Results are shown as *mean ± std*.

Model	Image	50 samples	100 samples	500 samples	1,000 samples
Capsule	Keeton Beach	**0.97 ± 0.009**	**0.98 ± 0.004**	**0.99 ± 0.002**	**0.99 ± 0.001**
	St George Sound	**0.93 ± 0.03**	**0.95 ± 0.02**	**0.98 ± 0.004**	**0.98 ± 0.004**
CNN	Keeton Beach	0.83 ± 0.03	0.88 ± 0.02	0.95 ± 0.01	0.96 ± 0.003
	St George Sound	0.81 ± 0.02	0.86 ± 0.02	0.93 ± 0.01	0.95 ± 0.001

Table 3. Regression errors (RMSE) by transfer learning and fine tuning with different number of subsamples from new locations. For each subsampling size, 5 experiments are conducted. Results are shown as *mean ± std*.

Method	Image	0 Samples	50 Samples Transfer Learning	50 Samples Fine Tuning	100 Samples Transfer Learning	100 Samples Fine Tuning	500 Samples Transfer Learning	500 Samples Fine Tuning	1,000 Samples Transfer Learning	1,000 Samples Fine Tuning
CNN	Keeton Beach	1.33	0.98±0.08	1.44±0.12	0.82±0.07	1.37±0.13	0.53±0.06	1.24±0.03	0.47±0.02	1.23±0.01
	St George Sound	0.66	0.32±0.05	0.46±0.01	0.29±0.02	0.47±0.01	0.26±0.02	0.30±0.02	0.22±0.01	0.31±0.04
Capsule	Keeton Beach	1.29	**0.44±0.05**	0.55±0.05	**0.35±0.04**	0.50±0.01	**0.27±0.01**	0.47±0.02	**0.25±0.02**	0.49±0.01
	St George Sound	1.11	0.45±0.11	**0.31±0.03**	0.39±0.09	**0.26±0.06**	0.28±0.03	**0.11±0.02**	0.26±0.03	**0.08±0.01**
Linear Regression	Keeton Beach	–	1.57±0.003		1.62±0.01		1.62±0.01		1.60±0.01	
	St George Sound	–	0.71±0.01		0.72±0.01		0.72±0.01		0.71±0.01	

4.5 Computational Complexity

All the experiments are conducted using a desktop computer with an Intel Xeon E5-2687W v3 @ 3.10 GHz (10 cores) and 64 GB RAM. On average, training the capsule network on the selected regions of one satellite image takes 85.39 s/epoch, whereas training the CNN model takes 13.17 s/epoch. Testing the capsule network on one entire image takes about 1.5 h, while testing CNN needs 0.42 h. Approximately, training and testing the capsule network takes 6.5 and 3.5 times longer as compared to CNN.

5   Discussions

The capsule network has proven to be the best deep learning model for seagrass distribution quantification in coastal water. The proposed model achieves LAI quantifications with a RMSE of 0.46, 0.07 and 0.11 at St. Joseph Bay, Keeton Beach and St. George Sound, respectively. On average, the RMSE is reduced by 0.02 with respect to the RMSE obtained by the convolutional neural network, and by 0.07 as compared to the linear model.

Note that all the three models use linear regression for LAI quantification. However, in both CNN and capsule network, seagrass LAI is quantified based on the new representations learned by the models. In contrast, the linear model directly uses pixel values in the multispectral image patch of size $5 \times 5 \times 8$ to quantify LAI. Both CNN and capsule network outperform the direct linear model, demonstrating that the learned representations by CNN and capsule network may contain more LAI related information and less noise to help the quantification. In addition, capsule network performs an end-to-end learning in which classification and regression are jointly optimized, which helps refine the representation learning process and achieves even better results than CNN.

The mappings of LAI index on whole images usually differ significantly from the mapping provided by the physics model. However, the physics model is not the ground truth and it is shown in the paper for visualization only. To compare the effectiveness of different models, we should focus on the RMSE obtained in the selected regions only as shown in Tables 1, 2 and 3. As a part of the project plan, more on-site validation will be conducted and the data obtained will be used as ground truth for model evaluation.

The seagrass vector in the new representations learned by the capsule network is supposed to represent properties of seagrass patches so that these cleaned representations are more stable and can better quantify LAI. The capsule network is able to achieve much better classification accuracies (Table 2) with 50 and 100 samples from the new locations. For LAI mapping, capsule network performs much better than CNN at Keeton Beach and slightly worse at St. George Sound but both models achieve very good LAI mapping. The performance of fine-tuning is inconsistent, it always makes the CNN model worse than the capsule network. For capsule network, it makes LAI prediction slightly worse at Keeton Beach but it improves the prediction at St. George Sound. Overall, the capsule network performs much better than CNN in transfer learning (Tables 2 and 3).

6   Conclusions

We presented a capsule network model for quantification of seagrass distribution in coastal water. The proposed capsule network jointly optimized regression and classification to learn a new representation for seagrass LAI mapping. We compared the representation learned by the capsule network with that by a traditional CNN model, and capsule network showed much better performances for LAI quantification in both regular learning and transfer learning. To the best of our knowledge, this is the first attempt to apply the capsule network for seagrass quantification in the aquatic remote sensing community.

References

1. Banerjee, D., et al.: A deep transfer learning approach for improved post-traumatic stress disorder diagnosis. In: 2017 IEEE International Conference on Data Mining (ICDM), pp. 11–20. IEEE (2017)
2. Breuer, L., Freede, H.: Leaf area index - LAI. https://www.staff.uni-giessen.de/~gh1461/plapada/lai/lai.html (2003). Accessed 4 Oct 2018
3. Chowdhury, M.M.U., Hammond, F., Konowicz, G., Xin, C., Wu, H., Li, J.: A few-shot deep learning approach for improved intrusion detection. In: 2017 IEEE 8th Annual Ubiquitous Computing, Electronics and Mobile Communication Conference (UEMCON), pp. 456–462. IEEE (2017)
4. Donahue, J., et al.: DeCAF: a deep convolutional activation feature for generic visual recognition. In: International Conference on Machine Learning, pp. 647–655 (2014)
5. Hemminga, M.A., Duarte, C.M.: Seagrass Ecology. Cambridge University Press, Cambridge (2000)
6. Hill, V., Zimmerman, R., Bissett, W., Dierssen, H., Kohler, D.: Evaluating light availability, seagrass biomass and productivity using hyperspectral airborne remote sensing in Saint Joseph's Bay, Florida. Estuaries Coasts **37**(6), 1467–1489 (2014)
7. Hinton, G., et al.: Deep neural networks for acoustic modeling in speech recognition: the shared views of four research groups. IEEE Sig. Process. Mag. **29**(6), 82–97 (2012)
8. Hinton, G., Sabour, S., Frosst, N.: Matrix capsules with EM routing (2018). https://openreview.net/pdf?id=HJWLfGWRb
9. Islam, K., Perez, D., Hill, V., Schaeffer, B., Zimmerman, R., Li, J.: Seagrass detection in coastal water through deep capsule networks. In: Chinese Conference on Pattern Recognition and Computer Vision. Sun-Yat Sen University (2018)
10. Krizhevsky, A., Sutskever, I., Hinton, G.E.: ImageNet classification with deep convolutional neural networks. In: Advances in Neural Information Processing Systems, pp. 1097–1105 (2012)
11. Ning, R., Wang, C., Xin, C., Li, J., Wu, H.: DeepMag: sniffing mobile apps in magnetic field through deep convolutional neural networks. IEEE (2018)
12. Oguslu, E., et al.: Detection of seagrass scars using sparse coding and morphological filter. Remote Sens. Environ. **213**, 92–103 (2018)
13. Pan, S.J., Yang, Q.: A survey on transfer learning. IEEE Trans. Knowl. Data Eng. **22**(10), 1345–1359 (2010)
14. Perez, D., et al.: Deep learning for effective detection of excavated soil related to illegal tunnel activities. In: IEEE Ubiquitous Computing, Electronics and Mobile Communication Conference (2017)
15. Perez, D., Li, J., Shen, Y., Dayanghirang, J., Wang, S., Zheng, Z.: Deep learning for pulmonary nodule CT image retrieval-an online assistance system for novice radiologists. In: 2017 IEEE International Conference on Data Mining Workshops (ICDMW), pp. 1112–1121. IEEE (2017)
16. Phinn, S., Roelfsema, C., Dekker, A., Brando, V., Anstee, J.: Mapping seagrass species, cover and biomass in shallow waters: an assessment of satellite multi-spectral and airborne hyper-spectral imaging systems in Moreton Bay (Australia). Remote Sens. Environ. **112**(8), 3413–3425 (2008)
17. Sabour, S., Frosst, N., Hinton, G.E.: Dynamic routing between capsules. In: Advances in Neural Information Processing Systems, pp. 3857–3867 (2017)

18. Short, F.T., Coles, R.G.: Global Seagrass Research Methods, vol. 33. Elsevier, Amsterdam (2001)
19. Wicaksono, P., Hafizt, M.: Mapping seagrass from space: addressing the complexity of seagrass LAI mapping. Eur. J. Remote Sens. **46**(1), 18–39 (2013)
20. Xi, E., Bing, S., Jin, Y.: Capsule network performance on complex data. arXiv preprint arXiv:1712.03480 (2017)
21. Yang, D., Yang, C.: Detection of seagrass distribution changes from 1991 to 2006 in Xincun Bay, Hainan, with satellite remote sensing. Sensors **9**(2), 830–844 (2009)
22. Yosinski, J., Clune, J., Bengio, Y., Lipson, H.: How transferable are features in deep neural networks? In: Advances in Neural Information Processing Systems, pp. 3320–3328 (2014)

Attention Enhanced ConvNet-RNN for Chinese Vehicle License Plate Recognition

Shiming Duan, Wei Hu, Ruirui Li[⊠], Wei Li, and Shihao Sun

Beijing University of Chemical Technology, Beijing 100029, China
ilydouble@gmail.com

Abstract. As an important part of intelligent transportation system, vehicle license plate recognition requires high accuracy in an open environment. While a lot of approaches have been proposed, and achieved good performance to some extent, these approaches still have problems, for example, in the condition of characters' distortion or partial occlusion. Segmentation-free VLPR systems compute the label in one pass using Long Short-Term Memory Network (LSTM), without individual segmentation step, their results tend to be not influenced by the segmentation accuracy. Based on the idea of Segmentation-free VLPR, this paper proposed an attention enhanced ConvNet-RNN (AC-RNN) for accurate Chinese Vehicle License Plate Recognition. The attention mechanism helps to locate the important instances in the step of recognition. While the ConvNet is used to extract features, the recurrent neural networks (RNN) with connectionist temporal classification (CTC) are applied for sequence labeling. The proposed AC-RNN was trained on a large generated dataset which contains various types of license plates in China. The AC-RNN could figure out the vehicle license even in cases of light changing, spatial distortion and partial blurry. Experiments showed that the AC-RNN performs better on the testing real images, increasing about 5% on accuracy, compared with classic ConvNet-RNN [8].

Keywords: Vehicle license plate recognition
Recurrent neural networks · Long Short-Term Memory Network
Attention

1 Introduction

As an important part of intelligent transportation system, vehicle license plate recognition (VLPR) has attracted considerable research interests. It is a useful technology for government agencies to track or detect stolen vehicles or collect data for traffic management and improvement. Due to its close relationship to public security, VLPR requires generalization and high accuracy in real applications.

© Springer Nature Switzerland AG 2018
J.-H. Lai et al. (Eds.): PRCV 2018, LNCS 11257, pp. 417–428, 2018.
https://doi.org/10.1007/978-3-030-03335-4_36

While a lot of works have been proposed on the topic of VLPR, the VLPR task is still challenging, not only because of the environmental factors such as lighting, shadows, and occlusions, but also because of the image acquisition factors such as motion and focus blurs. For Chinese license plate recognition, the situation is more complicated. They are composed of Chinese characters and numbers. Their colors and sizes may be different and their lengths are not necessarily fixed, even placed in two lines.

Traditional image processing method needs a series of processing steps, including localization, segmentation and recognition. Many of them depend on handcrafted features and could only work well under controlled conditions. These handcrafted features are usually sensitive to image noises, and may result in many false positives under complex backgrounds.

CNNs have achieved great success in various tasks including image classification, object detection and semantic segmentation [11]. CNNs containing deep neural layers can learn efficient representations from a large amount of training data. For the VLPR tasks, extended CNNs transform the one-to-many problem into a single-label classification problem by classifying one character at a time. This requires the task to firstly segment characters and then recognize them one by one. More recent work performs segmentation before classification and use CNN-BRNN [14] and CTC to achieve the state of the art results. The segmentation-free VLPR [8] focus on images from real-world traffic cameras and applies the ConvNet RNN to the VLPR tasks. Unfortunately, their method takes no consideration of Chinese license plate recognition and requires specific optimization for higher accuracy.

In this paper, we proposed an attention enhanced ConvNet-RNN for Chinese vehicle license plate recognition. It is one-pass, end-to-end neural network. The proposed AC-RNN has two improvements. The original ConvNet-RNN is actually not fit for the vehicle license plate recognition with weak semantic connections. Thus, a novel semantic enhance strategy is introduced which inserts some trivial null characters into labeled strings. Secondly, an attention mechanism is added to learn the weights map, helping the neural network to perform classification better. The two techniques are not individual with each other. They work together to get higher accuracy. Furthermore, to avoid overfitting caused by lack of data. We also proposed a data generation method and generated a dataset containing one million labeled images. In summary, this paper makes the follows contributions to the community:

- A novel semantic enhance strategy for Chinese VLPR.
- An attention enhanced ConvNet-RNN.
- A data generation method and a new dataset of Chinese VLP.

This paper is organized as thus, Sect. 2 presents related works about this paper and Sect. 3 provides the proposed neural network, In Sect. 4, a series of experiments will be presented and the conclusion will be shown in Sect. 5.

2   Related Works

2.1   Vehicle License Plate Recognition

Approaches for VLPR problems contain two stages, localization and recognition. The main work of this paper focus on the latter stage–recognition.

Plate localization aims to detect plates from images. Lots of work has been done for detection problems, for example, Faster RCNN [28] is known for its high precision of detection. YOLO [27] is famous for its speed of detection. Like a combination of Faster RCNN and YOLO, SSD [20] performs very well on both accuracy and speed. In [30], CPTN is designed for texts detection in natural images. Plate localization aims to detect plates rather than texts, therefore, a SSD model is applied in our project to detect plates.

Previous works on plate recognition include traditional image processing methods [1,2,12,13,15,25,26,31] and new deep learning approaches [3,16,18, 19,21,23,33]. Most of them need to detect and segment the characters out from a license plate image before recognition.

The recognition of plates typically contains two-stages as well. Segmentation extracts characters from license plate image; and classification distinguishes the segmented characters one by one. For example, in [12], Gou *et al.* propose Extremal Regions (ER) to segment characters from coarsely detected license plates. Restricted Boltzmann machines were applied to recognize the characters. In [33], the license plate is segmented into seven blocks using a projection method, after which, two classifiers are designed to recognize Chinese characters, numbers, and alphabet letters. In [18,23], two CNN models are used to recognize characters from plate image. Firstly, a binary deep network classifier is trained to confirm if a character exists. Another deep CNN is adopted for the task of character recognition. In [21], Liu *et al.* implement a CNN model which has shared hidden layers and two distinct softmax layers for the Chinese and the alphanumeric characters respectively.

In fact, character segmentation by itself is a challenging task since it is prone to be influenced by uneven lighting, shadows and noises in the images [18]. The plate cannot be recognized correctly if the segmentation is improper, even if we have a strong classifier for characters. Therefore, in this paper, VLPR is regarded as a sequence labeling problem, and our proposed method aims to recognize plates without segmentation.

2.2   ConvNet-RNN

One of the most popular methods for sequence-to-sequence problems is ConvNet-RNN (CRNN) [14]. ConvNet-RNN is proposed for image-based recognition in [29], Shi *et al.* integrate feature extraction, sequence modeling and transformation into a unified framework. CRNN is end-to-end trainable and can deal with sequence in various lengths, involving no character segmentation or horizontal scale normalization. CRNN has been popular since it is proposed, for example, in

[10], CRNN is adopted for offline handwriting recognition, in [7,32], CRNN provides a useful method for Optical Music Recognition (OMR), and in [6], CRNN is used for script identification in natural scene image and video frame.

CRNN is also applied to VLPR. In [8], CRNN is adopted for plate recognition with CTC. However, due to the weak correlation between characters in plate, classic CRNN does not work well on VLPR, therefore, this paper introduces the method of generating interval characters to strengthen the correlation between characters combined with a fixed length CTC.

2.3   Attention Model

Attention mechanism becomes more and more popular since being used in image classification by Mnih *et al.* [24]. In [4], Dzmitry *et al.* first introduce attention mechanism to neural machine translation (NMT). By learning different weights from the source parts to different target words, the trained Model can automatically search for parts of a source sentence that are relevant to a target word. In [22], Luong *et al.* show that how to extend RNN with attention mechanism. Global attention and local attention are introduced in natural language processing (NLP). After [4,22], attention mechanism is widely used in NLP tasks, including not only sequence-to-sequence models, but also various classification tasks. In [5], attention is used to allow a Recurrent Neural Network (RNN) to learn alignments between sequences of input frames and output label on the topic of Large Vocabulary Continuous Speech Recognition (LVCSR) system. In [9], Serdyuk adopted the attention mechanism for speech recognition. Attention is also used for OCR in [17].

3   The Proposed AC-RNN Framework

3.1   Network Architecture

The network architecture of AC-RNN is shown in Fig. 1. It contains three main parts: the ConvNet, the attention based RNN and the CTC. The AC-RNN takes plate images as input. Through deep convolutional neural layers, the AC-RNN learns a group of feature maps. It then departs the feature map into sequence feature blocks and sends them to Bi-LSTM RNN. After encoding and decoding training processes, pre-frame predictions are gotten. Then a length-fixed CTC is performed to classify the characters. The AC-RNN works consecutively in an end-to-end fashion which inputs a plate image and outputs the predicted labels.

3.2   Interval for Semantic Enhancement

LSTM is well known for its ability to capture long-range dependencies. Therefore, LSTM is widely used in voice recognition, Optical Character Recognition (OCR), text categories and so on. As often observed, the characters of vehicle license plate have semantic connections in the context. Since the LSTM is

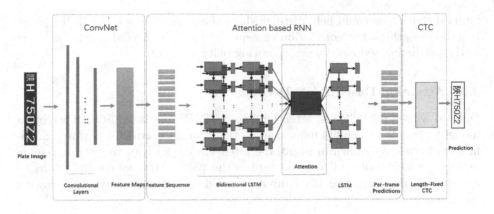

Fig. 1. Attention enhanced ConvNet-RNN.

directional, to make the best use of context information, the AC-RNN adopts a bidirectional LSTM. On the other hand, differed with language translation or OCR tasks, which the LSTM is intuitively fit for, the characters on a plate are weakly relevant. Following the rules, some characters are fixed according to the car properties while other characters may be generated randomly.

In order to strengthen the correlations between characters on a plate, characters named empty of sequence (EOS) are inserted at the intervals to the sequential labels when training the model.

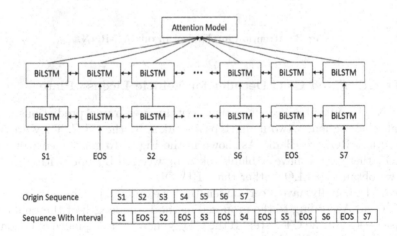

Fig. 2. Sample of interval character in sequence.

As shown in Fig. 2, the EOS participates in the training of the attention-based recurrent neural network. In the case of Chinese vehicle license plate, the AC-RNN adopts the rule that inserting the EOS at each interval between neighbouring pairs of characters showed with solid EOS labeled rectangles. The interval characters could help distinguishing the gaps of characters in the plate. It also strengthens the correlation of sequence that the LSTM need. The EOS in the prediction sequence needs removing before output.

3.3 Attention Based RNN Decoder

Differed with classic CRNN, attention based CRNN has an additional attention model to learn the weights map, helping the neural network to perform classification better. As shown in Fig. 3, the attention model tries to learn a weights map a_{ij}, which could tell how relevant is the part of the source hidden h_j to a target frame. Then the RNN input c_i could be calculated by the following equation.

$$c_i = \sum_{j=1}^{T_X} a_{ij} h_j \tag{1}$$

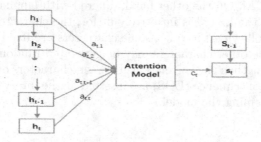

Fig. 3. Attention mechanism in our AC-RNN.

3.4 Length-Fixed CTC Decoder for Vehicle License Plate

The RNN will output a sequence that contains per-frame predictions. To get the final label sequence, two main steps are taken by the CTC. They are Merge Repeated and Remove Blank. As shown in the Fig. 4, to get the correct output 'HELLO', there must have a blank token between 'LL', and with this blank token, we obtain 'HELLO' rather than 'HELO'.

The VLPs usually have a certain length, for example, in China, the length of VLP is seven. According to the proposed method, the length of the final output result is checked in the CTC step. If the CTC generates a sequence of uncommon length, the AC-RNN will find the longest continuous sub strings without blank. This step is illustrated by label (2) in Fig. 4. In this situation, the AC-RNN will put a blank into the longest substring in force, which guarantees the right output. This step is illustrated by label (1) in Fig. 4.

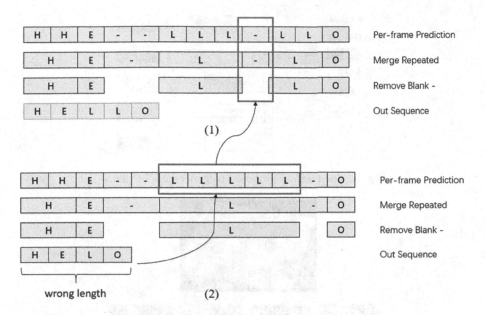

Fig. 4. Illustration of CTC progress.

4   Experiments

4.1   Experimental Environments

Our experiments are carried out on the 8-way GPU cluster, whose configuration is shown in Table 1. We design the experiments with caffe and try to compare general ConvNet-RNN and our AC-RNN with length-fixed CTC.

Table 1. Experimental environments.

Operating system	Red Hat 4.8.3-9
CPU	Intel(R) Xeon(R) CPU E5-2678 v3 @ 2.50 GHz
GPU	GeForce GTX TITAN X
Hard disk	1TB
cudnn	4.0.7
CUDA	7.0.27

4.2   Generated Datasets

On account of various reasons, it is always difficult to obtain VLP datasets, not to mention balanced datasets over the country. To avoid overfitting caused by lack of data and to enhance the robustness of our model, a data generation

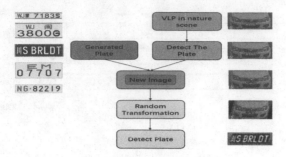

Fig. 5. The method proposed to generate VLP data.

Fig. 6. Examples of images generated by our method.

method is proposed. By this method, plenty of plate images are generated, which can be used both in VLP detection and VLP recognition.

As shown in Fig. 5, our method to generate data set is shown as following.

Step 1: A dataset from monitor cameras is necessary, with which some of lean VLPs will be detected by a detector. The remaining part without the plate will be used as background.

Step 2: Lots of VLPs with random character distribution will be plotted according to template from transportation department.

Step 3: The plates detected in step 1 will be replaced by plates from step 2, thus new images will be generated with nature backgrounds and manual plates.

Step 4: A series of transformations will be applied to these generated data, such as random scale, random blur, random rotate, random sharpen etc.

Step 5: After detected by a detector, our new VLP dataset will be ready.

By our method, datasets of VLP containing millions of images can be generated for detection and recognition. Some examples of our generated images are shown in Fig. 6.

4.3   Experiments and Results

In our experiments, dataset for training and valuation contains 400 thousand images collected from natural scene and 800 thousand images generated by our data generation method. A dataset from EasyPR containing 260 images is set for test, all these images are collected from natural scene. Some instances of the test dataset are shown in Fig. 7.

Fig. 7. Some instances in test dataset

The main work of this paper focus on the stage of recognition. As described in Sect. 3, contributions to network in this paper are semantic enhancement of plates, length-fixed CTC decoder and attention mechanism, therefore our contrast experiments are carried out on two different stages: The classic ConvNet-RNN with nothing enhanced and our AC-RNN. We test these models and summarize the results as Table 2. As shown in Table 2, compared with the classic ConvNet-RNN, our work in this paper makes an excellent improvement on accuracy.

Table 2. Evaluation results.

Comparison	Accuracy overall
Classic ConvNet-RNN	85.17%
AC-RNN	90.11%

A classic method to evaluate the performance of sequence labeling is to measure the percentage of perfectly predicted images in the test dataset, as shown in Table 2. Considering vehicle license plates in China contain a Chinese character and the repeated characters can only appeared in alphabets and numbers, the accuracy of the last six bits is calculated in Table 3. The accuracy of the Chinese characters is also listed in results. Meanwhile, some instances are given in Fig. 8.

Table 3. Evaluation results on our VLP dataset.

Comparison	Accuracy of last six bits	Accuracy of Chinese characters
Classic ConvNet-RNN	91.25%	88.97%
AC-RNN	95.44%	93.54%

As shown in Table 3 and Fig. 8, the classic ConvNet-RNN performs bad when text on a plate contains several same connected characters. As comparison, the AC-RNN proposed in this paper does not have this problem, and with attention mechanism, the AC-RNN performs better on recognition.

Test image	Ground truth	ConvNet-RNN	AC-RNN
	JI|A9J333	JI|A9J33	JI|A9J333
	渝BE7773	渝BE773	渝BE7773
	苏ANC818	苏AN0818	苏ANC818
	鲁A88888	鲁A8888	鲁A88888

Fig. 8. Some examples in experiments

5   Conclusion

In this paper, an attention enhanced ConvNet-RNN for Chinese Vehicle License Recognition, AC-RNN, is proposed. Compared with classic ConvNet-RNN, there are two improvements in AC-RNN. Firstly, intervals for semantic enhancement and length-fixed CTC decoder are firstly introduced to VLPR problems, in which intervals can strengthen the correlations between characters on a plate and a length-fix CTC decoder can perform better when there are several connected same characters on a plate. Secondly, attention mechanism is applied to learn a weights map, helping the neural network to perform classification better. Besides, a new method to generate datasets of VLP is proposed, thus, the overfitting caused by lack of data can be avoided.

References

1. Aboura, K., Al-Hmouz, R.: An overview of image analysis algorithms for license plate recognition. Organizacija **50**(3), 285–295 (2017)
2. Abtahi, F., Zhu, Z., Burry, A.M.: A deep reinforcement learning approach to character segmentation of license plate images. In: 2015 14th IAPR International Conference on Machine Vision Applications (MVA), pp. 539–542, May 2015. https://doi.org/10.1109/MVA.2015.7153249
3. Angara, N.S.S.: Automatic license plate recognition using deep learning techniques (2015)
4. Bahdanau, D., Cho, K., Bengio, Y.: Neural machine translation by jointly learning to align and translate. arXiv preprint arXiv:1409.0473 (2014)
5. Bahdanau, D., Chorowski, J., Serdyuk, D., Brakel, P., Bengio, Y.: End-to-end attention-based large vocabulary speech recognition. In: 2016 IEEE International Conference on Acoustics, Speech and Signal Processing (ICASSP), pp. 4945–4949. IEEE (2016)
6. Bhunia, A.K., Konwer, A., Bhowmick, A., Bhunia, A.K., Roy, P.P., Pal, U.: Script identification in natural scene image and video frame using attention based convolutional-LSTM network (2018)
7. Calvo-Zaragoza, J., Valero-Mas, J.J., Pertusa, A.: End-to-end optical music recognition using neural networks. In: Proceedings of the 18th International Society for Music Information Retrieval Conference, Suzhou, China, pp. 23–27 (2017)

8. Cheang, T.K., Chong, Y.S., Yong, H.T.: Segmentation-free vehicle license plate recognition using ConvNet-RNN (2017)
9. Chorowski, J.K., Bahdanau, D., Serdyuk, D., Cho, K., Bengio, Y.: Attention-based models for speech recognition. In: Advances in Neural Information Processing Systems, pp. 577–585 (2015)
10. Ding, H., et al.: A compact CNN-DBLSTM based character model for offline handwriting recognition with Tucker decomposition. In: 2017 14th IAPR International Conference on Document Analysis and Recognition (ICDAR), vol. 01, pp. 507–512, November 2017. https://doi.org/10.1109/ICDAR.2017.89
11. Girshick, R., Donahue, J., Darrell, T., Malik, J.: Rich feature hierarchies for accurate object detection and semantic segmentation. In: IEEE Conference on Computer Vision and Pattern Recognition, pp. 580–587 (2014)
12. Gou, C., Wang, K., Yao, Y., Li, Z.: Vehicle license plate recognition based on extremal regions and restricted Boltzmann machines. IEEE Trans. Intell. Transp. Syst. **17**(4), 1096–1107 (2016)
13. He, S., Yang, C., Pan, J.S.: The research of chinese license plates recognition based on CNN and length_feature. In: Fujita, H., Ali, M., Selamat, A., Sasaki, J., Kurematsu, M. (eds.) Trends in Applied Knowledge-Based Systems and Data Science, pp. 389–397. Springer, Cham (2016). https://doi.org/10.1007/978-3-319-42007-3_33
14. Hui Li, C.S.: Reading car license plates using deep convolutional neural networks and LSTMS (2016)
15. Hurtik, P., Vajgl, M.: Automatic license plate recognition in difficult conditions - technical report. In: Fuzzy Systems Association and International Conference on Soft Computing and Intelligent Systems (2017)
16. Laroca, R., et al.: A robust real-time automatic license plate recognition based on the YOLO detector. In: International Joint Conference on Neural Networks (2018)
17. Lee, C.Y., Osindero, S.: Recursive recurrent nets with attention modeling for OCR in the wild. In: Proceedings of the IEEE Conference on Computer Vision and Pattern Recognition, pp. 2231–2239 (2016)
18. Li, H., Wang, P., Shen, C.: Towards end-to-end car license plates detection and recognition with deep neural networks (2017)
19. Li, H., Wang, P., You, M., Shen, C.: Reading car license plates using deep neural networks. Image Vis. Comput. **72**, 14–23 (2018). https://doi.org/10.1016/j.imavis.2018.02.002, http://www.sciencedirect.com/science/article/pii/S0262885618300155
20. Liu, W., et al.: SSD: single shot multibox detector. In: Leibe, B., Matas, J., Sebe, N., Welling, M. (eds.) ECCV 2016. LNCS, vol. 9905, pp. 21–37. Springer, Cham (2016). https://doi.org/10.1007/978-3-319-46448-0_2
21. Liu, Y., Huang, H.: Car plate character recognition using a convolutional neural network with shared hidden layers. In: 2015 Chinese Automation Congress (CAC), pp. 638–643, November 2015. https://doi.org/10.1109/CAC.2015.7382577
22. Luong, M.T., Pham, H., Manning, C.D.: Effective approaches to attention-based neural machine translation. arXiv preprint arXiv:1508.04025 (2015)
23. Masood, S.Z., Shu, G., Dehghan, A., Ortiz, E.G.: License plate detection and recognition using deeply learned convolutional neural networks (2017)
24. Mnih, V., Heess, N., Graves, A., et al.: Recurrent models of visual attention. In: Advances in Neural Information Processing Systems, pp. 2204–2212 (2014)
25. Mubarak, H., Ibrahim, A.O., Elwasila, A., Bushra, S., Ahmed, A.: A framework for automatic license number plate recognition in sudanese vehicles (2017)

26. Pant, A.K., Gyawali, P.K., Acharya, S.: Automatic nepali number plate recognition with support vector machines. In: International Conference on Software, Knowledge, Information Management and Applications (2015)
27. Redmon, J., Divvala, S., Girshick, R., Farhadi, A.: You only look once: unified, real-time object detection. In: Proceedings of the IEEE Conference on Computer Vision and Pattern Recognition, pp. 779–788 (2016)
28. Ren, S., He, K., Girshick, R., Sun, J.: Faster R-CNN: towards real-time object detection with region proposal networks. In: Advances in Neural Information Processing Systems, pp. 91–99 (2015)
29. Shi, B., Bai, X., Yao, C.: An end-to-end trainable neural network for image-based sequence recognition and its application to scene text recognition. IEEE Trans. Pattern Anal. Mach. Intell. **39**(11), 2298–2304 (2017). https://doi.org/10.1109/TPAMI.2016.2646371
30. Tian, Z., Huang, W., He, T., He, P., Qiao, Y.: Detecting text in natural image with connectionist text proposal network. In: Leibe, B., Matas, J., Sebe, N., Welling, M. (eds.) ECCV 2016. LNCS, vol. 9912, pp. 56–72. Springer, Cham (2016). https://doi.org/10.1007/978-3-319-46484-8_4
31. Wang, J., Bacic, B., Yan, W.Q.: An effective method for plate number recognition. Multimed. Tools Appl. **77**(2), 1679–1692 (2018). https://doi.org/10.1007/s11042-017-4356-z
32. Wel, E.V.D., Ullrich, K.: Optical music recognition with convolutional sequence-to-sequence models (2017)
33. Zang, D.: Vehicle license plate recognition using visual attention model and deep learning. J. Electron. Imaging **24**(3), 033001 (2015)

Prohibited Item Detection in Airport X-Ray Security Images via Attention Mechanism Based CNN

Maoshu Xu, Haigang Zhang, and Jinfeng Yang[✉]

Tianjin Key Lab for Advanced Signal Processing,
Civil Aviation University of China, Tianjin, China
jfyang@cauc.edu.cn

Abstract. Automation of security inspections is crucial for improving the efficiency and reducing security risks. In this paper, we focus on automatically recognizing and localizing prohibited items in airport X-ray security images. A top-down attention mechanism is applied to enhance a CNN classifier to additionally locate the prohibited items. We introduce a high-level semantic feedback loop to map the targets semantic signal to the input X-ray image space for generating task-specic attention maps. And the attention maps indicate the location and general outline of prohibited items in the input images. Furthermore, to obtain more accurate location information, we combine the lateral inhibition and contrastive attention to suppress noise and non-target interference in attention maps. The experiments on the GDX-ray image dataset have demonstrated the efficiency and stability of the proposed scheme in both single target detection and multi-target detection.

Keywords: Prohibited item · Detection · Attention · CNN

1 Introduction

Airport security is an important guarantee for aviation safety. Prohibited item detection using X-ray screening plays a critical role in defending passengers from the risk of crime, and terrorist attacks [1]. However, during the security screening, uncontrollable human factors always reduce the accuracy and efficiency of inspection [2]. Establishing an efficient and intelligent security inspection system is crucial to promoting the safe operation of civil aviation and ensuring the safety of passengers. The core work of X-ray screening is to distinguish what type of the prohibited items and detect where they are. To achieve automatic security, the computer is required to replace the security inspector to answer the two questions of "What" and "Where". Automatic and intelligent security detection for X-ray images remains an open question. Most of challenges come from the following points: (1) different imaging modes; (2) clutter background; (3) angle variation of the items in imaging; (4) color variation caused by material difference of the items [3–5].

© Springer Nature Switzerland AG 2018
J.-H. Lai et al. (Eds.): PRCV 2018, LNCS 11257, pp. 429–439, 2018.
https://doi.org/10.1007/978-3-030-03335-4_37

In recent years, some deep neural networks have achieved remarkable performance in the areas of target recognition and detection. Compared with traditional algorithms, deep learning algorithms have stronger generalization ability and can achieve higher recognition accuracy. Motivated by the convolutional neural network (CNN), [1] has presented a strategy based on deep features to deal X-Ray image recognition problems on a public GDX-ray dataset. A deep multi-layer CNN approach is employed in [6] for the end-to-end entire feature extraction, representation and classification process, which achieves 98.92% detection accuracy. Usually, common CNNs can only complete the task of image classification. For object detection, the more complex the model is, the more labor-intensive supervision information is required. For example, several network architectures have good performance in object recognition and location such as single shot multibox detector (SSD) and faster region-based convolutional neural networks (Faster R-CNN). However, they all require strong supervision information for training, e.g., bounding boxes or segmentation masks. Collecting such a large amount of labeled data is often expensive and time-consuming. Especially for security images, the position of the prohibited items requires professional security personnel to mark. Taking into account this actual situation of security images, these methods cannot be effective in practical applications.

Recently, the work of Cao [7,8], Zhang et al. [9] provide a new idea for intelligent security inspection. Attention mechanism based CNN has achieved great detection performance on nature image set. For target recognition tasks, CNNs have strong anti-jamming and anti-blocking capabilities. For target localization tasks, the attention feedback mechanism can enable the network to achieve the prohibited item localization, while not requiring a strong supervised learning [7]. The attention mechanism can then find out which areas of the image can cause CNN to extract these features that activate the output node. This is very similar to the working mechanism of the human visual cortex: When dealing with these stimuli, we also know where these stimuli come from [8].

In this paper, we apply the model proposed by Cao [7] on the automatic prohibited item detection system to prove that the attention mechanism can also perform well on X-ray image processing. Considering the large amount of noise and interference between prohibited items in the security image, we combined the lateral inhibition [8] and contrastive attention [9] to establish a neuronal stimulus inhibition model. When performing the feed-back propagation, it can effectively suppress noise and interference. Furthermore, to make the algorithm suitable for the security X-ray image set, we optimized the two suppression methods. Finally, the semantic information of the target is mapped to the image space as an attention map, and we can know which areas of the image are most relevant to the target.

The main contributions of this paper are summarized as follows: (1) We introduce the semantic feedback model in CNNs and obtain a cursory target attention map. (2) To cope with noise and interference in the security image, we combine two neural suppression algorithms to establish a neuronal stimulus inhibition model. (3) To improve the practicality of our model, we develop a multi-target detection strategy. (4) We perform experiments on the GDX-ray dataset, and our method achieves significant performance in both single-target and multi-target detection.

2   High-Level Semantic Feedback Model

When searching for objects, the top-down attention of a person plays the role of regulating neurons in the visual cortex according to the current task and prior knowledge. Same as most attention models [7], we use a CNN to model visual cortex neurons and apply the high-level semantic feedback mechanism on the CNN framework. It can layer-by-layer calculate correlations between each layer neurons and CNN output semantic notes. As shown in Fig. 1, in the feed-forward propagation process of CNN, an X-ray security image of a gun is mapped to one-dimensional semantic space by a CNN classifier, and target category information is obtained. In the feed-back propagation, the semantic information is mapped to image space by semantic feedback model, and the attention map of the gun is shown in the input image.

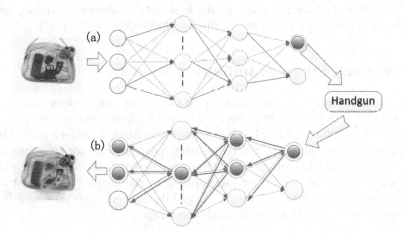

Fig. 1. Attention mechanism based model. (a) and (b) represent feed-forward and feed-back propagation for a convolutional neural network. (a) Given an input image, the output neuron corresponding to the predicted category is activated after the feed-forward propagation and represented by the red dot. (b) In the feed-back propagation, the red dots represent neurons positively related to the output neuron and are activated layer by layer. Finally, we can use the neurons that are activated in the input layer to obtain attention maps. (Color figure online)

The feedback model is much like the backpropagation in the training process. But the signal of the backpropagation changes to the semantic information of the output layer, not the value of loss function. On this basis, the correlation between each convolutional layer and semantic neurons can be calculated by deconvolute the output with the parameters of the convolutional layer, and is denoted as α^l. This backpropagation is performed from top to bottom as described in Eq. (1), where "$*$" represents deconvolution. In this way, the attention map of the targets is generated which marks the most relevant pixel region in the image to the semantic node, so as to achieve the positioning and segmentation of the targets, as shown in Fig. 2.

$$\alpha^{N-1} = x^N * w^{N-1} \qquad \alpha^{l-1} = \alpha^l * w^{l-1} \quad l = 2, 3, 4, \dots, N, \tag{1}$$

where x^l denotes the output of the layer, and x^N denotes the output of the network. w^l represents the convolution kernel parameters on layer l.

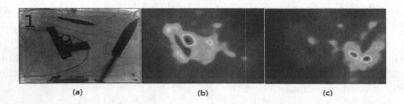

Fig. 2. Result by high-level semantic feedback model for different targets respectively. (a) The input image. (b), (c) Output maps for gun and knife respectively.

3   Neuronal Stimulus Inhibition Model

In the previous section, the attention maps are rather rough, often accompanied by noise and interference. It is because that the X-ray image has a complex background and clutter. Most kinds of noise come from the defect caused by the non-linearity of the network. Since activated patterns can not only be derived from target objects but also derived from background and disturbed objects, there will be a lot of non-target interference in the picture. In order to meet the requirements for precise location of prohibited item, we take the following measures to deal with these noises and interference.

3.1   Lateral Inhibition Mechanism

Lateral inhibition mechanism can enhance the contrasts between the neurons, and has provided good performance on natural images processing [8,10,11]. For further filtering the activated neurons, we apply the lateral inhibition mechanism on the top-down procedure of the CNN frame. Different from [8], in order to deal with a lot of noise in the security X-ray image, we use the output of the previous layer to normalize the suppression coefficient of the current layer. According to the distribution of the value in attention maps, we choose distribution cosine function to evaluation the inhibition values, such as Eqs. (2) and (3).

$$w_{ij}^{ave} = \frac{\cos(\overline{w_{ij}})}{\cos(\overline{x_{ij}})} \tag{2}$$

$$w_{ij}^{dif} = \frac{\sum_{uv} d_{uv} e^{-d_{uv}} \delta(w_{uv} - w_{ij})}{\cos(\overline{x_{ij}})}, \tag{3}$$

$$w_{ij}^{'} = \begin{cases} w_{ij} \ if \quad w_{ij} > (a * w_{ij}^{ave} + b * w_{ij}^{dif}) \\ 0 \quad if \quad w_{ij} < (a * w_{ij}^{ave} + b * w_{ij}^{dif}) \end{cases}, \tag{4}$$

where w_{ij} denotes an element in the normalized attention map of this layer at location (i, j). w_{ij}^{ave} denotes the mean inhibition coefficient, and w_{ij}^{dif} denotes the differential inhibition coefficient. w_{uv} denotes the elements in the sliding window centered on w_{ij}, and d_{uv} denotes the Euclidean distance between w_{uv} and w_{ij}. $\overline{w}_{ij}$ denotes the mean of the elements in the sliding window. x_{ij} denotes the outputs of layer $l - 1$. $w_{ij}^{'}$ denotes the new value of the element in the attention map.

Those two kinds of coefficients are standardized by a and b, which we setting $a = 0.2$ and $b = 0.8$. Under the combined effect of these two suppression methods, noise in the attention map can be well suppressed, as shown in Fig. 3. The results prove that the lateral inhibition mechanism has excellent performance in our model.

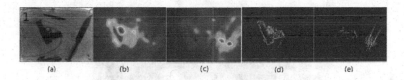

Fig. 3. Comparison between original attention map and the results of lateral inhibition. (a) The input images. (b), (c) Original attention maps for gun and knife respectively. (d), (e) Attention maps after lateral inhibition for gun and knife respectively.

3.2 Contrastive Top-Down Attention

The lateral inhibition model excels in suppressing noise, but when the security image contains multiple prohibited targets, the accuracy of the model is disturbed. In Figs. 3(d)(e), the attention map of a gun is disturbed by the lines around the gun, while the attention map of a knife is interfered by the gun. This is consistent with our previous discussions that other targets in the input image will interfere with the attention map. It has been proved in [9] that using the negation of the original weights of layer can obtain the next level of non-targets signal, and here it is denote as $P_1^{'}$ in Eq. (5).

$$P_1^{'} = EP(-W_1) = A_1 \bigotimes ((-W_1)^{+} (P_0/((-W_1)^{+T} A_1))), \tag{5}$$

where P_0 represents the probability correlation matrix in the top layer. $P_1^{'}$ represents the probability correlation matrix of the non-targets signal. W^{+} is the plus weight of the top layer, while $-W$ is the negation. A_1 is the response value of the second layer neurons. $EP()$ represents the function of $-W$ that calculate the non-targets signal.

Because there are too many sundries in the security X-ray images, even in the non-target signal, there are still some target signals. If we immediately subtract it from the semantic signal, the target signal in semantic information will be loss, as shown in Fig. 4(a). Instead of immediately subtracting P_1' from the semantic signal as the [9] did, we use the improved algorithm to obtain more complete semantic information in Eq. (6). In our method, after performing the lateral inhibition on P_1', the target signal in P_1' will be suppressed. When we subtract it from the semantic signal, the target signal can be better preserved, as shown in Fig. 4(b). In this way, we also complete the organic combination of the two algorithms, as shown in Fig. 5. We use contrast attention to remove non-target interference in semantic signal. Furthermore, we add lateral suppression layers in the top-down feedback path to optimize the contrast attention and suppress noise. As shown in Figs. 6(d)(e), it is obvious that compared with the contrastive attention algorithms, the combined algorithms has more powerful ability to suppress noise in the attention map.

$$S = Lat(EP(W_1)) - Lat(EP(-W_1)), \tag{6}$$

where S is the target signal. $Lat()$ is the lateral inhibition function.

(a)   (b)

Fig. 4. (a) The result of contrastive top-down attention method. (b) The result of our method

4   Multi-target Detection Strategy

Our model can be used not only for single-target detection but also for multi-target detection. In order to detect every type of threat targets in security X-ray images as much as possible, we designed the following multi-target inspection process:

(1) Given an X-ray image and perform forward to obtain probability values of various types of threat objects.
(2) Judge the objects with a probability value greater than r as the suspected targets, where r is determined in advance.

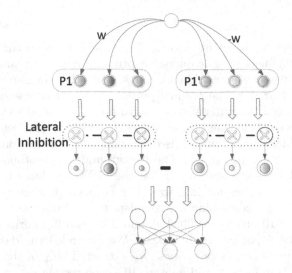

Fig. 5. Neuronal stimulus inhibition model. The red dot represents the target signal and the blue dot represents the non-target signal. The yellow dot represents the target signal in P_1' (Color figure online)

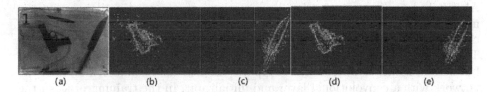

(a)   (b)   (c)   (d)   (e)

Fig. 6. Comparison between contrastive top-down attention maps and the results of combined algorithm. (a) The input images. (b), (c) Contrastive top-down attention maps for gun and knife respectively. (d), (e) Attention maps obtained by the combination of two algorithms.

(3) Activate the CNN output node corresponding to the target type and perform feed-backward propagation using feedback models.

(4) Obtain response-based attention maps for suspected object at the data layer and display it on the input image.

5   Experiments

To quantitatively demonstrate the effectiveness of the attention mechanism based CNN, we carry out the experiments on the GDX-ray dataset. As mentioned before, our model should answer two questions: what and where. So, we use the above security inspection strategy to verify the model's recognition and location capabilities.

5.1   Dataset

The security image data set used for training and testing in this paper comes from the GDX-ray dataset. The dataset captures single-target and multi-target X-ray security images of guns, knives, darts, and other dangerous goods from multiple angles. However, the original purpose of the database was created to study the traditional computer vision algorithms. If it is used to train the CNN model, there are the following disadvantages: (1) The samples set is very small. There are few single-target images used to train the classification network, and it is easy to cause overfitting; (2) The background is monotonous. Therefore, we performed data augmentation [12] on the GDX-ray dataset. We cut it to 2/3 of the security images original size. The cropped position is random, and we pick out 10 images containing the complete target from the cropped images. Then rotate these 10 images at, 90, 180, and 270° and flip horizontally. Finally one image can be expanded to 80 images. We expanded the data set to 5000 pictures containing 4 object categories. We extracted 90% of the pictures from the dataset as a training set, and another 10% as a testing set.

5.2   CNN Classifiers

Although data augmentation has been carried out, the existing data volume is not enough for the CNN network to fully learn the characteristics of various threat targets. So we use the transfer learning strategy to train the CNN model. The Google net which is pretrained with ImageNet 2012 training set is obtained from Caffe Model Zoo website. We replace the last fully connected layer of the network with a convolutional layer and initialize it. In the training process, the learning rate of the bottom network is set to 0.0001, and the learning rate of the top network is set to 0.001. After 30 iterations with batchsize set of 8, the network tends to convergence.

5.3   Experimental Results

Our model has achieved a classification accuracy of 97.6%. We apply the attention mechanism to single-target and multi-target detection. In order to better coordinate with the security inspector, we directly display the salience map of the target on the input image, 65% positioning is correct after judging by security professionals, as shown in Table 1.

When there is only a single target in the image, even if the gun's pose and the complexity of image background have changed as shown in Figs. 7(a)(b), the target salience map generated by our method can still provide accurate positioning. When there are multiple targets of the same kind in the image as shown in Figs. 7(c)(d), each target is effectively marked in the salience map. When there are multiple types of targets in the image, our model can generate a salience map for each type of target after the multi-target detection process proposed in Sect. 4.

Table 1. Detection accuracy of single-target detection.

Category	Recognition accuracy	Positioning accuracy
Revolver	95.6%	53%
Gun	98.3%	73.5%
Revolver	99.2%	79.3%
Knife	97.2%	54.1%

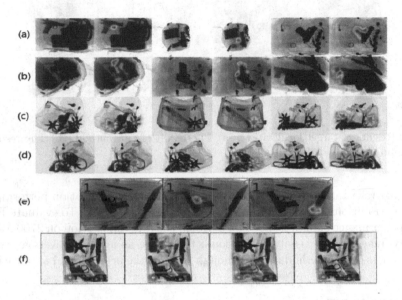

Fig. 7. Results of single-target and multi-target detection. (a), (b) Single-target salience maps. (c), (d) Salience maps of similar multiple targets. (e), (f) Multi-target salience maps.

To quantitatively evaluate the localization effectiveness of our model, we use the above salience map to generate the bounding box, as shown in Fig. 8, which preserves 99% energy of the salience map. Each bounding box in a testing image is compared with the ground-truth bounding box, and the IoU (Intersection over Union) is calculated by Eq. (7). We compare the localization performance of our attention model with the traditional deconvolution method in Table 2.

$$IoU = \frac{area(C) \bigcap area(G)}{area(C) \bigcup area(G)}, \tag{7}$$

where $area(C)$ is the area of candidate bound, and $area(G)$ is the area of ground-truth bound.

Our model can produce highly discriminative salience maps, which is essential for prohibited item detection. Due to the introduction of neuronal stimulus inhibition, the salience maps generated by high-level semantic feedback model

Table 2. Localization IoU of our attention model and the traditional deconvolution method.

Method	Localization IoU
Deconvolution	34.3%
Ours	56.6%

(a)   (b)

Fig. 8. Results of target localization. (a) The result of our method. (b) The result of deconvolution method.

are highly relevant to the target objects. We get better localization performance than the traditional deconvolution method, as shown in Fig. 8. To evaluate Real-Time performance of our method, we perform the target detection on 2700 X-Ray security images. It takes only 0.76 seconds to process an image on average. So the effectiveness of our method is good enough to meet the needs of real applications.

6   Conclusion

In this paper, we applied an Attention Mechanism based CNN model to achieve detection for prohibited item in airport security X-ray images. It can achieve recognition and location of prohibited item but only need weak supervision training. Our model jointly reasons the outputs of class nodes and the activation of hidden layer neurons during the feedback process. High level semantic is captured and mapped to the image space as an attention map after suppressing noise and interference.

During the inspection process, the CNN can tell the security inspectors the category of prohibited item. At the same time, the attention maps of the prohibited item can remind the security inspectors where the dangerous goods are, facilitating the reinspection. We believe that Attention Mechanism based Convolutional Neural Network provides a new direction for automated security.

Acknowledgments. This work was supported by the National Science Foundation of China Nos. 61379102, 61806208.

References

1. Mery, D., Svec, E., Arias, M., et al.: Modern computer vision techniques for x-ray testing in baggage inspection. IEEE Trans. Syst. Man Cybern. Syst. **47**(4), 682–692 (2017)
2. Mclay, L.A., Lee, A.J., Jacobson, S.H.: Risk-based policies for airport security checkpoint screening. INFORMS (1999)
3. Riffo, V., Mery, D.: Automated detection of threat objects using adapted implicit shape mode. IEEE Trans. Syst. Man Cybern. Syst. **46**(4), 472–482 (2017)
4. Franzel, T., Schmidt, U., Roth, S.: Object detection in multi-view X-ray images. Joint DAGM **7476**, 144–154 (2012)
5. Kundegorski, M.E., Akcay, S., Devereux, M., et al.: On using feature descriptors as visual words for object detection within X-ray baggage security screening. In: International Conference on Imaging for Crime Detection and Prevention 2016, vol. 12, no. 6 (2016)
6. Akcay, S., Kundegorski, M.E., Devereux, M., et al.: Transfer learning using convolutional neural networks for object classification within X-ray baggage security imagery. In: IEEE International Conference on Image Processing 2016, pp. 1057–1061 (2016)
7. Cao, C., Huang, Y., Yang, Y., et al.: Feedback convolutional neural network for visual localization and segmentation. IEEE Trans. Pattern Anal. Mach. Intell. **99**, 1 (2018)
8. Cao, C., Wang, Z., Wang, L., et al.: Lateral Inhibition-inspired Convolutional Neural Network for Visual Attention and Saliency Detection. Association for the Advancement of Artificial Intelligence (2018)
9. Zhang, J., Bargal, S.A., Lin, Z., et al.: Top-down neural attention by excitation backprop. Int. J. Comput. Vis. **17**, 1–19 (2016)
10. Wang, Q., Zhang, J., Song, S., et al.: Attentional neural network: feature selection using cognitive feedback. In: International Conference on Neural Information Processing Systems. MIT Press, pp. 2033–2041 (2014)
11. Arkachar, P., Wagh, M.D.: Criticality of lateral inhibition for edge enhancement in neural systems. Neurocomputing **70**(4–6), 991–999 (2007)
12. Krell, M.M., Seeland, A., Kim, S.K.: Data augmentation for brain-computer interfaces: analysis on event-related potentials data (2018)

A Modified PSRoI Pooling with Spatial Information

Yiqing Zheng$^{(\boxtimes)}$, Xiaolu Hu, Ning Bi, and Jun Tan

Sun Yat-sen University, Guangzhou, China
{zhengyq23,huxlu5}@mail2.sysu.edu.cn, {mcsbn,mcstj}@mail.sysu.edu.cn

Abstract. Position Sensitive RoI pooling in RFCN [5] is a RoI pooling that contains the position information. Each RoI rectangle will be devided into K × K bins by a regular grid. In this paper, we present a modified PSRoI pooling that contains spatial information. Every bin in PSRoI pooling is rescaled to 2×. With this proposed network, the spatial information around the bin will be added to predict the classifications. The weight outside the bin is simply set to 0.5 manually. We use ResNet101 backbone network to test our model on PASCAL VOC and MS COCO. We gain some improvement compared with RFCN [5] on the VOC and MS COCO Dataset.

Keywords: Modified PSRoI pooling · Spatial information

1 Introduction

Object Detection is a computer vision task that detects the objects in the images or videos. In this task, we should find out the objects and locate them. There may be one or more object in the images. It's difficult to locate the object which will be anywhere in the images. There are a series of methods to deal with the task. The methods based on DNN can be generally devided into 2 groups: (1) one-stage methods and (2) two-stage methods.

One-stage methods including YOLO [9] and SSD [10] perform more efficient than two-stage methods and are applied in real time object detection. One-stage methods generate the classification and the boxex information directly by regression, without region proposal network. Two-stage methods are based on RCNN [4] architecture, and improved to many other methods, like Fast RCNN, Faster RCNN, RFCN, Mask RCNN [1–3,5] and so on. In the two-stage methods, deep convolutional neural networks pretrained on Imagenet are used to extract feature maps, and then fine tuned through the backpropagation process. Two-stage methods can be devided to 2 subnetworks, region proposal network and prediction network. In common, two-stage methods perform better than one-stage methods in object detection. It has to be said that accuracy and speed are a pair of contradictions, and how to better balance them has been an important direction of the research of the target detection algorithm.

© Springer Nature Switzerland AG 2018
J.-H. Lai et al. (Eds.): PRCV 2018, LNCS 11257, pp. 440–445, 2018.
https://doi.org/10.1007/978-3-030-03335-4_38

In current research, some significant methods are proposed and perform well such as [3,8]. FPN [8] propose A topdown architecture with lateral connections is developed for building high-level semantic feature maps at all scales. The main idea is to build feature pyramid by using the multi-scale Pyramid shaped hierarchy inherent in the deep convolution network.And the feature pyramid creates a top-down architecture with a lateral connection to build high-level semantic feature maps on all scales. FPN is a general feature extractor as a general feature extractor. It is still important to use Pyramid to clearly solve the multiscale problem with the strong expressive ability and internal robustness of the scale. Mask RCNN [3] propose a additional path for object mask task, and it becomes the beseline of object detection.

Region proposal network (RPN) is a significant subnetwork that outputs many candidate boxes about objects. The boxes and features will be input into the RoI pooling. In the RoI pooling, the features in the boxes are extracted and reshaped to a preset scale by a special pooling layer with variable shape of filters. Many improvements are proposed, like Position Sensitive RoI pooling (PSRoI pooling) [5] and RoIAlign [3]. PSRoI pooling, proposed in the RFCN, encodes the position information with respect to a relative spatial position. RoiAlign uses bilinear interpolation to compute the exact values of the input features at four regularly sampled locations in each RoI bin. In this paper, a modified PSRoI pooling is proposed. Each bin in PSRoI pooling is scaled to 2× and includes more spatial information around the area. We use ResNet101 backbone network to test our proposed network. We get some improvement on the datasets.

2   Related Work

In the Object Detection algorithm based on the region proposal, Fast R-CNN [2] adds an ROI pooling layer after the last convolutional layer of the R-CNN [4]; the box regression is added to CNN training process; Softmax is used instead of SVM for classification, and end-to-end is also implemented. Faster R-CNN [1] uses RPN instead of Fast R-CNN's Selective Search method [2] to allow RPN and Fast R-CNN networks to share feature extraction networks. Mask R-CNN [3] adds FCN to generate corresponding MASK branches based on the original Faster R-CNN algorithm. The algorithm can be used to accomplish various tasks such as target classification, target detection, semantic segmentation, instance segmentation, and human pose recognition.

We know that classification requires features with translation invariance, and object detection requires accurate responses to the translation of the object. It can be seen that most CNNnet can do a good job in classification, but they are not very effective in detecting them. So for this problem, we find that methods such as Faster R-CNN [1] are convolutional before ROI pooling. They are translation-invariant, but once ROI pooling is inserted, the underlying network structure is no longer translation-invariant. Then position-sensitive score map proposed in RFCN [5] can integrate the object position information into ROI pooling, which can solve this problem well. At the same time, CoupleNet [6] introduced the global and context information of the proposal on the basis of the original RFCN [5], and improved the accuracy of detection by combining the information of part, global, and context. According to different layers of feature map, the advantages are different. A multi-scale convolutional neural network is proposed, and different-scale detectors are designed for different layers on the feature map [7]. Based on the RFCN network, this paper builds a modified position sensitive pooling to contain spatial information and achieve some improvement on some dataset.

3   Our Approach

3.1   PSRoI Pooling

Since our work is based on the PSRoI pooling [5], we first introduce the PSRoI pooling. In RFCN, the images are input into the backbone subnetwork, and extracted to feature maps. The feature maps then generate score maps and location information. In PSRoI pooling, score maps and candidate boxes are the inputs. The score maps have $K \times K \times (C+1)$ channels. We extract the sub-area of score maps according to the candidate boxes. The RoI is then divided to $K \times K$ bins. Refer to RFCN, the (i, j)-th bin$(0 \leq i, j \leq k - 1)$ operation in position-sensitive RoI pooling [5] is:

$$r_c(i, j | \Theta) = \sum_{(x,y) \in bin(i,j)} z_{i,j,c}(x + x_0, y + y_0 | \Theta)/n \tag{1}$$

Here $r_c(i, j)$ is the pooled response in the (i, j)-th bin for the c-th category, $z_{i,j,c}$ is one score map of the $k^2(C + 1)$ score maps, (x_0, y_0) denotes the top-left corner of an RoI, n is the number of pixels in the bin, and Θ demotes all learnable parameters of the network. When we compute the score of one bin, such as the top-left bin, we first find out the corresponding $C + 1$ score maps. We extract the sub-area of the bin and compute the average score as output. Then we vote to get the final score of the whole RoI of every class.

3.2   Our Modified Model

Refer to [6,7], using larger RoI which includes spatial information can help to improve the performent of the network. As seen in PSRoI pooling, scores is computed restricted in the bin. When computing the score in each bin, we rescale the size of the bin to $2\times$. Figure 1 is an example of our model. For the central bin of the PSRoI pooling, the original PSRoI pooling will compute the score for $C + 1$ classification in the corresponding RoI while our modified PSRoI pooling will compute the score for the $C + 1$ classification in the $2\times$ RoI. For example, (x_0, y_0, x_1, y_1) is the coordinate of one bin in the RoI. Then the weight of the bin is $x_1 - x_0$ and the height of the bin is $y_1 - y_0$. In our modified network, the coordiinate is set to $(x_0 - (x_1 - x_0)/2, y_0 - (y_1 - y_0)/2, x_1 + (x_1 - x_0)/2, y_1 + (y_1 - y_0)/2)$. With our modified, some area may be outside the image, we set the score equal to 0 outside the image. Therefore, we add the spatial information around the RoI which will improve the performent of the network. We set the weight of outside the bin equal to 0.5 manually. Then score of the (i, j)-th bin$(0 \leq i, j \leq k - 1)$ is modified to:

$$r_c(i, j|\Theta) = \sum_{(x,y) \in bin^*(i,j)} w \times z_{i,j,c}(x + x_0, y + y_0|\Theta)/2n \qquad (2)$$

where $bin^*(i, j)$ is the $2\times bin(i, j)$ and w is 1 where $(x, y) \in bin(i, j)$ and 0.5 where $(x, y) \notin bin(i, j)$.

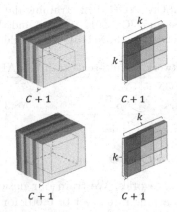

Fig. 1. The top figure shows the PSRoI pooling operation of the central bin. The bottom figure shows our modified model. The scale of the RoI is enlarge to $2\times$.

4 Experiments

4.1 Experiments on PASCAL VOC

PASCAL VOC has 20 object categories. The VOC 2007 and the VOC 2012 are widely used in object detection. We first train on the union set of VOC 2007 trainval and VOC 2012 trainval, and test on VOC 2007 test. We use ResNet101 backbone to compute the feature maps. And in the PSRoI pooling, every RoI is divided to $7 \times 7(K = 7)$. The multi-scale training strategy [11] is adopted here. Follow the RFCN [5], for each training iteration, we resize the image randomly to 400, 500, 600, 700 or 800. When testing, we only test on a single scale of 600 pixels. The strategy is adopted in following experiment. The learning rate of the network is set to 0.001 for the first 30k iterations and then set to 0.0001 for the rest with a mini-batch size of 8. We compare RFCN [5] and our network. The result is in Table 1.

Then we test on the VOC 2012. We train the network on the union set of VOC 2007 trainval, VOC 2007 test and VOC 2012 trainval. The parameter is the same as above. In the PSRoI pooling, every RoI is divided to $7 \times 7(K = 7)$. We compare with the result of RFCN [5], and our network has some improvement. Table 2 is the result.

Table 1. The results on PASCAL VOC 2007. Training data is the union set of VOC 2007 trainval and VOC 2012 trainval and the test data is VOC 2007 test. The backbone of the network is ResNet101.

Network	Multi-scale train?	mAP
RFCN [5]	No	79.5
RFCN [5]	Yes	80.5
Ours	No	79.8
Ours	Yes	80.6

Table 2. The results on PASCAL VOC 2012. Training data is the union set of VOC 2007 trainval, VOC 2007 test and VOC 2012 trainval and the test data is VOC 2012 test. The backbone of the network is ResNet101. The model is train multi-scale.

Network	Multi-scale train?	mAP
RFCN [5]	Yes	77.6
Ours	No	78.3

4.2   Experiments on MS COCO

MS COCO has 80 object categories. We train our network on the trainval and test on the test-dev. The learning rate is set to 0.001 for the first 110k iterations and 0.0001 for the rest. We use ResNet101 to compute the feature maps. in the PSRoI pooling, every RoI is divided to $7 \times 7(K = 7)$. The multi-scale training strategy [11] is adopted here. The result is in the Table 3. We find that our network have some improvement compared with RFCN [5].

Table 3. The results on MS COCO. Training data is the COCO trainval set and the test data is COCO test-dev set. The backbone of the network is ResNet101.

Network	Multi-scale train?	mAP@0.5	AP[0.5:0.95]
RFCN [5]	No	51.5	29.2
RFCN [5]	Yes	51.9	29.9
Ours	No	51.7	29.0
Ours	Yes	52.1	30.4

References

1. Ren, S., He, K., Girshick, R., Sun, J.: Faster R-CNN: towards real-time object detection with region proposal networks. In: NIPS (2015)
2. Girshick, R.: Fast R-CNN. In: ICCV (2015)
3. He, K., Gkioxari, G., Dollár, P., Girshick, R.: Mask R-CNN. In: ICCV (2017)

4. Girshick, R., Donahue, J., Darrell, T., Malik, J.: Rich feature hierarchies for accurate object detection and semantic segmentation. In: CVPR (2014)
5. Dai, J., Li, Y., He, K., Sun, J.: R-FCN: object detection via region-based fully convolutional networks. In: NIPS (2016)
6. Zhu, Y., Zhao, C., Wang, J., et al.: CoupleNet: coupling global structure with local parts for object detection. In: ICCV (2017)
7. Cai, Z., Fan, Q., Feris, R.S., Vasconcelos, N.: A unified multi-scale deep convolutional neural network for fast object detection. In: Leibe, B., Matas, J., Sebe, N., Welling, M. (eds.) ECCV 2016. LNCS, vol. 9908, pp. 354–370. Springer, Cham (2016). https://doi.org/10.1007/978-3-319-46493-0_22
8. Lin, T.-Y., Dollár, P., Girshick, R., He, K., Hariharan, B., Belongie, S.: Feature pyramid networks for object detection. In: CVPR (2017)
9. Redmon, J., Divvala, S., Girshick, R., Farhadi, A.: You only look once: unified, real-timeobjectdetection. In: CVPR (2016)
10. Liu, W., et al.: SSD: single shot MultiBox detector. In: Leibe, B., Matas, J., Sebe, N., Welling, M. (eds.) ECCV 2016. LNCS, vol. 9905, pp. 21–37. Springer, Cham (2016). https://doi.org/10.1007/978-3-319-46448-0_2
11. He, K., Zhang, X., Ren, S., Sun, J.: Spatial pyramid pooling in deep convolutional networks for visual recognition. In: Fleet, D., Pajdla, T., Schiele, B., Tuytelaars, T. (eds.) ECCV 2014. LNCS, vol. 8691, pp. 346–361. Springer, Cham (2014). https://doi.org/10.1007/978-3-319-10578-9_23

A Sparse Substitute for Deconvolution Layers in GANs

Juzheng Li[1], Pengfei Ge[1], and Chuan-Xian Ren[1,2(✉)]

[1] School of Mathematics, Sun Yat-sen University, Guangzhou 510275, China
{lijzh29,gepengf}@mail2.sysu.edu.cn, rchuanx@mail.sysu.edu.cn
[2] Shenzhen Research Institute, Sun Yat-sen University, Shenzhen 518000, China

Abstract. Generative adversarial networks are useful tools in image generation task, but training and running them are relatively slow due to the large amount parameters introduced by their generators. In this paper, S-Deconv, a sparse drop-in substitute for deconvolution layers, is proposed to alleviate this issue. S-Deconv decouples reshaping input tensor from reweighing it by first processing it with a sparse fixed filter into desired form then reweighing them using learnable one. By doing so, S-Deconv reduces the numbers of learnable and total parameters with sparsity. Our experiments on Fashion-MNIST, CelebA and Anime-Faces verify the feasibility of our method. We also give another interpretation of our method from the perspective of regularization.

Keywords: Generative adversarial networks · Sparsity · Deconvolution

1 Introduction

Generative adversarial networks (GANs [5]) have been a heated topic in the deep learning community since they provide a powerful framework that allows us to learn complex distributions in tasks where no explicit merits to apply such as image generation and manipulation. To this end various network architectures were designed, many of which have multiple generators with great depth [3,4,13]. Along with their mirrored counterparts, those generators introduce too many parameters making it slow to train GANs. There has been methods [6,8] focusing on substitutes with fewer parameters for convolution layers used in recognition tasks; however, to the best of our knowledge, no similar substitutes has been proposed for deconvolution layers in GANs.

In this paper, inspired by the success of introducing atrous convolution into semantic segmentation tasks [2], we propose a new building block of neural

C.-X. Ren—This work is supported in part by the Science and Technology Program of Shenzhen under Grant JCYJ20170818155415617, the National Natural Science Foundation of China under Grants 61572536, and the Science and Technology Program of GuangZhou under Grant 201804010248.

J.-H. Lai et al. (Eds.): PRCV 2018, LNCS 11257, pp. 446–456, 2018.
https://doi.org/10.1007/978-3-030-03335-4_39

networks called S-Deconv that functions similarly to a vanilla deconvolution layer but with controllable sparsity built within and fewer parameters to learn. These two properties are believed to helpful in terms of accelerating GANs during training. Our proposed method can be considered as a combination of fixed and learnable kernels. Although we adopt the similar setting of fixed kernel in [8], our approaches are fundamentally different. Firstly, the problem settings are not the same: generation and classification. Secondly, we use these fixed kernels as mean to reshape the input tensor reserving much of its information despite the sparsity, an encouraging result due to the nature of deconvolution while in [8], fixed kernels, followed by Sigmoid activation, were used to approximate the standard convolution layers.

2 Related Work

Generative Adversarial Networks. Being an upcoming technique in the unsupervised learning field, generative adversarial networks [5] provide a way to implicitly model distributions of high-dimensional data, for example, images and neural languages [9,10]. In general, a GAN can be well characterized by training two networks simultaneously in competition with each other. When a GAN is applied in image synthesis tasks, one can image that one of the networks is a forger whose specialty is to imitate master pieces while another is a expert whose majors in art. In this scenario, the forger G, or Generator in GAN terminology, will try its best to generate plausible art, or realistic images, from noises while the expert D, or Discriminator, will receive both fake and real art then try to identify which one is authentic and which one is not. In our experiments, we use WGAN [1], a variant of GAN approximates EM distance rather than JS distance, as our baseline model.

Local Binary Convolution. Local binary convolution (followed by a ReLU activation), an approximation of vanilla convolution which is also followed by a ReLU activation is proposed [8]. A LB-Conv consists of three parts: a convolution layer with fixed LB-kernels, a sigmoid activation and a standard 1×1 convolution. A LB-Conv kernels is many alike to a standard kernel used in convolution and deconvolution layers except that elements in a LB-kernel are only zero, one and negative one. We utilize this kind of kernels in our method for its sparsity and other desirable properties.

3 Our New Method

3.1 S-Deconv

Our new method is based on one observation that after a feature map which is passed to a deconvolution layer, two things happened *simultaneously*: (1) this tensor is reshaped and (2) new values are given by a weighted summation of old ones. We call them *reshapingphase* and *reweighingphase*. Due to this simultaneity, a kernel in a deconvolution layer must be lager enough to catch the surrounding of a pixel in the feature map. However this often leads to vain efforts since this kernel is operated on a feature map that is seriously padded with zeros. If we shrink the size of this kernel or enlarge the stride of it, it may receive more non-padded values giving more meaningful reweighing results; however, doing so will jeopardize reshaping results forcing us to add more layers. To address this dilemma, we trade simultaneity for freedom in designing kernels. This decoupling reshaping and reweighing results our proposed method, S-Deconv layer.

In S-Deconv, reshaping is done by fixing sparse kernels containing only -1, 1 and 0 and then reweighing is done by channel-wise weighted summations. To best utilize existing deep learning library, both phases in S-Deconv are implemented by vanilla deconvolution and convolution layers: reshaping phase can be considered as a deconvolution layer with fixed LB-kernels while reweighing phase can be considered as a convolution layer with 1×1 kernels. However, these two operations may increase the computational afford of GAN since S-Deconv works best with sparse matrix multiplication. We present our main operations in Algorithm 1 to have a clear understanding of how our method works in practice and make a comparison to vanilla deconvolution layers in Table 1. And in Eq. (1) we show the ratio of numbers of learnable parameters

$$\frac{\#Deconv}{\#Our\ Method} = \frac{p \times h \times w}{m} \tag{1}$$

and total parameters in Eq. (2)

$$\frac{\#Deconv}{\#Our\ Method} = \frac{p \times h \times w \times q}{p \times h \times w \times m \times (1 - \theta) + m \times q} \tag{2}$$

where p, q and m are numbers of input, output and intermediate channels, $h \times w$ is the size of deconvolution kernels and θ is the sparsity. Under mild settings, we can see that both ratios are lager than one, which indicates that our method uses fewer learnable and total parameters.

Algorithm 1. S-Deconv layer

Input: Tensor X; Fixed LB-Conv kernels K_{lb}; Learnable 1×1 Kernels $K_{1\times1}$.
Reshaping Phase: $X_{inter} = Deconv(X; K_{lb})$
Reweighing Phase: $Y = Conv(X_{inter}; K_{1\times1})$
Output: Y

We discuss some technical details as follows.

Why the Name? The name of our proposed method may be confusing. The meanings of "sparse" here are of two folds. First, weights in a S-Deconv layer are most zeros. Second, most of those weights need not to be learned.

Table 1. A comparison of our method and deconvolution

Layer	Components	Output
Vanilla deconvolution	Deconvolution	Feature map
Our method	Fixed deconvolution	Reshaped input
	1×1 convolution	Feature map

Drop-In Substitute. Given LB-Conv kernels and intermediate channel size, our method is a drop-in substitute for deconvolution layers. Our experiments show that replacing a deconvolution layer with a S-Deconv layer often require no changes in hyperparameter setting.

Why LB-Conv Kernels. When it comes to fixed hand-crafted kernels, there are many options including randomly initialized weights, among which we take LB-Conv kernels as our reshaping kernels for two reasons: (1) they have controllable sparse nature built within; (2) aside from zeros for sparsity, it contains only one and negative one which can help with persevering information.

Channels of Intermediate Feature Maps. After reshaping phase, input feature maps have been transformed into new feature maps we call intermediate feature maps which would be sent to reweighing. About the number of channels of those maps, it seems it should be as large as possible to best preserve information of the input ones; however, setting it too large will increase number of parameters to learn in reweighing phase, and experiments have shown that keeping the number of channels unchanged would be enough.

Runtime Analysis. In theory, our method should be faster due to its sparsity nature. However, the convolution operation we use to implement our method in the experiments are designed for sparse matrices in terms of forward, backward ans storage; thus the significant improvement of runtime is not observed in our pilot experiments. How to modify this operation would be our further work.

Relation with Other Methods. In [6], a vanilla convolution layer is decomposed into a channel-wise convolution and a point-wise convolution layer to save parameters. In [8], fixed kernels are constructed by a Bernoulli distribution of $(1, -1, 0)$. Our method shares certain similarity with these two methods, but our goals and approaches are different:

(1) We present a drop-in substitute that use the sparse nature of LB-Conv kernels and paddings in deconvolution which is not a approximation to deconvolution layers differencing from LB-Conv in [8]. And we do not intend to make our method an approximated deconvolution layer but a regularized one. See Sect. 3.2 for a regularization view.
(2) We aim to accelerate networks with sparsity which is different from [6].

3.2   A Regularization View

In this section, we interpret our method in a regularization perspective.
A deconvolution layer can be written as

$$Vec(Y)_{deconv} = K^T Vec(X) \tag{3}$$

where K^T is the kernel matrix used in deconvolution. In a S-Deconv setting, we would have

$$Vec(Y)_{our} = VB^T Vec(X) \tag{4}$$

where B is a fixed LB-Conv kernel matrix and V is a learnable 1×1 convolution kernel matrix. In a regularization perspective, we can see that we add regularization to kernels in standard deconvolution layers forcing their corresponding matrix K^T to be decomposed as matrix multiplication of V and B^T.

4   Experiments

To verify the feasibility of our method S-Deconv, we conduct several experiments of image generation on different datasets. We also show Inception scores to compare qualities of images generated by different generators used in our experiments.

4.1   Datasets and Preprocessing

Datasets used in our experiments are summarized as follows:

(1) Fashion-MNIST [12] is a Fashion version of MNIST dataset only with more complex data structure. It was proposed to be direct replacement for MNIST for benchmarking. We will focus on this dataset in terms of computing Inception scores since it is complex enough to show that our method can also work well on other datasets while not too complex that we have enough computational resources to obtain Inception scores with Monte Carlo method.
(2) CelebA [11] is a large scale real life dataset of face attributes, we use its face images in our experiments; since it's not a label dataset, we cannot report Inception scores.
(3) Anime-Faces[1] contains 143,000 anime styled images with more than 100 tags (attributes).

As for preprocessing, we resized all images into 64×64, and centralized them. Resizing may add extra difficulties but it can save us a lot of time reorganizing models.

---

[1] Dataset obtained from https://github.com/jayleicn/animeGAN.

4.2   Architectures and Hyperparameters Settings

We used a WGAN [1] with a five deconvolution layers generator and a mirrored discriminator as our baseline model. Batch Normalization layers [7] are used. Modifications made to verify the feasibility of our approach are replacing deconvolution layers with S-Deconv ones. Details of this architecture is presented in Fig. 1, where arrows indicate the directions of information flowing.

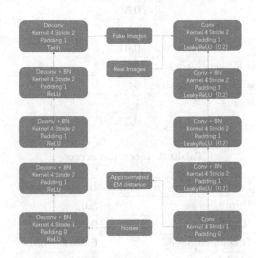

Fig. 1. Architecture of the baseline WGAN

All hyperparameters are kept unchanged for the same datasets in our experiments to avoid cherry-picking. We pay no attention to adjusting those hyperparameters to create very smart results. In contrary, we use some default settings that can be applied to many models and datasets to achieve not state-of- the-art but satisfying enough results to show that those models work. Details of those parameters are presented in Table 2[2]. The classifier used to compute Inception scores is built and trained by ourselves, the accuracy of which is a leaderboard performance.

4.3   Results

Feasibility. We focus on the results, Inception scores especially, of experiments on Fashion-MNIST dataset and show those scores in Table 3. Exact value of Inception score indicates nothing, and to show a clearer idea of how well models performed, we also compute the Inception scores of pure noises and real images.

From Table 3, we observe that by replacing a few deconvolution layers in our baseline model, the resulting models can actually generate images with higher

---

[2] Internal Coefficients: Ratio of internal channels and input channels in a SLBP layer. Density: Controlling the sparsity of SLBP layers.

Table 2. Hyperparameter sittings for three datasets

Hyperparameter	Fashion-Mnist	CelebA	Anime
Image size	64 × 64	64 × 64	64 × 64
Dimension of noise	100	200	200
Optimizer	RMSprop	RMSprop	RMSprop
Learning rate	0.0002	0.00005	0.00005
Beta	0.5	0.5	0.5
Batch size	64	16	16
Clipping	0.01	0.01	0.01
Basic channels for generators	64	128	128
Basic channels for discriminators	64	64	64
Internal coefficients	1	1	1
Density	0.5	0.5	0.5

Table 3. Inception scores

Source of evaluated images	Inception score
Pure nosies	3.02
Real images	9.67
Baseline model	6.6364
Model−1	6.9164
Model−1−2	6.6427
Model-1−2−3	6.7098
Model-1−2−3−4	1.4297
Model-1−2−3−4−5	1.0000

Inception scores which verifies the feasibility of our method. And there is a dramatic drop after $Model-1-2-3$ where the term $Model-1-2-3$ means the first three deconvolution layers has been replaced. This may be caused by over-regularization. Models with four or five S-Deconv layers would a small capacity since their learnable parameters are of a small number. Such capacities may not be enough to learn a complex image distribution.

Effects of Regularization. Experimental results in Table 3 verify the feasibility of our proposed S-Deconv method. Now we further investigate the regularization effect of different combinations of S-Deconv layers (in total $2^5 = 32$ cases). Table 4 shows Inceptions scores under different settings where array (0, 1, 0, 1, 0) means the second and fourth deconvolution layers being replaced by SLBP layers. Note that over regularization (4 or 5 layers replaced, 2 or 3 top layers

Table 4. More inception scores

Model	Inception score	Model	Inception score
0 0 0 0 0	6.6364	0 0 0 0 1	1.0000
0 0 0 1 0	6.8365	0 0 0 1 1	1.0000
0 0 1 0 0	6.7918	0 0 1 0 1	1.5593
0 0 1 1 0	6.5145	0 0 1 1 1	1.0000
0 1 0 0 0	1.0457	0 1 0 0 1	6.3385
0 1 0 1 0	6.4304	0 1 0 1 1	1.5357
0 1 1 0 0	6.8262	0 1 1 0 1	1.0000
0 1 1 1 0	1.0956	0 1 1 1 1	1.0000
1 0 0 0 0	6.9164	1 0 0 0 1	6.5662
1 0 0 1 0	1.0071	1 0 0 1 1	6.1790
1 0 1 0 0	4.7278	1 0 1 0 1	1.0000
1 0 1 1 0	1.0000	1 0 1 1 1	5.2147
1 1 0 0 0	6.6427	1 1 0 0 1	1.0075
1 1 0 1 0	1.0007	1 1 0 1 1	5.0681
1 1 1 0 0	6.7098	1 1 1 0 1	5.3925
1 1 1 1 0	1.4297	1 1 1 1 1	1.0000

replaced) would lead to catastrophic results since networks under such regularizations would not have sufficient model capacity to learn complex distributions.

Generated Images. We show some samples of images generated by $Model - 1$ and Baseline model as a comparison on all three datasets using hyperparameter

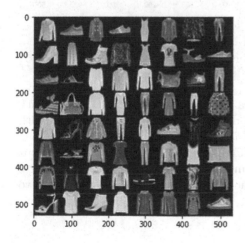

Fig. 2. Real Fashion-MNIST images

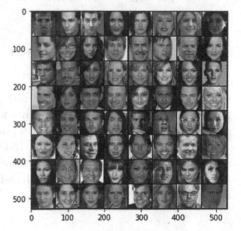

Fig. 3. Real CelebA images

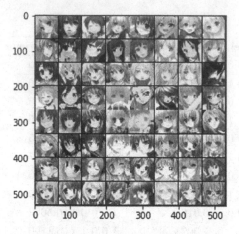

Fig. 4. Real Anime-Faces images

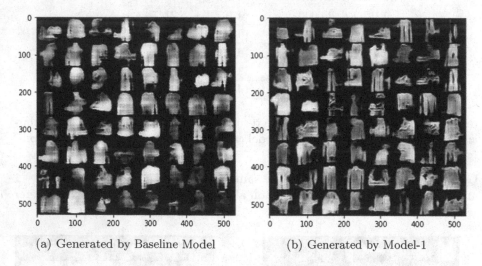

(a) Generated by Baseline Model   (b) Generated by Model-1

Fig. 5. Generated Fashion-MNIST images

settings described in Sect. 4.2. All images were generated during training with no hand-picking. Real images are provided for evaluation and comparison with generated images shown in Figs. 5, 6 and 7.

We can see that on Fashion-MNIST dataset, model equipped with our method clearly outperforms the baseline model as indicated by Inception Scores in Table 3. As for CelebA and Anime-Faces datasets, we believe that the two models perform very similarly.

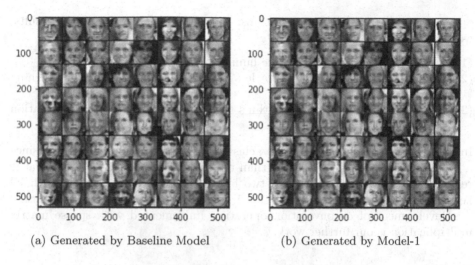

(a) Generated by Baseline Model   (b) Generated by Model-1

Fig. 6. Generated CelebA faces

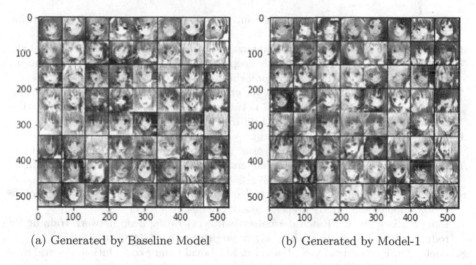

(a) Generated by Baseline Model   (b) Generated by Model-1

Fig. 7. Generated Anime Faces

5   Discussion

We have proposed S-Deconv, a sparse substitute for deconvolution layers in
GANs settings, and have shown that our method is feasible in practice. In experiments, we use WGAN as our baseline model and make modifications only on
generators since that WGAN add extra constraints to discriminators. However,
in other GAN architectures, such constraints are not needed, which means that
we can replace convolution layers in discriminators to further reduce parameters.
As we all know, neural networks are, in most cases, over-parameterized and the
search in parameter space is constrained by network structures and guided by

optimizers using SGD-based algorithms. Thus, to obtain better search results, we can

(1) design architectures that encode human pilot knowledge;
(2) design building blocks that are less redundant than stand deep learning layers;
(3) design new optimization algorithms that can make full use of information contained in data.

In this paper, our method should be classed into option (1) or option (2) since a S-Deconv layer is less redundant than a standard deconvolution layer that it replaces and can be considered as two layers (a deconvolution one with fixed kernels and a convolution one with 1×1 kernel size) taken place in sequence.

Development of deconvolution operation implemented with sparse matrix multiplication is our further work.

References

1. Arjovsky, M., Chintala, S., Bottou, L.: Wasserstein gan. arXiv preprint arXiv:1701.07875 (2017)
2. Chen, L.C., Papandreou, G., Kokkinos, I., Murphy, K., Yuille, A.L.: DeepLab: semantic image segmentation with deep convolutional nets, atrous convolution, and fully connected CRFs. arXiv preprint arXiv:1606.00915 (2016)
3. Denton, E.L., Chintala, S., Fergus, R., et al.: Deep generative image models using a Laplacian pyramid of adversarial networks. In: Advances in Neural Information Processing Systems, pp. 1486–1494 (2015)
4. Ghosh, A., Kulharia, V., Namboodiri, V., Torr, P.H., Dokania, P.K.: Multi-agent diverse generative adversarial networks. arXiv preprint arXiv:1704.02906 (2017)
5. Goodfellow, I., et al.: Generative adversarial nets. In: Advances in Neural Information Processing Systems, pp. 2672–2680 (2014)
6. Howard, A.G., et al.: MobileNets: efficient convolutional neural networks for mobile vision applications. arXiv preprint arXiv:1704.04861 (2017)
7. Ioffe, S., Szegedy, C.: Batch normalization: accelerating deep network training by reducing internal covariate shift. arXiv preprint arXiv:1502.03167 (2015)
8. Juefei-Xu, F., Boddeti, V.N., Savvides, M.: Local binary convolutional neural networks. In: 2017 IEEE Conference on Computer Vision and Pattern Recognition (CVPR), vol. 1 (2017)
9. Li, J., Monroe, W., Shi, T., Ritter, A., Jurafsky, D.: Adversarial learning for neural dialogue generation. arXiv preprint arXiv:1701.06547 (2017)
10. Liu, L., Lu, Y., Yang, M., Qu, Q., Zhu, J., Li, H.: Generative adversarial network for abstractive text summarization. arXiv preprint arXiv:1711.09357 (2017)
11. Liu, Z., Luo, P., Wang, X., Tang, X.: Deep learning face attributes in the wild. In: Proceedings of the IEEE International Conference on Computer Vision, pp. 3730–3738 (2015)
12. Xiao, H., Rasul, K., Vollgraf, R.: Fashion-MNIST: a novel image dataset for benchmarking machine learning algorithms. arXiv preprint arXiv:1708.07747 (2017)
13. Zhu, J.Y., Park, T., Isola, P., Efros, A.A.: Unpaired image-to-image translation using cycle-consistent adversarial networks. arXiv preprint arXiv:1703.10593 (2017)

Crop Disease Image Classification Based on Transfer Learning with DCNNs

Yuan Yuan[1], Sisi Fang[1,2(✉)], and Lei Chen[1(✉)]

[1] Institute of Intelligent Machines, Chinese Academy of Sciences, Hefei, China
fss135721@163.com, chenlei@iim.ac.cn
[2] University of Science and Technology of China, Hefei, China

Abstract. Machine learning has been widely used in the crop disease image classification. Traditional methods relying on the extraction of hand-crafted low-level image features are difficulty to get satisfactory results. Deep convolutional neural network can deal with this problem because of automatically learning the feature representations from raw image data, but require enough labeled data to obtain a good generalization performance. However, in the field of agriculture, the available labeled data in target task is limited. In order to solve this problem, this paper proposes a method which combines transfer learning with two popular deep learning architectures (i.e., AlexNet and VGGNet) to classify eight kinds of crop diseases images. First, during the training procedure, the batch normalization and DisturbLabel techniques are introduced into these two networks to reduce the number of training iterations and overfitting. Then, after training the pre-trained model by using the open source dataset PlantVillage. Finally, we fine-tune this model with our relatively small dataset preprocessed by a proposed strategy. The experimental results reveal that our approach can achieve an average accuracy of 95.93% compared to state-of-the-art method for our relatively small dataset, demonstrating the feasibility and robustness of this approach.

Keywords: Transfer learning · Deep learning · Image classification
DCNN · Crop diseases

1 Introduction

Crop disease is one of the important factors that affect food security [9,15]. It is reported that 50% of the yield losses are caused by crop diseases and pests [3]. Due to the wide variety of diseases, it is easy to misdiagnose only by artificial observation and experience judgment.

In the past few years, there has been a great progress in the area of crop disease image recognition since computer vision and machine learning was used. The most commonly used classification methods include support vector machine (SVM) [10,16], K-nearest neighbors (KNN) [8,19] and discriminant analysis [17]. For example, Tian, et al. [16] extracted the color and texture features of the

© Springer Nature Switzerland AG 2018
J.-H. Lai et al. (Eds.): PRCV 2018, LNCS 11257, pp. 457–468, 2018.
https://doi.org/10.1007/978-3-030-03335-4_40

lesion leaves and then used SVM with different kernel functions to identify 60 images including cucumber downy mildew and powdery mildew. Zhang, et al. [19] classified 100 images of five different corn diseases with KNN after the lesion area segmentation and feature extraction. Wang, et al. [17] used discriminant analysis to identify three different cucumber diseases of 240 images by combining color, shape and texture feature of leaf spots with environmental information. These previous studies have two principal problems. First, the number of samples in datasets is small (between 60 and 240 images). Second, it is necessary to segment the lesion area firstly and extract some specific features, which are always not easy for some kinds of crop diseases, such as cucumber powdery mildew, rice flax spot, etc. Meanwhile, the information of crop diseases cannot be represented entirely with the specific features.

Fortunately, deep convolutional neural network (DCNN), which can extract the deep feature of images by multiple convolution layer and pool layer, was adopted to deal with the above problems in recent years. In 2012, a large DCNN achieved a top-5 error of 16.4% for the classification of images into 1000 possible categories [6]. In the next few years, some DCNN architectures such as AlexNet, GoogLeNet [14] and VGGNet [11] were widely applied in the task of plant disease image recognition. Mohanty, et al. [7] trained a CNN to identify 14 crop species and 26 diseases of PlantVillage dataset, which demonstrated that the feasibility of the approach for disease classification based on the pre-trained model. Srdjan, et al. [12] and Brahimi, et al. [1] classified plant leaf disease images by fine-tuning CaffeNet and AlexNet, which obtained good results. We can see that the above methods are mainly based on the PlantVillage dataset with a large number of images and simple background.

Different from the above works, our crop disease dataset, including five kinds of rice diseases and three kinds of cucumber diseases, has two key issues, a relatively small number of images (less than 10,000 images) and complex background. Therefore, this paper proposes a novel method that employs the PlantVillage dataset to assist our crop disease dataset for classification based on one pre-processing strategy for our dataset and two networks, which are optimized by using the batch normalization and DisturbLabel technique during training.

2   Materials and Methods

2.1   Image Preprocessing

Two datasets are used in this paper. First, in order to obtain the pre-trained model, we use an auxiliary dataset that is collected from the open dataset PlantVillage [4], which contains 54306 images with simple background in 38 classes. Another one is the target dataset with complex background that is collected on sunny days, using the digital single lens reflex camera Canon EOS 6D. The original target dataset, which consists of 2 crop species with 8 different kinds of diseases, contains 2430 images with the inconsistent size. Figure 1 shows some examples from the original target dataset.

Fig. 1. Example of leaf images from original target dataset

Two pre-processing strategies of the target dataset called center crop and corner crop are used in this work. In center crop, we crop a 300×300 square region from the center of each image. Thus, most complex background can be removed and the image quantity is unchanged. In corner crop, we firstly crop center area to 512×512 resolution which keeps most complex background. And then we divide the image into four pieces with 256×256 resolution. Finally, we resize these images into two different sizes (227×227 pixels for AlexNet and 224×224 pixels for VGGNet) using bi-linear interpolation respectively. The pre-processing procedures are shown in Fig. 2. After conducting the above operations on each image and filtering the images with no lesion area, the original target dataset is eventually augmented to 9592 images.

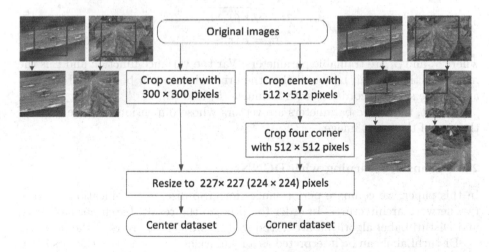

Fig. 2. Two strategies for image pre-processing

2.2   Batch Normalization

Batch normalization ensures that the inputs of layers always fall in the same range even though the earlier layers are updated and always leads to an obvious reduction in the number of training iterations and regularizes the model [5]. We calculate the mean and variance of $x_1 \sim x_n$ for each batch of n samples according to formulas (1) and (2):

$$\mu = \frac{1}{n} \sum_{i=1}^{n} x_i \tag{1}$$

$$\sigma^2 = \frac{1}{n} \sum_{i=1}^{n} (x_i - \mu)^2 \tag{2}$$

where μ and σ are the mean and variance of the data of current batch respectively. After normalized according to formulas (3), the parameter $\hat{x}_i$ is obtained whose mean is 0 and variance is 1:

$$\hat{x}_i = \frac{x_i - \mu}{\sqrt{\sigma^2 + \varepsilon}} \tag{3}$$

where ε is a small constant that is added to the variance to avoid zero-division. To avoid the change of feature distribution by data normalization, the reconstitution is needed to restore the original feature distribution.

$$y_i = \gamma_i \hat{x}_i + \beta_i \tag{4}$$

$$\gamma_i = \sqrt{Var[x_i]} \tag{5}$$

$$\beta_i = E[x_i] \tag{6}$$

where γ_i and β_i are trainable parameters, Var the variance function and E is the mean function. It can be found that the original data can be restored when γ_i and β_i are set in accordance with formulas (5) and (6).

In fact, the above parameters are vectors whose dimensions are the same as the size of the input image.

2.3   Transfer Learning with DCNNs

In this paper, we compare performances for crop disease classification between two network architectures. In order to optimize the result, batch normalization and DisturbLabel algorithm are introduced into different layers of the network.

DisturbLabel can be interpreted as a regularization method on the loss layer, which works by randomly choosing a small subset of training data, and intentionally setting their ground-truth labels to be incorrect [18]. So it can improve the network training process by preventing it from over-fitting. We assume that there are N samples in C classes in each batch given as $(x_n, y_n)_{n=1}^{N}$, where y_n is a corresponding label for a sample. When a sample x_n is determined to be disturbed with a certain probability γ which is a noise rate, its label y_n will be set to a new label $\widetilde{y}_n$ that is randomly chosen from $\{1, 2, \cdots, C\}$ according to formulas (7) and (8),

$$p_t = 1 - \gamma \cdot \frac{C-1}{C} \tag{7}$$

$$p_i = \gamma \cdot \frac{1}{C} \tag{8}$$

where t is the ground-truth label, $i \neq t$ and the range of γ which can be set according to different datasets and different networks is 0 to 1.

The first network we use is AlexNet, which is a DCNN successfully trained on roughly 1.2 million labeled images of 1,000 different categories from the ImageNet Large Scale Visual Recognition Challenge (ILSVRC) dataset. It consists of five convolution layers, followed by three fully connected layers (fc6 to fc8) and a softmax classifier. The first two convolution layers are each followed by a Local Response Normalization (LRN) and a max-pooling layer, and the last convolution layer is followed by a single max-pooling layer. Moreover, it uses the dropout regularization method [13] to reduce over-fitting in the fully connected layers and applies Rectified Linear Units (ReLUs) [2] for the activation of those and the convolutional layers. The second network we use is a modified version of the 16-layer model from the VGG team in the ILSVRC 2014 trained on the ImageNet dataset. In our paper, we denote it as VGGNet. The network consists of thirteen convolution layers followed by three fully connected layers (fc6 to fc8) and a softmax classifier. There is an obvious improvement on VGGNet with depth increase and very small convolution filters (3×3). The width of convolution layers is rather small, starting from 64 in the first layer and increasing by a factor of 2, until it reaches 512.

It will take a long time to converge when training a model for disease image classification by analyzing the structures of two networks. Thus, we consider adding batch normalization in final fully connected layers to reduce the number of iterations. To train a transfer learning model where the final fully connected layers (fc8) of two networks are replaced with a layer with 38 outputs corresponding to the 38 image categories of the PlantVillage dataset. The training is carried out by using mini-batch gradient descent where the batch size is set to 64. And the dropout ratio for the first two fully-connected layers is set to 0.5. The learning rate is initially set to 10^{-2}, and then decreased by a factor of 0.98. For random initialization, the weights are initialized from a normal distribution with the zero mean and 0.01 variance and the biases are initialized with zero. However, during the procedure of transfer learning, we take the following three measures.

1. The output of the final fully connected layer (fc8) is set to 8 to satisfy target dataset.
2. DisturbLabel algorithm are employed in the loss layer to improve the network training process by preventing it from over-fitting. Here, the batch size is set to 128.
3. And the weights of the final fully connected layer (fc8) for two networks is re-initialized.

The improved network architecture based on fine-tuning the pre-trained model with the PlantVillage dataset is shown in Fig. 3.

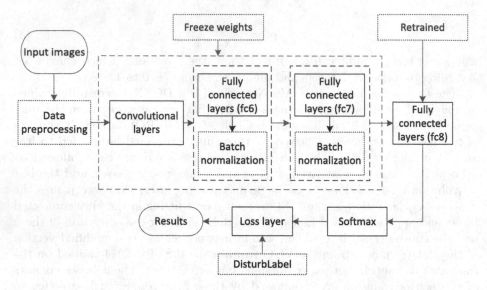

Fig. 3. The improved network architecture based on fine-tuning the pre-trained model

3   Experimental Results and Discussion

3.1   Experimental Setup

All the experiments are conducted on TensorFlow framework, which is a fast open source framework for deep learning. On a system equipped with three NVIDIA 1080Ti GPUs and a 64 G of memory, training a model on the PlantVillage dataset takes approximately fifteen hours depending on the architecture. For our approach, we make use of the PlantVillage dataset as an auxiliary dataset to train the pre-trained model for our target dataset containing eight kinds of crop diseases of 2430 original images.

We use the average accuracy as the evaluation index of the experiment result and calculate it according to formula (9):

$$Accuracy = \frac{1}{n_c} \sum_{i=1}^{n_c} \frac{n_{ai}}{n_i} \times 100\% \tag{9}$$

where n_c is the training number of each epoch, n_{ai} is the number of the sample predicted accuracy of each training and n_i is the number of the sample of each training.

3.2 The Pre-trained Model

During training the pre-trained models, for comparison, we train the models by using the PlantVillage dataset on two different network architectures. The dataset is split into two sets, namely training set (80% of the dataset) and validation set (20% of the dataset). Since the learning always converges well within 100 epochs based on the empirical observation, each of these experiments runs for 100 epochs, where one epoch is defined as the number of training iterations in which the neural network has completed a full pass of the whole training set. As Fig. 4(a) shows, between the AlexNet and VGGNet architectures, we can see that the classification results on the PlantVillage dataset of AlexNet is better than VGGNet. Meanwhile, Fig. 4(b) shows that there is no divergence between the validation loss and the training loss of these two network architectures, confirming that the over-fitting problem is not a contributor to the obtained results.

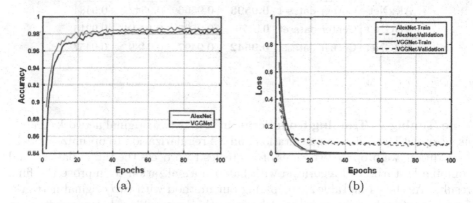

Fig. 4. (a) Comparison of validation accuracy by training on AlexNet and VGGNet with the PlantVillage dataset; (b) Comparison of train-loss and validation-loss by training on AlexNet and VGGNet with the PlantVillage dataset.

3.3 Transfer Learning

After obtaining the pre-trained model with the PlantVillage dataset, we carry out transfer learning based on this model. During fine-tuning, each target dataset (shortly written as Corner dataset and Center dataset) is also split into two sets, training set (80% of the dataset) and validation set (20% of the dataset). Based on the empirical observation, the number of iterations is set to 300 epochs. Then we compare the results of two networks by training models on the Center dataset and Corner dataset.

The Effect of γ on Accuracy. Because each target dataset has only a few thousands of images, we use DisturbLabel algorithm on the loss layer to reduce the over-fitting problem. Dropout rate is fixed to 0.5, since it has been proved that DisturbLabel cooperates well with dropout when dropout rate takes this value. On the one hand, we carry out the experiments on two datasets when noise rate γ is set to different values from 0.08 to 0.2 according to previous works. The results are shown in Table 1. For Center dataset, when γ takes 0.15, the validation accuracy of two networks can reach 94.97% and 95.14%, respectively. For Corner dataset, when γ takes 0.08, two networks achieve the highest accuracies of 95.93% and 95.42% respectively. Besides, we can see that overall experimental results of Corner dataset are better than Center dataset. On the other hand, we compare the results on two networks when γ is set to different values, showing that AlexNet performs better than VGGNet on the Corner dataset.

Table 1. Validation accuracies of different γ on different networks and datasets

Model	Dataset	$\gamma = 0.08$	$\gamma = 0.1$	$\gamma = 0.15$	$\gamma = 0.2$
AlexNet	Center dataset	0.9414	0.9181	**0.9497**	0.9239
AlexNet	Corner dataset	**0.9593**	0.9566	0.9542	0.9484
VGGNet	Center dataset	0.9179	0.9505	**0.9514**	0.9215
VGGNet	Corner dataset	**0.9542**	0.9497	0.9489	0.9457

Fine-Tuning vs Training from Scratch. These two original networks mainly use dropout layer, data augmentation and L2 regularization to optimize models. In addition, we propose two kinds of strategies to process the target dataset and combine DisturbLabel algorithm with batch normalization to improve the final results. As shown in Table 2, comparing our method with two original networks for fine-tuning the pre-trained model, our method can achieve better results than the two original networks on both Corner dataset and Center dataset.

Table 2. Validation accuracies of different methods on different networks and datasets

Model	Corner dataset	Center dataset
AlexNet (Our method) fine-tuning	**0.9593** ($\gamma = 0.08$)	**0.9497** ($\gamma = 0.15$)
AlexNet fine-tuning	0.9492	0.9100
AlexNet from scratch	0.9473	0.8924
VGGNet (Our method) fine-tuning	**0.9542** ($\gamma = 0.08$)	**0.9514** ($\gamma = 0.15$)
VGGNet fine-tuning	0.8613	0.8260
VGGNet from scratch	0.8520	0.8448

Furthermore, in order to ensure the availability of our method, transfer learning and training from scratch are compared, showing that transfer learning always yields better results. From Fig. 5(a) and (b), we can see that our method converge well within 300 epochs for two networks. And the performance of the training on the Corner dataset is more stable than on the other one. We think the reason is that the images in Corner dataset after data preprocessing is more than Center dataset.

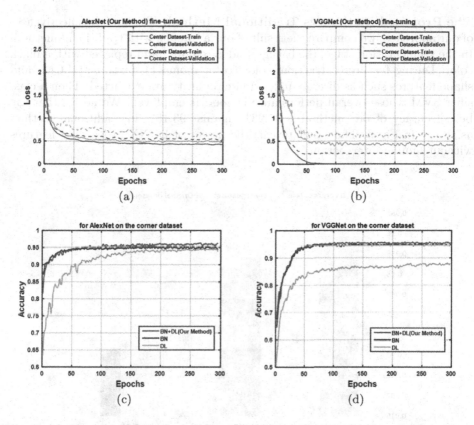

Fig. 5. (a) Comparison of loss on the two dataset for AlexNet; (b) Comparison of loss on the two dataset for VGGNet; (c) Comparison of validation accuracy for AlexNet with our method, BN and DL; (d) Comparison of validation accuracy for VGGNet with our method, BN and DL. (BN: batch normalization; DL: DisturbLabel)

The Effects of Batch Normalization and DisturbLabel. In order to know the effect of batch normalization or DisturbLabel on results, we show the performance of our method in Fig. 5(c) and (d), including the method only with the batch normalization and the method only with DisturbLabel algorithm for two networks on the Corner dataset. As we expect, there is a faster convergence by adding the batch normalization to the fully connected layers than only with DisturbLabel algorithm. Because batch normalization always results in a significant reduction in the required number of training iterations. Although our method lead to a slightly decrease of accuracy than the method only with the batch normalization at first, there is still an advantage on our method than two other methods after 80 epochs. Meanwhile, the method only with DisturbLabel algorithm which causes a decrease of accuracy and a slower convergence reveals the worst results.

The Proposed Method vs Traditional Method. To show the effectiveness of our approach, we compare the result of our approach with traditional method. In the segmentation stage, the background is removed and replaced with a black color. During features extraction, color (color moment), texture (GLCM) and shape features such as discrete index and circularity are extracted. Then a classifier SVM whose overall performance is good is employed. We notice that the best accuracy of our method is 95.93% against 93.15% in traditional method as shown in Fig. 6. The result reveals the power of DCNN in learning features without human intervention.

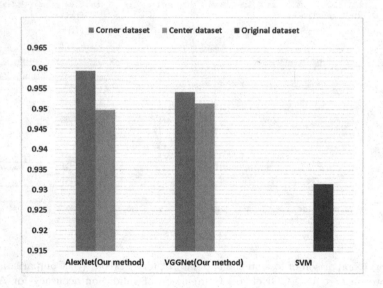

Fig. 6. Comparison of accuracy between our method and traditional method

4   Conclusion

The paper proposes a method which uses the open source dataset PlantVillage to combine transfer learning with two popular deep learning architectures AlexNet and VGGNet to classify eight kinds of crop diseases images, including five kinds of rice diseases and three kinds of cucumber diseases. First, the strategy of target dataset preprocessing can obviously augment the original target dataset. Second, the method combining batch normalization with DisturbLabel algorithm can better optimize these two networks. Comparing with original networks, the proposed method is able to achieve an average accuracy of 95.93%.

The experiment results reveal that using PlantVillage dataset to assist our target dataset for classification is feasible and AlexNet always performs better than VGGNet for target dataset with our method. Meanwhile, the proposed method provides one possibility for classification of relatively small disease dataset based on DCNNs and avoid the problem of spot segmentation. This work can provide the theoretical basis for the development of automatic identification system for crop diseases.

The work in this paper is still preliminary. In next work, how to select the more suitable auxiliary training dataset and obtain the more appropriate features will be studied. And comparisons with more deep learning architectures will also be considered.

Acknowledgments. The authors would like to thank the anonymous reviewers for their helpful reviews. The work is supported by National Natural Science Foundation of China (Grant No. 31871521), the Open Project of Key Laboratory of Agricultural Internet of Things, Ministry of Agriculture, China (2017AIOT-01) and the 13th Five-year Informatization Plan of Chinese Academy of Sciences (Grant No. XXH13505-03-104).

References

1. Brahimi, M., Boukhalfa, K., Moussaoui, A.: Deep learning for tomato diseases: classification and symptoms visualization. Appl. Artif. Intell. **314**, 1–17 (2017)
2. Glorot, X., Bordes, A., Bengio, Y.: Deep sparse rectifier neural networks. In: International Conference on Artificial Intelligence and Statistics, pp. 315–323 (2011)
3. Harvey, C.A., et al.: Extreme vulnerability of smallholder farmers to agricultural risks and climate change in Madagascar. Philos. Trans. R. Soc. Lond. **369**(1639), 20130089 (2014)
4. Hughes, D.P., Salathe, M.: An open access repository of images on plant health to enable the development of mobile disease diagnostics. Comput. Sci. (2015)
5. Ioffe, S., Szegedy, C.: Batch normalization: accelerating deep network training by reducing internal covariate shift, pp. 448–456 (2015)
6. Krizhevsky, A., Sutskever, I., Hinton, G.E.: ImageNet classification with deep convolutional neural networks. In: International Conference on Neural Information Processing Systems, pp. 1097–1105 (2012)
7. Mohanty, S.P., Hughes, D.P., Salath, M.: Using deep learning for image-based plant disease detection. Front. Plant Sci. **7**, 1419 (2016)
8. Prasad, S., Peddoju, S.K., Ghosh, D.: Multi-resolution mobile vision system for plant leaf disease diagnosis. Sig. Image Video Process. **10**(2), 379–388 (2016)
9. Sanchez, P.A., Swaminathan, M.S.: Cutting world hunger in half. Science **307**(5708), 357–359 (2005)
10. Semary, N.A., Tharwat, A., Elhariri, E., Hassanien, A.E.: Fruit-based tomato grading system using features fusion and support vector machine. In: Filev, D., et al. (eds.) Intelligent Systems 2014. AISC, vol. 323, pp. 401–410. Springer, Cham (2015). https://doi.org/10.1007/978-3-319-11310-4_35
11. Simonyan, K., Zisserman, A.: Very deep convolutional networks for large-scale image recognition. Computer Science (2014)

12. Srdjan, S., Marko, A., Andras, A., Dubravko, C., Darko, S.: Deep neural networks based recognition of plant diseases by leaf image classification. Comput. Intell. Neurosci. **2016**(6), 1–11 (2016)
13. Srivastava, N., Hinton, G., Krizhevsky, A., Sutskever, I., Salakhutdinov, R.: Dropout: a simple way to prevent neural networks from overfitting. J. Mach. Learn. Res. **15**(1), 1929–1958 (2014)
14. Szegedy, C., et al.: Going deeper with convolutions, pp. 1–9 (2014)
15. Tai, A.P.K., Martin, M.V., Heald, C.L.: Threat to future global food security from climate change and ozone air pollution. Nat. Clim. Change **4**(9), 817–821 (2014)
16. Tian, Y.W., Li, T.L., Zhang, L., Wang, X.J.: Diagnosis method of cucumber disease with hyperspectral imaging in greenhouse. Trans. Chin. Soc. Agric. Eng. **26**(5), 202–206 (2010)
17. Wang, X., Zhang, S., Wang, Z., Zhang, Q.: Recognition of cucumber diseases based on leaf image and environmental information. Trans. Chin. Soc. Agric. Eng. **30**(14), 148–153 (2014)
18. Xie, L., Wang, J., Wei, Z., Wang, M., Tian, Q.: Disturblabel: regularizing CNN on the loss layer. In: Computer Vision and Pattern Recognition, pp. 4753–4762 (2016)
19. Zhang, S.W., Shang, Y.J., Wang, L.: Plant disease recognition based on plant leaf image. J. Anim. Plant Sci. **25**(3), 42–45 (2015)

Applying Online Expert Supervision in Deep Actor-Critic Reinforcement Learning

Jin Zhang, Jiansheng Chen[(⊠)], Yiqing Huang, Weitao Wang,
and Tianpeng Li

Department of Electronic Engineering, Tsinghua University, Beijing, China
{jinzhang16, huang-yq17}@mails.tsinghua.edu.cn,
jschenthu@mail.tsinghua.edu.cn, wanweitao8@qq.com,
llltttppp@qq.com

Abstract. Deep reinforcement learning (DRL) has been showing its strong power in various decision making and controlling problems, e.g. Atari games and the game of Go. It is inspiring to see DRL agents to outperform even human masters. However, DRL algorithms require a large amount of calculation and exploration, making DRL agents hard to train, especially in problems with large state and action spaces. Also, most DRL algorithms are very sensitive to hyper parameters. To solve these problems, we propose A3COE, a new algorithm combining the A3C algorithm with online expert supervision. We applied it on mini-games of the famous real-time-strategy game StarCraft II. Results show that this algorithm greatly improved the agent's performance with fewer training steps while acquiring more stable training processes with a greater range of hyper parameters. We also proved that this algorithm works even better with curriculum learning.

Keywords: Deep reinforcement learning · Expert supervision
A3C · Curriculum learning

1 Introduction

1.1 Deep Reinforcement Learning and Its Weakness

Deep reinforcement learning, combining neural networks with traditional tabular reinforcement learning to improve its generalization ability, has been proved successful in multiple decision making problems: Atari games [1], the game of Go [2], and physic simulators [3]. However, DRL algorithms require enormous training steps and exploration data, and this problem becomes more serious when the state and action space is large. For example, Deepmind's Rainbow algorithm requires over 200 million frames of Atari game play to train an agent [1], and AlphaGo Lee used as many as 48 TPUs to train [2].

Although the convergence of traditional reinforcement learning algorithms like Q-learning have been proved mathematically [11], there is no evidence that these algorithms remain convergent when combined with neural networks. Also, evidence showed that most popular DRL algorithms are very sensitive to hyper parameters, and

---

The first author of this paper is an undergraduate

© Springer Nature Switzerland AG 2018
J.-H. Lai et al. (Eds.): PRCV 2018, LNCS 11257, pp. 469–478, 2018.
https://doi.org/10.1007/978-3-030-03335-4_41

even the randomly initialized network weights can affect the training process greatly [12]. This is definitely what we do not want to see: a reliable algorithm should be robust and reproducible. A natural idea is to make use of demonstrations, as human learn faster and better with demonstrations than exploring alone.

1.2   StarCraft II and Its Large Decision Space

Our experiment takes StarCraft II as the training environment and we use Deepmind's PYSC2 training platform. In PYSC2, the game's state is represented by 24 feature maps, with 17 main screen features, and the rest 7 minimap features. The game's actions are organized into 524 different action functions, each taking 0 to 2 parameters, and there are more than 10^8 possible actions in total. Compared with the game of Go, which has a state space of 19 * 19 * 5 (according to the training settings of [2]) and an action space of approximately 361, StarCraft II is obviously more complex. So we conclude that StarCraft II is a hard reinforcement learning problem, as it has a vast decision space, which will require considerable exploration to train an agent.

It is worth mentioning that StarCraft II is also difficult for its long time scale, strategy complexity and partial observations, but we do not discuss it because we avoid these problems in our environment choosing, to focus on the point we want to solve: the large decision space.

2   Backgrounds and Related Works

DRL algorithms are based on the concept of Markov Decision Processes (MDPs) [13]. An MDP can be described by a tuple $\{\mathcal{S}, \mathcal{A}, P, R, \gamma\}$, with $\mathcal{S}$ the set of states, $\mathcal{A}$ the set of actions, $P(s'|s, a)$ the transition probabilities, $R(s, a)$ the set of rewards, and a reward discount factor γ. Our aim is to find a good policy $\pi(s)$, which gives out the next action given the current state. Based on the rewards received each step, we can define the Q-value function and the V-value function as follows:

$$V^{\pi}(s) = \sum_{s' \in S} P(s'|s, \pi(s))[R(s, \pi(s)) + \gamma V^{\pi}(s')] \tag{1}$$

$$Q^{\pi}(s, a) = \sum_{s' \in S} P(s'|s, a)[R(s, a) + \gamma V^{\pi}(s')] \tag{2}$$

And these equations are known as the Bellman Equations. The aim of reinforcement learning is to find the optimal policy π^*, and π^* can be acquired with the following Bellman optimality equations:

$$V^*(s) = max_a E[R(s, a) + \gamma V^*(s')] \tag{3}$$

$$Q^*(s, a) = E\left[R(s, a) + \gamma \sum_{s'} P(s'|s, a) max_{a'} Q^*(s', a')\right] \tag{4}$$

Value-based DRL methods (e.g. DQN [14]) try to solve Eq. (4) and give optimal actions according to Q-values, while actor-based methods try to directly give the optimal action. In our experiment we use A3C, an actor-critic algorithm which contains a critic network to estimate V-values and an actor network to give actions. The critic network's loss and actor network's loss are designed as follows:

$$loss_c = (V_{actual} - V_{estimate})^2 \tag{5}$$

$$loss_a = -(V_{actual} - V_{estimate}) * \log(p(a|s)) + \beta * E_a \tag{6}$$

with $p(a|s)$ the possibility of taking action a under state s, E_a the entropy of the actions' possibilities ($\sum_{a \in A} p(a|s) * \log(p(a|s))$) and β a positive hyper parameter to encourage exploration.

In August of 2017, Deepmind released the PYSC2 platform with some baseline results using A3C. Although they tried various network structures, all of them took up to 300 million training steps to achieve good behavior in mini-games [8]. What's more, they hardly made any progress in full game and could not win the easiest built-in AI, even with shaped rewards. However, agents trained with human replay data managed to perform better and produced more units. That suggested that imitation learning may be a 'promising direction' for AI training. Their work proved that StarCraft II is now a challenging problem for DRL.

The idea of implementing demonstration data to pre-train network has been widely used, for example, on DQN [4], A3C [5], DDPG and ACER [6]. However, these work focuses on offline demonstration data, and little work looks on online expert data. In some cases, it may be convenient to give expert policy in the training process, e.g. mini-games in StarCraft II (you can easily hard-code an agent to give expert policies) and automatic driving (provided with images of roads, people can easily give the right action). Under these circumstances, training will be faster if we introduce online expert supervision than offline pre-training as it is more straightforward.

Curriculum learning is a training method to help speed up training. Human beings learn better if they learn easier tasks before hard ones, so it is possible to train networks with easier tasks in the beginning to acquire better performance. Results have proved that curriculum learning helps get better results in shape recognition and language modeling using neural networks [9]. In DRL, this method has also been used to train agents. For example, in the first-person shooting game Doom, curriculum learning has helped agents to perform better, and one agent using A3C and curriculum learning won the champion of Track1 in ViZ-Doom AI Competition 2016 [10].

3   Methods

3.1   Environment Settings

In our discussion we apply Collect Mineral Shards, a simple StarCraft II mini-game, as our training environment. In this task, the agent controls two units to reach and get the 20 mineral shards on the map to get scores. The units and mineral shards are all randomly placed on the map. We only consider controlling the two units together (that is, the two units receive the same instructions at the same time). We choose this task because it simplifies the state and action space, lowering the total number of actions to 4097 (64 * 64 possible destinations for the agent to move units to and one action to select the two units). It is also a small map which excludes camera moving, fog of war and partial observation. Also, we can discard unused feature maps, thus reducing the state space's dims to 64 * 64 * 5 (64 is the screen's resolution, and there are five feature maps involved). We use the default settings of making a decision every 8 frames, and an episode lasts for 120 s. In an episode, when all the mineral shards have been collected, the units and the mineral shards will be reset randomly until reaching the time limit. For reward shaping, the agent gets +1 for every mineral shard collected, and −0.001 for every action to encourage faster collections. This setting is similar to that in Deepmind's work [8] (Fig. 1).

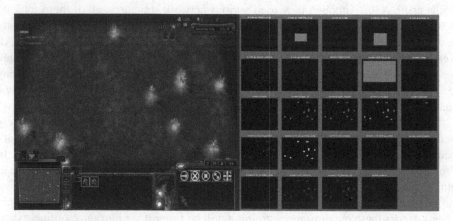

Fig. 1. A screenshot of Collect Mineral Shards (left) and the feature maps (right).

3.2 Asynchronous Advantage Actor-Critic

We are facing a reinforcement training task with a vast action space, so it is difficult to apply value-based DRL algorithms, in which one has to give an estimate of all the 4097 Q-values in one state while only a few Q-values are updated in one training step. So we decide to apply Deepmind's A3C [7] (Asynchronous Advantage Actor-Critic), an actor-critic method which avoid these problems. In A3C, the critic network estimates the V-value of the state while the actor gives out possibilities for taking each action. In the training process we used 64 asynchronous local threads to learn together, each of them sharing and updating parameters via a shared global net (Fig. 2).

For the network structure, we used convolutional neural networks similar to Deepmind's: two convolutional layers of 16, 32 filters of size 8 * 8 and 4 * 4 with strides 4 and 2, connected with two dense layers [8]. For spatial actions (e.g. choosing a point in the map), instead of outputting the possibility for choosing each point, we assume the points' coordinates to be normally distributed and output their means and variances. This setting introduces a nice prior, that is, destination points near the

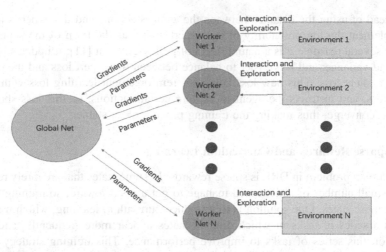

Fig. 2. Illustration of how A3C works. Notice that all worker nets work asynchronously, which avoids the relevance of experience data.

optimal point should also be good, and that should contribute to a more stable training process.

As for hyper parameter settings, all network weights are initialized with a variance scaling initializer with factor 0.5, and all the worker nets share two common Adam optimizers with the same learning rate (one for the critic net, and one for the actor net). The parameters are updated every 40 game steps.

3.3   Introducing Online Expert Supervision: A3COE

For this DRL task, we can easily hard-code an agent which performs nicely: always moving the units to the nearest mineral shard. This strategy may be sub-optimal under some circumstances, but it is still a strategy nice enough to learn from.

With this hard-coded agent, we can introduce expert supervision while training. For each training step, apart from feeding states, actions and rewards to the network, we also feed expert's action to the network, and to utilize this expert demonstration, we change the loss of the actor network (6) to:

$$\text{loss}'_a = -(V_{actual} - V_{estimate}) * \log(p(a|s)) + \alpha * \log(p(a_E|s)) + \beta * E_a \qquad (7)$$

where a_E represents the expert's actions, and α is a positive hyper parameter to control the degree of supervision. It is worth noticing that in this loss, β should be negative, for the network tends to enlarge variance to minimize the loss and an negative β encourages the network to converge. β was set positive in the original loss to encourage exploration, but we do not need to encourage it any more (for the supervision loss has already told us where to explore). We name this algorithm A3COE, which is short for Asynchronous Advantage Actor-Critic with Online Experts.

Instead of using the distance between the agent's actions and the expert's actions, we implement the log probability of the expert action as the form of the supervision loss for several reasons: it is a natural form of policy gradient [11]; it updates both the mean and variance; and it is easier to balance between the expert loss and the original policy gradient loss. This new loss combines reinforcement learning loss with supervision loss, and instructs the agent to explore certain actions, so this loss should be easier to converge, thus making the training process more stable.

3.4 Sparse Rewards and Curriculum Learning

One common problem in DRL is sparse rewards. In some states that are rarely reached, only a small number of actions will manage to get a good reward, so training will be slow in these states. One solution is to introduce curriculum learning, which manually designs a series of tasks in which difficult states appear more frequently, and trains agents on this series of tasks to improve performance. This training strategy is reasonable because it is similar to human's learning progress: to learn easy tasks first and then try harder ones.

In our experiment, we found that when there are few mineral shards left, the agent makes progress obviously slower, for these states (few mineral shards on the map) appear less frequently, and actions that acquire positive rewards are pretty rare under these states. So we applied curriculum learning to speed up training, designing maps of 2, 5, 10, 15 and 20 mineral shards in it, and set a score limit to decide which difficulty the agent should be trained with. Agents who get high scores will be trained with a more difficult map, while agents who fail to reach certain scores will be trained with easier maps. Detailed score settings are listed in the following chart (Table 1).

Table 1. Difficulties and score settings

Mineral shards on the map	Minimum scores required to enter next stage	Minimum scores required to stay in this stage
2	6	–
5	15	5
10	25	10
15	35	15
20	–	20

4 Results

4.1 A3C and A3COE

We tested the performance of A3C and A3COE in the Collect Mineral Shards task without curriculum learning. We set $\beta = -0.5$ and $\alpha = 5.0$ for A3COE and $\beta = 0.05$ for the original A3C. We tried three different learning rates and the results are in Fig. 3. The horizontal axis is the total episodes trained, and the vertical axis is the smoothed reward of each episode.

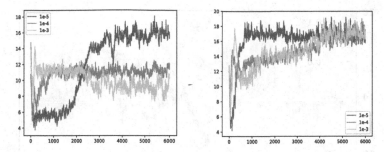

Fig. 3. Performances of the original A3C algorithm (left) and A3COE (right) with different learning rates.

The original A3C algorithm preformed just fine with a suitable small learning rate (1e−5), but with 1e−4 and 1e−3, the training process became unstable, and the agent was trapped in a local minimum, unable to perform better. In contrast, A3COE was more stable and performed nicely with all three learning rates. But the agent trained with the small learning rate still outperforms the other two in training speed.

Also, with a proper learning rate, A3COE learned very quickly, reaching the score of 18 at about 1,000 episodes, while the original A3C takes about 5,300 episodes. Supervision has speeded up the learning process as we expected.

4.2   Degree of Supervision

We also tested the influence of different supervision parameter α, also without curriculum learning, and the results are in Fig. 4. We can see that $\alpha = 1.0$ acquired the greatest learning speed, while the agent trained with $\alpha = 5.0$ performed slightly better in the end. The $\alpha = 0.1$ agent performed the worst, even unable to outperform the original A3C agent, and the $\alpha = 5.0$ agent was slower in the beginning because of overfitting. However, all of the A3COE agents outperformed the original one in training speed. So an appropriate parameter α will help A3COE to perform better.

4.3   Curriculum Learning

In the experiments showed below, agents learned significantly slower when they got a score of about 17, mainly because of sparse rewards. To boost training, we introduced curriculum learning and tested its effect.

We focused on the agent's ability to get a score more than 20 in a single episode, which means that the agent must overcome the states with sparse rewards and manage to collect all the mineral shards on the map, and that is exactly what we want curriculum learning to do. In the following statements, if an agent gets more than 20 points in an episode, we consider this performance to be 'nice', for it overcomes the hard state of having few mineral shards on the map. We trained four agents each taking a different training method, and all the agents were trained for 3,000 episodes. Then we tested them for 2,000 episodes each, and counted the times they got a score over 20. The results are in Table 2.

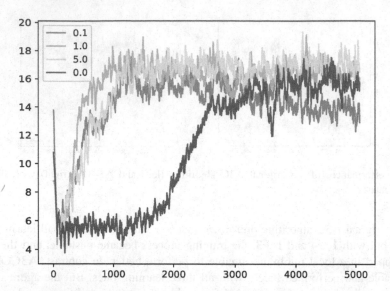

Fig. 4. Training agents with different supervision parameters.

Table 2. Performance of agents with different training methods

Agent training method	Times of getting over 20 points ('nice' performances) in 2,000 episodes
Original A3C without curriculum learning	34
Original A3C with curriculum learning	36
A3COE without curriculum learning	104
A3COE with curriculum learning	389

With supervision, curriculum learning indeed helped agents to overcome sparse reward dilemmas, enabling the agent to perform 'nicely' two times more frequently. However, the effect of curriculum learning in the original A3C case was rather weak, for the training without supervision was slow and the agent had not fully explored its policies.

4.4   Case Study

How does curriculum learning helps overcome sparse rewards? We inducted a case study to have a closer look. We tested the 'A3COE without curriculum learning' agent and the 'A3COE with curriculum learning' agent mentioned in Sect. 4.3 in two states: the first state is an 'easy' case with 20 mineral shards on the map and a large number of actions can get good rewards. And the other state is a 'harder' one with only two mineral shards on it. We recorded position of mineral shards, position of the units the agents control, and the first action chosen by the agents and the expert, and the results are shown in Fig. 5.

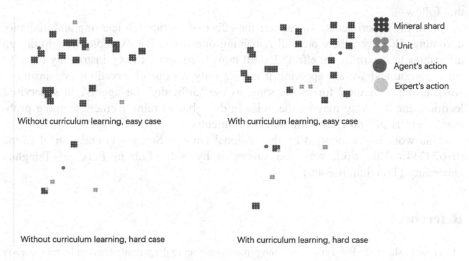

Fig. 5. The first action chosen by the agents in different states.

We can see that in the easy cases, it is acceptable to take actions different from the expert's for they will get good rewards as well, and so the two agents both performed nicely. However, in the hard sparse reward settings, few actions can get good rewards, so the agent without curriculum learning performed worse due to lack of exploration. In contrast, the agent with curriculum learning acted very similar to the expert because it had already been well-trained in sparse reward states.

5   Conclusions and Discussions

Human beings learn much faster with experts' instructions than exploring alone. Similarly, DRL algorithms that do not rely on expert data require a large amount of exploration, and supervision is a reasonable way to speed up training. In our experiment, supervised A3C outperforms the unsupervised algorithm, and is more stable as well.

In offline pre-training, the distributions of expert demonstrations and exploration experience may vary a lot, and that affects the effect of pre-training. However, online expert supervision is more flexible and reliable, and speeds up training much more directly. So in tasks which we can easily provide online expert policy, our method will train faster. Also, our method can deal with suboptimal expert demonstrations. After the agent performs nicely enough, we can train it with the original unsupervised method. As the suboptimal policy is more close to the optimal policy than random policies, this training process will be faster than completely unsupervised training. In that condition, our method serves as a kind of pre-training.

We observed a 'peak' in the training curve of supervised A3C algorithm with the learning rate 1e−4 and 1e−3 at about 400 episodes, but the score failed sharply after the peak before climbing up again slowly. Our explanation is that the actor network might be over-fitted at the beginning of training, and that causes the drop in the training scores that follow.

From the experiments, we can see the effect of curriculum learning and difficulty designing. However, there are still remaining questions. For example, how to design difficulties to maximize its effect? Up till now, there is no theory instructing on difficulty design, and we are applying it relying only on our observations and instincts. Also, is the 'difficulty' for us the same as the 'difficulty' for agents? In supervised learning, the difficulty may be the noise in data, but in reinforcement learning problems, there is still no clear definition for 'difficulty'.

This work was supported by the National Natural Science Foundation of China (61673234). This work was also supported by SaturnLab in FITC of Tsinghua University (Tsinghua iCenter).

References

1. Hessel, M., et al.: Rainbow: combining improvements in deep reinforcement learning. arXiv preprint arXiv:1710.02298 (2017)
2. Silver, D., et al.: Mastering the game of go without human knowledge. Nature **550**(7676), 354 (2017)
3. Duan, Y., Chen, X., Houthooft, R., Schulman, J., Abbeel, P.: Benchmarking deep reinforcement learning for continuous control. In: International Conference on Machine Learning, pp. 1329–1338 (2016)
4. Hester, T., et al.: Deep Q-learning from Demonstrations. arXiv preprint arXiv:1704.03732 (2017)
5. Cruz, J., Gabriel, V., Du, Y., Taylor, M.E.: Pre-training neural networks with human demonstrations for deep reinforcement learning. arXiv preprint arXiv:1709.04083 (2017)
6. Zhang, X., Ma, H.: Pretraining deep actor-critic reinforcement learning algorithms with expert demonstrations. arXiv preprint arXiv:1801.10459 (2018)
7. Mnih, V., et al.: Asynchronous methods for deep reinforcement learning. In: International Conference on Machine Learning, pp. 1928–1937 (2016)
8. Vinyals, O., et al.: StarCraft II: a new challenge for reinforcement learning. arXiv preprint arXiv:1708.04782 (2017)
9. Bengio, Y., Collobert, R., Weston, J.: Curriculum learning. In: Proceedings of the 26th Annual International Conference on Machine Learning, vol. 60, no. 1, pp. 41–48 (2009)
10. Wu, Y., Tian, Y.: Training agent for first-person shooter game with actor-critic curriculum learning. In: 5th International Conference on Learning Representations (2016)
11. Sutton, R.S., Barto, A.G.: Reinforcement learning: an introduction. IEEE Trans. Neural Networks **9**(5), 1054 (1998)
12. Henderson, P., Islam, R., Bachman, P., Pineau, J., Precup, D., Meger, D.: Deep reinforcement learning that matters. arXiv preprint arXiv:1709.06560 (2017)
13. Sutton, R.S., Barto, A.G.: Introduction to Reinforcement Learning, vol. 135. MIT Press, Cambridge (1998)
14. Mnih, V., et al.: Human-level control through deep reinforcement learning. Nature **518** (7540), 529 (2015)

Shot Boundary Detection with Spatial-Temporal Convolutional Neural Networks

Lifang Wu, Shuai Zhang, Meng Jian[✉], Zhijia Zhao, and Dong Wang

Faculty of Information Technology, Beijing University of Technology, Beijing, China
lfwu@bjut.edu.cn, zhangshuai0212@emails.bjut.edu.cn, jianmeng648@163.com,
zhaozhijia0229@163.com, dwang@nlpr.ia.ac.cn

Abstract. Nowadays, digital videos have been widely leveraged to record and share various events and people's daily life. It becomes urgent to provide automatic video semantic analysis and management for convenience. Shot boundary detection (SBD) plays a key fundamental role in various video analysis. Shot boundary detection aims to automatically detecting boundary frames of shots in videos. In this paper, we propose a progressive method for shot boundary detecting with histogram based shot filtering and C3D based gradual shot detection. Abrupt shots were detected firstly for its specialty and help alleviate locating shots across different shots by dividing the whole video into segments. Then, over the segments, gradual shot detection is implemented via a three-dimensional convolutional neural network model, which assign video clips into shot types of normal, dissolve, foi or swipe. Finally, for untrimmed videos, a frame level merging strategy is constructed to help locate the boundary of shots from neighboring frames. The experimental results demonstrate that the proposed method can effectively detect shots and locate their boundaries.

Keywords: Shot boundary detection · Shot transition
Video indexing · Convolutional neural networks
Spatial-temporal feature

1 Introduction

With the development of multimedia and network technologies, a large amount of videos are uploaded to the internet, rapid video understanding and content-based retrieving become serious problems. To complete content-based video retrieval, that is, to quickly and efficiently retrieve the user's desired video content from the video database, the first task is to structure the unstructured video sequence. Typically, a top-down multi-level structure model can be used to hierarchically represent video. The top layer is the video layer, which is composed of multiple different scenes; Following is the scene layer, which is composed of a plurality of shot segments that are related to each other in terms of content; The third layer

© Springer Nature Switzerland AG 2018
J.-H. Lai et al. (Eds.): PRCV 2018, LNCS 11257, pp. 479–491, 2018.
https://doi.org/10.1007/978-3-030-03335-4_42

is the shot layer, which consists of multiple consecutive frames; the bottom is the frame layer, which is the smallest unit of video.

A video shot is defined as a sequence of frames taken by a single camera. The quality of shot boundary detection will affect the efficiency of video retrieval and video semantic analysis. Shot boundary detection, also known as shot transition detection, is the basis of video retrieval. Shot transition refers to the transformation from one continuous video image sequence to another. These transformations can be classified into two main categories: abrupt and gradual shot transition, which is shown in Fig. 1. An abrupt shot change completed between two frames, while gradual transitions occur over multiple frames. Gradual transition can be further classified into dissolve, swipe, fade in and fade out.

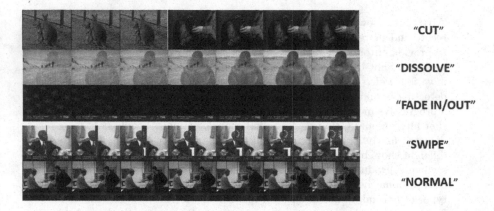

"CUT"

"DISSOLVE"

"FADE IN/OUT"

"SWIPE"

"NORMAL"

Fig. 1. Cut and gradual shot change.

Until now great efforts have been made in SBD, but most of them focus on abrupt shot change detection. Considering that two frames have great dissimilarity, these approaches usually extract features of consecutive frames and measure the similarity between features; When similarity exceeds a threshold, then an abrupt transition is detected. Compared with abrupt transition, gradual transition is more difficult because a gradual shot transition usually consists of a few frames and the difference between adjacent frames is not obvious. Traditional SBD techniques analyze hand-crafted features. The pixel comparison method is the simplest shot boundary detection algorithm and the theoretical foundation of most other algorithms. By comparing the density values or color difference values in adjacent video frames, this method is to calculate the absolute sum of the pixel differences and compare them with the threshold [1]. Obviously, this method is very sensitive to the motion of objects and cameras. Thus [2] uses a 3×3 filter to smooth the image, then traverses all the pixels in the image, and counts the number of pixel points where the pixel value difference is greater than a certain threshold, which is treated as the frame of the two frames. Compared to template matching methods based on global image feature (pixel difference) comparison methods, block-based comparison methods [3] use local features to increase the robustness to camera and object motion. When the shot changes, the edges between frames of different shots also change. Zabih et al. proposed the use of Edge Change Ratio to detect the shot boundary [4]. Individual edge features are not suitable for detecting shot boundaries because sometimes the edge is not clear. Some studies have shown that edge features can be a good complement to other features. Because the edge features are insensitive to brightness changes, Kim and Heng avoid the false detection of shot boundaries caused by flashlight by detecting the edge features of candidate shot boundaries, and does not significantly increase the computation time [5,6]. Among the shot boundary detection algorithms, the histogram method is a method that is frequently used to calculate the difference between image frames [7]. Zhang et al. [2] compared the two methods of pixel values and histograms and found that the histogram can meet the requirements of the speed and accuracy of video edge detection. Ueda uses color histogram change rates to detect shot boundaries [8]. In order to improve the difference between two video frames, the author proposed to use x^2 histogram to compare the color histogram differences between two adjacent video frames [9]. There are several ways to calculate the difference between two histograms. Some studies have shown that the Manhattan distance and the Euclidean distance are simple and effective frame difference calculation methods [10]. Zuzana uses mutual information to calculate the similarity of images, the larger the mutual information, the more similar the two images are [11].

Compared with abrupt shot transition, gradual shot transition is more difficult because a gradual shot transition usually consists of a few frames and the difference between adjacent frames is not obvious. The dual threshold method [12] is a classic method of shot detection which requires setting two thresholds. But it has a major problem: the starting point of the gradual is difficult to determine. The basic principle of the optical flow method [13] is that there is no optical flow when the gradual transition is happening, and the movement of the camera should be suitable for a certain type of optical flow. This method can achieve better detection results, but its calculation process is quite complicated.

The methods mentioned above were relied on low-level features of visual information. Recently, the use of deep neural network has attracted extensive attention from researchers, and it has also achieved a major breakthrough in both accuracy and efficiency compared to traditional manual feature methods. However, relatively few studies have applied deep learning to the field of shot boundary detection. [14] present a novel SBD framework based on representative features extracted from CNN which achieves excellent accuracy. [15] present a CNN architecture which is fully convolutional in time, thus allowing for shot detection at more than 120x real-time. [16] presents DeepSBD model for shot boundary detection and build two large datasets, but did not distinguish the specific gradual shot type. Inspired by these works, we first use the histogram method to detect the abrupt shots; Based on this, C3D model is employed to extract time domain features and achieve gradual shot detection.

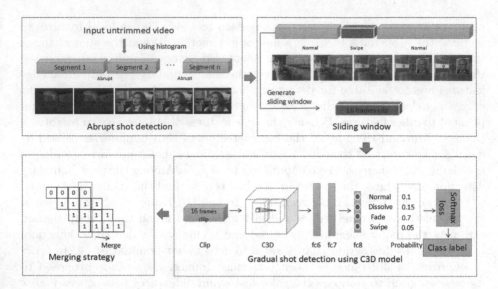

Fig. 2. Framework of the proposed method.

In this work, we investigate spatial and temporal features of videos jointly with a deep model and proposed shot boundary detection with spatial-temporal convolutional neural networks. Figure 2 illustrates the framework of the proposed shot boundary detection method. The proposed method implements shot boundary detection in a progressive way of detecting abrupt and gradual shots. The abrupt shots are firstly extracted from the whole video with histogram base shot filtering. Then, C3D deep model is constructed to extract features of frames and distinguish shot types of dissolve, swipe, fade in and fade out, and normal. The main contributions of this work are summarized as follows:

- Considering different changing characteristics of abrupt shots from gradual shot, a progressive method was proposed to distinguish abrupt and gradual shots separately.
- Joint spatial and temporal feature extraction with C3D model help effectively distinguish different gradual shot types from video segments.
- We further develop a frame level merging strategy to determine temporal localization of shot boundaries.

2   Proposed Method

In this section, we describe the details of the proposed progressive method for shot boundary detection. As illustrated in Fig. 2, the proposed method performs shot boundary detection in a hierarchical manner. Histogram based abrupt shot filtering is employed to detect abrupt shots, which further help divide the whole video into segments with the abrupt frames as boundaries. Then, a 16 frames sliding window is conducted with 87.5% overlap, which will be the inputs of C3D model. Next, C3D model extracts spatial-temporal features of sequential frames from the segments to assign clips with a shot type of dissolve, swipe, fade in and fade out, and normal. Last, a frame level merging strategy is proposed to well locate shot boundaries.

Table 1. Utilization popularity of different features in shot boundary Detection algorithms [17].

Luminance and color	Histogram analysis	Edge	Transformation coefficients (DCT,DFT etc.)	Statistical measurement	Motion analysis	Object detection
4	28	3	7	16	13	2
8%	56%	6%	14%	32%	26%	4%

2.1 Abrupt Shot Detection

Considering imbalance of frames of abrupt shot compared with the other gradual shot, in this work we intuitively construct a hierarchical progressive framework to detect abrupt shot firstly and distinguish the other shot type with a deep model. According to [17], more than 50 investigation works were published on shot boundary detection from 1996 to 2014 with various feature descriptors. [17] provided a summary of utilization popularity summarization on feature descriptor in shot boundary detection as Table 1, which indicated that histogram based shot analysis is the most popular feature with 56% utilization rate compared with traditional luminance and color, edge, transformation coefficients, statistical, motion and object based descriptors. Therefore, we employ histogram in abrupt shot detection considering the lack of frames of the abrupt shot type for feature learning. Then we perform histogram based abrupt shot filtering by measuring difference of neighboring frames. Indeed, researches in similar domains have indicated that the simple Manhattan distance metric is highly effective. We conduct histogram based abrupt shot filtering with Manhattan distance to measure the difference of neighboring frames as follows.

$$D_{Manhattan}(H_i, H_j) = \sum_{k=1}^{binNum} |h_{ik} - h_{jk}| \tag{1}$$

where H_i and H_j denote histograms of the $i-$th frame and $j-$th frame of an video, h_{ik} is the value of the k−th bin of the histogram H_i, and binNum is the number of bins of the histogram. In this work, we take 64 bins for each channel of R,G,B. The smaller the distance is, the more similar the histograms of the two frames are. Otherwise, the difference between the two frames is greater. If the difference between frames exceeds a given threshold, the two frames is treated as an abrupt shot.

2.2 Gradual Shot Detection

Pre-processing. With the detected abrupt shot frames, the whole video has been divided into several segments of frames. As mentioned in the proposed framework, the divided segments are given to a deep learning model C3D for feature extraction and shot type classification. The networks are set up to take video clips as inputs and predict the shot category which belong to 4 different shot types, i.e., dissolve, swipe, fade in and fade out, and normal. All video frames are resized into 128×171. Videos are split into variable length−overlapped 16−frame clips which are then used as input to the network. The input dimensions are $3 \times 16 \times 128 \times 171$. We also use jittering by using random crops with a size of $3 \times 16 \times 112 \times 112$ of the input clips during training.

Fig. 3. A varied-length sliding window used for sampling video clips.

Sliding Window. Considering that the length of each gradual shot transition type is different, we need to select the clip length of each type and the step size of the window according to the length of the shot type. Therefore, we calculate the length of the gradual transition events used by TRECVid 2003-2007. The statistical results show that the average length of SWIPE, DIS and FOI are 12.5, 21.9 and 29.9 frames, respectively. Therefore, 16 frames used by Trans [18] is the appropriate length. Based on the length of different events, a sliding window with step size of 2, 7, 5 is used to sample the video clips to ensure the equalization of the samples, as shown in Fig. 3.

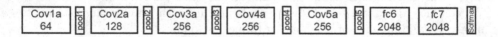

Fig. 4. The structure of C3D model for spatial temporal feature learning.

C3D Based Gradual Shot Detection. Most previous works for detecting gradual shots are mainly based on hand crafted features. These low level visual features are lack of describing ability on high level semantic information. Feature extraction based on deep neural network is favored by researchers because it can better reflect the information of the data itself and does not require researchers to have a large number of domain related information as manual features. The shot transition features that need to be extracted are in time series, so the solution to the SBD task is more dependent on the extracted temporal features. Therefore, we use a three dimensional CNN–C3D mode to extract temporal features automatically. Compared with a two–dimensional CNN, Three–dimensional CNN not only divides video into frames, but also applies convolution kernel to both spatial domain and temporal domain. Combining with each other, the video features can be obtained better. As depict in Fig. 4, the C3D mode includes five convolution layers, five pool layers, two fully connection layers to learn features, and one softmax layer to provide the predicted class. The number of convolution kernels of the five convolution layers is 64, 128, 256, 256, and 256, the optimal size of the convolution kernel is $3 \times 3 \times 3$, After one convolution operation, the features are downsampled by one pooling operation to gradually reduce the scale of feature map, reduce the difficulty of training and improve the accuracy of training. In this paper, the convolution kernel size of the pooling layer from the second to the fifth are $2 \times 2 \times 2$, while that of the first layer is $1 \times 2 \times 2$, so that in the early stage, the time domain information in the network can be preserved to the maximum extent. After several convolution and pool operations, the feature map is abstracted into a 2048 dimensional feature vector to mark the classification information of the sample.

Post-processing. We tested on both trimmed videos and untrimmed videos. For trimmed videos, we used a method similar to video classification, which took a part of the sample as test set and got the classification result; For untrimmed videos, We proposed frame level merging strategy, which is shown in Fig. 5. After detecting the location of the abrupt shot and divide the video into video segments, we conduct temporal sliding windows of 16 frames with 87.5% overlaps over the video segment. We visualize the output of the model's softmax layer so that we get a classification result every 16 frames, which take the label with the highest probability as the prediction label for this video clip; Then each frame in the video clip is given the same label as the video clip, so that each frame will be combined with the results of multiple clips to get a prediction result. Each frame will have a maximum of 8 labels, we take label with maximum amount as the frame label.

3   Experiment

TRECVid Dataset. From 2001 to 2007, NIST held a competition from 2001 to 2007 and provided data sets and shot type labels for the contest. The data for each year have been a representative, usually random, sample of approximately 6 h of the video The origins and genre types of the video data have varied widely from the initial NIST and NASA science videos in 2001, to the Prelinger Archive's antique, ephemeral video, to broadcast news from major US networks in the mid–1990's to more recent Arabic and Chinese TV news programming. Editing styles have changed and with them the shot size and distribution of shot

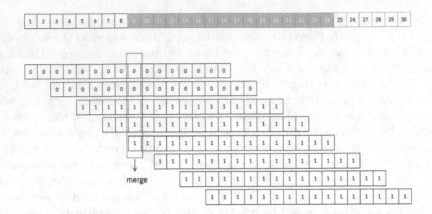

Fig. 5. Frame level merging strategy, where the frames 9 to 24 represent a gradual shot change. By moving sliding window with 87.5% overlap, Each frame will be combined with the results of multiple clips to get a prediction result. Each frame will have a maximum of 8 labels, we take label with maximum numbers as the frame label.

transitions types. The TRECVid dataset is not public available and requires an application from NIST to obtain it. We collected all the SBD related dataset from the year 2003 to 2007.

Implementation Details. The proposed framework is built on the deep learning model of caffe C3D. The whole network is trained from scratch and the parameter are set as mini-batch size of 20, base learning rate to 1×10^{-4}, momentum to 0.9, weight decay to 5×10^{-5}, and maximum number of training iterations to 60000. The learning rate is divided by 10 every 10000 iterations. All experiments are conducted on Nvidia Titan X GPU with Intel(R) Xeon(R) CPU E5-2683 v3 @ 2.00GHz, running a Ubuntu 14.04 LTS environment and python 2.7.12.

Abrupt Shot Change Detection. For abrupt shot detection, We took 10 videos from the TRECVid data set for testing. The threshold is set to 0.2, which is based on the results of the experiment. Detecting results are partly shown in Table 2 (due to limitation of length). The overall F score is 0.899, which is effective; What's more, the execution time took only 0.11 of real time, which is very fast.

Gradual Shot Change Detection. For gradual shot change detection, we use five years of data from the TRECVid competition to train and test. The data of TRECVid 2005 is used for testing and is not included in the training set. By sampling windows with different lengths, the data set is sample-equalized. The number of training set, verification set, and testing set are 7015, 2618, and

Table 2. The results of abrupt shot detection using the histogram comparison method.

Video	Total transition	Detected	Misdetected	Recall	Precision
BG_2408	121	100	2	82.64%	98%
BG_9401	90	79	7	87.78%	92%
...	...	...	...	...	...
BG_14213	111	91	3	81.98%	97%
BG_34901	224	204	20	91.07%	91%
Total	1146	1019	97	88.92%	91%

2752 video segments, respectively, and the ratio is roughly 3:1:1. Table 3 is data distribution of the data set.

Table 3. Data distribution of the data set.

Shot Type	Train	Val	Test
NOR	1799	677	630
DIS	1821	543	752
FOI	1847	670	504
SWIPE	1548	728	866

The results of the shot detection after trimming are shown in Table 4. The results show that the proposed method can effectively extract and identify the time domain features of different shot transition types. The average detection accuracy is 89.4%.

Table 4. Confusion matrix for trimmed video.

	NOR	DIS	FOI	SWIPE	Accuracy
NOR	528	12	18	72	83.81%
DIS	32	618	60	42	82.18%
FOI	0	0	493	11	97.82%
SWIPE	10	11	23	822	94.97%

Further, we tested on untrimmed video of TRECVid 2005. The frame level comparison results are shown in Table 5, where the overall detection accuracy is 88.8%. For more intuitive representation, we randomly selected several segments, as shown in Fig. 6, where the x-axis indicates the frame number, and the y-axis indicates shot types. The labels 0, 1, 2, 3, 4 represent normal shots, dissolves, fades, swipes, and abrupt shots respectively.

It is easy to find that the accuracy of localizing might affects the results to some extent. In this regard, we have performed statistics on localizing accuracy of TRECVid 2005 data set. The results are shown in Fig. 7. Where the x-axis represents the degree of overlap, and the y-axis represents the proportion of each gradual shot change type. Experiments show that the overlapping degree between the prediction result and Groundtruth is centered on 0.9-1, and the overlap degree of FOI is all greater than 0.6. This indicates that this method not only can identify different shot types, but also can accurately locate events.

Table 5. Confusion matrix for untrimmed video.

	NOR	DIS	FOI	SWIPE	CUT	Accuracy
NOR	374769	11785	2571	30011	112	89.39%
DIS	771	6482	351	1877	44	68.05%
FOI	67	66	1918	68	26	89.42%
SWIPE	205	147	553	2720	18	74.66%
CUT	97	27	25	42	3059	94.12%

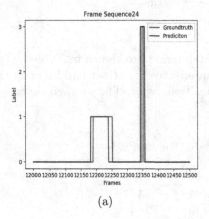 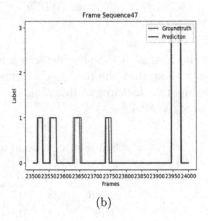

(a)   (b)

Fig. 6. Frame level comparison. The x-axis indicates the frame number, and the y-axis indicates shot types; The red line represents the Groundtruth result, and the blue line represents prediction result by our model. (Color figure online)

We use Trecvid 2005 data as a test set and compare it with other methods. The comparison results are shown in Table 6. The Best TRECVid performer [19] make use of support vector machine classifiers (SVMs) to help detect either cuts or gradual transitions and use color features to train the classifier, and the accuracy is 78.6%. In comparison, Our method extracts the deep features that

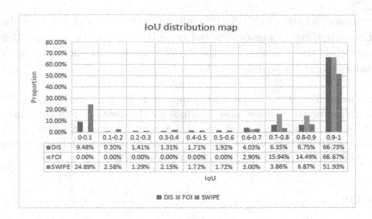

Fig. 7. IoU distribution of test video, where the x-axis represents the degree of overlap and the y-axis represents the proportion of events.

combine the relationships between frames through convolutional neural network, which improves the result by nearly 10%; Compared with the results of another deep learning model LSTM, Our proposed method increases the accuracy by 18%; DeepSBD [16] divides the shot transition types into abrupt transition, gradual transition and no-transition. Instead, the progressive framework we used first detects abrupt shots and only distinguish three types of gradual transition and no-transition, which effectively avoid the misdetection caused by the abrupt shots which lack of time domain information and increase the accuracy by 4%.

Table 6. Comparing against different techniques.

MODEL	Accuracy
CNN+LSTM	0.708
Best Trecvid Performer	0.786
DeepSBD	0.844
OURS(untrimmed)	**0.888**
OURS(trimmed)	**0.894**

4   Conclusion

In this paper, we have proposed a progressive method for shot boundary detection task. Our method employs histogram comparison method to detect abrupt shot changes, which effectively avoid the misdetection caused by the abrupt shots which lack of time domain information. Moreover, C3D model performs to extract temporal features and distinguish different types of gradual shot transitions. The experiments are conducted on TRECVid data set and the results demonstrate that the proposed method are feasible and effective for detecting shot boundaries and its position.

Acknowledgements. This work was supported in part by Beijing Municipal Education Commission Science and Technology Innovation Project under Grant KZ201610005012, in part by Beijing excellent young talent cultivation project under Grant 2017000020124G075 and in part by China Postdoctoral Science Foundation funded project under Grant 2017M610027, 2018T110019.

References

1. Wang, J., Li, J., Gray, R.: Unsupervised multiresolution segmentation for images with low depth of field. IEEE Trans. Pattern Anal. Mach. Intell. **2**(5), 99–110 (2002)
2. Zhang, H., Kankanhalli, A., Smoliar, S.: Automatic partitioning of full-motion video. Multimed. Syst. **1**(1), 10–28 (1993)
3. Lefèvre, S., Vincent, N.: Efficient and robust shot change detection. J. R.-Time Image Process. **2**(1), 23–34 (2007)
4. Zabih, R., Miller, J., Mai, K.: Feature-based algorithms for detecting and classifying scene breaks. Proc. ACM Multimed. **7**(2), 189–200 (1995)
5. Sang, H., Kim, R.: Robust video indexing for video sequences with complex brightness variations (2002)
6. Wei, J., Ngan, K.: High accuracy flashlight scene determination for shot boundary detection. Signal Process. Image Commun. **18**(3), 203–219 (2003)
7. Feng, H., Yuan, H., Wei, M.: A shot boundary detection method based on color space. In: Proceedings of the International Conference on E-Business and E-Government, pp. 1647–1650. IEEE (2010)
8. Ueda, H., Miyatake, T., Yoshizawa, S.: IMPACT: an interactive natural-motion-picture dedicated multimedia authoring system. Proc. Chi **7**(7), 343–350 (1991)
9. Nagasaka, A., Tanaka, Y.: Automatic video indexing and full-video search for object appearances. Ipsj J. **33**, 113–127 (1992)
10. Cheng, C., Lam, K., Zheng, T.: TRECVID2005 Experiments in The Hong Kong Polytechnic University: Shot Boundary Detection Based on a Multi-Step Comparison Scheme. TREC Video Retrieval Evaluation Notebook Papers (2005)
11. Cernekova, Z., Pitas, I., Nikou, C.: Information theory-based shot cut/fade detection and video summarization. IEEE Trans. Circuits Syst. Video Technol. **16**(1), 82–91 (2005)
12. Wang, J., Luo, W.: A self-adapting dual-threshold method for video shot transition detection. In: Proceedings of the IEEE International Conference on Networking, Sensing and Control, pp. 704–707. IEEE (2008)
13. Zhang, H., Wu, J., Zhong, D.: An integrated system for content-based video retrieval and browsing. Pattern Recognit. **30**(4), 643–658 (1997)
14. Xu, J., Song, L., Xie, R.: Shot boundary detection using convolutional neural networks, In: Proceedings of Visual Communications and Image Processing, pp. 1–4. IEEE (2016)
15. Gygli, M.: Ridiculously Fast Shot Boundary Detection with Fully Convolutional Neural Networks (2017)

16. Hassanien, A., Elgharib, M., Selim, A.: Large-scale, fast and accurate shot boundary detection through spatio-temporal convolutional neural networks (2017)

17. Pal, G., Rudrapaul, D., Acharjee, S.: Video shot boundary detection: a review. In: Satapathy, S., Govardhan, A., Raju, K., Mandal, J. (eds.) Emerging ICT for Bridging the Future - Proceedings of the 49th Annual Convention of the Computer Society of India CSI Volume 2. Advances in Intelligent Systems and Computing, vol. 338, pp. 119–127. Springer, Heidelberg (2015). https://doi.org/10.1007/978-3-319-13731-5_14

18. Du, T., Bourdev, L., Fergus, R.: Learning spatiotemporal features with 3D convolutional networks, pp. 4489–4497 (2014)

19. Smeaton, A., Over, P., Doherty, A.: Video shot boundary detection: seven years of TRECVid activity. Comput. Vis. Image Underst. 114(4), 411–418 (2010)

Built-Up Area Extraction from Landsat 8 Images Using Convolutional Neural Networks with Massive Automatically Selected Samples

Tao Zhang and Hong Tang[✉]

Beijing Key Laboratory of Environmental Remote Sensing and Digital Cities,
Beijing Normal University, Beijing 100875, China
201721480054@mail.bnu.edu.cn,
{hongtang, tanghong}@bnu.edu.cn

Abstract. Extraction of built-up area (e.g., roads, buildings, and other Man-made object) from remotely sensed imagery plays an important role in many urban applications. This task is normally difficult due to complex data in the form of heterogeneous appearance with large intra-class variations and lower inter-class variations. In order to extract the built-up area of 15-m resolution based on Landsat 8-OLI images, we propose the convolutional neural networks (CNN) which built in Google Drive using Colaboratory-Tensorflow. In this Framework, Google Earth Engine (GEE) provides massive remote sensing images and preprocesses the data. In this proposed CNN, for each pixel, the spectral information of the 8 bands and the spatial relationship in the 5 neighborhood are taken into account. Training this network requires lots of sample points, so we propose a method based on the ESA's 38-m global built-up area data of 2014, Open Street Map and MOD13Q1-NDVI to achieve rapid and automatic generation of large number of sample points. We choose Beijing, Lanzhou, Chongqing, Suzhou and Guangzhou of China as the experimentation sites, which represent different landforms and different urban environments. We use the proposed CNN to extract built-up area, and compare the results with other existing building data products. Our research shows: (1) The test accuracy of the five experimental sites is higher than 89%. (2) The classification results of CNN can be very good for the details of the built-up area, and greatly reduce the classification error and leakage error. Therefore, this paper provides a reference for the classification and mapping of built-up areas in large space range.

Keywords: Extract built-up area · CNN · Landsat 8 image · Generate samples Google Earth Engine · Google Colaboratory

1 Introduction

Built-up area refers to the land of urban and rural residential and public facilities, including industrial and mining land, energy land, transportation, water conservancy, communication and other infrastructure land, tourist land, military land and so on.

This work was supported by the National Key R&D Program of China (No. 2017YFB0504100).

J.-H. Lai et al. (Eds.): PRCV 2018, LNCS 11257, pp. 492–504, 2018.
https://doi.org/10.1007/978-3-030-03335-4_43

Built-up is one of the most important elements of land use, and plays an extremely important role in urban planning. In the process of urban development, on the one hand, the expansion of the built-up area provides suitable sites for industrial production, economic activities, and people living. On the other hand, the built-up area has profoundly changed the natural surface of the region, and then affects the natural processes of heat exchange, hydrological process and ecosystem [1].

Built-up area extraction based on remote sensing image has always been a research hotspot. In [2–4], normalized difference building index (NDBI), index-based build-up index (IBI) and texture-derived built-up presence index (PanTex) are separately proposed in order to extract buildings. But these methods have strong dependence on threshold selection, and how to find the suitable threshold is very difficult. In recent years, very high resolution and hyperspectral images have been gradually used in building extraction. Many methods which are based on morphological filtering [5], spatial structure features [6], grayscale texture features [7], image segmentation [8] and geometric features [9] have been applied to building extraction. But these methods are difficult to consider spectral information and spatial structure information at the same time. With the rapid development of convolution neural network and deep learning, especially the excellent performance of deep convolution neural network on ImageNet contest [10–13], CNN has shown great advantages in image pattern recognition, scene classification [14], object detection and other issues. More and more researchers have applied CNN to remote sensing image classification. In [15–17], CNN of different structures have been used for building extraction. In [24], Deep Collaborative Embedding (DCE) model integrates the weakly-supervised image-tag correlation, image correlation and tag correlation simultaneously and seamlessly for understanding social image. These studies were based on open data sets within small range and ground truth, which made great progress in the methodology. However, there are few researches on image classification in large areas. For 15-m built-up area extraction based on CNN in large region, there are three key issues: (1) Acquisition and preprocessing of huge Landsat 8-OLI images. (2) Generate a large number of accurate sample points applied to train CNN. (3) CNN framework using multiband-spectral and spatial information simultaneously. In this paper, we study these three points and try to find a solution.

A typical pipeline for thematic mapping from satellite images consists of image collection, feature extraction, classifier learning and classification. This pipeline works more and more difficult along with increasing of mapping geographical scope or spatial resolution of satellite images. The difficulty originates from the inefficiency of data collection and processing and the ineffectiveness of both classifier learning and prediction. One could be partly relieved from the inefficiency of the traditional pipeline by using the data on the Google Earth Engine (GEE). A multi-petabyte catalog of satellite imagery and geospatial datasets have been collected in GEE and freely available to everyone [18]. Some functions of geo-computation are also available to users by online interface or offline application programming interfaces. However, many advanced functions of machine learning are still out of the GEE, for example deep learning technologies.

So we introduce an effective way to rapid extract built-up areas by making full use of huge data on the GEE, high speed computation of the Google Cloud Storage (GCS) and the contemporary machine learning technologies within Google Colaboratory (Colab). As shown in Fig. 1, GCS can be used as a bridge between the GEE and

Colab. First of all, Landsat 8 images on the GEE are selected and preprocessed, e.g., cloud mask and mosaicking. Massive training samples are automatically selected from low-resolution land-cover production using a preset rule. Then, a Convolutional Neural Network (CNN) is designed based on the TensorFlow using Colab. Finally, the CNN is trained and utilized to rapid mapping of built-up areas within the GCS using the Landsat 8 images and training samples transferred from the GEE.

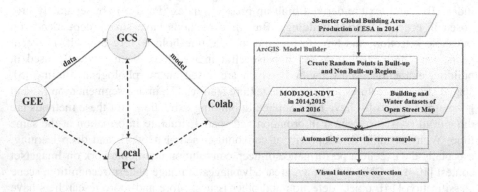

Fig. 1. Flowchart of extracting built-up area   **Fig. 2.** Sample generation and correction

2 Study Area and Data

China has vast territory, complex and changeable climate types, and different landforms in different regions. In order to train a CNN with strong universality and robustness, the choice of Landsat 8 images needs to consider multiple regions and multi time period. In this paper, we choose Beijing, Lanzhou, Chongqing, Suzhou and Guangzhou as the experimental region, as shown in Table 1: the five regions represent the situation of the cities under different climates and landforms in China. We chose Landsat 8 images on GEE, taking into account the large amount of cloud cover in spring and autumn, so the date of image is mainly in summer. And in order to ensure data quality, the cloud coverage of each image is less than 5%. The image of each region was preprocessed by mosaicing and cutting on GEE. Finally, in each region, the size of image at 15-m resolution is 12000 * 12000. As shown in Fig. 3, A, B, C, D and E are the five experimental region numbers selected respectively. The false color (7, 6, 4 band combination) shows that the quality of the data is good and meets the requirements.

The training and testing samples are automatically selected from the 38-m global built-up production of ESA in 2014 [21]. Based on the ArcGIS-Model Builder tool (Fig. 4 is the model created), a large number of sample points are automatically generated, filtered and corrected. As shown in Fig. 2, the detailed process includes three steps: (1) Randomly select 20 thousand sample points in each experimental area. (2) Use the buildings and water data sets of Open Street Map (OSM) in China and

Tabel 1. The information of Landsat 8 images in the five experimental region

Code	Test sites	Characteristics	Climates	Path/row	Date	Cloud cover (%)
A	Beijing	The political center, the mega city, the buildings are densely distributed	The semi humid continental monsoon climate in the north temperate zone	122/32	2015-08-15	0.1
				122/33	2015-06-12	0.43
				123/32	2015-04-16	0.25
				123/33	2015-05-18	0.44
				124/31	2015-09-14	0.05
				124/32	2015-05-25	0.06
				124/33	2015-08-13	0.72
B	Lanzhou	City in the gobi. Buildings are distributed along the river	The temperate continental climate	130/34	2015-10-10	0.27
				130/35	2015-10-10	0.07
				130/36	2015-07-06	1.48
				131/34	2015-06-11	0.37
				131/35	2015-06-11	0.76
C	Chongqing	The terrain is undulating. Buildings are distributed in valley and low-lying land	Subtropical monsoon humid climate	127/39	2016-05-16	0.92
				127/40	2016-06-17	2.11
				128/39	2014-08-06	2.92
				128/40	2014-08-06	3.76
D	Suzhou	Too many rivers and lakes. The distribution of buildings is broken	Subtropical monsoon ocean climate	118/38	2015-08-03	0.33
				118/39	2015-08-03	0.5
				119/38	2015-10-13	4.37
				119/39	2015-10-13	1.01
E	Guangzhou	Pearl River Delta, Developed economy, Complex building types	Subtropical oceanic monsoon climate	122/43	2015-10-18	0.03
				122/44	2015-10-18	1.15
				123/43	2015-04-16	0.14
				123/44	2015-04-16	0.09

MOD13Q1-NDVI data to filter and correct the selected sample points. The aim is to modify the built-up sample points in the vegetation area and the water body into non-built-up sample points, and to modify the non-built-up sample points in the built-up area into the built-up sample points. (3) Combine with ArcGIS Online Image for manual correction. Finally, accurate sample points of built-up area and non-built-up area are obtained. For each experimental region, the corrected sample points were hierarchically divided into training samples and test samples at 50% ratio. Table 2 shows the number of samples that will eventually be used for training and testing.

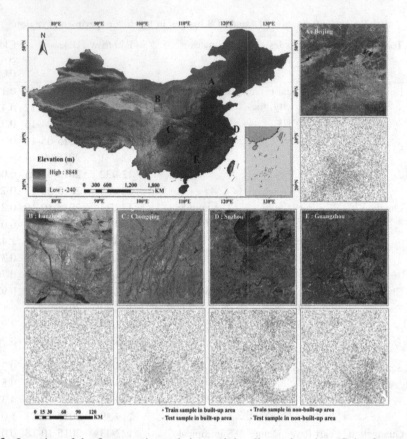

Fig. 3. Location of the five experimental sites and the all sample points (Color figure online)

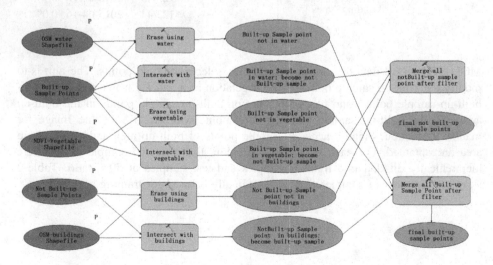

Fig. 4. Correct error sample points by ArcGIS Model Builder

Table 2. The final number of training and testing samples

Test sites	Training samples		Testing samples		Sum
	Built-up area	Non built-up area	Built-up area	Non built-up area	
A	4973	5026	4973	5026	19998
B	4760	5000	4762	4999	19521
C	4906	5017	4905	5017	19845
D	4950	5042	4950	5043	19984
E	4955	5038	4954	5037	19984

3 The Proposed CNN

There are multiple spectral bands in Landsat 8 OLI sensors. Many empirical indexes have been shown to be effective to characterize land-cover categories by a combination of a subset Landsat bands, for example the Normalized Urban Areas Composite Index [19] and normalized building index [3]. In addition, Yang et al. have shown that the combination of a subset of spectral bands can promote the classification accuracy of convolutional neural networks [20]. This motivate us to use the networks as shown in Fig. 5, which consists of input layer, convolution layer, full-connected layer and output layer.

As for the input layer, all of the first seven bands of the Landsat 8 OLI images are up-sampled to 15 m using the nearest neighborhood sampling. Then the up-sampled seven bands are stacked with the panchromatic band. In the 15-m resolution image, the size of the building is generally less than 5 pixels. For each pixel, the 5-neighborhood is considered, which means the size of image patch is 5 * 5 * 8. So an image patch with 8 bands and 5 * 5 neighborhood centered on each sample is inputted into the neural

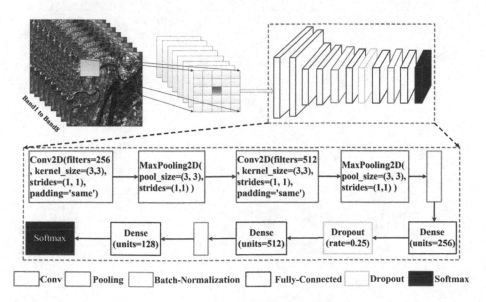

Fig. 5. The proposed CNN framework

network. Within the convolutional layer, there are two convolution and two max-pooling layers, which aim to extract spectral features and spatial features, even more high-grade features. In the fully-connected layer, we use three fully-connected layers. In order to prevent over fitting, one batch-normalization layer and a dropout layer are added. The output layer consists of a soft max operator, which outputs two categories. In the whole network, we use the popular function called Rectified Linear Unit (ReLU) solving the vanishing gradient problem for training epochs in the network.

4 Experiments and Data Analysis

There are a total of 44717 training sample points, including 24544 built-up area samples and 20173 non built-up area samples. We divide the training samples into training set and validation set according to the ratio of 7:3. For the CNN, we input training data and set up some hyper-parameters. The batch size was set to 128 and the epoch was set to 200. We use cross entropy as the loss function and use stochastic gradient descent (SGD) as the optimizer to learn the model parameters. The initial learning rate of SGD is set to 0.001. When the learning rate is no less than 0.00001, the learning rate decreases exponentially with the increase of training epoch-index. The calculation formula of the learning rate is as follows:

$$initial\_lrate = 0.001$$
$$if(lrate < 0.00001) : lrate = 0.00001$$
$$else : lrate = initial\_lrate * 0.5^{\frac{1+n}{10}}$$

In this formula, 'Initial_lrate' represents the initial learning rate, 'lrate' represents the learning rate after each iteration, and 'n' indicates the epoch of iteration.

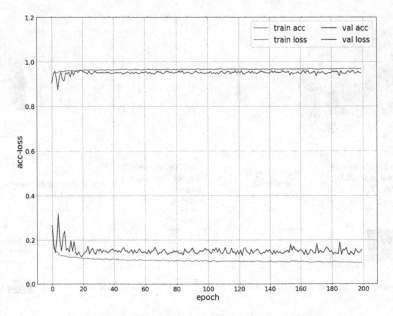

Fig. 6. Accuracy and loss in the training process

As shown in Fig. 6, after the thirtieth epoch, the model tends to converge, and the values of training accuracy and verification accuracy are stable at 0.96 and 0.95, but the value of training loss and verification loss still slows down slowly. At the thirtieth epoch, the time is 50 min. When the 200 epochs is completed, it takes 368 min. Using the trained network to classify the five experimental sites, and calculate the classification accuracy and loss value of the test samples. As shown in Table 3, the test accuracy of the five experimental sites is higher than 0.89, and it can be seen from Fig. 7 that the result of extracting built-up area is very good. The test accuracy of Chongqing and Lanzhou is the highest, 0.95 and 0.94 respectively, while the test accuracy of Suzhou and Guangzhou is lower, and their values are 0.92 and 0.91 respectively. Beijing has the lowest test accuracy, only 0.89. According to our priori knowledge, Beijing is a mega city, and the buildings are densely distributed and ground surface coverage is mixed and complex. So there are great difficulties to classify built-up and non-built-up area accurately.

Table 3. The test accuracy loss in the five experimental sites

Experimental site	A	B	C	D	E
Test accuracy	0.89	0.95	0.94	0.92	0.91
Test loss	0.37	0.20	0.24	0.23	0.34

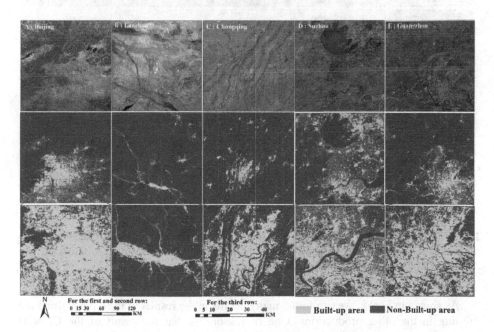

Fig. 7. Results of built-up area by CNN in the five experimental sites

5   Discussion

5.1   Qualitative Comparison

For the sake of qualitative comparison, we compare the results of the proposed CNN with that of Global-Urban-2015 [22], GHS-BUILT38 produced by ESA [21] and GlobalLand30 [23] in the C experimental site: Chongqing. Three small regions with the size of 1000 * 1000 pixels are separated from the Chongqing region, numbered as 1, 2 and 3 in Fig. 8.

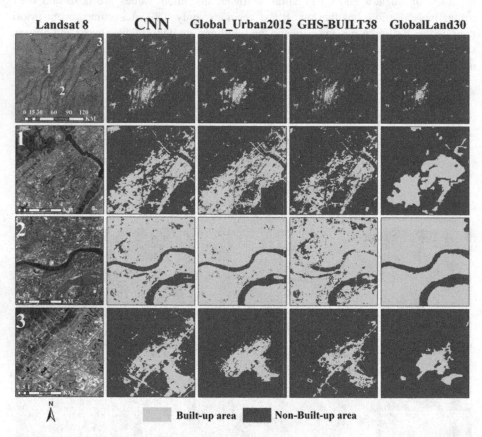

Fig. 8. The classification results. The first column shows the experimental images and their three sub-regions. The other columns exhibit the classification results of CNN, Global_Urban 2015, GHS-BULT 38, and GlobalLand 30, respectively.

As shown in Fig. 8, we can found many details in the results of the CNN, which are missing in the other productions. One of reasons is that the result of the CNN is produced from satellite images with higher spatial resolutions. Consequently, within the urban area, non-built-up area, e.g., water and vegetation in the dense buildings, can be discriminated from built-up area within the Landsat 8 images. Meanwhile, in the suburbs, small size of built-up areas and narrow roads become distinguishable from the background. Another reason is due to the higher classification accuracy of the CNN.

5.2   The Proposed CNN VS VGG16

We choose Beijing as experimental site, and compare the results of the proposed CNN with VGG16 [11]. As shown in Fig. 9, We reserve the weight of the convolution layers and the pooling layers of VGG16, and reset the top layers including the full connection layers, BatchNormalization layer and softmax layer. We use Colab-keras to achieve transfer learning and fine-tuning of VGG16. As for VGG16, the channels of input data must be 3, and the size must be greater than 48 * 48, so the neighborhood of 5 * 5 is up-sampled to 50 * 50 by nearest neighbor sampling. Since the original image has 8 bands and cannot be directly input to VGG16, we fuse panchromatic and multispectral bands by Gram-Schmidt Pan Sharpening to obtain the fusion image with 15 m resolution having 7 bands. Then we take three bands in two ways: (1) The first three principal components are taken after principal component analysis; (2) The 432 bands representing RGB are taken directly.

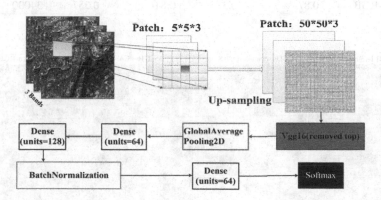

Fig. 9. Transfer learning and fine-tuning of VGG16

We set the ratio of training samples and validation samples to 7:3 for training the proposed CNN and VGG16. The accuracy and loss of the training process are shown in Fig. 10.

We recorded training accuracy, training loss, test accuracy, test loss, and the training time of 200 epochs. We can see from Table 4 that the accuracy of the proposed CNN is significantly better than that of VGG16, and the training time is greatly shortened. In Fig. 11, the classification effect of the proposed CNN is obviously greater than that of VGG16, and the extraction of built-up area is more detailed and accurate.

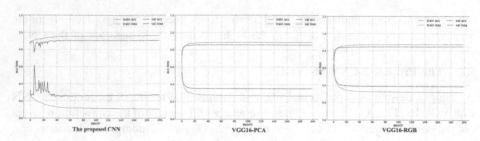

Fig. 10. Accuracy and loss in the training process of the proposed CNN, VGG16-PCA and VGG16-RGB

Table 4. The accuracy and loss of the proposed CNN, VGG16-PCA and VGG16-RGB

CNN-strategy	Train accuracy	Train loss	Test accuracy	Test loss	Training time (s)
The proposed CNN	0.968	0.102	0.901	0.262	4000
VGG16-PCA	0.886	0.266	0.842	0.321	36000
VGG16-RGB	0.873	0.316	0.816	0.357	34000

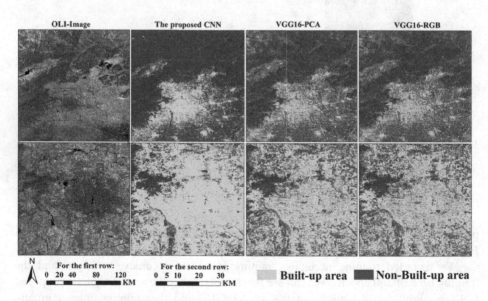

Fig. 11. Results of built-up area by the proposed CNN, VGG16-PCA and VGG16-RGB

6 Conclusion

In this paper, we build a simple and practical CNN framework, and use the automatic generation and correction of a large number of samples to realize the 15-m resolution built-up area classification and mapping based on the Landsat 8 image. We selected five typical experimentation sites, trained a better universal network, and classified the data of each experimentation site. The results show that all the test accuracy is higher than 89%, and the classification effect is good. We compared the CNN classification results with the existing built-up data products, which showed that the classification results of CNN can be very good for the details of the built-up area, and greatly reduced the classification error and leakage error. We also compared the results of the proposed CNN with VGG16, which indicated that the classification effect of the proposed CNN is obviously greater than that of VGG16, and the extraction of built-up area is more distinct and accurate. Therefore, this paper provides a reference for the classification and mapping of built-up areas in a wide range. At the same time, this paper also has the shortage that the choice of experimentation site is only in China and we fails to carry out experiments and verification on a global scale.

References

1. Chen, X.H., Cao, X., Liao, A.P., et al.: Global mapping of artificial surface at 30-m resolution. Sci. China Earth Sci. **59**, 2295–2306 (2016)
2. Zha, Y., Gao, J., Ni, S.: Use of normalized difference built-up index in automatically mapping urban areas from TM imagery. Int. J. Remote Sens. **24**(3), 583–594 (2003)
3. Xu, H.: A new index for delineating built-up land features in satellite imagery. Int. J. Remote Sens. **29**(14), 4269–4276 (2008)
4. Pesaresi, M., Gerhardinger, A., Kayitakire, F.: A robust built-up area presence index by anisotropic rotation-invariant texture measure. IEEE J. Sel. Top. Appl. Earth Obs. Remote. Sens. **1**(3), 180–192 (2009)
5. Chaudhuri, D., Kushwaha, N.K., Samal, A., et al.: Automatic building detection from high-resolution satellite images based on morphology and internal gray variance. IEEE J. Sel. Top. Appl. Earth Obs. Remote. Sens. **9**(5), 1767–1779 (2016)
6. Jin, X., Davis, C.H.: Automated building extraction from high-resolution satellite imagery in urban areas using structural, contextual, and spectral information. EURASIP J. Adv. Signal Process. **2005**(14), 745309 (2005)
7. Pesaresi, M., Guo, H., Blaes, X., et al.: A global human settlement layer from optical HR/VHR RS data: concept and first results. IEEE J. Sel. Top. Appl. Earth Obs. Remote. Sens. **6**(5), 2102–2131 (2013)
8. Goldblatt, R., Stuhlmacher, M.F., Tellman, B., et al.: Using Landsat and nighttime lights for supervised pixel-based image classification of urban land cover. Remote Sens. Environ. **205**(C), 253–275 (2018)
9. Yang, J., Meng, Q., Huang, Q., et al.: A new method of building extraction from high resolution remote sensing images based on NSCT and PCNN. In: International Conference on Agro-Geoinformatics, pp. 1–5 (2016)
10. Krizhevsky, A., Sutskever, I., Hinton, G.E.: ImageNet classification with deep convolutional neural networks. In: International Conference on Neural Information Processing Systems, vol. 60, no. 2, pp. 1097–1105 (2012)

11. Russakovsky, O., Deng, J., Su, H., et al.: ImageNet large scale visual recognition challenge. Int. J. Comput. Vis. **115**(3), 211–252 (2015)
12. Szegedy, C., et al.: Going deeper with convolutions. In: 2015 IEEE Conference on Computer Vision and Pattern Recognition (CVPR), Boston, MA, USA, pp. 1–9 (2015)
13. He, K., Zhang, X., Ren, S., Sun, J.: Deep residual learning for image recognition. In: 2016 IEEE Conference on Computer Vision and Pattern Recognition (CVPR), Las Vegas, NV, United States, pp. 770–778 (2016)
14. Castelluccio, M., Poggi, G., Sansone, C., et al.: Land use classification in remote sensing images by convolutional neural networks. Acta Ecol. Sin. **28**(2), 627–635 (2015)
15. Vakalopoulou, M., Karantzalos, K., Komodakis, N., et al.: Building detection in very high resolution multispectral data with deep learning features. In: Geoscience and Remote Sensing Symposium, vol. 50, pp. 1873–1876 (2015)
16. Huang, Z., Cheng, G., Wang, H., et al.: Building extraction from multi-source remote sensing images via deep deconvolution neural networks. In: Geoscience and Remote Sensing Symposium, pp. 1835–1838 (2016)
17. Makantasis, K., Karantzalos, K., Doulamis, A., Loupos, K.: Deep learning-based man-made object detection from hyperspectral data. In: Bebis, G., et al. (eds.) ISVC 2015. LNCS, vol. 9474, pp. 717–727. Springer, Cham (2015). https://doi.org/10.1007/978-3-319-27857-5_64
18. Gorelick, N., Hancher, M., Dixon, M., et al.: Google earth engine: planetary-scale geospatial analysis for everyone. Remote Sens. Environ. **202**, 18–27 (2017)
19. Liu, X., Hu, G., Ai, B., et al.: A normalized urban areas composite index (NUACI) based on combination of DMSP-OLS and MODIS for mapping impervious surface area. Remote Sens. **7**(12), 17168–17189 (2015)
20. Yang, N., Tang, H., Sun, H., et al.: DropBand: a simple and effective method for promoting the scene classification accuracy of convolutional neural networks for VHR remote sensing imagery. IEEE Geosci. Remote Sens. Lett. **5**(2), 257–261 (2018)
21. Martino, P., Daniele, E., Stefano, F., et al.: Operating procedure for the production of the global human settlement layer from landsat data of the epochs 1975, 1990, 2000, and 2014. JRC Technical report EUR 27741 EN. https://doi.org/10.2788/253582
22. Liu, X., Hu, G., Chen, Y., et al.: High-resolution multi-temporal mapping of global urban land using landsat images based on the Google earth engine platform. Remote Sens. Environ. **209**, 227–239 (2018)
23. Chen, J., Chen, J., Liao, A., et al.: Global land cover mapping at 30 m resolution: a POK-based operational approach. ISPRS J. Photogramm. Remote. Sens. **103**, 7–27 (2015)
24. Li, Z., Tang, J., Mei, T.: Deep collaborative embedding for social image understanding. IEEE Trans. Pattern Anal. Mach. Intell. **PP**(99), 1 (2018)

Weighted Graph Classification by Self-Aligned Graph Convolutional Networks Using Self-Generated Structural Features

Xuefei Zheng[1,2], Min Zhang[1], Jiawei Hu[2], Weifu Chen[1(✉)], and Guocan Feng[1]

[1] School of Mathematics, Sun Yat-sen University, Guangzhou, China
alexandrap@163.com, Zhangjmin@gdpu.edu.cn,
{chenwf26,mcsfgc}@mail.sysu.edu.cn
[2] Tencent-CDG-FIT, Shenzhen, China
jessejwhu@tencent.com

Abstract. Directed weighted graphs are important graph data. The weights and directions of the edges carry rich information which can be utilized in many areas. For instance, in a cashflow network, the direction and amount of a transfer can be used to detect social ties or criminal organizations. Hence it is important to study the weighted graph classification problems. In this paper, we present a graph classification algorithm called Self-Aligned graph convolutional network (SA-GCN) for weighted graph classification. SA-GCN first normalizes a given graph so that graphs are trimmed and aligned in correspondence. Following that structural features are extracted from the edge weights and graph structures. And finally the model is trained in an adversarial way to make the model more robust. Experiments on benchmark datasets showed that the proposed model could achieve competitive results and outperformed some popular state-of-the-art graph classification methods.

Keywords: Graph classification · Graph convolutional networks
Graph normalization · Structural features · Adversarial training

1 Introduction

Many data, such as social networks, cash flow networks or structures of proteins, can be naturally represented in the form of graphs. Graphs can be simply classified into directed graphs and undirected graphs, based on whether nodes are connected by directed or undirected edges. For examples, cash flow networks are directed graphs, since money is transferred from one account to another; protein-protein interaction networks are undirected graphs, where undirected edges are used to characterize the interaction between protein molecules. One of the most important types of graph is weighted graph, in which each edge is associated with a numerical weight. Since it is natural to measure the relationship between

© Springer Nature Switzerland AG 2018
J.-H. Lai et al. (Eds.): PRCV 2018, LNCS 11257, pp. 505–516, 2018.
https://doi.org/10.1007/978-3-030-03335-4_44

nodes based on edge weights, weighted graphs have been widely used to store network objects. Given a collection of weighted graphs, the work considers how to classify the graphs. Unlike grid data, there are several challenges in graph classification:

- Graphs usually differ in size, i.e., the number of nodes and the number of edges of graphs are different;
- the nodes of any two graphs are not necessarily in correspondence, which, however, is critical in comparing graphs;
- although sub-structures are basic elements for classifying graphs, how to use the structural information in graph classification is still an open problem.

In the past decades, Support Vector Machines (SVMs) have been shown the great power in classification [15]. When applying SVMs to graph classification problems, the core issue is how to define kernels for graphs. The most popular way to define graph kernel is based on subgraphs [13, 16]. In summary, those algorithms first recursively decomposed a graph into subgraphs, then counted how many times each given subgraph occurred in the graph, and finally kernel functions were defined to measure the similarity between the vectors of the subgraph-occurring frequencies. The major limitation of those algorithms is the high computational complexity, due to the decomposition of the graph, which restricts the graph kernels only suitable to small number of subgraphs with few nodes.

Recently, convolutional neural networks (CNNs) have achieved great success in many fields [7, 8]. Traditional CNNs are designed for grid data, and there is an implicit order of the components. Hence, a receptive field can be moved in particular directions. However, graph data don't have such specific ordering and it is necessary to redefine convolution operators for graph data. Many researches tried to extend CNNs for graph data. One of the popular approaches is to generalize the convolution in the graph Fourier domain [3, 4]. The basic procedure of those algorithms was first to do the eigenvalue decomposition of the Laplacian matrix of a graph, and the first d eigenvectors were then used as the filters parameterized by diagonal matrices whose diagonal elements were related to the eigenvalues of the graph Laplacian matrix. Although the definition of spectral graph convolution in this way is attractive and the experimental results reported are significantly improved, it was time-consuming (the computational complexity is $\bigcirc(n^2)$, where n is the number of nodes of a graph) to calculate the eigenvectors of the Laplacian matrix, in particular for large-scale graphs. Meanwhile, those methods assumed that the input vertices were in correspondence so that the nodes could be easily transformed into a linear layer and fed to a convolutional architecture. For handling general graph data (with different nodes and edges), Niepert et al. [11] proposed an algorithm called PATCHY-SAN to extract locally connected regions from graphs using the Weisfeiler-Lehman algorithm [18] for graph labelling so that the nodes of graphs were ordered and convolution can be implemented as traversing a node sequence and obtain convincing classification accuracy. One of the drawbacks of PATCHY-SAN is that graph labelling methods are usually not injective and PATCHY-SAN used a software named NAUTY [9] to break ties between same-label nodes, which will weaken the ordering meaning and lead to eliminating important nodes.

In this paper, we present a new kind of graph convolutional networks (GCNs) for weighted graph classification. Since the proposed model could learn the order of the nodes of a graph by itself based on the importance which is measured by PageRank and degree centrality, we call the model Self-Aligned GCN (SA-GCN). According to the order of the nodes, SA-GCN trims graphs into the same size so that a correspondence of the vertices across input graphs could be fixed. Following that graphs could be compared directly. In contrast to existing GCNs, SA-GCN also considers structural features extracted from edge weights and graph global structure, which are usually neglected by other models but contain rich discriminative information for classification. Another problem could be solved by SA-GCN is small-dataset problem. As it is well-known, due to huge of parameters, a neural network tends to be overfitting if there is lack of training samples. SA-GCN tries to solve this problem by adversarial training which in essence is a way to augment training samples by adding particular noise to existing training samples but has been proved efficient for increasing the robustness of a model [6].

2   Self-Aligned Graph Convolutional Networks

In this section, we will introduce the novel Self-Aligned Graph Convolutional Networks (SA-GCNs). First we will introduce the basic notations, and we will introduce the three elements (graph normalization, structural feature generation and adversarial training) in sequence.

Let $G(V, E, A, W)$ denote a graph G with nodes $V = \{v_1, \ldots, v_n\}$, edges $E = \{e_1, \ldots, e_m\}$, adjacent matrix A and weight matrix W. Here each edge $e = (u, v) \in V \times V$ is a ordered pair for directed graphs and is unordered pair for undirected graph. $A_{ij} = 1$ represents that there is an edge from v_i to v_j and $A_{ij} = 0$ means there is no edge connecting v_i and v_j. If $A_{ij=1}$, v_i and v_j are called adjacent. Let $\mathcal{N}_1(v)$ denote the node set whose elements are adjacent to node v, and $\mathcal{N}_1(v)$ can be treated as the first-order neighborhood of node v. W_{ij} is the sum of all weights associated with $e(v_i, v_j)$. Obviously, if G is an undirected graph, both A and W are symmetric matrices. Define the degree of node v_i as $d_i = \sum_{j=1}^n W_{ij}$, and degree matrix as $D = diag(d_1, \ldots, d_n)$ and then Laplacian matrix can be defined as $L = D - W$. For directed graphs, the indegree of a vertex is the number of head ends adjacent to the vertex, and the outdegree of the vertex is defined as the number of tail ends adjacent to the vertex. We denote the indegree and the outdegree of node v_i as $d^{in}(v_i)$ and $d^{out}(v_i)$ or simply as d_i^{in} and d_i^{out}. Details of graph theory can be referred to Ref. [5].

2.1   Graph Normalization

In order to compare the graphs, we should impose an order on the vertices across input graphs. Intuitively, nodes should be ordered based on their importance in a graph. In this paper, PageRank and degree centrality are used to measure the importance of nodes, according to which graphs are trimmed into fixed size. Breadth-first search (BFS) is used to find the k-most-important neighbors of each selected vertex to form the neighborhoods as the receptive fields so that convolution operators can be easily implemented.

Node Ranking. Node ranking is the basis of graph normalization, and there are many criteria to measure the importance of a node in a graph. In this work, we chose PageRank (PR) [12] and degree centrality (DC) [10] as our node ranking criteria, as both of these methods are highly effective and efficient in characterizing the importance of a node in a graph, and they can be easily extended to weighted graphs.

– **PageRank.** PageRank is originally designed to use link structure to rank web pages, but can be easily extended to any directed graphs. The algorithm first assigns every node the same initial value as its PR value, then in each iteration splits the PR value of every node equally among the nodes that it points to. After each iteration, the PR value of node v_i is updated by

$$PR_i(t) = \sum_{j=1}^{n} A_{ji} \frac{PR_j(t-1)}{d_j^{out}} \tag{1}$$

When there is a node with outdegree 0, Eq. (1) won't work. In order to handle this problem, a damping factor p $(0 < p < 1)$ is added to denote the probability that a node would split its PR value among all nodes in the graph, and $1 - p$ denotes the probability that a node would split its PR value among the nodes it points to. The update equation is changed to:

$$PR_i(t) = (1 - p) \sum_{j=1}^{n} A_{ji} \frac{PR_j(t-1)}{d_j^{out}} + \frac{p}{n} \tag{2}$$

– **Degree Centrality.** Degree is a simple but effective measure to reflect node importance. For an undirected graph, the degree of node v_i is the number of nodes that are directly connected with v_i through edges. The degree centrality of a node in an undirected graph is defined as

$$DC(i) = \frac{d_i}{n-1}, \tag{3}$$

where n is the number of nodes in the graph. Hence, $n - 1$ is the largest possible degree of a node. For a directed graph, since each node has indegree d_i^{in} and outdegree d_i^{out}. The degree centrality can be defined as:

$$DC(i) = \frac{d_i^{out}}{n-1} \tag{4}$$

It should be noted that degree centrality only reflects the local influence of a node, but doesn't consider the global structure of a graph and the quality of the neighbors of a node. Therefore, degree centrality is seldom used alone as the ranking criterion.

To rank the nodes in a graph, we first compute both the PageRank values and the degree centralities of the nodes in a graph. Then we rank the nodes based on their PageRank values, and break the ties based on the degree centralities, and eventually obtain a node ranking without ties. In the experiments, the first w important nodes were chosen to form a fixed-size ordered node sequence (denoted by P). For weighted graphs, the edges between nodes have not only directions but also weights. In general, some edges are more important than others, which means those edges are more useful. To extend PageRank to weighted graphs, we just need to change the PR value splitting strategy in the iterations. Instead of equally splitting the PR value of a node among the nodes it points to, each neighboring node get a proportion of its PR value which is defined by the edge weight divided by the sum of weights on all edges leaving the current node.

Neighborhood Generation. After we have generated the ordered sequence P with w important nodes, we consider generate the receptive field (i.e., the neighborhood) for each vertex in P. Algorithm 1 depicts the procedure. First, $\forall v_i \in P$, we use node v_i as a starting point and apply breadth-first search(BFS) to find its neighbors iteratively with an increasing distance from v_i and add them to set N_i. It should be noted that inside the while loop, the distance from v_i increases 1 in each iteration and the adjacent sets $\mathcal{N}_1(v)$ of the neighboring nodes are unified into the neighborhood N_i until there are more than k nodes in set N_i or there are no more unexplored nodes to be added into set L_i. Here $|L_i|$ represents the number of unexplored nodes in L_i. Second, the nodes in N_i are sorted by their path distance from v_i in an ascending order, and their PR values and degree centralities are in sequence used to break the ties if they occur. Finally, the top k nodes are selected to form the neighborhood of v_i's.

---

1   **Input:** $PR, DC, P = \{v_1, ..., v_w\}, k$
2   **Output:** for every node v_i generate a regularized neighborhood N_i^{sorted}
1:   **for** $i = 1$ to w **do**
2:      $N_i = [v_i]$
3:      $L_i = [v_i]$
4:      **while** $|N_i| < k$ and $|L_i| > 0$ **do**
5:         $L_i = \cup_{v \in L_i} \mathcal{N}_1(v)$
6:         $N_i = N_i \cup L_i$
7:      **end while**
8:      **if** $N_i < k$ **then**
9:         Fill $k - |N_i|$ elements in N_i with 0
10:     **end if**
11:     $N_i^{sorted} =$ the top k nodes of N_i sorted by firstly the distance to node v_i in an ascending order, secondly PR value, and thirdly DC value.
12:     **return** N_i^{sorted}
13: **end for**

Algorithm 1: Neighborhood Generation

Figure 1 demonstrates two classes of graphs before and after the proposed graph normalization.

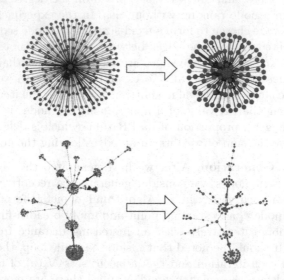

Fig. 1. Two classes of graphs before and after graph normalization. The blue one is a gamble community, and the star network structure was preserved after graph normalization. The red one is a pyramid scheme community, and the hierarchical structure was kept after graph normalization.

2.2   Node Feature Generation

After graph normalization, we consider how to extract structural features for each node from a graph. In this work, two kinds of structural features were used in the experiments:

– **PageRank and Degree Centrality.** The PR values and the degree centralities defined in Sect. 2.1 are useful structural features, as both of them could characterize the relationship between the central vertex and its neighbors.
– **Spectral Embedding.** While PageRank and Degree Centrality could reflect the local structures of a graph, spectral embedding contains the global information for graph partition [14,17]. In this work, spectral embedding based on Laplacian Eigenmaps [2] was used in the experiments, which is defined to solve the optimization problem

$$\min_{Y^T DY=I} \frac{1}{2} \sum_{i,j} \|y_i - y_j\|^2 W_{ij} = trace(Y^T LY). \tag{5}$$

It can be proved that the optimal solution of (5) is the eigenvectors corresponding to the top K smallest eigenvlues of the random-walk normalized

Laplacian matrix $\hat{L} = I - D^{-1}W$, where K is the dimensions of the embedding space.

After we have computed the spectral embedding, each node is associated with c attributes ($c = K + 2$). Hence, the size of the input tensor to the convolutional network is $w \times k \times c$, where w is the number of selected important points, k is the size of the node neighborhood, and c is the number of channels.

2.3   Adversarial Training

After graph normalization and node feature generation, each graph is represented by a 3-dimension fixed size ordered tensor, that is, graphs are in correspondence. The input tensor for each graph is of dimension $w \times k \times c$, which can be imagined as an image in size $w \times k$ with c channels. We apply a $k \times 1$ convolutional filter with stride 1 on the tensors, and the rest of the architecture can be an arbitrary combination of convolution, pooling and fully connected layer. Softmax layer is used for the final classification. Assume that the input tensor of CNNs is x, the corresponding label is y, and θ is the parameter set, the loss function of SA-GCN is defined as:

$$J_1(\theta, x, y) = -logP(y|x; \theta) \tag{6}$$

However, as we know, CNNs need to be trained with large datasets to avoid overfitting, but the datasets in the graph classification problems usually quite small. In order to train a robust model, we introduce the adversarial training objective into SA-GCN to make our model more robust and less prone to over-fitting. The adversarial training objective is defined as [6]

$$J_2(\theta, x + r, y) = -logP(y|x + r; \theta), \tag{7}$$

where r is defined as

$$r = -\epsilon sign(\nabla_x logP(y|x; \theta)). \tag{8}$$

Thus, the objective function can be defined as the weighted average of J_1 and J_2

$$\tilde{J}(\theta, x, y) = \alpha J(\theta, x, y) + (1 - \alpha)J(\theta, x + r, y), \tag{9}$$

where $\alpha \in [0, 1]$ is a trading coefficient. This cost function can be viewed as actively adding a most destructive perturbation on the input and forcing the model to learn more robust feature to overcome the perturbation. We denote the model with adversarial training SA-GCN$^+$

In summary, SA-GCN consists of three steps: (1) graph normalization, (2) node feature generation and (3) CNNs classification with adversarial training. We show the SA-GCN architecture in Fig. 2

3   Experiment

3.1   Data Description

The performance of the proposed model was tested on two types of datasets. The first type of datasets is a real cash flow networks. It contains four classes

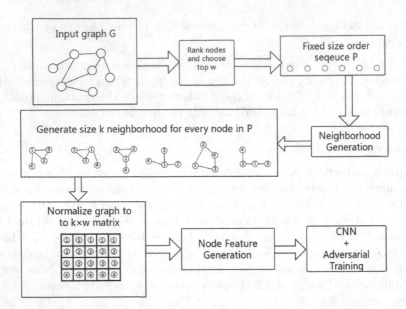

Fig. 2. Architecture of SA-GCN.For input graph G, firstly perform graph regularization with two steps of node ranking and neighborhood generation and rearrange graph to a $w \times k$ matrix, secondly generate structural feature of graphs as node feature, and lastly trains CNNs with adversarial training using node features as input.

of financial communities (pyramid scheme, illegal foreign exchange, gamble and Wechat-sale group) in total of 1944 networks. Each community is represented by a weighted graph without node information. The number of nodes of a graph varies from 100 to 3000.

The second type of datasets consists of 7 standard benchmark datasets described in line 2 to 4 of Table 3. Among them, PTC, NCI1, NCI109 and PROTEINS are bioinformatic datasets, and COLLAB, IMDB_B and IMDB_M are social network datasets. These benchmark datasets have node information, and edge features are discrete or nonexistent.

3.2 Experimental Setting

All experiments were implemented on the Tensorflow platform [1] with a single NVIDIA Titan X GPU. To compare with other models, we performed 10-fold cross validation on all datasets and repeated the experiments 10 times and reported the average prediction accuracies and standard deviations. For SA-GCN, we use $w = 100$, $k = 5$ on all datasets. For PSCN [11], DGCNN [20], and DGK [19] on standard benchmark datasets, we report the best results from the papers. For DGCNN on weighted graph dataset, We set the k of SortPooling such that 60% graphs have nodes more than k, and used weight matrix instead of 0/1 adjacent matrix, and used degree centrality as node information to extend DGCNN to weighted graph classification.

Table 1. Comparison of accuracy results with different node features

Node features	SA-GCN	SA-GCN$^+$
PageRank	*84.77 ± 2.05*	*85.81 ± 2.39*
Degree centrality	*86.58 ± 2.92*	*87.50 ± 1.61*
Spectral embedding	*82.38 ± 3.61*	*83.49 ± 2.82*
All three	*89.20 ± 1.46*	***90.80 ± 1.40***

3.3 Node Feature Selection

In this section we compared the performance of three types of node features: PageRank, degree centrality and spectral embedding with the partitions of 3. We used the same graph normalization process to rearrange graph nodes to an ordered tensor, and used PR, DC values and spectral embedding respectively as the only node feature to train CNNs. The first 3 rows of Table 1 list the results and show that degree centrality is the best out of the three. The reason behind it maybe that cash flow networks have fewer hierarchies so that the number of immediate neighbors could reflect more information of a graph. The fourth row in Table 1 shows when using all three types of node features our model reached the accuracy of 89.20%, which is higher than using either single kind of node features. The reason behind it is that these three different node features reflect different structural information of nodes. Therefore, all features could make contribute to the classification and achieved the highest accuracy.

Table 2. Compare with other methods on weighted graph dataset

Method	Accuracy
DGK	*62.47 ± 2.56*
DGCNN	*84.59 ± 0.79*
SA-GCN	*89.20 ± 1.46*
SA-GCN$^+$	***90.80 ± 1.40***

Table 2 lists the result of our model comparing with DGK [19] and DGCNN [20], and shows that SA-GCN and SA-GCN$^+$ performed better than the other two algorithm on weighted graph datasets. DGK is based on deep graph kernel, and couldn't utilize edge features, hence the bad performance. DGCNN is a CNNs based method like ours, but with a different regularization process and feature extracting mechanis. DGCNN use degree centrality as node feature, and achieve higher accuracy than SA-GCN with PR value or spectral embedding as node features, but have lower accuracy than SA-GCN with degree centrality. On the one hand, these results show that degree centrality is indeed a better node feature for these datasets and shows that SA-GCN can extract more useful information than DGCNN from the same node features.

3.4   Adversarial Training

In this section we compared our model with or without adversarial training, denoted by SA-GCN$^+$ and SA-GCN respectively. Results are listed in the first and second column of Table 1 and show that adversarial training could enhance the performance of every combination of node features, and when using all three node features and adversarial training, SA-GCN$^+$ achieved the best results.

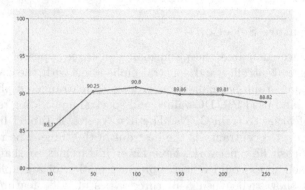

Fig. 3. Set w to 10, 50, 100, 150, 200 and 250 respectively, and report the model's average accuracy. The horizontal axis is x, and the vertical axis is the corresponding accuracy. Model achieve the highest accuracy when $w = 100$.

3.5   Parameter Analysis

In this section we analyzed the choice of parameters in the graph normalization process. The most important parameter is w, which indicates how many nodes to keep in a graph. For cash flow network dataset, there are four classes of graphs in total of 1944 and each graph have nodes number between 100 and 3000. We chose $w \in \{10, 50, 100, 150, 200, 250\}$, $k = 5$ as parameter and train our model respectively for 10 times and report average accuracy in Fig. 3. The line chart shows that parameter w has a relatively small influence on the accuracy of the model. Accuracy didn't go up as w increase, which indicates that keeping more nodes of a graph doesn't provide the model with more useful information for classification; with the increase of w, accuracy slightly come down, this indicates that extra node information can be seen as noise and be deleted from the graph, which further validate the effectiveness of graph regularization process. When $w = 10$, accuracy shows acute drop, which means too little nodes are kept in the regularization process and therefore the performance of classification suffers. Accuracy reach the highest point when $w = 100$, hence is chosen as the optimal w of SA-GCN.

3.6   Compare with Others

We compared SA-GCN$^+$ with 2 CNNs based methods (DGCNN [20] and PATCHY-SAN denoted as PSCN [11]) and 1 graph kernel based method (Deep Graphlet Kernel, DGK [19]) on 7 standard benchmark datasets, the results were listed in Table 3. SA-GCN$^+$ achieves the highest accuracy on PROTEINS, COL-LAB, PTC, NCI109 and IMDB_B, and has highly competitive on other two datasets, which proves that our model works well on unweighted graph despite the fact that it is designed for weighted graph.

Compared to DGCNN and PSCN, the differnce lay between the graph regularization mechanism we chose. PSCN uses Weisfeiler-Lehman algorithm and external software to order and chose nodes. But the Weisfeiler-Lehman algorithm sorted nodes by it's structural role and doesn't reflect the importance of a node, which means nodes which are more important in a graph could be excluded in the process. DGCNN uses graph convolutional network to extract node features and rank and choose the nodes according to these features, which means the ranking would be refined through the process of training, which is the greatest strength of this method. The drawback is that the edge feature and the structural features of graph (like the partitions) aren't fully utilized. The strength of SA-GCN is that we fully extract information from edge features and graph structural features and use them to the fullest extend to regularize graph and introduce them as node feature. Furthermore, we use adversarial training to resolve the overfitting problem and make our model more robust.

Table 3. Compare with other method on benchmark datasets. SA-GCN$^+$ achieved state of the arts on PROTEINS, COLLAB, PTC, NCI109 and IMDB_B.

Dataset	PTC	NCI1	NCI109	PROTEINS	COLLAB	IMDB_B	IMDB_M
Size	344	4110	4127	1113	5000	1000	1500
Classes	2	2	2	2	3	2	3
Avg. nodes	25.5	29.8	29.6	39.1	74.49	19.77	13
PSCN	62.29 ± 5.68	76.34 ± 1.68	-	75.00 ± 2.51	72.60 ± 2.15	71.00 ± 2.29	45.23 ± 2.84
DGCNN	58.59 ± 2.47	74.44 ± 0.47	-	75.54 ± 0.94	73.76 ± 0.49	70.03 ± 0.86	47.83 ± 0.85
DGK	57.32 ± 1.13	62.48 ± 0.25	62.69 ± 0.23	71.68 ± 0.50	73.09 ± 0.25	66.96 ± 0.56	44.55 ± 0.52
SA-GCN$^+$	62.93 ± 3.26	71.63 ± 0.61	68.86 ± 1.17	76.06 ± 2.04	74.02 ± 1.50	72.40 ± 1.84	45.76 ± 2.03

4   Conclusion

In this paper, we proposed a GCN-based model for weighted graph classification called SA-GCN. Experimental results on several popular datasets showed that the proposed model outperformed some state-of-the-art models, which indicated the advantages of the proposed model.

Directions for future work include using alternative node features and develop a criterion to compare the effectiveness each type of node features; combing the graph regularization process with the neural network, so that both part can be trained simultaneously.

Acknowledgements. This work is partially supported by the NSFC under grants Nos. 61673018, 61272338, 61703443 and Guangzhou Science and Technology Founding Committee under grant No. 201804010255 and Guangdong Province Key Laboratory of Computer Science.

References

1. Abadi, M., et al.: TensorFlow: a system for large-scale machine learning. In: OSDI 2016, pp. 265–283 (2016)
2. Belkin, M., Niyogi, P.: Laplacian eigenmaps for dimensionality reduction and data representation. Neural Comput. **15**(6), 1373–1396 (2003)
3. Bruna, J., Zaremba, W., Szlam, A., Lecun, Y.: Spectral networks and locally connected networks on graphs. In: International Conference on Learning Representations (2014)
4. Defferrard, M., Bresson, X., Vandergheynst, P.: Convolutional neural networks on graphs with fast localized spectral filtering. In: Advances in Neural Information Processing Systems, pp. 3844–3852 (2016)
5. Diestel, R.: Graph Theory, 3rd edn. Springer, Heidelberg (2006)
6. Goodfellow, I., Shlens, J., Szegedy, C.: Explaining and harnessing adversarial examples (2015)
7. LeCun, Y., Bottou, L., Bengio, Y., Haffner, P.: Gradient-based learning applied to document recognition. Proc. IEEE **86**(11), 2278–2324 (1998)
8. LeCun, Y., Bengio, Y., Hinton, G.: Deep learning. Nature **521**, 436–444 (2015)
9. McKay, B., Piperno, A.: Practical graph isomorphism, II. J. Symb. Comput. **60**, 94–112 (2014)
10. Newman, M.: Networks: An Introduction. Oxford University Press, Oxford (2010)
11. Niepert, M., Ahmed, M., Kutzkov, K.: Learning convolutional neural networks for graphs. In: Proceedings of the 33rd International Conference on Machine Learning, pp. 2014–2023 (2016)
12. Page, L., Brin, S., Motwani, R., Winograd, T.: The PageRank citation ranking: bringing order to the web. Technical report, Stanford InfoLab (1999)
13. Shervashidze, N., Borgwardt, K.M.: Fast subtree kernels on graphs. In: Advances in Neural Information Processing Systems, pp. 1660–1668 (2009)
14. Shi, J., Malik, J.: Normalized cuts and image segmentation. IEEE Trans. Pattern Anal. Mach. Intell. **22**(8), 888–905 (2000)
15. Vapnik, V.: Statistical Learning Theory. Wiley, New York (1998)
16. Vishwanathan, S., Schraudolph, N., Kondor, R., Borgwardt, K.: Graph kernels. J. Mach. Learn. Res. **11**(Apr), 1201–1242 (2010)
17. Von Luxburg, U.: A tutorial on spectral clustering. Stat. Comput. **17**(4), 395–416 (2007)
18. Weisfeiler, B., Lehman, A.A.: A reduction of a graph to a canonical form and an algebra arising during this reduction. Nauchno-Tech. Informatsiya **2**(9), 12–16 (1968)
19. Yanardag, P., Vishwanathan, S.: Deep graph kernels. In: Proceedings of the 21th ACM SIGKDD International Conference on Knowledge Discovery and Data Mining, pp. 1365–1374. ACM (2015)
20. Zhang, M., Cui, Z., Neumann, M., Chen, Y.: An end-to-end deep learning architecture for graph classification (2018)

Author Index

Printed in the United States
By Bookmasters